PERSONAL FINANCIAL MANAGEMENT

Stanley B. Block
Texas American Bank/Fort Worth Chair of Finance
Texas Christian University

John W. Peavy III
Chairman, Department of Finance
Southern Methodist University

John H. Thornton
Professor of Insurance
North Texas State University

Photo Credits

Chapter 1 Page 12, New York Stock Exchange / page 20, © 1981, Rosner, Stock, Boston. **Chapter 2** Page 48, Antman, The Image Works. **Chapter 3** Page 58, AP/Wide World (all photos). **Chapter 4** Page 113, Druskis, Taurus. **Chapter 5** Page 142, Carey, The Image Works / page 158, © Druskis, Taurus. **Chapter 6** Page 180, Carey, The Image Works / page 192, Gans, The Image Works. **Chapter 7** Page 232, Grunnitus Studios / page 242, Courtesy of IBM / page 244, Courtesy of IBM / page 245, Courtesy of IBM / page 251, Courtesy of Apple Computer, Inc. **Chapter 8** Page 276, Grunnitus Studios. **Chapter 9** Page 314, © 1976, Hrynewych, Stock, Boston. **Chapter 12** Page 398 (top left), Courtesy Dictaphone Corp.; (top right), Courtesy, Pitney Bowes; (bottom), Courtesy Dictaphone Corp. / page 422, Courtesy, Prudential-Bache. **Chapter 13** Page 458, Courtesy, Fidelity Investments. **Chapter 14** Page 477, Figure 14.4, Brody, Stock, Boston / page 486, James McGoon **Chapter 16** Page 554, Grunnitus Studios.

Sponsoring Editor: John Greenman
Development Editor: Mary Lou Mosher
Project Editor: Carla Samodulski
Text and Cover Design: Barbara Bert/North 7 Atelier
Cover and Part Photos: Joel Gordon
Text Art: Vantage Art, Inc.
Photo Research: Mira Schachne
Production Manager: Jeanie Berke
Production Assistant: Beth Maglione
Compositor: Ruttle, Shaw & Wetherill, Inc.
Printer and Binder: R. R. Donnelley & Sons Company
Cover Printer: Lehigh Press

PERSONAL FINANCIAL MANAGEMENT

Library of Congress Cataloging in Publication Data

Block, Stanley B.
Personal financial management.

Includes bibliographies and index.
1. Finance, Personal. I. Peavy, John W.
II. Thornton, John H. III. Title.
HG179.B555 1988 332.024 87-19088
ISBN 0-06-040789-1

87 88 89 90 9 8 7 6 5 4 3 2 1

PERSONAL FINANCIAL MANAGEMENT

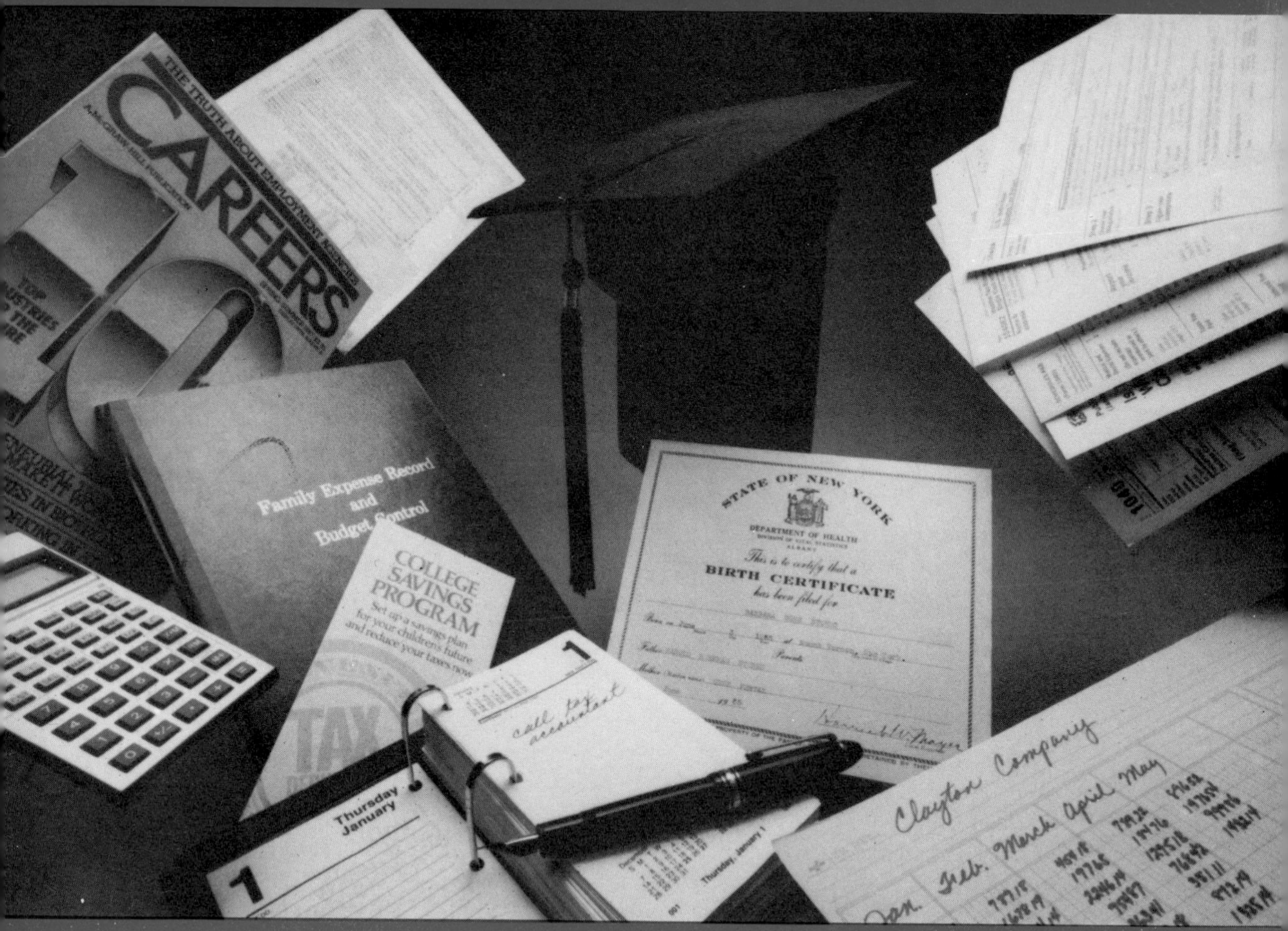

HARPER & ROW, PUBLISHERS, New York
Cambridge, Philadelphia, San Francisco, Washington,
London, Mexico City, São Paulo, Singapore, Sydney

Contents

Real-World Applications

To the Instructor

Although *Personal Financial Management* adopts a decidedly modern approach to personal financial planning and management, we have made clarity of presentation our foremost objective in writing this book. We want the reader to come away from the book with a full understanding of the major points and analytical procedures we present. Such topics as budgeting, tax computation, leasing versus purchasing, auto ownership costs, insurance settlement procedures, and bond valuation are covered in a fairly sophisticated and detailed manner, but one that the willing student can easily follow. We also go into present-value analysis, but we are very careful to take the student with us.

The content of the text is influenced somewhat by the authors' philosophy of teaching. We know today's students can be turned on by good, up-to-date material supported by concrete applications from the real world. We also consider it important to present relevant examples involving a variety of life-styles. We use abundant illustrative situations dealing with single parents, college students, unmarried professionals, and two-wage-earner families, as well as the classic one-wage-earner/one-homemaker family.

Organization of the Text

We have followed a lifetime planning orientation in organizing the text. Part One starts with how to establish personal goals and objectives, which leads into career planning, budgeting, and tax planning. In the next two parts, we explore the processes of using financial services and purchasing housing and consumer durables. Once assets are acquired, they must be protected through insurance and redeployed through investments, so these are the next two major topics discussed in Parts Four and Five. In the final section of the book, Part Six, we introduce the student to the importance of retirement and estate planning, emphasizing that these issues cannot be separated from the topics presented earlier.

Notable Content Features

Personal Financial Management reflects the most recent changes affecting financial planning. An entire chapter is devoted to the effect of the Tax Reform Act of 1986 on tax planning. Furthermore, the effects of this legislation are developed in our coverage of investments, retirement planning, the establishment of trusts, and many other areas. Also, the use of personal computers is described in some detail in the appendix to Chapter 7, and specific computer applications or programs are suggested at the ends of many of the chapters. The changes in the structures of financial institutions and the products they offer are also highlighted, since the services that banks or savings-and-loans provide today are so dissimilar to what they offered only a decade ago. In the same way, the text takes full account of changes in risk management tools and investment products.

Pedagogical Features

To make the book eminently teachable, the six parts of the text are introduced by brief **preview essays** on what will be discussed in each part, and each chapter is preceded by a list of **learning objectives.** The **questions** at the ends of chapters closely relate to these objectives. In addition, there are **two cases at the end of each chapter** that help to reinforce the learning process. Throughout the text we also provide reference materials and stress the importance of additional **sources of information** from the government and the private sector that are potentially helpful to the reader. We want students to be able to put their hands on the right material for making decisions, rather than merely to memorize facts.

Ancillary Materials

One of our major objectives was to develop a comprehensive support package for the students and instructors using the textbook. The supplements include:

- **Instructor's Manual** by the authors. Answers to the end-of-chapter questions and cases are provided, along with learning objectives and teaching strategies.
- **Test Bank** by Cherie Mazer. This test-item file consists of 400 objective questions, with answers, and 100 case problems with full solutions.
- **Harpertest.** The test bank questions will be available in a computerized format for use with IBM and Apple personal computers.
- **Study Guide** by Gayle M. Ross of Copiah-Lincoln Junior College. Each chapter includes learning objectives, a chapter outline in which blanks are to be filled in by the student to complete the outline sentences, objective self-test questions (including true-false, multiple-choice, and matching), and case problems. All answers are given in the guide.
- **Student Practice Set** by Gayle M. Ross. Using this unique study aid, the student handles the finances of the mythical Johnson family. Fifteen assignments cover such areas as a personal balance sheet, monthly budgets, checkbook entries and reconciliation, figuring loan payments, and even the purchase of common stock. The Practice Set contains all the necessary blank forms to complete the assignments. Full solutions are provided in a separate instructor's manual.

- **Transparency Masters.** A separate section at the back of the instructor's manual contains over 50 transparency masters of (1) key text figures and tables and (2) answers to the end-of-chapter case problems.
- **Computer Software.** Available through Harper & Row is a program from Sierra On-Line, a California software firm, entitled "Smart Money™: The Comprehensive Financial Manager." This menu-driven program constructs budgets, records expenditures, balances checking and credit card statements, calculates declining balances for loans and annuities, and with the addition of a printer, prints balance sheets, budget reports, and even graphs. It is available in IBM and Apple versions, and can be ordered through your Harper & Row sales representative. Demonstration disks are free of charge.

Acknowledgments

The authors are deeply indebted to the following reviewers, whose remarks were often incisive and had an important influence on the development of the final text: Michael J. Ahern III, University of Toledo; Robert J. Angell, University of North Carolina—Greensboro; H. Kent Baker, The American University; Andrew Cao, KCBA, The American University; P. R. Chandy, North Texas State University; Sharon Garrison, East Tennessee State University; Carol Z. Green, Metropolitan Technical Community College, Omaha; Carole J. Makela, Colorado State University; Craig C. Milnor, Clark Community College; Gayle M. Ross, Copiah-Lincoln Junior College; and Grant J. Wells, Ball State University.

We wish to express our special thanks to John Greenman and Mary Lou Mosher of Harper & Row for the high level of professionalism they brought to the project. Finally, we are particularly grateful to our families for their patience and support throughout the development of this text.

Stanley B. Block
John W. Peavy III
John H. Thornton

To the Student

Did you know that if as a working person you put $2000 a year (tax-free) into a retirement account, and if you do this from the time you are 20 to the time you are 70 and the money grows at 10 percent, you will have accumulated $2,323,817? Did you know that many millionaires virtually escape estate taxes because of careful tax planning? Did you know that you might pay an 8 percent commission to buy a mutual fund (investment fund) if you do not know what you are doing, but you will pay nothing if you are knowledgeable?

Unlike a course in chemistry, history, or even accounting, the material in this text covers real problems and the solutions to those problems. The issues discussed are not trivial, and understanding the proper approaches to financial questions requires some work. But the potential payoff goes beyond a good grade in the course to the acquisition of skills that you can draw on over a lifetime.

Here is another example of an important thing to know: Virtually every bank, savings and loan, insurance company, stockbroker, car dealer, or real estate agent charges an average price for each service performed. They, in turn, depend on those customers who are not cost conscious or knowledgeable to subsidize those who are. To the extent that you are paying more for your checking services than necessary or accepting less than the market rate for your savings dollars, you are providing funds for a smarter, more discerning customer. This course in personal financial management forces you to come to grips with many issues such as these.

You will study many exciting areas of finance in this book. The nature of U.S. financial markets has changed more in the last five years than in almost any time in our history. For example, there has been a massive deregulation of financial institutions (such as banks and savings and loans), and they compete not only for customers but also for their own continued existence. Recently the stock market has had some of its largest daily movements, both up and down, in decades. We are also in an era of internationalization. Did you know that the biggest stock exchange in the world is no longer on Wall Street in New York, but in Tokyo? Did you know that the Tax Reform Act of 1986 has made many conventional investments obsolete?

In short, while you are getting your academic credits for this course, you will also be getting useful information that can lead to future financial success.

About the Authors

Stanley B. Block holds the Texas American Bank/Forth Worth Chair of Finance in the M. J. Neeley School of Business at Texas Christian University. He received his undergraduate degree in business at the University of Texas, Austin, an M.B.A. at Cornell, and a Ph.D. at Louisiana State University. He is a chartered financial analyst. Dr. Block is the coauthor of five other books in finance and has written two dozen journal articles. He is on the board of directors of the Financial Management Association. His areas of specialization include corporate and personal finance, and investments.

John W. Peavy III is chairman of the finance department at Southern Methodist University. He took his undergraduate business degree at Southern Methodist, an M.B.A. at the University of Pennsylvania, and a doctorate at the University of Texas, Arlington. Dr. Peavy is a chartered financial analyst, chartered financial consultant, and chartered life underwriter. His special areas of concentration include investments, portfolio management, and financial planning. He has written or coauthored over 20 articles in professional journals, as well as two other books.

John H. Thornton is professor of insurance at North Texas State University. He graduated from the University of the South, and received both an M.B.A. and a Ph.D. at Georgia State University. He is a chartered life underwriter. Dr. Thornton has taught in the areas of risk management, and life and property insurance. He is author or coauthor of numerous journal articles. He is currently president-elect of the American Risk and Insurance Association.

PERSONAL FINANCIAL MANAGEMENT

Financial planning and management are inescapable; the only real issue is whether you perform these functions well. You must select a career path, pay your bills, file tax returns, select a place to live, determine a mode of transportation, protect against unforeseen losses, and invest excess funds. The question is, do you want to try to control the key financial factors in your environment or be a victim of circumstance?

Of course, a *desire* to do well in managing your financial affairs is not enough. You must also have sufficient knowledge so that you can make and implement your plans.

In Chapter 1, we discuss the first key step in financial planning: to establish the goals and objectives that are important to you (and to your family unit if you are married). The worst mistake you can make is to imitate somebody else's goals or objectives. You must assess what is right for you and then proceed down that path. A very important consideration is the career you wish to follow, and a number of helpful suggestions and information

THE ENVIRONMENT FOR FINANCIAL DECISION MAKING

1 Planning for the Future
2 Developing Budgets and Financial Statements
3 Preparing for Personal Income Taxes

sources are offered in this chapter.

Since you, like most people, are probably faced with financial constraints, you need to develop a facility for budgeting and resource allocation. In Chapter 2, you will learn how to develop skills in budgeting and how to construct and read a personal financial statement. You will also find out the importance of the human dimension that is part of every financial decision. Certainly, for some of us, money is meant to be spent, while others of us are nest egg builders.

Almost every financial decision has a tax-related aspect, and in Chapter 3 you will learn how to prepare a tax return and work out strategies to minimize your tax burden. You will also become familiar with the Tax Reform Act of 1986 and its implications for financial planning. Since many of the rules of the game have changed, you will want to make sure that you are playing by the right rules when you fill out your tax return. ■

1 Planning for the Future

After studying this chapter, you should:

- Appreciate the importance of financial planning in meeting lifelong objectives
- Identify the key elements in the process of goal setting
- Separate out short-term, intermediate, and long-term financial goals
- Understand the nature of the changing economic and political environment in which financial planning must take place
- Appreciate the importance of career selection as the first important step in personal and financial planning
- Identify the characteristics of a successful entrepreneur
- Understand the role of the professional financial planner in aiding others in the planning process

The typical college graduate will make a million and a half dollars during his or her lifetime. Some will eventually end up with a beautiful home, a well-funded retirement plan, ample cash for travel, and a large estate for their heirs. Others with the same lifetime income will end up depending on Social Security payments or a small private pension fund and will continually ask themselves, where did it all go?

Neither of those outcomes will depend upon pure luck. As the old saying goes, luck comes when preparedness and opportunity get together. Thousands of events influence your life, and you can control most of them. Nowhere is this more evident than in the area of personal financial planning. You can choose your career path after college, you can invest in whichever stocks and bonds you desire, you can buy the insurance policies that you want, you can select the certified public accountant (CPA) or financial planner of your choice, and so on. Furthermore, you do not need any great inherent talents to accomplish most of these tasks.

Nevertheless, only 2 percent of the population reaching age 65 is financially independent. The reason in many cases is only too evident. Major decisions were made by chance or happenstance rather than through careful planning. A stock was bought on a hot tip, an insurance policy was purchased from a friend who happened to be in the business, an exorbitant price was paid for a major purchase because alternatives were not explored, or a budget and retirement plan were too much trouble to set up. All of the above are common causes for failure to meet long-term financial objectives.

It is not our intent in this book to make you a millionaire—although anyone who puts $2000 a year into an individual retirement account (IRA) for his or her entire working life is almost assured of that fate. Furthermore, we realize that the pursuit of wealth is not necessarily the most noble objective in life. Material possessions are certainly only one measure of a person's well-being and quite likely not the most important. But the fact is, financial planning and management are inescapable. If you put your money into a low-yielding savings account, you have made a decision to accept a lower return than might be available elsewhere. If you rent instead of purchase, you are betting that inflation will not cause home prices to go up in the future. If you don't buy disability or life insurance, you have decided to absorb the risk of possible losses rather than pass it on to another party.

In reading this book, you will be forced to come to grips with the many decisions that have to be made. You are probably relatively young, and this is the best time to think about financial planning. You truly are in a position to influence your financial well-being. Some of the issues discussed in the text will have immediate importance to you, whereas others will take on greater meaning as you progress through your family life and career. In either case, now is the time to start thinking about all these issues. We want you never to become too comfortable with your financial plan or your method of managing your money. We want you to constantly wonder if you are paying too much in taxes, or if you are paying an 8½ percent commission to buy a mutual fund when others are smart enough not to pay a commission, or if you're acquiring a home mortgage that has restrictive provisions that a savings and loan down the block does not require. We certainly cannot answer all questions for you, but we can help you develop a lifelong pattern of asking questions and encourage you to develop a small dose of cynicism in evaluating the financial products that will be offered to you.

THE SETTING OF GOALS

The first step in financial planning is to assess your own goals and objectives. For some people, the goal will be the accumulation of great wealth. For others, goal setting will be weighted more heavily toward financial security. Clearly, your family situation will play a role in your goal planning. If you have financial dependents, you will have a greater need for stability of income and protection against unforeseen events. As you set financial goals now or in the future, keep some important guidelines in mind.

1. Do a Careful Self-Assessment. Before you determine what you want to achieve, you must determine what is important to you personally. Some people have a compelling need to succeed. Leisure time is of little use to them, so to plan long summer vacations or retirement at age 65 is a wasted task. To retire a dynamic trial lawyer or a dedicated researcher in biochemistry is like putting a racehorse out to pasture.

Most people have more balanced goals: They want to accumulate a certain measure of wealth and still enjoy the fruits of their labor. In choosing your own goals, remember that following someone else's path is a useless exercise. Your best friend may desire to achieve financial independence at age 50, while living in an exciting major metropolitan area and vacationing in Europe at every opportunity. He or she may further decide not to have a family. This approach may not fit you at all.

2. Involve Others in the Process. This second factor takes on greater importance as you become part of a family unit. This means including your spouse and children, when they are old enough to participate, in the decision process. Also, the term *involve* does not mean to dictate or proclaim your intentions. It implies a sharing of ideas, thoughts, plans, and goals. The problems related to cooperative (and noncooperative) efforts in family financial planning and budgeting are covered in Chapter 2.

3. Separate Out Your Goals by Time. As indicated in Table 1.1, goals may be **short-term, intermediate,** or **long-term** in nature. Short-term goals should be fairly specific, whereas longer-term objectives require greater flexibility. Don't be afraid to pinpoint the age at which you hope to achieve a goal or the dollar amount involved. The numbers are meant to be flexible.

Actually, the time dimension of our goals is consistent with the financial life cycle we all go through. When in college, our most immediate objective is normally to complete our education and to earn enough funds to stay financially afloat. Our intermediate goals coincide with our working years, in which we settle into a career, perhaps purchase a home, and begin an investment program. Our long-term goals relate to the latter stages of the financial life cycle, where the emphasis is on retirement and travel for most people. Others, of course, may choose to work throughout their lives.

4. Prioritize Your Goals. If you are like most people, you will not be able to achieve all the goals to which you aspire. The best approach is first to consider all things possible and then to line up those items that are truly important to you.

Box 1.1 A SUCCESS STORY: THE IMMIGRANT PRINCE

Ellis Island

I was 12 when my father met me at Ellis Island. I made the trip alone, in steerage. My mother died right after I was born, in 1907, and my father left Italy a few months later, so I didn't really know him at all. The only way I had of recognizing him was a photo I carried with me from Sicily. He met me at the boat carrying a pair of knickers—I'll never forget this—and insisted right away that I put them on. I was wearing these tight pants with three buttons down the front, and I said to him, forget it, I'm not going around looking like some Arab. In school, you see, we'd read that Arabs wore knickers, all the way down to their ankles. He told me everyone would laugh at me in those tight pants. Well, I said, I'm sorry, but I'm not wearing any knickers. Put them on, he said. So I put them on—but over my other pants, you know. Then we went home.

Joseph Pellegrino

In the four decades from 1880 to 1920, more than 26 million immigrants made the voyage from the Old World to the New. They came from small towns and farms, factories and urban ghettos; they came from Ireland and from Poland, from Russia, Rumania, and a dozen other sovereign states. They came from Italy—more than 2 million of them in the years spanning 1901 to 1910 alone. Mostly poor and ill-educated, they came to an America long on possibilities and short on guarantees.

One of these immigrants was Joseph Pellegrino, age 12, a native of Mastretta, Sicily. Pellegrino's father, a stonecutter by trade, had himself emigrated to the United States in 1908, finding work on the Rockefeller estate near the banks of the Hudson River. When he could afford it, he sent for his only child, meeting him at Ellis Island and taking him home to a third-floor walk-up in lower Manhattan.

Young Joseph spoke no English and left school for good in the eighth grade. With few skills to fall back on, he soon found his calling as a hustler and street vendor, selling everything from shopping bags and shoeshine stands to Coney Island frozen custard. By the time he reached his early twenties, his father was dead, a victim of lung disease. Joseph scraped together $12,000 in savings from a variety of enterprises and sank it into a grocery-store partnership with two fellow immigrants from Mastretta.

The business thus established was a paradigm of how commerce evolved in the ethnic pockets of urban America circa the 1920s: neighbor to neighbor, bloodline to bloodline, immigrant to immigrant. But Joseph Pellegrino's destiny far transcended that of the prototypical small-time immigrant entrepreneur. Today, at age 79, "JP" is the incumbent—and as yet unretired—board chairman of the Prince Co., an enterprise established by fellow Sicilians and built by Pellegrino, with the help of family and colleagues, into the largest independently owned manufacturing company of its kind in the United States.

Independence, an idea much on the nation's mind this July, has meaning for companies as well as countries. From the neighborhood grocery to today's $200-million-a-year business, Pellegrino and Prince have faced virtually every opportunity—and obstacle—a man and a company can confront. In simple terms, theirs is a classic American success story; yet little of their story translates into easy simplicities. Filled with catastrophic setback and vicious ethnic rivalry, it dramatizes the effects of old loyalties, new opportunities, and intergenerational conflict on a business and a family coming of age in twentieth-century America.

SOURCE: Joseph P. Kahn, "The Immigrant Prince." Reprinted with permission, *INC.* magazine (July 1986).

Table 1.1 TIME CONSIDERATION FOR FINANCIAL GOALS (LIFE-CYCLE APPROACH)

Short-term	Intermediate	Long-term
Complete education Maintain positive balance in checking account Get summer job Buy used car Repay loan Establish minimum insurance coverage	Find permanent job or start own business Purchase home Set up comprehensive insurance coverage Begin setting up fund for children's college education Begin investment program Begin contributing to retirement program	Accumulate x dollars in wealth Retire at age x Travel x months of the year

5. Reassess Your Goals. We all change with the passage of time, so it is important to reevaluate your goals. Perhaps an item that you thought was essential when you were 20 is no longer as important a decade later. Also, lifestyles change with the arrival of children, a divorce, or an untimely death. We are not suggesting that you become a rudderless ship in the sea, but simply that you reevaluate what you truly want from time to time. Perhaps some hidden or seemingly unachievable goals will become possible with the passage of time.

6. Chart Your Progress in Meeting Your Goals. This procedure can be as formal or informal as you desire. For financially oriented objectives, a fairly formalized system can be developed (see Chapter 2 on budgeting, for example). For more subjective goals, such as getting a job or buying a home, a highly formalized system of review is not very realistic or probably even necessary. You know where you stand without filling in a table or chart. There are enough really important records to keep in the overall process of financial planning without engaging in meaningless exercises.

THE CHANGING ENVIRONMENT FOR FINANCIAL PLANNING

Financial planning must be done within the context of the economic environment. This would not be a particularly difficult task if it were not for the fact that economic and political circumstances are constantly changing. Someone doing financial planning in the late 1970s would have been particularly concerned about high rates of inflation and the need to maintain purchasing power. A heavy emphasis would have been placed on the accumulation of tangible assets (real estate, precious metals, collectibles) that go up in value with inflation.

Furthermore, the maximum tax rate in the late 1970s was 70 percent, and that high rate had to be a major influence on each investment decision.

By the mid- to late 1980s, the U.S. economy had shifted from a high-inflation to a low-inflation environment. Financial assets, such as stocks and bonds, became primary outlets for investments. Furthermore, the maximum individual tax rate shifted to the 20 to 30 percent range, making tax considerations less critical in investment decisions.

No doubt the economic environment will change many times again in the 50 to 60 years during which you will be doing financial planning. If we look at the past 50 to 60 years, we see a severe depression, a major world war and two other significant conflicts, a half dozen recessions, unprecedented prosperity in the 1960s, and the previously mentioned high inflation rate of the late 1970s. The economic environment changes in major ways, although over long periods of time history tends to repeat itself. Therefore, you should not be overly influenced by *current* economic conditions in doing long-range financial planning. Professional financial planners as well as individuals tend to get swept away by the current economic concern (inflation, disinflation, high interest rates, low interest rates, and so on) and make long-term decisions based on what turn out to be short-term phenomena. A good financial planner must recognize the impermanent nature of the economy and build in some flexibility that will allow for a reasonable measure of success in changing environments.

Key Economic and Political Influences

Some of the most important economic and political influences of the late 1980s are listed in Table 1.2. Most of these will be covered in one form or another throughout this book, so they are not discussed at length here. A few items, however, are worthy of observation.

First, with the tax reform legislation of 1986 and the **deregulation** of such industries as banking, the brokerage industry, and the airline industry, more and more responsibility is being placed on the individual to make his or her own decisions. The government is no longer dictating that every bank or savings and

Table 1.2 IMPORTANT ECONOMIC AND POLITICAL INFLUENCES IN A CHANGING ENVIRONMENT

Tax Reform	Inflation	Stock prices
Deregulation	Disinflation	Interest rates
	Federal deficits	Oil prices
	Foreign trade deficits	Real GNP
	High individual and corporate debt	Balance of payments
	Bankruptcies	International dependence

loan pay the same interest rate or that a given investment be allowed a large tax write-off. Your success or failure as a consumer/investor will fall much more heavily on your own shoulders. Furthermore, those who fail can expect less in the way of aid or protection by the federal government. Therefore, an understanding of personal financial planning is more important than ever before.

Second, the economic environment of the 1970s and 1980s had an unprecedented level of volatility in major financial variables. As an example, let's examine Figure 1.1, which covers the movement of short-term interest rates over a long period of time. The prime rate is the rate at which a bank's most credit-worthy customers may borrow, and the commercial paper rate is the interest rate at which large corporations borrow in the market. These definitions are not very important for now; the main factor to observe in the figure is simply the movement of short-term interest rates over time.

Note the relative stability of interest rates between 1940 and 1970; then observe the extremely rapid rate of change from 1970 on. Not only are the rates

Figure 1.1 PATTERNS OF INTEREST RATE CHANGE

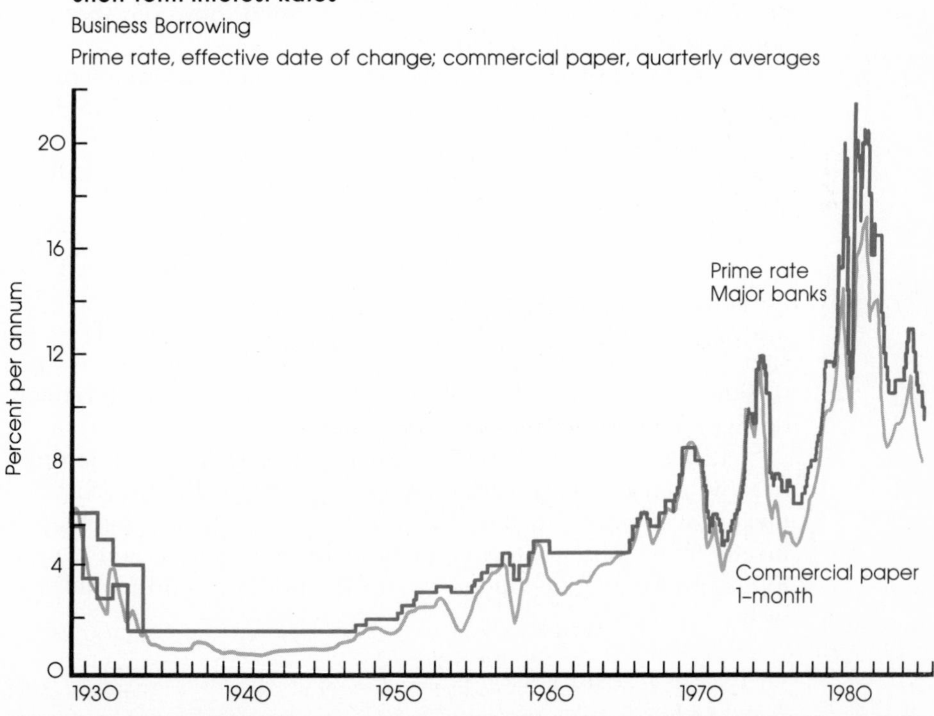

SOURCE: *1985 Historical Chart Book,* Board of Governors of the Federal Reserve System, p. 99.

much higher, but they change by as many as eight percentage points in a given year. Clearly, a financial planner in the years 1960–1965 had a much easier task than a financial planner in the early 1980s.

These highly **volatile interest rates** have important consequences for decision making. Because long-term interest rates (those on bonds or mortgages) tend to track the same general pattern as short-term rates, someone who signed a home mortgage in 1980 was paying an interest rate two or three times higher than a home buyer a decade or two before, and also a much higher rate than a home buyer a few years later. In addition, deregulation has further increased the burden or opportunity for decision making in this area. In the late 1980s, you can either agree to a *fixed*-rate mortgage and stay with it for the next 20 or 30 years (or however long you own the home), or you can go to a variable-rate mortgage that regularly adjusts the interest rate to current market conditions. Obviously, your outlook for future interest rates will have a major impact on your decision.

Another highly volatile economic index can be seen in Figure 1.2. Note that consumer prices as measured by the consumer price index were relatively stable between 1952 and 1970, but observe the extreme patterns of price movement since 1970.[1] Much of the price volatility can be linked to changing energy prices. In 1973–1974 as well as 1979–1980, we had major increases in oil prices. To the extent that oil prices stay at a permanently low level, perhaps the volatility in price changes is under control. Keep in mind, however, that history tends to repeat itself over long periods of time.

A final point about the changing economic environment is that the U.S. economy is now much more dependent on worldwide conditions than ever before. An economic or stock market study based solely on events in the U.S. economy ignores a significant part of the picture. The same is true for individual financial planning.

The outlook for U.S. industry is now heavily dependent on the ability of U.S. firms to export their products overseas. To the extent that the Western European or Japanese economies are weak or there are trade barriers set up against U.S. products, overseas shipments may be limited. To appreciate the significance of this point, consider that such companies as Dow Chemical, Exxon, Gillette, Mobil, Colgate Palmolive, and Chase Manhattan all generate 50 percent or more of their revenues in foreign markets.

Foreign imports into the United States also have a strong positive and negative impact. Imports from Japan, Korea, and other low-cost producers often mean lower prices to the U.S. consumer. Foreign competition, however, also means fewer jobs in steel, apparel, office equipment, and a number of other industries for longtime members of the work force and for college graduates as well.

[1] The change in rates of inflation also helps to explain the changing levels of interest rates shown in Figure 1.1.

Figure 1.2 **CHANGES IN CONSUMER PRICES**

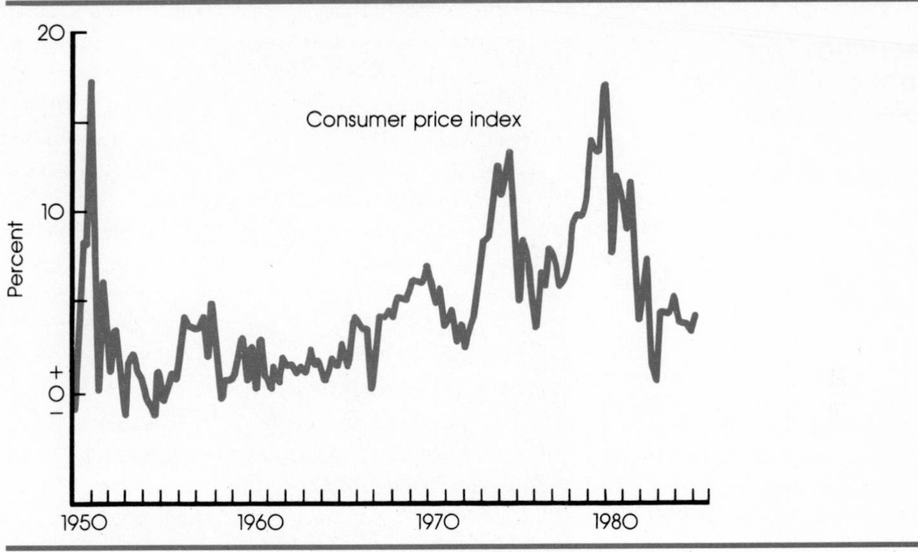

SOURCE: *1985 Historical Chart Book,* Board of Governors of the Federal Reserve System, p. 37.

One of the ways in which U.S. dealings with foreign countries are influenced is through the value of the U.S. dollar in foreign markets relative to the Japanese yen, the German mark, the Swiss franc, and other major currencies. Although the mechanics of foreign-market trading are beyond the scope of this book, the important point is that key *domestic* economic decisions are often made by the president, the Congress, and the Federal Reserve Board with a sharp eye on *international* markets. For example, U.S. interest rates may be kept at artificially high or low levels to influence the value of the dollar in overseas trading or to attract foreign capital to the United States. In doing your financial planning, you do not have to be an expert in international affairs, but you should have at least some sensitivity to worldwide events.

YOUR CAREER AND PLANNING FOR THE FUTURE

Probably your most important financial planning decision concerns your career. If you are to acquire the financial resources necessary to make other decisions, you first must choose your primary method of wealth accumulation.

The career path you choose will normally determine how you will spend eight hours of each working day for the rest of your life. The 90,000 hours that the average person works in a lifetime exceeds all other activities, except possibly

Box 1.2 EXCERPT FROM THE *OCCUPATIONAL OUTLOOK HANDBOOK*

Securities and Financial Services Sales Workers

Nature of the Work

Securities Sales Workers. Most investors—whether they are individuals with a few hundred dollars or large institutions with millions to invest—call on securities sales workers when buying or selling stocks, bonds, shares in mutual funds, or other financial products. Securities sales workers often are called *registered representatives, account executives,* or *brokers.*

When an investor wishes to buy or sell securities, sales workers may relay the order through their firms' offices to the floor of a securities exchange, such as the New York Stock Exchange. There, securities sales workers known as *brokers' floor representatives* buy and sell securities. If a security is not traded on an exchange, the sales worker sends the order to the firm's trading department, which trades it directly with a dealer in the over-the-counter market. After the transaction has been completed, the sales worker notifies the customer of the final price.

sleep. Your job will determine how wealthy you are and, to a large measure, how happy you are.

Many students take the matter of career selection too lightly. To some people, it is simply a matter to be considered when they get to their senior year and finally begin the interviewing process. Even those who choose a major early in their college careers often do so without careful study or insight. Perhaps their parents think it's a good idea, or their roommate is going in that direction, or they had a class or professor that they really enjoyed. Students sometimes dedicate less time to career selection than they do to determining whether they should take economics at 8:30 on Tuesday and Thursday or psychology at 9:00 on Monday, Wednesday, and Friday.

As is true of almost any other decision-making process, the first step is to assess your own interests and talents and the second step is to determine the actual opportunities that exist (or are likely to exist) in the marketplace in the future.

Securities sales workers also provide many related services for their customers. Depending on a customer's knowledge of the market, they may explain the meaning of stock market terms and trading practices; offer financial counseling; devise an individual financial portfolio for the client including securities, life insurance, tax shelters, mutual funds, annuities, and other investments; and offer advice on the purchase or sale of a particular security.

Employment

Securities and financial services sales workers held about 81,000 jobs in 1984. In addition, a substantial number of people in other occupations sold securities. These include partners and branch office managers in securities firms as well as insurance agents and brokers offering securities to their customers.

Securities sales workers are employed by brokerage and investment firms in all parts of the country. Many of these firms are very small. Most sales workers, however, work for a small number of large firms with main offices in big cities (especially in New York) and approximately 14,000 branch offices in other areas.

Financial services sales workers are employed by banks, savings and loan associations, and other credit institutions.

Job Outlook

The number of securities sales workers is expected to grow much faster than the average for all occupations through the mid-1990's. Most job openings, however, are expected to be created by workers who transfer to other jobs, retire, or stop working for other reasons. Due to the highly competitive nature of securities sales work, many beginners leave the field because they are unable to establish a sufficient clientele. Once established, however, securities sales workers have a relatively strong attachment to their occupation because of high earnings and the considerable investment in training.

Sources of Additional Information

Further information concerning a career as a securities sales worker is available for $1 from: Securities Industry Association, 120 Broadway, New York, N.Y. 10271.

SOURCE: *Occupational Outlook Handbook,* Washington, D.C.: U.S. Government Printing Office, 1986–1987, pp. 263–265.

In evaluating your own interests, you should ask yourself such questions as the following:

> Do you enjoy working with people, or do you prefer working alone?
>
> Are you a risk-taker, or do you prefer stability and predictability?
>
> Are you a self-starter, or do you prefer to work in a well-defined environment?
>
> Are you primarily motivated by money, prestige, a sense of helping others, or perhaps other factors?
>
> Are you willing to travel, or do you prefer to settle into one place?
>
> Do you wish to do graduate work as is required in certain fields, or do you want to begin work as soon after college as possible?

These merely represent a short sample of questions. You may wish to visit the counseling or career placement office at your school to investigate the possibility of going through a more thorough evaluative process. While many people change their career directions a number of times during their lifetime—and this is certainly acceptable and often wise—many of the false starts could have been avoided if more exploratory work had gone into the first decision. It is not enough simply to know what you like to do, and it is not enough simply to know where the best career opportunities are; you must match the two. To train for a Ph.D. in Romance languages may give one great psychic pleasure, but little or no income. Similarly, a $20,000–$30,000 starting salary in accounting or engineering may ensure the financial well-being of some students, but not the psychological well-being if their heart is in social work, music, or other areas.

Determining Job Opportunities

The best way to prudent decision making is through knowledge of opportunities. One of the best places to start is the ***Occupational Outlook Handbook,*** published by the U.S. Department of Labor. It can be found in most libraries or university counseling and career placement centers. It is almost mandatory reading for one who wishes to explore a wide variety of career choices. Over 200 career paths are covered under 20 different major headings. You can read about becoming anything from a purchasing agent to a nuclear engineer to a rabbi. An excerpt from one of the 200 fields is presented in Box 1.2. It is best just to scan the information for now, but keep in mind there are 200 career paths similar to this that are covered, so you may want to focus on your area(s) of interest. In each case training, working conditions, job outlook, earnings potential, and sources of additional information are covered.

A representative sample of relative salary levels of different career paths is presented in Table 1.3. Obviously these are only general indicators; some individuals make considerably more or less than the average indicated for the category, depending on training, hours worked, and special skills. A truly talented lawyer may make over $1 million a year, whereas another attorney may only make enough to pay the rent and hire a part-time secretary. Nevertheless, the great majority of practitioners in a given field fall reasonably close to the mean, so the relative comparisons do possess some degree of validity.

A key ingredient in career planning is identifying those career options that offer the best potential for the future. In Figure 1.3, at the top we see the outlook for 12 key industries through 1995. Computers, high technology, health care, recreation services, banking, publishing, communications, and retailing look particularly good. Negative growth is expected in such areas as textile manufacturing, food and beverage supply functions, and auto making.

Very closely aligned to the material at the top of Figure 1.3 are the data at the bottom. Here the emphasis is strictly on *occupations* rather than industries. Most of the fast-growing occupations relate to computers and high technology, but note the growth in the need for paralegals, medical assistants, and travel agents. Stenographers lead the category of the five most rapidly shrinking oc-

Table 1.3
SELECTED OCCUPATIONS AND AVERAGE MIDCAREER EARNINGS LEVELS

Career	Estimated midcareer annual income
Doctor	$105,000
Dentist	68,000
Attorney	65,000
Stockbroker	64,000
Bank officer	50,000
Engineer	44,000
Accountant	42,000
Computer programmer	34,000
Buyer	30,000
Registered nurse	24,000
Computer operator	24,000
Public relations specialist	23,000
Photographer	23,000
Dental hygienist	21,000
Secretary	18,000
File clerk	13,000

SOURCE: Selected data from the U.S. Department of Labor, Bureau of Labor Statistics, 1986.

cupations. Their numbers will decline by 40 percent due to sophisticated word-processing systems.

The *Occupational Outlook Handbook* contains a ten-page section entitled "Tomorrow's Jobs: An Overview." According to that section, the service industries (such as accounting, computer programming, marketing, interior design) will continue to grow, while the manufacturing industries will decrease in importance. The service industries accounted for 35 percent of the work force in 1959. By 1995, the percentage is expected to grow to 70 percent. Also, related data indicate the importance of college training. College graduates, despite their later entry into the job market, earn about $600,000 more during their working lifetime than non-college graduates.

The Changing Nature of the Work Force

With the emergence of the two-wage-earner family and the acceptance of the single-female life-style, women are becoming a much more important factor in the workplace. At first women were begrudgingly accepted into male-dominated

Figure 1.3 **JOBS FOR THE FUTURE: WHERE THE JOBS WILL BE**

A look ten years ahead by the government's Bureau of Labor Statistics shows more shifts coming in job opportunities. The number of Americans making goods in 1995 is expected to change little, but the number providing services will swell by an estimated 14 million. Women, who ten years ago held two of every five jobs, are expected to make up nearly half the work force.

Outlook in Key Industries

	Expected Jobs in '95	Change from '84		Expected Jobs in '95	Change from '84
Retailing	21,287,000	+16%	Textiles, apparel	1,581,000	−18%
Health care	8,332,000	+29%	Computers, electronics	1,559,000	+35%
High tech	7,730,000	+28%	Leisure, recreation services	1,525,000	+27%
Banking, financial	5,723,000	+19%	Food, beverages	1,474,000	−10%
Printing, publishing	1,751,000	+20%	Public utilities	1,177,000	+13%
Communications	1,585,000	+17%	Auto making	828,000	− 4%

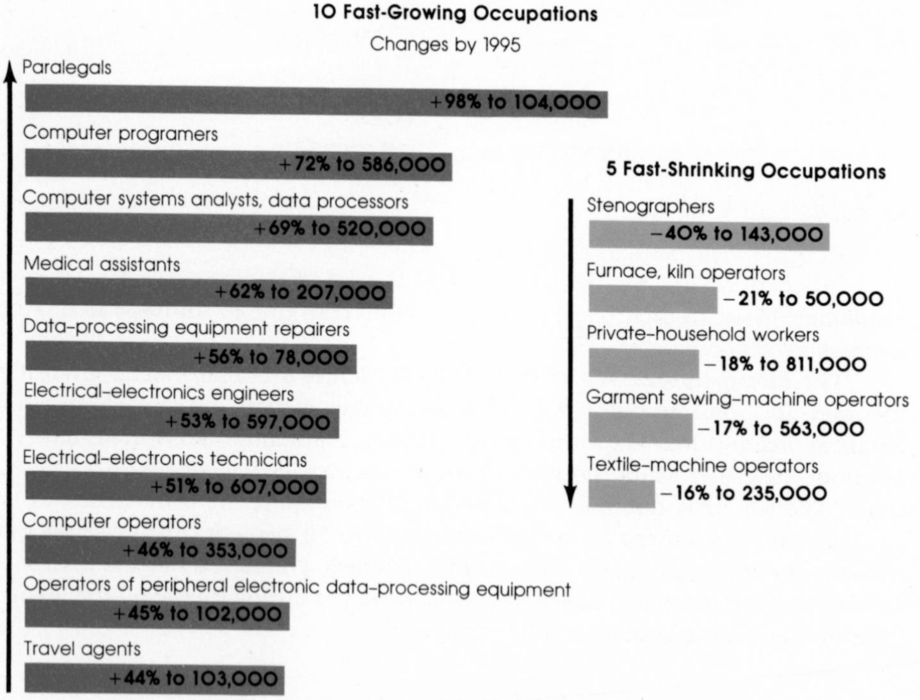

10 Fast-Growing Occupations

Changes by 1995

Paralegals	+98% to 104,000
Computer programers	+72% to 586,000
Computer systems analysts, data processors	+69% to 520,000
Medical assistants	+62% to 207,000
Data-processing equipment repairers	+56% to 78,000
Electrical-electronics engineers	+53% to 597,000
Electrical-electronics technicians	+51% to 607,000
Computer operators	+46% to 353,000
Operators of peripheral electronic data-processing equipment	+45% to 102,000
Travel agents	+44% to 103,000

5 Fast-Shrinking Occupations

Stenographers	−40% to 143,000
Furnace, kiln operators	−21% to 50,000
Private-household workers	−18% to 811,000
Garment sewing-machine operators	−17% to 563,000
Textile-machine operators	−16% to 235,000

Note: Projected employment based on moderate growth of economy and labor force. Industry employment includes wage and salary workers, the self-employed, and unpaid family workers.

SOURCE: Copyright, 1985, *U.S. News & World Report.* Reprinted from issue of December 23, 1985, p. 45.

Table 1.4 WOMEN EMPLOYEES AS A PERCENTAGE OF TOTAL WORKERS

Occupation	PERCENTAGE OF WOMEN IN THE OCCUPATION		
	1950	1970	1981
Accountant	14.9	25.3	38.5
Bank officer/manager	11.7	17.6	37.5
Bank teller	45.2	86.1	93.5
Bookkeeper	77.7	82.1	91.1
Engineer	1.2	1.6	18.8
Manager-administrator	13.8	16.6	27.5
Nurse, registered	97.8	97.4	96.8
Physician	6.5	8.9	13.7
Secretary/typist	94.6	96.6	96.3
Teacher: college, university	22.8	28.3	35.2
Teacher: elementary, secondary	74.5	70.4	70.6

SOURCE: U.S. Department of Labor, *Time of Change: 1983 Handbook on Women Workers*, 1983 (Bulletin 298).

professions, but now they have established their ability to perform on an equal basis. Salaries for women, however, are still at a level of only 60 percent of those for men.

In Table 1.4, we see percentages of women workers to total workers in selected occupations and the changes that have taken place over time. The most significant changes have occurred in accounting, banking, management, engineering, and medicine.

The future importance of women in the work force can also be judged by the increasing number of women who are receiving master of business administration degrees (MBAs). As indicated in Figure 1.4, over 20,000 women received MBAs in 1986.[2] Whereas the ratio of male to female MBAs was 7:1 in 1976, by 1986 it was close to 2:1.

Women also continue to be important participants in the workplace in nursing, teaching, and many other fields. Furthermore, education in such areas as business and home economics has made women more capable managers of households and stronger participants in the work environment.

The Entrepreneur and the Work Force

Not all people choose to join the work force as employees. Some decide to strike out on their own. If they are successful, they are called **entrepreneurs.** Dramatic

[2] The value is actually a projection.

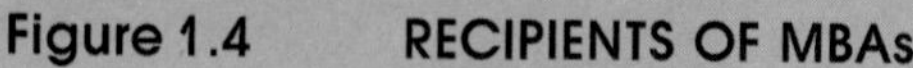

Figure 1.4 RECIPIENTS OF MBAs

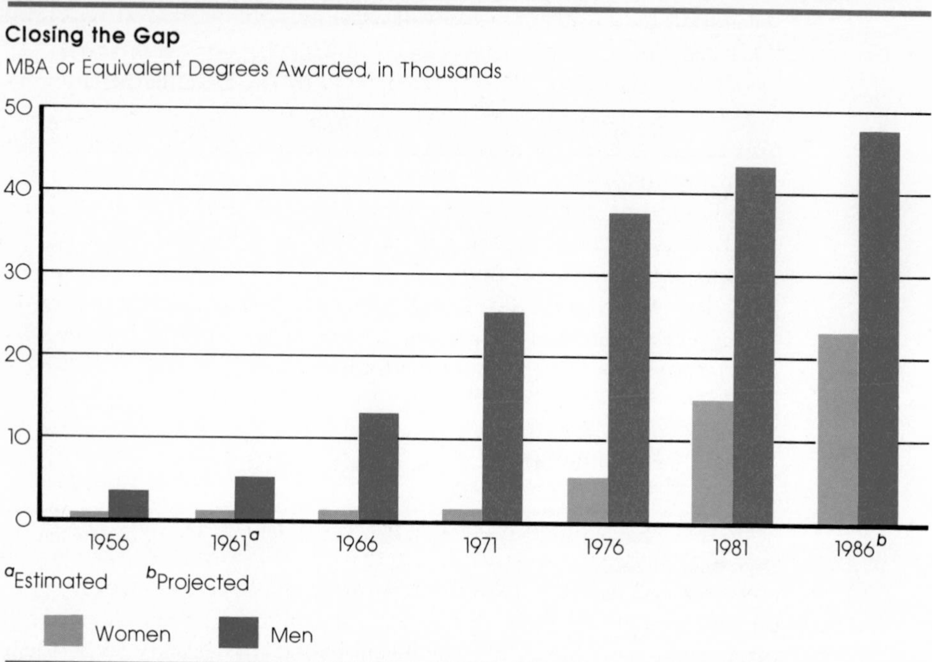

SOURCE: "Corporate Women Careers." Reprinted by permission of *The Wall Street Journal,* © Dow Jones & Company, Inc., March 24, 1986, p. 116.

examples include H. Ross Perot, the billionaire founder of Electronic Data Systems (later acquired by General Motors), and Steven Jobs, the founder of Apple Computer. There are obviously many other success stories.

It is difficult to characterize entrepreneurs as a group, but they do share some common attributes. First, almost by definition entrepreneurs are self-starters. They do not need anyone to motivate them or set quotas for them. Second, they are risk takers. People who are only comfortable with a guaranteed monthly paycheck probably do not have entrepreneurial tendencies.

Though many people think of entrepreneurs as being highly creative or inventive, such qualities are not an essential prerequisite. The true test of an entrepreneur is whether he or she can assemble the necessary financial resources and properly direct the activities of others.

Some people think of entrepreneurs as being loners or recluses who cannot blend in well with others. A classic example is Howard Hughes—a titan of the airline, oil service, and movie industries—who eventually withdrew from society. For the most part, however, this is not the case. The most important skills of a successful entrepreneur are likely to relate to interacting successfully with others. The key factor, though, is that entrepreneurs do not wish to participate in a structural environment such as a large bank, a CPA firm, or government. They want to determine their own destiny.

Finally, many people wonder whether entrepreneurial talent is inborn or developed over time. It's doubtful whether anyone truly knows the answer. More than 300 colleges and universities now teach courses on entrepreneurship to undergraduates and MBAs. Although certain skills and refinements can be taught in the classroom, such as how to develop a pro forma financial statement or how to approach a bank for funding, it's also likely that many skills and attributes of entrepreneurs are inborn. Perhaps you recognize those skills in classmates or friends of your family. Entrepreneurs are not afraid to fail, and they are willing to go for personal financial gain in a big way. It is probably true that if men or women such as J. Paul Getty (Getty Oil), Charles Tandy (Tandy Corporation), or Mary Kay Ash (Mary Kay Cosmetics) were born many times over, they would find a way to amass a fortune each and every time. Their drive and skills are far more important than their individual products.

ADVICE ON PERSONAL FINANCIAL PLANNING

There are approximately 200,000 **personal financial planners** prepared to help you in your financial planning activities. These include lawyers and CPAs with a special interest in this area, insurance agents, stock brokerage firm representatives, and other individuals who specialize in financial planning. Financial planning assistance is one of the fastest growing and least regulated fields in the United States. If you eventually decide to seek outside help in your own financial management activities, choose very carefully. There are far more pretenders than there are experts.

A skilled financial planner should be able to help you integrate all the various elements that go into long-term financial planning—budgeting, insurance, tax planning, retirement, estate planning, and so on. The planner must be enough of a generalist to see how many diverse elements interrelate and enough of a specialist to be able to answer specific questions or at least to know where to find answers to tough questions on taxes, insurance, and other key areas.

How do you go about selecting a financial planner if you are so inclined? If you live in a small town of 50,000 or less, you will probably find a handful of people listed under "Financial Planning Consultants" in the phone book. A city of half a million will have 100 or more listed in the yellow pages.

There are two primary factors you should consider when selecting a financial planner: (1) background and qualifications and (2) method of compensation.

Background and Qualifications of Financial Planners

A financial planner should be willing to give you information on his or her education, professional certification, areas of specialization, prior work experience, and references. Anyone who is in the business for the long term already

Box 1.3 WHAT TO EXPECT FROM YOUR CAREER COUNSELOR

It's sad but true. Many college graduates today approach the job market and the business world with a lack of knowledge that makes interviewers wince. They act as if they never had contact with a career counselor. Many of them cannot articulate their goals and lack the skills for critical thinking and decision-making. Many have not developed the capacity for self-insight. Too often, when asked, "If you could describe the job you would like, what would it be?" students give mundane replies such as, "Any entry-level position, a training program or something in this area."

When asked how they chose their college or why they chose a particular major, their answers are frequently not as concise as they should be. It soon becomes apparent to the recruiter that the job applicant has not given much thought to his or her career, let alone interviewing techniques.

The professional recruiter or line manager politely thanks the applicant for his or her cooperation and a rejection letter is routinely sent. The job seeker continues to stumble through the job search for what seems an interminable period of time. When a position is finally secured, it usually represents a job to pay the bills rather than a quality position which serves as the foundation for a fruitful career.

The sad fact is that many college students put off career planning until it is time to graduate. This is like putting off studying for a major exam until the night before it is taken. Many students repeat the same procedure when the job hunt begins. They seek career counseling at the last minute. To make matters worse, in many colleges courses are not given for credit in career planning. Without such mandatory courses, many students bypass or ignore this critically important function until they are overwhelmed by the job search. It must also be pointed out that the career counseling function is severely understaffed in many colleges, creating an additional problem for students.

Now for the questions at hand: What should I expect from my career counselor? and What should I expect of myself when it comes to planning my career?

There is a dictum in the Marine Corps training program for officer candidates called the five Ps. It says: "Prior planning prevents poor performance." If you were engaged in a military operation, you wouldn't wander into the jungle without a map and compass, or without a plan. If you did, chances are you would not survive.

The same standards apply to the job jungle. In many cases there are more people than there are jobs, and the competition is fierce. To reach your objective, you must have a plan. You must market your skills. How you do it and how much preparation goes into your marketing plan depends on you. The wise individual will start career planning well in advance of graduation.

Approach the career counselor at college and in all probability you will find a trained professional who is more than willing to assist you. Career counselors will help you explore and articulate your career goals. They can assist in clarifying your long-range plans and work with you as your college career unfolds.

Another critical area in which your career counselor can help is the activities in which you choose to participate. Selecting activities that will enhance your growth is more advantageous to your overall career development than haphazardly choosing them.

The business world wants well-rounded individuals rather than those with just high grade-point averages. It takes more than skills to get a job in today's competitive marketplace. Having a degree is not enough. You are going to have to pass through a behavioral window in which a professional recruiter and/or line manager will assess your confidence, ability to sustain and build on relationships, maturity, and motivation. Traits such as flexibility, organizational skills, judgment, and the ability to handle a heavy work load will also be taken into consideration. Your participation in extracurricular activities will give the recruiter additional information about the extent to which you possess these particular traits.

Career counselors can help you find internships and cooperative education programs. Such work-study schedules can be invaluable to your career development and should be pursued. They will give you an advantage over those without such experience when it comes to competing for a job.

Matching your area of academic concentration to internships and cooperative programs will give you a practical understanding of the business world and the skills necessary for success: to communicate effectively, to organize your work load, to adapt to new technology, to be a leader, and to increase your value as an employee.

Your career counselor is your link to such valuable information and programs. He or she will map contingency plans by suggesting alternate directions. The path to success often leads in many directions. For example, if you are an English major, your career counselor may have you research the field of human resources and all its possibilities—employment, wage and salary administration, benefits, training and development, and manpower planning—as well as public relations or publishing.

As you approach your senior year, you should not be scrambling over a wide front, but approaching the final stage of your plans with your career counselor. You will be writing an effective resume, learning how to conduct a letter campaign, plotting an effective job strategy with contingency plans, and sharpening your interviewing skills by role-playing. Your career counselor can also help you effectively communicate your skills in those important job interview situations.

Don't wait. Establish a rapport that will enable you to talk frankly with your career counselor now. He or she can give you a good start in your job quest and help you turn your aspirations and career goals into reality.

For Additional Information

Job & Career Building by Richard Gehrmann and Peter Arnold. Ten Speed Press. 241 pages; $6.95.

The Harvard Guide to Careers by Martha P. Leape. Harvard Press. 223 pages; $6.95.

SOURCE: William Leonard, "What to Expect from Your Career Counselor." Reprinted from Spring/Summer 1986 issue of *Business Week CAREERS* by special permission, © 1986 by McGraw-Hill, Inc.

has this type of information available, so it is no imposition to request background information. A truly professional financial planner should be supplying you with this type of data almost as you walk through the door (types of appropriate certification are further mentioned in Chapter 2).

Generally, what you wish to avoid is one who is highly inexperienced or is a glorified salesperson parading as a financial planner. Financial planners are often sole practitioners, but those who employ a few related support people in their office are likely to be well established and have a wider range of talents in such areas as tax planning, insurance, and stock portfolio management. In this particular instance, we are not referring to larger CPA or law firms, but to those that have as their sole mission the art of financial planning.

Methods of Compensation

Financial planners may work on a fee basis or a commission basis or a combination of the two.

The advantage of **fee-based compensation** is that fee-based financial planners have no product to sell. Presumably their only concern is to make the very best decision possible for you. The disadvantage is that your total costs of doing business may be somewhat higher. You are paying both a consultant fee to the financial planner and a full commission to those who will eventually execute your financial plan. Furthermore, even when there is only a fee involved, you cannot be completely sure that your "independent" financial planner is not favoring one brokerage house or insurance company over another. In some cases, firms selling financial products may give kickbacks—from free research, lavish travel to meetings, split commissions, and so on—to the financial planner. Nevertheless, fee-based financial planning probably offers the best opportunity for comprehensive, objective financial management. The fee may range anywhere from $150 to $10,000 or more. It depends on the client's needs and the extent and nature of the client's assets. There may also be small annual charges for a review and adjustment of strategies.

Planners who receive **commission-based compensation** or who work on a fee-plus-commission basis tend to be less expensive. If there is a fee involved along with the commission, chances are the fee will be smaller than normal because of the income supplement provided by the commission. Naturally, you have to be more on guard when the financial planner is receiving part of his or her total return from your purchase of a given product. Nevertheless, this does not necessarily mean that bad decisions are being made. A commission-oriented financial planner may have a wide enough package of products to appropriately satisfy your needs. But be particularly suspicious when one product (such as a mutual fund or insurance policy) is being pushed to the exclusion of others.

The most important consideration in any type of financial arrangement is that all forms of compensation be established at the outset. You should know what you are expected to pay and what services you will receive. Also, if the financial planner has a special relationship with another firm selling financial products, that should be divulged at the beginning of the relationship.

There is one last source of potential expertise in financial planning that you should consider, and that is yourself. To the extent that you are willing to take additional courses in finance and insurance and stay up-to-date on economic developments and tax law changes, you may be able to service your own needs (with only limited help from others). It all depends on how you want to allocate your time.

WHAT YOU WILL LEARN FROM THIS BOOK

In the remaining chapters, you will work toward building up your financial planning skills. In the rest of Part One, we look at the process of budgeting. We also examine the impact of tax laws on your financial planning decisions, particularly in light of the tax reform legislation that was passed in 1986.

Parts Two and Three deal with your role as a consumer of financial services and a purchaser of major products. We discuss operations of the banking system as they apply to you as a consumer and show how credit influences your lifestyle. We also look into the variables that affect key purchases during your lifetime and give you new insights into the process of buying an automobile, a personal computer, or a home.

In Part Four, we examine how you can protect yourself and your property through insurance. The topic is approached from the viewpoint of managing the risk exposure that is inevitable for all of us. After reading this material, you should be a better informed consumer of property, health care, and life insurance.

The topic of investments is covered in Part Five, and there are plenty of dos and don'ts. You will be exposed to the ins and outs of stocks and bonds, mutual funds, options, commodities, and collectibles as investments. In Chapters 11 through 14, you learn to ask the right questions and develop some historical perspective about what works and what doesn't. You can acquire a reasonable measure of sophistication within a relatively short time.

In Part Six, we complete the life-cycle orientation of the book. Whereas in Part One we talk about setting goals and career considerations, and in the intermediate parts we talk about spending and investing, in the last two chapters, we discuss retirement and estate planning. As you accumulate some measure of wealth, you must have a plan for enjoying it during retirement and passing it on to your heirs.

SUMMARY

The first step in taking control of your financial future is to establish appropriate goals or targets. All too often people act on impulse; they buy a stock on a hot tip or an insurance policy from a friend. Careful long-term planning can insure that even someone with modest resources and earning capability can reach a measure of financial comfort during his or her lifetime. Of course, those with substantial resources may achieve even greater wealth through tax planning and a careful selection of investment alternatives.

In setting goals, you should do a careful self-assessment, involve others in the process, separate out your goals by time, prioritize your goals, and chart your progress toward meeting your objectives.

In doing overall financial planning, you must be sensitive to the changing economic environment, directing a sharp eye to inflation and disinflation and their impact on your investments and standard of living. Other key items are government taxing policy, deregulation, federal deficits, and international developments. Generally the government has been less involved in the affairs of the average citizen in the last decade, and this has placed greater responsibility on the individual for careful financial planning.

The first major step you may have to make in planning for the future is to determine the career route you wish to follow. Although flexibility in choosing a career is desirable, many people take this responsibility too lightly and end up going in many different directions before they find the proper occupation. You can avoid poor initial decisions through better knowledge of yourself and of job markets. You should take maximum advantage of any career counseling facilities your college or university has as well as such sources as the *Occupational Outlook Handbook*, published by the U.S. Department of Labor. You should begin planning well before your senior year.

If you want outside help in the broad spectrum of financial planning (budgeting, insurance, tax planning, retirement planning, and so on), you may employ the services of a professional planner. There is unequal quality in this industry of up to 200,000 participants, so be particularly sensitive to the financial planner's education, credentials, and method of compensation.

KEY TERMS

commission-based compensation
deregulation
entrepreneurs
fee-based compensation
intermediate goals
long-term goals
Occupational Outlook Handbook
personal financial planners
short-term goals
volatile interest rates

SELECTED READINGS

Bureau of Labor Statistics. *Occupational Outlook for College Graduates.* Washington, D.C.: U.S. Government Printing Office, annual edition.

Bureau of Labor Statistics. *Occupational Outlook Handbook.* Washington, D.C.: U.S. Government Printing Office, annual edition.

Business Week's Guide to Careers. Selected issues.

The College Placement Annual. Bethlehem, Pa.: College Placement Council, Inc., annual edition.

"Jobs of the Future." *U.S. News & World Report,* December 23, 1985, pp. 40–44.

"Picking a Planner." *Kiplinger's Changing Times Financial Services Directory,* Washington, D.C., 1986.

"A Special Report: Financial Planning." *Wall Street Journal,* December 2, 1985, Section 4.

QUESTIONS

1 What are the key steps (guidelines) in setting financial goals?

2 Give an example of a short-term, an intermediate, and a long-term goal.

3 Were tangible investments as important in the mid- to late 1980s as they were in the late 1970s? Give the reasoning behind your answer.

4 How important should the current economic environment be in making long-term financial planning decisions?

5 Explain how the tax reform legislation of 1986 and the deregulation of a number of industries have placed greater responsibility on the individual to make his or her own appropriate financial planning decisions.

6 Have interest rates become more or less volatile since 1970? Comment.

7 What would be the consequence of having signed a long-term fixed-rate mortgage in 1980?

8 Explain how foreign imports into the United States have a strong impact on the consumer as well as the work force.

9 Why is it not enough simply to know what you would like to do for a career?

10 What type of information is contained in the *Occupational Outlook Handbook,* published by the U.S. Department of Labor?

11 Using data from Table 1.3, rank order the following occupations based on midcareer earnings levels.

Dental hygienist
Engineer
Registered nurse
Accountant
Attorney
File clerk
Doctor

12 Suggest three *industries* that are expected to experience increases in jobs between now and 1995. Suggest three industries that will experience losses in jobs. What is anticipated to be the fastest-growing *occupation*?

13 How has the ratio of male to female MBAs changed from 1976 to 1986?

14 What are some common characteristics of entrepreneurs?

15 Suggest various elements that a financial planner should be able to integrate into a long-term financial plan.

16 What is the advantage and disadvantage of employing a financial planner on a fee basis?

17 When should you be particularly suspicious of a commission-based financial planner?

2

Developing Budgets and Financial Statements

After studying this chapter, you should:

- Be able to construct a detailed monthly budget
- Understand the major concepts that are part of a personal balance sheet
- Appreciate the importance of the *human* dimension in establishing and following budgets
- Be able to better anticipate personal financial problems before they occur
- Appreciate how alternative life-styles influence budgeting
- Understand the difference in consumption patterns between high- and low-income families
- Appreciate the advantages and limitations of a personal computer in financial planning

Imagine a large corporation without a **budget.** Every time an executive needs to take a business trip he or she merely jumps on a plane and heads to the appropriate destination. The same is true for purchasing raw materials and hiring employees. Everyone acts on his or her own accord. At the end of the year, the profits and losses are determined and the cash balance is computed. If you were a stockholder in the firm or a banker lending money to the company, you would be uncomfortable with such policies. The company could literally be on the threshold of bankruptcy and not even know it. Perhaps a new wing is being added to the plant at the very time the firm cannot meet its financial obligations on its existing facility.

In many respects, an individual or family unit that fails to engage in financial planning faces the same problems and dilemmas. A new car is impulsively purchased off the showroom floor when there is not adequate cash flow to meet current obligations, or a hastily arranged spring vacation may mean there is not sufficient cash to cover the increase in fall tuition. Just as a business firm must anticipate and plan for its financial obligations, so must the individual or family unit. The consequence of no planning or poor planning is misallocation of resources. Often people live like kings or queens for the first 20 days of the month and like paupers for the remainder (for some the period of royalty is considerably shorter).

The principles of financial planning and budgeting are not difficult to understand. Nevertheless, they may be difficult to implement when there is a family unit involved, with multiple personalities interacting in the process. The financial skills and tools are much easier to acquire than the human relations skills. Often in a marriage one spouse is highly disciplined while the other is more carefree. In such cases, an attempt to agree on and then follow a budget can create an explosive situation. For that reason, compromise is essential to the budgetary process. No one personality should dominate the process. Furthermore, too much financial reporting and discipline can be as bad as none at all. If the budget becomes a financial straitjacket, then it has failed to serve its purpose. All participating parties must be comfortable with the budget.

KNOWLEDGE ABOUT YOURSELF

As you begin the budgeting process, it's good to know something about yourself. Do you tend to buy or save and how do you feel about these activities? Do you feel compelled to make certain purchases or are you happy only when saving every possible dollar? Once you have a feel for your own personality, you are in a better position to compensate for your normal tendencies. If you are a hoarder/saver, you may wish to loosen up a little. If you are a free spender, then some degree of frugality may be indicated. The idea is to maximize your mental wealth as well as your financial wealth.

In the rest of the chapter, we examine how one's wealth is measured through a **personal balance sheet** and the actual process for developing and monitoring a budget. We also examine actual data on how families across the country spend their funds, budgetary considerations for alternate life-styles, the potential use of personal computers in budgeting and financial planning, and the use of outside experts.

PERSONAL BALANCE SHEET

Before you actually begin to develop a budget, you must take inventory of your current wealth. For the typical college student, this can be done very quickly. Nevertheless, the purpose of this book is to prepare you for lifelong planning,

Table 2.1
PERSONAL BALANCE SHEET: STEVE AND SUSAN KLINE

Assets	
Financial assets:	
Checking account	$ 400
Savings account	4,000
IRA	2,500
Cash value of life insurance	500
Mutual fund shares	1,700
Total financial assets	$ 9,100
Nonfinancial assets:	
Furniture and appliances	$ 4,000
Automobiles	8,000
Jewelry	1,350
Clothing	1,500
Books	200
Collectibles	1,500
Home	65,000
Business assets	2,500
Other assets	1,200
Total nonfinancial assets	$85,250
Total assets	$94,350
Liabilities and Net Worth	
Short-term liabilities:	
Charge account balances	$ 800
Utility bills	150
Medical bills	200
Total short-term liabilities	$ 1,150
Installment loans:	
Automobile	$ 6,000
Furniture and appliances	2,000
Total installment loans	$ 8,000
Long-term liabilities:	
Home mortgage	$55,000
Total liabilities	$64,150
Net worth	$30,200
Total liabilities and net worth	$94,350

so let's move the calendar out a few years. We will examine a two-person family unit, with the assumption that both parties have been out of college for three years and have begun to accumulate some amount of wealth. Their personal balance sheet is shown in Table 2.1. We'll call the couple Steve and Susan Kline.

Steve is a quality control engineer for an aerospace company. Susan has a degree in interior design and is beginning a small consulting business. In examining their personal balance sheet, you must keep in mind some key factors about a financial statement of this nature.

Current Market Values

First, the values on a personal balance sheet are stated on the basis of current market value. This is very different from a business balance sheet, in which values are generally stated on the basis of original cost (less depreciation[1]). Actually, the personal balance sheet tends to be more meaningful than that of a corporation. The guiding principle behind the business balance sheet is that values must be objectively determined and, therefore, they must be established through actual transactions. This often leads to misleading reporting. For example, a plant that was purchased ten years ago in a booming section of a community would still be recorded on the business balance sheet at its original cost (less depreciation). The reason for the demand for objectivity in business financial reporting is that accountants and financial analysts do not fully trust each other's judgment. Therefore, they want to see an actual recorded transaction before they accept a value on the balance sheet.

For purposes of a personal balance sheet, we are free of the constraint of only showing original cost. However, that presents the added burden of accurately reflecting current market value. In most instances, it's simply a matter of being true and honest with yourself. In other instances, you may be using your financial statements as part of a presentation to a bank, savings and loan, or other financial institution in order to acquire a loan. In such cases, honest assessment is even more important.

Assets

In examining the personal balance sheet of Steve and Susan Kline as presented in Table 2.1, we first of all observe the **assets** section. This represents the items they own. Their ownership interests are broken down into **financial assets** and **nonfinancial assets**. Financial assets include cash, near-cash items, or financial documents that represent a claim to assets. The latter would include such items as stocks, bonds, mutual fund shares, and insurance policies. There generally is no problem in valuing financial assets. Because they are in cash or in a form for which a quotation is readily available, their value is easily determined.

Nonfinancial assets include all the other assets that the Klines own. Nonfinancial assets are sometimes referred to as real assets and consist of tangible

[1] Depreciation is the systematic writing off of the original cost of an asset over the life of the asset for business reporting purposes. An asset that is purchased for $10,000 and has a ten-year life would be written down to $9000 after one year, $8000 after two years, and so forth. This assumes equal or straight-line depreciation. There are also many other forms of depreciation.

items that can be seen (real estate), held (books), worn (jewelry, clothes), and so on. The valuation of nonfinancial assets is a much more difficult task than the valuation of financial assets. Keep in mind that the emphasis is on current market value. An asset (such as furniture) that was purchased a year ago has probably undergone a change in value. Even an asset that is purchased today may have an immediate change in value. The minute you drive a new car off the lot it declines in value by 10 to 20 percent (unless there is a shortage of the model). Of course, not all assets decline in value with the passage of time. Some assets, such as a home, jewelry, and collectibles (for example, silver and stamps) may actually appreciate over time. In the case of the Klines' balance sheet, we shall assume that the home listed at $65,000 was purchased 18 months ago at $59,000 and has appreciated by $6000. We shall also assume that the jewelry and collectibles have enjoyed modest appreciation.

While we have had mild inflation of 3 to 4 percent in the mid- to late 1980s, some assets that were purchased 20 years ago have greatly increased in value. Allowing for a 6 percent annual increase in price, a house that was purchased 20 years ago for $40,000 now has a value of $128,280. At a continued 6 percent rate of increase in the future, it would have a value of $411,390 in 20 years.

In the appraisal of assets, clothing usually has the largest decline from the original purchase price. Second-hand clothing is generally worth one-third to one-fourth of the original purchase price.

Most people who set up a personal balance sheet are able to reasonably determine their own values for nonfinancial assets. You can, for instance, get automobile values from advertisements in the paper and housing values from comparable property in the neighborhood that has been sold. Of course, in some cases you may have to call in an appraiser to measure value. If you own a unique piece of jewelry or art, an outside appraiser may be the only feasible source for valuation. As is true of all forms of financial planning, you must weigh the benefits against the costs. It is hardly appropriate to spend $75 to appraise a $150 item.

One question to be considered is whether you should include the **transactions cost** of selling an asset when you record the value. For example, the Klines' home is listed at $65,000, but if they were to sell it, they might well have to pay a commission as part of the transaction. If the commission were 6 percent, $3900 would go to a real estate agent and the Klines would only net $61,100. Generally such costs are *not* subtracted out in showing value. Nevertheless, you should remain sensitive to such factors in viewing a balance sheet. A house that is listed for $65,000 is not the equivalent of $65,000 in cash dollars.

In assessing the Klines' overall asset position, we see that it is heavily weighted toward nonfinancial assets. Of the $94,350 in assets, $85,250 are nonfinancial. This amount represents 90.4 percent of their holdings. This is not unusual for a young couple who own their home. However, at different stages in their life cycle, this ratio can be expected to change. As they build up substantial retirement funds in the formative years of their earning power, their financial assets can be expected to increase in importance. Actually the key issue is not so much the mix between financial and nonfinancial assets as it is the relationship between financial assets and short-term liabilities. In this regard, the Klines are in good shape. Financial assets of $9100 greatly exceed short-term liabilities ($1150).

Liabilities and Net Worth

Now that we have established the fact that the Klines have $94,350 in assets, the next important question is, who provided the financing for these assets? The financing of an asset can take two different forms:

1 **Liability**—the financing is provided by a creditor or supplier. This is a form of debt or credit extension.
2 **Net worth**—the financing is provided by the owners. This may be in the form of personal salary or profits used to finance assets. There is also an increase in net worth when assets appreciate in value.

Assets on the balance sheet are always equal to the liabilities plus the net worth:

$$\text{Assets} = \text{liabilities} + \text{net worth} \tag{2.1}$$

In the case of the Klines, we show

$$\$94{,}350 = \$64{,}150 + \$30{,}200$$

We could also transfer our terms to indicate

$$\begin{aligned} \text{Net worth} &= \text{assets} - \text{liabilities} \\ \$30{,}200 &= \$94{,}350 - \$64{,}150 \end{aligned} \tag{2.2}$$

The objective in personal financial management is not to maximize your assets, but to maximize your net worth. For example, assume that through some unusual set of circumstances, the Klines were able to borrow a million dollars to acquire a shopping center. They would now have over a million dollars in assets. Are they millionaires? Hardly. Their net worth has not changed by one cent. Using Equation 2.2, we show

$$\begin{aligned} \text{Net worth} &= \$1{,}094{,}350 - \$1{,}064{,}150 \\ &= \$30{,}200 \end{aligned}$$

The lesson is not to judge people's wealth by the assets they own, but by how they are financed. A person driving a $35,000 Mercedes financed by a $28,000 bank loan has less wealth than a person driving a $10,000 Chevrolet with a clear title.

In examining the Klines' liabilities, we see that they currently have $64,150 in debts. However, only $1150 are short-term in nature and these are well covered by the Klines' financial assets. The rest of their liabilities are longer-term in nature and directly related to the purchase of assets. If they continue to maintain their earning power, there should be no major problems. Of course, if there were the loss of a job, or a major drain on cash balances, that would be quite another matter.

Their net worth of $30,200 indicates that they are beginning to build up a modest nest egg. Earlier we stipulated that net worth is increased by building up assets through ownership funds rather than debt. Over the long term, appreciation in asset values may also provide an important increase in net worth. You may recall the earlier example of the home that increases from $40,000 to $411,390 over 40 years as a result of 6 percent inflation. We might also assume that the debt (or mortgage) on the home went from $30,000 to zero over the same time period. Even if the owners of this home had not saved another penny, they would have enjoyed a $401,390 increase in net worth.

	Assets –	Liabilities =	Net Worth
Final net worth	$411,390 –	0	$411,390
Initial net worth	$ 40,000 –	30,000	10,000
Increase in net worth			$401,390

DEVELOPING THE BUDGET

Now that the Klines have constructed their personal balance sheet and determined their net worth, they can move on to the budget. They should keep foremost in mind the process of developing financial objectives discussed in Chapter 1. They must relate their planned expenditures to such goals as maximizing net worth, providing adequate liquidity to meet unexpected events, setting aside adequate savings to meet long-term retirement needs, and providing adequate financial protection in the event of death. Many of these considerations will be factored into the analysis as we work through the process of budget construction.

The normal **planning horizon** for a budget is one year. The following steps are taken:

1. Determine income on a monthly basis
2. Determine total expenses on a monthly basis
3. Determine how cash shortfalls or excess funds will be managed

Determination of Income

Let's assume that Steve Kline has an annual salary of $28,000. This translates to $2333 per month, but his take-home pay, after deductions for Social Security, federal income taxes, and a number of other minor items, is $1860. He also anticipates a $500 bonus in December. Susan is in the process of starting an interior decorating business on a part-time basis. As is true of most new ventures, there will be a deficit in the first few months of operation. When a business first begins, there is generally not enough revenue to cover advertising, telephone

Table 2.2 PROJECTED MONTHLY INCOME: STEVE AND SUSAN KLINE

	Jan.	Feb.	Mar.	Apr.	May
Salary (take-home pay)	$1,860	$1,860	$1,860	$1,860	$1,860
Bonus					
Susan's profit or loss	(400)	(400)	(350)	(250)	(150)
Total	$1,460	$1,460	$1,510	$1,610	$1,710

and utility expenditures, rent, and many other miscellaneous items. We'll assume that Susan's business venture will show a deficit for the first six months and begin earning a profit in the last six months of the year. Since Susan is also taking some graduate courses on a part-time basis, the business venture will keep her quite busy. The Klines' projected monthly income pattern for the full year is presented in Table 2.2.

Determination of Expenditures

Before their expenditure pattern can be fully developed, the Klines must review their goals and objectives. We shall assume that they wish to give primary attention to maintaining adequate cash reserves to meet unforeseen contingencies as well as set aside funds to meet long-term retirement objectives. Also, they want to begin expanding their family in two years and hope that Susan's business will be going well enough by then to allow her to bring in a partner who can help out while Susan is altering her life-style. Furthermore, they want to include some recreation in their activities and intend to take a one-week trip during the year.

While in the process of developing numbers to cover their normal operating expenses as well as set aside funds toward their goals, the Klines are well advised to look at national income data on average family expenditures. Although they will not follow these values in any rigorous sense, the numbers provide an interesting background for all financial planners. Available data are presented in Table 2.3. The government information is shown for a family of four and is broken down between three different income levels. The low level represents an equivalent 1986 income level of $18,725, the intermediate level is $31,047, and the high level is $46,509.[2] Notice that for the low-income family, food and medical care expenditures make up a combined total of 39.1 percent of the budget. The same expenditures account for only 23.3 percent of the high-income family

[2] These values were arrived at by taking Bureau of Labor Statistics information for 1981 (the last year it was compiled for family budgets) and adjusting it forward by the annual rate of inflation. This is a common practice when the government fails to update its own information.

June	July	Aug.	Sept.	Oct.	Nov.	Dec.	Total
$1,860	$1,860	$1,860	$1,860	$1,860	$1,860	$1,860	$22,320
						500	500
(100)	150	200	400	500	600	650	850
$1,760	$2,010	$2,060	$2,260	$2,360	$2,460	$3,010	$23,670

budget. If we were observing a really high-income family (over $100,000), these expenditures would normally account for less than 10 percent of their budget. We also see in Table 2.3 that the high-income family spends somewhat more percentagewise on housing and considerably more on personal income taxes. The latter is due to the nature of the tax structure in the United States (the more you make, the higher your tax bracket). If travel and entertainment were shown in the table, we could also observe that the percentage expenditure for these items expands rapidly as income increases. Also, high-income families are more likely to save and invest a portion of their income. This is not so much a matter of strategy or timing, as it is an economic fact of life. Poor families are often forced into dissaving (spending more than they take in) because the costs of necessities exceed their annual cash inflow.

Table 2.3 **ANNUAL BUDGET FOR FOUR PERSON FAMILY AT DIFFERENT LEVELS OF LIVING (PERCENTAGE BREAKDOWN)**

	Low	Intermediate	High
Food	29.7	23.0	19.3
Housing	18.4	21.8	22.1
Transportation	8.6	9.3	8.1
Clothing	6.1	5.2	5.1
Personal care	2.5	2.0	1.8
Medical care	9.4	5.7	4.0
Other family expenditures	4.1	4.8	5.3
Other items	4.0	4.0	4.6
Social Security and disability	6.8	6.7	5.2
Personal income taxes	10.4	17.5	24.5
Total budget	100.0	100.0	100.0

SOURCE: Percentage values computed from "Family Budgets," *Monthly Labor Review*, February 1982, p. 44.

Cost-of-living considerations vary not only by income level, but by different geographical areas of the country. We see in Table 2.4 the differences in **cost-of-living indexes** between various metropolitan areas.

The average cost of living for U.S. urban areas is 100. Thus, we would say that Dallas is 11 percent below the average and Anchorage is 26 percent above. These values tend to be strongly influenced by the cost of housing accommodations, particularly the cost of renting. If you were comparing two job offers, one in Atlanta and one in New York City, you would need to make approximately 26 percent more in New York City just to come out even.

$$\frac{\text{Cost of living—New York City}}{\text{Cost of living—Atlanta}} = \frac{116}{92} = 1.26$$

Thus a \$20,000 job offer in Atlanta is roughly comparable to a \$25,200 job offer in New York City (\$20,000 × 1.26). An executive making \$90,000 a year in Atlanta might require \$113,400 to maintain his or her standard of living in New York City (\$90,000 × 1.26). If the move were from Dallas to Honolulu, the \$90,000-a-year executive would need to ask for \$127,800.

$$\frac{\text{Cost of living—Honolulu}}{\text{Cost of living—Dallas}} = \frac{126}{89} = 1.42$$

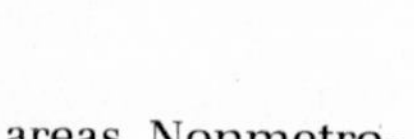

$$\$90{,}000 \times 1.42 = \$127{,}800$$

Note that the data in Table 2.4 only apply to metropolitan areas. Nonmetropolitan areas generally have about a 10 percent lower cost of living. Thus Spring-

Table 2.4 RELATIVE COST-OF-LIVING INDEXES FOR SELECTED U.S. CITIES

City	Index	City	Index
Dallas, Texas	89	Cincinnati, Ohio	100
Atlanta, Georgia	92	Cleveland, Ohio	101
Houston, Texas	93	Minneapolis–St. Paul	102
St. Louis, Missouri	96	Seattle–Everett	102
Kansas City, Missouri	96	Buffalo, New York	104
Pittsburgh, Pennsylvania	97	Philadelphia, Pennsylvania	103
Denver, Colorado	98	Milwaukee, Wisconsin	106
Los Angeles–Long Beach	98	San Francisco, California	107
San Diego, California	98	Washington, D.C.	108
Detroit, Michigan	99	Boston, Massachusetts	113
Baltimore, Maryland	99	New York, New York	116
U.S. urban	100	Honolulu, Hawaii	126
Chicago, Illinois	100	Anchorage, Alaska	126

field, Illinois; Waco, Texas; Ardmore, Oklahoma; and other similar communities can be expected to be well below the national average. For truly rural areas, the cost of living is even lower.

Also, we observe the effect of inflation on the cost of various items from 1967 through 1986 in Table 2.5.

Observe that in the 19-year period, the cost of "all items" (the first category) has gone up by over 200 percent from the base value of 100. Though not specifically shown in the table, the annual percentage increase is slightly over 6 percent. This rate of inflation is heavily influenced by the rapid price increases in the late 1970s and early 1980s (observe the values for the "all items" category of 11.5 percent in 1979, 13.5 percent in 1980, and 10.2 percent in 1981). Since 1983, however, inflation has moderated substantially. While no one can accurately predict the future, if inflation is at 3 percent, 20 years from now a $10,000 car will cost $18,060, at 6 percent inflation it will cost $32,070, and with 10 percent inflation it will cost $67,270. The effect of inflation is indeed important.

Also note in Table 2.5 that the cost of medical care has far outstripped all other major categories. It is up to 433.5 (a gain of over 300 percent from its base value of 100 in 1967). Housing costs have also grown rapidly, while "apparel and upkeep" is the slowest growth category. In the latter case, foreign competition has had a moderating effect on price increases. Though not shown in the table, the cost of a college education has roughly tracked the "all items" category. The cost of a four-year college education at a state university is now about $25,000, but it will increase to $45,150 in 20 years at 3 percent inflation, to $80,175 at 6 percent inflation, and to $168,175 at 10 percent inflation. You can roughly double these figures for the cost of a private university education.

The Klines' Expenses

Having observed various sources of economic data, let's return to the analysis of the Klines' monthly spending pattern. The Klines have been out of school and married for three years. They can partially rely on prior data to construct their budget for the coming year. Based on their past experiences, their knowledge of typical family spending patterns, and their goals and plans for the future, they have developed the anticipated monthly expenditure plan shown in Table 2.6.

The expenditure part of the budget is broken down into three categories. The first category includes fixed items that cannot be eliminated from the budget such as mortgage payments and utilities. The second category includes flexible, discretionary items such as charitable contributions and recreation, and the third category is composed of retirement income contributions.

We are now ready to merge the projected monthly income in Table 2.2 with the projected monthly expenditures in Table 2.6. The output is shown in Table 2.7.

Table 2.5 CONSUMER PRICE INDEX FOR 1967–1985

YEAR	ALL ITEMS		FOOD AND BEVERAGES		HOUSING		APPAREL AND UPKEEP		TRANSPORTATION		MEDICAL CARE		ENTERTAINMENT		OTHER GOODS AND SERVICES	
	Index	Percent change	Index	Percent change	Index	Percent change	Index	Percent change	Index	Percent change	Index	Percent change	Index	Percent change	Index	Percent change
1967	100.0	—	100.0	—	100.0	—	100.0	—	100.0	—	100.0	—	100.0	—	100.0	—
1968	104.2	4.2	103.6	3.6	104.0	4.0	105.4	5.4	103.2	3.2	106.1	6.1	105.7	5.7	105.2	5.2
1969	109.8	5.4	108.8	5.0	110.4	6.2	111.5	5.8	107.2	3.9	113.4	6.9	110.0	5.0	110.4	4.9
1970	116.3	5.9	114.7	5.4	118.2	7.1	116.1	4.1	112.7	5.1	120.6	6.3	116.7	5.1	115.8	5.8
1971	121.3	4.3	118.3	3.1	123.4	4.4	119.8	3.3	118.6	5.2	128.4	6.5	122.9	5.3	122.4	4.8
1972	125.3	3.3	123.2	4.1	128.1	3.8	122.3	2.1	119.9	1.1	132.5	3.2	126.5	2.9	127.5	4.2
1973	133.1	6.2	139.5	13.2	133.7	4.4	126.8	3.7	123.8	3.3	137.7	3.9	130.0	2.8	132.5	3.9
1974	147.7	11.0	158.7	13.8	148.8	11.3	136.2	7.4	137.7	11.2	150.5	9.3	139.8	7.5	142.0	7.2
1975	161.2	9.1	172.1	8.4	164.5	10.6	142.3	4.5	150.6	9.4	168.6	12.0	152.2	8.9	153.9	8.4
1976	170.5	5.8	177.4	3.1	174.6	6.1	147.6	3.7	165.5	9.9	184.7	9.5	159.8	5.0	162.7	5.7
1977	181.5	6.5	188.0	8.0	186.5	6.8	154.2	4.5	177.2	7.1	202.4	9.6	167.7	4.9	172.2	5.8
1978	195.3	7.6	206.2	9.7	202.6	8.6	159.5	3.4	185.8	4.9	219.4	8.4	176.2	5.1	183.2	6.4
1979	217.7	11.5	228.7	10.9	227.5	12.3	166.4	4.3	212.8	14.5	240.1	9.4	187.6	6.5	196.3	7.2
1980	247.0	13.5	248.7	8.7	263.2	15.7	177.4	6.6	250.5	17.7	267.2	11.3	203.7	8.5	213.6	8.8
1981	272.3	10.2	267.8	7.7	293.2	11.4	186.6	5.2	281.3	12.3	295.1	10.4	219.0	7.5	233.3	9.2
1982	288.6	6.0	278.5	4.0	314.7	7.3	190.9	2.3	293.1	4.2	326.9	10.8	232.4	6.1	257.0	10.2
1983	297.4	3.0	284.7	2.2	322.0	2.3	195.6	2.5	300.0	2.4	355.1	8.6	242.4	4.3	286.3	11.4
1984	307.6	3.4	295.2	3.7	329.2	2.2	199.1	1.8	313.9	4.6	377.7	6.4	251.2	3.6	304.9	6.5
1985	322.2	4.7	301.8	2.2	343.3	4.3	205.0	3.0	319.9	1.9	401.2	6.2	260.1	3.5	322.7	5.8
1986	328.4	1.6	311.8	3.3	360.2	4.9	207.8	1.4	307.5	−3.7	433.5	8.1	274.1	5.4	346.4	7.3

SOURCE: "Current Business Statistics: Consumer Prices," *Monthly Labor Review*, February 1987, p. 75.

Table 2.6 PROJECTED MONTHLY EXPENDITURES: STEVE AND SUSAN KLINE

	Jan.	Feb.	Mar.	Apr.	May	June	July	Aug.	Sept.	Oct.	Nov.	Dec.	Total
Fixed	$ 525	$ 525	$ 525	$ 525	$ 525	$ 525	$ 525	$ 525	$ 525	$ 525	$ 525	$ 525	$ 6,300
Home mortgage	170	170	170	170	170	170	170	170	170	170	170	170	2,040
Utilities	270	270	270	270	270	270	270	270	270	270	270	270	3,240
Groceries	30	30	30	30	30	30	30	30	30	30	30	30	360
Medical care	80	80	80	80	80	80	80	80	80	80	80	80	960
Clothing	100	100	100	100	100	100	100	100	100	100	100	100	1,200
Gas & auto upkeep	205	205	205	205	205	205	205	205	205	205	205	205	2,460
Payments on auto loans													
Payments on other	70	70	70	70	70	70	70	70	70	70	70	70	840
installment loans	35	35	35	35	35	35	35	35	35	35	35	35	420
Life insurance	350	0	0	0	0	0	0	0	350	0	0	0	700
Tuition and books	70	70	60	60	60	60	60	60	60	60	65	65	750
Total	$1,905	$1,555	$1,545	$1,545	$1,545	$1,545	$1,545	$1,545	$1,895	$1,545	$1,550	$1,550	$19,270
Flexible													
Charitable contributions	$ 50	$ 50	$ 50	$ 50	$ 50	$ 50	$ 50	$ 50	$ 50	$ 50	$ 50	$ 50	$ 600
Recreation[a]	100	100	100	100	100	100	100	100	100	100	100	100	1,200
Summer vacation	0	0	0	0	0	1,000	0	0	0	0	0	0	1,000
Other													
Provision for retirement	0	0	0	1,000	0	0	0	0	0	0	0	0	1,000
Total	$2,055	$1,705	$1,695	$2,695	$1,695	$2,695	$1,695	$1,695	$2,045	$1,695	$1,700	$1,700	$23,070

[a] Dining out, weekend trips, tennis club, etc.

Table 2.7 PROJECTED TOTAL BUDGET: STEVE AND SUSAN KLINE

	Jan.	Feb.	Mar.	Apr.	May	June	July	Aug.	Sept.	Oct.	Nov.	Dec.	Total
Total monthly income (Table 2.2)	$1,460	$1,460	$ 1,510	$ 1,610	$ 1,710	$ 1,760	$ 2,010	$ 2,060	$ 2,260	$ 2,360	$2,460	$3,010	$23,670
Total monthly expenditures (Table 2.6)	$2,055	$1,705	$ 1,695	$ 2,695	$ 1,695	$ 2,695	$ 1,695	$ 1,695	$ 2,045	$ 1,695	$1,700	$1,700	$23,070
Surplus or deficit	$ (595)	$ (245)	$ (185)	$(1,085)	$ 15	$ (935)	$ 315	$ 365	$ 215	$ 665	$ 760	$1,310	
Cumulative surplus or deficit	$ (595)	$ (840)	$(1,025)	$(2,110)	$(2,095)	$(3,030)	$(2,715)	$(2,350)	$(2,135)	$(1,470)	$ (710)	$ 600	$ 600

Surplus or Deficit

In Table 2.7, we see both the monthly surplus or monthly deficit and the **cumulative surplus** or **cumulative deficit.** For example, there is a deficit of $595 in January followed by a deficit of $245 in February, bringing the cumulative two-month deficit up to $840. The cumulative deficit grows to a maximum value of $3030 in June and then declines each month until December, when it actually becomes a surplus of $600. The main variable contributing to the deficits in the first part of the year are the losses in Susan's business. Reviewing Table 2.2, you can see that these losses run from $400 down to $100 during the first part of the year. As her business turns profitable in the second half of the year, however, the profits contribute to a surplus cash position each month from July through December, as can be seen in Table 2.7. As previously indicated, a $600 cumulative surplus is achieved in December.

The first question we must ask is, can the Klines really afford the cumulative deficit of $3030 in the first six months of the year? We must return to their personal balance sheet in Table 2.1. Since they had $400 in their checking account and $4000 in their savings account at the first of the year, it appears that they have enough of a cash cushion to absorb the losses. One of the advantages of a budget is to help see the problem areas before they arise. The Klines have identified their cash shortfall problems and, in all likelihood, can manage them. They still may want, however, to return to the projected monthly expenditures in Table 2.6 and search for additional ways to reduce their cash outflows in the first part of the year.

The fixed items do not offer much opportunity for revision or reduction, so we can look at the flexible expenditures. Note, for example, that there is $1000 allocated for a vacation in June. If the vacation is deferred until later in the year, the cumulative deficit can be reduced by $1000 in June and it will peak out at $2030 rather than $3030. Even if the Klines decide to take their vacation in June they may choose to spend less than $1000 on it. Along these same lines, it may be appropriate to reduce the recreational expenditures to half the currently designated amount of $100 per month for the first six months of the year. This reduction would provide another $300 in funds (6 × $50). Furthermore, all charitable contributions might be made in the second half of the year. The full annual amount of $600 would still be given, but the contributions would begin in July. This would postpone $300 in contributions for the first six months. The provision for the retirement payment in April is assumed to be to an individual retirement account (IRA) and cannot be deferred past April for tax purposes. In any event, it is not a likely candidate for change. The other suggested changes would reduce the anticipated deficit for June by $1600.

Postpone vacation	$1000
Reduce recreation	300
Defer charitable contributions	300
Reduction to cumulative deficit in the first six months	$1600

If these steps are taken, the cumulative deficit in June will be reduced to $1430.

Original cumulative deficit—June	$3030
Reduction in deficit for first six months	1600
Revised cumulative deficit—June	$1430

With the Klines showing a beginning cash balance of $4400 in checking and savings, a $1430 reduction in funds during the first six months would leave them with a cash cushion of approximately $3000. Furthermore, by the end of the year they will have a surplus of $600, so their total cash balance will be up to $5000.

Original checking account balance (Table 2.1)	$ 400
Original savings account balance (Table 2.1)	4000
Cumulative surplus in funds (Table 2.7)[3]	600
Year-end funds	$5000

The $5000 should provide ample reserves to meet rainy-day contingencies in the future.

As we saw earlier, it was Susan's new business venture that put the strain on funds at the first of the year. It is that same business venture, however, that offers the Klines a real opportunity for financial gain in the future. By December, the business is projected to be generating $650 a month in profit, and that figure may well increase in the future. This may allow the Klines to build up their contingency funds and a retirement nest egg. Furthermore, the Klines anticipate that the part-time business venture can be continued even as they begin to raise a family.

Of course, in a worst-case scenario the business venture may never get off the ground. In that event, the Klines would probably cut their losses by discontinuing the operation after the first six months. They appear to have the financial flexibility to take the risk. They further realize there is more uncertainty associated with a business venture than with a fixed salary. Nevertheless, this uncertainty can be reflected in upside potential as well as downside losses.

ESTABLISHING BUDGETARY CONTROLS

Once the budget is established, the next step is to set up adequate measurement and **budgetary control devices** to determine if budget targets are being met. A monthly worksheet is presented in Table 2.8.

Large **variances from the budget** should be noted and corrective measures taken where appropriate. For example, the Klines have $100 budgeted for monthly gas and auto upkeep (Table 2.6). If the actual expenditure is $125, the

[3] The surplus would be $300 larger if there were a $300 permanent reduction in recreational expenses. This would bring year-end funds up to $5300.

Table 2.8 BUDGET CONTROL WORKSHEET

Category	Planned amount	Actual amount	Variance
Income			
Salary	______	______	______
Bonus	______	______	______
Profit or loss	______	______	______
Other	______	______	______
Expenditures			
Home mortgage	______	______	______
Utilities	______	______	______
Groceries	______	______	______
Medical care			
Clothing	______	______	______
Gas and auto upkeep	______	______	______
Payments on other installment loans	______	______	______
Life insurance	______	______	______
Tuition and books	______	______	______
Other expenditures	______	______	______
Charitable contributions	______	______	______
Recreation	______	______	______
Summer vacation	______	______	______

Klines must determine if the variance is caused by an increase in gasoline prices, an auto repair, or simply use of the automobiles beyond the normal amount. A word of caution is necessary when implementing a control system. Nothing can destroy a family's budgetary process faster than excessive or overbearing control procedures. The family members must respect each other's needs, and some degree of variance from the plan must be accepted as the family unit moves from a textbook exercise to actually living through a budget. As we suggested at the beginning of the chapter, the human relations skills are more important than the financial skills in developing and implementing a budget.

Maintaining Records

A key element in any budget is the maintenance of adequate records. Actually, certain documents should be retained not only for budgetary considerations, but for tax purposes, for safety and security reasons, and for establishing your rights as a consumer. Important documents include the following:

1. Canceled checks
2. Monthly bank statements

3. Regular paychecks and annual W-2 forms
4. Sales slips for credit or major cash purchases
5. All tax deductible items whether paid for by check, credit, or cash
6. Annual information on interest paid to you by a financial institution (form 1099-INT)
7. Prior-year tax returns (for at least three years)
8. All credit card numbers (in the event of loss so that immediate notification of the credit card company can take place)
9. Information on valuables—description and appraisals
10. Warranties, contracts, and service policies
11. Automobile and home titles (the original may be in the hands of the lender, but you should have a copy)
12. Rental or lease agreements
13. Investment records for stocks, bonds, mutual funds, and so forth
14. Loan agreements
15. Insurance policies
16. Wills
17. Birth certificates

Although not all of these items may apply to you, for those that do, you must maintain adequate documentation. You forfeit a large part of your rights when you cannot document a claim.

It is also essential that you maintain your records in an orderly fashion. The best procedure is probably to combine a filing cabinet system in your home with a lockbox at the bank. Everyday records should be placed in labeled manila folders in a filing system at home. Items that are difficult to replace, such as birth certificates or stock certificates, should be kept in a lockbox at the bank.

Generally, you should not keep a will in a lockbox because it may be difficult for your survivors to gain access to the document upon your death. Of course, if you have more than one copy, you can keep one at home and one in the bank lockbox (but be sure to destroy outdated wills so there will be no confusion).

Whatever your system is, you should tell others who are involved with you about it. It does you little good to have an elaborate filing system or lockbox if no one knows where the records are. For married couples, each spouse should have a key to the family lockbox.

THE BUDGETARY PROCESS AND ALTERNATIVE LIFE-STYLES

Although most of the discussion has been directed to a typical young married couple, the same basic principles of financial planning apply to a single person, a divorcée with a family, and so on. The same procedure of establishing a workable plan and then tracking progress against that plan still applies. The working single adult probably has the easiest situation. He or she is likely to have ample funds to meet everyday expenses and does not have to work with a second party. The working single parent is likely to have the most difficult time.

Although the potential for two-party disagreements is not present, an acute shortage of funds can be an even greater problem. The problem is further compounded when court-ordered obligations by an ex-spouse are not met. It is particularly important that a single parent maintain adequate budgetary procedures because the issue may no longer be whether a summer vacation is taken, but whether the rent is paid. The establishment of spending priorities is no longer an optional exercise; it is now a necessity.

College students are also prime candidates for putting a budget together and establishing control procedures. The income and expense items are likely to be quite different from those of Steve and Susan Kline, but the same principle of anticipating needs remains important. Typical items that can impact a college student's life are shown in Table 2.9. After you complete the chapter, you may wish to review the table for items that apply to you. The budget can be developed for a number of months. There also is a case problem devoted to the college student at the end of the chapter. Furthermore, the single-parent and two-wage-earner family unit are given consideration in problem material.

SMART SPENDING

Whatever your current life-style, you will wish to spend your funds in as prudent a fashion as possible. One important consideration is the timing of your purchases. Actually, there are optimum months in the year for purchases. Table 2.10 presents a suggested list of the best months to purchase certain items in order to minimize costs. You may or may not agree.

The primary emphasis in Table 2.10 is to buy items at the end of the season or in the off-season. Of course, there is a certain loss of psychic pleasure in buying items that will not be worn or used until next year. Nevertheless, with careful planning, you can get much more mileage out of your money. Clearly, the suggestions in Table 2.10 are not for everyone. If you aspire to have the latest wardrobe, you may get caught in an out-of-style item. But opportunities to buy at a 50–60 percent discount should generally not be overlooked.

COMPUTER SUPPORT FOR FINANCIAL PLANS

The personal computer can be of great help to you in the budgetary process. Instead of keeping handwritten records, you can convert your data to a flexible computer disk. With the use of the proper software, your computer can perform all the necessary calculations in a matter of seconds. You can also ask it "what if" questions such as, "What will happen to my cumulative surplus or deficit if utility expenses go up by 10 percent or tuition payments increase in September by $200?" Generally a computer can answer such questions almost instantaneously and provide an immediate printout of a new budget. Computers are also quite effective in allowing you to do longer-range planning because of the ease of data storage and calculations.

Table 2.9 POTENTIAL ITEMS IN A COLLEGE STUDENT'S BUDGET

Category	Planned amount	Actual amount	Variance
Income			
Revenue from part-time job			
Funds from parents			
Scholarship, grants, financial aid			
Interest on savings			
Drawdown on savings			
Sale of textbooks			
Tax refund			
Total income			
Personal expenses			
Dormitory room or apartment			
Clothes			
Food			
Medical and dental expenses			
Recreation and dating			
Auto or transportation expenses			
Telephone			
Other utility expenses			
Bank charges			
Alcohol or cigarettes			
Vacation			
Other personal expenses			
Total personal expenses			
College-related expenses			
Tuition			
Fees			
Books			
Supplies			
Sorority or fraternity dues			
Other college-related expenses			
Total college-related expenses			
Total expenses			
Total deficit or surplus			

Table 2.10 BEST TIME OF YEAR FOR SELECTED PURCHASES

Months	Purchases
Late December to early January	Next year's Christmas presents and Christmas cards; personal computer
January, February	Winter clothing (be cautious about style changes for next year)
March	Jewelry
April	Vacation
July, August	Summer clothing
August	New automobile
October	Vacation
November	Furniture and appliances
December	New home

Of course, computers are not necessarily appropriate for everyone. Unless there is a fairly large volume of data, the start-up cost and time may be difficult to justify. Some major considerations related to personal computer purchases are presented in Appendix 7A.

Computer Information

There are some excellent computer software packages for budgeting and personal finance planning. *PC World,* a popular computer magazine, selected *Managing Your Money* as the best personal financial software for 1985. It costs about $200, and it is produced by Micro Education Corporation of America (285 Riverside Ave., Westport, Connecticut 06880). Well over 50,000 copies have been sold. The software package is very user friendly. Instead of sending users to printed pages for answers to questions in using the program, *Managing Your Money* provides electronic pages near the program sections they describe. The software has a budget and check module, a tax estimator, an insurance planner, a financial calculator, a portfolio manager, and a personal balance sheet.

Another suggested software package is titled *Smart Money™: The Comprehensive Financial Manager.* It is available in IBM and Apple versions from Sierra On-Line, Inc. (Coarsegold, California 93614), and costs about $80. The package is unusually complete, and is designed with text or picture menus that eliminate the need to memorize commands. It can track assets and liabilities in as many as 200 accounts, record expenditures, construct and track monthly budgets, balance bank statements, calculate declining balances, project future balances, perform investment analyses, and (for those computers with printing capabilities) print out reports, amortized schedules, graphs, and even customized checks.

Detailed reviews of many more personal finance software packages can also be found in the *Book of IBM Software* (approximately $20) and the *Book of*

Box 2.1 *CONSUMER REPORTS* LOOKS AT A FINANCIAL PLAN

"Chances are the expert help for your changing life is right at Sears," trumpets a Sears TV commercial. If there was expert help at Sears, we couldn't find it.

Dean Witter, a major brokerage house, is part of the Sears Financial Network. "We do financial plans, but my personal opinion is that they could cost you a lot of money and might not be the best choice," said a Dean Witter account executive in a Sears store in Hicksville, N.Y. "We are test-marketing something but it doesn't mean the plan is working yet. I don't think it should be sold. You have to pay for the financial plan and the investments, so why do both?" she asked.

Nevertheless, she sent a questionnaire, which our reporter filled out. Later the account executive called to say she doubted that our reporter could buy a financial plan from Dean Witter, but she'd send the questionnaire to the firm's planning center in California anyway. The center indeed said that a financial plan was not appropriate for our couple. Instead a financial consultant sent 14 recommendations to help our couple accomplish its goals.

The recommendations were a scatter-shot approach to investing. They did not consider our couple's risk tolerance—which was understandable since the questionnaire didn't ask about it. Nor did the recommendations try to reallocate our couple's portfolio.

SOURCE: "Looking for Mr. Goodplan." from *Consumer Reports,* January 1986, p. 42.

Apple Software (approximately $25). Both are published by Arrays, Inc. (11223 S. Hindry Ave., Los Angeles, California 90045).[4]

FINANCIAL PLANS DEVELOPED BY FINANCIAL SERVICE FIRMS

Almost certainly, at some point in your life you will be asked to fill out a financial planning form for a stockbroker, an insurance company, or some other firm offering financial services. The plans run the gamut from the simple to the highly sophisticated. Some are free to customers, whereas others are fee-based. Among the better-known plans are

IDS/American Express Personal Financial Analysis
E. F. Hutton Money Allocation Program
Merrill Lynch Financial Pathfinder
Prudential-Bache Securities Total Financial Planning Overview
Sears/Dean Witter Reynolds Personal Financial Planner
The Banker's Life Company of Iowa Financial Profiles Analysis
Chemical Bank Personal Financial Plan

As you may recall from Chapter 1, as many as 200,000 people are engaged in providing financial planning services. If you decide to seek professional assistance in setting goals, establishing a budget, defining long-term retirement objectives, and so on, you should generally turn to a financial planner who is properly certified. Examples of certifying organizations include the **Institute of Certified Financial Planners** (ICFP), the **International Association for Financial Planning** (IAFP), the **Institute of Chartered Financial Analysts** (ICFA), and the **American College** (Chartered Financial Consultant). As indicated in Chapter 1, the services to be provided should be clearly delineated and fees or commissions should be established at the outset. There are far more people providing financial advice than you could ever hope to utilize or pay for, so ask for credentials and choose carefully if you decide to choose at all.

SUMMARY

An individual or family unit faces many of the same problems as a business in allocating scarce financial resources. Therefore, budgeting and financial planning are important. Without adequate control devices, funds are often arbitrarily spent for less important items, and then important purchases cannot be made.

The people participating in the budgetary process must know their own strengths and weaknesses. Some people have a tendency toward free spending,

[4] For an excellent article on this topic, see "Computerline: Financial Planning Programs for Investors," *Personal Investor,* January 1986, pp. 102–103.

whereas others are hoarders. Furthermore, human relations skills in working with others are essential, as is the ability to compromise. If one party attempts to dominate the process, it will not work.

You must first assess your personal wealth. The personal balance sheet forces you to determine what you own and how your assets are being financed. Total assets minus total liabilities equals net worth. Personal assets should always be measured on the basis of current market value, not original cost. Assets such as housing and collectibles often increase in value beyond their original purchase price, whereas automobiles and clothing normally decline. You can increase your net worth just as easily through appreciation in asset values as through earnings or interest.

Once your personal balance sheet is drawn up, you are in a position to begin the budgetary process. The budget must relate to the financial and personal objectives you have set for yourself and your family unit (if you are married). Your budget should show monthly income and monthly expenses, broken down into items that are fixed and items that are flexible. You should determine the deficit or surplus for each month and track the cumulative deficit or surplus over an entire 12-month period. Shortfalls may force you to cut back expenditures. The real value of a budget is that it helps you anticipate needs and problems. Even when you foresee problems, you can feel confident that you are meeting issues head-on.

You must have reporting and control devices to measure variance away from the stated budget. Although this process is as important as establishing the budget, the reporting procedures should not be so detailed or onerous that they cause the participants to abandon the process.

If you are so inclined, you can use computer software to support and enhance the budgetary process. There are user friendly packages that help with record maintenance, tax computation, and so forth. Also, many firms in the financial services industry have developed forms and questionnaires that help in establishing short- and long-term planning strategies. Finally, there are individuals who specialize in providing financial planning services. If you use these services, you must carefully assess the cost and effectiveness of the product being offered.

KEY TERMS

American College
asset
budget
budgetary control devices
cost-of-living index
cumulative deficit
cumulative surplus
financial asset
Institute of Certified Financial Planners
Institute of Chartered Financial Analysts
International Association of Financial Planning
liability
net worth

nonfinancial asset
personal balance sheet
planning horizon
transactions cost
variance from the budget

SELECTED READINGS

Bronson, Gail. "Personal Budgeting for Hard Times." *Money,* May 1982, pp. 157–167.

"Computerline: Financial Planning Programs for Investors." *Personal Investor,* January 1986, pp. 102–103.

"Family Budgets." *Monthly Labor Review,* February 1982, pp. 44–46.

Gurney, Kathleen. "The Hoarding Hang-up." *Personal Investor,* November 1985, pp. 76–78.

"Make a Budget for Your Inflation Rate." *Changing Times,* October 1982, pp. 45–54.

Tuhy, Carrie. "Winning the Budget Battle." *Money,* October 1982, pp. 74–78.

QUESTIONS

1 Explain why there can be difficulty in budgeting and financial planning in a family environment.

2 Comment on the statement, "There can never be too much financial reporting and discipline in the budgeting process."

3 Are assets on a personal balance sheet generally listed at cost or current market value? How does this differ from a business balance sheet? Why do businesses use the particular approach that they do?

4 Distinguish between financial and nonfinancial assets and give two examples of each.

5 Suggest approaches that can be used to determine values for nonfinancial assets.

6 Your next-door neighbors have doubled the assets they own in the last two years, yet they are poorer than ever. Explain the possible reasoning behind this statement.

7 If inflation causes the value of your property to go up during a time period in which you do not increase your new investments in assets or your debt, will your net worth go up, go down, or remain the same?

8 Contrast the relative importance of expenditures for (a) food, (b) medical care, (c) housing, and (d) personal income taxes for low- and high-income families.

9 Explain why high-income families save more of their income than low-income families.

10 Using Table 2.5 as your data source, indicate which category of items has

gone up the most and which category the least over the 19-year period. What is the reason for the slowest growth index?

11 Explain how large cumulative budget deficits will affect the personal balance sheet.

12 What is meant by the term *budget variance?* Should a budget variance always be immediately corrected?

13 Why are budgetary problems often most acute for the working single parent?

14 What is a basic principle that often goes with "smart spending" policies?

15 What advantages do computers offer to personal financial planning? Are they appropriate in all cases?

16 What are four organizations that certify individuals as having some competence as financial planners?

17 The Arnolds have assets of $120,000 and liabilities of $70,000. Use the original data for each part of this question; that is, each question is separate from the other.

a What is their net worth?

b If their assets go up by 25 percent while their liabilities go up by 15 percent, what will their net worth be? Remember to use the original data only.

c If their assets go up by 30 percent while their liabilities go down by 10 percent, what will their net worth be?

d If their assets go down by 5 percent while their liabilities increase by 60 percent, what will their net worth be?

18 Assume that you are considering a job in either Boston or Atlanta. The job in Boston pays $25,000 a year and the job in Atlanta pays $19,000 a year. After cost-of-living differences are adjusted for, which job provides the better standard of living potential. Use the data in Table 2.4 to help do your calculations.

19 Jean Taylor is a single working mother with a 7-year-old son. She is only able to work 25 hours a week because of her responsibility to her young child. Refer to Table 2.3 and indicate which five categories of expenditures are likely to be most important to her. There is no one right answer; merely use your best judgment.

CASE PROBLEMS

2.1 Carol Hilton is a junior at a large state university. She has just completed a course in personal financial management and has decided to draw up a budget for the coming academic year of September to May.

She has $1600 in her bank account from her summer job as a lifeguard at a local country club. She will receive $150 a month from her parents. She also has a part-time job as a grader and tutor in accounting, for which the department pays her $45 a month. Furthermore, she makes another $110 a month working part-time at the university bookstore.

Her tuition is $1500 a year. Because Carol is an outstanding student, she receives a scholarship that reduces her tuition by 40 percent. Her tuition payments are paid in equal amounts in September and January. Other university fees, which are paid in the same two months, are $125 in September and $135 in January. Her expenses for books will be $150 in September and $180 in January. Room and board are paid for monthly and average $225 per month. All other expenses, including clothing and transportation, are $140 per month.

a How much will Carol have in the bank at the end of September?

b Compute her monthly deficit for October.

c If she wants to be at a break-even level on a monthly basis (income equals expense) and her parents agree to give her another $35 a month, how much of a raise will she need to request from the accounting department? Use the data from October to answer this question.

d Carol had $860 in her bank account at the beginning of January. How much will she need to borrow (if at all) to pay her bills for the month and have a bank balance of $200? Assume that she has the added income from her parents and the raise from the accounting department.

2.2 Bill and Michelle Brewer have been married for five years. Bill is a life insurance salesman and Michelle is an assistant basketball coach at a college preparatory school. Their anticipated total monthly income for the next six months is as follows:

January	$3200	March	$2900	May	$3400
February	$3500	April	$3700	June	$4100

Their total expenses over the next six months are

January	$3400	March	$4700	May	$2800
February	$4000	April	$3500	June	$2200

a Prepare a projected budget similar to Table 2.7.

b If they have $2000 in the bank at the beginning of the year, will they have to borrow money during the course of the year? If so, how large will the loan have to be and in what month?

c If 20 percent of their expenditures are flexible (discretionary) and can be eliminated, what will be the cumulative surplus or deficit at the end of March?

3

Preparing for Personal Income Taxes

After studying this chapter, you should:

- Be able to prepare a simple tax return
- Understand the impact of the Tax Reform Act of 1986 on tax preparation and financial planning
- Appreciate distinctions between the different types of filing status—individual, joint, and unmarried head of household
- Understand how to read and use the tax tables
- Identify tax planning strategies that will minimize your overall tax obligations
- Understand the implications of the tax laws on different types of life-styles
- Appreciate what is normally involved in a tax audit

A reasonably successful person may pay 25 percent of his or her income to the federal government in the form of taxes. Based on a 365-day year, this taxpayer works the first 91 days of the year for the benefit of the government. It will be the first of April before the individual begins personally benefiting from the fruits of his or her labor. Of course, this is only part of the story. There is also a Social Security tax, officially known as the Federal Insurance Contributions Act (FICA) tax. Since this tax is 7.15 percent on income of up to approximately $44,000, it presents an additional tax burden. Seven percent of a 365-day year represents an additional 26 days. So now the person in our example has worked for the benefit of the federal government up to April 27.

If you think it is now time for a vacation, hold off on the plans. There are more taxes to be paid. Many states have their own income taxes. Furthermore, states and localities may have sales taxes. Also, property owners will pay local property taxes (particularly on real estate). Although some of these taxes are deductible for the purpose of computing federal taxes, the burden of state and local taxes still remains large. It is not unusual for 15 percent of a person's income to go for this purpose. On a 365-day year, this represents another 55 days. It will now be June 21 before our taxpayer has earned enough to satisfy the taxing power of the federal, state, and local governments.

Only now can the individual truly begin earning funds to share with his or her family, to give to charity, or to spend on a car or a vacation. The interesting part of the story is that even with this enormous tax support, the federal government is running a deficit of $150 billion to $200 billion a year and is trillions of dollars in the red. On a smaller scale, many state and local governments face the same bleak picture.

Before you get too discouraged, you should realize that the maximum individual tax rate was as high as 90 percent from World War II to the early 1960s and as high as 70 percent as recently as 1981. Currently, the maximum individual tax rate is only 33 percent. The changes are illustrated on the top line of the graph in Figure 3.1. Also, as you will see later in the chapter, many people are exposed to only a 15 percent federal tax and some to none at all.

Furthermore, you do have some opportunity to control your fate in paying taxes. For example, the interest you pay on a home mortgage is a tax deductible item for federal income tax purposes; the interest you pay on an auto loan is not.[1] In terms of interest received, if one is paid interest on a municipal bond (a bond issued by a state or local government authority), the interest is exempt from taxes. That same dollar amount of interest paid by the federal government or a corporate issuer is fully taxable. If you live in a state that has a high income tax burden (such as New York or Massachusetts), you will feel an additional income tax burden at the local level. If you live in a state with no personal income tax (such as Texas), you will feel none.[2] The point is that there are opportunities to reduce your tax burden, no matter how onerous it may seem.

In this chapter, we shall first review the most important provisions of the federal income tax laws as they apply to you. The primary emphasis will be on the impact of the Tax Reform Act of 1986. We will go through the process of preparing a tax return and then look at the effect of the tax laws on people with different life-styles. We will also consider ways to minimize the tax burden and discuss whether you should use outside help in the tax preparation process.

THE TAX REFORM ACT OF 1986

The **Tax Reform Act of 1986** was the most sweeping piece of tax legislation passed in over three decades. Though you need not become a tax historian, you

[1] Actually, consumer interest as a tax deductible expense is being phased out between 1987 and 1990.

[2] Of course, you may still be subject to a large sales or property tax.

Figure 3.1 **MAXIMUM FEDERAL INCOME TAX RATES**

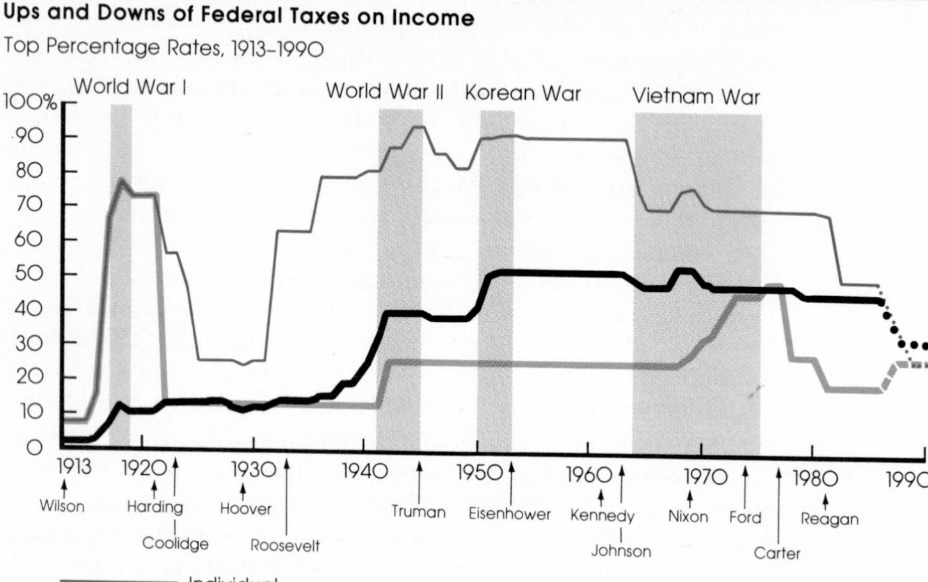

SOURCE: Reproduced by permission of *The Wall Street Journal* © Dow Jones & Company, Inc., August 18, 1986, p. 10.

should be aware of the key changes that were put in place and that will affect your future tax obligations. We will touch on them lightly for now, but their implications will become increasingly obvious as we examine the process of completing and filing a tax return.

- The number of tax brackets was reduced from 15 to 3. The range of tax brackets was changed from 11 to 50 percent to 15 to 33 percent. The government only highlights the 15 and 28 percent brackets in the new law, but the 33 percent bracket is very real for upper-income taxpayers.
- The use of **tax shelters** was sharply curtailed. A tax shelter is an investment that generates a loss for tax purposes. Tax shelters are frequently found in the real estate, oil and gas, and equipment-leasing industries. The intent was to reduce the use of tax shelters, primarily by the wealthy, and to use the proceeds to lower tax rates for everyone.
- The use of tax deductible expenses was reduced somewhat. For example, sales tax expenses and interest on consumer loans are being phased out

as tax deductible expenses. However, many tax deductible items for individuals still remain, such as property taxes, moving expenses, alimony payments, and casualty and theft losses.

- There is a much tougher alternative minimum tax on the wealthy. The alternative minimum tax is simply a second way to compute tax obligations after adding back in any specially treated items for tax purposes (such as income on certain forms of municipal bonds that are not normally taxed). You do not need to understand any of the details, only the concept that the very wealthy will generally be subjected to a much tougher alternative minimum tax of 21 percent regardless of what the normal tax computation procedure would indicate.
- Individuals will be able to take much larger deductions for themselves and their families simply as a result of being claimed as a **personal exemption.** Do not let that term throw you; a personal exemption simply means that everyone is entitled to one deduction of approximately $2000 as a result of being appropriately claimed on a tax form. Prior to tax reform, the value of the personal exemption was $1080. The result of the higher personal exemption, as well as other rules to be discussed later, is that 6 million more poor people will no longer have to pay taxes.
- All investment income is now taxed the same.[3] Before tax reform, income from an investment that increased in value and was held for at least six months was taxed at only 40 percent of the normal tax rate. For example, if your normal tax rate were 25 percent, your tax rate from the previously described long-term capital gain would only be 10 percent (40 percent × 25 percent). As a result of the new tax law, income on a savings account or similar investment is taxed at the same rate as profit from a stock that has doubled in value. Some individuals suggest that because of this feature, people are going to be less willing to take risks.

- The ability to split income between parents and children is now sharply reduced. Many wealthy parents have directed a part of their income to their children because the latter were taxed at a lower rate (they were not in the upper brackets as their parents were). Under the Tax Reform Act of 1986, if a child is under 14 years of age, any of the parents' income over $1000 that is passed on to the child is taxed at the parents' rate regardless of whose tax return it ends up on.

These are some of the most important features of the Tax Reform Act of 1986.[4] As you can see, the emphasis was on reducing many forms of tax deductible items for the purpose of lowering everyone's tax rates. The Tax Reform

[3] Of course, many forms of municipal bonds still have tax-exempt income. The emphasis here is on the capital gains versus ordinary income treatment.

[4] Many other features of the act will be discussed after more complicated terms and concepts are introduced, such as the standard deduction, the use of individual retirement accounts, and the earned income credit.

Box 3.1 SEVEN WHO MADE TAX REFORM HAPPEN

Bill Bradley
drafted a visionary "fair tax" plan in 1982 that proposed curtailing many tax breaks in exchange for sharply lowered rates. That plan moved the issue from academia to the political arena. The New Jersey Democrat played a key role in drafting the Senate Bill.

Jack Kemp
realized in 1982 that the supply-side formula of rate cuts without offsetting revenue increases could no longer be sold. The Buffalo (N.Y.) congressman came up with his own base-broadening plan as a counter to Bradley's, and built a reform constituency among Republicans.

James A. Baker III
as White House chief of staff, persuaded Reagan to make tax revision an issue in the 1984 campaign. As Treasury Secretary, he modified a radical proposal drawn up by then–Treasury Secretary Donald T. Regan to make it salable. Baker then guided the plan through Congress.

Richard Darman
oversaw the drafting of the Administration's tax plan. By pitching tax reform as a "populist" issue, the Deputy Treasury Secretary made it intellectually respectable for Republicans to support a big hike in corporate taxes. He also forged a bipartisan strategy.

Ronald Reagan
pushed reform to the top of his second-term domestic agenda. By embracing the issue, the President used his great personal popularity to sway a reluctant business community, Republican Party, and House Democratic leadership to support reform.

Dan Rostenkowski
was the first Democratic leader to see tax reform as a political lever for the party. The Illinois Democrat's tough personality and close ties to Speaker Tip O'Neill allowed him to push the measure through his Ways & Means Committee and the House floor.

Bob Packwood
began the process as a fan of tax breaks. With the bill near death in his Senate Finance Committee, the Oregon Republican took a big gamble, calling for even lower rates than Reagan had proposed. The plan rescued the Senate bill—and became the basis for the final draft.

SOURCE: Reprinted from September 1, 1986 issue of *Business Week* by special permission, © 1986 by McGraw-Hill, Inc.

Table 3.1
AVERAGE TAX CUTS UNDER THE TAX REFORM ACT OF 1986

Income class (in thousands)	Tax cut (%)
Less than $10	−65.7
$10–$20	−22.3
$20–$30	−9.8
$30–$40	−7.7
$40–$50	−9.1
$50–$75	−1.7
$75–$100	−1.0
$100–$200	−2.4
$200 and above	−2.3
Total	−6.1

SOURCE: Joint Taxation Committee, U.S. Congress.

Act was also intended as a vehicle to ensure that everyone paid their fair share through the tougher standards of the alternative minimum tax. The general impact of the act on various income groups is illustrated in Table 3.1. The main beneficiaries are the lower-income groups. The reason that all groups benefit by an average of 6.1 percent is that business taxes were raised by $120 billion over five years to help pay for the reduction in individual income taxes. This is not to imply that all individuals will come out ahead; on a case-by-case basis about one-fourth of the population will pay more in taxes. These are primarily individuals who were the largest users of tax shelters in the old tax code and are now having to pay more as a result of losing their write-offs. Also, some middle-income taxpayers will get caught in an unintended squeeze from various new provisions in the tax code. As we go through the different life-style examples later in the chapter, you will get a better idea of who gains and who loses.

BASIC PRINCIPLES OF TAX COMPUTATION

Keeping the key elements of tax reform in mind, we now turn our attention to the basic principles of tax computation. We will consider the following steps:

1 Determine filing status
2 Determine gross income
3 Compute adjusted gross income
4 Determine the deductions
5 Compute taxable income

6 Apply the appropriate tax rate
7 Subtract tax credits
8 Determine the amount owed

Determine Filing Status

Generally a person or family reports their income to the federal government under one of three categories:

1 Individual return
2 Joint return
3 Unmarried head of household return

An individual return normally carries the highest tax burden, as you can see in Table 3.2. That is to say, the tax rates become higher at lower levels of income. Tax tables will be explained in greater detail later in the chapter and in Appendix 3A. A **joint return,** filed by a husband and wife, carries the lowest tax burden. For example, you can see in Table 3.2 that the 33 percent tax rate does not come into play on a joint return until taxable income is $71,900. For an individual return, the 33 percent bracket starts at $43,150. Both spouses do not have to be working to file a joint return.[5]

In addition to filing individually or jointly, a single person may elect to file as an **unmarried head of household.** As you can see in Table 3.2, the tax burden for an unmarried head of household is less than that for an individual (the higher rates take place at higher income levels). In order to qualify for an unmarried head of household status, a single person must meet all the following rules:

1 Not be married at the *end* of the year
2 Be a U.S. citizen or resident alien during the entire year
3 Maintain a household for the entire year for a child or dependent relative (grandchild, foster child, stepchild, parent, and so on)
4 Pay more than half the cost of the household that is maintained

We have been discussing the three major categories under which people can file their tax returns. However, not everyone is required to file. Generally, if your income is $5000 or less, you may not be required to submit a tax return. The rules change annually, so you need to check the *Federal Income Tax Forms and Instructions* booklet provided by the Internal Revenue Service (IRS). The booklet can be acquired from the IRS and is available at most post offices. If you are not certain of your filing status or have other questions for the IRS, a list of IRS phone numbers by state is provided in Appendix 3B.

[5] Where there are two working spouses, each may choose to use a "married filing separately" return to avoid parlaying their income into upper brackets. This only happens a relatively small percentage of the time.

Table 3.2
TAX RATES UNDER THE TAX REFORM ACT OF 1986[a] (BASED ON TAXABLE INCOME)

Single

$0–$17,850	15% of the amount
$17,850–$43,150	28% of the amount over $17,850
$43,150–$89,560	33% of the amount over $43,150

The third bracket is extended by $10,920 per personal exemption. After that point, it reverts back to 28 percent.

Married (joint return)

$0–$29,750	15% of the amount
$29,750–$71,900	28% of the amount over $29,750
$71,900–$149,250	33% of the amount over $71,900

The third bracket is extended by $10,920 per personal exemption. After that point, it reverts back to 28 percent.

Unmarried head of household

$0–$23,900	15% of the amount
$23,900–$61,650	28% of the amount over $23,900
$61,650–$123,790	33% of the amount over $61,650

The third bracket is extended by $10,920 per personal exemption. After that point, it reverts back to 28 percent.

[a] The taxable income figures are subject to change with inflation after 1988. For example, the upper end of the first bracket for singles may be extended to $18,000 or higher.

Dependents. Another matter of importance related to your filing status is the number of **dependents** that you can claim. The issue tends to be very important on a joint return or unmarried head of household return. Each person claimed as a dependent qualifies for a *personal exemption* deduction, which is $1950 in 1988 and $2000 in 1989.[6] Prior to tax reform, the personal exemption was only $1080. We can readily see that a family of four has $7800 (4 × $1950) of deductions right off the top in 1988. For this reason the Tax Reform Act of 1986 was labeled as a form of pro-family legislation.

A person who files a single return can automatically claim himself or herself as a personal exemption and take the $1950 deduction, so the number of dependents only becomes more involved when there are other family members or a divorce has split up the family unit.

To claim another as a dependent (and get the personal exemption deduction), a taxpayer must pass a number of tests.

[6] The amount will be further adjusted for inflation after this time period.

1 *Relative or member-of-household test:* The party must be a relative or a member of the household.[7]

2 *The support test:* The taxpayer claiming the dependent must provide more than half the dependent's support. For children of divorced or separated parents there are special rules that allow for the claim of a dependent with less than 50 percent support. However, keep in mind that only one parent can claim a child as a dependent. Also, if another party claims you as a dependent, you cannot take the personal exemption yourself.

3 *The income test:* To be claimed as a dependent a person must receive less than $1000 of gross income. However, this rule is waived if the potential dependent is under 19 years of age or was enrolled as a full-time student any five months of the year.

4 *Citizen or resident test:* The dependent must be a citizen or resident of the United States (the definition is expanded somewhat to include Mexico).

The tax reform law also specifies that every taxpayer claiming a dependent who is at least 5 years old must obtain a Social Security number for that dependent. That number must be reported on the tax return on which a personal exemption for the dependent is claimed. To obtain a Social Security number for a dependent child, a parent must submit Form SS-5 with a copy of the child's birth certificate to the Social Security Administration.

The discussion up to now has dealt with determining the filing status and identifying the number of dependents that can be claimed. We shall assume that these issues have been resolved and it is time to go on to figuring your income, your expenses, and the amount you actually owe. In the balance of this section we'll discuss a number of tax principles and rules. If there are one or two items you do not understand, keep reading. There are more items discussed than you could hope to remember the first time through. But keep in mind that at the end of the section, we will go through a complete analysis applying all these principles. This should allow you to develop a reasonable degree of confidence in tying together the basic elements of the personal income tax. If you work the problems and short cases at the end of the chapter, you may even be in a position to give limited advice to friends and relatives. Let's start the process.

Determine Gross Income

Gross income is generally composed of all of a person's sources of income. For a joint return, both the husband's and wife's income should be included. Major items that may be included are

Wages, salaries
Interest

[7] In many cases, of course, a relative may also be a member of the household, but this is not essential.

Dividends
Business income
Capital gains (profits from investments)[8]
Rents, royalties, partnerships
Unemployment compensation
Alimony received
Other income (taxable pension distributions, taxable Social Security benefits)

For a few of these items, such as interest income over a minimal amount ($400), business income, capital gains, and rents, other schedules must supplement the reported amounts to prove the accuracy of the number. For example, if you have capital gains (profits from investment), you must fill out an accompanying schedule showing each investment. The IRS has ways of cross-checking your numbers through reports that banks, brokerage houses, and others file, so it is essential that you keep accurate records and report honestly.

When you add up all sources of income, you arrive at gross income. A simple example would be

Wages, salaries	$28,500
Interest income	1,500
Gross income	$30,000

Compute Adjusted Gross Income

From gross income, the taxpayer is allowed to deduct a few special items to arrive at **adjusted gross income.** These are not regular personal or business expenses, which are covered later, but special deductions that Congress and the IRS have singled out for deduction. Under the Tax Reform Act of 1986, the number of such deductions has been reduced or lessened in amount in recognition of the fact that taxpayers now enjoy much lower tax rates.[9]

Currently allowable deductions are primarily restricted to contributions to individual retirement accounts (and other forms of retirement plans) as well as alimony payments. An **individual retirement account (IRA)** allows a taxpayer to deduct $2000 from taxable income and invest the funds at a bank, savings and loan, brokerage house, mutual fund, or other financial institution. The funds are normally placed in interest-paying instruments, such as certificates of deposit, or common stock. Not only is the $2000 allowed to be deducted from gross income to reduce current taxes, but the income earned on the funds is allowed

[8] As previously indicated, capital gains are now fully taxable, as would be true of any income. Previously, 60 percent of long-term capital gains could be excluded from tax computations, so the tax rate was only 40 percent of the taxpayer's normal tax rate.

[9] Some of the old adjustments, such as moving expenses and employee business expenses, are now covered under the itemized deductions section of the tax return rather than as adjustments to gross income. The marital deduction feature is eliminated completely.

to grow tax-free until withdrawn at retirement. A single individual may qualify for a deduction of $2000; a couple filing a joint return may qualify for a $2250 deduction if there is only one working spouse, but potentially $4000 if there are two working spouses. The Tax Reform Act of 1986 established some additional income rules for qualifying for the IRA deduction, and because they can get complicated, they are covered in a later section of the chapter. IRAs are also discussed in Chapter 15.

If you have an allowable adjustment (such as an IRA), you deduct it from the *gross income* figure computed under the last heading to arrive at *adjusted* gross income, and you are ready to move on. An example is:

Wages, salaries	$28,500
Interest income	1,500
Gross income	$30,000
IRA contribution	2,000
Adjusted gross income	$28,000

Determine the Deductions

In determining deductions, you must decide whether you wish to *itemize* your tax deductible expenses or not. If you choose to show **itemized deductions,** you list out each allowable expense and total up the deductions.

As an alternative to actually listing the expenses, you may simply take a single lump-sum deduction that applies to the category in which you fall. This deduction is known as the **standard deduction.** The standard deduction that pertains to different classes of filers is presented in Table 3.3.[10]

Let's assume for now that we have a family of four filing a joint return without any further additions for age considerations or blindness. The standard deduction will be $5,000, as shown in Table 3.3.

The key question then becomes, Are the family's actual deductible expenses higher or lower than this? If they are higher than this, let's say $8000, then the family will choose not to use the standard deduction of only $5000, but will itemize or write out their $8000 of expenses on the tax form. If the expenses are lower than the standard deduction of $5000, then the family will quickly decide not to itemize or claim their own individual deductions, but simply take the standard deduction of $5000. The process is depicted in Figure 3.2. Because the standard deduction was increased substantially in the Tax Reform Act of 1986, many taxpayers are electing to take the standard deduction rather than go through the tedious process of itemizing deductions.

Nevertheless, if one has substantial deductions to itemize, then this route should be followed. Only certain types of expenses are allowed for itemized deductions, and we shall discuss these. Also, many expenses that at one time were eligible deductions no longer are. Falling into this category are sales tax

[10] These values are adjusted for inflation after 1988.

Table 3.3 THE STANDARD DEDUCTION FOR DIFFERENT CATEGORIES OF FILERS

Single	$3000
Married (joint)	5000
Unmarried head of household	4400

The standard deduction is further increased for the aged and blind. It is increased by $600 for each qualifying person on a joint return and $750 for each qualifying person on a single or unmarried head of household return. If a person or persons in a family fall into these categories, you check the boxes below.

65 and over	You	☐	Your spouse	☐
Blind	You	☐	Your spouse	☐

You then add up the boxes that are checked. If there are two people over the age of 65 filing a joint return, the standard deduction would be increased to $6200, as indicated below.

	1 box	2 boxes	3 boxes	4 boxes
Single	$3750	$4500		
Married (joint)	5600	6200	$6800	$7400
Unmarried head of household	5150	5800		

expenses and interest on consumer loans, such as interest on auto and home appliance loans and credit card interest. Actually, the deductibility of some of these expenses is being phased out over a number of years. For example, 40 percent of consumer interest expense is deductible in 1988, 20 percent is deductible in 1989, 10 percent in 1990, and none thereafter. But keep in mind that if you do not take itemized deductions and use the standard deduction instead, the loss of these deductions does not directly affect you.

Let's look at the most important items that can be deducted as part of the itemized deduction process:

Medical and dental expenses (if over 7.5 percent of adjusted gross income).

State and local taxes (excluding the sales tax). This category would primarily include state and local income and property taxes.

Home mortgage interest. Unlike consumer interest, this item is fully deductible on an itemized return. For this reason some people are actually

Figure 3.2 **DECIDING WHETHER TO ITEMIZE OR TAKE THE STANDARD DEDUCTION**

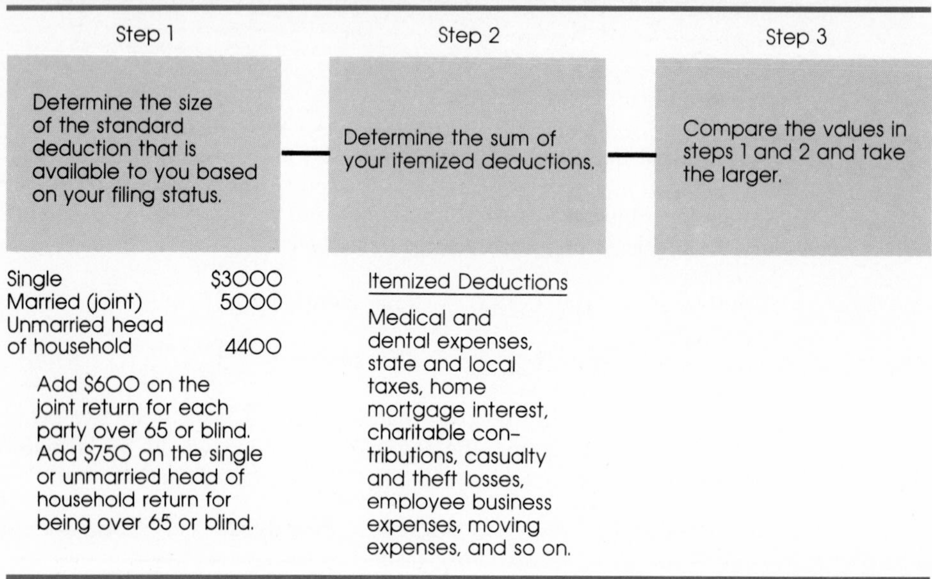

borrowing money on their home to create home mortgage interest to pay for consumer purchases such as a car or vacation. You can only deduct interest on a home mortgage to the extent that the loan does not exceed the purchase price of the home plus improvements. One exception to this rule is if the proceeds are being used for medical or educational purposes.

Charitable contributions. These can only be deducted if you take itemized deductions. Before the Tax Reform Act of 1986, they were deductible to all parties.

Casualty and theft losses in excess of 10 percent of adjusted gross income plus $100.

Employee business expenses and miscellaneous business deductions. This category includes such items as professional journals, union dues, tax preparation fees, and investment fees, as well as deductions related to a job such as a home computer and an automobile partially used on the job. Actually, these expenses are only deductible to the extent that they exceed 2 percent of adjusted gross income.[11]

Moving expenses.

[11] Before the Tax Reform Act of 1986, most of these items were *fully* deductible. Furthermore, they were available whether the taxpayer itemized expenses or not. Most could be taken as a deduction to gross income to get adjusted gross income.

Let's assume that a family of four arrives at the following figures for itemized deductions. They have an adjusted gross income of $28,000.

Medical and dental expenses ($2150)	
Amount minus 7.5% of adjusted gross income	
$2150 − (7.5% × $28,000) =	
$2150 − $2100 =	$ 50
State and local taxes	1100
Home mortgage interest	4300
Charitable contributions	450
Casualty and theft losses	0
Employee business expenses ($680)	
Amount minus 2% of adjusted gross income	
$680 − (2% × $28,000) =	
$680 − $560 =	120
Moving expenses	0
Total itemized deductions	$6020

Since the total itemized deductions of $6020 exceed the $5000 standard deduction, the family is advised to take the itemized deductions. Clearly, if they had not owned a home and paid $4300 in mortgage interest, they would be much better off taking the $5000 standard deduction. That's because their itemized deductions would only be $1720 ($6020 − $4300). After we subtract the itemized deductions (or the standard deduction), we arrive at *taxable income before personal exemptions.* An example would be as follows:

	Itemized deductions		Standard deduction
Wages, salaries	$28,500	or for a family	
Interest income	1,500	using the	
Gross income	$30,000	$5,000 stan-	
IRA contribution	2,000	dard deduc-	
Adjusted gross income		tion	
Itemized deductions	$28,000		$28,000
Taxable income before personal exemptions	6,020		5,000
	$21,980		$23,000

Compute Taxable Income

Now that we have computed taxable income before personal exemptions, we subtract the personal exemptions (or dependents' deduction) to obtain the appropriate value for taxable income. It is important to remember that whether itemized deductions or the standard deduction was used, the taxpayer still is entitled to use the personal exemption deductions. You may recall from our prior discussion that the personal exemption deduction is $1950 in 1988 and

$2000 in 1989. Thus in 1988, an individual gets a $1950 deduction, a married couple with no children $3900, and a family of four $7800 (4 × $1950). This value is subtracted from taxable income before personal exemptions to arrive at taxable income.

For the family of four example that we have been following, their taxable income will be

Taxable income before personal exemptions	$21,980
Personal exemptions	7,800
Taxable income	$14,180

Also observe that a family of four that has no deductions besides the standard deduction and personal exemptions will have zero tax liability unless their income is over $12,800 in 1988.

Standard deduction (joint)	$ 5,000
Personal exemptions (4 × 1,950)	7,800
Total automatic deductions	$12,800

The number will be even higher in later years as the size of the standard deduction and personal exemption are adjusted upward for inflation.

Apply the Appropriate Tax Rate

The appropriate tax rate is then applied to taxable income. Look at Table 3.4, which reproduces a portion of Table 3.2. Since the taxable income in the example we have been using is $14,180 on a joint return, a tax rate of 15 percent will apply. Actually, at this relatively low level of income, a 15 percent tax rate will apply to any of the three filing classifications (single, joint, or unmarried head of household).

Using the tax rate of 15 percent, we arrive at a tax obligation of $2127.

Taxable income	$14,180
Tax rate	15%
Tax obligation	$ 2,127

In terms of tax rates, note that the rate of 15 percent does not go up for a joint filing until a family has an income of $29,750. Furthermore, keep in mind that a family of four can automatically deduct $12,800 in the form of a standard deduction and personal exemptions. This means that they, in effect, must earn over $42,550 ($29,750 + $12,800) to be forced out of the 15 percent bracket. It is for this reason that the great majority of the population will be in the 15 percent bracket. A similar analysis can be done for individuals or unmarried heads of households.

Let's use Table 3.4 again to make sure we understand the computations.

Table 3.4 TAX RATES

Rate	Single	Married (joint)	Unmarried head of household
15%	$0–$17,850	$0–$29,750	$0–$23,900
28%	$17,850–$43,150	$29,750–$71,900	$23,900–$61,650
33%	$43,150–$89,560	$71,900–$149,250	$61,650–$123,790

Assume an unmarried head of a household has a taxable income of $100,000. What will the tax be? The tax obligation is computed in Table 3.5. In this case, we take 15 percent of $23,900 or *$3,835*. We then take the difference between $23,900 and the next bracket of $61,650, which equals $37,750, and multiply this value by 28 percent. This gives us an additional *$10,570* in taxes. Finally we take $100,000 and subtract the beginning value of the last bracket of $61,650 and arrive at $38,350. This value multiplied by 33 percent yields *$12,656*. The total tax in all three brackets is $26,811.

Subtract Tax Credits

There are circumstances in which taxpayers may be able to use a **tax credit** to partially or fully offset their tax obligation after it is computed. These credits apply to 10–20 percent of the population.

The most important is the **earned income credit,** which is available to low-income workers, with dependents, who maintain a household for the dependents. Earned income is generally from wages and salary, not from interest or dividends, which are considered investment income. Under the Tax Reform Act of 1986, an earned income credit of 14 percent can be applied to the first $5714 of *earned income* for those low-income workers who qualify. This represents a possible credit of up to $800.[12] The ability to use the credit is phased

[12] Note that the credit is applied to earned income before the standard deduction or personal exemptions are subtracted.

Table 3.5 TAX OBLIGATION

On first $23,900	$23,900 × 0.15 =	$ 3,585
On $23,900 to 61,650	37,750 × 0.28 =	10,570
Between $61,650 and 100,000	38,350 × 0.33 =	12,656
		$26,811

out if there is total income over $9000 and ceases altogether at $17,000. Assume that a mother working part-time to support her child had earned income of $5000. She would qualify for an earned income credit of $700 (14 percent × $5000). This $700 credit could be used to offset any tax obligation or even to create a refund or subsidy from the government. If she had a $100 tax obligation,[13] the $700 earned income credit would mean that she would have her $100 tax obligation canceled and receive a refund of $600. The earned income credit is sometimes referred to as a negative income tax. It is used to provide funds to needy working people with one or more dependents.

There are other special credits that are available for child and dependent care expenses as well as for the elderly and disabled who meet special qualifications for need. The child and dependent care credit is especially valuable to a working parent who must pay child care expenses in order to generate income. Any of the basic tax guides cited at the end of this chapter can be consulted to see if one qualifies for a special tax credit.

Determine the Amount Owed

The next step is to subtract any tax credits from the computed tax obligation. In the example we've been using, we'll assume that no tax credit applies, so the tax owed is equal to the tax obligation of $2127 previously computed.

Because of **tax withholding,** chances are that the family in our example has already paid an amount close to this value to the IRS over the course of the year in which the funds were earned. That is because the IRS operates on a pay-as-you-go basis in terms of tax payments. If you are employed by another, your paycheck will reflect a regular deduction in pay toward meeting your anticipated payments for the year. You are required to file a Form W-4 with your employer. This form is used to determine the amount that should be withheld from your paycheck. The amount withheld is based on your income, the number of dependents you declare, and other sources of income. Under the Tax Reform Act of 1986, the intent of the W-4 form is not only to withhold directly against your salary, but to withhold against other forms of income as well so that what is withheld will match as closely as possible what you owe at the end of the tax year. Also, if you are in business for yourself, you may be required to make quarterly tax payments in anticipation of your tax obligation for the year. If your estimated business tax is at least $500, you should follow this procedure.

Let's assume in the example above that the family with the tax obligation of $2127 had paid $2000 during the course of the year toward their tax obligation. Their tax obligation to be paid on April 15 of the following year would be $127.

Tax obligation	$2127
Amount withheld	2000
Amount owed	$ 127

[13] The tax obligation at this low level could result because taxable child support payments were received.

Table 3.6
GROSS INCOME FOR TED AND ALICE HAILEY

Salary—Ted Hailey	$17,270
Salary—Alice Hailey	17,450
Interest	680
Dividends	250
Capital gains	350
Total income	$36,000

Of course if $2400 had been withheld, they would get a welcome refund of $273.

Tax obligation	$2127
Amount withheld	2400
Tax refund	$ 273

BRINGING THE PROCESS TOGETHER

We shall now go through a complete example that brings together the elements we have just discussed. Ted and Alice Hailey are both employed, and they have a combined income of $36,000 per year. Each contributes approximately half to this sum. The income figures are shown in Table 3.6. They have a young son, Todd, who will start kindergarten next year. They will file a joint return, and because they are both working and earning at least $2000, they are each entitled to set aside $2000 in an IRA. They are allowed three personal exemptions for the family members of $1950 each and a standard deduction of $5000 as a married couple filing jointly. Their tax deductible expenses are shown in Table 3.7.

Table 3.7
TAX DEDUCTIBLE EXPENSES FOR TED AND ALICE HAILEY

Medical and dental expenses	$ 800
State and local taxes	1300
Home mortgage interest	4750
Charitable contributions	300
Employee business expenses (job-related personal computer used at home)	900

The material from Table 3.6 and Table 3.7 is combined with the other facts that have been stated to determine their tax obligation in Table 3.8.

A few special comments are necessary in interpreting the data shown in Table 3.8. First, the Haileys are itemizing their deductions rather than taking the standard deduction of $5000 because their itemized deductions of $6610 exceed this amount. Second, note under itemized deductions that there is no write-off allowed for medical and dental expenses of $800 because the sum does not exceed 7.5 percent of adjusted gross income of $32,000. Seven and a half percent of adjusted gross income is equal to $2400, so the medical expenses are $1600 less than this amount. For this reason, a zero is entered for medical and dental expenses.

Also note that employee business expenses of $900 are more than 2 percent of adjusted gross income ($640 = 2 percent × $32,000), so a $260 deduction is allowed.

When total itemized deductions are subtracted from adjusted gross income, the remaining value is $25,390 for taxable income before personal exemptions. Since three personal exemptions can be claimed, a deduction of $5850 is allowed, providing the Haileys with taxable income of $19,540. Using Table 3.4 to find the appropriate tax rate, we determine that for a joint filing, the 15 percent tax rate applies up to a taxable income level of $29,750. Since the Haileys' taxable income is only $19,540, the 15 percent rate clearly applies. Multiplying the 15 percent rate by $19,540 gives the taxes owed of $2931. Since the Haileys will have wages withheld throughout the year (and perhaps made quarterly payments as well), they may have already paid in full the amount of the obli-

Table 3.8 TAX ANALYSIS FOR TED AND ALICE HAILEY

Gross income			$36,000
IRA contributions			4,000
Adjusted gross income			$32,000
Itemized deductions:			
Medical and dental expenses	$800 − (7.5% × $32,000)		
	$800 − $2,400 = $ −1,600	$ 0	
State and local taxes		1,300	
Home mortgage interest		4,750	
Charitable contributions		300	
Employee business expenses	$900 − (2% × $32,000)		
	$900 − $640 = $260	260	
Total itemized deductions			$ 6,610
Taxable income before personal exemptions			$25,390
Personal exemptions (3 × $1,950)			5,850
Taxable income			$19,540
Taxes owed (15% × $19,540)			$ 2,931

gation. To the extent that they have underpaid or overpaid, they may need to make a small payment or may be entitled to a small refund. Note that the Haileys did not qualify for a tax credit of any sort. In problems at the end of the chapter you will have an opportunity to fill in tables comparable to Table 3.8, so you should become familiar with how various items affect a tax return. For now we shall examine two more examples of how tax laws affect payment obligations for people in different situations. We shall first examine an unmarried head of household who is in a low-income bracket. Then we'll evaluate the tax status of a wealthy attorney who had sheltered large amounts of income prior to the passage of the Tax Reform Act of 1986.

Alternative Life-Styles—Unmarried Head of Household

Joan Fleming divorced her husband three years ago and received custody of their 9-year-old son, Allen. She has earned income this year of $6500 from working part-time. The balance of her time is devoted to her son. She also receives $2400 a year in alimony payments (which must be shown as income for tax purposes) and $4800 in child support payments (which do not have to be included in income). She has no other forms of income, and she is not participating in an IRA because she is short on funds.

Her total expenses that qualify for itemized deductions are only $1350. This number is low because she is renting an apartment and does not have large mortgage interest payments or property taxes to deduct. Unfortunately, she has large rental payments to make, but these are not tax deductible. Because her itemized deductions are small, she examines Table 3.3 to see if she would not be better off using a standard deduction rather than itemized deductions. With a standard deduction of $4400 allowed for an unmarried head of household, she definitely will take this route in preference to itemized deductions. She also will be allowed two personal exemptions for herself and her son (she has indicated to her former husband that she might allow him to take the personal exemption for their son if he would increase the child support payments). She also will be allowed an earned income credit by the IRS. The tax analysis is presented in Table 3.9.

Note that Joan has taxable income of $600. Applying the appropriate tax rate of 15 percent from Table 3.4, we see that her tax obligation is only $90. However, she qualifies for an earned income credit because she is a low-income worker—with a dependent—who maintains a household. The credit can be taken for up to 14 percent of the first $5714 of earned income or $800. Since she earned $6500, she clearly qualifies for the full $800. There is also a special credit for child and dependent care expenses that the government offers, but Joan provides her son's after-school care, so she incurs no such expenses.

Note that Joan has a negative tax obligation of $710. This means she will receive a refund from the government for this amount plus any additional funds that may have been withheld from her salary. Joan might even consider filing a Form W-5 to get the payment of her credit before the end of the taxable year.

Table 3.9 TAX ANALYSIS FOR JOAN FLEMING

Salary	$6500
Alimony received	2400
Adjusted gross income	$8900
Standard deduction	4400
Taxable income before personal exemptions	$4500
Personal exemptions (2 × $1950)	3900
Taxable income	$ 600
Taxes owed (15% × $600)	$ 90
Earned income credit	800
Tax	($710)

Alternative Life-Styles—Wealthy Attorney

Norman Barrister is a successful lawyer. Last year his salary and earnings were $160,000. He married for the third time the last week in December and will file a joint return.

Because he owns two homes, his itemized deductions are quite large and total $21,800. Therefore, he will itemize his deductions rather than take the standard deduction. He also invested $200,000 in a real estate deal in 1985 with the intention of taking an annual $20,000 deduction on this tax shelter for the next decade. However, with the passage of the Tax Reform Act of 1986, such deductions are disallowed. Actually, the disallowance is phased in over five years. In 1988, he can still use 40 percent of his $20,000 annual write-off, or $8000. By 1991, he will not be able to use any. The overall tax analysis for Norman Barrister is presented in Table 3.10.

Table 3.10 TAX ANALYSIS FOR NORMAN BARRISTER

Salary and earnings	$160,000
Tax shelter loss	8,000
Gross income	$152,000
Itemized deductions	21,800
Taxable income before personal exemptions	$130,200
Personal exemptions (2 × $1,950)	3,900
Taxable income	$126,300
Taxes owed (see computation that follows)	$34,217

The computation of taxes owed is based on tax rate information in Table 3.4. We use the married (joint) return column in that table to get the rates:

On the first $29,750	29,750 × 0.15 =	$ 4,463
On $29,750–$71,900	42,150 × 0.28 =	11,802
$71,900–$126,300[a]	54,400 × 0.33 =	17,952
		$34,217

[a] Note we do not need to go all the way up to the upper limit of the third bracket in the table.

One can only hope that Norman Barrister made sufficiently large quarterly payments during the course of the year to cover this tax obligation.

MINIMIZING TAXES UNDER THE TAX REFORM ACT OF 1986

The main intent of the Tax Reform Act of 1986 was to eliminate most special deductions and abuses of the tax code and to reward taxpayers with lower tax rates. Thus, many favored techniques for reducing or eliminating taxes are no longer available or at least are restricted. For example, the use of real estate and equipment-leasing tax shelters to generate paper losses is greatly restricted (as Norman Barrister found out in our last example).

The use of *income averaging* has also been eliminated. Under income averaging a taxpayer could average his or her taxable income over a number of years and apply the appropriate tax rate to the *averaged* income. The tax burden is often less than that on nonaveraged income if there has been a great increase in reported income. For example, a salesperson might have made $15,000 a year for three years and then hit a big sale and made $100,000 in the fourth year. Formerly, the values could be averaged together to determine the appropriate tax rate instead of simply applying a very high rate to the last year.

With so many of these old favored techniques gone, what is left? Municipal bonds (bonds issued by state and local governments) still carry tax exempt (nontaxed) interest payments. Under the Tax Reform Act of 1986, however, the issuing agency must be using the funds for public purposes rather than to subsidize private-interest projects (such as a major league baseball park). Before one purchases a municipal bond, he or she should confirm its tax-exempt nature with the salesperson. Generally, an investor should be at least in the 28 percent tax bracket to justify the purchase of municipal bonds because they pay lower interest rates than other bonds.

Most of the tax benefits of home ownership were also left intact in the Tax Reform Act of 1986. That is, home mortgage interest and property taxes can still be deducted. For this reason, a home represents one of the best tax shelters still available. The same cannot be said for the purchase of automobiles, personal computers, furniture, and so on. For such purchases, interest as a tax deductible expense is being phased out through 1990 (40 percent is deductible in 1988, 20 percent in 1989, 10 percent in 1990). Of course, there may be other very good, non-tax-related reasons to make these purchases.

Perhaps the best tax write-off or shelter under the new tax laws is the previously described individual retirement account (IRA). As earlier mentioned, an individual may qualify for a deduction of $2000 a year, and a couple filing a joint return may qualify for a $2250 deduction if there is only one working spouse and $4000 if there are two working spouses. An unmarried head of household is treated the same as an individual for purposes of utilizing an IRA. There are a number of rules that must be followed in using an IRA. First of all, the individual or joint filer must have *earned income* at least equal to the intended contribution to an IRA. Thus an individual who only earned $1500 is limited to that amount as a deduction. You may wonder why such a low-income person would desire an IRA. The reason could be that he or she also received $50,000 in unearned income from a family trust.

Another important rule applies to whether the person (or persons) participates in a pension or retirement plan at work. If an individual or married couple do not participate in such a plan at work, they are qualified to take an IRA deduction regardless of the upper level of their income as long as they have earned income at least equaling the IRA contribution. However, what if either an individual or a husband or wife participates in a retirement plan at work? Then the ability to use an IRA depends on an upper limit on income. Individuals with overall income up to $25,000 may still take the deduction, but the deduction is phased out between income levels of $25,000 to $35,000. For married couples, the IRA deduction may be taken for income levels up to $40,000, but is phased out between $40,000 and $50,000. The phaseout provision under both circumstances is presented in Table 3.11.

One final point; even if you are disallowed from taking a tax deductible contribution to an IRA, you may still choose to make a *non*-tax deductible IRA contribution. The IRS will allow you to accumulate the interest or profit on the account tax-free until you withdraw the funds at retirement. Though you do not get the advantage of the initial deduction, you still accumulate income on a tax-free basis until it is withdrawn.

HELP IN PREPARING YOUR TAX RETURN

At the beginning of this chapter, we talked about the days in the year that one must work just to pay taxes. You may need to work a few more days to pay for the additional cost of tax preparation fees.

Of course, not everyone will choose to hire a tax preparation service or certified public accountant (CPA) to fill out his or her tax form. If you enjoy this type of activity, you can fill out the form yourself. You can also have the IRS assist you by phone or at a local IRS office. The IRS will even figure your tax for you if you have adjusted gross income of $50,000 or less and do not take itemized deductions. Keep in mind that the IRS issues important publications such as

Table 3.11 PHASEOUT OF ALLOWABLE IRA CONTRIBUTIONS FOR TAXPAYERS IN A WORK-RELATED PENSION PLAN

INDIVIDUAL		JOINT FILING		
Income level	Maximum IRA deduction	Income level	Married, 1 spouse works	Married, 2 spouses work
$25,000	$2,000	$40,000	$2,250	$4,000
26,000	1,900	41,000	2,138	3,800
27,000	1,700	42,000	1,913	3,400
28,000	1,500	43,000	1,688	3,000
29,000	1,300	44,000	1,463	2,600
30,000	1,100	45,000	1,238	2,200
31,000	900	46,000	1,013	1,800
32,000	700	47,000	788	1,400
33,000	500	48,000	563	1,000
34,000	300	49,000	338	600
35,000	100	50,000	113	200
over $35,000	0	over $50,000	0	0

Your Federal Income Tax and *Federal Income Tax Forms and Instructions.* You must request the former, but the latter is sent to you with your federal income tax form.

Of course, you may not want to be overly dependent on the IRS. Actually, their task is to collect the maximum tax dollar possible. For this reason, you may wish to engage the services of a tax preparation firm such as H & R Block or even a CPA. A general guideline is to attempt to fill out the tax form yourself if you feel comfortable with the process; if not, look to a local or national tax preparation firm that does mass production type work for a relatively low fee ($10 to $50) if your return is relatively simple. If your financial affairs are complicated, you will probably want to use the services of a CPA. The fee will likely start at $100 and could be much larger depending on circumstances. Of course, the reputation of anyone you use must be checked out in advance.

Regardless of what route you take in tax preparation, you can find help in a number of nongovernmental publications on tax planning. Examples include J. K. Lasser's *Your Income Tax* (Simon & Schuster), H & R Block's *Income Tax Workbook,* The Research Institute of America's *Individual Return Tax Guide,* and The Commerce Clearing House *Tax Guide.* All come out annually and can normally be purchased at bookstores.

Also, keep in mind the importance of maintaining good records for tax preparation. You should keep documentation on all income and any expenses that could possibly be tax deductible. The best way to maintain proper records is to keep canceled checks and invoices of purchase. It is best to segregate your checks on a monthly basis into normal expense categories, particularly if you think you might want to itemize deductions. Although at first you only have to send the IRS a few items with your tax return, such as your W-2 earnings form, you need all the backup information in your files in case the IRS later decides to examine your financial information in more depth. Also, if you employ a professional tax preparer, he or she will want to see evidence of your records before signing your return.

A Tax Audit

A **tax audit** is a term that strikes fear into the hearts of taxpayers. It simply means that the IRS wants to see more of your records to validate your income or deductions. In most cases, there is no cause for great concern by the taxpayer.

There are two types of audits that you may have to face. The first is the random or "black bean" audit. This simply means that your tax identification number (Social Security number) was randomly selected by the IRS's computer for a routine investigation of your tax return and supporting records. The IRS is likely to look at every item on your tax return, but under a random audit it has no reason to suspect you of any wrongdoing.

The second type of audit is a directed investigation into a special item on your tax return that appears to be unusual or out of line for your income level. Perhaps you have only $10,000 of income but have made an unusually high charitable contribution of $2,000. Examples of deductions for a typical family based on income levels are shown in Table 3.12.

If your return is being audited, you may simply be asked to send in additional information to the IRS to clear up the matter or you may be required to meet with an IRS agent to review the matter. Your tax preparer also normally participates in the process. The key to dealing with potential audits is to keep good records and to act honestly. Also, keep in mind that if you are acting in good faith, there is no reason to be passive in defending your deductions. In many cases, the IRS merely wishes to see the logic and justification behind what you have done. If the IRS rules against you, you can pay up and go about your

Table 3.12 AVERAGE ITEMIZED DEDUCTIONS

	ADJUSTED GROSS INCOME ($000)					
	20–25	25–30	30–40	40–50	50–75	75–100
Medical expenses	$1554	$1387	$1405	$1872	$2741	$5900
Taxes	1791	2195	2690	3437	4711	6833
Interest	3016	3298	3778	4679	6259	9187
Contributions	734	797	900	1113	1553	2697

SOURCE: Internal Revenue Service, U.S. Department of the Treasury, 1985.

business or appeal the ruling to higher levels in the IRS system or in the federal courts. Of course, if you suspect that someone in your family has acted fraudulently, you should obtain legal representation immediately in order to minimize the damage.

OTHER FORMS OF TAXATION

As we mentioned at the beginning of the chapter, there are other forms of taxes besides the federal income tax. The Social Security or FICA tax was 7.15 percent of salary up to $43,800 in 1987, so a person was subject to a maximum tax of $3131.70 in that year. The rate and amount subject to taxation go up regularly. This tax, unlike many state and local taxes, is not a deductible item for purposes of computing the federal income tax.

State and Local Taxes

State and local taxes vary so much by locale that it is difficult to generalize. The three primary kinds of taxes on the local level are income, sales, and property taxes. State and local taxes are normally 5 to 15 percent of income, sales taxes 3 to 6 percent of purchases, and property taxes 1 to 3 percent of property value. State and local income and property taxes are tax deductible for federal income tax purposes (if you itemize), whereas sales taxes are not.

You should consider the taxing power of a state before you locate there. A *Money* magazine story showed a ranking of the 50 states and the District of Columbia and indicated that the five highest-taxing areas are New York, Massachusetts, the District of Columbia, Maryland, and Wisconsin. The five lowest from the bottom up are Wyoming, Louisiana, Nevada, Tennessee, and Florida.[14] Of course, it is entirely possible that high-tax states also provide particularly effective health and human services.

In any event, you should include FICA, state and local taxes, and any other taxes appropriate to your circumstances when computing the total tax burden that applies to you.

SUMMARY

The tax environment changed radically with the passage of the Tax Reform Act of 1986. The main impact was to eliminate most tax shelters and many deductions and to reward the taxpayer with lower overall tax rates. The number of tax brackets was reduced from 15 to 3 and the tax rates went from 11–50 percent to 15–33 percent. Also, the size of the standard deduction was raised substantially, which meant far fewer people would choose to itemize their deductions. Finally, the size of the personal exemption was almost doubled, meaning large

[14] Sarah E. Button, "States that Tax the Most and Least," *Money,* February 1983, pp. 76–77.

families are almost assured of paying less taxes. The benefits of tax reform primarily fall to the low-income groups as indicated in Table 3.1, but many others will also be beneficiaries. The primary losers are those who formerly used large tax shelters in real estate, equipment leasing, and other areas to protect their income from taxation.

In preparing your tax return, you must determine your filing status. You may generally file as an individual, as a married couple on a joint return, or as an unmarried head of household (some married couples may choose to file separate returns in the hope of lowering their overall tax burden). The filing status determines the income bracket for the 15, 28, and 33 percent tax rates. The size of the standard deduction is also different for those in different filing categories.

One of the major decisions a taxpayer must make is whether to itemize deductions or to take the standard deduction. Because tax reform raised the standard deduction and eliminated some other deductions, many more taxpayers are choosing to use the standard deduction rather than itemizing each expense item by item. Nevertheless, the use of itemized deductions will still remain important for many homeowners because of the large size of such tax deductible housing expenses as home mortgage interest and property taxes.

There are few tax shelters remaining after the Tax Reform Act of 1986, but among the best is the use of tax-exempt public-purpose municipal bonds. The utilization of an individual retirement account (IRA) is also attractive, but there are some restrictions for those in a work-related retirement plan. The ability to use a tax deductible IRA is restricted to $35,000 of total income for individuals (actually the phaseout in the deduction begins at $25,000) and $50,000 for joint return filers (the phaseout starts at $40,000). For those not participating in a work-related retirement plan, a tax deductible IRA contribution is available regardless of income level.

A key question for you as a taxpayer is whether to prepare the return yourself or use an outside party. For uncomplicated returns, you can learn a lot about the tax code by trying the process yourself. An alternative is to use a local or national tax preparation service. For more complicated returns, a CPA is recommended.

KEY TERMS

adjusted gross income
dependent
earned income credit
gross income
individual retirement account (IRA)
itemized deductions
joint return
personal exemption
standard deduction
tax audit
tax credit
Tax Reform Act of 1986
tax shelter
tax withholding
unmarried head of household

SELECTED READINGS

Button, Sarah E. "States That Tax the Most and Least." *Money,* February 1983, pp. 76–77.

"How Tax Reform Affects You." *Newsweek,* August 25, 1986, pp. 18–22.

Osserman, R. A. "How to Negotiate a Settlement with the IRS—After the Audit." *Practical Accountant,* February 1982, pp. 47–54.

Seixas, Suzanne, and Leslie Laurence. "What Tax Reform Will Do to Four Typical Families," *Money,* October 1986, pp. 118–130.

The Tax Revolution: A New Era Begins. New York: Deloitte, Haskins and Sells, 1986.

Regular Annual Publications (Tax Guides)

Commerce Clearing House *Tax Guide.*

H & R Block's *Income Tax Workbook.*

J. K. Lasser's *Your Income Tax* (Simon & Schuster).

Tax Research of America's *Individual Tax Return Guide.*

"Your Federal Income Tax," Publication 17 (Internal Revenue Service).

QUESTIONS

1 Compare the current maximum tax rate for individuals with past levels of maximum rates for individuals.

2 How did the Tax Reform Act of 1986 change the number of tax brackets and the range the brackets covered?

3 What is a tax shelter? In what industries are tax shelters frequently found?

4 Write down which of the following expenses are eliminated or phased out from being tax deductible under the Tax Reform Act of 1986:

property taxes
moving expenses
sales tax expense
alimony payments
interest on consumer loans
casualty and theft losses

5 What income group is likely to be the main beneficiary of the Tax Reform Act of 1986? Who might end up paying more taxes?

6 What four requirements must one satisfy to file as an unmarried head of household?

7 What is the dollar amount of the personal exemption deduction in 1988? in 1989? If another party claims you as a personal exemption for purposes of taking the deduction, can you also take the personal exemption deduction yourself?

8 What is an individual retirement account? How large a deduction can an individual take? What about a married couple filing a joint return if there is only one working spouse? How large is the potential IRA deduction if there are two working spouses?

9 Explain the difference between itemizing deductions and taking the standard deduction. If an unmarried head of household has itemized deductions of $3800, should he or she take the standard deduction?

10 What is meant by the statement that the IRS collects taxes on a pay-as-you-go basis in terms of taxpayer obligations?

11 Why is a renter less likely to itemize deductions than a homeowner?

12 Why are municipal bonds an advantageous investment under the tax laws? What types of municipal bonds qualify for special tax treatment under the new tax laws?

13 Interest on consumer loans is being phased out as a tax deduction expense. Indicate the schedule for the phasing out. (That is, what percent a year will remain deductible?)

14 If you are an individual who participates in a retirement plan at work and has an income of $40,000, can you still establish a tax deductible IRA on your own? What about if you have an income of $200,000 but do not participate in a retirement plan at work? Can you set up a tax deductible IRA on your own?

15 Suppose you do not participate in a retirement plan at work. Your sole source of income ($10,000) is from interest on bonds that your grandmother provided. Can you open up a tax deductible IRA account?

16 If you decide not to fill out a tax form yourself, whom can you look to for potential help (excluding the IRS)?

17 What is the difference between a random audit and a directed audit?

18 Compute the tax obligation on a single tax return for each of the following taxable income levels:

a $15,000
b $38,000
c $87,200

19 You are figuring the tax return for an unmarried head of household who is 68 years old. How large a standard deduction can he or she take?

20 Assume the following expenses:

Medical and dental expenses	$2500
State and local taxes	1200
Home mortgage interest	4000
Charitable contributions	500
Employee business expense	500
Moving expenses	500

Also assume that adjusted gross income is $20,000. How large will the itemized deductions be?

21 A 25-year-old junior executive has the following expenses:

Medical and dental expenses	$ 900
State and local taxes	1000
Sales taxes	900
Charitable contributions	700
Employee business expenses	1800
Moving expenses	900

Assume that adjusted gross income is $30,000.

a How large will the itemized deductions be? Only include those items that are tax deductible under the Tax Reform Act of 1986.

b Should this individual use the itemized deductions or the standard deduction?

c If this were a joint return instead of a single return, would your answer to part b change?

22 A family of five takes the standard deduction and five personal exemptions ($1950 each in 1988). On an income of $13,500, will they pay any taxes? Do the necessary calculations and explain your answer.

23 A young, widowed mother has $8800 of taxable income. To partially offset her tax obligation, she has an earned income credit of 14 percent on $4000 of her income.

a Compute her tax obligation on $8800 (before the credit).

b What is the value of her earned income credit?

c How much will she have to pay in taxes?

d If $1200 were withheld from her wages during the year, would she receive a refund the following year? If so, what would be the size of the refund?

24 Compute the tax obligation for a married couple with two children by using the following data to fill in the table below:

Total salaries	$32,000
Interest income	1,000
IRA contributions	4,000
Medical and dental expenses	2,300
State and local taxes	1,400
Home mortgage interest	3,600
Charitable contributions	250
Employee business expenses	650

Personal exemptions equal $1950 per person. The couple is going to itemize their deductions rather than take the standard deduction.

1. Total salaries	32.000
2. Interest income	1.000
3. Total income	33.000
4. −IRA contributions	4.000
5. Adjusted gross income	29.000

Itemized deductions:

6. Medical and dental expenses
Deduction for medical and dental expenses (line 6 minus 7.5% of line 5)
7. State and local taxes
8. Home mortgage interest
9. Charitable contributions
10. Employee business expenses
Deduction for employee business expenses (line 10 minus 2% of line 5)
11. Total itemized deductions
12. Taxable income before personal exemption (line 5 minus line 11)
13. Personal exemptions (4 × $1950)
14. Taxable income (line 12 minus line 13)
15. Taxes owed (tax rate from Table 3.4 times line 14)

25 Compute the tax obligation for Janice Arnold, M.D., by using the data to fill in the table below. Dr. Arnold is single.

Total earnings	$95,000
Interest income	4,000
IRA contribution	2,000
Medical and dental expenses	400
State and local taxes	6,000
Home mortgage interest (condominium)	9,000
Charitable contributions	1,800
Employee business expense	1,000

Her personal exemption equals $1950 in 1988. She is going to itemize deductions rather than take the standard deduction.

1. Total earnings
2. Interest income
3. Total income
4. −IRA contribution
5. Adjusted gross income

Itemized deductions:

6. Medical and dental expenses
Deduction for medical and dental expenses (line 6 minus 7.5% of line 5). Enter 0 if negative
7. State and local taxes
8. Home mortgage interest
9. Charitable contributions
10. Employee business expense
Deduction for employee business expense (line 10 minus 2% of line 5). Enter 0 if negative.
11. Total itemized deductions
12. Taxable income before personal exemption (line 5 minus line 11)
13. Personal exemption (1 × $1950)

14. Taxable income (line 12 minus line 13) __________
15. Taxes owed (tax rates from Table 3.4 times line 14) __________

26 Indicate the maximum IRA contribution that would be allowed under the following circumstances. All income is assumed to be earned.

a Individual, with retirement plan at work, earns $27,000.
b Individual, without retirement plan at work, earns $38,000.
c Married couple, with one spouse working, earns $45,000. They do not have a retirement plan at work.
d Married couple, with both spouses working, earns $49,000. They participate in retirement plans at work.

CASE PROBLEMS

3.1 In March 1988, Lisa Gomez is considering the purchase of a car. She currently works as a fashion consultant. She checks out a book from the library on purchasing an automobile that was written in 1984. The book says you can deduct the sales tax and the interest on an auto loan for tax purposes. She then remembers the lecture that Professor Quick gave on personal income taxes at State U. In checking her notes she determines that the sales tax deduction was eliminated by the Tax Reform Act of 1986 and that under the same legislation, consumer interest deductions are only 40 percent deductible in 1988, 20 percent deductible in 1989, 10 percent deductible in 1990, and none thereafter.

The proposed new auto purchase is for $12,000. The state sales tax is 5 percent. Furthermore, the interest payments on the auto loan will be $1200 in 1988, $800 in 1989, $500 in 1990, and $200 in 1991.

a For each year from 1988 to 1991, indicate separately the amount of tax deductible expenses that Lisa could claim based on the rules in place *before* and *after* the Tax Reform Act of 1986.
b Does your answer to part a tend to influence the maximum amount that Lisa might be able to justify for an auto purchase?
c If Lisa had intended to take the standard deduction regardless of your analysis, how important are the losses of these tax deductible write-offs?

3.2 Earl "The Tank" Simmons has just signed a pro football contract with the New York Bulldogs. His first-year salary is $80,000. He is seriously considering marrying Nancy Willis, who is still a senior in college. Since his financial adviser considers the tax ramifications of all of Earl's decisions, he will first of all determine Earl's taxable income for a joint return as well as a single return. He will also compute the taxes owed under each of these circumstances.

a In determining taxable income for the joint return, allow two personal exemptions of $1950 and a standard deduction for a joint filing. Exclude all other deductions.

In determining taxable income for a single return, allow one personal exemption of $1950 and the appropriate standard deduction for a single filing. Exclude all other deductions.

b Having determined taxable income for a joint and single return in part a, compute the tax obligation under both of these circumstances.

c If both parties on a joint return each earned about the same amount (say in the low twenties), would it still be advantageous to have a joint return? You do not need to supply a numerical answer. This is more of a thought question. But you may wish to refer to Table 3.4 to help you in the thought process.

Appendix 3A

Computing the Tax Burden for Upper Income Levels

Understanding the Phaseout of the 15 Percent Bracket and the Loss of Personal Exemptions

One of the least understood features of the Tax Reform Act of 1986 is how the law affects upper-income taxpayers. However, this material is not essential to understanding the tax law in general so you can bypass the appendix if the material is not of interest to you.

To formally begin the discussion, Table 3.2 on tax rates is reproduced as Table 3A.1.

Attention should be directed to the married (joint return) brackets and rates, although the same principles apply to individuals and unmarried heads of households. There are two important provisions in the tax law that affect upper-income taxpayers.

Phaseout of the 15 Percent Bracket

There is a 5 percent surtax built into the table, which automatically takes place between income levels of \$71,900 and \$149,250. This bracket is referred to as the third bracket or 33 percent bracket and covers \$77,350 (\$149,250 − \$71,900). Five percent of \$77,350 equals \$3867, which is the maximum amount of the surtax. Adding \$3867 to the normal tax obligation is exactly the same as eliminating the 15 percent tax bracket for upper-income taxpayers. As you can see in Table 3A.1, the 15 percent tax bracket applies to \$29,750 of income for joint filers. If 28 percent were applied instead of 15 percent on the first \$29,750 of income, \$3867 more in taxes would be required, as shown in the following calculations.

First bracket at 28%		First bracket at 15%	
\$29,750		\$29,750	
× 28%		× 15%	
\$ 8,330	−	\$ 4,463	= \$3,867

Table 3A.1
TAX RATES UNDER THE TAX REFORM ACT OF 1986 (BASED ON TAXABLE INCOME)

Single

$0–$17,850	15% of the amount
$17,850–$43,150	28% of the amount over $17,850
$43,150–$89,560	33% of the amount over $43,150

The third bracket is extended by $10,920 per personal exemption. After that point, it reverts back to 28 percent.

Married (joint return)

$0–$29,750	15% of the amount
$29,750–$71,900	28% of the amount over $29,750
$71,900–$149,250	33% of the amount over $71,900

The third bracket is extended by $10,920 per personal exemption. After that point, it reverts back to 28 percent.

Unmarried head of household

$0–$23,900	15% of the amount
$23,900–$61,650	28% of the amount over $23,900
$61,650–$123,790	33% of the amount over $61,650

The third bracket is extended by $10,920 per personal exemption. After that point, it reverts back to 28 percent.

Instead of eliminating the first bracket for high-income taxpayers, the surtax is created in a third bracket. The consequence is exactly the same. An additional tax of $3867 is paid.

Loss of Personal Exemptions Benefits

The government also desired to take the value of personal exemptions away from taxpayers with very high incomes. For example, for those filing a joint return with income above $149,250, one continues to pay the 5 percent surtax on $10,920 of income for each personal exemption claimed. This represents an added tax of $546. This number is exactly equal to the value of a personal exemption in 1988 in terms of tax savings; that is, a personal exemption is worth $546 (28 percent × $1950). By continuing the surtax on $10,920 of income for each exemption, the government is essentially eliminating the value of the exemption for upper-income taxpayers. A wealthy taxpayer claims the personal exemption, but the benefit is offset or neutralized through the additional surtax.

Appendix 3B

IRS Phone Numbers by State

To Call IRS Toll-Free for Answers to Your Federal Tax Questions, Use Only the Number Listed Below for Your Area

Caution: *"Toll-free" is a telephone call for which you pay only local charges with no long-distance charge. Please use a local city number only if it is not a long-distance call for you. Otherwise, use the general toll-free number given.*

We are happy to answer questions to help you prepare your return. But you should know that you are responsible for the accuracy of your return. If we do make an error, you are still responsible for the payment of the correct tax.

To make sure that IRS employees give courteous responses and correct information to taxpayers, a second IRS employee sometimes listens in on telephone calls. No record is kept of any taxpayer's name, address, or social security number.

If you find it necessary to write instead of calling, please address your letter to your IRS District Director for a prompt reply. Make sure you include your social security number or taxpayer identifying number when you write.

The IRS has a telephone service called Tele-Tax. It provides automated refund information and recorded tax information tapes on about 150 topics covering such areas as filing requirements, dependents, itemized deductions, and tax credits. Tele-Tax is available 24 hours a day, 7 days a week, to taxpayers using push-button (tone signaiiing) telephones, and Monday through Friday, during office hours, to taxpayers using push-button (pulse dial) or rotary (dial) phones.

ALABAMA
Call 1-800-424-1040

ALASKA
Anchorage, 276-1040
Elsewhere in Alaska, call operator and ask for Zenith 3700

ARIZONA
Phoenix, 257-1233
Tucson, 882-4181

ARKANSAS
Call 1-800-424-1040

CALIFORNIA
Please call the telephone number shown in the white pages of your local telephone directory under U.S. government, Internal Revenue Service, Federal Tax Assistance.

COLORADO
Denver, 825-7041

CONNECTICUT
Call 1-800-424-1040

DELAWARE
Wilmington, 573-6400

DISTRICT OF COLUMBIA
Call 488-3100

FLORIDA
Jacksonville, 354-1760

GEORGIA
Atlanta, 522-0050

HAWAII
Oahu, 546-8660
All other islands, 1-800-232-2511

IDAHO
Call 1-800-424-1040

ILLINOIS
Chicago, 435-1040

INDIANA
Indianapolis, 269-5477

IOWA
Des Moines, 283-0523

KANSAS
Call 1-800-424-1040

KENTUCKY
Call 1-800-424-1040

LOUISIANA
Call 1-800-424-1040

MAINE
Call 1-800-424-1040

MARYLAND
Baltimore, 962-2590
Prince George's County, 488-3100
Montgomery County, 488-3100

MASSACHUSETTS
Boston, 523-1040

MICHIGAN
Detroit, 237-0800

MINNESOTA
Minneapolis, 291-1422
St. Paul, 291-1422

MISSISSIPPI
Call 1-800-424-1040

MISSOURI
St. Louis, 342-1040

MONTANA
Call 1-800-424-1040

NEBRASKA
Omaha, 422-1500

NEVADA
Las Vegas, 388-6291

NEW HAMPSHIRE
Call 1-800-424-1040

NEW JERSEY
Newark, 622-0600

NEW MEXICO
Call 1-800-424-1040

NEW YORK
Bronx, 732-0100
Brooklyn, 596-3770
Buffalo, 855-3955
Manhattan, 732-0100
Nassau, 294-3600
Queens, 596-3770
Rockland County, 997-1510
Staten Island, 732-0100
Suffolk, 724-5000
Westchester County, 997-1510

NORTH CAROLINA
Greensboro, 274-3711

NORTH DAKOTA
Call 1-800-424-1040

OHIO
Cincinnati, 621-6281
Cleveland, 522-3000

OKLAHOMA
Call 1-800-424-1040

OREGON
Portland, 221-3960

PENNSYLVANIA
Philadelphia, 574-9900
Pittsburgh, 281-0112

PUERTO RICO
San Juan Metro Area, 753-4040
Isla DDD, 753-4549

RHODE ISLAND
Providence, 274-1040

SOUTH CAROLINA
Call 1-800-424-1040

SOUTH DAKOTA
Call 1-800-424-1040

TENNESSEE
Nashville, 259-4601

TEXAS
Austin, 472-1974
Corpus Christi, 888-9431
Dallas, 742-2440
El Paso, 532-6116
Ft. Worth, 335-1370
Houston, 965-0440
San Antonio, 229-1700

UTAH
Salt Lake City, 524-4060

VERMONT
Burlington, 658-1870

VIRGINIA
Bailey's Crossroads, 557-9230
Richmond, 649-2361

WASHINGTON
Seattle, 442-1040

WEST VIRGINIA
Call 1-800-424-1040

WISCONSIN
Milwaukee, 271-3780

WYOMING
Call 1-800-424-1040

Note: If there is no number listed for your specific area, please call 1-800-424-1040.

Telephone Assistance
Services for Deaf Taxpayers Who Have Access to TV/Telephone—TTY Equipment

Hours of Operation

8:00 A.M. to 6:45 P.M. EST (Filing Season)

8:00 A.M. to 4:30 P.M. EST (Nonfiling Season)

Indiana residents, 1-800-382-4059

Elsewhere in U.S., including Alaska, Hawaii, Virgin Islands, and Puerto Rico, 1-800-428-4732

Toll-Free "Forms Only" Telephone Numbers

If you only need to order tax forms and publications and do not have any tax questions, please call the number listed below for your area. If there is no telephone number listed for your state or specific area, please refer to the toll-free telephone numbers listed above.

ALABAMA
Call 1-800-241-3860

ALASKA
Anchorage, 276-4368

ARIZONA
Phoenix, 257-9722
Tucson, 882-0730

CONNECTICUT
Call 1-800-225-0717

FLORIDA
Call 1-800-241-3860

GEORGIA
Atlanta, 221-6023
Elsewhere in Georgia, 1-800-282-6689

HAWAII
Honolulu, 546-7300

MAINE
Call 1-800-225-0717

MARYLAND
Baltimore, 962-0801

MASSACHUSETTS
Boston, 367-1040
Elsewhere in Massachusetts, 1-800-892-0288

MICHIGAN
Detroit, 237-0794
Residents in Area Code 313, 1-800-462-9910
Elsewhere in Michigan, 1-800-482-0828

MINNESOTA
St. Paul, 224-7461

MISSISSIPPI
Call 1-800-241-3860

MISSOURI
Kansas City, 421-2330
St. Louis, 231-6505

MONTANA
Call 1-800-547-4960

NEBRASKA
Omaha, 221-3321
Elsewhere in Nebraska, 1-800-642-8278

NEVADA
Las Vegas, 388-6516

NEW HAMPSHIRE
Call 1-800-225-0717

NEW JERSEY
Camden, 966-7200
Hackensack, 342-1211
Newark, 622-5550
Paterson, 278-0339
Trenton, 393-0900
Elsewhere in New Jersey, 1-800-242-0249

NEW YORK
Albany, 1-800-225-0717
Bronx, 732-0240
Brooklyn, 596-3610
Buffalo, 847-1510
Manhattan, 732-0240
Nassau County, 294-3700
Rockland County, 997-1410
Staten Island, 732-0240
Suffolk County, 724-8836
Westchester County, 997-1410
Western New York, 1-800-462-1860

NORTH CAROLINA
Call 1-800-241-3860

OREGON
Portland, 221-3933
Elsewhere in Oregon, 1-800-452-1996

PENNSYLVANIA
Allentown, 866-2914
Philadelphia, 627-7373
Pittsburgh, 281-0137

RHODE ISLAND
Call 1-800-225-0717

SOUTH CAROLINA
Call 1-800-241-3860

TENNESSEE
Call 1-800-241-3860

UTAH
Salt Lake City, 524-4368

VERMONT
Call 1-800-225-0717

WASHINGTON
Seattle, 442-5100
Elsewhere in Washington, 1-800-542-7890

WISCONSIN
Milwaukee, 291-3244
Elsewhere in Wisconsin, 1-800-242-9699

SOURCE: Internal Revenue Service, U.S. Department of the Treasury.

If you are sometimes confused by the claims of cereal or detergent manufacturers, just wait until you see what financial institutions have in store for you. Although you may already have a checking or savings account, that does not ensure that you are getting the best deal for your money. To the extent that you are paying more for your checking services than necessary or accepting less than the market rate for your savings dollar, you are subsidizing a smarter, more discerning customer. All financial institutions (banks, savings and loans, credit unions, and so on) are partially dependent on the apathy of a segment of the population to meet their total objectives. We hope that you will not be part of this segment.

In Chapter 4, you will be exposed to the ins and outs of using bank services. There are many different kinds of checking accounts: a no-minimum checking account, a regular checking account, a NOW account, a super NOW account, and so on. To determine which is best for you, you should explore the material in the chap-

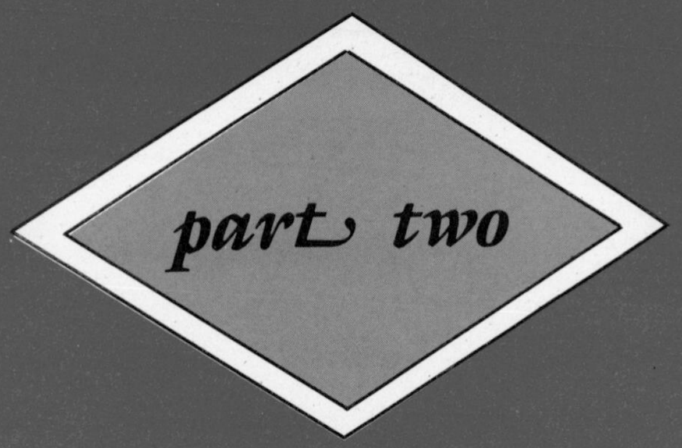

THE ENVIRONMENT FOR FINANCIAL SERVICES

ter. Also, the rate of return you receive on a savings instrument depends on the quoted rate of interest, the compounding method, the interest-crediting procedure, and other factors as well. Federal regulatory agencies require full disclosure of the procedures used by financial institutions, but this disclosure has little meaning if you are not well informed on financial matters.

Chapter 5 is exclusively devoted to the use (or misuse) of credit. We first explore sources of credit such as charge accounts, bank credit cards, and travel and entertainment cards. We also help you read and interpret the monthly statement for a charge or credit account so that you know the procedures and fees involved. Also, when you borrow cash, you have many potential options such as a bank, a consumer finance company, a savings and loan, a credit union, an insurance company, and even a pawnshop. In Chapter 5 we discuss all of these as well as the procedures for computing the annual percentage rate (APR) on the loan. ■

4

Using Commercial Bank Services

After studying this chapter, you should:

- Understand the importance of banks
- Know how to select, open, use, and benefit from a checking account
- Be able to compute the costs associated with maintaining a bank account
- Understand the types of special services available from banks and other financial institutions
- Appreciate the role of savings accounts and know how to use these accounts
- Know how to obtain a bank loan

The more than 14,000 commercial banks in this country offer a wide variety of financial services to American consumers. In recent years the number of these services has expanded tremendously. Today, many banks aim to be financial supermarkets—offering virtually every financial service that a consumer may desire. In the past, banks were primarily viewed only as places to deposit and borrow money; the consumer had to rely on different financial institutions to obtain other financial services. Now, however, you can find banks that offer almost any personal financial service. Through your bank you can pay your bills, obtain a credit card, execute stockbrokerage transactions, and receive financial counseling. These services are in addition to the more traditional bank deposit and lending activities.

Because of the explosion in the number of financial services offered, many banks proclaim to be one-stop personal finance centers. In addition, several nonbank financial institutions, such as credit unions, mutual savings banks, and savings and loan associations, have expanded their available services to the extent that they seriously challenge banks as financial supermarkets. At the same time, personal financial planning has become more complex. As a consumer, you are confronted with a seemingly endless array of financial services and products. You will most likely want to use several of these services and products to assist in the management of your financial affairs. If you are like most consumers, however, you are probably unsure about how to select the services that are most beneficial to you.

In this chapter we discuss several important banking considerations:

1 How to select, open, use, and benefit from a checking account
2 The costs associated with maintaining a bank account
3 The types of special services available from banks
4 The role of savings accounts and how to use these accounts
5 How to obtain a bank loan

ESTABLISHING CHECKING ACCOUNTS

About four out of every five Americans have a **checking account.** Next to cash payments, writing checks is the most frequently used method for making payment. The typical individual writes 24 checks each month and maintains an average checking account balance of almost $1000. Table 4.1 shows the importance of checking accounts. In July 1986, checking account balances at commercial banks totaled $288.3 billion. At the same time, other types of checkable accounts contained another $203.9 billion. Checking accounts are offered by a wide variety of financial institutions including commercial banks, savings and loan associations, mutual savings banks, and credit unions. Because of the similarity of these accounts among the various institutions, we confine our discussion to checking accounts at commercial banks. We begin with a discussion of how to select a checking account.

Selecting a Checking Account

You should have no difficulty in opening a checking account. At most banks you can accomplish this task in only a few minutes. Before you open an account, however, you should devote considerably more time to two other matters. First, you should compare banks to determine the one most suitable for you. Second, you need to select the most appropriate type of checking account for your needs.

Choosing a Bank. You will want to compare banks to determine which one is the best for you. To make an intelligent choice, you should consider three factors: convenience, cost, and services provided. Considering the frequency with which you are likely to use banking services, it is important to select a bank that

Table 4.1
BALANCES IN VARIOUS DEPOSIT-TYPE ACCOUNTS, JULY 1986

Type of account	Amount ($ billions)
Checking account at commercial banks	288.3
Other checking accounts[a]	203.9
Savings accounts	
At commercial banks	133.4
At thrift institutions	197.8
Time deposits	
Small (under $100,000)	883.2
Large ($100,000 and above)	446.5
Money market mutual funds	276.9

[a] Consists of NOW, super NOW, credit union share draft, and demand deposits at thrift (nonbank) institutions.

SOURCE: *Federal Reserve Bulletin,* Washington, D.C.: Board of Governors of the Federal Reserve System, October 1986.

gives you easy access to these services. You do not necessarily have to live or work near your bank, but you should be sure that you can readily make deposits and withdrawals. Often this can be done through bank branches or automated teller machines. Other services can often be obtained via mail or telephone.

You should compare the cost of services at different banks. These costs vary considerably. Some banks offer "free checking" privileges where the depositor pays no service charge when a specified minimum or average account balance is maintained. Other banks charge a monthly **service fee** regardless of the amount of your account balance. Many banks impose additional fees for checking account activities. A **clearing fee** may be charged for each check written against your account. You may also be required to pay a charge for printing your personalized checks or for inquiring about the current balance in your account. Many other checking-related fees may exist. It is important that you know about these costs before opening a checking account. Then you can estimate the annual cost of your checking account based upon the average number of checks you anticipate writing each month.

Banks offer numerous financial services. These services differ from bank to bank. Some banks offer only basic deposit and lending arrangements, but others provide an abundance of financial services. Depending on the bank you choose, you may be able to obtain a large number of varied services including credit cards, financial counseling, and professional money management. The services that appeal to you the most may largely influence your selection of a bank.

Remember, although your first inclination may be to choose the bank nearest your home or office, you should also consider cost and service factors before making your final decision.

Types of Checking Accounts. After you have selected a bank, you need to determine what kind of checking account is most appropriate for your needs. Regular checking accounts rank among the oldest and most popular forms of payment. Recently, however, new forms of checking accounts have emerged. In 1980, the federal government authorized credit unions to issue interest-bearing share drafts, and in 1981, it allowed banks and savings and loans to issue interest-bearing negotiable order of withdrawal (NOW) accounts. In the following section we discuss the types of checking accounts. These alternatives include regular accounts, no-minimum accounts, NOW accounts, super NOW accounts, and share drafts. Table 4.2 compares typical features of these accounts.

Regular Account. The **regular checking account** offers unlimited checking services. The cost of this type of account depends on the number of transactions in a month and the minimum balance maintained during the month. Monthly service and transaction fees are not charged when a specified minimum balance is maintained. This minimum amount varies among banks, but most banks require about a $500 minimum to waive fees. When the minimum balance is not maintained, the bank imposes a monthly service fee and charge for each check written. Although these charges vary, most banks assess a $3 to $5 monthly service fee and between 20 cents and 25 cents for each check written during the month. Some banks may waive these fees for certain groups such as college students or senior citizens. The minimum balance may be determined using one of two methods: lowest daily balance or average daily balance.

Lowest daily balance: Your bank may set your minimum balance to equal the **lowest daily balance** at any time during the month. Your monthly service charge is based on that lowest balance, regardless of how much money you keep in your checking account during the rest of the month.

Average daily balance: Under the **average daily balance** method, your bank calculates the average amount of money you maintain in your account each day. That average determines the amount of your monthly service fee. A brief example shows how service fees may vary between these two methods.

Suppose your bank imposes the following monthly service fees: $3 for a minimum balance between $300 and $500 and $5 for amounts less than $300. A minimum balance exceeding $500 evokes no service fee. We assume that your daily account balance is $600 for the first 10 days, $200 for the next three days, and $900 for the remaining 17 days of the month. Your minimum balance using the lowest daily balance method equals $200 because that is the lowest amount observed for any day during the month. Based on the fee schedule, a $5 monthly fee is imposed. If, on the other hand, your bank uses your average daily balance to calculate the minimum balance, the result will be different. The average daily balance equals $730, determined as follows: ($600 × 10/30) + ($200 × 3/30) + ($900 × 17/30). Accordingly, you pay no monthly service fee because your average

Table 4.2 TYPICAL FEATURES OF CHECKING ACCOUNTS

Type of account	Minimum to earn interest	Interest rate (%)	Minimum to avoid fees	Monthly service charge	Per-check charge
No-minimum	NA	NA	NA	$3.00	$ .25
Regular checking	NA	NA	$ 500	3.00	.25
NOW	$ 100	5.25	1000	5.00	.25
Super NOW	2500	6.50	2500	5.00	.25
Share draft	237	5.90	300	3.00	.15

NA = not applicable.

SOURCE: From *The Bank Book—How to Get the Most for Your Banking Dollars* by Naphtali Hoffman and Stephen Brobeck, copyright © 1986 by Consumer Federation of America. Reprinted by permission of Harcourt, Brace, Jovanovich, Inc.

daily balance exceeds the $500 minimum threshold. Table 4.3 summarizes the results.

No-Minimum Account. You may find that you need to write only a few checks each month. In this case you may not want to keep a large balance in your account. A **no-minimum account** may best satisfy your needs. The bank charges a monthly service fee, regardless of the balance in your account, and an additional fee for each check written. The primary advantage of this type of account is that the monthly service fee is typically lower than the monthly fee on a regular account. If you write checks infrequently, this account may be less expensive to maintain than a regular account.

NOW Account. Until 1981, banks were not allowed to pay interest on checking accounts. Currently, however, most banks offer interest-bearing checking accounts. These are **negotiable order of withdrawal,** or **NOW,** accounts. When minimum balances are kept, the interest earned is usually 5 to 5¼ percent. If somewhat higher balances are maintained, monthly service and transaction fees are waived. NOW account minimums are usually higher than those on regular checking accounts. When the minimums are not met, the fees are also generally higher.

Table 4.3 DETERMINING THE MONTHLY SERVICE FEE

Method	Minimum balance	Monthly service fee
Lowest daily balance	$200	$5.00
Average daily balance	730	None

Super NOW Account. **Super NOW accounts** closely resemble NOW accounts but pay a higher interest rate if a larger minimum balance is maintained. Although some financial institutions require a $1000 minimum balance, most require $2500. Unlike NOW accounts, super NOW accounts do not have a fixed maximum interest rate. Rather, interest rates are allowed to fluctuate. Recently the typical super NOW interest rate was about 6 percent. Most institutions treat super NOW accounts as NOW accounts during months when the minimum balance is not achieved. As a result, if your balance falls below the super NOW minimum, you continue to earn interest and avoid transaction fees as long as the NOW account minimum is met.

Share Drafts. Many credit unions offer interest-bearing **share drafts.** These accounts are essentially the same as NOW accounts offered by banks and savings and loans. Most credit unions offering share drafts impose no service charges or transaction fees, regardless of the size of the account. Furthermore, most credit unions require no minimum balance to earn interest on these accounts. Among those that require a minimum, the required balance is small, recently averaging less than $250. The average interest rate paid on share draft accounts typically is slightly higher than those paid on regular NOW accounts, but somewhat less than the rates offered on most super NOW accounts.

Package Plan Account. Many banks now offer a **package plan** which provides a combination of services for a single fee. Services provided under a typical package plan include the following: unlimited check writing, personalized checks, overdraft protection, free travelers checks and cashiers checks, a safe deposit box, and preferred interest rates on personal loans. Package accounts make sense for people who use virtually every type of bank service, but few individuals really need all these services. If you do not make extensive use of many bank services, you will probably find that the additional expense of a package account is not justifiable.

Opening a Checking Account

Once you have selected a bank and determined the type of checking account you want, you are then ready to open the account. To do so you must complete information and signature cards, decide on a single or joint account, select checks, and make an initial deposit.

Information and Signature Cards. To open a checking account you must complete an **information card** that gives your name, address, telephone number, occupation and employer, and other pertinent facts. You must also sign a **signature card.** The bank compares the signature on checks written on your account to the signature on this card to ensure the authenticity of the checks. A sample signature card completed by Alan and Janet Berry is presented in Figure 4.1.

Figure 4.1 SAMPLE OF SIGNATURE CARD

INTEREST, TIME AND CHARGES:

a ANNUAL INTEREST RATE ______ %
b COMPOUNDED ______
c ANNUAL YIELD ______ %
d ASSUMED DAYS/ANNUM ______
e STATEMENT CYCLE ______
f DAILY CUT-OFF TIME ______
g MAINTENANCE FEE $______
h FEE PER WITHDRAWAL ITEM $______
i INSUFFICIENT FUNDS ITEM $______
j OVERDRAFT ITEM $______
k RETURNED DEPOSIT ITEM $______
l STOP-PAYMENT REQUEST $______
m STOP-PAYMENT RENEWAL $______
n CHECKS (PER ______) $______

EXPLANATION:

A DORMANT ACCOUNT FEE of $______ will be charged each ______ if for ______ (previous) there is no activity or other indication in writing from you of an interest in this Account

TYPE OF ACCOUNT — PERSONAL:

☐ INDIVIDUAL
☒ JOINT - WITH SURVIVORSHIP
☐ JOINT - NO SURVIVORSHIP
☐ ______
☐ TRUST
  ☐ SEPARATE AGREEMENT
  ☐ BENEFICIARIES NAMED HEREIN
☐ PAY-ON-DEATH (BENEFICIARIES NAMED HEREIN)

DATE ______ BY ______
INITIAL DEPOSIT $ ______
OCCUPATION(S) ______
TELEPHONE NO S ______
OTHER BANKING ______

TRUST OR PAY ON DEATH BENEFICIARY DESIGNATION
NAME ______
ADDRESS ______
NAME ______
ADDRESS ______

TYPE OF ACCOUNT — BUSINESS:

☐ SOLE PROPRIETORSHIP
☐ PARTNERSHIP
☐ CORPORATION - FOR PROFIT
☐ CORPORATION - NOT FOR PROFIT
☐ ______

BUSINESS COUNTY AND STATE OF ORGANIZATION ______
AUTHORIZATION DATED ______

(Name and address of someone who will always know your whereabouts)

NAME AND ADDRESS

ACCOUNT NUMBER
NUMBER OF SIGNATURES REQUIRED FOR WITHDRAWAL:

SIGNATURES - THE UNDERSIGNED AGREE(S) TO THE TERMS STATED ON THE FRONT AND BACK OF THIS FORM, and acknowledge(s) receipt of at least one copy on the date stated.

(1) X ______
(2) X ______
(3) X ______

☒ CHECKING ☐ NOW ☐ SAVINGS

☐ **TAXPAYER I.D. NUMBER - MY CORRECT TAXPAYER IDENTIFICATION NUMBER IS:**

☐ **BACKUP WITHHOLDING - I AM NOT SUBJECT TO BACKUP WITHHOLDING EITHER BECAUSE I HAVE NOT BEEN NOTIFIED THAT I AM SUBJECT TO BACKUP WITHHOLDING AS A RESULT OF A FAILURE TO REPORT ALL INTEREST OR DIVIDENDS, OR THE INTERNAL REVENUE SERVICE HAS NOTIFIED ME THAT I AM NO LONGER SUBJECT TO BACKUP WITHHOLDING.**

☐ **EXEMPT RECIPIENT - I AM AN EXEMPT RECIPIENT UNDER THE INTERNAL REVENUE SERVICE REGULATIONS. (SEE INSTRUCTIONS.)**

SIGNATURE - BY SIGNING BELOW I CERTIFY UNDER PENALTIES OF PERJURY THE STATEMENTS CHECKED IN THIS BOX.

X ______

ACCOUNT AGREEMENT AA-SC-A

SOURCE: Courtesy of Banker's Systems, Inc., 1985.

Single or Joint Account. A **single account** is opened by only one person. Only that individual can write a check on the account. A **joint account** can be opened in the name of any two people, but usually this is done for a husband and wife. With a joint account both people sign the signature card, as is the case for the Berrys in Figure 4.1. Either person can write a check on the joint account. Married couples often use a joint account with the right of survivorship. This type of account allows both parties to draw on the account, and if one party dies, the other can continue to use the account. If, on the other hand, the deceased person had a single account, the surviving partner could not obtain access to those funds until the deceased's estate had been probated.

Check Selection. Most banks offer several types of **check**s. Checks come in different colors and with various designs and may cost a few dollars to purchase. You may obtain either personalized or plain checks. You will receive some temporary checks when you initially open your account. These checks are not personalized but will have your new account number printed on them.

Initial Deposit. You must make an initial deposit to open your new account. Some banks require a minimum deposit generally ranging from \$25 to \$50 to open an account, but many other banks do not have a minimum requirement.

Using a Checking Account

Now that you have opened a checking account, you are ready to use it. To use the account properly, you must understand how to write checks, endorse checks, make deposits, and record all transactions. You should also understand the check-clearing process.

Writing Checks. Check writing requires a relatively small effort. Nevertheless, you must take certain precautions to prevent your check from being altered or forged. When you write a check, you enter the name of the person or vendor to whom you are making payment (the payee) on the appropriate line. It is usually safer to make a check payable to a specific person or vendor. If lost, a check made payable to cash can be readily cashed by anyone who finds the check. The amount of the check is entered both in numbers and in writing. If these amounts differ, the written amount takes legal precedence. You should always date and serially number (if not already prenumbered) your checks. Sign the check exactly as you signed the signature card. Your bank compares these signatures; a difference might cause the bank to reject the check. Most checks provide a space where you can enter the reason for which the payment was made. An example of a personal check written by Janet Berry appears in Figure 4.2. In this case a plain check was used. If a personalized check had been used, Janet's name and address would appear in the upper left-hand corner of the check. Note that Janet has correctly entered all necessary information on this check. By entering "groceries" in the "for" space, Janet has made a permanent

Figure 4.2 SAMPLE CHECK

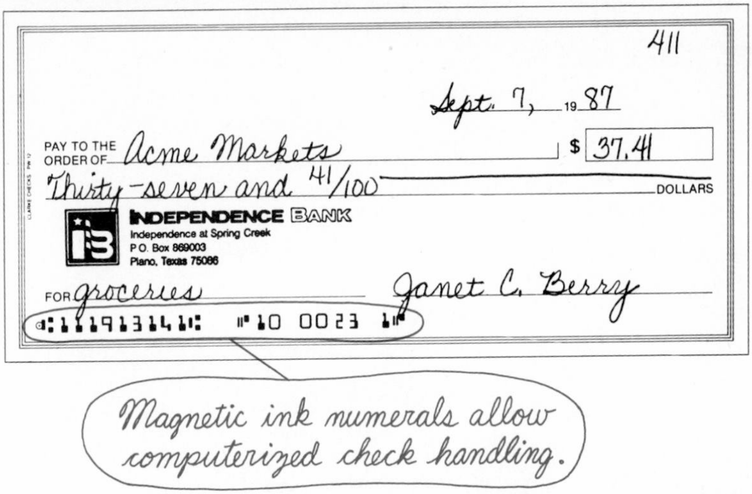

411

Sept. 7, 19 87

PAY TO THE ORDER OF Acme Markets $ 37.41

Thirty-seven and 41/100 DOLLARS

INDEPENDENCE BANK
Independence at Spring Creek
P.O. Box 869003
Plano, Texas 75086

FOR groceries Janet C. Berry

⑆111913141⑆ ⑈10 0023 1⑈

Magnetic ink numerals allow computerized check handling.

SOURCE: Courtesy of Independence Bank, Plano, Texas.

record of the reason for which she wrote this check. Janet has also numbered the check in the upper right-hand corner to facilitate record-keeping. She should also enter the number and purpose of the check in a **checkbook ledger** at the time it is written. This information may be useful for tax and budgeting purposes.

Endorsing Checks. When you receive a check signed by another party, you can designate still another party to receive payment through a process called **endorsement.** There are several forms of endorsement, of which four kinds are most commonly used. Examples of each form of endorsement appear in Figure 4.3.

Blank Endorsement. Under a **blank endorsement** the payee (the person to whom the check is payable) signs his or her name on the back of the check. Once endorsed in this manner, the check can be cashed by anyone who gets possession of it. This is the most commonly used and least restrictive form of endorsement.

Special Endorsement. With a **special endorsement** the payee endorses the check over to a specific person to whom the check is to be paid. The payee then signs the back of the check. But that new person to whom the check is endorsed may then endorse the check over to yet another party. This is done by writing on the back "Pay to the order of" followed by the most recent party's name and signed by the original endorsee.

Restrictive Endorsement. When the payee endorses the check to an-

Figure 4.3 COMMON FORMS OF CHECK ENDORSEMENT

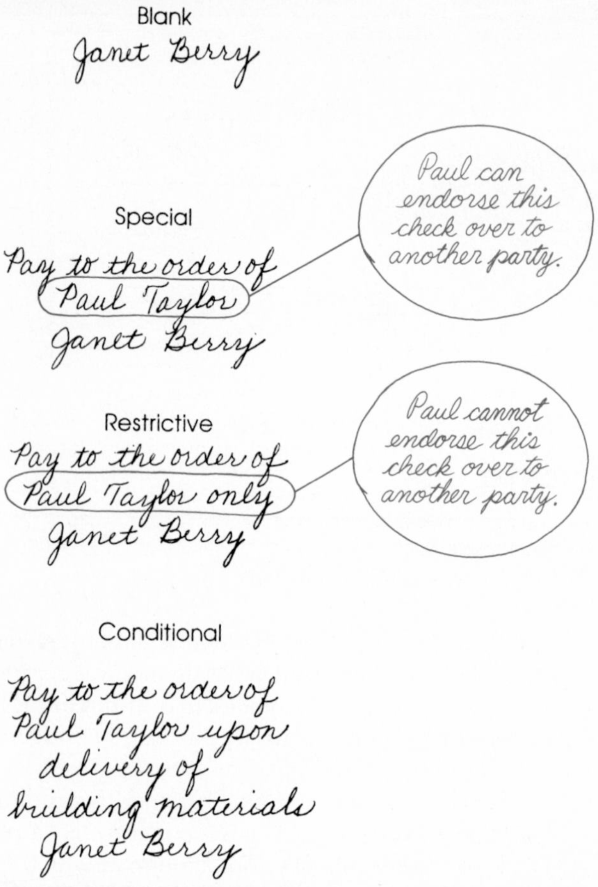

other party "only," a **restrictive endorsement** has occurred. This restriction prevents the check from being endorsed over to another party. Only the original endorsee can cash the check.

Conditional Endorsement. A **conditional endorsement** places some condition on the endorsement. The intent is to prevent the check from being cashed prior to the condition being satisfied. Although the condition is not legally binding, it does make further negotiation of the check impossible.

Making Deposits. You must follow three steps to make a **deposit.** The first step is to fill out a deposit slip listing each item you plan to deposit separately. Your bank provides deposit slips for your use. When you receive your checks,

Figure 4.4 SAMPLE DEPOSIT SLIP

INDEPENDENCE BANK

DEPOSIT SLIP

			Dollars	Cents
Independence Bank, Plano, Texas 75023				
Date	September 13, 1987	CASH Currency		
		Coins		
Name	Alan B. Berry	CHECKS	586	21
Address	123 Main St.			
	Plano, TX	TOTAL from reverse side		
Signature for Less Cash		TOTAL		
		Less Cash Received		
Account Number	119 214 9	Net Deposit	586	21

#0-411 (9-83)

⑆1119131416⑆

SOURCE: Courtesy of Independence Bank, Plano, Texas.

you should also receive a supply of deposit slips. A sample plain deposit slip is shown in Figure 4.4. If you use personalized checks, you will also receive personalized deposit slips. You must then endorse all checks to be deposited. This is the second step. You may want to use a special endorsement, such as "Pay to the order of First Bank," or a restrictive endorsement, such as "For deposit only," to guard against the loss or theft of endorsed checks.

The final step is to present the deposit to your bank to be credited to your account. This can be done in any of several ways. Many individuals prefer to make deposits in person at their bank during normal bank hours. Others may choose to make deposits at a drive-in window, a remote automatic teller machine, a night depository slot, or by mail. Regardless of the manner in which you make deposits, you should insist on a receipt for each deposit so that you have proper confirmation in the event the bank makes an error in crediting your account.

Check Clearance. Your check has cleared when your bank receives and makes payment for the face amount on it. **Check clearance** usually takes from one to three days if the payee is in the same city as your bank. The process may take longer if the payee is in another city, but some states limit how long a bank can hold a check before clearing it.

Banks have an efficient, computerized clearing system. This efficiency results largely from the use of magnetic ink character recognition (MICR). With this procedure your checks and deposit slips are encoded with numbers iden-

Figure 4.5 MONTHLY BANK STATEMENT

INDEPENDENCE BANK
P.O. Box 869003 • Plano, Texas 75086

ALAN B. BERRY OR
JANET C. BERRY
123 MAIN STREET
PLANO, TEXAS 75000

PAGE 1

STATEMENT DATE
OCT 01, 1987

DIRECT INQUIRIES TO CUSTOMER SERVICE 214-000-0000

CHECKING ACCOUNT SUMMARY

PREVIOUS STATEMENT WAS DATED 09/01/87			BALANCE WAS	521.86
DEPOSITS AND OTHER CREDITS	2	TRANSACTIONS,	TOTALING	587.69
CHECKS AND OTHER DEBITS	11	TRANSACTIONS,	TOTALING	424.78
BALANCE ON STATEMENT DATE				684.27

CHECKS PAID

DATE	AMOUNT	NUMBER	DATE	AMOUNT	NUMBER
09/10	37.41	411	09/18	27.09	417
09/12	42.06	412	09/21	63.20	418
09/14	21.93	413	09/26	27.14	420*
09/16	3.00S		09/29	9.00	421
09/17	46.82	415*	09/30	14.50	422
09/17	132.63	416			

* INDICATES A SKIP IN CHECK SEQUENCE ON THIS STATEMENT

DEPOSITS ADDED

DATE	AMOUNT	DATE	AMOUNT	DATE	AMOUNT
09/15	586.21	09/30	1.48I		

D = AUTOMATIC DRAFT S = SERVICE CHARGE
I = INTEREST DEPOSIT OD = OVERDRAFT

SOURCE: Courtesy of Independence Bank, Plano, Texas.

tifying the routing of the check, the bank, and the account number. These numbers appear in the lower left-hand corner of a check, as shown on the Berrys' check in Figure 4.2. These numbers are machine-read and transmitted to a computer. The computer sorts the checks and deposits and transmits the appropriate information to the account records. This process enables banks to clear checks and deposits more rapidly than previously possible.

Account Reconciliation

Your bank will provide a monthly statement listing all transactions occurring within your account. You should compare the dollar balance shown on the monthly statement with the dollar balance in your checkbook ledger. This procedure is known as **account reconciliation.** Figure 4.5 shows an example of a monthly bank statement for Alan and Janet Berry. An example of the Berrys' checkbook ledger appears in Figure 4.6. By reconciling your account as soon as you receive the monthly statement, you can detect any errors that may have occurred and verify the accuracy of your account records. You must determine six amounts before reconciling your account: the balance shown on the bank statement, the balance according to your checkbook, service charges, interest earned in your account, outstanding checks, and deposits in transit. Once you have identified these items, you can proceed to reconcile your account by calculating an adjusted bank balance and an adjusted checkbook balance.

Adjusted Bank Balance. You can compute an adjusted bank statement balance using the following steps:

1. Obtain the ending cash balance shown on your monthly bank statement.
2. List **deposits in transit.** These are deposits you have made that have not yet been added to your account.
3. List all **outstanding checks**. These are checks you have written that have not been cashed by the bank.
4. Calculate the adjusted cash balance in your bank account as follows: adjusted cash balance equals ending bank balance *plus* deposits in transit *minus* outstanding checks.

Adjusted Checkbook Balance. Follow these steps to calculate an adjusted checkbook balance:

1. Obtain the ending cash balance appearing in your checkbook.
2. Determine the amount of service charges incurred by your account.
3. Ascertain the amount of interest earned in your account.
4. Use the following procedure to calculate the adjusted cash balance in your checkbook: adjusted cash balance equals ending checkbook balance *minus* service charges *plus* interest earned.

The adjusted cash balances for your bank account and your checkbook should be equal. If the two are not equal, an error exists. In that case you should recheck your and the bank's computations to find the error and make the necessary correction.

Figure 4.6 CHECKBOOK LEDGER

BE SURE TO DEDUCT ANY PER CHECK CHARGES OR MAINTENANCE CHARGES THAT MAY APPLY

DATE		CHECK NUMBER	CHECKS ISSUED TO OR DEPOSIT RECEIVED FROM	AMOUNT OF DEPOSIT	✓	AMOUNT OF CHECK	BALANCE
							521 36
9	7	411	Acme Markets		✓	37 41	483 95
9	8	412	James Wilson, D.D.S.		✓	42 06	441 89
9	10	413	Payway Drugs		✓	21 93	419 96
9	10	414	Texaco			27 74	392 22
9	13	—	Deposit	586 21			978 43
9	14	415	Municipal Power		✓	46 82	931 61
9	14	416	Ready Appliances		✓	132 63	798 98
9	14	417	Central Water Works		✓	27 09	771 89
9	17	418	Sears		✓	63 20	708 69
9	19	419	United Fund			50 00	658 69
9	23	420	Varsity Book Store		✓	27 14	631 55
9	25	421	Best's Parking		✓	9 00	622 55
9	26	422	Golden Bakery		✓	14 50	608 05
9	29	423	Sunshine Savings			417 27	190 78
9	29	—	Deposit	125 00			315 78
10	1	424	City Gas Co.			28 42	287 36
			Service charge			3 00	284 36
			Interest	1 48			285 84

Adjusted balance

Ending amount

An Example. We use the Berrys' bank account for the month of September 1987 to illustrate how to reconcile an account. Their ending bank account balance on the statement date is $684.27 (Figure 4.5). After comparing their checkbook ledger to the monthly statement, the Berrys found the following checks were outstanding:

Check Number	Amount
414	$ 27.74
419	50.00
423	417.27
424	28.42
Total	$523.43

In addition, they discovered that their $125.00 deposit dated September 29, 1987, was still in transit. As a result, their adjusted bank balance is

$285.84 =	$684.27 +	$125.00 −	$523.43
Adjusted Bank Balance	Bank Statement Balance	Deposit in Transit	Outstanding Checks

The Berrys' checkbook ledger shows an ending amount of $287.36 (Figure 4.6). During the month a $3.00 service charge was made and $1.48 interest was earned. Therefore, their adjusted checkbook balance is

$285.84 =	$287.36 −	$3.00 +	$1.48
Adjusted Checkbook Balance	Checkbook Ledger Balance	Service Charges	Interest Earned

Since the adjusted bank balance equals the adjusted checkbook balance, the Berrys know that their account is accurately reported.

SPECIAL CHARGES

We have already mentioned that most banks charge a monthly service fee and an amount for each check written. In addition, banks often impose charges for special services such as check purchases, overdrafts, check holds, stop payments, canceled check truncation, and balance inquiries.

Check Purchases

Most banks charge a fee for providing checks. There are several different types of checks. The cost of checks varies from bank to bank and usually depends on whether the checks are personalized or printed on special paper. The cost of the least expensive checks generally ranges from $3 to $5 per hundred. In our example, the Berrys chose to minimize their cost by acquiring unpersonalized checks on plain paper. Because this expense is relatively small, it should not be your primary consideration in choosing a bank account.

Box 4.1 BANKS BY OTHER NAMES: WHO OFFERS WHAT SERVICES

	Commercial Banks[a]	Savings Institutions[a]	Credit Unions
Checking	Regular checking plus interest-bearing NOW and Super-NOW accounts, automatic teller machines	NOW and Super-NOW accounts, automatic teller machines	Interest-bearing share-draft accounts that resemble conventional checking accounts, automatic teller machines
Saving	Passbook and statement savings, certificates of deposit and money-market deposit accounts	Passbook and statement savings, certificates of deposit and money-market deposit accounts	Passbook savings, certificates of deposit, money-market deposit accounts and vacation and Christmas Club accounts
Loans	Personal secured and unsecured loans, automobile and home improvement loans, first and second mortgages and home-equity lines of credit	Personal secured and unsecured loans, automobile and home improvement loans, first and second mortgages and home-equity lines of credit	Small personal secured and unsecured loans, automobile and home improvement loans and first and second mortgages
Brokerage	Discount stock and bond brokerage but no direct investment advice; banks may lease space to brokers.	Discount and full-service stock and bond brokerage	Discount stock and bond brokerage at a few larger credit unions
Insurance	Credit life and credit disability insurance; travel, accident, life and health policies through credit cards; banks may also lease space to independent insurance companies.	Credit life and credit disability insurance, property and casualty and life and health insurance	Credit life and credit disability insurance, group life and auto insurance

[a] Federally chartered.

	Finance Companies	Brokerage Firms	Retailing Chains[b]
Checking	Not offered in finance company offices, but parent corporations may own consumer banks.	Checking as part of an asset management account at full-service and a few discount firms; some offer automatic teller machines.	Regular checking plus interest-bearing NOW and Super-NOW accounts at consumer banks or banks that rent space in local stores
Saving	Not offered in finance company offices, but parent corporations may own consumer banks.	Money-market funds and certificates of deposit from full-service and some discount firms	Savings accounts, certificates of deposit and money-market deposit accounts through asset management accounts at Sears, consumer banks or banks that rent space in local stores
Loans	Personal secured and unsecured loans, automobile and home improvement loans and second mortgages	Home-equity lines of credit at full-service firms and margin loans at both full-service and discount firms	Personal secured and unsecured loans, automobile and home improvement loans, first and second mortgages at consumer banks or banks that rent space in local stores; home-equity lines of credit and auto loans through Sears
Brokerage	Not offered	Full-service and discount stock and bond brokerage	Full-service brokerage through Sears and discount brokerage at four K Mart stores in Indiana
Insurance	Credit life and credit disability insurance	Fixed and variable annuities and single-premium life insurance at full-service firms	Life, health and property and casualty insurance through Penney's and Sears' insurance companies, K Mart's insurance services division or through local agents that rent space in 17 Kroger stores; fixed and variable annuities and single-premium life insurance through Sears

[b] J.C. Penney Co., K Mart, Kroger Co. and Sears Roebuck & Co.

(continued)

Box 4.1 (cont.) BANKS BY OTHER NAMES: WHO OFFERS WHAT SERVICES

	Commercial Banks[a]	Savings Institutions[a]	Credit Unions
Credit Cards	American Express Gold Card, MasterCard and Visa	American Express Gold Card, MasterCard and Visa	Visa and sometimes Mastercard
Other	Investment management and counseling, estate planning and tax planning usually through trust department or private banking division; financial planning services on a fee basis at some banks or through leasing space to independent advisers	Investment counseling, estate planning, retirement planning and tax preparation	Budget counseling, investment counseling and retirement planning

[a] Federally chartered.

Overdrafts

An **overdraft** occurs when you write a check for an amount greater than your current bank account balance. The treatment of overdrafts varies from bank to bank and often depends on the relationship between the bank and the check writer. In many instances the bank stamps the check "insufficient funds" and returns the overdrawn check to the person to whom it was written. The account

	Finance Companies	Brokerage Firms	Retailing Chains[b]
Credit Cards	MasterCard and Visa through consumer bank susidiaries of parent corporations	American Express Gold Card, Gold MasterCard and Visa debit cards through asset management accounts	MasterCard and Visa through J.C. Penney consumer bank . . . and Discover through Sears . . .; Visa debit card through asset management accounts at Sears
Other	Tax preparation	Investment counseling and management, estate planning and retirement planning at full-service firms	Investment counseling and management, real estate brokerage and tax preparation at Sears; real estate brokers lease space in five K Mart stores.

[b] J.C. Penney Co., K Mart, Kroger Co. and Sears Roebuck & Co.

SOURCE: *Money,* September 1985, pp. 80–81.

of the person writing the check is charged a penalty fee which usually ranges from $10 to $15. On the other hand, if a strong relationship exists between the bank and the check writer, the bank will usually make payment on the check and obtain reimbursement at a later time. A penalty fee is normally charged, but the check does not bounce and the check writer's creditworthiness is not harmed. Most banks offer prearranged lines of credit to ensure against overdrafts.

Check Holds

Banks typically place a **check hold** on deposits for a period of time before releasing funds to the depositor's account. The length of the holding period usually depends on the distance between the bank on which the check was written and the bank where the check was deposited. Greater distances are generally associated with longer holding periods. Check holds vary considerably, ranging from no delay when a check is written on the same bank at which the deposit is made to as many as 10 days on out-of-state checks. Check holds cause considerable expense and irritation to consumers who, believing funds are available, write checks that then bounce. This potential problem can be avoided by selecting a bank that is willing to release deposited funds in a short period of time. The issue of check holds is one of major concern to consumer groups and no doubt will generate new legislation in the future.

Stop Payments

Your checks may have been lost or stolen, or you may have paid for defective merchandise by check. These are instances where you may desire to **stop payment** on a check. A bank usually requires you to complete a form identifying the check by number, date, amount, and person to whom issued. Most banks allow stop payments to be initiated over the telephone, as long as a written order soon follows. A sample stop payment form appears as Figure 4.7. Written

Figure 4.7 STOP PAYMENT FORM

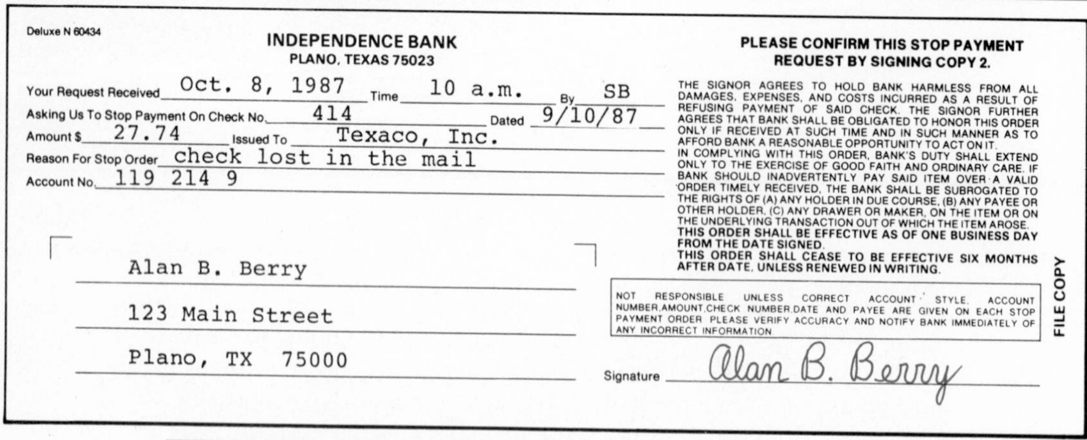

Deluxe N 60434

INDEPENDENCE BANK
PLANO, TEXAS 75023

Your Request Received Oct. 8, 1987 Time 10 a.m. By SB
Asking Us To Stop Payment On Check No. 414 Dated 9/10/87
Amount $ 27.74 Issued To Texaco, Inc.
Reason For Stop Order check lost in the mail
Account No. 119 214 9

Alan B. Berry
123 Main Street
Plano, TX 75000

PLEASE CONFIRM THIS STOP PAYMENT REQUEST BY SIGNING COPY 2.

THE SIGNOR AGREES TO HOLD BANK HARMLESS FROM ALL DAMAGES, EXPENSES, AND COSTS INCURRED AS A RESULT OF REFUSING PAYMENT OF SAID CHECK. THE SIGNOR FURTHER AGREES THAT BANK SHALL BE OBLIGATED TO HONOR THIS ORDER ONLY IF RECEIVED AT SUCH TIME AND IN SUCH MANNER AS TO AFFORD BANK A REASONABLE OPPORTUNITY TO ACT ON IT.
IN COMPLYING WITH THIS ORDER, BANK'S DUTY SHALL EXTEND ONLY TO THE EXERCISE OF GOOD FAITH AND ORDINARY CARE. IF BANK SHOULD INADVERTENTLY PAY SAID ITEM OVER A VALID ORDER TIMELY RECEIVED, THE BANK SHALL BE SUBROGATED TO THE RIGHTS OF (A) ANY HOLDER IN DUE COURSE, (B) ANY PAYEE OR OTHER HOLDER, (C) ANY DRAWER OR MAKER, ON THE ITEM OR ON THE UNDERLYING TRANSACTION OUT OF WHICH THE ITEM AROSE.
THIS ORDER SHALL BE EFFECTIVE AS OF ONE BUSINESS DAY FROM THE DATE SIGNED.
THIS ORDER SHALL CEASE TO BE EFFECTIVE SIX MONTHS AFTER DATE, UNLESS RENEWED IN WRITING.

NOT RESPONSIBLE UNLESS CORRECT ACCOUNT STYLE, ACCOUNT NUMBER, AMOUNT, CHECK NUMBER, DATE AND PAYEE ARE GIVEN ON EACH STOP PAYMENT ORDER. PLEASE VERIFY ACCURACY AND NOTIFY BANK IMMEDIATELY OF ANY INCORRECT INFORMATION.

Signature Alan B. Berry

FILE COPY

SOURCE: Courtesy of Independence Bank, Plano, Texas.

stop payments often remain in effect for six months or longer, but telephone orders usually expire within two weeks. When a bank receives a stop payment order, it instructs its tellers not to make payment on the specific check. Fees for stop payments vary among banks but usually range from $10 to $15 per check.

Canceled Check Truncation

Most banks still return canceled checks. Customers like to receive their canceled checks because they provide a better record of transactions than do monthly statements. However, many banks have been trying to truncate this service. This means that the bank retains the canceled checks and provides customers with a monthly statement showing check numbers and amounts. Truncation saves banks both the time and expense of mailing canceled checks to customers. Some banks automatically impose truncation, but other banks give customers the option of receiving their canceled checks, sometimes for a fee. Banks with truncated accounts charge a fee (often $2 to $3) to customers requesting copies of canceled checks.

Balance Inquiries

Traditionally banks provided account balances over the telephone to account holders at no charge. However, a growing number of banks now charge a fee to answer a telephone inquiry about your account balance. The typical fee charged for this service is $1 to $2. Still other banks now refuse to provide this information over the telephone.

SPECIAL SERVICES

Banks offer a variety of special services and conveniences. These include credit lines, bill-payer services, automatic teller machines, safe deposit boxes, debit cards, and trust services.

Credit Lines

Your bank may provide you with a **credit line,** an amount that you can automatically borrow if you write a check for more than your account balance. A credit line covers overdrafts and thus allows you to avoid the expense and inconvenience of a bounced check. The amount of a credit line varies considerably, typically ranging from $500 to $7500. As a general rule, smaller credit lines are easier to obtain. If you use your credit line to cover an overdrawn account, you will be charged interest on the borrowed amount. Interest rates on these loans typically range from 12 to 18 percent. Some banks may also assess a monthly service fee or per-loan fee when the credit line is used.

Bill-Payer Services

Some banks allow customers to authorize payment for continuing obligations such as utility bills, insurance premiums, rent payments, and mortgage payments. This is known as an automatic draft. The authorization is typically initiated over the telephone. The bank automatically pays for these obligations from the customer's checking account balance. A small fee is usually charged for each transaction, but in many instances this fee is less than the cost of postage. In addition, this service provides a convenience to the customer.

Automatic Teller Machines

Many banks provide **automatic teller machines (ATMs),** stand-alone computer terminals at which customers can make deposits, withdrawals, and other basic transactions. ATMs operate every day at every time, thus providing full-time banking services to customers. As an added convenience, banks often place these terminals in special locations such as shopping centers, grocery stores, and office buildings. Some banks may charge a small fee for each ATM transaction. ATMs can pose a security problem because someone may try to illegally access your account. Here are seven rules to follow when using ATMs:[1]

1 Do not write your identification code number or name on your ATM card or on any paper you carry in your wallet or purse. Although this may seem obvious, a surprisingly large number of consumers unthinkingly record their personal identification number (PIN) or personal identification code (PIC) in a place accessible to a thief. Instead, memorize the code.

2 Do not use an ATM if there is significant risk of theft. For example, do not withdraw cash at night from an exposed, poorly lighted machine located in a high-crime area.

3 When using an ATM, make certain to conceal your PIN or PIC as you enter it. Sometimes thieves pretend they are ATM customers to try to see your identification code, then pick your pocket to obtain your ATM card.

4 Do not make cash deposits. There is no verifiable record of this deposit—only the receipt you have created—so you run the risk of losing your deposit if the bank makes an error or a bank employee steals your cash. The risk of depositing checks is much less, since cashed checks remain as a record.

5 When you make a deposit or withdrawal, make certain you get a receipt and check its accuracy. Institutions operating ATMs are required to provide you with this record. Make certain to complain if you do not receive one, or if it is inaccurate.

6 Compare these receipts with your monthly statements to check for potentially costly bank errors. Call any discrepancies to the attention of the bank.

7 If your ATM card is lost or stolen, immediately inform the bank. If this loss or any unauthorized transaction is reported within two days, you are liable only for losses up to $50. After two days your liability increases to $500.

[1] Naphtali Hoffman and Stephen Brobeck, *The Bank Book,* New York: Harcourt Brace Jovanovich, 1986, pp. 29–30.

Safe Deposit Boxes

A **safe deposit box** is a container in a bank's vault that can be used to keep jewelry and valuable papers, including securities, contracts, and titles. Although the annual rental fee averages about $15, large boxes may rent for more than $100 per year. A safe deposit box has two locks. You receive the key to one lock and the bank retains the key to the other lock. Both keys must be used to open the box. This arrangement protects the contents of the box from theft.

Debit Cards

A **debit card** can be used to make purchases at stores that have special point-of-sale terminals and with automatic teller machines. When a debit card is inserted into a store's terminal and certain information about the specific purchase is entered, the amount of the purchase is electronically transferred from the customer's account to the store's account. Debit cards eliminate the need for cash or checks. Although the use of debit cards is not widespread, their eventual acceptance in the market could lead to the much publicized "checkless society" where transactions would be settled immediately via an electronic transfer of funds among accounts.

Trust Services

Most large and many smaller banks offer trust services through their trust departments. **Trust services** include managing your assets; maintaining records pertaining to your assets; performing custodial services such as collecting dividends, interest, and royalty payments; and buying and selling assets. A trust department may also serve as the trustee of your assets or the executor of your will (these functions are discussed in Chapter 16). Banks charge a fee for performing these services. Because these fees vary from bank to bank, you should shop around to ensure that you are paying a reasonable fee for the services you receive.

Special Types of Checks

Checks are a convenient and safe way of paying for purchases. Most merchants will accept your check if it is drawn on a local bank and you can provide proper identification. You may not find the same willingness to accept your check if you make a purchase in another city. The merchant has no way to determine that your check is good and may refuse to sell to you unless you can make a guaranteed payment. Although there are several ways to make guaranteed payment, the most common involve the use of cashier's checks, certified checks, and traveler's checks.

Cashier's Check. You can purchase a **cashier's check** from a bank. The check is backed by the promise of the issuing bank and thus is readily accepted in

Box 4.2 AVOID LOSING MONEY WHEN YOUR BANK GOOFS

Want to make some easy money? I'm embarrassed to tell you how simple it is: Just stake out your bank, and . . . keep a sharp eye on everything it does to your account. You may be surprised how much money—your money—falls through the cracks.

Bank clerks and computers make mistakes—a lot of them. Most can be corrected quickly, but only if you notice them! It's hard to miss a big blunder in your checking account because your checks will start bouncing, but small errors can easily get by if you're not careful. Here are the main mistakes to watch for—and how to correct them:

Cash

How many times have you cashed a check in a hurry, then walked away without counting the money? Maybe you really believe the teller is always right. Or maybe you're intimidated by the line of people behind you. Whatever the reason, you're not alone. Millions of people do the same thing, but it's very risky.

If a teller accidentally short-changes you, your only hope of recovering the money may be to discover it immediately. One woman moved aside to count her cash and came up $20 short. But when she went back to complain, it was too late. Tellers aren't allowed to pay extra money on a customer's say-so; after all, she could have slipped the "missing" $20 into her pocket while no one was looking.

Rule #1. Always count your money before leaving the window. If you discover an error later, give your name, address and account number to both the teller and the manager. If the teller winds up the day with the right amount of extra cash, you'll be reimbursed.

Deposits

Adding machines are no guarantee against mistakes. "Last month," one reader wrote, "I gave a teller three checks—for $525, $37.50 and $44.75—plus a deposit slip for $500. The balance was to be paid in cash. She carefully counted out $82.25 and gave it to me—but I was due to get $107.25. If I hadn't worked it out on my own calculator I'd have been out $25."

Errors often creep into savings accounts too. "I was once credited with $100 when I deposited $1,000," a friend told me. Fortunately she spotted the error and got it corrected before leaving the window. What if a mistake is made the other way—$1,000 credited when only $100 was deposited? Don't spend the money! In the world of finance, there's no finders keepers. Anything mistakenly put into your account will be unceremoniously yanked away.

Rule #2. Don't rely on the bank to make all the calculations. Do your own arithmetic in advance—and take the figures with you. Double-check your bank book as well as the cash for accuracy.

Automated Tellers

Electronic machines goof just like humans. They accept cash and checks that never get credited to the right accounts, and they short-change customers too. You may ask for $100, for example, and get a withdrawal receipt for that amount—but receive only $80 in cash.

Rule #3. Never deposit cash into an ATM. It's impossible to prove how much you put into the envelope, so losses are difficult to recover. Checks are easier to find or replace—especially if you have a receipt showing when and where the deposit was made.

any transaction. You give the bank an amount equal to the face amount of the check plus a service fee in exchange for the cashier's check. The fee, which usually ranges from $1 to $2 per check, may sometimes be waived for regular customers. Since the check is payable to a specific vendor, it is a convenient and safe way to make payment.

Rule #4. Report all errors immediately. Some banks have telephones next to ATMs for that purpose. If there's no such phone, call or visit the bank. Fast action gives your complaint more credibility. *For help:* Leave your name, address, account number, amount of your loss and the location of the ATM with a bank employee, then put the same information in a letter. You'll have to wait until the accounts are balanced, but if the machine is over by the sum you reported, you should get your money.

Deposit Slips

"It always amazes me to see the trash baskets near ATM machines overflowing with deposit slips," says Dan Buser of the American Bankers' Association. "If the bank credits a deposit incorrectly, how would the customer know?" Banks do make mistakes, even on computerized statements. If you don't keep deposit slips as a double check, it's a cinch that you're going to eventually lose some money.

Stopping Payment

If you write a check you later regret, call your bank and request payment be stopped. Your account will be flagged right away, but you must also give written authorization—usually by filing a stop-check form. Despite the high fee for this service (often $7 to $15), there's no guarantee. If the check slips through, you must prove it's the bank's fault to make a claim (although you may be able to recover the fee you paid in vain). The rules should be spelled out clearly on the stop-check form.

Forgeries

If someone forges your signature on a check and the bank cashes it, you're entitled to be reimbursed 100 percent. It doesn't matter that you hadn't reported the loss of your blank checks (although you should have) or that you kept them with credit cards bearing your signature. It is the bank's absolute duty to guard against forgeries. If a forged signature looks like your handwriting, the bank will have it verified by an expert. It will also go through its own systems to find out which teller accepted the check and what proof of identity was used.

Monthly Statements

It's essential to go over your bank statement every month to be sure that all deposits and withdrawals are accurate and the fees are right. (Keep a list of the current fees on hand so there's no doubt.) If you're allergic to balancing your checkbook, it's low-risk to trust the computer's addition once you've ascertained that the entries are correct. But a few minutes with a calculator could turn up an erroneous entry you overlooked.

Careful examination of her statement is how one woman learned why two of her checks had bounced; the paycheck she'd deposited had never been credited. She sent a copy of her deposit slip in a frosty letter to the bank manager. She demanded that he find the missing check, write letters to her creditors explaining that the checks were bounced in error, rescind the bounced-check charges and credit her $6.50 for the interest she had to pay on an overdue account. The bank not only did all that, it also sent her a letter of apology.

SOURCE: Jane Bryant Quinn, *Woman's Day,* November 5, 1985, p. 16.

Certified Check. You can make your check out to a specific payee and take it to your bank for certification. After deducting the face amount of the check plus a small fee from your account, the bank stamps its certification on the front of the check. This is a **certified check.** The bank guarantees that your check is good. As a result, certified checks are widely accepted as a means of payment.

Traveler's Check. People who are away from home often use **traveler's checks** to satisfy their cash needs. Traveler's checks are issued by several large financial institutions and may be purchased at commercial banks in denominations ranging from $10 to $1000 per check. A fee of about $1 per $100 of checks usually prevails, but some banks provide traveler's checks at no charge. Because they have the backing of a large financial institution, most traveler's checks are readily accepted at airlines, hotels, restaurants, and department stores throughout the world. All institutions issuing these checks guarantee to replace any lost or stolen checks.

SAVINGS ACCOUNTS

Savings accounts once dominated in the competition for consumers' short-term funds. In the past decade, however, a large number of competitive outlets for your money have emerged, including NOW and super NOW accounts, money market demand accounts, and money market funds.[2] Nevertheless, even in the face of increasing competition, savings accounts at commercial banks and thrift institutions accounted for $331.2 billion at mid-year 1986. This means that savings accounts hold more of consumers' money than any other short-term investment alternative except time deposits (primarily certificates of deposit).

Individuals find savings accounts attractive for three primary reasons. First, savings accounts are convenient. You can open one easily at the same financial institution where you have your checking account. Second, savings accounts pay interest on your money, so you can earn a return on your temporary investment. Finally, your savings deposits can be converted to cash quickly and thus provide a ready source of funds. Most people do not use savings accounts for long-term investments. Savings accounts provide a safe way of storing highly liquid, temporary funds, whereas longer-term investments in stocks, bonds, and real estate tend to be riskier and often promise a higher return. In this section of the chapter we discuss several important considerations about savings accounts.

Computing Interest on Savings

One of your primary incentives to place money in a savings account is to earn interest on your funds. Banks and other financial institutions quote a nominal or **stated rate of interest** on savings accounts. Until April 1986, regular savings accounts were subject to interest rate restrictions. Now, however, banks are free to pay any interest rate they want on savings accounts. Rates may vary among institutions so you should shop for the best rate before opening a savings account.

[2] We discussed NOW and super NOW accounts earlier in this chapter. Chapter 11 contains a description of money market demand accounts and money market funds.

You may find that many banks quote the same rate of interest on savings accounts. For example, many banks currently offer a 5 percent stated interest rate. The actual amount of interest your savings account earns, however, may vary among these banks, even though they quote the same interest rate. To find out how much interest your account will earn, you must determine the true or effective rate of interest. The **effective rate of interest** is the actual rate at which your money earns interest and may differ from the stated rate of interest. Three considerations affect the effective rate of interest: the compounding period, the time the bank credits your account for deposits received, and the method of computing interest.

Compounding Period. The effective rate of interest on your savings account depends on the frequency in which interest is compounded. **Compounding** interest enables you to earn interest not only on your original deposit but also on interest accumulated from period to period. Thus, compounding allows you to earn interest on interest. If your account earns interest at 5 percent compounded semiannually, your bank credits your account for interest earned every six months. For the first six months you earn interest only on your original deposit. If you deposited $1000, then your interest would equal $25 ($1000 × 5 percent × ½ year) and your new principal amount would be $1025 ($1000 original deposit + $25 interest). Your interest for the second six months would be $25.63 ($1025 × 5 percent × ½ year). The increase in interest from the first period to the second is attributable to earning interest on accumulated interest. Table 4.4 shows this relationship. You can plainly see that the greater the frequency at which interest is compounded (the shorter the compounding period), the larger will be the dollar amount of your interest earnings and the higher your effective rate of interest.

Interest-Crediting Period. A credit occurs when money is added to your account balance, such as when you make a deposit or earn interest on the account. Savings account interest is generally credited either monthly or quarterly. The amount of interest your account earns depends to a large extent on the timing of the credits to your account. The sooner a deposit is credited to your account, the more interest you earn. Banks have different policies concerning the crediting of accounts, and these policies can significantly affect the amount of interest you receive. Most banks adhere to one of the following three policies:

1. If the bank receives your deposit after the beginning of the **interest crediting period** (usually the beginning of a month or quarter), you do not earn any interest for that period.
2. If the bank receives your deposit within a specified period, called a **grace period,** you earn interest on that amount for the entire period. If your deposit arrives after the grace period, no interest is earned for the

Table 4.4 INTEREST EARNED FOR DIFFERENT COMPOUNDING PERIODS ON $1000 AT A 5 PERCENT STATED RATE

Year	COMPOUNDING PERIOD			
	Annually	Quarterly	Weekly	Daily
1	$1050.00	$1050.94	$1051.25	$1051.27
2	1102.50	1104.47	1105.13	1105.16
3	1157.63	1160.74	1161.76	1161.82
4	1215.51	1219.86	1221.30	1221.39
5	1276.28	1282.00	1283.90	1284.01
Effective rate	5.000%	5.094%	5.125%	5.127%

period. Grace periods seldom exceed 10 days (such as the first 10 days of the month).

3 If the bank receives your deposit at any time during the period, you earn interest from that date until the end of the period. Thus, even if your deposit arrived only one day before the period's close, you would receive one day's interest.

Method of Computing Interest. The method a bank uses to compute interest affects the amount of interest a savings account earns. This computation is often the most important determinant of the amount of interest a savings account earns. Competing banks posting the same stated rate of interest and compounding period may compute significantly different interest earnings. To see how these earnings can vary, let's look at an example: the savings account of a person named Susan Strickland.

The Situation. Susan Strickland has a savings account at the First State

Table 4.5 ACCOUNT TRANSACTIONS DURING SEPTEMBER

Date	Deposits	Withdrawals	Account balance
September 1	—	—	$ 0
September 8	$5000	—	5000
September 15	2000	—	7000
September 23	—	$4000	3000
September 30	3000	—	6000

Bank. Her deposits and withdrawals in the account during the month of September appear in Table 4.5. The account pays interest at a 5 percent stated rate, compounded monthly. Her bank allows a 10-day grace period for crediting deposits to savings accounts. The amount of interest earned depends on the interest computation method used. Methods in common use are the low balance; first-in, first-out; last-in, first-out; and day of deposit to day of withdrawal. We now examine each of these methods.

Low Balance. The **low-balance method** pays interest only on the smallest amount of money in the account during the entire month. In our example, the smallest account balance is $3000. The account would earn $12.50 in interest for the month, calculated as follows:

$12.50	=	$3000 ×	5%	× 1/12 year
Interest		Low Balance	Stated Interest Rate	Time Period

Even though Susan had as much as $7000 in her account for a portion of the month, she earns interest only on her $3000 minimum balance.

First-in, First-out. Under the **first-in, first-out (FIFO) method,** any withdrawals during the period are deducted from the initial balance and then from subsequent deposits in the order made. This method causes loss of interest on the earliest deposits rather than only from the date of withdrawal. As a result, the amount of interest paid is less than under any other alternative. In our example, Susan would lose interest on $4000 of her September 8 deposit as the result of the September 23 withdrawal. Therefore, only $1000 of that deposit is eligible to earn interest during September. Since the remaining deposits occurred after the grace period (first 10 days of the month) and thus are not credited to the account for interest computation purposes, Susan's account earns interest only on that $1000, as follows:

$4.17	=	$1000 ×	5%	× 1/12 year
Interest		FIFO Balance	Stated Interest Rate	Time Period

Last-in, First-out. The **last-in, first-out (LIFO) method** deducts any withdrawals during the period from the latest deposits before the withdrawal. This approach is more favorable to the consumer than the FIFO method because the interest lost from withdrawals comes from the most recent deposits. Therefore, the amount of interest lost is minimized. In our example, the $4000 withdrawal on September 23 is partially offset by the $2000 deposit on September 15. The remaining $2000 of this withdrawal is then deducted from the deposit of $5000 made on September 8. As a result, $3000 of Susan's initial deposit (the

Table 4.6 INTEREST EARNED USING DAY OF DEPOSIT TO DAY OF WITHDRAWAL TECHNIQUE

Balance period	Balance eligible to receive interest	Stated interest rate (%)	Time period	Interest[a] earned
9/8 to 9/14	$5000	5	7/360[b]	$ 4.86
9/15 to 9/22	7000	5	8/360	7.78
9/23 to 9/29	3000	5	7/360	2.92
9/30	6000	5	1/360	0.83
			Total interest earned	$16.39

[a] Interest earned *equals* balance eligible to receive interest *times* stated interest rate *times* time period.

[b] Financial calculations are normally based on 360 days rather than 365. Some financial institutions, however, now use 365 days.

only deposit made within the first-10-day period) remains to earn interest for the entire month, as follows:

$12.50 =	$3000 ×	5%	× 1⁄12 year
Interest	LIFO Balance	Stated Interest Rate	Time Period

This amount compares favorably to the $4.17 under the first-in, first-out method and thus clearly illustrates the importance of the interest computation method.

Day of Deposit to Day of Withdrawal. Interest is paid on funds from the day deposited until the day withdrawn. The 10-day grace period rule does not apply to this method. Under the **day of deposit to day of withdrawal method** you earn interest for the actual number of days your money is in the account. This technique is the most favorable to the consumer and the most common one in use. The calculation of interest for Susan's account depends on her daily balances shown in Table 4.5. The interest on these balances, shown in Table 4.6, totals $16.39 for September.

We summarize the amount of interest earned in Susan Strickland's savings account under each of the four computational techniques, as follows:

Computational technique	Interest earned
Low balance	$12.50
First-in, first-out	4.17
Last-in, last-out	12.50
Day of deposit to day of withdrawal	16.39

The day of deposit to day of withdrawal technique produces the highest return, whereas the first-in, first-out method yields the lowest return. In this example, the interest earnings vary widely depending on the computational method used. You can clearly see the importance of choosing a savings account that computes interest in the way that benefits you the most.

Minimum Balance to Earn Interest. Some banks impose minimum-balance requirements for savings accounts to earn interest. If the account balance falls below this minimum requirement, no interest is earned. Any of three methods may be used to determine an account's balance. Under the first method, the average daily account balance for the interest-crediting period is used. The second method uses the lowest account balance at any time during the period. Under the first two methods, no interest is paid if at any time during the period the appropriate account balance falls below the minimum requirement. A third method pays interest on each day the minimum requirement is met. The last method is the most favorable to consumers, whereas the second method is least desirable. Although many banks have no minimum-balance requirements, some have minimums as high as $500.

Insurance

Most savings deposits are insured by an agency of the federal government.[3] This insurance protects the depositor's account against failure of the financial institution for up to some maximum dollar amount. The insured institution pays a small fee for this insurance coverage, but the depositor does not have to pay for this insurance. Since not all financial institutions participate in deposit insurance, you should be careful in selecting a depository institution. You may want

[3] You can obtain a free booklet, *Your Insured Deposit,* by writing the Federal Deposit Insurance Corporation, 550 17th Street, N.W., Washington, D.C. 20429. This booklet describes and provides examples of insurance coverage on different types of accounts at insured banks.

Table 4.7 INSURED SAVINGS INSTITUTIONS

Savings institution	Insuring agency	Insurance coverage[a]
Commercial bank Mutual savings bank	**Federal Deposit Insurance Corporation (FDIC)**	$100,000
Savings and loan association	**Federal Savings and Loan Insurance Corporation (FSLIC)**	$100,000
Credit union	**National Credit Union Association (NCUA)**	$100,000

[a] Per depositor.

to find out if the financial institution where you keep your savings is federally insured. Table 4.7 shows the federal insuring agencies and current insurance limits per depositor.

Some institutions do not provide federal insurance coverage. They may, instead, offer private insurance. You should be aware that reserves in the private insurance funds typically amount to about 2 percent of insured deposits. Hence one or two major failures or a general panic by depositors could quickly deplete a fund. Over the last decade, privately insured depositors in seven states have lost money or been denied access to it temporarily because of inadequate insurance. By contrast, nobody has ever experienced a loss in a federally insured account, except in some instances where the amount on deposit exceeded the maximum insurance coverage.

DIFFERENT TYPES OF LOANS

In addition to using a bank as a place to keep your money, you may at some point want to borrow money from a bank. Banks lend money to a variety of customers, as indicated in Table 4.8, and offer several types of loans. These include lines of credit, signature loans, installment loans, and mortgage loans.

Table 4.8
OUTSTANDING LOANS AT COMMERCIAL BANKS, DECEMBER 1985

	Amount outstanding (billions)[a]
Commercial and industrial	$ 501.5
Real estate	423.3
Individual	294.8
Security	45.4
Nonbank financial institutions	33.4
Agricultural	36.0
State and municipal	52.8
Foreign banks and institutions	16.4
Lease financing receivables	18.8
Other	40.5
Total	$1,462.9

[a] Excludes loans to domestic commercial banks.

SOURCE: *Federal Reserve Bulletin,* Washington, D.C.: Board of Governors of the Federal Reserve System, December 1986.

Line of Credit

A bank may give a commitment to an individual to borrow funds up to some maximum amount for a given time period, typically one year. This is a **line of credit.** You may borrow any amount up to the maximum limit without having to obtain additional approval from the bank. You pay interest only on borrowed amounts. If you do not use the line of credit, no interest is charged. Your bank may charge a small commitment fee, usually ½ percent on the unused credit balance. Therefore, if you borrow $600 against a $1000 line of credit, you will be charged interest on $600 and a commitment fee on the unused $400 balance.

A line of credit is a convenient source of credit. Many large businesses have lines of credit in the millions of dollars. This form of credit, however, sees limited use among individuals. Banks extend standard lines of credit only to the most creditworthy customers, so someone just entering a career and having limited financial experience will probably not qualify for this kind of loan.

Signature Loan

A **signature loan** is an unsecured loan made only on the belief that the borrower will repay the bank. The bank does not have claim to specific collateral. Only the borrower's promise to pay secures the loan. Signature loans are generally made only to the most creditworthy individuals. The bank carefully evaluates a customer's financial capabilities and credit history before granting this type of loan. Most signature loans are made to existing bank customers who are known for their strong credit standing.

Signature loans are almost always extended for a period of one year or less, most often three or six months. Therefore, these loans provide temporary financing sources. Banks hesitate to renew signature loans, so you should be careful not to borrow more than you can repay in a short period of time. Although signature loans fulfill only temporary financing needs, they can prove advantageous to the borrower for several reasons. First, these loans require a minimum amount of paperwork and documentation, largely because no collateral is involved. Second, customers with strong credit standings can readily obtain these loans. Third, signature loans typically have lower effective interest rates. Because only the most creditworthy customers receive these loans, the risk of default is lower.

Installment Loan

When you borrow money through an **installment loan,** you must repay it through a series of equal monthly payments. Installment loans are often obtained to purchase an automobile or make home improvements. Banks generally require collateral on these loans. Smaller installment loans made to finance items such as appliances, medical bills, or educational expenses may be made on an unsecured basis, depending on the borrower's creditworthiness. An example of an installment loan application appears in Figure 4.8.

Figure 4.8 SAMPLE LOAN APPLICATION

BANK USE ONLY
DATE ____
LOAN OFFICER ____

INDEPENDENCE BANK

PERSONAL BANKING LOAN REQUEST

THANK YOU FOR COMING TO INDEPENDENCE BANK. YOUR PERSONAL BANKER HAS BEEN SPECIALLY TRAINED TO HANDLE YOUR BANKING NEEDS. PLEASE COMPLETE THE INFORMATION BELOW TO HELP US SERVE YOU BETTER.

PERSONAL INFORMATION

NAME | BIRTHDATE | HOME PHONE | BUSINESS PHONE | HOW LONG IN CITY?

STREET ADDRESS (APT. #) | BUYING ☐ RENTING ☐ OTHER ☐ | LANDLORD OR MORTGAGE COMPANY | MONTHLY PAYMENT OR RENT $

CITY & STATE ZIP | HOW LONG AT THIS ADDRESS? | MARRIED ☐ UNMARRIED ☐ SEPARATED ☐ | NO. OF DEPENDENTS | SOCIAL SECURITY NO. | TEXAS DRIVER'S LICENSE NO.

YOUR BANK'S NAME AND ADDRESS CK. ACCT. NO. ____ SVGS. ACCT. NO. ____ | YOUR PREVIOUS ADDRESS | HOW LONG?

NEAREST RELATIVE NOT LIVING WITH YOU | RELATIONSHIP | RELATIVE'S ADDRESS | CITY | STATE & ZIP | PHONE NO.

PERSONAL REFERENCE (OTHER THAN RELATIVE) | REFERENCE'S ADDRESS | CITY | STATE & ZIP | PHONE NO.

PERSONAL INCOME & EMPLOYMENT

MY EMPLOYER IS: (Name & Address) | DATE EMPLOYED | POSITION OR TITLE | MONTHLY INCOME $

MY PREVIOUS EMPLOYER WAS: (Name & Address) | HOW LONG? | POSITION OR TITLE | INVESTMENT, RENTAL OR MISC. BUSINESS INCOME | PER MONTH $

Alimony, child support, or separate maintenance income need not be revealed if you do not wish to have it considered as a basis for repaying this credit obligation. | MONTHLY

☐ I choose to disclose such income. ____ (Initials of Applicant)

☐ I have no such income, or I choose not to disclose it as a basis for repaying this credit obligation. ____ (Initials of Applicant) $

IS SUCH INCOME RECEIVED PURSUANT TO A WRITTEN AGREEMENT OR COURT DECREE? ☐ YES ☐ NO | HOW LONG RECEIVED? | HOW OFTEN RECEIVED? | TOTAL MONTHLY INCOME $____

NAME & ADDRESS OF PERSON MAKING ALIMONY, CHILD SUPPORT, OR MAINTENANCE PAYMENTS

HOW MUCH LIFE INSURANCE $ | NAME OF COMPANIES | CASH VALUE $ | AMOUNT BORROWED AGAINST INSURANCE $

CURRENT DEBTS & CREDIT REFERENCES

PLEASE LIST BELOW ALL BANKS, SAVINGS & LOAN, FINANCE & MORTGAGE COMPANIES, CREDIT UNIONS, MERCHANTS & INDIVIDUALS YOU NOW OWE.

	TO WHOM OWED	ACCOUNT NUMBER	ORIGINAL BALANCE	PRESENT BALANCE	MONTHLY PAYMENT
MASTERCARD			$	$	$
VISA					
AUTOMOBILE LOAN					
REVOLVING ACCOUNT					
HOME MORTGAGE					
INSTALMENT LOAN OR ACCT.					
INSTALMENT LOAN OR ACCT.					

ADDRESS AND DESCRIPTION OF REAL ESTATE OWNED (OTHER THAN HOME) | MORTGAGE COMPANY | PURCHASE PRICE $ | BALANCE OWING $ | MONTHLY PAYMENT $

HAVE YOU EVER APPLIED WITH US FOR CREDIT? ☐ YES-WHEN? ☐ NO | HAVE YOU EVER BEEN BANKRUPT OR HAD ANY JUDGMENTS OR GARNISHMENTS AGAINST YOU? ☐ YES-WHEN? ☐ NO | ARE YOU A COMAKER, ENDORSER, OR GUARANTOR ON ANY NOTE OR ACCOUNT? WHERE? AMOUNT $

SPOUSE INFORMATION

Spouse information need not be revealed unless you reside in, or the collateral offered will be located in, the State of Texas or other community property state, or your spouse will use or pay for this account.

NAME OF SPOUSE | BIRTHDATE | ADDRESS (If Different From Yours) | SOCIAL SECURITY NO.

SPOUSE EMPLOYED BY: (Name & Address) | BUSINESS PHONE | DATE EMPLOYED | POSITION OR TITLE | MONTHLY INCOME $

Your spouse's alimony, child support, or separate maintenance income need not be revealed if you do not wish to have it considered as a basis for repaying this credit obligation. | MONTHLY

☐ I choose to disclose such income. ____ (Initials of Applicant)

☐ My spouse has no such income, or I choose not to disclose it as a basis for repaying this credit obligation. ____ (Initials of Applicant) $

SPOUSE'S OTHER INCOME (Describe) | AMOUNT OF OTHER INCOME $ PER

SIGNATURES

I WISH TO BORROW $ FOR MONTHS FOR THE PURPOSE OF:

I OFFER THE FOLLOWING COLLATERAL TO SECURE THIS CREDIT:

NOTICE: The Creditor may cause a credit investigation to be made concerning your character, general reputation, personal characteristics, and mode of living among your friends, neighbors, associates, consumer reporting agencies, and other sources to be considered a part of this Application. You have the right to make a written request for a complete and accurate disclosure of information concerning the nature and scope of an investigative report, if such a report is obtained by the Creditor.

I certify that the above information is accurate and complete.

x ____ x ____ Date ____

#L-134 (9-83)

SOURCE: Courtesy of Independence Bank, Plano, Texas.

Installment loans usually require more paper work and legal formality than signature loans, especially if collateral is involved. Also, banks sometimes extend these loans to customers with less established credit records. As a result, the effective interest cost of these loans tends to be higher than for signature loans. Installment loans are sometimes confusing to consumers, largely because the stated interest rate on these loans may differ significantly from the effective interest rate. In order to reduce confusion, the federal government requires the lender to inform the customer of the effective interest cost before granting an installment loan. The calculation of the effective rate of interest on installment loans is discussed in Chapter 5.

Mortgage Loan

A **mortgage loan** is usually a long-term installment loan used to finance the purchase of real estate. A detailed discussion of this type of loan appears in Chapter 6. These loans are collateralized by the acquired real estate. Previously, mortgage loans primarily were made by mutual savings banks and savings and loan associations, but commercial banks have now become active in the mortgage lending area. Until recently, banks hesitated to lend funds for long periods of time because most of their funds came from short-term checking deposits. Now, however, a greater proportion of banks' funds come from time deposits, and thus most banks are comfortable in granting mortgage loans. When shopping for a mortgage loan, you should not overlook your bank as a possible source of funds. Mortgage lending to individuals has become a common bank activity.

SUMMARY

The number of financial services offered by commercial banks has grown substantially in recent years. As a result, many banks proclaim to be one-stop personal financial centers. Checking accounts remain the most used bank product, with about 80 percent of American adults having such an account. Before you open a checking account, you should compare banks to determine which one offers the most suitable account for you. After selecting a bank, you must decide what kind of checking account is most appropriate. Regular checking accounts remain the most popular alternative, but you will also want to consider no-minimum accounts, NOW accounts, super NOW accounts, share drafts, and package plans.

Before opening an account, you should become familiar with the mechanics for writing checks, endorsing checks, and making deposits. The process of opening a checking account is relatively simple. Once you have opened your account, you will receive a bank statement itemizing all transactions each month. To verify the account balance, you should reconcile the bank statement with the checkbook ledger. This procedure will detect errors in either the bank statement or your checkbook ledger.

In addition to a monthly service fee and an amount for each check written, banks often impose charges for services such as check purchases, overdrafts, check holds, stop payments, canceled check truncation, and balance inquiries. Banks also offer a variety of special services and conveniences. Many banks provide ongoing credit lines to their most creditworthy customers. Some banks have arrangements through which routine bills can be paid directly from the customer's account. Banks also offer special conveniences such as automated teller machines (ATMs), safe deposit boxes, debit cards, and trust services. There are several ways to make guaranteed payment, including the use of cashier's checks, certified checks, and traveler's checks.

Savings accounts, although no longer dominating in the competition for consumers' short-term funds, remain an important investment alternative. The popularity of these accounts is largely attributable to convenience, payment of interest, and ease of conversion to cash. The amount of interest earned on a savings account depends on the effective rate of interest. This rate is largely influenced by the compounding period, the time the bank credits an account for interest, and the method of computing interest. Most savings accounts are insured for up to $100,000 by an agency of the federal government.

Banks lend money to many different kinds of customers. Through numerous arrangements a bank may give a commitment to an individual to borrow funds up to some maximum amount for a given period, usually one year. This is a line of credit. Signature loans are unsecured and typically made only to the most creditworthy customers for a short term. Money lent through an installment loan arrangement requires repayment through a series of equal monthly payments. These loans are usually secured. Banks are increasingly making more mortgage loans. These are long-term, collateralized loans used to finance the purchase of real estate.

KEY TERMS

account reconciliation
automatic teller machine (ATM)
average daily balance
blank endorsement
cashier's check
certified check
check
checkbook ledger
check clearance
check hold
checking account
clearing fee
compounding
conditional endorsement
credit line
day of deposit to day of withdrawal method
debit card
deposit
deposits in transit
effective rate of interest
endorsement
Federal Deposit Insurance Corporation (FDIC)

Federal Savings and Loan Insurance Corporation (FSLIC)
first-in, first-out (FIFO) method
grace period
information card
installment loan
interest-crediting period
joint account
last-in, first-out (LIFO) method
line of credit
low-balance method
lowest daily balance
mortgage loan
National Credit Union Association (NCUA)
negotiable order of withdrawal (NOW) account
no-minimum account
outstanding check
overdraft
package plan
regular checking account
restrictive endorsement
safe deposit box
savings account
service fee
share draft
signature card
signature loan
single account
special endorsement
stated rate of interest
stop payment
super NOW account
traveler's check
trust services

SELECTED READINGS

"Credit Unions: Are They Better Than Banks?" *Consumer Reports*, February 1986, pp. 108–111.

Dreyfus, Patricia A. "How Safe Are Your Savings?" *Money*, May 1985, pp. 56–59.

Hoffman, Naphtali, and Stephen Brobeck. *The Bank Book*. New York: Harcourt Brace Jovanovich, 1986.

"How to Bank Today." *Changing Times*, August 1985, pp. 27–33.

"How Safe Is Your Money?" *Changing Times*, August 1985, pp. 34–37.

Rock, Andrea. "Where to Put Your Cash Now." *Money*, December 1986, pp. 81–86.

QUESTIONS

1 What is a checking account? Which institutions offer these accounts?

2 Compare the key features of each of the following kinds of checking accounts: (a) regular account, (b) NOW account, and (c) share draft account.

3 How does a super NOW account differ from a regular NOW account? Explain why an individual might prefer a super NOW account to a regular NOW account.

4 Distinguish between a single and a joint checking account. Explain why a married couple might prefer a joint account to separate single accounts.

5 What information should be contained on a written check? What is the difference between a plain check and a personalized check?

6 Identify and describe each of the four forms of check endorsement.

7 Briefly describe the procedure involved in the account reconciliation process.

8 What is an overdraft? Explain what happens when a check is returned for "insufficient funds."

9 Differentiate between a check hold and a stop payment. Provide an example of each.

10 What is a credit line on a checking account? How does a credit line protect against bounced checks? Describe the expenses associated with a credit line.

11 What is an automated teller machine (ATM)? What is the primary advantage of an ATM?

12 Briefly describe the key features of each of the following special types of checks: (a) cashier's check, (b) certified check, and (c) traveler's check.

13 What is a savings account? Explain the reasons for the popularity of savings accounts.

14 Identify the three considerations that affect the effective rate of interest you earn in a savings account. Explain how each consideration affects your interest earnings.

15 Briefly describe the four methods that may be used to determine the savings balance on which interest is earned. Which method is most favorable to the account holder? the least favorable?

16 Distinguish among (a) FDIC, (b) FSLIC, and (c) NCUA deposit insurance. Do all banks and savings institutions offer deposit insurance? Explain.

17 Differentiate among the following types of loans: (a) line of credit, (b) signature loan, and (c) installment loan.

18 If you deposit $10,000 in a savings account for five years, how much more will you have after five years if interest is compounded daily rather than annually? The stated interest rate is 5 percent. Use Table 4.4 to help determine your answer.

19 You invest $5000 at an 8 percent rate for two years. Interest is compounded semiannually.

a How much will you have after the first six months? Multiply $5000 × 0.08 × ½ (year). Add this value to the beginning $5000.

b How much will you have after the first year? Multiply your answer in part a by 0.08 × ½. Add this value to the answer to part a.

c How much will you have after 1½ years? Continue the process.

d How much will you have after two years? Continue the process.

CASE PROBLEMS

4.1 Jim and Maxine Lawton have a joint checking account at the Service Bank and Trust. Each month the Lawtons reconcile their bank statement. They recently received their bank statement for the period June 16, 1987, to July 15, 1987. This bank statement and the Lawtons' checkbook ledger appear on page 133.

Bank Statement
Jim and Maxine Lawton
1415 Azalea Trail
Dallas, Texas

Statement Period: June 16, 1987 to July 15, 1987	
Opening Balance:	$277.54
Checks and Other Debits:	571.16
Deposits and Other Credits:	751.81
Ending Balance:	458.19

Date (1987)	Checks and other charges	Deposits and other credits
June 17	$ 36.20	
June 24	15.24	
June 26	49.00	
June 29	45.21	
July 2	300.00	$750.00
July 6	94.37	
July 13	27.14	
July 15	4.00 S	1.81 I

S = service charge; I = interest deposit.

Jim and Maxine Lawton
Checkbook Ledger

Date (1987)	Check number	Description	Check amount	Deposit amount	Account balance
Beginning balance					277.54
June 16	208	Steak & Ale—entertainment	36.20		241.34
June 22	209	Southwestern Bell—telephone	15.24		226.10
June 22	210	Dallas Power & Light—utilities	33.95		192.15
June 24	211	Varsity Books—textbooks	49.00		143.15
June 25	212	Safeway—groceries	45.21		97.94
June 30	—	Deposit—Maxine's salary		750.00	847.94
June 30	213	Lakewood Apartments—rent	300.00		547.94
July 3	214	J.C. Penneys—clothing	94.37		453.57
July 10	215	Acme Cleaners—laundry	27.14		426.43
July 14	216	Allstate—auto insurance	334.90		91.53
July 14	—	Deposit—Jim's salary		750.00	841.53

a Write down the ending bank balance from the bank statement.
b Write down any deposit shown in the Lawton's checkbook that does not show up in the bank statement. This represents a deposit in transit.
c Write down any checks shown in the Lawton's checkbook that do not show up in the bank statement. These represent checks outstanding.
d Calculate the Lawton's adjusted cash balance in their bank account as follows: ending cash balance plus deposit in transit minus checks outstanding.
e Write down the ending checkbook balance.
f Calculate the Lawtons' adjusted cash balance for their checkbook as follows: ending checkbook balance minus service charges plus interest deposited.

Note: The answers to part d and part f should be equal if you have correctly reconciled the two statements. If they are not equal, please reexamine your work.

4.2 David and Pam Barnett have recently moved to Memphis, Tennessee, and are shopping for the financial institution that offers the most attractive terms on a savings account. They have identified four institutions, each offering a 6 percent effective rate of interest, but each using a different method for determining the amount on which the interest is paid. The Barnetts decide to determine how much interest each institution would have paid on their prior month's savings account. They write down the following information:

Date (1987)	Deposits	Withdrawals	Account balance
June 1	—	—	$ 0
June 5	$3000	—	3000
June 15	2000	—	5000
June 17	—	$3000	2000
June 29	3000	—	5000

a Determine the amount of interest that would be earned under the low-balance method. (Multiply the low balance times 6 percent times 1⁄12.)
b Determine the amount of interest that would be earned under the first-in, first-out method (if any). Assume there is a 10-day grace period, meaning interest can only be earned on deposits used for computation that fall within the first 10 days of the month.
c Determine the amount of interest that would be earned under the last-

in, first-out method. Assume once again that there is a 10-day grace period. Multiply the appropriate balance times 6 percent times 1⁄12.

d Determine the amount of interest that can be earned under the day of deposit to day of withdrawal method. June is a 30-day month. Follow the procedures shown in Table 4.6.

e Which alternative will be most advantageous to the Barnetts?

5

Establishing Consumer Credit

After studying this chapter, you should:

- Appreciate the basic types and sources of consumer credit
- Understand the need to use credit wisely
- Know where to obtain a consumer loan
- Understand how to compute the true cost of consumer credit
- Be able to distinguish between features associated with single-payment and installment loans
- Understand the various techniques used by lenders in processing a loan application
- Identify the basic provisions contained in consumer credit legislation

Americans have become so accustomed to using credit to make purchases that our economy is often called a credit economy. Only rarely do American consumers use cash to buy homes, automobiles, or major appliances. Instead, we tend to rely on credit to make these and other purchases. The amount of credit used varies substantially among individuals. Some people use credit only to pay for sudden and unexpected emergencies. Others may use credit to finance major purchases. Still others may use it for all kinds of expenditures, including food, clothing, and entertainment.

Clearly, credit has become an important part of the American way of life. Although the use of credit in this country dates back to colonial days, attitudes toward credit have changed considerably since then. Your grandparents may have taken a very cautious approach toward the use of credit. Chances are, however, that you are less hesitant to borrow money. During the past 35 years

Figure 5.1 CONSUMER CREDIT OUTSTANDING PER CAPITA, 1950–1985

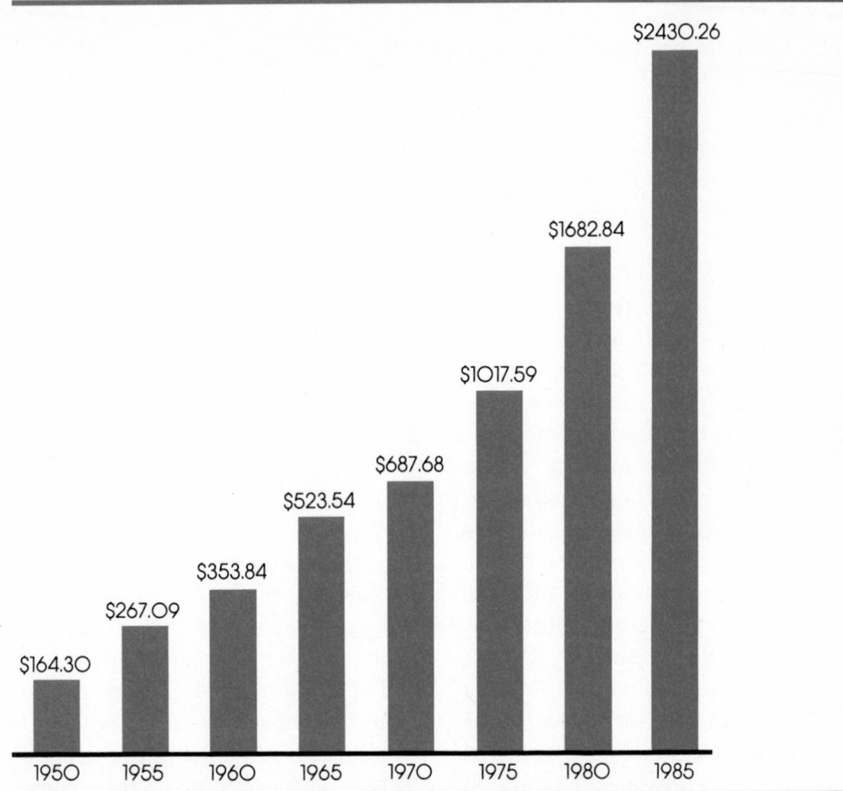

SOURCE: *Economic Report of the President*, Washington, D.C.: U.S. Government Printing Office, 1986.

the use of consumer credit has become considerably more widespread. As shown in Figure 5.1, the amount of consumer credit outstanding per person in the United States soared from only $164.30 in 1950 to $2430.26 in 1985—almost a 15-fold increase. The increase in the use of credit was especially high during the past decade. As a result, the amount of consumer credit outstanding in this country now exceeds one-half trillion dollars.

In this chapter, we present several important topics pertaining to the use of consumer credit:

1 The reasons for borrowing
2 The basic types of consumer credit
3 Where to obtain a consumer loan
4 Rules and regulations that protect the borrower

5 How to determine the true cost of credit
6 How to apply for a consumer loan

REASONS FOR BORROWING

By using credit, you increase your current purchasing power. Of course, you must repay borrowed money, so any increase in purchasing power is a temporary one. Your overall ability to buy is not changed; only the timing of your purchases is altered. You must pay a finance fee to obtain the use of another person's money. This fee is essentially a rental fee for the use of money. Because you must pay a finance charge, your total purchasing power is actually reduced. Nevertheless, the *prudent* use of credit may allow you to enhance your overall standard of living.

Borrowing may occur for many reasons. You may be confronted with an unexpected medical expense or suffer a loss of income during a temporary period of unemployment. Although you should have savings set aside to meet these emergencies (as discussed in Chapter 2), your savings may be insufficient to meet such contingencies. In this case you may find it necessary to borrow. You may also decide to borrow for nonemergencies.

Some people use credit to live beyond their means. The easy availability of credit causes some individuals to borrow to pay for vacations, entertainment, and luxury items. Although this approach may produce immediate enjoyment, it can cause serious financial problems later. When a person consumes these goods and services immediately, all that remains is an ever-growing amount of debt. Some borrowers develop a tendency for impulsive buying. These people often buy on credit without carefully evaluating the repercussions of the purchase. The person using this strategy is gambling on the receipt of a future financial windfall. If that windfall fails to materialize, the debt-burdened person will have to partially forgo future consumption.

You may desire to borrow to finance expenditures for major durable goods. Unlike goods and services that are consumed immediately, these products provide benefits for many years. The use of credit allows you to obtain the services of these products immediately, even though you do not have the cash to pay for the entire outlay. As long as the payments for the product approximately coincide with the consumption of the product, you should not necessarily be hesitant to borrow. For example, you may finance a new automobile with a four-year loan. If you plan to use that car for those four years, then you have synchronized your payments and usage. Therefore, credit can prove most helpful in allowing you to acquire expensive consumer products because you can spread the payments over a long time period instead of having to make an immediate cash payment for the entire purchase price.

You may have other legitimate reasons for borrowing money. Many people use credit cards as a matter of convenience. Credit cards are readily available, are easy to use, and allow you to make purchases even when your cash account is low. You may also use credit for investment purposes. Although investments made with borrowed funds tend to be riskier, they may produce handsome returns if your selection and timing are accurate.

An important principle to keep in mind is that a good credit record is one of the most important personal assets you can have. It is not easily achieved, and it can be very quickly lost. If you are late or irresponsible in meeting your obligations, this fact will be quickly transmitted throughout the financial and retail community. When you really need the money, it may not be available.

BASIC TYPES AND SOURCES OF CONSUMER CREDIT

In this section we discuss the two basic types of consumer credit: open-account credit and cash credit. We also describe the primary sources of each kind of credit.

Open-Account Credit

Open-account credit involves the use of credit by an individual to finance a specific transaction. A key feature of this type of credit is that the credit is approved and extended before any transaction is made. A wide variety of charge accounts and credit cards are available to most consumers who desire to buy on open account. In most instances the store or financial institution allows credit purchases or borrowing up to a specified limit. The consumer can borrow any amount as long as the **credit limit** is not exceeded and payments are made as agreed. Traditionally, open-account credit was designed for small, recurring transactions such as clothing purchases at a retail store or gasoline purchases at a service station. Recently, however, some credit cards have allowed consumers to make much larger purchases. Bank credit cards occasionally offer credit limits of several thousand dollars. We now discuss the two main forms of open-account credit: charge accounts and credit cards.

Charge Accounts. Charge accounts are available through individual businesses, such as department stores, drugstores, or public utilities. You can use your charge account only to make purchases through the particular business offering the account. Two primary types of charge accounts exist: regular charge accounts and revolving charge accounts.

Regular, or 30-Day, Charge Accounts. Several types of businesses offer **regular, or 30-day, charge accounts** to simplify consumer purchases. These accounts are provided for consumer convenience and are not designed to offer credit for any extended period. Payment is usually due 10 to 30 days after the billing date. If payment is made within the allotted grace period, no finance charge is imposed. Most charge accounts set a limit on the amount that can be charged. Because payment must be made within a short time period after the purchase, charge accounts do not differ considerably from paying cash. Convenience is the main reason for the existence of these accounts.

Revolving, or Open-End, Charge Accounts. **Revolving, or open-end, charge accounts** allow you to purchase goods and services up to a specified credit limit. As long as this limit is not exceeded and required minimum payments are made, you can continue to purchase merchandise using this type of charge account. This type of account differs from a regular charge account primarily because it does not require the full repayment of the outstanding balance at regular intervals. The **line of credit,** or maximum amount of credit you are permitted at any point in time, depends on your creditworthiness. A finance charge, often 1½ percent monthly, is imposed on any unpaid balance. Revolving charge accounts are usually found at department stores and major oil companies.

Credit Card Accounts. **Credit cards** are offered by a wide variety of businesses. Some credit cards can be used only at the retail outlets of the issuer; other cards, however, are accepted by businesses throughout the world.

Here are ten important precautions to take when using credit cards:[1]

1. Sign your cards as soon as they arrive.
2. Keep your cards in a safe place and carry them separately from your wallet.
3. Keep, in a secure place, a record of your card numbers and expiration dates, and the phone number and address of each card company.
4. Save all records of purchases. Always destroy or void carbon copies of transactions and the carbon paper that made the copies.
5. Never give your credit card numbers out over the phone unless you are sure of a company's legitimacy.
6. Avoid signing a blank receipt.
7. Notify card companies in advance of a change of address.
8. Never lend your cards to anyone.
9. Notify card companies immediately if cards are lost or stolen. (If you do so, your liability under federal law is only $50 per card.)
10. Open billing statements promptly and reconcile your card accounts each month.

There are three important types of credit cards.

Bank Credit Cards. The most popular credit cards are the **bank credit cards** issued by a group of affiliated financial institutions. MasterCard and Visa are the two major bank credit cards (see Table 5.1). The many MasterCard and Visa accounts are generally not administered at a central location; rather, individual accounts are handled by one of the many issuing financial institutions. Nevertheless, a bank credit card, regardless of the location of the issuing institution, is acceptable at millions of businesses worldwide.

[1] From *The Bank Book—How to Get the Most for Your Banking Dollars* by Naphtali Hoffman and Stephen Brobeck, copyright © 1986 by Consumer Federation of America. Reprinted by permission of Harcourt, Brace, Jovanovich, Inc.

Table 5.1 THE USE OF CREDIT CARDS

Type of credit card	Number of cardholders	Number of retail outlets
Bank cards		
MasterCard	103 million	4.3 million
Visa	124 million	4.4 million
Travel and entertainment cards		
American Express	21.3 million	1.2 million
Carte Blanche	0.3 million	N/A
Diners Club	5 million	0.8 million

N/A = not available.

SOURCE: "Which Credit Card for You," *Changing Times,* November 1985, pp. 105–107. Reprinted with permission from *Changing Times* Magazine, © 1985 Kiplinger Washington Editors, Inc. This reprint is not to be altered in any way, except with permission from *Changing Times.*

As a bank credit cardholder you will be assigned an upper credit limit. The size of this limit depends upon your income, net worth, and credit history. Although limits typically range from $500 to $1500, higher limits are available. You can continue to make purchases (and in some instances receive cash advances) as long as you do not exceed your credit limit and make required monthly minimum payments. If you pay the entire balance within the specified 25- to 30-day grace period, no finance charge is imposed.

Travel and Entertainment Cards. The primary use of **travel and entertainment credit cards** is to pay for food, lodging, and entertainment expenses. American Express, Carte Blanche, and Diners Club are the three major types of travel and entertainment cards. As you can see in Table 5.1, these cards are not as prevalent as bank credit cards. Several reasons account for the smaller number of these cards. First, travel and entertainment cards usually impose more stringent qualification standards than do bank credit cards (but they also typically have higher credit limits). Second, these cards typically require annual fees ranging from $30 to $50, whereas bank card fees rarely exceed $20 a year. Finally, fewer retail establishments accept travel and entertainment cards.

These cards have maximum credit limits and generally require that the entire balance be paid off within 30 days. The amount of cash advances available through travel and entertainment cards is limited when compared to most bank credit cards. As a result, these cards are frequently used to pay for business as opposed to personal transactions.

Retail Store and Oil Company Cards. Retail store and oil company cards are designed to make purchases more convenient for consumers. These

Box 5.1 EASING THE COST OF PLASTIC MONEY

Are interest rates on credit cards at long last coming down? The People's Bank in Bridgeport, Conn., currently charges 11.5 percent on purchases—a far cry from its 17 percent rate at the beginning of the year. Home Plan Savings & Loan in Des Moines charges 12.9 percent. A card from Simmons First National Bank in Pine Bluff, Ark., carries an 11 percent rate.

If you are willing to shop around, bargains can be found. But don't expect wholesale changes anytime soon. "The big banks' rates are stuck in cement," says Robert Heady, publisher of *Bank Rate Monitor.* Heady says the average card rate is a hefty 18.82 percent.

Banks blame billing and processing costs, losses and fraud. More to the point, institutions such as Citibank, Chase Manhattan and Bank of America can still assess card holders 19.8 percent because consumers keep charging, oblivious to the burden their plastic imposes. Credit-card debt is $118 billion, points out credit expert Spencer Nilson—up from $97 billion at the end of 1983.

You can fight back, however. Analyze your card usage and shop for the most appropriate features. What is the interest rate, and is it fixed or variable? What is the annual fee? Will you be charged transaction fees? Are you allowed the usual grace period—typically 25 to 30 days from date of purchase—during which no interest accrues? Some issuers of lower-interest-rate cards, such

cards can be used only in the retail outlets of the respective issuers. Most of these cards allow purchases up to a specified limit. The cardholder can repay the entire balance within the 25- to 30-day **grace period** and thus avoid any finance charge. Alternatively, the repayment may be extended up to 36 months, but unpaid balances incur a 1 to 1½ percent monthly finance charge.

Example of Open-Account Credit

Some kinds of open credit can be used only at the issuing store or its branches. Exxon and Sears charge cards are examples of credit that can be used only at the retail outlets of the respective card issuers. Other cards typically allow the consumer to make credit purchases at a large variety of businesses. Bank cards (Visa and MasterCard) and travel and entertainment cards (American Express, Carte Blanche, and Diners Club) are examples. Figure 5.2 shows an example of

as Banc Texas in Dallas and Society for Savings in Hartford, Conn., do not offer that float.

People who pay off their balance every month need a card with a grace period and a low annual fee regardless of interest rate. Those who maintain a card balance need a low rate. If you shop both ways, carry one of each type of card.

Does your credit union offer a credit card? According to Howard Cosgrove of the Credit Union National Association, those that do have been dropping rates, and few assess annual fees. Many credit unions begin charging interest when a purchase is posted to your account, but the trend has been to add, not do away with, the grace period. Members who keep their savings at Southern Credit Union in Chattanooga can get a 12.9 percent card.

Here are some other ways to beat the high cost of credit:

The same bank that charges you 19.8 percent when you put that $4,000 living-room suite on your MasterCard may give you a personal loan for up to 6 percentage points less. Chase Lincoln First in Rochester, N.Y., charges Visa customers 19.5 percent but offers 36-month personal unsecured loans at 13.35 percent. Connecticut National Bank in Hartford lends funds for 14 percent. A three-year loan at New York City's Amalgamated Bank costs 12 percent.

Consider borrowing against your whole-life insurance policy. Interest rates now run 8 to 10 percent.

Home-equity credit lines could become more popular if the new tax law forbids deducting interest on consumer debt and does not restrict the deduction for mortgage interest. Rates are favorable—prime rate plus 1 to 3 percentage points—but they are usually variable. Also, closing costs can bite.

If you have a brokerage account, consider borrowing on margin, using your securities as collateral. Interest rates are between 8.5 and 9.5 percent, says Percy Dubbin of Piper Jaffray & Hopwood in Minneapolis.

You can also look into a loan from savings or retirement plans your company may have. Interest rates charged are typically prime rate or slightly above. Another advantage: The interest you repay accrues to your own account.

There's much you can do to minimize the money that goes into your bankers' pockets. If enough people did so, maybe credit-card interest rates would finally come down from the ceiling.

SOURCE: Copyright, 1986, *U.S. News & World Report.* Reprinted from issue of August 11, 1986, p. 46.

a monthly Visa statement. We examine this statement to show how open credit works. Several key amounts, rates, and dates appear on this statement. Five relevant items appear on the top row of this statement. Reading from left to right across this row, these items are as follows:

Total Credit. The total amount of available credit for this account is $3500. This is the credit limit. The Visa cardholder is authorized to make credit purchases up to this amount without having to request further credit approval. Most bank card accounts have lower credit limits than this, but other accounts may be approved with higher limits.

Unused Credit. The individual purchases posted on this statement illustrate the wide variety of credit purchases that can be made with a bank credit card. For this month, purchases were made for books, clothing, medical services, and

Figure 5.2 MONTHLY BANK CARD STATEMENT

(1) (2) (3) (4) (5)

PLEASE DETACH AND RETURN TOP PORTION WITH YOUR PAYMENT

ACCOUNT NUMBER	YOUR REVOLVING CREDIT LINE FOR PURCHASES AND CASH ADVANCES: TOTAL CREDIT	UNUSED CREDIT	CLOSING DATE	PAYMENT DUE DATE	MINIMUM PAYMENT
	$3,500.00	$2,371.62	05-08-86	06-02-86	$56.00

POSTING DATE	REFERENCE NUMBER	DATE	DESCRIPTION OF TRANSACTION			$ AMOUNT
0415	14628006105118967223037	0412	NOAH'S ARK INC	DALLAS	TX	55.18
0415	14628006105118967223003	0412	NOAH'S ARK INC	DALLAS	TX	88.52
0416	10608740519		PAYMENT - THANK YOU			622.35CR
0417	42333304161060145 9	0412	TAYLORS INC NO 2	DALLAS,	TX	20.00
0421	14619006111900309130670	0412	VARSITY BOOK STORE INC	DALLAS	TX	62.85
0421	42333304181070799 4	0415	GEORGE E ORM DD	DALLAS	TX	89.00
0423	14658006113112328126883	0418	ROTHSCHILD MENSWEAR	DALLAS	TX	333.13
0424	14408746114134335112923	0418	DESIGNERS DEN INC.	DALLAS	TX	391.56
0425	439900042423NHNLEA	0419	PICKWICK BOOKS	DALLAS	TX	28.64
0502	944800050181206118	0424	DEPT OF TREASURY	WASHINGTON	DC	59.50
	***********************		FIRST CITY POINTS EARNED		226	
	***********************		FIRST CITY POINTS AVAILABLE		1,277	

BALANCE PRIOR TO 07-01-83 | BALANCE PRIOR TO 09-01-85

SUMMARY OF TRANSACTIONS	PREVIOUS BALANCE	- PAYMENTS AND CREDITS	+ PURCHASES AND ADJUSTMENTS	+ CASH ADVANCES	+ FINANCE CHARGE	= NEW BALANCE
BEFORE 09-01-85	$.00	$.00	$.00	$.00	$.00	$.00
AFTER 09-01-85	$622.35	$622.35	$1128.38	$.00	$.00	$1128.38
TOTAL	$622.35	$622.35	$1128.38	$.00	$.00	$1128.38

TO AVOID ADDITIONAL FINANCE CHARGE PAY NEW BALANCE BY PAYMENT DUE DATE. (6)

FINANCE CHARGE SCHEDULE

RANGE OF BALANCES	MONTHLY PERIODIC RATE	ANNUAL PERCENTAGE RATE	BALANCE SUBJECT TO FINANCE CHARGE	METHOD OF CALCULATION OF BALANCE SUBJECT TO FINANCE CHARGE
	BALANCES PRIOR TO 09-01-85 *	**		SEE REVERSE SIDE
ENTIRE BALANCE	BALANCES AFTER 09-01-85 1.65%	19.80%	$.00	SEE REVERSE SIDE METHOD D

*PERIODIC RATE MAY VARY.

FIRSTCITY

YOU MAY CALL THIS NUMBER FOR INFORMATION OR TO REPORT LOSS OR THEFT. HOWEVER, BILLING RIGHTS ARE PRESERVED ONLY BY WRITTEN INQUIRIES.

1-800-641-7878

MINIMUM PAYMENT DUE	
PAST DUE AMOUNT	$.00
REVOLVING CREDIT MINIMUM	$56.00
MINIMUM PAYMENT	$56.00

**RATE NEXT MONTH'S STATEMENT 14.10%

PAGE 1 OF 1 **APPLIES TO BALANCES BETWEEN 7/1/83 - 9/1/85

FORWARD BILLING INQUIRIES TO
FIRST CITY-SIOUX FALLS NA
P. O. BOX 5091
SIOUX FALLS, SD 57117

SOURCE: Courtesy of First City—Sioux Falls, South Dakota.

even a collector coin set from the U.S. Treasury. These purchases total $1128.38. Because this account has a $3500 credit limit, a total of $2371.62 of unused credit remains ($3500 − $1128.38).

Closing Date. Transactions are posted to the account on the day received by Visa, not on the actual purchase date. The closing date represents the last date that a transaction will be included on that particular monthly statement. You may make a credit card purchase before the closing date, but if that transaction does not arrive at the Visa office by the closing date, it will not appear on that month's statement.

Payment Due Date. Payment on this account must be made on or before June 2, 1986, to keep the account current. The account becomes delinquent if payment is not made by that date. The entire balance does not have to be paid by the closing date, but at least the minimum payment must be made.

Minimum Payment. Most charge accounts and credit cards do not require the payment of the entire outstanding balance. Rather, these open accounts require a minimum payment that is equal to some specified percentage of the outstanding balance. In this example, the $56.00 minimum payment equals 5 percent of the new balance (rounded to the nearest dollar). If at least $56.00 is paid by the June 2, 1986, payment due date, the customer's account remains in good standing. Finance charges will be imposed on any unpaid balances.

Determining the New Balance. The determination of the new account balance is shown under "Summary of Transactions" in the middle of Figure 5.2. The new balance is calculated as follows:

New Balance	=	Previous Balance	−	Payments and Credits	+	Purchases and Adjustments	+	Cash Advances	+	Finance Charge
$1128.38	=	$622.35	−	$622.35	+	$1128.38	+	0	+	0

The new balance is equal to the unpaid portion of any previous balance plus amounts for new purchases, cash advances, and finance charges. In this example, the $622.35 previous balance was entirely paid off during the month. If any portion of that amount was not paid, a finance charge would be imposed on the unpaid balance. The annual percentage rate of interest charged on this account is shown to be 19.80 percent (or 1.65 percent monthly). However, the statement shows that this annual percentage rate is scheduled to decline to 14.10 percent for the next month. Finance charges are also imposed on any cash advances. The calculation of finance charges and annual percentage rates of interest are discussed in detail later in this chapter.

Cash Credit

Cash credit is obtained through an actual loan. Unlike open credit, which is typically used for a specific consumer purchase, cash credit may be extended for many reasons and can be obtained from a wide variety of lenders. You may want to take out a cash loan to pay for a new refrigerator, especially if the seller does not offer open credit. Some people use cash credit to pay for a vacation or remodeling a home. Others may obtain a cash loan to pay off other outstanding loans. In some instances **loan consolidation,** or the combination of several different loans into a single loan, can reduce your overall finance charges (by using cheaper sources of financing) and at the same time eliminate much cumbersome paperwork.

Sources of Cash Credit. Commercial banks remain the largest provider of consumer credit, with almost one-quarter trillion dollars of consumer installment credit outstanding (see Figure 5.3). We discussed the role of banks in extending cash credit in Chapter 4. Other sources of cash credit include consumer finance companies, credit unions, life insurance companies, savings and loan associations, and pawnshops. We briefly examine each of these sources.

Figure 5.3 CONSUMER INSTALLMENT CREDIT BY TYPE OF LENDER, 1985 (IN MILLIONS)

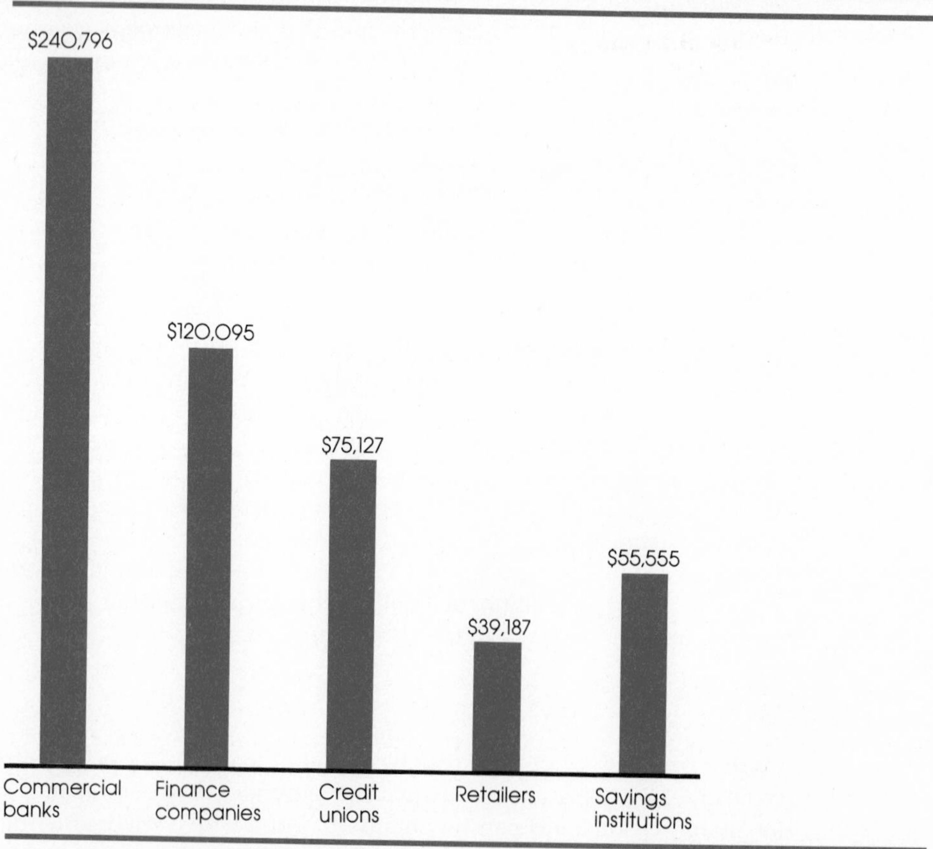

SOURCE: *Federal Reserve Bulletin,* Washington, D.C.: Board of Governors of the Federal Reserve System, July 1986.

Consumer Finance Companies. The primary activity of consumer finance companies is to make small loans to qualified individuals. These companies often make loans to consumers without an established credit history. The loans are either personal installment loans or second mortgages. Most personal loans are made on a secured basis, but occasionally an unsecured loan is made. The maximum amount of a loan made by a consumer finance company is regulated by state law.

Loans from consumer finance companies are often easy to obtain. In some instances the consumer can receive borrowed funds on the same day the application is made. However, these types of loans are generally more costly than loans from other sources. Interest rates may range from 12 to 36 percent per year. There is some justification for these high interest rates. Many individuals who borrow from consumer finance companies are poor credit risks and cannot obtain credit from other sources. As a result, higher collection fees and bad-debt expenses occur among these customers. Also, most consumer loans are made in small amounts but still require the same investigative and processing expenses of larger loans.

Credit Unions. A credit union is a state or federally chartered organization formed to provide savings and lending services to its members. Credit union members must have a common bond, such as working for the same employer or belonging to the same club. Credit unions can make loans only to members. Most loans are either personal installment loans or second mortgages and may be made on either a secured or an unsecured basis. In addition, many credit unions make credit card loans. Most credit union loans are made in small amounts, averaging about $2000 per loan. Rarely is a loan exceeding $10,000 made.

Credit union loans are usually less expensive than other types of loans. All federal and most state-chartered credit unions are limited to a 21 percent maximum interest rate; in most instances, however, the actual rate charged is much less than the maximum rate, typically ranging from 8 to 12 percent. These lower rates are made possible because credit unions are nonprofit organizations with minimal operating costs and relatively low costs of funds. Credit unions also tend to make lower-risk loans than do other financial institutions. As a general rule, credit unions offer a lower cost of credit than other sources of consumer loans.

Life Insurance Companies. You may obtain a loan on certain types of life insurance policies (which are discussed in detail in Chapter 10). These policies offer a savings function as well as providing a death benefit. The amount of savings accumulated in the policy is known as the cash value. You can borrow against the cash value of your policy at any time. Previously, state laws often limited the maximum interest rate on these loans to 8 percent, but the recent trend is to allow life insurance companies to charge the market interest rate on these loans.

Consumers often overlook this source of credit. However, a loan against the cash value of your life insurance policy can provide an attractive financing alternative. Furthermore, the procedure for acquiring this type of loan is relatively simple. When you borrow against the cash value of your policy, you are really borrowing your own money. Therefore, no credit investigation is required; as a policyholder you automatically qualify for the loan. All you must do is contact your insurance company and request the appropriate form for borrowing. After completing the form and returning it to the company, you will soon receive the loan proceeds. Interest on the loan will be added to your regular premium payment or billed to you annually. Because there is no maturity date on these loans, consumers tend not to repay them. You can suffer adverse financial repercussions if you neglect to account for this expense in your budget. Also, if the loan is not repaid, the amount of the loan is deducted from the insurance payout at time of death.

Savings and Loan Associations. Savings and loan associations and mutual savings banks primarily make mortgage loans. If you want to obtain funds, you may want to consider a second mortgage loan on your home to obtain funds because the finance charges on such loans are tax deductible. Whereas, beginning in 1987, finance charges on other consumer loans are being phased out as a tax deductible expense. These savings associations have recently expanded their lending activities to include loans made on consumer durables such as televisions, ranges, and washers and dryers. These loans are made on a secured basis. Some of these savings institutions also make smaller consumer loans using passbook savings for collateral.

Pawnshops. An individual who cannot obtain a loan from any other source may turn to a pawnshop. Loans can be obtained from pawnshops by pledging certain types of merchandise, such as jewelry, guns, and television sets. Most pawnshops do not lend more than 50 percent of the appraised value of pledged goods, because many borrowers default on these loans. The pawnshop then sells the property to pay off the delinquent loan balance. Most borrowers who use pawnshops have low incomes and few assets. Because of the high amount of credit risk and the costs associated with handling these typically small loans, finance charges are usually very high. The high costs of these loans should discourage all but the most desperate borrower.

CONSUMER CREDIT LEGISLATION

Although most lenders employ fair credit practices, there nevertheless are some lenders who attempt to take advantage of the unwary consumer. Many federal regulations and laws pertaining to consumer lending exist to protect you from the unscrupulous lender. Ten of these regulations and laws are summarized below.

Regulation AA (Consumer Inquiries and Complaints)

Sets forth procedures for investigating and processing complaints by a consumer in relation to the denial of credit.

Regulation B (Equal Credit Opportunity)

Prohibits discrimination against a credit applicant on the basis of race, sex, color, marital status, religion, age, receipt of public assistance, and national origin in any credit transaction.

Regulation BB (Community Reinvestment)

Forbids the arbitrary consideration of geographic factors or redlining in granting credit within the financial institution's local community. Redlining consists of blanket refusal to grant credit within circumscribed (redlined) neighborhoods deemed by the bank to be in physical and economic decline.

Regulation C (Home Mortgage Disclosure)

Details reporting requirements of geographical data on mortgages to enable regulators to detect redlining practices.

Regulation E (Electronic Funds Transfer)

Limits consumer liability for unauthorized use of lost credit or debit cards. Controls issuance of cards and specifies information to be supplied to the consumer in using electronic transfer devices.

Regulation Z (Truth-in-Lending)

Requires that consumers be given meaningful and consistent information on the cost of credit. Certain nonprice information must also be disclosed.

Fair Housing Act

Prohibits discrimination in housing and housing credit on the basis of race, color, religion, national origin, or sex. This act preceded passage of the Equal Credit Opportunity Act, which defined several additional bases of discrimination. The act prohibits redlining housing credit.

Fair Credit Reporting Act

Grants consumers access to their credit bureau records, and entitles them to check the source of information and its accuracy. Denials of credit by banks on the basis of credit bureau information must be reported to consumers.

Fair Credit Billing Act

Gives consumers legal rights pertaining to credit disputes. Protects consumers from creditors' actions while a bill is in dispute.

Real Estate Settlement Procedures Act

Requires a detailed statement of settlement costs on real estate transactions and reporting of borrowers' rights in the granting of mortgage credit.

Most of this legislation deals with disclosure of credit information, credit denial and discrimination, credit disputes, errors in credit billing, and protection against collector harassment. There are also similar state laws in many parts of the country.

Disclosure of Credit Information

For many years there was no standard amount of information that lenders were required to disclose to consumers. Information provided borrowers was often incomplete and confusing. Congress believed that too many abuses by creditors were the result of poor credit information. The **Truth-in-Lending Act** and the associated **Regulation Z** of the Federal Reserve System became effective in June 1969 and required the disclosure of key credit information in straightforward language. The most important provision of this act requires lenders to "clearly and conspicuously" disclose both the dollar amount of finance charges and the annual percentage rate on all loans and to do so before the credit is extended. With this information, you can make valid comparisons among the various sources of credit.

The **finance charge** is the total dollar amount of the cost of credit. The interest cost of the loan is the most obvious example of a finance charge. However, the finance charge also includes other expenses such as points[2] or credit insurance premiums. The lender must also disclose prepayment penalties, charges made if the borrower defaults, and any collateral requirement. The Truth-in-Lending Act also provides a standard way for calculating the **annual percentage rate (APR),** or true rate of interest, on the loan. The APR is the percentage rate of interest the borrower pays on the average loan balance outstanding.

The original Truth-in-Lending Act imposed such complicated reporting requirements that many consumers were confused with the highly technical disclosure statement. Because of the difficulty in interpreting credit information, many consumers simply ignored the information. Congress recognized this problem and in 1980 passed the **Truth-in-Lending Simplification and Reform Act.** This act reduced disclosure requirements and required lenders to use standard, easy-to-understand disclosure statements. Figure 5.4 contains a sample Truth-in-Lending Disclosure Statement. On this form you can see space to provide the annual percentage rate and finance charge prominently displayed in bold boxes in the upper left-hand portion of the statement.

Credit Refusal and Discrimination

The **Equal Credit Opportunity Act** of 1971 contains provisions that address credit refusal and discrimination. If you have been denied a loan you can ask the creditor why, and this act requires the creditor to tell you the specific reason for the denial. A general response, such as reporting that you did not rank high enough on the creditor's credit scoring program, is not acceptable. Some common reasons that are valid for rejecting a loan application include the following:

[2] Points refer to an extra payment to the lender that is frequently used with home mortgages. For example, two points (percent) on a $50,000 home loan would mean that the lender would receive a $1000 initial fee (0.02 × $50,000).

Insufficient income
Inadequate collateral
Insufficient credit history
Delinquent credit obligations
Poor credit references
Excessive obligations
Incomplete credit application

In October 1975, the Equal Credit Opportunity Act was extended to prevent a creditor from discriminating on the basis of sex or marital status when considering a credit application. The act requires that women be treated the same as men. This means that creditors must regard the income of women in exactly the same way as they treat the income of men. The act was further expanded in 1977 to make it illegal to discriminate among borrowers based on age, race, religion, or national origin. Therefore, you cannot be denied credit because you belong to a particular religion or have reached a certain age.

Access to Credit Information

Many lenders pay a fee to be a member of a **credit-reporting agency,** which gives them access to any credit information in the agency's files. The information retrieved from these files often becomes a significant factor in determining the creditworthiness of a loan applicant. Because of the importance creditors attach to this credit information, you may want to determine the accuracy of your credit file. Effective April 1971, the **Fair Credit Reporting Act** allows you to review your credit file. Because this act requires a credit file to contain only accurate, relevant, and recent credit information, the credit reporting agency is legally required to reinvestigate any information you claim to be erroneous. If the agency does not change the disputed information, you have the right to include your refutation in the file.

The **Fair Credit Billing Act** gives the consumer legal rights pertaining to credit disputes. If you question the accuracy of a bill, you have 60 days to notify the creditor in writing. The creditor must respond in 30 days and resolve the dispute in 90 days. The creditor is legally prohibited from taking any action to impair your credit while the account is in dispute. If, after investigating the disputed account, the creditor still claims the charge is valid, he or she may report the account as delinquent. In such a case, the creditor's report must also indicate that the account is disputed and must tell you where the report has been filed.

Protection Against Harassment

Some creditors employ collection agencies to collect delinquent loans. These collectors occasionally resort to extreme measures. You may have heard about instances where a collector threatened a delinquent borrower or made abusive

Figure 5.4 SAMPLE TRUTH-IN-LENDING DISCLOSURE STATEMENT

TRUTH-IN-LENDING
SEPARATE DISCLOSURE STATEMENT

BANK:
INDEPENDENCE BANK
Independence and Spring Creek Parkways
Plano, Texas
Date of Loan Transaction ______________

BORROWER:
Name Richard T. Friedman
Address 116 Highland Road
Plano, Texas
Account Number 863 207

ANNUAL PERCENTAGE RATE The cost of your credit as a yearly rate.	FINANCE CHARGE The dollar amount the credit will cost you.	AMOUNT FINANCED The amount of credit provided to you or on your behalf.	TOTAL OF PAYMENTS The amount you will have paid after you have made all payments as scheduled
14% %	$ 7%	$ $1,800.00	$ 1,926.00

Your **Payment Schedule** will be:

Number of Payments	Amount of Payments	When Payments Are Due
12	$ 160.50	10th of the month
	$	
	$	
	$	

Demand: ☐ If this box is checked, this obligation is, as an alternative to the above-recited payment schedule, due and payable on demand.

Variable Rate: ☐ **If this box is checked, the interest rate may increase during the term of this transaction if the "Prime Rate" of Independence Bank (the "Bank") increases (such Prime Rate being at any date the rate of interest per annum then most recently established by the Bank as its prime rate on commercial loans). Any increase may take the form of higher payment amounts or a larger amount due at maturity or both.**

If your loan were for $12,000.00 at 15% for twelve (12) months, in monthly payments of $1,000.00 plus accrued interest (the amount of such interest varying from $152.88 to $12.33), and the rate increased to 15.25% in 1 month, each of your regular payments would increase (by an amount varying from $2.26 to $ .20). If your loan were for $12,000.00 at 15% for 90 days and the rate increased to 15.25% in 30 days, your payment due at maturity would increase by $4.93.

Security: You are giving a security interest in:
☒ the goods or property being purchased ☐ (brief description of other property). personal computer
☐ the home being improved

Collateral securing other loans with the Bank may also secure this loan.

Filing Fees: $__________

Late Charge: ☒ If this box is checked and a payment is late, you will be charged 5% of the payment.

Prepayment: ☒ If you pay off early, you will not have to pay a penalty, and you ☒ may ☐ will not be entitled to a refund of part of the Finance Charge.

See your contract documents for any additional information about nonpayment, default, any required repayment in full before the scheduled date, and prepayment refunds and penalties.

*means an estimate

Insurance: Credit life insurance and credit disability insurance are not required to obtain credit, and will not be provided unless you sign and agree to pay the additional cost.

Type	Premium	Term	Signature of Maker
Credit Life			I want credit life insurance x__________
Credit Disability			I want credit disability insurance x__________

Property Insurance: ☐ If this box is checked, property insurance is required in connection with the promissory note. You may obtain such property insurance from anyone you want that is acceptable to Bank. You have the option of furnishing the required insurance either through existing policies of insurance owned or controlled by you or of procuring and furnishing equivalent insurance coverages through any insurance company authorized to transact business in Texas.

Richard T. Friedman

Itemization of the Amount Financed of $ 1,800

Amount given to you directly	$ 1,800
Amount paid on your account	$ 0
Amount paid to others on your behalf:	
To Public Officials or Government Agencies	$
To Insurance Company	$
For Credit Report	$
To __________	$
__________	$
Prepaid Finance Charge	$

The undersigned hereby acknowledge(s) receipt of a copy (copies) of this Disclosure Statement, with all essential blanks filled in, prior to execution of the promissory note.

April 22, 1987 (Date Disclosure Received) — Sam H. Phillips (Signature)

April 23, 1987 (Date Disclosure Received) — Martin Gomez (Signature)

#L-133 (9-83)

SOURCE: Courtesy of Independence Bank, Plano, Texas.

phone calls at unreasonable hours. Because of the unreasonable collection tactics used by some collection agencies, the **Fair Debt Collection Practices Act** was passed. Effective March 1978, you are protected against abusive collection practices. Specifically, a bill collector is prohibited from subjecting you to any of the following abuses:

Using abusive language to coerce you to make a payment

Calling you at unreasonable hours or making excessive calls

Threatening to notify your employer or friends that you have not paid your bills

Using false pretenses to gain entry to your home with the intent of identifying or taking something of value

Attempting to collect more than is owed

Sending you misleading letters that appear to be from a government agency or court of law

THE EFFECTIVE COST OF CREDIT

Until 1969, when the Consumer Credit Protection Act, or Truth-in-Lending Act, became effective, most consumers could not determine the effective interest cost of a loan. Since that act took effect, however, all lenders have been required to disclose both the dollar amount of finance charges and the annual percentage rate (APR) of interest. The APR is determined by dividing the dollar amount of finance charges by the average loan balance for a specified time period and, therefore, is the effective, or true, cost of credit. The primary advantage of the APR is that it can be used to compare the cost of competing loans. You may find that loans with the same stated interest rates may have different finance charges and APRs. Therefore, it is important to understand how a loan's APR is calculated. We first describe the APR calculation for single-payment loans and next explain the APR computations for installment loans.

Calculating APRs for Single-Payment Loans

The simple interest method and the discount method may be used to calculate the finance charges and APRs on single-payment loans.

Simple Interest Method. Under the **simple interest method** the amount of the finance charge is calculated on the average loan balance outstanding for the length of time the money is borrowed. An example can be used to illustrate how this method works. Assume John White borrows $2000 for two years from the State National Bank at a 10 percent stated interest rate. The annual finance charge on this loan is computed as follows:

$$\text{Annual Finance Charge} = \text{Outstanding Loan Balance} \times \text{Stated Annual Interest Rate}$$

$$\$200 = \$2000 \times 10\%$$

The annual finance charge is paid at the end of each year. The APR for a loan using the simple interest method is calculated by dividing the annual finance charge by the outstanding loan balance. In this example the APR equals 10 percent, calculated as follows:

$$\text{APR} = \text{Finance Charge} \div \text{Outstanding Loan Balance}$$

$$10\% = \$200 \div \$2000$$

You may have noticed that the APR on this loan is the same as the stated interest rate. When the simple interest method is used, the APR always equals the stated interest rate.

Discount Method. The amount of the finance charge is subtracted in advance from the amount of money lent in the **discount method.** Therefore, the borrower does not receive the entire principal amount of the loan. Rather, the loan is discounted, or reduced, by the total amount of finance charges. The finance charge on a single-payment discount loan is calculated exactly the same as for the simple interest loan. Using the previous example, the total finance charges over the life of the loan are $400 ($200 annual finance charge × 2 years).

Although the yearly finance charge is the same for the simple interest and discount method, the APR for the two methods will always be different. The difference is attributable to the timing of the payment of the finance charge. For the simple interest method, finance charges are generally paid at the end of each year or at the time the loan matures, whereas under the discount method the finance charges are deducted at the time the loan is made.

For the previously described two-year loan to John White, the annual finance charge is $200. Total finance charges of $400 are subtracted from the principal amount of the loan to determine the net amount the borrower receives. In this example, the borrower receives only $1600 ($2000 principal amount − $400 finance charges). The same APR formula as used for the simple interest method yields a 12.5 percent APR for the discount method.

$$\text{APR} = \text{Annual Finance Charge} \div \text{Outstanding Loan Balance}$$

$$12.5\% = \$200 \div \$1600$$

Table 5.2 compares the finance charges and APRs for this example under the simple interest and discount methods. The APR using the discount method is 25 percent higher than the APR employing the simple interest method on this

Table 5.2 COMPARISON OF TOTAL FINANCE CHARGES AND APRs ($2000 SINGLE-PAYMENT LOAN FOR TWO YEARS)

Method	Total finance charges	Stated interest rate (%)	Annual percentage rate (%)
Simple interest	$400	10.0	10.0
Discount	400	10.0	12.5

single-payment loan, even though both loans are for the same dollar amount and have the same stated interest rate.

Calculating APRs for Installment Loans

Having explained the simple interest and discount methods for determining APRs for single-payment loans, we next turn to installment loans. We describe the simple interest and add-on methods of calculating APRs on installment loans.

Simple Interest Method. An installment loan requires regular periodic payments of both principal and interest. Under the simple interest method, interest is charged only on the principal amount of the loan outstanding. Therefore, as the loan balance decreases, so does the interest payment. We return to the John White example to show how to calculate the APR on an installment loan using the simple interest method. Let's assume that John decides to borrow the same $2000 at the same 10 percent stated interest rate. However, in this instance John decides to borrow on a one-year installment loan basis. The terms of the loan require equal monthly payments. The monthly payments can be calculated with the assistance of a hand-held calculator or can be obtained from installment loan tables.[3] For simplicity, we present the monthly payments in Table 5.3. As shown, each payment equals $175.83 and represents both interest and principal payments. The amount of interest paid each month gradually declines as the outstanding loan balance is reduced. Each month's interest payment is calculated by multiplying the outstanding loan balance at the beginning of the month by the monthly stated interest rate (the annual interest rate divided by 12). For example, the first month's $16.67 interest charge is computed as follows:

[3] Appendix 5.A shows the finance charge per $100 of amount financed for various interest rates (APRs) and loan maturities. This appendix also shows how to compute the monthly payment on an installment loan.

Table 5.3 INSTALLMENT LOAN PAYMENTS

(1) Month	(2) Outstanding loan balance	(3) Monthly payment	(4) Monthly interest	(5) Principal repayment
1	$2000.00	$ 175.83	$ 16.67	$ 159.16
2	1840.84	175.83	15.34	160.49
3	1680.35	175.83	14.00	161.83
4	1518.52	175.83	12.65	163.18
5	1355.34	175.83	11.29	164.54
6	1190.80	175.83	9.92	165.91
7	1024.89	175.83	8.54	167.29
8	857.60	175.83	7.15	168.68
9	688.92	175.83	5.74	170.09
10	518.83	175.83	4.32	171.51
11	347.32	175.83	2.89	172.94
12	174.38	175.83	1.45	174.38
Totals		$2109.96	$109.96	$2000.00

$$\text{Monthly Interest} = \text{Outstanding Loan Balance} \times \text{Monthly Stated Interest Rate}$$

$$\$16.67 = \$200 \times (10\% \div 12)$$

Table 5.3 shows how the monthly payments are divided into interest and principal components. Over the life of the loan, total payments equal $2109.96 of which $109.96 represents interest and the remaining $2000 represents the repayment of the principal. Because the stated interest rate is applied only to the amount of loan outstanding, the APR will always equal the stated rate for an installment loan using the simple interest method. In this case the APR equals 10 percent, the same as the APR for the simple interest method for a single-payment loan. Although the APRs are the same for these single-payment and installment loans using the simple interest method, there is one major difference between these two types of loans. With the single-payment loan, John White has the use of the $2000 principal amount for the entire duration of the loan. Under the installment method, however, John must make periodic principal repayments before the loan matures. In this example, John's average installment loan balance outstanding over the one-year term is only $1099.60.[4]

[4] The average loan balance outstanding is determined by summing the outstanding loan balance for each month (column 2 in Table 5.3) and dividing by the number of months in the repayment period (12 in this example).

Add-On Method. With the **add-on method** total finance charges are calculated by multiplying the original loan balance by the stated interest rate. Assume that John White agrees to the same $2000 installment loan as previously described with only one difference in terms: that finance charges are computed using the add-on method instead of the simple interest method. In this instance, total finance charges are computed to be $200 as follows:

$$\text{Total Finance Charges} = \text{Original Loan Balance} \times \text{Stated Interest Rate}$$

$$\$200 = \$2000 \times 10\%$$

The finance charges are added to the principal amount, and the total is divided by the number of payments to be made to obtain the amount of the monthly payment. In this example, the monthly payment equals $183.33 ([$2000 + $200] ÷ 12).

The APR computations for the add-on method are considerably more complex than for other methods. The following formula, called the ***N-ratio method,*** can be used to calculate an approximate APR on an installment loan using the add-on method.

$$\text{APR} = \frac{M(95N + 9)C}{12N(M + 1)(4P + C)}$$

where

APR = annual percentage rate
M = number of payments yearly
N = number of payments over life of loan
C = total finance charges
P = principal amount of loan

In this example, $M = 12$, $N = 12$, $C = \$200$, and $P = \$2000$. Therefore, the APR equals 17.96 percent, calculated as follows:

$$\text{APR} = \frac{12[(95)(12) + 9](\$200)}{(12)(12)(12 + 1)[(4)(\$2000) + 200]}$$

$$= \frac{\$2{,}757{,}600}{\$15{,}350{,}400} = 17.96\%$$

Table 5.4 on page 160 shows the substantial difference in the APR calculated under the simple interest and add-on methods. Before you borrow money, the lender must disclose the APR. If you understand the various methods for determining the amount of finance charges, you will be better prepared to negotiate a loan that best serves your interests. An uninformed consumer may pay unexpectedly high finance charges when obtaining credit.

Box 5.2 BORROWING MONEY TO SAVE MONEY

The same low interest rates that make some types of savings less attractive—money market funds and bank certificates of deposit, for example—make borrowing money more appealing. And as banks, brokers, and "financial supermarkets" compete, you can borrow most economically if you shop carefully among a variety of loan arrangements.

Familiar with finance company ads that suggest a "consolidation" loan to keep creditors off your back? At first glance, that might look like the objective of an Equity Access loan offered by Merrill Lynch & Co. (Other lenders offer it, too. Whatever the name, it's basically a line of credit secured by a second mortgage on your home.) But far from being a last resort for an overextended borrower, says Charles A. Humm, a Merrill Lynch vice-president, the idea of the loan is to help you save money. You do that by preparing now to borrow according to your anticipated cash flow needs over the next few years.

Humm shows how it can work if you already have a number of outstanding loans: a \$25,000 second mortgage at 16¼%, a \$10,000 unsecured personal loan at 16%, \$8,000 in credit card charges at 20%, and a \$10,000 car loan at 14%—all adding up to \$53,000 outstanding at a weighted average rate of 16.4%. If you take out a single \$53,000 loan when the going rate is 12%,

APPLYING FOR CREDIT

Not everyone qualifies for credit. Lenders carefully evaluate your creditworthiness before extending credit. **Creditworthiness** is defined as the probability, as perceived by the lender, that you will be able to repay the loan. A lender prefers to make loans only to individuals who are very creditworthy. This does not mean that the lender must believe that your probability of repayment is 100 percent. In this world of uncertainty, lenders often make loans when there is less than 100 percent chance of repayment. For example, if the lender perceives a 95 percent repayment probability, the loan will often be made. However, if the repayment probability is only 70 percent, the loan will probably be considered

for example, you would save $2,340 in interest in one year.

Getting one large loan to replace several small ones will become much more popular if tax reform ends consumer deductions for all but mortgage interest, experts say.* If the equity is worth $100,000, for example, you can get a line of credit for about 75% of that amount. (The maximum line available: $2 million.) You dip into your credit line as needed by using a special credit card or checks. On any amount you borrow, and for only as long as the money is borrowed, Merrill Lynch charges an interest rate 2 percentage points above the prime rate, or 10.5% at today's 8.5% prime. (Elsewhere, you may find rates varying by a half-point or so, sometimes depending on whether you are a "favored" customer.) And you pay a 2% origination fee—that's $1,500 on your $75,000 line—plus an annual fee of $35 or so in most states.

* With the passage of the Tax Reform Act of 1986, this is now the case.

Prepay Tuition with a Loan

This kind of arrangement, Humm notes, lets you borrow $1 for a day, $1,000 for a week, or $10,000 for a school year—and pay only a day, week, or year's worth of interest. As you pay back the borrowed principal, periodically or in a lump sum, you can keep borrowing up to the maximum. The credit line runs 10 years, so you don't have to apply for a new loan and undergo a credit check each time you need money. Here's one way you might come out ahead: Where a college permits it, you could borrow enough at today's low rate to prepay four years of tuition, rather than wait to borrow enough to cover each year's costs, perhaps at progressively higher interest rates. Says Humm: "A credit line makes it possible to plan your borrowing the way a corporation does—going long-term or short-term to get the best deal."

"By Far the Cheapest Way to Borrow"

Typically, where a stockbroker is in the picture, you are restricted from using funds borrowed in this manner to buy securities. A margin account at your broker, though, lets you borrow to invest in the market. Many brokers will lend you cash from the account for other purposes, too. You can draw up to 50% of the value of the equities in your account (often a higher amount on Treasury securities). And you pay off the loan at an interest rate that's a point or two above the broker loan rate, the rate brokers pay to borrow. That rate has been running below 8%. "It's by far the cheapest way to borrow," says Brent B. Erensel, senior banking analyst at Dean Witter Reynolds Inc.

SOURCE: Reprinted from June 16, 1986, issue of *Business Week* by special permission, © 1986 by McGraw-Hill, Inc.

too risky and therefore rejected. Consumer lenders expect some bad debts to occur. If credit was extended only to the most creditworthy individuals, lenders would forfeit the business of many potential borrowers who would repay their loans on a timely basis.

When applying for credit, you will normally be asked to supply information about your current bank account, your current and previous residence, your work history, and any other credit you currently have outstanding. Of course, not everyone has a positive response to all these questions, so a careful evaluation of your repayment potential will be necessary.

Although the various lenders may have different credit standards, it is useful to know about the important factors that credit analysts generally observe

Table 5.4 COMPARISON OF TOTAL FINANCE CHARGES AND APRs ($2000 MONTHLY INSTALLMENT LOAN FOR ONE YEAR)

Method	Total finance charges	Stated interest rate (%)	Annual percentage rate (%)
Simple interest	$109.96	10.00	10.00
Installment	200.00	10.00	17.96

in deciding whether or not to approve a loan. We examine three techniques for analyzing an individual's creditworthiness: (1) internal analysis made by a credit analyst, (2) credit scoring, and (3) external credit information.

Internal Credit Analysis

A credit analyst follows certain guidelines to determine the creditworthiness of loan applicants. These guidelines vary among lenders, but usually involve some combination of the following five criteria (often known as the five C's).

Capacity. Your earning power determines your capacity to borrow. Your ability to repay a loan is largely dependent on the amount of cash flows you generate each year. Therefore, creditors closely observe your recurring income streams to assess your creditworthiness.

Capital. Your capital is the total value of your financial resources less any amounts you owe. In the event you experience financial difficulties that cause your cash flows to decline, the lender can look to the sale of your assets to satisfy a claim.

Character. Creditors want to make sure that you are committed to the timely repayment of your obligations. Therefore, they look to your character as an indication of your creditworthiness. Your past history in honoring financial commitments provides a basis for evaluating this important characteristic.

Collateral. Creditors often insist that you pledge specific assets, or **collateral,** to secure a loan. For example, when you buy a new automobile, the lender will probably require you to pledge your automobile as collateral. If you default on the loan, the creditor repossesses the car. The car is then sold and the proceeds are applied against the loan.

Conditions. The state of the overall economy and the availability of money to lend are conditions that creditors consider before making loans. When the

Box 5.3 SAMPLE CREDIT-SCORING SYSTEM

	Points
1. Own or rent principal residence	
(a) Owns/buying	40
(b) Rents	8
(c) No answer	8
(d) Other	25
2. Time at present address	
(a) Under 6 months	12
(b) 6 months–2 years	15
(c) 2–6½ years	22
(d) Over 6½ years	35
(e) No answer	12
3. Time with present employer	
(a) Under 1½ years	12
(b) 1½–3 years	15
(c) 3–5½ years	25
(d) Over 5½ years	48
(e) Retired	48
(f) Unemployed with alimony/child support/public assistance	25
(g) Homemaker	25
(h) Unemployed—no public assistance	12
(i) No answer	12
4. Applicant's age	
(a) Under 45 years	4
(b) 45 years or older	20
(c) No answer	4
5. Banking reference	
(a) Checking and savings	60
(b) Checking	40
(c) Savings	40
(d) Loan and checking and/or savings	30
(e) Loan only	10
(f) None given	10
(g) No answer	10
6. Major credit card/dept. store	
(a) Major CC(s) and department store(s)	40
(b) Major CC(s) only	40
(c) Department store(s) only	30
(d) None	10
7. Finance company reference	
(a) One	15
(b) Two or more	10
(c) None	5
(d) No answer	10
8. Income	
(a) \$0–10,000	5
(b) \$10,000–15,000	15
(c) \$15,000–30,000	30
(d) Over \$30,000	50
9. Monthly payments	
(a) \$0–100	35
(b) \$100–300	25
(c) Over \$300	10
(d) No payments	45
(e) No answer	10
10. Derogatory ratings	
(a) No investigation	0
(b) No record	0
(c) Two or more derogatory	−20
(d) One derogatory	0
(e) All positive ratings	15

SOURCE: George H. Hempel, Alan B. Coleman, and Donald G. Simonson, *Bank Management: Text and Cases,* New York: Wiley, 1986, p. 418.

economy is weak and money is difficult to obtain, creditors may be less inclined to make loans. Under these circumstances your loan application may be rejected, whereas in a more favorable economic environment your loan might be approved.

Credit Scoring

Some lenders assign points to various loan applicant characteristics. The points are added to determine an applicant's total score, which is then compared with a predetermined accept-reject score. Credit is extended to applicants whose scores equal or exceed the accept-reject score, and credit is denied those whose scores fail to achieve this amount. This process is known as **credit scoring.** Box 5.3 presents an example of one lender's credit-scoring system. Each characteristic is assigned a different weight, so one factor, such as banking reference, may have more importance than another, for example, applicant's age.

The objective of credit scoring is to predict whether a borrower is creditworthy. The primary advantage of this system is that it objectively weighs numerous important characteristics. Credit scoring, however, has several disadvantages. First, it relies on historical data and might be obsolete in detecting current predictors of creditworthiness. Second, the lender's experience and insight in appraising a borrower's ability and willingness to pay are ignored. In some instances the borrower's character can be a valuable input in the lending decision. Finally, the relative importance of the observed characteristics may change over time. The weights in the credit-scoring system must be carefully monitored on a continuous basis for the system to provide useful decisions. Because of these limitations, many lenders use both credit scoring and their own judgment to arrive at lending decisions.

External Credit Information

We have already mentioned the role of the credit reporting agencies. These agencies are usually operated on a local basis. Ownership is typically in the hands of local banks and merchants. A local credit reporting agency collects credit information from its members on people living in the area and makes this information available to members for a small fee. Many local agencies are linked together nationally through computer networks, so a member can obtain credit information from almost any part of the United States. These agencies are excellent sources of credit information but do not analyze the information or make credit rankings. The bank or merchant must perform those tasks.

SUMMARY

The use of credit to make consumer purchases has grown tremendously since 1950. Only a generation ago many Americans were reluctant to use credit. Today, however, American consumers are less hesitant to borrow money. Consumers often view credit as a means to improve their overall standard of living. Some consumers take a very cautious approach toward the use of credit, borrowing only to pay for sudden and unexpected emergencies. Others may use credit more aggressively to pay for daily obligations like food, clothing, and entertainment. The key factor regarding credit is that borrowed money must be repaid. Your overall ability to buy is not changed; only the timing of your purchases is altered. The overuse of credit today may adversely affect your future living standard.

The popularity of consumer credit has been accompanied by an increase in the availability of credit. Two primary sources of consumer credit exist: open account and cash credit. Open-account credit is used to finance a specific transaction. Credit is preapproved under this type of credit. Charge accounts, available through individual businesses, and credit cards are the two main forms of open-account credit.

Cash credit is not preapproved and must be obtained through an actual loan. Cash credit may be extended for many reasons and can be obtained from a wide variety of lenders. Foremost among these lenders are commercial banks, consumer finance companies, credit unions, life insurance companies, savings and loan associations, and pawnshops. The availability, amount, and cost of credit vary considerably among the various lenders, so you must carefully shop to find the loan best suited for your specific need.

Although most lenders employ fair credit practices, there are some lenders who attempt to take advantage of the unwary consumer. Many regulations and laws exist to protect you from unscrupulous lenders. These laws generally pertain to the disclosure of credit information, credit denial and discrimination, credit disputes, errors, and protection against collector harassment.

Before you take out a loan, you should determine its effective interest cost. Because this determination is often complex, federal law now requires that all lenders disclose both the dollar amount of finance charges and the annual percentage rate (APR) of interest. The APR is calculated by dividing the dollar amount of finance charges by the average loan balance over a specified time period. Therefore, the APR is the effective cost of credit and can be used to compare the cost of competing loans. Given the importance of the APR, it is useful to understand how this rate is calculated. The method of calculating the APR for a single-payment loan differs from that for installment loans. The simple interest method and the discount method may be used to calculate the finance charges and APRs on single-payment loans. An add-on method of calculating APR on installment loans yields a considerably different rate than the simple interest method.

You should understand how lenders evaluate your creditworthiness. This will help you to determine how good a loan prospect you are. Lending standards vary among lenders, but most lenders use one or more of the following techniques to determine the creditworthiness of loan applicants: internal credit analysis, credit scoring, or external credit information. Internal credit analysis usually revolves around the evaluation of some combination of the five C's (capacity, capital, character, collateral, and conditions). Some lenders assign points to various loan applicant characteristics. The applicant's credit score determines whether a loan is accepted or rejected. Finally, external credit rating bureaus may be used to determine a loan applicant's creditworthiness.

KEY TERMS

add-on method
annual percentage rate (APR)
bank credit card
cash credit
collateral
credit card
credit limit
credit reporting agency
credit scoring
creditworthiness
discount method
Equal Credit Opportunity Act
Fair Credit Billing Act
Fair Credit Reporting Act
Fair Debt Collection Practices Act
finance charge
grace period
line of credit
loan consolidation
N-ratio method
open-account credit
regular or 30-day charge account
Regulation Z
retail store and oil company cards
revolving or open-end charge account
simple interest method
travel and entertainment credit card
Truth-in-Lending Act
Truth-in-Lending Simplification and Reform Act

SELECTED READINGS

The Arithmetic of Interest Rates. New York: Federal Reserve Bank, 1984.

"Credit Cards: Where the Deals Are." *Changing Times,* July 1986, pp. 75–76.

"Prestige Credit Cards: Those Pricey Plastics." *Changing Times,* April 1986, pp. 95–96.

Quinn, Jane Bryant. "Getting the Credit You Deserve." *Woman's Day,* October 21, 1986, p. 24.

Wasik, John F. "How to Beat the High Cost of Money." *Consumers Digest,* August 1985, pp. 19–22.

"Which Credit Card for You?" *Changing Times,* November 1985, pp. 105–107.

QUESTIONS

1 What are the primary advantage and the primary disadvantage of borrowing?
2 What is open-account credit? Identify and describe the two primary forms of open-account credit.

3 Explain how a regular, or 30-day, charge account differs from a revolving, or open-end, charge account.

4 Briefly describe the three most commonly used types of credit cards.

5 Explain how the new account balance is determined on the monthly statement for a bank credit card.

6 What is cash credit? How does cash credit differ from open-account credit?

7 Identify the main providers of cash credit.

8 What is a Truth-in-Lending Disclosure Statement? Why is the information provided on this statement important to a borrower?

9 Describe the federal consumer credit legislation that pertains to (a) disclosure of credit information, (b) credit refusal and discrimination, (c) access to credit information, and (d) protection against harassment.

10 What is a finance charge and why is it important?

11 How is a single-payment loan different from an installment loan?

12 Compare the stated interest rate and the effective interest rate. Explain which of these rates is more meaningful to the borrower.

13 Describe the two methods that may be used to calculate the annual percentage rate on a single-payment loan.

14 Describe the add-on method of calculating finance charges on an installment loan. Why might a borrower disapprove of this method?

15 Identify and briefly describe the five criteria (five C's) a lender may evaluate in determining the creditworthiness of a prospective borrower.

16 What is credit scoring? How might the credit score affect a loan applicant's ability to borrow?

17 Ray Larsen wants to know the new balance on his bank credit card. At the end of the previous month, Ray's account balance was $422.47. During the most recent month he paid $200 on the account and charged purchases of $307.61 to his bank credit card. He also incurred a $4.87 finance charge for the month on the account's unpaid balance. Calculate the new balance on Ray's bank credit card account.

18 Single-payment loan—simple interest: Compute the annual finance charge on a $5800 loan at 8.375 percent interest.

19 Single-payment loan—discount method: A two-year loan of $3800 will have $300 a year of finance charges, which will be discounted.

a What is the outstanding loan balance (the amount of funds initially provided to the borrower)?

b What is the annual percentage rate (APR)?

20 Installment loan—simple interest: A $4000, 12-month installment loan is based on simple interest of 15 percent.

a How much will the dollar monthly interest be in the first month?

b What is the annual percentage rate (APR) on this loan?

21 Installment loan—add-on method: A one-year $3000 installment loan is made using the add-on method. Payments are to be made monthly. The total finance charges are $330. Use the *N*-ratio method to determine the annual percentage rate (APR) on the loan.

CASE PROBLEMS

5.1 Martha Schilling, a senior journalism major at State University, believes that a personal computer will be greatly beneficial during her final college year and in the early years of her professional career. She therefore decides to purchase a new personal computer, complete with a printer and the necessary software. After considerable shopping, she finds the best available price for the entire package is $3000. Martha currently does not have enough cash to purchase the computer setup but believes she can save the needed amount over the next two years.

Because she sees immediate benefits from the use of the computer, she decides to borrow the $3000 in the form of a single-payment loan with a two-year maturity. Martha has contacted two lenders, each of whom will make her a single-payment loan. The terms offered by each lender are as follows:

1. First State Bank will lend a stated loan amount of $3615 at 8½ percent interest on a discount basis. The entire principal amount will come due at the end of two years.
2. Third State Bank will lend $3000 at a 10 percent simple interest rate. The loan will be due at the end of two years.

- **a** Determine the amount Martha will receive in loan proceeds under each of the two alternatives.
- **b** Specify the loan amount Martha will have to repay at the end of two years under each alternative.
- **c** Calculate the annual finance charges that Martha will pay under each loan. (In each case multiply the stated loan amount in the problem by the stated interest rate.)
- **d** Compute the annual percentage rate (APR) on each of the loans. (Divide the answer in part c by the answer in part a.)
- **e** Which loan should Martha select? Explain the reason(s) for your choice.

5.2 John Chang, a successful salesman, is contemplating the purchase of a new, state-of-the-art audio/video system for $2500. At the present time John has only $500 in savings that he can use toward the purchase of the system, and he wants to finance the remaining $2000 with a one-year installment loan. He has two alternatives for borrowing this amount:

1. Acme Finance Company offers a $2000, one-year installment loan requiring equal monthly payments. The loan has a 10 percent annual simple interest rate.
2. Fidelity State Bank offers a $2000 installment loan requiring 12 equal monthly payments at a 6 percent stated rate of interest. Finance charges are calculated using the add-on method.

a Determine the finance charges on each of the above loans. (See Appendix 5A to determine this amount for the Acme loan. Multiply the value in the table by 20.)

b Determine the monthly payment required on each of the loans offered John. (See the discussion in Appendix 5A to determine this amount for the Acme loan.)

c Calculate the annual percentage rate (APR) on each loan. (*Hint:* Use the *N*-ratio method for the Fidelity loan.)

d Which loan should John select?

$ 3.000

2year

1) $ 3615 8 1/2 i discount loans

2) $3000 10% simple interest.

Appendix 5A

Finance Charges on Monthly Installment Loans (Simple Interest Method)

Maturity of loan (months)	ANNUAL PERCENTAGE RATE					
	9%	10%	11%	12%	13%	14%
12	$ 4.94	$ 5.50	$ 6.06	$ 6.62	$ 7.18	$ 7.74
24	9.63	10.75	11.86	12.98	14.10	15.23
36	14.48	16.16	17.86	19.57	21.30	23.04
48	19.45	21.75	24.06	26.40	28.77	31.17
60	24.55	27.48	30.45	33.47	36.52	39.61
72	29.79	33.39	37.05	40.76	44.53	48.36

Determining the Finance Charge

The table shows the finance charge per $100 of the amount financed at various interest rates (APRs) and installment loan maturities. On $100 for 36 months at 10 percent, for example, the charge is $16.16 (circled). To find the finance charge on a loan of, say, $2500 for the same time period at the same interest rate (36 months, 10 percent), you simply multiply the value in the table for $100 by 25:

$25 \times \$16.16 = \$404$

Determining the Monthly Payment

The amount of the monthly payment on an installment loan can be computed using the following formula:

$$\text{Monthly payment} = \frac{\text{total finance charge} + \text{total amount of loan}}{\text{total loan periods in the loan}}$$

For the $2500 loan in this example, the monthly payment is calculated as follows:

$$\text{Monthly payment} = \frac{\$404 + \$2500}{36}$$

$$= \frac{\$2904}{36}$$

$$= \$80.67$$

The largest single purchase you are likely to make in your lifetime is a home. Twenty years ago, you simply picked out a house and signed a fixed-rate mortgage. You now must be much more sophisticated. First you must determine if you want a house, a condominium, or some other type of living arrangement that has come on the market. Next you must determine whether you want a fixed-rate mortgage, an adjustable-rate mortgage (ARM), a graduated-payment mortgage (GPM), a growing-equity mortgage (GEM), a rollover mortgage (ROM), or a shared-appreciation mortgage (SAM). If those terms sound like Greek, please be assured they will be translated to simple English in Chapter 6, which covers the topic of housing.

In Chapter 6, you will also be forced to go through the process of determining whether renting or buying is better for you, now or in the future. Obviously, owning a house ties up more of your cash and forces

PLANNING FOR MAJOR EXPENDITURES

you to make a long-term commitment (which may not prove very satisfactory if conditions change), but there are substantial tax advantages and you have a hedge against inflation.

More immediately relevant to you may be the purchase of an automobile. In Chapter 7, we go through the steps of shopping for the best deal. Discussion material in the chapter and excerpts from *Consumer Reports* will give you a feel for the dealer's cost and how much room there is to negotiate in a typical purchase. As is true in many other types of financial arrangements, if you pay too much, that simply allows the dealer to subsidize the more astute purchaser who is sufficiently knowledgeable to demand the bottom price.

As was true of housing, you should also consider the lease versus purchase decision for an automobile, and there is ample material in Chapter 7 to help you establish an appropriate decision model. We also consider how to finance a car if you decide to buy, whether to buy a new or used car, and how best to sell or trade your car.

Actually, the many factors

mentioned about automobiles apply as well to other consumer durables, such as furniture and appliances. Once the basic analytical techniques are in place, they can be applied to many different types of purchases. Of particular interest to some readers is the discussion of the purchase of personal computers in Appendix 7A. If you are a first-time purchaser or a frustrated previous purchaser, you will have an excellent opportunity to expand your general knowledge of personal computers, examine hardware versus software decisions, and learn the importance (or unimportance) of brand names. ■

6

The Housing Decision

After studying this chapter, you should:

- Understand the primary considerations involved in selecting a house
- Know how to determine the affordability of a house
- Understand the advantages and disadvantages of renting
- Be able to compare renting versus purchasing
- Appreciate the considerations involved in buying your first home
- Know how to finance a home
- Understand what is involved in selling your home

Selecting a house or other form of housing will probably be one of the most important decisions you make. You may find that housing-related expenditures consume 20 to 35 percent of your gross income. The largest financial outlay you ever make may well be for your home. With these kinds of financial requirements, it is not surprising that most people regard the home as a cornerstone of American life.

Your housing decision goes far beyond the effect on your pocketbook. It determines the availability of shopping, cultural, and entertainment activities near you. It also affects the amount of time you must spend commuting to work and the schools your children will attend. Because this decision determines your neighborhood, it may significantly influence your social contacts and the friends your children make. For these reasons and more you will want to make an intelligent and deliberate housing choice.

Most Americans prefer to own their own homes. As a practical matter, however, many people find they cannot afford a home and thus choose to rent. This is particularly true of young families who have not yet accumulated the financial resources to buy a home.

We discuss several important housing-related decisions in this chapter:

1 The fundamental considerations involved in renting
2 The key factors pertaining to the selection of a house
3 How to determine the affordability of a house
4 The comparison of the rent and purchase decisions
5 The considerations involved in buying your first home
6 How to finance the purchase of a home
7 Understanding the factors involved in selling a home

CONSIDERATIONS INVOLVED IN RENTING

With the median cost of a new home now approaching $85,000, many people find housing unaffordable. You may also find a house too costly for your budget. Possibly you cannot come up with sufficient funds to make the required down payment. Or you may not be able to qualify for a large enough mortgage loan to allow you to purchase. You may decide for various nonfinancial reasons not to purchase a home. Maybe you are unsettled in your job situation or expect to be transferred to another city soon. Or perhaps you do not want to assume the significant responsibilities associated with home ownership. In such situations, you will probably choose to rent rather than buy. Before renting, you should be aware of the obligations a rental agreement imposes on you. You should also be acquainted with the advantages and disadvantages of renting and how to compare the costs of renting and purchasing.

Lease Agreement

When you rent an apartment, duplex, condominium, or other type of housing unit, you will usually be required to sign a **lease agreement.** This is a written contract that sets forth the rights and obligations of both the landlord (the **lessor**) and the renter (the **lessee**). Because the agreement legally binds you to fulfill these obligations, you should clearly understand the provisions of the contract before entering into it. Most lease agreements state the amount of rent, frequency and timing of rental payments, deposit requirements, payment of expenses, any restrictions, and other terms of the agreement.

Rent. The lease agreement states the amount of rent due, the frequency of payment (usually monthly) and the date the rent is due (for example, the first day of each month). The agreement may require you to prepay the last month's rent to protect the landlord in case you move before the agreement expires. Late-payment penalties may also be stipulated.

Deposit. A deposit may be required to provide for repairs to the rental unit when you leave. The amount of the deposit varies, but landlords often require a deposit equal to one month's rent. If you maintain the unit reasonably well, most of your deposit should be refunded when you vacate. No matter how clean you leave the unit, however, the landlord will probably retain some portion of the deposit to cover cleaning costs. The landlord has final judgment on any amounts to be refunded, so a written statement of any damages existing prior to your occupancy may help you avoid losing the entire amount deposited when you leave.

Expenses. The lease agreement should also specify who bears the costs of utilities, maintenance and repairs, insurance, trash collection, and other expenses.

Restrictions. Any restrictions on the use of the property should be clearly set forth in the lease agreement. These restrictions may apply to pets, children, overnight guests, noise, subleasing, and alterations to the property.

Terms. Most lease agreements run for either six months or one year, although some are for as long as five years. A long-term lease affords the renter the benefit of knowing that monthly payments will be fixed for a long time. The lease should also state what happens when it expires. In some cases a new lease agreement must be negotiated for an additional term. In other cases you may not be required to sign a new lease; rather you proceed on a month-to-month basis. Such an agreement implies that the renter continues to accept the terms of the original lease. A major difference, however, is that under a month-to-month agreement, the landlord can raise your rent on a monthly basis.

Advantages and Disadvantages of Renting

Renting can provide several important advantages. First, when you rent you do not have to make a down payment as you do when you buy. Renting also gives you greater flexibility. When your lease expires, you are free to leave, and you have none of the expenses involved with selling a house. Renting also requires less maintenance and repairs on your part: The landlord takes care of these items. Community living often gives the tenant access to amenities, such as swimming pools and tennis courts, that would be unavailable to the homeowner. Another advantage may be the restrictions on type of tenant or activities. These restrictions may appeal to the renter who wants to be isolated from certain types of people or activities. Some young unmarrieds, for example, prefer "singles only" apartments, where one such apartment community advertises that "life is fun, fast, and exciting."

Renting can have a number of disadvantages, many of them financial. As a renter, you do not obtain any ownership interest as a result of rent payment, nor do you participate in any real estate price increases. You are also vulnerable to periodic rent increases. In addition, you get none of the tax deductible benefits provided to homeowners. You may also be restrained from certain activities because of lease restrictions. Noisy neighbors, uncooperative landlords, and poor security may also be disadvantages of renting.

SELECTING A HOUSE

Your specific needs and desires are the most important considerations in making a housing choice. You must clearly define and rank these considerations before you can make an intelligent housing decision. The first consideration that may come to mind is the cost of the house. Indeed, affordability is an important factor. But a house is much more than an investment. You may make a better decision if you initially evaluate the numerous nonfinancial aspects of a home. After defining your specific needs and desires, you should determine how a particular house would satisfy those considerations.

Location

You may have heard about the three most important rules of selecting real estate: location, location, location. Many experts agree that you simply cannot overstate the importance of location when making a housing decision. Some real estate agents will tell you that location matters more than the house itself. Not only does the location of your home affect your personal life-style, it may also influence the value of your home. Some communities enjoy more rapid real estate appreciation than others. You may believe this to be a moot point. After all, if your job is in Houston, you cannot very well benefit from housing price increases in Boston. However, you will still find that certain communities within a city may show far greater price appreciation potential than others. Often the qualities that make a particular community most desirable to you are the same factors that affect the prices of houses in that location. To find the right neighborhood, you should evaluate a community along several dimensions.

Schools. A strong school system is the foundation of a desirable community. Your investigation should focus on several school-related statistics. You should find out the percentage of high school seniors that go on to college. Anything substantially exceeding the national average of 54 percent is favorable. You will also want to know average student scores on national tests and how these compare to the averages at nearby school districts.[1] Another important factor is the local support for public schools. Does the community have a favorable record of providing financial support? Finally, a physical inspection of school facilities, a check on the districting of students, and informal inquiries about a school's reputation and teachers' credentials will yield useful information about a neighborhood's value.

Municipal Services. Important municipal services should be available. The answer to the following questions should tell you if a community's municipal services meet your expectations. Does the community seem clean and well

[1] The nationwide averages on the verbal and math portions of the Scholastic Aptitude Test (SAT) were 427 and 472, respectively, in 1986.

maintained? Are police and fire protection efficient and readily available? Are roads properly maintained and sufficient to accommodate traffic? Is the neighborhood on the sewer line? Are public utilities (electric, gas, water, and sewer) available and at reasonable rates? Is there reliable mass transportation? Do neighbors organize to tackle local problems such as neighborhood crime, landscaping and maintenance of common areas, and restrictions of undesirable additions? Only by answering these questions can the prospective homeowner make an educated judgment about a community's merits.

Amenities. The availability of attractive amenities can make a noticeable difference in your family's quality of life. A location's desirability depends on the recreational and cultural facilities that are nearby. The presence of a topflight local library, cultural facility, or park may provide numerous opportunities to enhance the quality of your life-style. You should also check to see if good shopping and service facilities are close at hand and if adequate playgrounds are available for your children.

Ambience. A casual drive through a community can give you a very distinct idea about the appeal of the neighborhood. Such a drive will probably reveal all you need to know about the community's zoning. Careless zoning erodes property values; you do not want to find junkyards or mobile homes mingling with single-family homes. You should investigate the zoning on any vacant property. If that open pasture that surrounds the community you are exploring has been zoned for light industry, you may want to steer clear of the area. Your visit will also reveal if the houses and yards seem well maintained. Also, areas where all houses are priced approximately the same are usually more desirable. Houses of lesser value tend to pull down the value of more elaborate homes.

Affordability

After you have considered the nonfinancial aspects of a home, you must decide how much you can afford to pay for a home. You may have a rough idea of how much you can spend, but if you are buying your first home, your idea of what to spend for a house may not be realistic. Several kinds of expenditures must be considered to determine how much house you can afford. These expenditures are

Down payment
Mortgage points
Closing costs
Mortgage payment
Homeowner's insurance
Property taxes
Maintenance and operating expenses

Down Payment. The **down payment** is the initial amount of cash you must invest to purchase a house. This payment represents your initial equity, or ownership interest, in your new home. Like most buyers, you may choose to finance most of the purchase price of your home. Lenders, however, generally will require you to put up some equity by investing part of your own money. The amount of down payment required varies among lenders, type of mortgage, and property type. Lenders often use a **loan-to-value ratio** to quote the maximum amount of financing allowed on a particular property. This ratio expresses the percentage of the property's value that you can borrow from the lender. The higher this ratio is, the more you can borrow and the less you have to invest in the down payment.

In recent years, some lenders have been willing to finance with a loan-to-value ratio as high as 95 percent. Other lenders may insist on an 80 percent maximum loan-to-value ratio. These contrasting ratios cause a sizable difference in the amount of the down payment you must make. For example, assume that you buy a house for $80,000. You will be required to make only a $4000 down payment by the lender quoting the 95 percent loan-to-value ratio. The lender using an 80 percent ratio, however, will require a down payment of $16,000. Usually a first-home buyer has not had enough time to accumulate a significant cash reserve and therefore may find a high loan-to-value ratio (low down payment) more desirable.

Mortgage Points. Lenders usually charge a fee known as **mortgage points** at the time they grant a mortgage loan. Points are an up-front charge for borrowing money. A point is 1 percent of the amount of the mortgage loan. Hence, one point on a $65,000 loan is $650; four points on that loan equals $2600. To a lender, points are compensation for processing and completing a loan. Often, however, the amount of points charged varies according to the availability of loanable funds. For example, a lender may charge one or two points when there is a plentiful supply of funds. On the other hand, when loanable funds are scarce, the lender may demand a greater number of points to make the loan.

Closing Costs. **Closing costs** are the expenses beyond the purchase price of a home. The buyer typically pays most of these expenses at the settlement of the purchase. Closing costs include expenditures for a title search, title insurance, appraisal fees, attorney's fees, termite inspection, and recording fees. In some instances the seller can be persuaded to pay some of the closing costs. Rarely, however, can the buyer avoid all of these costs. Some closing costs may be negotiable so you will want to compare costs among competing sources. Closing costs are often related to the amount of your down payment; a smaller down payment generally causes the lender to demand higher closing costs. Table 6.1 shows the estimated cost differences between a 10 percent and 20 percent down payment. Closing costs typically average from 3 to 5 percent of the cost of a house.

Table 6.1 HOW THE DOWN PAYMENT AFFECTS CLOSING COSTS

Closing cost[a]	DOWN PAYMENT PERCENTAGE	
	20%	10%
Loan application fee	$ 100–$ 300	$ 100–$ 300
Loan origination fee	800	900
Points (1–3)	800– 2400	900– 2700
Mortgage insurance	—	450– 900
Title search and insurance	485	525
Attorney's fees	500– 1500	500– 1500
Homeowner's insurance	500	500
Home inspection	150– 300	150– 300
Mortgage tax	575	650
Survey	125– 300	125– 300
Recording fee	40– 60	40– 60
Total	$4075–$7220	$4840–$8635

[a] Based on a $100,000 house in New York state.

SOURCE: *Money Guide/Your Home*, 1985, p. 40.

Mortgage Payment. Your **mortgage payment** represents the regular interest payments on your loan and the systematic repayment of the principal on that loan. The amount of your monthly mortgage payment depends on three things: the amount of the loan, the maturity of the loan, and the interest rate. A change in any of these three items can significantly affect the amount of your payment. Assume, for example, that you are considering a $65,000, 30-year maturity mortgage loan. If you finance at a 12 percent interest rate, your monthly payment equals $669. A 9 percent interest rate on that same loan costs only $521 monthly. Although the $148 monthly difference may not seem that important, over the life of this mortgage you would pay $53,352 less in total interest charges by financing at 9 percent as opposed to 12 percent. Clearly the choice of the mortgage loan is one of your most crucial financial decisions.

Homeowner's Insurance. In addition to interest and principal costs, most mortgage payments include **homeowner's insurance** premiums. Homeowner's insurance ranges from basic policies that safeguard your home only from named perils such as fire, windstorm, and hail to "all-risk" coverage that insures against such calamities as your water pipes bursting or your roof collapsing. Premiums on these policies vary depending on factors such as the age of the house, location, type of construction (brick versus frame, and so on), and type of coverage. Also, premiums differ among the various insurers. In general, annual

Box 6.1 MORTGAGE SHOPPING BY COMPUTER

The promise is tantalizing: instead of trekking around town in search of a mortgage, you can arrange for one without ever leaving your real estate agent's office. He punches a few keys on a desktop computer and up pops the most attractive available loan. This is known as computerized mortgage origination. In some cases, the computer cannot only sort through various types of loans to come up with the best rate and terms for which you would qualify but also accept your application, give you a conditional commitment subject to a credit check, and process the loan.

The convenience of borrowing by computer is very appealing, and the number of companies offering the service is steadily increasing. But does electronic mortgage shopping live up to its promise? For now, the answer is maybe. The computer can uncover attractive rates, but you may be able to do better on your own.

A *Money* Guide reporter compared the terms of loans offered by traditional lenders with those of two firms specializing in computerized mortgage origination in the Baltimore–Washington, D.C. area. The goal was to find the best $80,000 mortgage on a hypothetical $100,000 house. The two firms were Mortgage Resources Corp. in Towson, Md. and PRC LoanExpress in Falls Church, Va. Mortgage Resources, a subsidiary of O'Conor Piper & Flynn

insurance costs average about 0.25 and 0.50 percent of a home's market value. Therefore, insurance on an $80,000 home would cost between $200 and $400 per year. (Homeowner's insurance is discussed in more detail in Chapter 8).

Property Taxes. Local governments levy **property taxes** to support schools, police and fire departments, and other local services. These taxes may also be added to your monthly mortgage payment. The amount of property taxes varies considerably from one community to another. Some experts use a 1 percent rule

Realtors, is among 1,500 real estate brokers and mortgage companies nationwide that use Shelternet, by far the largest of the half-dozen national loan origination programs. PRC uses its own computer system that links 40 lenders with 300 real estate offices in metropolitan Washington, D.C.

After their computers digested an application that reported an income of $50,000 and savings of $25,000, the two firms' printers spit out long lists of possible mortgages. Neither concern would divulge the names of the lenders. PRC frets that borrowers would go directly to the lender offering the best deal, thus evading the firm's origination fee of 1% of the mortgage amount. So PRC waits until the loan application has been submitted before telling customers who the lender is. Customers are also charged $27.50 for a credit report and $150 for an appraisal. Shelternet's funds come mostly from savings and loan associations, and borrowers learn the identity of their lender at closing. Shelternet's fees run about $200.

Money Guide looked at the terms on a one-year adjustable-rate loan and a 30-year fixed-rate loan. The computer-originated loans were compared with those offered by traditional lenders as surveyed by the Peeke Report for the week of Jan. 21, 1985. Both PRC loans were competitive in the metropolitan Washington, D.C. area, as was Shelternet's fixed-rate loan in Baltimore. However, Shelternet's ARM terms did not match those of local lending institutions or PRC.

Shelternet's ARM, an atypical 29-year loan, carried an initial rate of 10½%, plus points equaling 3¾% of the loan amount, or $3,000. There were caps on future rate increases of two points a year and five points over the life of the loan and a profit margin for the lender of 2¾% of the loan amount. Monthly payments in the first year: $735.47. In Baltimore, about half the lenders offered better rates and lower points. Most had lower profit margins too.

A PRC customer could get an ARM package consisting of a 9½% first-year rate, four points, or $3,200, caps of two points a year and 4½ points over the life of the loan, and a 2½% profit margin. Monthly payments: $672.68. By shopping diligently among local lenders, you could have found more favorable terms at Dominion Mortgage Funding in McLean, Va. Seven other lenders listed in the Peeke Report had loans with terms as good as PRC's or better.

For a 30-year fixed-rate mortgage, Shelternet offered 12¾% plus 2¾ points, or $2,200. Monthly payments: $869.35. Four of 80 Baltimore lenders had better deals. For example, Germania Federal offered a 12½% loan, with 2½ points, or $2,000. PRC weighed in with a 12½% mortgage rate but with four points, or $3,200. Monthly payments for both were $853.82. In metropolitan Washington, there were no better rates offered. Seven of 62 firms did have fewer points.

The moral: touch as many bases as possible when looking for the best mortgage rate.

SOURCE: *Money Guide/Your Home,* 1985, p. 34.

of thumb to estimate property taxes. These taxes are imposed on the appraised value of a home. Thus a home with an $80,000 appraised market value might incur $800 in property taxes per year, that is, $80,000 × 0.01.

Maintenance and Operating Expenses. No matter how well you maintain your home, it is likely that some problems will eventually occur. Painting, repairs, lawn maintenance, and other expenses confront almost every homeowner. Typically these expenses are directly related to the size and age of the home. Older and larger homes simply cost more to maintain. You may save on maintenance and repairs if you are handy around the house and take a do-it-yourself approach.

Operating expenses also affect your cost of ownership. The payments necessary for utilities such as electricity, gas, water, trash collection, and sewage can be substantial. These costs can vary significantly among houses because of differences in the size of the house, energy efficiency of the home, type of heating and air conditioning, and other factors. Also, utility rates vary in different parts of the country. In one area, electricity may be less expensive, but in another area, gas may be the better buy. Before buying, you should carefully investigate the costs of operating your home. Too many new homeowners commit every possible dollar to the down payment and mortgage payments, only to find that they then cannot afford to meet routine maintenance and operating expenses.

How Much House Can You Afford?

We have briefly discussed the costs that face the homeowner. We now address the crucial question: How much house can you afford? The answer to this question depends on two key considerations: the amount of down payment you can make and the size of the mortgage loan you can arrange. The sum of these two items gives you an approximate price you can afford.

Determining Your Down Payment. The amount of money you originally invest influences the amount of house you can afford. Therefore, it's important to determine your down payment. You can use the following four-step procedure to calculate the amount you have available for a down payment.

Step 1: Calculate your net worth (see Chapter 2). Exclude personal assets (auto, clothes, jewelry, and so on) from your calculations.

Step 2: Decide how much of an emergency fund you need. Three to six months' net income is recommended.

Step 3: Estimate closing costs. These costs may run 3 to 5 percent of the purchase price.

Step 4: Subtract the amount of your emergency fund and closing costs from your net worth. This is the money you have for a down payment.

Determining Your Mortgage Loan. Once you have determined how much of a down payment you can make, you can estimate the size of the mortgage loan for which you qualify. The following three additional steps allow you to calculate the size of the mortgage loan you can obtain.

Step 5: Add up all your expenses including the estimated nonmortgage costs of a new house. Subtract them from your total income.

Step 6: Divide the amount in step 5 by 12 to determine the monthly payments you can afford.

Table 6.2 MONTHLY MORTGAGE PAYMENTS, 30-YEAR LOAN

Mortgage amount	ANNUAL INTEREST RATE					
	9%	10%	11%	12%	13%	14%
$ 50,000	$402	$439	$476	$ 514	$ 553	$ 592
55,000	442	483	524	566	608	652
60,000	483	527	571	617	664	711
65,000	521	570	619	669	719	770
70,000	563	614	667	720	774	829
75,000	603	658	714	771	830	889
80,000	642	702	762	823	885	948
85,000	683	746	809	874	940	1007
90,000	723	790	857	926	996	1066
95,000	763	834	905	977	1051	1126
100,000	804	878	952	1029	1106	1185

Step 7: Consult Table 6.2. Find the prevailing interest rate. Go down that column until you find the figure that most closely corresponds to the amount you arrived at in step 6. Then see what mortgage amount that figure indicates.

Your Price Range. By following the previous step-by-step procedure, you should now know how large a down payment you can afford and the amount of the mortgage loan you can accommodate. Now comes the final step.

Step 8: Add the amount of the down payment you can afford (see step 4) to the size of the mortgage loan you can handle (see step 7). This total gives you an idea of the house price you can afford. Case 6.1 at the end of this chapter will give you an opportunity to apply these eight steps to a home purchase for a married couple.

Rules of Thumb

Lenders often apply rules of thumb to determine how much you can afford to pay for a house. These guidelines allow you to quickly obtain an idea of the approximate amount you can spend or borrow. The following are two popular rules of thumb:

Rule 1: The purchase price of a home should not exceed 2½ times your annual gross (pretax) income.

Rule 2: The amount of your monthly mortgage payment should not exceed 25 to 28 percent of your before-tax monthly pay.

Under the first rule of thumb, if you earn $30,000 you can afford a $75,000 home ($30,000 × 2½). If your monthly pay equals $2500, the second rule of thumb indicates that your monthly mortgage payment should be limited to between $625 (25 percent of gross monthly pay) and $700 (28 percent of pay). These guidelines provide only a rough idea about the amount of home and mortgage you can afford. Your personal circumstances may suggest a deviation from the recommended amounts.

Using a Real Estate Agent

If you venture out to buy a house on your own, you will soon discover that most sellers are represented by **real estate agents** (**brokers**). These agents can also assist you in your search for a house. A properly selected broker can facilitate your house search. Because there are over one million real estate agents in this country, you will want to make sure that you select one that best fits your needs. Your home purchase is likely to be the biggest expenditure of your life, so you should be careful to select a broker who is knowledgeable enough to guide you.

An agent should be up to date on the specific housing market in which you are interested and locate properties that are suitable for you. Also, an agent can advise you on the advantages and disadvantages of a property and judge how reasonable a seller's asking price is. A good agent knows how to arrange satisfactory financing and how to close the transaction. Through the aid of a competent real estate broker, you can find the right house and save a lot of time, effort, and money.

In dealing with an agent, you should remember that the agent is employed by the seller. Agents typically earn a commission of 6 percent of the selling price of a home, and this amount is paid by the seller. A conflict of interest can arise because the agent's main responsibility is to get the highest possible price for the seller. Further, some agents may apply high-pressure sales tactics to make a quick sale. This type of broker is in the minority and should be avoided. Instead you should use a broker who has your best interests in mind. There are plenty of reputable, qualified brokers who are eager to accommodate the needs of both the buyer and the seller. Here is a checklist with helpful suggestions for selecting the right broker for you:[2]

1. Ask friends for recommendations.
2. Get referrals from the local Board of Realtors and branches of national franchises and attend open houses.
3. Question the agent about the housing market in the neighborhood that interests you.

[2] *Money Guide/Your Home*, 1985, p. 30.

4 Ask if the agent has access to a multiple-listing service so that you can be sure of seeing as many houses as possible.
5 Establish a price range with the agent so he will not show you houses you can't afford.
6 Wait for the seller's counteroffer before you tell the agent that you'd be willing to pay more for the house.
7 Consider hiring a buyer's broker to assist you in your search. He will represent you, thus ensuring you against conflicts between the buying agent and the selling agent.

Taking Title

When you buy a house, you will receive a deed. The **deed** is the legal document that transfers the ownership of the house from one person to another. The deed is prepared by the seller's attorney and signed by the seller. After the transaction is closed, the deed is recorded with the county in which the property is located. This recording makes public your ownership of the property. Your ownership interest is not protected unless you record the deed. There are three main kinds of deeds.

Warranty Deed. With a **warranty deed,** the seller guarantees there are no defects in the title to the property being sold. If defects arise later, the buyer may be able to sue the seller for damages. In cases where the seller acquires **title insurance** against such defects, any damages must be paid by the title company unless the defects were caused by the seller. This is the most desirable type of deed for the buyer.

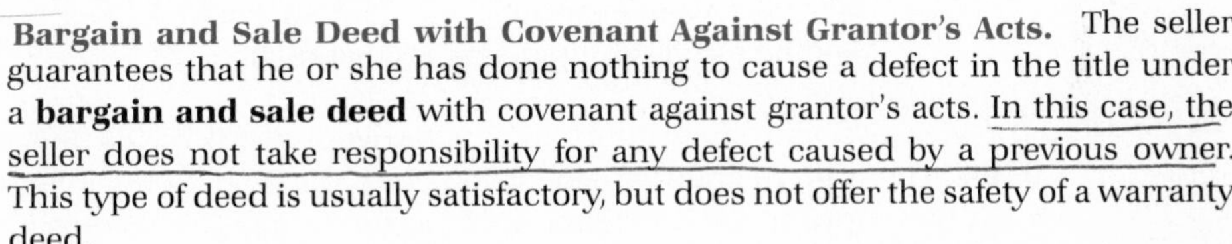

Bargain and Sale Deed with Covenant Against Grantor's Acts. The seller guarantees that he or she has done nothing to cause a defect in the title under a **bargain and sale deed** with covenant against grantor's acts. In this case, the seller does not take responsibility for any defect caused by a previous owner. This type of deed is usually satisfactory, but does not offer the safety of a warranty deed.

Quitclaim Deed. In a **quitclaim deed** the seller only maintains that he or she is transferring whatever title is owned. No guarantee is made about defects. Quitclaim deeds are commonly used in some regions, but because of their lack of guarantees you should be cautious when using this type of deed.

Rental Versus Purchase Decisions

We have reviewed the relative advantages and disadvantages of both the rental and ownership alternatives. However, we still need another input to make the rent-or-purchase decision. That input is a comparison of the cost of renting with the cost of buying. While the rent-purchase decision should rarely be based only on financial considerations, nevertheless a financial comparison of the costs of renting with the costs of buying is an important and necessary part of the overall decision. The following example provides a specific outline for determining whether to rent or buy.

The Situation. Let's assume that you are planning a move to a new city. One of your earliest and most important decisions is to select the housing unit in which you will reside. After several visits to your new city, you have reduced your housing choice to two specific alternatives.

Alternative 1 is an attractive garden apartment rental unit. The following terms apply:

Lease term = one year
Rent = $600 per month
Utilities = $100 per month
Personal insurance = $100 annually
Maintenance, repairs, and property insurance are paid by the landlord.

Alternative 2 is a 10-year-old house located in a popular suburban area. The following facts pertain to this alternative:

Purchase price = $80,000
Down payment = $15,000
Mortgage terms = 10 percent interest; 30-year life
Property insurance = $400 annually
Property taxes = $800 annually
Utilities = $1600 annually
Maintenance and repairs = $800 annually

Because you know that either alternative will provide the life-style you desire, you want to know which option costs the least. In the following financial analysis we provide a systematic method for comparing the costs of renting to the costs of owning.

The Comparison. One of the main advantages of renting is that the landlord pays for maintenance and repairs, property insurance, and property taxes. The only expenses confronting you as a renter are rent, utilities, and insurance on your personal property. Table 6.3 shows that these rental costs equal $8500 annually. Alternatively, the expenses associated with purchasing the suburban home are considerably greater. The home buyer must make the mortgage payments and all home-related expenses including those for insurance, taxes, maintenance and repairs, and utilities. These yearly purchase costs total $11,190 (as shown in Table 6.3), or $2690 more than the costs of renting.

Your first impression may be that to rent is considerably less expensive

Table 6.3 COMPARISON OF RENTAL AND PURCHASE COSTS

Rental alternative	
Costs	
Rent ($600 × 12)	$ 7,200
Insurance	100
Utilities	1,200
Total rental costs	$ 8,500
Purchase alternative	
Costs	
Mortgage payment ($65,000 at 10%, 30 years)	$ 6,840[a]
Interest = $6500[b]	
Principal = $340[b]	
Property insurance	400
Property taxes	800
Maintenance and repairs	800
Utilities	1,600
Interest lost on down payment funds ($15,000 × 0.05 return)	750
Total purchase costs	$11,190

[a] Using Table 6.2, the monthly payment for a 30-year $65,000 loan at 10% is $570. Multiplying this amount by 12 gives an annual payment of $6840.

[b] The approximate amount of interest paid is determined by multiplying the amount owed on the loan at the beginning of the period by the annual interest rate ($65,000 × 0.10 = $6500). The remainder of the annual payment is principal repayment. In this example, the annual payment is $6840, the interest is $6500, and the principal repayment is $340.

than to purchase. This is not necessarily true. We must consider the several savings generated by the purchase alternative before we arrive at a final conclusion. The financial benefits of home ownership include (1) equity buildup, (2) tax savings, and (3) potential price appreciation.

Equity Buildup. A portion of each mortgage payment is for the repayment of principal. After this partial loan repayment, you will owe less on your home. Thus your equity increases. This compares to the rental alternative in which none of your payment builds equity. In our previous example, $340 of your $6840 in first-year mortgage payments is principal repayment. Of course, in each subsequent year the amount of **equity buildup** gradually increases. Because this amount builds equity, it represents a kind of forced savings that adds to your net worth and therefore is deducted from the total costs of the purchase alternative.

Tax Savings. Two important home ownership expenses are tax de-

Figure 6.1 HOUSING PRICES, 1974 TO 1985

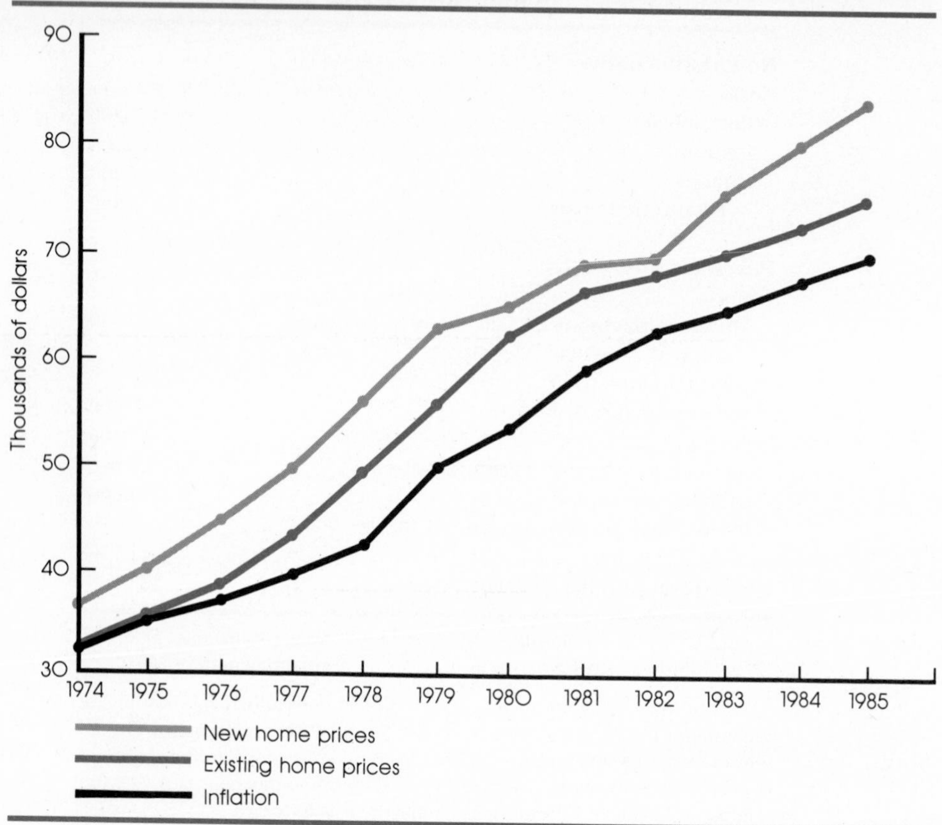

SOURCE: *Federal Reserve Bulletin,* various issues, 1975–1986.

ductible: mortgage interest and property taxes. These payments produce savings by reducing your income tax bill.[3] The amount of savings depends on your tax rate. Assume, for example, that your tax rate is 30 percent. In the previous example, you obtain a significant tax reduction because of the deductibility of mortgage interest and property taxes. This tax savings in the first year is calculated as follows: \$6500 (mortgage interest) + \$800 (property taxes) = \$7300 (tax deduction) × 0.30 (tax rate) = \$2190 (tax savings). Thus the first-year tax benefit associated with purchasing a home is \$2190. There are similar benefits in later years. None of the rental payment is tax deductible.

Potential Price Appreciation. For most Americans, the ownership of a

[3] These savings apply only to individuals who itemize deductions on their annual income tax form. They are not available to nonitemizers.

home has been a very effective inflation hedge. During the 1970s and early 1980s, when inflation was high, housing prices soared. For example, between 1974 and 1985 the price of goods and services as measured by the consumer price index slightly more than doubled. Over the same period, however, the median housing price in the United States nearly tripled. Figure 6.1 graphically portrays this relationship. Although the large price increases of the 1970s and early 1980s are not likely to be repeated, more moderate housing price appreciation is still visible. An increase in your home's value adds to your equity without any cash outflow on your part. Of course, a renter cannot participate in any real estate appreciation.

The Rent-Purchase Decision Reconsidered

You recall that our original analysis in Table 6.3 showed that purchase costs exceeded rental costs by $2690 a year. In Table 6.4, we recalculate the cost of purchasing the house; this time we make allowance for purchase-related financial benefits. Immediately you can see that the equity buildup and tax savings reduce the net cost of buying the home by $2530 a year. Still, however, the net purchase cost of $8660 slightly exceeds the annual rental cost of $8500 shown in Table 6.3

Does this revised analysis indicate that you would still be better off financially by renting the garden apartment? Not necessarily. One more factor must be included: potential price appreciation. If you assume the house's price will not appreciate, renting remains the most attractive alternative. But what if you believe the house will appreciate even a modest 2 percent each year? A different story emerges. That 2 percent price gain translates into a $1600 value increase ($80,000 × 0.02)—another form of equity buildup. Table 6.4 shows the final

Table 6.4 CALCULATING NET PURCHASE COSTS

Total purchase costs (Table 6.3)			$11,190
Savings			
Equity buildup from principal repayment		$ 340	
Income tax savings:			
Mortgage interest ($6500 × 0.30)	1,950		
Property taxes ($800 × 0.30)	240		
		$2,190	
Total savings			$ 2,530
Net purchase cost (before appreciation)			$ 8,660
Price appreciation (estimated at 2%)			
($80,000 × 0.02)			$ 1,600
Net purchase costs			$ 7,060

results. The net purchase cost declines to $7060, now considerably less than the $8500 rental cost. After accounting for all benefits, the purchase option becomes financially more desirable.

YOUR FIRST HOME

Owning a home has always been an important part of the American dream. In colonial days enterprising individuals could obtain land free by agreeing to cultivate it and build a home on it. Hard work and the desire to own a home enabled this country to expand from an unexplored frontier to a civilized nation in less than a century. At the very foundation of that progress was home ownership. Even today, home ownership serves as a reward for diligence and success and is a cornerstone of our way of life.

The importance we place on owning a home is confirmed by the fact that currently two-thirds of all American families own their own home. As a first-time home buyer, however, you may be concerned about your ability to finance this acquisition. Housing prices are no longer bargains. Gone are the days such as in 1926 when Sears Roebuck sold its Honor-Bilt kit houses for as little as $475, or in 1942 when Frank Lloyd Wright designed two-bedroom $4000 houses for Detroit auto workers. The 1986 median price of a new home was $85,000.

You are not alone in your financial concern. At this time, approximately 42 million Americans are between the ages of 25 and 34, the years when most of us buy our first homes. Fortunately, the current circumstances indicate that prospects for home ownership for these young people are more promising than at any time since the 1970s. The U.S. League of Savings Institutions reports that first-time buyers now account for 41 percent of annual home sales, up from only 13.5 percent in 1981. Specifically, current circumstances involving mortgage loan rates, cost efficiency, and housing supply are attractive.

Mortgage Rates

A decline in interest rates means your cost of buying a home drops substantially. In the early 1980s the average mortgage rate rose as high as 16 percent. These unprecedented rates caused mortgage payments to escalate to levels that most first-time home buyers could not afford. Now, with rates settling in around 10 percent, you can more easily afford a home. On a $65,000, 30-year mortgage loan, for example, the monthly cost falls from $876 at 16 percent to $570 at 10 percent—a 35 percent decline in your monthly mortgage expense. This meaningful savings, coupled with rising real incomes, means that more young people can afford mortgage payments.

Cost Efficiency

As housing prices increased, builders responded by downsizing the typical home. These new homes are more affordable to the new buyer. In 1978, newly constructed homes had a median floor space of 1655 square feet. Today that median size has dropped below 1500 square feet. Home builders have also cut housing amenities to hold down new-housing costs. Fewer new residences have fireplaces, garages, basements, or more than two bedrooms than in 1978. Alternative housing has also aimed at reducing costs. New condominiums have a median of 1150 square feet, thus offering a much cheaper housing alternative.

Supply

The number of new housing units has increased substantially, ensuring an ample supply to accommodate housing needs. In 1986, new housing units passed the 2 million mark for the very first time. Another 3½ million existing units were sold during 1985. Clearly, the supply of housing is at an all-time high.

ALTERNATIVE HOUSING FORMS

A wider array of housing forms than ever before is available for Americans. These different housing forms vary substantially in size, cost, and living accommodations. Not all housing forms are suitable for your particular needs, so it is important that you examine the alternatives to determine the ones that are best for you. As a newlywed, you may decide that a two-bedroom, one-bath condominium is suitable. But if you plan to have children soon, you might decide that a larger single-family house is more appropriate. We now discuss the various housing forms.

Single-Family Houses

The single-family house continues to be the most popular housing choice for Americans. It provides privacy, adequate space, durability, prestige, and potential financial benefits. You may want to purchase an existing (preowned) house, buy a new development house, or custom build a house to suit your specific needs and desires.

Existing Houses. An older home often offers several benefits to the homeowner. Older houses provide the pleasant environment where most people grew up. Often these homes are located in mature neighborhoods that have established residents. Many houses over ten years old have higher-quality materials and better construction than newer houses. You can often find thicker walls, full basements, lavish woodwork, high ceilings, and large rooms. Existing houses tend to be less expensive than new homes. In 1985, the median price of an existing home was $75,100, as compared with almost $85,000 for a new dwelling of comparable size. There are other financial advantages to older houses. You might be able to assume the previous owner's low-interest mortgage, and you can estimate the cost of operating the house by asking to see utility bills. Also,

Box 6.2 HINTS FOR THE SAVVY HOME BUYER

You may be a whiz at spotting bargains in clothes or food, but if you haven't bought many houses in your lifetime, you may not know a bad buy when you see it. Here are some smart questions to ask yourself, whether you're considering an old house or one that's brand-new:

1. How much will it cost to get the house into shape? Don't take the seller's or broker's guess. Call in a general contractor or remodeler to get an estimate for knocking down that living-room wall, adding a deck or installing the extra bathroom your family needs.

Make sure your written agreement with the owner specifies that the sale is contingent on the findings of a professional house inspector you hire. If the roof leaks or the plumbing has to be replaced, make the owner pay or call off the sale.

2. What will your fuel bills be? The owner should be able to show you fuel and utility bills for the last twelve months. Sometimes a builder or developer of a new house can supply estimates based on studies he commissions from the local utility or an independent engineering firm.

3. What will come with the house? Anything that can be removed without serious damage to the structure belongs to the owner. If you want the stove, refrigerator, laundry equipment, window air conditioners, awnings, draperies or chandeliers, list them in your agreement to buy.

Model homes are often loaded with optional features, such as fireplaces, flagstone entry

property taxes may be lower in an established neighborhood where streets, public utilities, schools, and sewers already exist.

On the other hand, an older house can be expected to have higher maintenance costs than a new home of similar size. Often the heating and air conditioning systems in older homes are inadequate and expensive to repair. Also, the house may not be able to accommodate a heavy load of contemporary appliances.

New Houses. One of the biggest advantages of a new house is that it generally appreciates in value faster than an old home. New homes are usually built in areas where the population is growing. Local building codes require the instal-

floors, built-in vacuum systems and top-of-the-line appliances that are not included in the basic price. Ask for the options list.

4. How will the place look when you move in? Every homeowner knows that cosmetic touches—a paint job, tidied-up lawn, vases of flowers—help sell a house. But developers take cosmetics one step further. They'll decorate model homes with small-scale furniture and lots of mirrors to make rooms appear larger than they really are. They'll limit traffic through the house, so spaces never seem crowded. They'll put in expensive landscaping—mature trees, brick walks, sod lawns—to give the house "curb appeal." If you want to see the *real* house, ask for a tour of an unfurnished or not-quite-completed model.

5. What's in it for the real-estate broker? No matter how friendly you become with the agent who takes you from house to house, always remember that agents represent sellers, not buyers. Their interest is in getting you to sign a contract in the quickest possible time. They may give you some hints about how low a bid the owner is likely to accept, because they'd rather make the sale than let you slip through their fingers. But don't count on them to reveal all the house's flaws or give you realistic estimates of the cost to set them right. And if you're hovering between a house that's listed with other brokers (who may share the commission) and one that's exclusive with a single agent, guess which one he or she will urge on you?

6. Could the property be contaminated? This is tricky to answer, but there are some checks you can make: Have the water supply tested for bacteria count and toxic chemicals. Ask your state's Department of Environmental Protection if there is any information on file about possible industrial waste or chemical contamination of the land. Inquire at the town clerk's office to determine if the house was built on landfill and what kind of fill was permitted.

7. Can I count on the builder? When you buy a house that hasn't been built yet, check the builder's reputation. Find out what other developments he has put up, then visit them and talk to the homeowners. Get the name of his bank, and question an officer of that bank about the builder's financial soundness. Write or call the Better Business Bureau and your state Attorney General's office and Department of Consumer Protection to find out if there are any complaints about him on file. The last thing you want to do is put your money in the hands of a sloppy producer, a near-bankrupt or a slow deliverer.

SOURCE: Hubbard Cobb, *Woman's Day,* July 23, 1985, p. 110.

lation of energy-saving heating and electrical equipment, insulation, and weather stripping, thus ensuring that a new home will be energy-efficient. You also get modern fixtures and appliances with a new home. The most significant drawback of a new home is that you cannot know how well everything will work. The foundation has not had time to settle, and there is no evidence about how expensive the home is to maintain. You should look for signs of high-quality construction. Signs of shoddy workmanship may indicate that the house was poorly constructed. On the other hand, evidence of high-quality construction, such as double-panel windows, neatly finished carpentry, and attractive amenities, is a good sign that the house is well constructed. You may also want a builder warranty against structural flaws to provide assurance of high-quality construction. Almost one-third of new houses have such warranties.

Custom Homes. Most of us would like to build a unique, architect-designed home to fulfill our most elaborate dreams. In this way you can be assured of having that special study you always wanted or a fireplace in your bedroom. Unfortunately, however, very few can afford this kind of luxury. The National Association of Home Builders estimates that a custom-built house costs up to 30 percent more than a comparable development house, even if you design the house yourself. If you use an architect, his or her fee will cost another 10 to 15 percent. You may also find custom building to cause numerous headaches because of disputes with the builder, the uncertainty of costs, and the seemingly endless decisions that must be made. Also, a very creative custom home may be a poor investment if it is so unique that it is not readily resalable.

Model Homes. Some builders offer model display homes, which are already completed units ready to sell. In many instances you may negotiate with the builder to have a home built in the general format of the display model, but custom ordering it with the special features you want. This alternative allows you to buy at a lower price than for a typical custom home, but still enables you to specify certain important features.

Condominiums

A **condominium** can be an apartment unit, attached townhouse, or house among a cluster of houses. The owner receives title to an individual unit in a group of units and shares possession of such common facilities as swimming pools, lakes, and tennis courts. Buyers enjoy the advantages of traditional home ownership: They arrange their own mortgages, are entitled to tax deductions, and are free to sell their property at any time. Condominium owners are typically assessed monthly fees to pay their proportionate share of maintaining common facilities.

Condominiums are usually less expensive than existing single-family houses because they tend to be built in a way that better utilizes land and lowers construction costs. However, condominiums are not likely to appreciate as much as single-family houses. Many cities currently have a substantial oversupply of these units. Market experts estimate that in Houston, for example, over half of all condominiums remain unsold or vacant.

Cooperative Apartments

In a **cooperative apartment** you own shares in an entire dwelling complex. Usually your ownership interest is proportionate to the living space you occupy in the complex. Therefore, if your apartment occupies 3 percent of the living area of the complex, then you would have to own 3 percent of the outstanding shares. Cooperative members are assessed a monthly charge to cover maintenance, upkeep, debt service, insurance, taxes, and a reserve fund. Although residing in a cooperative closely resembles apartment living, you have the potential advantage of your shares appreciating in price if you are in a well-located, quality complex. You should carefully examine the terms of ownership before buying. The board of directors controls many activities and may impose restrictions on subletting, resale, pets, children, and entertainment.

Factory-Built Houses

A **factory-built, or manufactured, house** is partially or totally built in a factory as opposed to on the homesite. Once assembled, these houses often look just like dwellings built from the ground up on the site. Because this housing form offers the advantages of faster construction and lower cost, more and more people are selecting this alternative. In 1985, for example, approximately one-third of all new housing units were partially or totally fabricated in factories and then shipped to the sites where the units were assembled.

Second Homes

More Americans now purchase a second home. A second home may be a regular house, condominium, or cooperative apartment. The primary attraction of a second home is the recreational or restful environment that it offers. In today's fast-paced world, a second home allows you to escape the pressures often associated with day-to-day living. Of course, you cannot expect to spend all your time in a second home and may desire to lease the home during periods when you do not use it. If you spend less than two weeks per year in your second home (or less than 10 percent of the number of days during the tax year it is rented), you can classify the home as an investment and therefore qualify for attractive tax breaks such as deductibility of depreciation, insurance, maintenance and operating expenses, and public utility expenses that otherwise are not allowed.

FINANCING YOUR HOME

Only the person with exceptionally large financial resources can afford the full purchase price of a house. Savings banks, savings and loan associations, mortgage companies, and life insurance companies frequently lend money for real estate purchases. The amount you can borrow from these lenders depends on your personal financial situation, the appraised value of the property you want to buy, the location, interest rate levels, and the availability of funds. The most common way to borrow money to help you purchase a home is to obtain a mortgage loan.

Mortgage Loans

A **mortgage loan** is a formal agreement under which you, as the home buyer, agree to repay on a regular basis the principal amount of the loan plus interest. The most important provision of a mortgage loan is that the property you are borrowing money to buy becomes the security (collateral) for the loan.

A mortgage loan typically consists of two parts. The **promissory note** is the written agreement between the lender and borrower stating how much money is owed and how this amount is to be repaid. The note should carefully specify the principal amount of the loan, the interest rate, the frequency of payment, and the maturity of the loan. The **mortgage** is a separate document that provides the lender with a claim on the property as security for the loan. If the borrower does not satisfy the repayment requirements of the loan, the lender can legally take hold of the property in order to protect his or her financial interest.

Because a mortgage loan is necessary to accommodate most real estate transactions, most sale contracts contain a conditional clause that makes the actual transfer of title subject to the buyer's obtaining a mortgage loan. Upon agreement to make the loan, the lender will usually give the borrower a **letter of commitment** summarizing the provisions of the loan. This letter allows the buyer to proceed immediately with the closing. If, as a prospective buyer, you are unable to obtain a mortgage loan, you are released from your obligation to purchase the house—but only if the contract for sale contained this conditional clause.

Types of Mortgages

Until the 1970s, shopping for the best mortgage loan simply entailed finding the loan with the lowest interest rates. Most mortgage loans had fixed monthly payments and a 30-year maturity. Soaring interest rates in the late 1970s and early 1980s dramatically changed the market for mortgage loans. Because of high interest rates, many home buyers could not afford the steep monthly payments that accompanied traditional mortgage loans. As a result, innovative lenders began to offer a wide array of new kinds of mortgage loans in an attempt to better accommodate borrowers. Now you must sort through an abundance of financing alternatives before you can determine the best way to borrow money to purchase a house. Globe Mortgage Company of Hackensack, New Jersey, for example, recently offered 28 different types of mortgage loans—thus illustrating the complexity of the financing decision now confronting you. Although we cannot describe every alternative, the following are among the most popular types of mortgage loans.

Fixed-Rate Mortgage. The **fixed-rate mortgage** ranks as the most popular form of financing a home. Under this alternative both the interest rate and the monthly payment are fixed over the life of the mortgage. Most fixed-rate mortgages have an original maturity of 30 years. Recently, however, many lenders who grew nervous about making such long-term commitments have aggressively marketed shorter-maturity (especially 15 years) fixed-rate loans. Lenders often enhance the appeal of these shorter loans by offering them at lower interest rates (often one-quarter to one-half percent less) than the traditional 30-year version. Table 6.5 reveals that a borrower would save approximately $100,000 of interest on an $80,000 loan by choosing the shorter-maturity alternative. However, to secure this saving the borrower must be prepared to make larger monthly payments. In this example, the monthly payment on the 15-year loan equals $847, compared to only $702 a month for the 30-year alternative.

The primary appeal of a fixed-rate mortgage is that you know with certainty the amount of your monthly payment obligation. This type of loan is particularly well suited for a young family with a limited budget. This family needs to know the exact amount of their monthly payment because they cannot afford the risk of an unexpected payment increase which may occur with other types of mortgage loans. Some fixed-rate mortgages require a **balloon payment** at a specified future time. This is a lump-sum cash payment that typically pays off the remaining balance on the mortgage loan in full before the stated term of the mortgage. For example, you may obtain an $80,000 30-year mortgage at a 10 percent fixed interest rate with a $40,000 balloon payment due in 10 years. Although your monthly payments, based on a 30-year schedule, will be considerably less than under a 10 percent, 10-year loan, you will have to make a $40,000 cash payment at the end of 10 years to pay off the loan. Only the most disciplined saver should consider a mortgage with a large balloon payment. If you do not have the needed cash at payment time, you must either sell the house or refinance at a new interest rate which may exceed your prior fixed rate.

Adjustable-Rate Mortgage (ARM). Instead of a fixed interest rate, an **adjustable-rate mortgage (ARM)** loan offers an interest rate that goes up or down based on an index to which the loan is pegged. Accordingly, the amount of your monthly mortgage payment fluctuates in direct proportion to the interest rate. Lenders tie ARMs to a number of indexes, but the most commonly used are based on Treasury securities. For example, an ARM tied to the six-month Treasury bill rate would have its interest rate adjusted every six months from the loan's origination date in line with the current Treasury bill rate.

Table 6.5 THE LURE OF A 15-YEAR MORTGAGE

	30-Year loan at 10%	15-Year loan at 9¾%
Number of payments	360	180
Payment size	$702	$847
Total interest cost	$172,720	$72,460

Lenders often view shorter-maturity loans more favorably than longer-term loans and thus may be willing to charge a slightly lower interest rate on the shorter loan. In this loan we assume the lender charges ¼ percent less for a 15-year as opposed to a 30-year loan.

As shown, by borrowing for 15 years instead of 30, the buyer would save over $100,000 in interest costs over the life of the loan.

ARMs became very popular during the high-interest-rate days of the early 1980s. Fixed-rate mortgages soared as high as 15 percent or more, but some ARMs were offered with initial interest rates considerably lower. As interest rates declined, however, ARMs became less popular. Experts say that when the difference between fixed and variable rates is less than two percentage points, borrowers tend to favor fixed-rate mortgages.

An ARM usually allows a home buyer to obtain a mortgage loan at a lower initial monthly payment than under the fixed-rate alternative. But if interest rates continue to increase, the monthly payments on this loan can become very substantial. Many borrowers, stung by rising payments combined with stagnant property values, defaulted on these loans. Because of the uncertainty about the amount of future payments, this type of loan is best suited for a person whose income is likely to increase substantially. If your income grows faster that payment increases, then the financial sting from an ARM diminishes.

Graduated-Payment Mortgage (GPM). Under a **graduated-payment mortgage (GPM)** loan the amount of the monthly payments can be tailored to satisfy the borrower's needs. Monthly payments are set to start out low but get larger later. The interest rate and the maturity of the loan are fixed. Often the interest rate is slightly higher than on a conventional fixed-rate loan.

A GPM appeals to first-time home buyers who cannot afford the high initial monthly cost of a fixed-rate loan. This loan enables the new home buyer to pay a smaller initial payment to be offset by larger future payments that come at a time when the borrower can reasonably anticipate to be making higher earnings. Some GPMs allow **negative amortization** in the early years, which means that for some period of time the principal amount of your loan increases instead of diminishing. Many financial advisers warn against this feature because it can put you on the road to perpetual debt.

Growing-Equity Mortgage (GEM). A **growing-equity mortgage (GEM)** loan offers a fixed interest rate over the life of the loan, but has monthly payments that are scheduled to increase by a specified percentage each year. The initial payment on a GEM loan is the same as the payment on a conventional mortgage loan of the same amount. In subsequent years, however, the monthly payment will increase by 5 to 7½ percent annually. These growing payments repay the loan more rapidly than under the traditional fixed-rate mortgage. At a 7½ percent annual payment increase, a loan will be repaid in approximately 10 years as compared to the 30 years required under the traditional fixed-payment option.

A GEM is ideal for home buyers who expect their incomes to rise and who also desire to use some of this additional income to repay their home loan more rapidly. Because of the accelerated repayment schedule, most lenders offer these loans at a slightly lower interest rate than on a fixed-rate mortgage loan.

Rollover Mortgage (ROM). A **rollover mortgage (ROM)** loan offers a fixed interest rate and fixed monthly payments for a specified period of time. At the end of that period, the entire loan is renegotiated, or rolled over. This means that every aspect of the loan—including the principal amount, interest rate, and maturity—is renegotiated. Most ROMs are rolled over every five years.

If interest rates change from the time you originate the loan to the time of the first rollover, then you can expect that interest rate change to be reflected in your new mortgage loan terms. Therefore, a decline in interest rates causes your monthly payment to decline, but an increase in rates produces a higher payment. The key advantage of the ROM lies in its flexibility. At stated intervals you can tailor the loan to suit your needs. You have the opportunity to adjust the principal or maturity without incurring the expenses of refinancing. Or you can pay off the entire loan without penalty.

Shared-Appreciation Mortgage (SAM). Under a **shared-appreciation mortgage (SAM)** loan, the lender agrees to charge you a lower interest rate (possibly three to four percentage points less) than for a traditional loan. In return, you agree to give the lender a share (typically one-third) in any appreciation in the property's value. This arrangement is designed to make a home more affordable. A first-time home buyer who could not afford the high interest payments on a traditional mortgage might be able to accommodate a SAM loan. However, these loans have disadvantages. The new homeowner forfeits some of any gain in property value. Also, lenders usually require the payment of accumulated gains in the property's value after a specified period of time. If the borrower cannot make a cash payment for that portion of the appreciation, the home must be sold.

Second Mortgage. Even though you already have a mortgage loan on your home, you may obtain another mortgage on it if you can find a lender who will assume the risk. This is a **second mortgage.** A lender under a second mortgage has a **subordinated claim** to the property. This means that the second mortgage lender can receive payment only after the first mortgage lender's entire claim has been satisfied. Assume, for example, that you borrowed $50,000 from the Ready Savings and Loan Association to buy your home and gave the company a first mortgage as security. Later you decide to add a new room to the house and obtain a $12,000 loan from the Willing Mortgage Company, giving them a second mortgage. If you default on the first mortgage loan, Ready can foreclose the loan and sell the property to satisfy its claim. Willing can satisfy its claim only if Ready sells the property for more than it is owed, in which case Willing can recover what it can from the surplus.

Conventional, Insured, and Guaranteed Loans

Most mortgage loans are made directly between the borrower and lender. These are known as **conventional mortgages**. There is no governmental participation in the form of loan insurance or guarantees. Therefore, the lender assumes the entire risk of default on this type of mortgage. The lender often requires a down payment of 20 percent or more to lower the default risk. History indicates that generally a borrower with a high initial equity tends to be a high-quality credit risk. Of course, the high down payment requirement on conventional mortgages makes home ownership unaffordable to many would-be buyers.

The federal government, through the Federal Housing Administration (FHA), extends lenders mortgage insurance on many low-down-payment loans. The FHA does not make mortgage loans; it only provides mortgage insurance to private lenders. **FHA mortgage insurance** enables an individual to buy a home with a smaller down payment than required to obtain a conventional loan. The borrower pays a one-half percent annual premium on the unpaid loan balance to acquire this insurance. If the homeowner defaults on the FHA-insured mortgage loan, the FHA reimburses the lender for the resulting loss up to a specified maximum. As a general rule, the maximum insurance coverage equals approximately the national median home sales price. This insurance limitation means that FHA insurance is not much help to the person buying an expensive home, but it can be beneficial to an individual purchasing a home priced at the national median amount or less.

Another federal agency, the Veterans Administration (VA), provides **VA loan guarantee**s on mortgage loans made to qualified veterans. A VA guaranteed loan is similar to an insured loan because the VA guarantees to reimburse the lender for any loss resulting from the borrower's inability to pay. A borrower can usually make a smaller down payment and possibly pay a lower interest rate than on a conventional loan. However, unlike with an insured loan, an individual obtaining a VA guaranteed loan does not have to pay an insurance premium. Rather, the guarantee acts as a reward to those who have been in the military services.

Refinancing a Mortgage Loan

You may remember the very high interest rates of the late 1970s and early 1980s. During these days many home buyers had to lock in a 15 percent or even higher interest rate to obtain a mortgage loan. As interest rates fell, these high-rate loans in many instances became attractive refinancing candidates.

If a mortgage contains a **prepayment provision,** the borrower can pay off part or all of the outstanding amount of the loan before the due date without a penalty. This feature is desirable to the borrower during times of falling interest rates or when he or she wants to resell a home without a mortgage on it. Some mortgages carrying a prepayment provision also impose a hefty **prepayment penalty** on any amount that is paid off early. All FHA and VA loans have clauses allowing prepayment without penalty, but many conventional loans attach substantial penalties, often 1 to 2 percent of the loan's outstanding balance, to prepayments.

You may think you will benefit by obtaining a new mortgage loan that has a lower monthly payment than your current loan requires. But the decision is more involved than that. To analyze the attractiveness of refinancing, you have to take into account all the costs associated with obtaining a new loan. Closing costs may total 3 to 5 percent of the loan amount and you may have to pay a 1 to 2 percent prepayment penalty. Also, the lender may require you to make a larger down payment. Typically, you cannot borrow as large a percentage of a

Table 6.6 INTEREST RATE REDUCTION NEEDED TO JUSTIFY REFINANCING[a]

Refinancing costs as a percent of new loan amount	NUMBER OF YEARS				
	2	4	6	8	10
1	0.875	0.500	0.375	0.375	0.250
2	1.875	1.125	0.875	0.750	0.625
3	2.875	1.750	1.250	1.125	1.000
4	3.875	2.250	1.750	1.500	1.375
5	4.875	2.875	2.250	1.875	1.750

[a] Based on a 15 percent fixed-rate mortgage with 28 years remaining until maturity.

home's value when you refinance as you could for the original mortgage (though, of course, the house may have increased in value). Once you have all this information, the decision of whether to refinance or not is relatively simple.

For example, assume you are investigating whether it is desirable to refinance your 15 percent fixed-rate mortgage of $75,000. You find that you will incur $3000 (0.04 × $75,000) in refinancing costs. Does refinancing make fiscal sense? The answer to your question depends on two key factors: (1) the new mortgage rate and (2) how much longer you expect to own your home. Say you plan to stay in your present home another four years. You can determine how much lower your mortgage rate should be to justify refinancing by referring to Table 6.6. Assume your refinancing costs are 4 percent of the loan amount, so you read across the 4 percent row to the column under four years. The corresponding number of 2.25 means that your mortgage rate must decline by at least 2.25 percentage points to make refinancing worthwhile. Therefore, your new mortgage rate should be below 12.75 percent to justify refinancing.

SELLING YOUR HOME

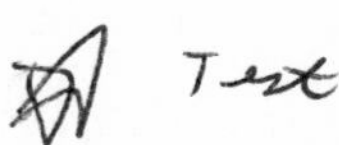

Most of this chapter has been devoted to buying a house. However, many of us will eventually be confronted with the task of selling our home. The way you approach this task can make a sizable difference in the dollar amount you receive for your home. The following checklist gives five dos and don'ts for selling a home.[4]

1 Have as few people in the house as possible when it is shown. This puts the buyer at ease and gives him a chance to absorb clearly the advantages of your property.

[4] *Consumer's Digest,* December 1985, p. 37.

Box 6.3 IF YOU DECIDE TO REFINANCE YOUR HOME

When does it pay to refinance a mortgage?

In general, when current interest rates are at least 2 percentage points below the rate on your existing home loan. . . . Mortgage rates now are averaging 9½ to 10 percent for a 30-year, fixed-rate loan. Charges have fallen to as low as 9¼ percent on 15-year loans, and 8¼ percent on 30-year adjustable-rate mortgages (ARM's).

When you cut your mortgage rate by at least 2 points, you can usually recoup the expense of a new loan in two years. Thus, if you will be moving in a year or so, refinancing isn't a good idea.

How much does it cost to refinance?

Closing expenses will probably equal 4 to 6 percent of what you borrow. You may pay more than you did when you took out your first mortgage, because there's no property seller to share the burden. If you're getting a new loan from your current lender, some expenses may be waived—for example, the cost of a new title search.

Don't closing costs vary by state and lender?

That's right. However, the Mortgage Bankers Association says most borrowers can expect the following charges: A property-appraisal fee of $100 to $300; a title-search and title-insurance fee, $450 to $600; a credit-report fee, $20 to $50; lawyer's fee, $75 to $200, and a recording fee, $6 to $50. You also may be asked to prepay your homeowner's-insurance premium or put in escrow a year's worth of property taxes. By far, your biggest expense will be the points or prepaid interest you must give the lender at closing. Points are calculated as a percentage of the mortgage balance.

How many points must I pay?

That varies, too. Still, you should count on paying 2½ to 3½ percent on loans charging the prevailing interest rate. The points are tax-deductible.

Will I be hit with a prepayment penalty on my old loan?

Only if your mortgage contract includes such a provision. Many

---

2 Keep pets out of the way. Most people like dogs and cats but they are a distraction. Chain the dog in the backyard, if possible.
3 Let the salesman talk. Be polite, but do not strike up a conversation with the potential buyer. The salesman needs the complete attention of the potential buyer to increase his interest in the sale.
4 Never apologize for the appearance or condition of your home. It will only call the buyer's attention to something he might otherwise have overlooked.
5 First sell the house. Do not try to sell any furniture, rugs or drapes. It complicates the sale and detracts from the interest created in the house. If a buyer does want to purchase some furnishings, the salesman will ask about them.

There are other important factors to consider when you decide to sell.

Preparing Your Home

Your home's first appearance to a potential buyer makes an indelible impression. Few home buyers will look past peeling paint and cluttered closets in evaluating

conventional fixed-rate loans require the borrower to pay 1 to 2 percent of the outstanding mortgage principal if the mortgage is paid off early. However, such clauses are forbidden in loans backed by the Federal Housing Administration and the Veterans Administration and are rarely found in adjustable-rate loans.

Can I borrow the money to pay the closing costs?

Yes. Many lenders will let you roll the bulk of these costs into the loan, but you probably will have to pay for the property appraisal, a credit check and application fee—if any—out of your own pocket.

What type of mortgage should I get?

You have three basic choices: A 30-year, fixed-rate loan; a 15-year fixed loan or an adjustable-rate loan amortized over 30 years. ARM's give the best break on interest, but if rates rise, so do payments.

Christopher Croft of Bailard Biehl & Kaiser, a financial advisory firm in San Mateo, Calif., argues that fixed-rate loans are newly attractive. "People have a good opportunity to lock in a low mortgage rate," says Croft. "This is a good time to switch from a variable-rate loan to a fixed-rate loan."

When applying for a new mortgage, should I lock in the current interest rate or let the interest rate float until the closing date in hopes that rates decline further?

Your best bet may be to go ahead and lock in today's terms. If rates fall during the processing period—typically 30 to 60 days—ask your lender to drop the rate. The lender knows you're free to shop elsewhere and will probably offer a better deal. If the answer is "no," take your business across the street. You may lose your application fee, but you'll still be ahead.

the attractiveness of a home. Attractively presented homes tend to sell faster and at higher prices. The dollar you spend on enhancing your home's sales appeal can be more than returned through a higher sales price. To determine how to use your money, try to put yourself in a buyer's shoes. In this way you can touch up the little things that can affect that all important first impression. You probably will not want to make major changes such as reshingling the roof or an entire paint job because it is unlikely that you will recoup these expenditures through a higher sales price. But small outlays for painting the trim, replacing broken shingles, and cleaning up the yard could produce a more appealing home that will yield a much higher selling price.

Selling on Your Own

You may be tempted to sell your home yourself in order to save the customary 6 percent brokerage fee. If you decide to go it alone, you must be prepared to work hard. You should be willing to research selling prices of comparable homes in the neighborhood, determine a fair price, become acquainted with the numerous financing alternatives, implement an advertising campaign, and deal with potential buyers. To accomplish all these tasks, you must be highly motivated, have a schedule that allows you to show the house, and be an excellent salesperson who can bargain and negotiate. Most people are happy to pay for the skill and service of a real estate agent to relieve themselves of the pressure of trying to sell their home alone. As a result, fewer than 10 percent of homes are sold directly by the owner. A good agent will research the market, help set a price, advertise the home, make showings, arrange financing, qualify buyers, and set up closing transactions. Further, an agent may be able to get a better price for your home and sell the property more quickly.

SUMMARY

The decision to buy a home has a substantial impact on both your standard of living and your pocketbook. Accordingly, this is a decision that should be made only after careful planning. You should first consider how a house accommodates such nonfinancial factors as the quality of schools, availability of municipal services and amenities, and ambience of the neighborhood. The next step is to consider how much you can afford to pay for a home. In deciding how much to pay you should consider the following expenditures: (1) the down payment, (2) mortgage points, (3) closing costs, (4) the mortgage payment, (5) homeowner's insurance, (6) property taxes, and (7) maintenance and operating expenses.

You may find a house too costly for your budget, or you may decide for nonfinancial reasons that homeownership is not desirable. In this case you may choose to rent rather than buy. Before renting, however, you should examine the obligations a rental agreement imposes. You should also know about the advantages and disadvantages of renting and how to compare the costs of renting and purchasing.

Even if you decide to purchase housing, your decision is still a complex one. Today, a larger number of housing forms than ever before are available. These different housing forms vary considerably in size, cost, and living accommodations. Although the single-family home remains the most popular housing alternative, you may want to consider condominiums, cooperative apartments, and factory-built houses. An increasing number of Americans are also electing to purchase a second home.

The way in which you finance your home purchase can make a substantial difference in the overall cost of your home. The most common way to borrow money to buy a home is to obtain a mortgage loan. The fixed-rate mortgage remains the most popular form of financing a home. However, the recent wide swings in interest rates have caused lenders to offer a greater variety of mortgage loan alternatives. You should examine the suitability of each of these financing alternatives. If you qualify for a government insured or guaranteed loan, you may be able to finance at a lower interest rate or with a smaller down payment.

If you are like most Americans, you will eventually be confronted with the task of selling your home. The steps you take to prepare your home for sale can substantially influence the sales price. Attractively presented homes tend to sell faster and at higher prices. You should also decide whether to sell your home yourself or to select a real estate agent to handle the sale for you.

KEY TERMS

adjustable-rate mortgage (ARM)
balloon payment
bargain and sale deed
closing costs
condominium
conventional mortgage
cooperative apartment
deed
down payment
equity buildup
factory-built, or manufactured, house
FHA mortgage insurance
fixed-rate mortgage
graduated-payment mortgage (GPM)
growing-equity mortgage (GEM)
homeowner's insurance
lease agreement
lessee
lessor
letter of commitment
loan-to-value ratio
mortgage
mortgage loan
mortgage payment
mortgage points
negative amortization
prepayment penalty
prepayment provision
promissory note
property taxes
quitclaim deed
real estate agent (broker)
rollover mortgage (ROM)
second mortgage
shared-appreciation mortgage (SAM)
subordinated claim
title insurance
VA loan guarantee
warranty deed

SELECTED READINGS

"Before You Buy: Hire a Home Inspector." *Better Homes and Gardens*, May 1986, p. F8.

De Palma, Anthony. "Deciding Whether to Rent or Buy." *New York Times Financial Planning Guide*, September 14, 1986, pp. 21–24.

Dreyfus, Patricia. "How to Get the Right Mortgage." *Money*, July 1986, pp. 105–110.

Money Guide: Your Home. New York: Time, Inc., 1985.

"Nail Down What That House Is Really Worth." *Changing Times*, March 1986, pp. 61–63.

Sheridan, Dan. "Strategies for Buying and Selling a House." *Consumers Digest*, December 1985, pp. 35–37.

"Time to Refinance Your Mortgage?" *Consumer Reports*, October 1986, pp. 646–649.

QUESTIONS

1. List and briefly discuss the important factors you should consider in selecting a house to purchase.
2. Explain why the location of a house may affect its price. Describe the important factors you should evaluate in selecting the location of a house to purchase.
3. Describe each of the several kinds of expenditures that must be considered to determine how much house you can afford.
4. What are the primary closing costs associated with obtaining a mortgage loan? Approximately how much would you expect to pay in closing costs for a $75,000 house if you make a 20 percent down payment?
5. The Jacobs have a gross annual income (pretax) of $30,000. Use a rule of thumb to estimate how much they can spend on a house.
6. What are the major advantages of renting? What are the disadvantages?
7. Comment on this statement: "Income tax laws favor ownership rather than renting."
8. Two of the financial benefits of ownership are equity buildup and potential price appreciation. Describe each of these considerations and explain how each may benefit the homeowner.
9. Explain why circumstances are more favorable now for new families to buy homes.
10. Compare the relative advantages and disadvantages between purchasing a new house and an existing house.
11. The adjustable-rate mortgage (ARM) has become more popular in recent years. Explain how an ARM differs from a fixed-rate mortgage. Under what circumstances does a borrower benefit from having an ARM rather than a fixed-rate mortgage? Explain.
12. Describe a graduated-payment mortgage (GPM) and a growing-equity mortgage (GEM). Explain why a borrower might find (a) a GPM or (b) a GEM attractive? What type of borrower do you think would like each of these mortgages?
13. What is meant by negative amortization? Can you think of an example where negative amortization would be acceptable?
14. Explain the circumstances under which you might want to refinance your mortgage. How would the existence of a prepayment penalty affect your decision?
15. Why would an individual consider an FHA or VA mortgage? How do they differ?

CASE PROBLEMS

6.1 Tom and Claire Russo are contemplating the purchase of a house. Before beginning their search for a house, the Russos want to know the price range in which they should be looking. Their personal balance sheet shows a net worth (excluding personal effects) equaling $36,000. Their projected budget shows an annual income of $36,000 and annual expenditures of $30,200 (including the estimated nonmortgage costs of a new home). They want to keep at least six months' income available as an emergency fund. Assume the closing costs on a loan will be $3000.

a Estimate the dollar amount the Russos have available to make a down payment on a house. Use the first four steps in the procedure shown in the section entitled, "How Much House Can You Afford?"

b Estimate the dollar amount the Russos can afford to borrow through a mortgage loan. Use the next three steps in the same section to determine this answer. Assume an annual interest rate of 9 percent.

c How much can the Russos afford to pay for a house? Use Step 8.

d By how much would an increase in the mortgage loan interest rate to 10 percent affect the amount the Russos could pay for a home?

6.2 Mike and Sherry Courtney are planning a move to a new city. One of their major decisions is whether to rent an apartment unit or purchase a home of comparable size and quality. The apartment leases for $400 monthly with an estimated $60 monthly utilities expense and $100 annually for personal insurance.

The house would cost $60,000 with a $10,000 down payment requirement. The remainder could be financed through a 9 percent, 30-year mortgage loan. In addition, the Courtneys would incur the following annual expenses if they purchase the house:

Property insurance	$300
Property taxes	700
Maintenance and repairs	550
Utilities	800

a Calculate the pretax total annual rental costs and total annual purchase costs. Follow the analysis shown in Table 6.3. In the process, use Table 6.2 to determine the monthly mortgage value and multiply this by 12. Further assume that 5 percent interest could have been earned on funds provided for the down payment.

b Explain how income tax considerations affect the comparison of rental costs and purchase costs.

c Indicate the equity buildup at the end of the first year for home ownership.

d Calculate the tax savings for home ownership in the first year. The tax rate is 30 percent.

e Assuming a 3 percent increase in value due to inflation, how much price appreciation will home ownership provide in the first year?

f Combine the values computed in parts c, d, and e with the total purchase costs computed in part a. Determine the net purchase costs. Follow the analysis shown in Table 6.4.

g How has the lease versus home ownership decision changed between part a and part f of this case?

7

Purchasing Consumer Durables

After studying this chapter, you should:

- Understand the importance of planning in buying consumer durables
- Appreciate the steps involved in planning a major purchase
- Appreciate the key considerations involved in buying an automobile
- Understand how to finance an automobile
- Be able to assess the costs of automobile ownership
- Know how to buy or sell a used car
- Apply wise shopping procedures to furniture, appliances, and computers

In Chapter 6 we discussed the major considerations involved in buying a house. In this chapter we examine other major consumer expenditures such as those made for automobiles, furniture, and appliances. Because of the rapidly growing use of personal computers, we also present a detailed discussion of how to evaluate and purchase this product in a separate appendix to this chapter. All of the items discussed in the chapter and in the appendix are known as **consumer durables** because of their lengthy service periods, importance to consumers, and relatively high costs. When combined, expenditures for consumer durables can have a major impact on your budget. Careful planning is a necessity when you are contemplating buying these items. You cannot expect to make intelligent purchases unless you follow an organized and thorough approach.

To explain what you need to know before making major expenditures, this chapter examines the following in regard to purchasing an automobile:

1 The importance of planning
2 The steps involved in planning a major purchase
3 The key considerations involved in buying an automobile
4 How to finance an automobile
5 The costs of automobile ownership
6 How to buy or sell a used car

We also briefly consider some of these same factors as they apply to other consumer durables such as furniture and appliances and, in the appendix, personal computers.

THE PLANNING PROCESS

Have you ever bought something suddenly or unexpectedly? Maybe you couldn't resist the temptation of a new set of golf clubs, or possibly it was a stylish designer dress that caused you to suddenly part with your money. At some time or other, most of us have made such an impulse acquisition. But can you envision making an impulse purchase of a new $15,000 automobile? Very few people would confess to such an extravagant action. Yet recent studies show that more than one out of five new-car purchases are made by individuals during their first visit to an automobile dealership. Although this approach may save some time and bother, we question whether these impulse shoppers obtain the best product for their money.

In this chapter we emphasize the importance of planning before you make a purchase. Proper planning not only allows you to buy at a better price, but it also ensures that you buy exactly what you need. Imagine the frustration of the impulse buyer who pays too much for something only to discover later that he or she has no use for that product!

Planning is a key component of the financial makeup of you and your family. With proper planning, your dollars will stretch further and you will be assured that you buy only what you need. Listed here are six planning steps that interact to guide you to intelligent purchase decisions.

1 Determine how much you can spend.
2 Identify your needs.
3 Conduct research.
4 Shop for the best buy.
5 Negotiate a price.
6 Arrange financing.

In the following paragraphs we review each of these steps as they relate to the purchase of an automobile. This same planning framework can be used for other major consumer purchases.

DETERMINING HOW MUCH TO SPEND ON AN AUTOMOBILE

You may want that new Mercedes, but it would be foolish to buy it without first consulting your budget. One of the important expenditures included in your budget is automobile-related expenses. In Chapter 2 we observed that Steve and Susan Kline had budgeted the following annual automobile expenses:

Payments on automobile loans	$2460
Gasoline and automobile upkeep	1200
Total automobile budget	$3660

Therefore, the Klines, after carefully considering all their other expected expenses and their desired savings amount, determined that they can spend $3660 a year on an automobile. Unfortunately, this amount isn't enough to buy a new Mercedes, but it does give the Klines an idea of the kind of cars they can afford. By adhering to their budget, Steve and Susan will not fall into the same trap that many other car buyers do: buying a lavish new car only to find that after making car-related expenditures, little is left for other necessities. In your lifetime, you most likely will expend more on automobiles than on any other consumer durable. Considering the expenses involved, you should carefully budget for this product before you begin to shop.

Identifying Your Needs

Not all cars accommodate your needs and desires. In identifying your needs, you will not only want to consider the practical aspects of ownership, but you will also want to incorporate your tastes and preferences. Three basic criteria are important in determining the best car for you to buy: size, body style, and options.

Size. There are four general auto size groups: subcompacts, compacts, intermediates, and full-size or standard cars.

Subcompacts These are the smallest cars of all, seating two adults quite comfortably, but with room in back for small children only. They are especially suitable for in-town driving, because of their maneuverability in traffic and in parking. Due to their less powerful engines, subcompacts do not perform as well on the highway and cannot be overloaded with optional equipment. Their size makes them vulnerable in an accident. Their biggest advantage? Economy!

Compacts Compact cars are somewhat larger and higher-priced than subcompacts as a rule, and will accommodate four adults comfortably for short periods of time. They make a satisfactory all-round car for small families. Compacts are also easy to handle and are among the less expensive cars to own and operate, for they get good mileage and have lower depreciation, insurance, and repair costs.

Intermediates These have lower mileage and higher upkeep expenses, but provide more space and comfort for the money. They are large enough to easily accommodate six adults, and perform well both in city traffic and on the highway.

Full-size or standard Cars of this type, which include the luxury models, are the largest of all. They are the most expensive to own and operate because of their high initial cost, upkeep, depreciation, insurance rates, and lower mileage. They usually offer greater riding comfort, power, and stability than do the smaller cars, so are more suitable for extensive highway and long-distance driving. On the other hand, their bulk makes them more difficult to manage in city traffic.[1]

Selecting the car size that is best for you is one of the most crucial decisions you can make. You should consider all of the following factors when making this choice: number of people who must ride in the car, cost of purchase and operation, and safety. Larger cars usually cost more and are more expensive to operate; however, they accommodate more passengers and generally provide greater safety in case of an accident.

Body Style. Once you have decided on a car size, you must next select a body style. There are six popular body styles:

Sedans (4-door and 2-door) Vehicles in this class are designed to carry several passengers, making them good family cars. They are solidly built, with central side pillars that provide extra stability in case of an accident. Two-door sedans cost slightly less and have a more streamlined appearance, but getting in and out of the back seat is more difficult. Parents of young children often prefer them because there are no rear doors to be accidentally opened.

Hardtops (4-door and 2-door) Hardtops are similar in size and style to sedans, but lack side pillars. This results in an appealing, sporty look and unobstructed side vision. Because the smooth, uncluttered look of hardtops is generally more popular, they usually have a higher resale value than sedans.

Station wagons These are utility cars that hold more people than comparable sedans. They are particularly suitable for those who frequently carry several passengers. The large amount of space in the rear makes them ideal for hauling large items, shrubbery, camping gear, lumber, or bags of groceries. They are several hundred pounds heavier than sedans in the same make and series, and are less maneuverable in traffic. With a higher price tag and lower gas mileage, station wagons are more expensive to own and operate.

Hatchbacks Hatchbacks are designed with a hinged rear window that provides access to a large, flat storage area created when the rear seat is folded down. At such times a subcompact or compact becomes, in effect, a small station wagon. These models are valued by people who have an occasional need for cargo space but no need for the extra seating capacity or power of a standard-size wagon.

[1] *Your Automobile Dollar,* Money Management Institute, Household Financial Services, 1979, p. 11.

Convertibles Once seen frequently, convertibles have declined in popularity. They have been phased out of most domestic car lines, but are available in some foreign makes that meet federal safety standards. The poorer insulation of convertibles results in noisier, less comfortable rides that are hotter in summer, cooler in winter. Their occupants are also more vulnerable in an accident.

Sports cars Popularly regarded as "fun" cars, sports cars generally seat only two people and offer little storage space. They are perhaps the least practical of all body types. Since some of the higher-priced models offer superior engineering qualities and finely tooled, powerful engines, they hold special appeal for automobile buffs. Even the lighter-weight, less expensive models provide status and delight along with transportation, and their sleek continental lines attract many an admiring eye.[2]

You can generally find most of these body styles in any size automobile. This decision can be very confusing to the average consumer. The Ford Escort, for example, comes in a total of 15 styles or models. Therefore, you will want to carefully investigate the body styles available in your desired car size. You may find several styles that fit your needs. Do not narrow your choice too much. If your heart is set on a single model, you are likely to overpay for it because you may not bargain as aggressively.

Options. After choosing size and body style, you must next decide what options you want.[3] An option is a discretionary feature that can be added at an extra cost to the buyer. New cars come with such a variety of options that you can easily spend $2000 or more on them. It is easy to get carried away in the showroom if you have not already determined the options appropriate for you. Often a model's costlier styles include special features in the base price. These features are either unavailable in a lower-price car or available only as an option. Sometimes it is cheaper to buy a high-line model than to add the same equipment to a lesser model (assuming, of course, that you want those features). If you have the time and patience, you will usually find it cheaper to order a lower-line car with only the desired equipment than to buy a fully equipped car off the dealer's lot that has many features you cannot use.

Conducting Research

Once you have decided on the kinds of automobiles that best fit your needs, you may be eager to head for the showroom. Before you make that trip, however, you should investigate each of the automobile models you are considering. At your local library, you can find several helpful publications that routinely rate new and used automobiles along several dimensions. A review of appropriate articles in publications such as *Consumer Reports, Consumers Digest, Car and*

[2] *Your Automobile Dollar,* Money Management Institute, Household Financial Services, 1979, p. 12.

[3] A description and evaluation of the most common automobile options are given in the annual issue of *Consumer Reports* published in April.

Driver, and *Changing Times* will provide you with extensive information about the relative advantages and disadvantages of many car models. In particular, you should obtain relative rankings for the models you are considering for the following factors:

Overall reliability
Road performance
Comfort and convenience
Fuel economy
Maintenance and repair record
Availability of options
Price
Resale value

All of this information is readily available. A well-informed consumer is more likely to make an intelligent and economical purchase, so the time you spend researching the cars you are considering for purchase will be well spent.

Shopping for the Best Deal

Now that you have an idea of the models that are most suitable for you and have done the basic research on those models, it is time to visit some automobile showrooms. Your primary objective is to look at the automobiles and their related features. This is not the time to test-drive a car or close a deal. You only want to see how the cars look and get a general idea of the prices and options. Avoid high-pressure sales pitches at this time by telling the salesperson you are only shopping around. Take brochures—you can study them later at home. Also, you will want to rate the models you like. It is easy to overlook an important consideration, so you may want to bring along a checklist to ensure that you evaluate each pertinent feature.

After you have made your initial visit to the showrooms, it is time to evaluate your findings. You should review the brochures and your list of candidates. In the process you should also rate the dealers. You may call your local Better Business Bureau to find out about the dealers' reputations. You can take your time, away from the pressures of the showroom, to decide which cars seem most appropriate.

Once you have limited your alternatives, prepare to test-drive the finalists. A test drive should include both city and highway driving: The customary drive around the block is too short and the conditions are too unvarying to provide much useful information.

Try to test-drive all your finalists in a single day. This allows you to make more direct comparisons. When you complete these test drives, you can objectively determine the final ranking of your preferences. You probably will find more than one acceptable candidate. That's fine, you don't have to narrow your list to only one final choice. In fact, if you still have several acceptable candidates, your next step—negotiating a price—will be easier and more effective.

Negotiating a Price

Once you have decided what car you want, it is time to negotiate the price. The **manufacturer's suggested list price**—the price shown on the sticker pasted on the window—is unrealistic. The true price is whatever you can negotiate. The dealer will often offer you a discount from the posted price, but unless you know the dealer's cost, you have a substantial bargaining handicap. The $300 or $400 discount the dealer offers may still mean a price that is considerably above the dealer's cost. Only if you know the dealer's cost can you bargain effectively. Several newsstand publications, such as *Edmund's New Car Prices,* provide information on a dealer's cost. Or, for a nominal fee, *Consumer Reports* will send you the dealer cost and list price on almost any model.[4] An example of this service is shown as Figure 7.1. This listing also gives prices for all available options, thus allowing you to determine exactly what the dealer's cost for a particular car and options is.

As a general rule, the dealer markup is 11 to 12 percent on subcompacts, 13 to 15 percent on compacts and intermediates, and 16 to 20 percent on full-size cars. The markup on options is generally 15 percent.

After you have obtained this important dealer cost information, you are ready to negotiate with the dealer. Before you approach the dealer, you should have a list containing dealer cost for the car and all the options you want. A simple and effective way to negotiate is to ask the dealer to tell you the minimum acceptable markup over invoice price. For most domestic cars, this should amount to $200 to $400. On luxury models and during times of short supply, however, this markup can be higher. If the minimum markup is much over $400, you can assume that the dealer is not interested in making low-margin sales. In that situation you must either go to another dealer or resign yourself to a relatively high price. On the other hand, if the dealer is willing to sell the car at, say, $250 over cost, add that amount to the cost you have already determined. The resulting figure should be your firm offering price for the car.

How Much to Pay: An Example

Figure 7.1 shows a *Consumer Reports* Auto Price Service printout that gives the dealer's cost and retail (list) price for a 1987 Buick Century Limited sedan and available options. The base retail price for the car is $11,593, or 15.9 percent more than the dealer's cost of $10,004.76. The car comes equipped with certain standard features, such as power brakes and steering and automatic transmission. These standard items are included in the car's base price—there is no added charge for them. You also have the choice of many optional features. Any of these items you select will cost you extra. For example, if you want power windows you must be prepared to pay between $242 (dealer's cost) and $285

[4] *Consumer Reports* Auto Price Service, P.O. Box 570, Lathrup Village, Michigan 48076. You will need to send them complete information about the make, model, and style of the car. The price for this service is $11 for one car, $20 for two cars, $27 for three cars, and $7 for each additional car over three. A check or money order must accompany your order.

Figure 7.1 A COMPARISON OF DEALER COST TO LIST PRICE

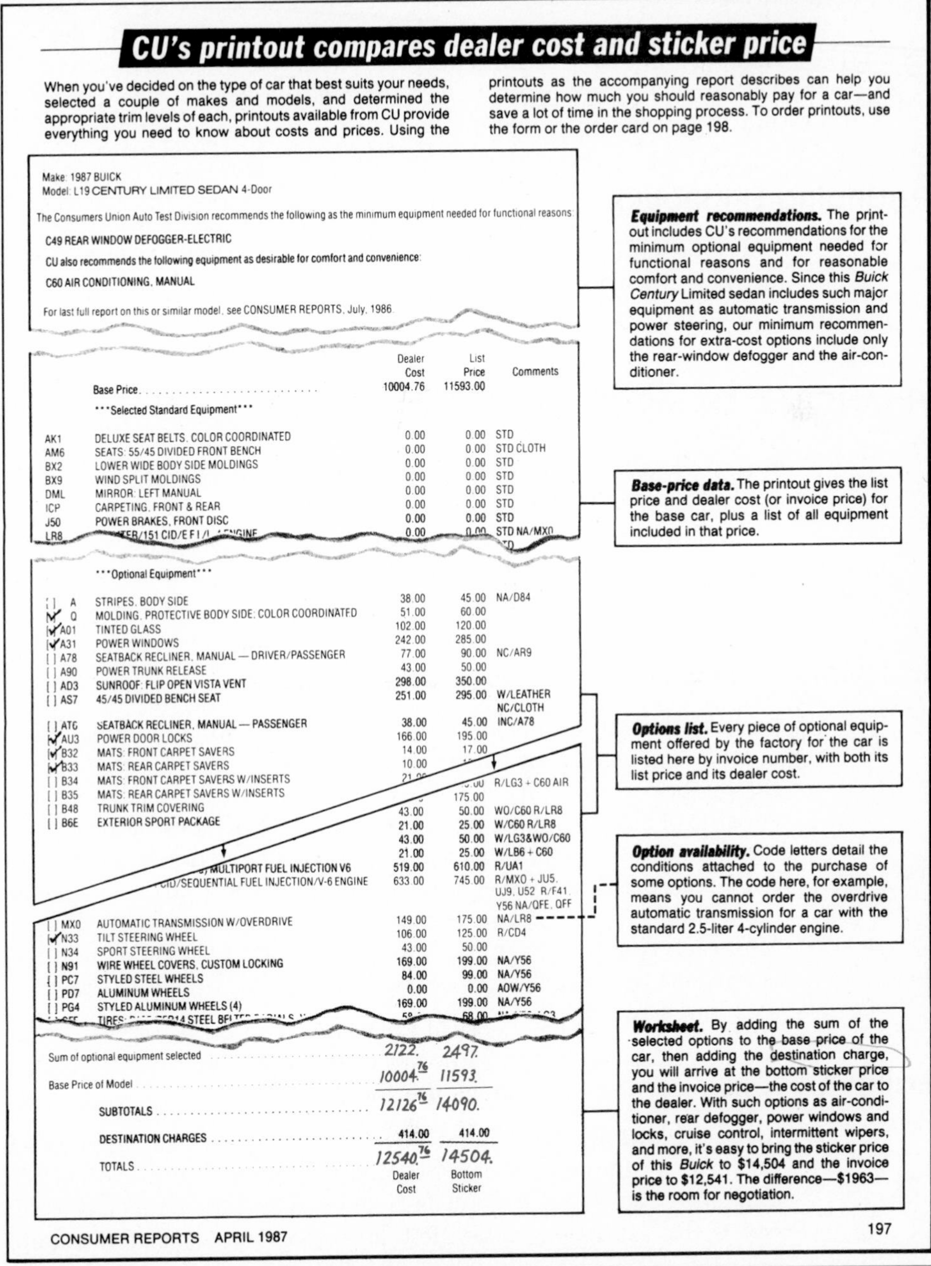

CU's printout compares dealer cost and sticker price

When you've decided on the type of car that best suits your needs, selected a couple of makes and models, and determined the appropriate trim levels of each, printouts available from CU provide everything you need to know about costs and prices. Using the printouts as the accompanying report describes can help you determine how much you should reasonably pay for a car—and save a lot of time in the shopping process. To order printouts, use the form or the order card on page 198.

Make: 1987 BUICK
Model: L19 CENTURY LIMITED SEDAN 4-Door

The Consumers Union Auto Test Division recommends the following as the minimum equipment needed for functional reasons:

C49 REAR WINDOW DEFOGGER-ELECTRIC

CU also recommends the following equipment as desirable for comfort and convenience:

C60 AIR CONDITIONING, MANUAL

For last full report on this or similar model, see CONSUMER REPORTS, July, 1986.

Equipment recommendations. The printout includes CU's recommendations for the minimum optional equipment needed for functional reasons and for reasonable comfort and convenience. Since this *Buick Century* Limited sedan includes such major equipment as automatic transmission and power steering, our minimum recommendations for extra-cost options include only the rear-window defogger and the air-conditioner.

		Dealer Cost	List Price	Comments
	Base Price	10004.76	11593.00	
	Selected Standard Equipment			
AK1	DELUXE SEAT BELTS, COLOR COORDINATED	0.00	0.00	STD
AM6	SEATS: 55/45 DIVIDED FRONT BENCH	0.00	0.00	STD CLOTH
BX2	LOWER WIDE BODY SIDE MOLDINGS	0.00	0.00	STD
BX9	WIND SPLIT MOLDINGS	0.00	0.00	STD
DML	MIRROR: LEFT MANUAL	0.00	0.00	STD
ICP	CARPETING, FRONT & REAR	0.00	0.00	STD
J50	POWER BRAKES, FRONT DISC	0.00	0.00	STD
LR8	[illegible]ER/151 CID/E F I/[illegible] ENGINE	0.00	0.00	STD NA/MX0

Base-price data. The printout gives the list price and dealer cost (or invoice price) for the base car, plus a list of all equipment included in that price.

		Dealer Cost	List Price	Comments
	Optional Equipment			
[ ] A	STRIPES, BODY SIDE	38.00	45.00	NA/D84
[✓] Q	MOLDING, PROTECTIVE BODY SIDE: COLOR COORDINATED	51.00	60.00	
[✓] A01	TINTED GLASS	102.00	120.00	
[✓] A31	POWER WINDOWS	242.00	285.00	
[ ] A78	SEATBACK RECLINER, MANUAL — DRIVER/PASSENGER	77.00	90.00	NC/AR9
[ ] A90	POWER TRUNK RELEASE	43.00	50.00	
[ ] AD3	SUNROOF: FLIP OPEN VISTA VENT	298.00	350.00	
[ ] AS7	45/45 DIVIDED BENCH SEAT	251.00	295.00	W/LEATHER NC/CLOTH
[ ] ATG	SEATBACK RECLINER, MANUAL — PASSENGER	38.00	45.00	INC/A78
[✓] AU3	POWER DOOR LOCKS	166.00	195.00	
[✓] B32	MATS: FRONT CARPET SAVERS	14.00	17.00	
[✓] B33	MATS: REAR CARPET SAVERS	10.00	[illegible]	
[ ] B34	MATS: FRONT CARPET SAVERS W/INSERTS	21.[illegible]		
[ ] B35	MATS: REAR CARPET SAVERS W/INSERTS			
[ ] B48	TRUNK TRIM COVERING			
[ ] B6E	EXTERIOR SPORT PACKAGE			

		Dealer Cost	List Price	Comments
			[illegible]	R/LG3 + C60 AIR
			175.00	
		43.00	50.00	WO/C60 R/LR8
		21.00	25.00	W/C60 R/LR8
		43.00	50.00	W/LG3&WO/C60
		21.00	25.00	W/LB6 + C60
	[illegible] MULTIPORT FUEL INJECTION V6	519.00	610.00	R/UA1
	[illegible] CID/SEQUENTIAL FUEL INJECTION/V-6 ENGINE	633.00	745.00	R/MXO + JU5, UJ9, U52 R/F41, Y56 NA/QFE, QFF
[ ] MX0	AUTOMATIC TRANSMISSION W/OVERDRIVE	149.00	175.00	NA/LR8
[✓] N33	TILT STEERING WHEEL	106.00	125.00	R/CD4
[ ] N34	SPORT STEERING WHEEL	43.00	50.00	
[ ] N91	WIRE WHEEL COVERS, CUSTOM LOCKING	169.00	199.00	NA/Y56
[ ] PC7	STYLED STEEL WHEELS	84.00	99.00	NA/Y56
[ ] PD7	ALUMINUM WHEELS	0.00	0.00	AOW/Y56
[ ] PG4	STYLED ALUMINUM WHEELS (4)	169.00	199.00	NA/Y56
[ ] [illegible]	TIRES: [illegible]14 STEEL BELTED RADIALS [illegible]	5[illegible]	68.00	[illegible]

Options list. Every piece of optional equipment offered by the factory for the car is listed here by invoice number, with both its list price and its dealer cost.

Option availability. Code letters detail the conditions attached to the purchase of some options. The code here, for example, means you cannot order the overdrive automatic transmission for a car with the standard 2.5-liter 4-cylinder engine.

Sum of optional equipment selected	2122.	2497.
Base Price of Model	10004.76	11593.
SUBTOTALS	12126.76	14090.
DESTINATION CHARGES	414.00	414.00
TOTALS	12540.76	14504.
	Dealer Cost	Bottom Sticker

Worksheet. By adding the sum of the selected options to the base price of the car, then adding the destination charge, you will arrive at the bottom sticker price and the invoice price—the cost of the car to the dealer. With such options as air-conditioner, rear defogger, power windows and locks, cruise control, intermittent wipers, and more, it's easy to bring the sticker price of this *Buick* to $14,504 and the invoice price to $12,541. The difference—$1963—is the room for negotiation.

CONSUMER REPORTS APRIL 1987 197

(list price) for them (see Figure 7.1). Let's assume that you choose $2497 retail value of optional equipment, thus raising the list price of the car to $14,090. This compares to the dealer's cost of $12,126.76 for the car—a 16.2 percent markup. Armed with this information, you are now ready to negotiate. You may, for example, decide to offer the dealer $300 over cost. If the dealer accepts your offer, you pay $12,426.76.[5] This price saves you $1663.24 as compared to the car's list price. The net result is that the dealer receives a 2.5 percent markup—not the 16.2 percent original markup.

Arranging Financing

After you have negotiated a deal for a car, you are ready to arrange financing. Because financing considerations are so involved, we devote the next section of this chapter to that important topic.

FINANCING AN AUTOMOBILE

If you are like most Americans, you will want to borrow some money when you buy a car. Very few of us pay cash for the entire purchase price of a car. In this section, we examine the important considerations concerning financing an automobile. We begin by describing the three types of loans that are generally used to finance the purchase of a car: installment, balloon, and single-payment.

Installment Loans

An **installment loan** is the most common type of automobile loan ($37.5 billion outstanding at year-end 1986) and requires equal monthly payments over some set period of time (usually 36, 48, or 60 months). Each installment payment consists of both principal repayment and interest. The earliest payments include heavy interest costs, but as the loan's balance is gradually paid off subsequent payments contain smaller interest amounts and larger principal repayments. For example, on a $10,000, 48-month installment loan with a 10 percent interest rate, each monthly payment amounts to $254. The first month's payment includes $83 of interest expense; however, the last payment (month 48) has only a $2 interest cost.

Balloon Loans

Under a **balloon loan** you borrow a fixed amount—say $10,000—and pay interest on this full amount. Repayments of principal, however, are figured on the difference between the loan's face amount and the expected resale value of the car. If the estimated value after four years is $4000, for example, you make

[5] You will also have to pay a destination charge of $414, which raises the cost of the car to $12,840.76 before payment of license fee and sales tax.

principal payments on only $6000 (the difference between the $10,000 purchase price and the $4000 resale value). This type of loan can reduce the amount of your monthly payment by 20 percent or more. When the loan term expires, you can either return the car to the lending institution and walk away or keep the car and pay the lender its resale value (the balloon) in cash.

Single-Payment Loans

With a **single-payment loan,** the entire loan amount must be repaid in one lump sum. This type of loan requires the borrower to exercise disciplined budget control in order to accumulate the cash necessary to repay the loan at maturity. Most lenders are reluctant to make this kind of auto loan because the amount owed stays constant but the value of the collateral (the car) steadily declines. If the borrower defaults, the lender may not be able to sell the repossessed car for an amount sufficient to pay off the loan.

Sources of Financing

The terms on auto loans can vary considerably from one lender to another. It is wise to shop for the best auto loan just as you would shop for the best car buy. Automobile dealers, commercial banks, consumer finance companies, and credit unions are the most commonly used financing outlets. A brief discussion of each source follows.

Automobile Dealers. Most major dealers are prepared to provide financing. The dealer does not directly finance your automobile purchase, but passes the loan on to an affiliated finance company such as Chrysler Credit Corporation, Ford Motor Credit Company, or General Motors Acceptance Corporation. A typical loan through a dealer is of the installment variety and requires a modest down payment. Terms such as interest rate and maturity vary on these loans. Often during slow sales periods these automobile finance companies offer special low-rate loans as incentives to entice people to buy new cars.

Commercial Banks. Many commercial banks are active lenders on automobiles. A bank requires a down payment and secures the loan by a lien on the car so that the car itself is the collateral for the loan. Interest rate requirements, length of loan, and the amount of down payment differ considerably among commercial banks. Some banks offer a better rate to their regular customers. Therefore, you may be able to save a percentage point or so by using your own bank.

Consumer Finance Companies. You will probably want to approach a consumer finance company for an auto loan only after you have exhausted other possible sources of financing. These companies generally extend credit to individuals with unestablished or poor credit ratings. As a result, you can expect their interest rates to be higher than those of many other sources of financing.

Credit Unions. If you belong to a credit union, you may be able to obtain an attractive auto loan. Because they are nonprofit entities, credit unions generally offer lower interest rates to their members than can be obtained from other financing sources. You can usually arrange either installment or single-payment loans through your credit union. Further, smaller loans often can be unsecured. Some credit unions even provide members the opportunity to buy automobiles through wholesale dealers at wholesale prices.

Shopping for a Loan

The terms on automobile loans offered by the various sources of financing can vary substantially. Many automobile dealers offer big financial incentives and some offer preapproved credit on certain models. Consequently, you will want to actively shop for the financing package that best fits your needs. An intelligent shopper can save meaningful amounts of money by obtaining the most attractive loan. Note these important points to consider when shopping for an auto loan:

1. *Do* talk with a loan officer at your bank or credit union before you head for the dealers. He'll be able to tell you how much you owe on your present car and help you figure out how much you can afford to borrow for a new one.
2. *Don't* simply compare monthly payments and Annual Percent Rates (APRs) between loan sources. You need to calculate the *total* cost of the loan.
3. *Do* find out whether your bank or credit union will offer a better rate because you're a customer.
4. *Do* check the incentives from auto companies.
5. *Don't* overlook preapproved loans. Sometimes, car manufacturers offer preapproved credit on certain models; if this applies to the car you want, it may be the easiest way to get a loan.
6. *Do* be prepared to have a co-signer if you haven't taken out a loan in your name before, or if your credit is overextended. The co-signer must agree to repay the loan if you default.
7. *Don't* automatically take credit life insurance along with the loan. If you are healthy and less than 45–50 years old, you may very well be better off using that same money to buy term life insurance, instead.[6]

Costs of Financing

We have seen that most auto loans are made on an installment basis. On these loans, your total interest cost can amount to a substantial sum. For example, if you borrow 80 percent of the cost of a new $12,500 automobile and repay the loan over four years, your total interest cost on this $10,000 loan at a 10 percent yearly rate amounts to $2174. That interest expense adds a lot to the overall cost of your car.

Because total interest costs can vary so much among loans, it becomes important for you to understand the mechanics of an automobile installment

[6] *Family Circle,* May 6, 1986, p. 30.

Table 7.1 MONTHLY PAYMENTS AND INTEREST COSTS

		36 MONTHS		48 MONTHS		60 MONTHS	
APR	Loan amount	Monthly payment	Total interest	Monthly payment	Total interest	Monthly payment	Total interest
9%	$ 6,000	$191	$ 869	$149	$1167	$125	$1473
	8,000	254	1158	199	1556	166	1964
	10,000	318	1448	249	1945	208	2455
10%	6,000	194	970	152	1305	127	1649
	8,000	258	1293	203	1739	170	2198
	10,000	323	1616	254	2174	212	2748
11%	6,000	196	1072	155	1444	130	1827
	8,000	262	1429	207	1925	174	2436
	10,000	327	1786	258	2406	217	3045
12%	6,000	199	1174	158	1584	133	2008
	8,000	266	1566	211	2112	178	2678
	10,000	332	1957	263	2640	222	3347

loan. Three factors affect the total amount of interest you pay over the life of a loan: the amount you borrow, the interest rate, and the length of the loan.

Most new-car loans today are repaid over 48 months, or in some instances 60 months. The duration of the repayment period is a crucial determinant of the total amount of interest you will pay. Although a longer repayment period lowers your monthly payments, it causes your total interest costs to increase. Table 7.1 shows this relationship. For example, the total interest costs on a $10,000 loan at a 10 percent **annual percentage rate (APR)** amounts to $1616 for 36 months, as opposed to $2748 for 60 months.[7] The longer repayment period costs you $1132 more over the life of the loan, even though the amount borrowed and the APR are the same.

In determining total interest cost, the APR is less of a factor than the duration of the loan. A difference of two or three percentage points between two otherwise identical loans has less effect on the amount of the monthly payment and the total interest cost than a difference of 12 months in the repayment period. Your budget largely determines the length of your repayment period. If you can afford slightly higher monthly payments with a shorter repayment

[7] APR is an abbreviation for annual percentage rate which is the true rate of interest on a loan. It takes into account the fact that the balance of the loan declines as the loan is repaid. A more complete discussion of APR appears in Chapter 5.

period, you will pay out less over the life of the loan. For example, Table 7.1 shows that the difference in the monthly payments between two $10,000 loans with a 10 percent APR—one for 36 months and one for 48 months—is $69 ($323 versus $254). If you can afford that additional amount each month, you will pay $558 ($1616 versus $2174) less in total interest over the duration of the loan.

LEASING AN AUTOMOBILE

In recent years, people have increasingly chosen to lease rather than purchase new cars. Today approximately one-fourth of all cars are leased, compared with less than one in 25 in 1970. You must evaluate many considerations before deciding whether leasing or purchasing is better.

Leasing Features

You can lease from leasing companies, automobile dealers, or commercial banks. Although leases can be arranged to cover almost any time period you desire, most leases run two to five years. There are two types of leases available to individuals. A **closed-end lease** requires you to pay a fixed monthly payment. At the end of the term you just walk away from the car. Under an **open-end lease** you still make a fixed monthly payment, but your final cost depends on the car's resale value. If at the end of the lease term the car sells for more than the leasing company estimated, you receive that extra money as a refund. If it sells for less, you must pay the difference. The monthly payment under an open-end lease is usually $15 to $40 less than for a comparable closed-end lease because you assume the risk of fluctuation in the leased car's final market value.

Comparing Lease and Purchase Costs

You may have seen an advertisement from an automobile leasing company claiming that because the monthly lease payment is lower than the monthly loan payment on the same car, the lease alternative is financially more attractive. Do not be misled by such claims. Comparing a lease payment to a loan payment makes no more sense than comparing the price of a new Rolls Royce to that of a Chevrolet and concluding that all foreign cars are more expensive than American cars. The following example provides a guideline for comparing the costs of purchasing and leasing.

Lease-Purchase Analysis: An Example

Bert and Mary Arnold were recently married and now want to obtain a new full-size car. The Arnolds estimate that they will use the car for four years. Because they have not yet saved enough money to make a cash purchase of the car, the Arnolds want to know whether they should buy the new car using borrowed money or lease the car. Therefore, they have the following two alternatives.

Alternative 1: The Arnolds' automobile dealer offers a new midsize car for $12,500 with a $2,500 cash down payment and a $10,000 installment loan (48 months, 10 percent APR).

Alternative 2: A local automobile leasing company quotes a $270 monthly payment for a closed-end lease on the same car. The leasing company pays sales taxes, but the Arnolds must make all other payments associated with owning and operating the car. The company also requires a security deposit amounting to two monthly payments.

The Comparison. We now directly compare the net cost of buying versus leasing an automobile. Under either alternative the Arnolds must pay the costs of gasoline, oil, maintenance, repairs, insurance, and the license. Therefore, we ignore these costs in the comparison because they will be the same under either alternative. Table 7.2 presents the computations pertaining to this comparison. The top part of the worksheet gives the costs of purchasing and the bottom part shows the costs of leasing.

As shown, the monthly installment loan payments over the four-year period comprise the largest expenditure when purchasing a car. The monthly payment of $254 was determined by referring to Table 7.1. At the end of the loan's term, total payments will have amounted to $12,192. An additional $2500 is spent on the down payment. Two other costs pertain to this purchase. A 5 percent state sales tax equals $625 and, assuming a 5 percent after-tax return, the forgone interest on the $2500 down payment totals $539 (if the car had not been bought, interest could have been earned on this amount). Combining all these purchase-

Table 7.2 COMPARING AUTOMOBILE PURCHASE AND LEASING COSTS

Purchase costs	
Down payment	$ 2,500
Total installment loan payments (48 months × $254[a])	12,192
Sales tax on $12,500 purchase price at 5%	625
Interest forgone on $2500 down payment at 5% after-tax rate for four years	539
Total cost of purchasing	$15,856
Less: Resale value of car at the end of 4 years	5,000
Net cost of purchasing car	$10,856
Lease costs	
Total lease payments (48 months × $270)	$12,960
Interest forgone on $540 security deposit at 5% after-tax rate for 4 years	116
Net cost of leasing car	$13,076

[a] Value determined in Table 7.1 for a $10,000 loan for 48 months at 10 percent APR.

Table 7.3 AUTOMOBILE RESALE VALUE AS PERCENTAGE OF PURCHASE PRICE

Type of automobile	First year	Second year	Third year	Fourth year	Fifth year
Subcompact	84	73	63	53	43
Compact	82	69	59	49	40
Midsize	78	63	50	40	32
Large	76	58	45	34	28

SOURCE: U.S. Department of Transportation.

related costs produces a $15,856 total cost. However, at the end of four years the Arnolds will own the car outright and can then sell it at the fair market value. Table 7.3 shows that after four years a midsize car should retain about 40 percent of its original purchase price. This amount ($12,500 × 40 percent = $5,000) reduces the net purchase cost to $10,856.

The primary leasing expenses are the 48 monthly payments at $270 each. These payments total $12,960. In addition, the Arnolds forfeit the interest that they would have earned on the $540 security deposit. The security deposit itself is not a cost of leasing because this amount is returned to them at the expiration of the lease. Therefore, the net cost of leasing for four years is $13,076.

In this instance the Arnolds should elect to buy the car instead of lease. Total purchase costs ($10,856) are $2,220 less than total lease costs ($13,076). This example presents a realistic picture of the relative costs. In general, leasing is 20 to 25 percent more expensive than buying over a four-year period. There are exceptions, but generally the longer you drive a car, the more expensive leasing becomes. By making a lease-purchase cost comparison, you can determine the most advantageous financial arrangement.

Some people believe that leasing or owning offers special tax breaks. That notion is wrong. The costs of business driving are tax deductible and personal driving costs are not—no matter how you hold the car. Actually, it used to be that owning a car for personal driving did offer a special advantage over leasing: The sales tax and interest payments were tax deductible. With the passage of the Tax Reform Act of 1986, these deductions were eliminated (or substantially phased out) for personal automobiles, so no real tax advantage exists.

COSTS OF OWNING AND OPERATING AN AUTOMOBILE

When considering the cost of owning and operating an automobile, you may first think of the monthly installment payment. However, owning a car entails many more expenses. Before you purchase a car, you should carefully determine the total costs of operating it. In this section we briefly discuss the primary types of expenses encountered in owning an automobile.

Automobile expenses fall into two basic categories. **Fixed costs** do not change with the number of miles driven. Examples of fixed costs include depreciation, interest, and insurance premiums. Your car depreciates in value even if you never drive it out of the garage. Likewise, you must continue interest payments whether or not you drive. **Variable costs** vary directly with the number of miles driven. For example, you pay for gasoline only if you drive your car. The more miles you drive, the higher your gasoline bill. Maintenance and repairs are other variable-cost items.

The major expenses you must consider in operating a car are (1) depreciation, (2) interest, (3) insurance, (4) gasoline, and (5) maintenance and repairs.

Depreciation

Most consumer durable goods decline in value over a period of time, and automobiles are no exception. This erosion process is called **depreciation.** In general, the longer you own a car, the more its value depreciates. However, depreciation does not occur at a constant rate. As soon as you drive a new car off the showroom floor, you incur what is known as the **cost of acquisition.** That cost amounts to the difference between the amount you paid for the car and its immediate resale value. In some instances, this cost can total as much as 20 percent of the original purchase price. This is especially true for larger models.

After that immediate decline in a car's value, depreciation continues but at a slower rate. The largest depreciation is in the first year of ownership. After that, the rate of depreciation gradually declines. Once you have owned a car for several years, the decrease in market value for one more year of ownership is relatively small.

Referring back to Table 7.3 we emphasize that the resale value of an automobile declines over time. You can see that the depreciation rate for the first year is large. For example, a typical midsize car loses 22 percent of its value in the first year of ownership. Of course, much of this first-year value decline is due to the cost of acquisition. In the fifth year, however, the same car's value declines only eight percentage points. You may also notice that smaller cars generally depreciate less rapidly than the larger vehicles. After five years, a large model retains only 28 percent of its original value, but a subcompact still retains 43 percent of its initial price.

Interest

If you borrow money to buy a car, you will have to pay interest. Most auto loans are repaid in equal installments so that the amount of interest paid per year gradually declines until the loan is paid off. We discussed this important cost of ownership earlier in this chapter, and you might refer back to that section (Financing an Automobile) to determine how this expense will affect your purchase decision.

Insurance

Automobile insurance is a necessary cost of owning a car. Many states require you to be insured before you drive. As the costs of claims have risen, so has the cost of insurance. We discuss this important item in Chapter 8.

Gasoline

Once a relatively inexpensive item, gasoline has increased in cost in recent decades. Many consumers have responded to this increased cost by downsizing their automobile purchases—that is, by buying smaller cars that get better gasoline mileage. You can also reduce gasoline costs by driving less, driving at slower speeds, or tuning up your auto more often. At a price of $1 a gallon, for example, a typical midsize automobile costs about 5¢ per mile for gasoline.

Maintenance and Repairs

The amount you are likely to spend on maintenance and repairs is closely related to the number of miles driven. Older models with higher mileages tend to cost more to maintain than newer cars. In early 1987, for example, *Consumer Reports* estimated the average maintenance and repair costs for a typical automobile to vary according to the model year as follows:[8]

AVERAGE REPAIR COST PER MODEL YEAR[a]

1981	1982	1983	1984	1985
$430	$380	$300	$210	$110

[a] No estimate is given for 1986 models because most of their repair costs should be covered under warranty. The costs of accident repairs, tires, and batteries are omitted.

As shown, the average cost of maintaining a relatively new 1985 model is approximately one-fourth of the expense of caring for a 1981 model. You should also know that some models, on average, tend to require more maintenance and repairs than others. In your research you should check the repair records of earlier models for signs of the kinds of problems that might develop in a current model.

[8] Copyright 1987 by Consumers Union of United States, Inc., Mount Vernon, NY 10553. Excerpted by permission from *Consumer Reports,* April 1987, p. 248.

Analyzing the Costs of Ownership

You may be surprised to see how expensive owning and operating an automobile is. You may think that once you have paid for the car all that is left are expenses for gasoline, an occasional oil change, and an even less frequent tire change. Nothing could be further from the truth. Interest, insurance, taxes, licenses, and maintenance and repairs are substantial expenses. You must account for all of these expenses when estimating the cost of owning a car. The following case example provides an illustration of how to determine the cost of owning an automobile.

Cost of Owning an Automobile: An Example. After comparing the costs of leasing and purchasing, Bert and Mary Arnold decide to buy the $12,500 *midsize* automobile previously described. Although they have determined that buying is the least costly alternative, they do not know exactly how much it will cost to operate that car each year. You will recall that we intentionally ignored the costs of gasoline, oil, licenses, insurance, and maintenance and repairs because these payments are the same under either alternative. To determine the total costs of operating the auto, however, we must consider all costs involved in owning and operating the car.

We previously identified the primary costs of driving. Now we present a numerical example to illustrate the Arnolds' estimated costs of driving for each of their first five years of ownership. These costs may be slightly different for you because insurance, gasoline, and maintenance and repair expenses may vary in different parts of the country. Nevertheless, the following illustration provides a guideline for estimating the total expenses of driving a car 15,000 miles a year:

1 *Depreciation.* By referring back to Table 7.3, we can determine the amount of depreciation for each of the first five years of ownership. This yearly amount is calculated as follows:

   Value of the auto at the beginning of the year *minus*
   the auto's value at the end of the year *equals*
   annual depreciation

   For example, the first year's estimated depreciation is $2750, determined as follows:

   $12,500 (original purchase price) *minus*
   $ 9,750 (resale value after one year, or
   $12,500 *times* 78 percent) equals $2,750

   Subsequent years' depreciation is calculated in the same way.

2 *Interest.* In this example, the Arnolds borrow $10,000 on a 48-month installment basis at a 10 percent APR, which produces a $254 monthly payment. The interest portion of the monthly payment gradually de-

creases over time. In their first year of ownership, for example, the Arnolds pay $900 of interest expense, but by the fourth year their interest cost is only $144. The principal repayment component of the monthly payment is not an expense because this amount builds equity in the car.

3 *Insurance.* We base the Arnold's annual insurance expense on a non-business-use automobile with $100 deductible comprehensive, $250 deductible collision, $100,000/$300,000 liability, and $25,000 property damage coverage (see Chapter 8 for a more detailed description of these coverages). This kind of coverage currently costs about $450 annually. We assume this cost to remain the same over the five-year analysis period. Actually, the collision portion of the coverage will gradually decline as the car depreciates, but we assume this decline is offset by price increases in other components of the coverage.

4 *License Fee.* The license fee is based on the weight of the auto. The current average license fee for a midsize car is about $50 a year, but this fee may vary greatly from state to state. Because the car's weight presumably remains the same, this expense does not change from year to year.

5 *Personal Property Taxes.* A personal property tax is charged based upon the car's estimated market value. Because the car's resale value gradually declines, this expense will become smaller each year. For a new midsize car this tax is about $40 in the first year of ownership but is estimated to fall to $16 by the fifth year. This expense may also differ considerably among states.

6 *Gasoline.* We assume that the cost of gasoline will be $1.00 per gallon for each of the next five years and that the Arnolds' new car averages 20 miles per gallon (5¢ gasoline cost per mile). If they drive 15,000 miles each year, the annual gasoline expense equals $750. That is, you multiply the gasoline cost of 5¢ per mile by 15,000 miles to arrive at $750. Of course, this amount can change considerably if gasoline prices vary or if you drive a different number of miles than assumed in this example.

7 *Oil.* We assume the Arnolds spend $40 a year on oil for their car. If maintained properly, the car should not use much more oil as it grows older. A neglected car, however, will experience substantial cost increases for this item.

8 *Maintenance and Repairs.* Maintenance and repair expenses are small on a new automobile, especially while it is still under warranty. The first-year expenditure for this category may total only $150. However, as the Arnolds' car ages, they can reasonably expect more things to go wrong. Older cars simply cost more to maintain than new ones.

Explanation of Cost of Ownership Calculations. In Table 7.4 we itemize the Arnolds' costs of owning an automobile for each of the first five years. You will notice that total expenses decline noticeably in the second and third years, but

Table 7.4 COSTS OF OWNING AND OPERATING AN AUTOMOBILE: BERT AND MARY ARNOLD

	YEAR OF OWNERSHIP				
	One	Two	Three	Four	Five
Fixed expenses:					
Depreciation	$2750	$2125	$1375	$1250	$1000
Interest	900	670	421	144	0
Insurance	450	450	450	450	450
License fee	50	50	50	50	50
Personal property tax	40	31	24	20	16
Total fixed expenses	$4190	$3326	$2320	$1914	$1516
Variable expenses:					
Gasoline	$ 750	$ 750	$ 750	$ 750	$ 750
Oil	40	40	40	40	40
Maintenance and repairs	150	275	400	550	900
Miscellaneous	150	175	200	250	325
Total variable expenses	$1090	$1240	$1390	$1590	$2015
Total expenses	$5280	$4566	$3710	$3504	$3531
Cost per mile (15,000 miles)	35.2¢	30.4¢	24.7¢	23.4¢	23.6¢

then remain roughly the same for the next two years. The first year, it costs 35.2¢ per mile to operate the car; more than half of this cost is depreciation. This example illustrates three important relationships:

1 Depreciation gradually declines. The longer you own the car, the less the annual depreciation cost.
2 If the car is financed with an installment loan, the interest expense grows smaller each year.
3 In general, the older the car becomes, the greater are maintenance and repair expenditures.

The net result of this analysis is that a new car is expensive to operate in the first year, mainly because of the large decline in the car's resale value. After that year, the cost of operating a car usually declines for several years. At some point in time, however, a car will become more expensive to operate. This is because increasing maintenance and repair expenses more than offset the decline in depreciation and interest costs. For example, Table 7.4 shows that the Arnolds' cost of operating their car increases slightly in year five after having declined in each of the prior three years. Over the entire five-year period, the car's estimated operating costs average 27.5¢ per mile.

Operating Costs and Car Size

We determined that Bert and Mary Arnold would spend about 27.5¢ per mile yearly to operate their new midsize car for the first five years. The Arnolds may want to compare their cost estimate to the national cost average for operating a car. Table 7.5 shows the average cost of operating automobiles of various sizes. This table reveals that, on average, a midsize automobile costs an estimated 27.8¢ per mile each year to operate—very close to the Arnolds' 27.5¢ per mile annual average. An important relationship emerges from the information in this table: Smaller cars cost less to operate than larger ones. For example, these estimates show that a full-size auto is about one-third more expensive to operate than a subcompact. Therefore, if your budget is stretched too thin, you may want to consider downsizing the car you plan to buy.

BUYING A USED CAR

You may find that the average $11,000 retail price of a new car is somewhat beyond your budget. If so, you may do like 17 million people did in 1986—buy a used car. A used car may afford you the opportunity to buy a more luxurious or better-equipped car than you might be able to obtain otherwise. But you must be careful. Many used cars have serious problems. You will want to take steps to avoid someone else's "lemon." If you are willing to devote some time and effort to the selection process, you can probably find an attractive and reasonably priced used car. There are five basic steps you should follow in evaluating a used car: (1) Determine the model that best fits your needs, (2) find the best selling source, (3) inspect the car, (4) obtain an outside evaluation, and (5) determine a fair price.

Table 7.5 COST OF OWNING AND OPERATING AN AUTOMOBILE (CENTS PER MILE)[a]

Size of car	Taxes and fees	Depreciation	Maintenance & repairs	Tires	Gasoline	Insurance	Parking	Total
Subcompact	1.4	5.9	4.5	0.4	4.3	4.9	0.9	22.7
Compact	1.6	7.3	3.9	0.4	4.5	4.3	0.9	23.3
Midsize	1.8	8.6	4.5	0.5	5.5	5.6	0.9	27.8
Large	2.2	9.6	5.1	0.7	6.8	4.9	0.9	30.6

[a] Estimates (1984) based on vehicle operated in Baltimore, Maryland, area with an assumed life span of 12 years and 120,000 miles.

SOURCE: U.S. Federal Highway Administration, *Cost of Owning and Operating Automobiles and Vans,* periodic.

Determining the Best Model

Before you begin to shop for a used car, you should determine what model best fits your needs. Your budget will partially determine your needs, but you will want to consider other factors. Are you looking for an economy auto to drive to work? Do you need a large car or station wagon to transport your family? Are you seeking out that special sports car to project a certain image? Let the answers to these and other pertinent questions guide you to the proper model. If you know what kind of car you want, you can save many frustrating hours of looking at cars that are of no interest to you.

Finding a Seller

Generally, there are two sources of used cars: private sellers and used-car dealers. You can locate private sellers through newspaper ads, word of mouth, bulletin boards, and so forth. Often, a private seller will offer a better price than a used-car dealer. The private seller usually wants to sell a car more quickly than a dealer. Also, the private seller is probably not as aware of prevailing prices as a dealer would be. On the other hand, a used-car dealer displays many used cars in one location, thus making comparison shopping more convenient. A dealer usually has service facilities available to repair cars. In some cases, a used-car dealer may offer a 90-day warranty on the cars it sells. This warranty may cost extra or may be included in the purchase price. Either way, this feature protects you against major problems that you did not detect during the initial inspection.

Inspection

Once you find a car you like, you should carefully inspect its condition. You may feel very uncomfortable about this inspection, and with good reason. Many sellers will not give you the complete details about a car's condition. Therefore, you must conduct a careful inspection of the car to make sure you are getting what you bargain for. You can learn a lot by performing a thorough, common-sense examination. This process must include a test drive for you to make a reasonable assessment of the car's condition. Fortunately, you do not have to be a mechanical genius to perform a careful inspection. Figure 7.2 illustrates eight important areas you must consider before buying a used car. Of course, you may also want to inspect other areas before making your final decision.

Outside Evaluation

You may not be very confident about your ability to inspect a used car, or you may not have the time or inclination to conduct such an activity. In such an instance, you may hire a professional mechanic to examine the car. Although this independent analysis may cost you $50 or so, it may uncover a deficiency

Figure 7.2 EIGHT CRUCIAL USED-CAR CHECKPOINTS

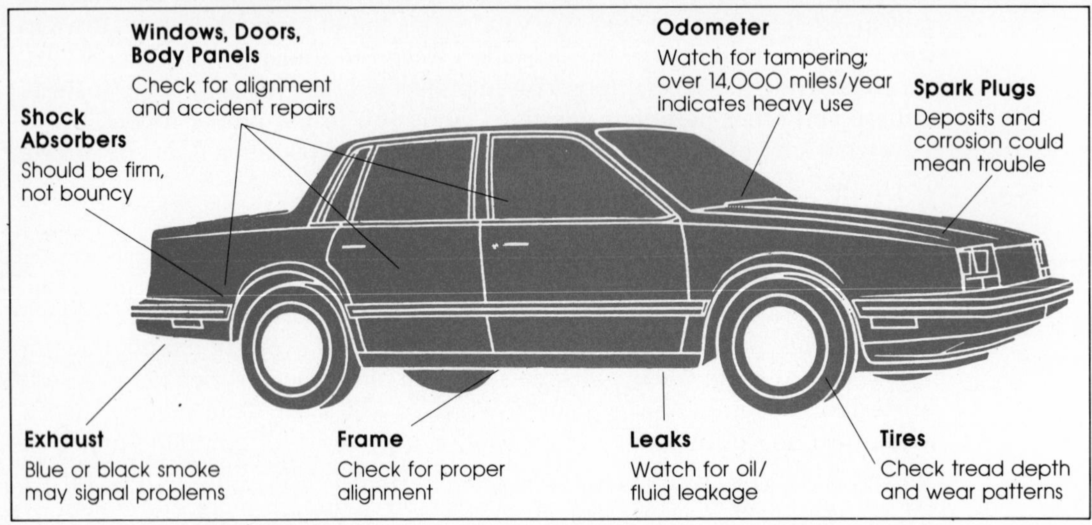

SOURCE: *Consumers Digest*, April 1986, p. 46.

that could save you several hundred dollars. You can take the car to a local electronic diagnostic center that, for $15 to $25, will analyze vital components and give you a summary report.

Determining a Fair Price

Even if you find a "creampuff" of a used car, you will want to buy it only if the price is reasonable. Check the local newspaper ads to determine the asking prices of comparable models. The National Automobile Dealers Association (NADA) publishes the *Official Used Car Guide.*[9] This monthly guide shows the average retail, average loan, and average trade-in values for each domestic and imported vehicle. It also provides information on the effect of different mileages on the value of various cars and on the value of extra equipment such as air conditioning, automatic transmission, and stereo tape deck. Your local bank or public library will probably have a copy of this publication.

SELLING YOUR CAR

Eventually the time comes when you want to sell your car. You may decide that you can get a better price by trying to sell the car yourself rather than trading

[9] This guide can be obtained through the NADA, 8400 West Park Drive, McLean, Virginia 22102.

the car in on a new model. To obtain the best price for your car you should consider the following:

1 *Appearance.* No one wants a dirty car. You get an advantage by offering a car that is neat and clean. The time taken to wash and wax the car and clean the interior is usually rewarded with a better sales price. Be sure you clean under the hood; a filthy engine is a major buyer turnoff.
2 *Condition.* Your car should be in proper working order. The few dollars spent to restore your car to good condition can be an excellent investment. This is especially true about obvious defects such as a broken air conditioner or a failing battery. You may be able to save by making minor repairs yourself.
3 *Price.* Determine a fair market price. You cannot sell your car for more than it is worth. Be careful not to underprice the car. Many savvy used-car buyers are looking for a bargain at your expense. A quick check of used-car dealers will reveal their asking prices. You will also want to consult the NADA *Guide.*
4 *Advertising.* Word of mouth is an excellent and inexpensive advertising method, as is the use of free bulletin boards at school or work. Classified ads in local newspapers are reasonably priced and reach the largest audiences, especially on the weekends. The more people who know your car is for sale, the better is your chance of finding the right buyer.

BUYING FURNITURE AND APPLIANCES

After your home and car, your next largest expenditures may be for furniture and appliances. Because the costs of furniture and appliances can be large, you should carefully plan before making these purchases. You will probably make a much wiser selection if you follow the six-step planning process we introduced earlier in this chapter. A brief explanation of how each step in this process may affect your decision to buy furniture and appliances follows.

Your Spending Allowance

When you visit a furniture or appliance store, you will probably see many items that would fit nicely in your home. The temptation to buy may be great. But you should carefully examine the effect of any purchase of furniture and appliances on your overall budget. Ideally, you will have already prepared an annual budget that allocates a portion of your income to the purchase of these items. By keeping within your budget, you can be confident that you will still have enough money for other necessary purchases. Also, if you limit your furniture and appliance purchases to a predetermined, fixed amount, you will more likely have the discipline to shop for those products that best satisfy your needs. You may want to refer to Chapter 2 to review key budgetary considerations.

Box 7.1 BEFORE YOU SELL YOUR CAR

When Nattadis Diskul began advertising his 1984 Camaro Z28 earlier this month, he was confident that selling the fully loaded T-top sports car for $10,500 would be a breeze. He was asking only what the "blue book," a catchall name for several used-car price guides, said the car was worth at retail. Diskul thought it would be tougher to sell his '79 Dodge Omni with 60,000 miles and a repair history that would make a mechanic's mouth water.

But in the first five days, not one buyer materialized for the Camaro—now on the market in Washington, D.C., for $9,500—and it looks like the lemon might be easier to unload than the peach.

Diskul's woes tell a lot about today's used-car market and why hordes of owners are trying to sell their cars themselves. The recent flurry in new-car buying, induced by rock-bottom financing rates, rebates and other incentives, has swollen dealers' inventories of used cars. So many cars are on the market that dealers are offering an average $500 to $1,000 less on trade-ins than they were earlier in the year. "I'm flooded with junk," complains Frank Berger, resale manager at a Scottsdale, Ariz., Cadillac dealership.

Regardless of the glut, the best way to get the most for your used car may well be to do what Diskul is having trouble doing—sell it yourself. The effort can be a monumental hassle, but the private market usually reaps the highest price. Selling outright to a dealer

Satisfying Your Needs

Not all furniture and appliances satisfy the same consumer needs. For example, a refrigerator would be more important to a newlywed couple than would the latest model video recorder. Unfortunately, most of us do not have sufficient resources to buy all the furniture and appliances we want. Rather, we must be selective in our purchases. Some decisions are relatively easy. For example, you know that you need basic items such as a range, refrigerator, bed, and table and chairs. You may think you need other items such as a color television set and a microwave oven. Time devoted to ranking the importance of furniture and appliances in satisfying your needs is wisely spent.

for cash usually brings in the least, and a trade-in yields something in between.

Before putting a car on the market, know how much it is worth at both retail and wholesale and how much you still owe on it. "People think trading in an '85 or '84 car on a new one is like refinancing their house at a lower interest rate," says Frank Gutierrez, used-car manager at a Dublin, Calif., dealership. "It doesn't work that way. The car depreciates, the house appreciates." Thus, a 1984 model might be worth $6,000 in trade-in while the owner still owes $8,000 in payments.

To price your car, start with the retail value in the blue book, which often means the *NADA* (National Automobile Dealers Association) *Official Used Car Guide,* available at many public libraries and banks. Some people advise setting the price between the retail and wholesale levels. Check your price against listings for similar cars advertised in your area. Prices vary by region.

If you're selling a late-model car, be ready to accept less than the listed retail value. The larger the incentives on new cars, the less inclined consumers are to buy 1985s or 1984s. Notes Bob Gurney, sales manager for Firestone Chrysler-Plymouth in Downey, Calif.: A used 1985 Chrysler Fifth Avenue sells for about $14,000 with financing at about 13 percent. A new Fifth Avenue costs $16,000 to $17,000, but financing is only 4.8 percent. "We're talking almost the same figures, so why would anyone want the used car?" asks Gurney.

In today's market, older cars often stand a better chance of being bought than do newer ones. Says Gurney: "I'm selling a lot more used cars in the $4,000-to-$5,000 range than I've ever sold."

Hassles in Store

Don't discount the headache element when unloading your wheels. Before you dive in, make sure your car lives up to its billing; savvy buyers won't deal until the car has passed muster with a mechanic. Then, decide if you want to take calls at the office, many of which won't result in anything but conversation. Are you prepared to stay home weekends and put up with a string of no-shows? Do you want strangers coming to your home?

There is a personal-risk element, too. If you're selling a high-priced car, say a Mercedes, or if you live alone, experts advise selling your car from a public lot such as a gas station during daylight hours to reduce the danger of robbery.

Finding an interested buyer isn't enough. There's still the question of payment. A prospective purchaser might be put off by the high interest rates on used-car loans—usually 13 or 14 percent nowadays. The older the car, the higher the financing rate will be.

SOURCE: Copyright 1986, *U.S. News & World Report.* Reprinted from issue of October 20, 1986.

Conducting Research

Many of the same sources that provide important buying information on automobiles also give evaluations on other consumer durables. A visit to your local library will enable you to gather valuable data about virtually any type of consumer durable. All too often an individual omits this important step only to find later that he or she has made a poor purchase. Armed with information gathered from your research, you are much more likely to make a wise and economical purchase. You may also wish to research any service contracts associated with the potential purchase. With a **service contract,** you pay an annual premium in exchange for the seller's or manufacturer's agreement to repair the item at

Box 7.2 ARE SERVICE CONTRACTS WORTH IT?

You have finally made up your mind—this car is exactly what you want. But no sooner do you decide than the salesperson poses a troubling scenario: As good as it may be, the car could fall apart after your warranty expires. Why take the chance? An "extended-service contract" will protect you.

Extended-service contracts, also known as extended warranties, are sold on everything from automobiles to videocassette recorders to computers. Hundreds of retailers, manufacturers and independent underwriters have a stake in the business. Jack Gillis, author of *The Car Book,* estimates that the service contract is one of the most profitable "options" a car dealer sells, after financing.

Sellers gamble that revenue will exceed the cost of claims. Usually they win the bet. For that reason—and because it is broached most often as an afterthought—the extended-service contract should be approached with a large degree of skepticism.

Think of a service contract as insurance—you pay a "premium" as protection against expensive breakdowns. Then try to analyze the likelihood of facing these expenses, and compare that with the cost of the contract. General Electric charges around $30 for a year's contract on one new refrigerator. That seems cheap, but refrigerators are hardy appliances that may remain trouble-free for decades. Solid-state electronics products, if they don't break down while under warranty, are apt to last indefinitely.

Consider the value of the product and how intensively it is used. Warrantech Corporation in New York sells a three-year contract on television sets for $80. An outrageous expense for someone who is rarely at home, it may seem reasonable to a family of TV addicts.

Sometimes, the prospect of product failure is so daunting that a contract can make sense, provided you know exactly what services you are buying. Cars—mechanically complex and expensive to repair—are cases in point. Ford sells about 100 different plans. They can cost as little

little or no cost in the future. It offers you protection against expensive repairs.

Finding the Best Buy

Even after you determine which items of furniture or appliances best satisfy your needs, you still have work to do to find the best buy. You will want to follow these steps:

1 Investigate the various brands, models, and features to determine which best satisfy your needs and fall within your budget. Consumer magazines, such as *Consumers Digest,* can help your investigation. Visits to local stores and dealers to visually inspect the products can provide important information.
2 After completing your investigation, reduce your alternatives to two or three brands or models that best conform to your needs. You should become especially knowledgeable about these brands or models before making the final purchase.
3 Shop for the best buy. Prices vary substantially for most furniture and

as $240 for three years and as much as $1,335 for five years. The advantage is that buyers will know at the outset that they never need worry about at least some repair costs. But virtually every auto plan exempts whole categories of repairs from coverage—batteries, tires, brake pads, clutches and other wear-and-tear items.

Should you decide to purchase such peace of mind, study the documents before you sign. Contracts vary widely in what they cover and how service is rendered. Here are some questions that bear asking:

- How does the service contract dovetail with warranty coverage? There's little point in a contract from date of purchase on a product that carries a warranty.
- How reliable is the company backing the contract? "It should have considerable reserves," warns Joel San Antonio, head of Warrantech. "It shouldn't be paying claims today with funds it took in yesterday."
- What is excluded? If a part or the cost of labor is not explicitly included, you should expect to pay for it yourself.
- Is there a deductible? Each one paid adds to your cost of the contract. For autos, deductibles typically are $25 to $75 per visit.
- Where can you get service? How will billing be handled? Ford prefers that you return to your dealer, although you can get help at any of 6,100 outlets. The dealer bills the company. GM reimburses for work done at any shop. If your GE dishwasher acts up while under contract, a technician will come to you.

Obviously, there are no hard-and-fast rules. You're best off using some common sense, taking a few days to determine your tolerance for risk and decide without being rushed. It's a rare buyer of a service contract who gets back more than he or she puts in.

SOURCE: Copyright 1986, *U.S. News & World Report.* Reprinted from issue of July 7, 1986.

appliances. You will want to consider both retailers and discounters. You may also find that the item you desire can be purchased cheaper through a mail-order catalog. Assume that you decide to buy a new bedroom set. After careful deliberation, you conclude that the Henredon Scene One bedroom set best satisfies your needs. This set retails for $7583. Can you get a better price? Table 7.6 provides the answer. The price ranges are large. In this case you can buy the bedroom set through a catalog for $2799—63 percent less than the retail price. Clearly, it pays to shop for expensive items of furniture and appliances.

Negotiating a Price

After you have found the specific item you want, it is time to negotiate a price. Furniture and appliance dealers (including some discounters) will often bargain. In some cases all you have to do is ask to get the dealer to lower a price. In other instances the dealer may be more reluctant to change a posted price. Sometimes you can obtain a much better price if you settle for a floor model or last year's model. Dealers frequently make sizable concessions to sell these items. Finally, you may want to consider used furniture or appliances. These items

Table 7.6 PRICES FOR HENREDON SCENE ONE BEDROOM SET (1986)

Source	Price	In-home delivery	Total
Discounters			
Blackwelder's	$3565	$230	$3795
Country Furniture	3847	300	4147
Retailers			
Marshall Field (regular)	$7583	$ 15	$7598
Marshall Field (sale)	4545	5	4560
Catalog			
Spiegel	$2799	None	$2799

SOURCE: *Consumers Digest*, March 1986, p. 43.

generally have long lives and, therefore, the wear they show may be more than offset by the more favorable price.

Arranging Financing

If you do not have enough cash available to pay for an item of furniture or an appliance, you will probably have to borrow money to make the purchase. Many lenders, such as commercial banks, consumer finance companies, and credit unions, stand ready to make installment loans on these purchases. These types of loans are discussed in detail in Chapters 4 and 5. In some instances the dealer from whom you buy may have credit available. In addition, many dealers extend special terms that may allow you to buy without obtaining credit. Some furniture and appliance dealers offer "30-60-90 day" terms, which require the payment for the merchandise in three monthly installments without interest. You will want to investigate the available financing alternatives because financing costs can vary considerably among the various lending sources.

SUMMARY

Since the purchase of consumer durables can have a major impact on your budget, you should plan carefully before you buy. There are six important steps in planning a major consumer expenditure: (1) determine how much you can spend, (2) identify your needs, (3) conduct research, (4) shop for the best buy, (5) negotiate a price, and (6) arrange financing. With proper planning, your dollars will stretch further and you will be assured that you buy only what you need.

Next to your house, your automobile will probably be your most expensive acquisition. Prices for the same model can vary substantially among dealers, so it is even more important for you to research and shop for the best deal and negotiate a favorable price. The financing package you arrange can also make a sizable difference in the overall cost of a car. You will want to examine each of the three main types of car loans (installment, balloon, and single-payment) and each of the several sources of financing.

The costs of operating an automobile may vary among the different models and makes. Both fixed and variable costs must be evaluated to determine how much it costs to operate your car. Some people may find leasing to be a more attractive alternative than buying. By performing a lease-purchase analysis, you can determine which alternative is best for you. You may also want to consider the potential savings associated with the purchase of a used car.

Other major consumer assets, such as furniture and appliances, have important implications for your budget. Because they are relatively expensive items, when planning your purchases you should carefully consider such factors as costs, need satisfaction, durability and reliability, operating and maintenance costs, and appearance.

KEY TERMS

annual percentage rate (APR)
balloon loan
closed-end lease
consumer durables
cost of acquisition
depreciation
fixed costs
installment loan
manufacturer's suggested list price
open-end lease
service contract
single-payment loan
variable costs

SELECTED READINGS

"Buying Guide." *Consumers Digest,* published annually in November–December issue.

Consumer Reports Annual Automobile Buying Guide, published in April of each year by the editors of *Consumer Reports.*

"Deals on Wheels: Get the Best Car for Your Money." *Family Circle,* November 5, 1985, pp. 73–77.

"Great Furniture, Great Prices." *Consumers Digest,* March 1986, pp. 42–45.

"How to Get the Best New Car Deal." *Better Homes and Gardens,* May 1986, pp. 91–94.

"Service Contracts: Hype or Help?" *Changing Times,* August 1986, pp. 69–74.

"Used Cars: Good Bets and Bad." *Consumer Reports,* April 1985, pp. 248–250.

QUESTIONS

1 Identify the six steps that a consumer should follow in planning a major consumer expenditure.

2 Should you normally test-drive an automobile when you are in the *early* stages of shopping for the best deal?

3 What are the normal markups for subcompacts, compacts and intermediates, and full-size cars? What is the normal markup on options?

4 How much over dealer invoice should you generally expect to pay?

5 Describe the general characteristics of an installment loan and a balloon loan for an auto purchase.

6 Identify the most commonly used financing outlets on automobile loans.

7 Identify the three factors that interact to determine the total amount of interest paid over the life of an automobile loan.

8 Does the length of an auto loan or the APR tend to have a greater impact on total interest paid?

9 Compare a closed-end lease and an open-end lease. Which lease usually has a lower monthly payment? Why?

10 In recent years, which types of automobiles have depreciated the least during the initial few years of ownership? You may want to refer to Table 7.3.

11 Identify the major expenses that must be considered in operating a car. Explain how these expenses may change as the car ages.

12 In which year in the life of a car are operating costs, as defined in the chapter, usually the highest? Explain.

13 In general, the costs of owning an automobile decline in the second and third years of ownership, but then remain approximately the same for the next few years. Explain the three underlying relationships that are responsible for this pattern of yearly costs.

14 Identify the steps to follow in evaluating a used car.

15 What are three possible outlets for purchasing furniture and appliances? Which tends to be the cheapest?

16 What do the terms "30-60-90 day" mean for a furniture or appliance loan?

17 You wish to purchase a new $10,000 automobile and propose to borrow 80 percent of the cost at a 9 percent annual interest rate. Compare the amount of monthly payment and the amount of total interest paid over the life of the loan for a 36-month and a 60-month installment loan. Use Table 7.1 to answer this question.

18 You are going to borrow $10,000 on an auto loan. Indicate which of the following two alternatives will provide the smaller amount of total interest: a 36-month installment loan at 12 percent interest or a 48-month installment loan at a 10 percent interest. Once again, use Table 7.1 in your analysis.

19 Assume you are going to buy a compact car for $8000. Indicate the dollar resale value and depreciation (loss in value that takes place) over each of the first five years. Refer to Table 7.3 to do your analysis.

CASE PROBLEMS

7.1 Bob and Linda Swanson are considering the purchase of a new midsize car for $10,000. They plan to own and operate the car for five years. The Swansons note that state sales taxes on the purchase equal 5 percent. The automobile dealer offers them an installment loan with the following terms: 20 percent down payment and an $8000 loan with a 60-month life and a 9 percent annual percentage rate. The interest forgone on the funds tied up in the down payment will be $431. The car is expected to retain 32 percent of its resale value after five years.

Before they make the purchase, the Swansons want to investigate the costs of leasing the same car. The Mobile Leasing Company offers them a five-year closed-end lease at $180 monthly. A $500 security deposit is required. The leasing company pays sales taxes, but the Swansons must make all other payments associated with owning and operating the car. Follow the general procedures in Table 7.2 to:

- **a** Calculate the net cost of owning the car over the five-year period. In your calculations omit those expenses that are the same for both the purchase and lease alternatives, that is, gasoline, oil, maintenance, repairs, insurance, and license.
- **b** Calculate the net cost of leasing the car over the five-year period. The interest forgone on the funds tied up in the security deposit will be $108. In your calculations omit those expenses that are the same for both alternatives.
- **c** Should the Swansons purchase or lease the car? Explain.
- **d** Would your answer to part c above change if the car's resale value (after five years) was only 20 percent of the purchase price? Explain, showing calculations to justify your answer.

7.2 Morris and Lynn Cohen plan to buy a new $12,000 full-size automobile. After checking their current financial situation, the Cohens find that they have cash available to make a $2000 down payment. They also will pay a 5 percent state sales tax. The automobile dealer agrees to finance the remaining $10,000 with a 48-month installment loan at a 10 percent annual percentage rate.

The annual interest and principal payments on this loan are as follows:

Year	Interest	Principal
1	$900	$2,148
2	670	2,378
3	421	2,627
4	144	2,847

The Cohens estimate they will drive the car 15,000 miles yearly and get 20 miles per gallon of gasoline. The car is expected to depreciate at the same rate as typical large automobiles (see Table 7.3). In addition, they estimate the following expenses associated with owning the car:

Insurance (annual)	$500
Maintenance and repairs (annual)	200[a]
Oil (annual)	50
License (annual)	50
Personal property tax ($60 in year 1 and $46 in year 2)	
Gasoline (90¢ per gallon)	
Miscellaneous (annual)	200[b]

[a] Expected to increase 75 percent yearly.
[b] Expected to increase 50 percent yearly.

a Calculate the total fixed expenses incurred during each of the first two years of owning the new car. Follow the general procedure in Table 7.4.
b Calculate the total variable expenses incurred during each of the first two years of ownership.
c Calculate the cost per mile of owning and operating the car for the two years.
d Why does the cost per mile go down between the first and second year?
e How does the first-year total cost compare to that in Table 7.5 for a car of comparable size?

Appendix 7A

Purchasing a Personal Computer[1]

In an academic environment, have you ever been bombarded with too many facts and figures? That feeling is not restricted to the classroom. We are living in the Information Age. Computers have assisted many businesses and individuals through this time by helping them make better, more productive, and more profitable decisions.

If you own a personal computer, you may have used it to prepare for the college entrance exams, to write your papers, or to take an occasional break from the grind by playing a game. The last two uses may never leave you. Whether or not you own such a device, this appendix will help you to expand your knowledge of computers. In earlier chapters we have already discussed budgets, income taxes, and decision models. Businesses and individuals alike turn to the computer for these and many more uses.

WHAT IS A PERSONAL COMPUTER?

A **personal computer** is an electronic device used by *one* person to assimilate information (see Figure 7A.1). Think of a personal computer as you would your record player or compact disc player. The unit itself is tangible. You can see it and touch it. It has a physically hard appearance, but it can do nothing without records or compact discs. Yes, you can see and feel them, too, but you cannot read the words or listen to the music implanted on them. That transformation is reserved for the player.

Much the same is true of personal computers. The unit sitting on your desk—the CPU, the monitor, the disk drives, and the printer—is the **hardware**. The program disks that you created or bought are the **software**. The software gives the hardware purpose and the hardware brings life to the software.

[1] This appendix was developed by C. Kent Harrington in consultation with the authors. Mr. Harrington is the owner of C. Kent Harrington and Co., a management consulting firm, and president of Information Basics, Inc.

Figure 7A.1 IBM PERSONAL COMPUTER

SOURCE: IBM Corporation.

What Are the Major Hardware Components?

CPU. The central processing unit, or **CPU,** is the brain of the computer. It performs all the calculations and analyses. All processing is performed in its memory, just as all information processing takes place in our brains. Some computers have larger memory capacities, just as some people are endowed with higher IQs.

The computer's memory is classified into two different categories: RAM and ROM. Random-access memory, or **RAM,** is the type of memory usually associated with the processing capacity of a computer. It permits the user to read or write information to the CPU—in other words, to record information in the computer's brain.

The larger the memory or RAM of a personal computer, the more information it can process. But when RAM is used, the information is not stored permanently. Once the power is turned off or a particular program is stopped, the CPU "forgets" everything. It is necessary to reload or restart the process before the CPU will "remember" the facts. Fortunately, it can process new information very quickly.

Although the computer goes through many logical steps to make a decision, what is important to you is the decision it reaches. It is not our purpose in this appendix to teach you how the computer uses electronic impulses in a series of mathematical computations to produce answers. Any attempt to explain the process in detail would cloud your appreciation of what the computer can do.

Read-only memory, or **ROM,** is similar to RAM but is typically used to store software that might be frequently used by the computer. It is continuously accessible and must not be reloaded into RAM. In other words, it does not infringe on the limited memory capacity, which does all the processing.

Capacity is measured in terms of bytes. A **byte** is the equivalent of an alphabetic character or number. One **K** is equal to 1024 bytes. One megabyte, or **Meg,** is 1 million bytes. The same measurement technique is used whether talking about memory or storage.

CRT or Monitor. The cathode ray tube (CRT) or monitor or television set, if you will, allows you to see what is going on in the mind of the computer. The monitor can be either color or **monochrome,** single-color (usually green or amber letters on a black background).

Storage. Information is read into the CPU from storage devices called disks. When you want to see the information stored on a disk, you place the disk into a **disk drive,** which transmits the contents of the disk onto the CPU. The disks act like filing cabinets or drawers in a desk. When you want to know how much money is in your checking account, you retrieve the checkbook from your desk. Assuming you always put it back, it will always be there. Likewise, assuming you always store your documents or files on the disks, they will always be there. The information can be in the form of programs or data, that is, your own budget, tax information, or term paper.

The most common disk is the **floppy disk,** as shown in Figure 7A.2. It is about the size of a compact disc or a 45 rpm record. It is flexible and somewhat delicate. If you look closely at one, you can see grooves on the disk, similar to those on records, where information is recorded.

Hard disks are being used in greater numbers as their price declines. The difference between a hard disk and a floppy is that the **hard disk** is fixed in place in the computer, is not removable like the floppy, and can hold many times more information than a floppy. Whereas a floppy may contain 1.2 Meg,[2] a hard disk may hold as much as 250 Meg, with 10- to 30-Meg capacities being most common.

The same technology that has given us compact digital discs is providing optical disk systems with minimum capacities of 250 Meg. With this seemingly unlimited storage capacity, the only limitation facing personal computers appears to be their ability to process that amount of information in an efficient manner.

[2] A Meg is equal to 1 million alphabetic characters.

Figure 7A.2 FLOPPY DISKS

SOURCE: IBM Corporation.

Keyboard. The **keyboard** is the means by which you communicate with the computer. An example of an IBM keyboard is shown in Figure 7A.3. Instructions are issued or information is entered on the typewriterlike keys. The major visible difference from a typewriter is the presence of cursor keys and, possibly, function keys.

The cursor keys move the cursor (indicator of current location on the monitor) up or down or right or left. On a typewriter you must erase or white out to make a correction. Using the computer, you simply move the cursor to the spot and retype.

Function keys are not common to all computers, but they are to a majority. A function key is used to perform a given task, which might otherwise require typing several instructions. It may be preprogrammed or assigned by you.

Printer. Quality and speed of printing are the determining factors in selecting a printer. Available alternatives include dot matrix, letter quality, and laser. Examples of the first two are shown in Figure 7A.4.

The output of a **dot matrix** is usually discernible. Each letter is composed of a series of dots; however, as technology has improved, dot matrix has approached what is known as **letter quality,** the equivalent of material typed on a traditional typewriter.

Previously, a letter-quality printer required either a daisywheel—preformed letters on the tips of a wheel giving it the appearance of a daisy flower—or a

Figure 7A.3 IBM COMPUTER KEYBOARD

SOURCE: IBM Corporation.

thimble—letters on the edge of a device similar in appearance to a sewing thimble.

New laser technology has closed the gap between dot matrix and letter quality even more. In effect, a **laser** printer uses a copier technique to print a page at a time rather than a letter or character at a time. The result is a letter-quality document with a speed improvement over a letter-quality printer, which prints one page every two minutes, and a dot matrix, which prints two pages every one minute. Laser printers produce only the noise of a personal copier while printing eight to ten pages every minute. As with hard disks, you will see laser printers in greater numbers as costs continue to decline.

What Are the Major Software Categories?

Operating Systems. **The operating system** assumes the intermediate responsibility of interpreting the software requirements for the hardware. This system has also served as a standardization tool for software developers. In the early days of personal computers, the Control Program for Microcomputers (CP/M) operating system dominated. But with IBM's introduction of the IBM Personal Computer, a shift took place to the Disk Operating System (DOS), now the most widely used. AT&T has touted UNIX as the next system.

Each of these operating systems directs the computer to perform its duties in a different fashion. In other words, an application program—for example, in accounting—written to operate on a computer running the DOS operating system would not operate on one running UNIX. But how is a program written in

Figure 7A.4 DOT MATRIX VERSUS LETTER QUALITY PRINTING

Before: ABCDEFGHIJKLMNOPQRSTUVWXYZabcdef
After: ABCDEFGHIJKLMNOPQRSTUVWXYZabcdef

the first place? A **program** is a logical sequence of instructions that directs the computer to solve specific problems or to manipulate data.

Programming Languages. Different languages are used to give instructions to the computer. Some may seem as foreign as Greek or Russian. Though the names—such as BASIC, Pascal, COBOL, and Fortran—may be familiar, their dialect may not be. An example of a program listing in BASIC is presented in Figure 7A.5.

Application Programs. A program may be developed to perform any logical processing function, but why reinvent the wheel? For that reason, software companies have written accounting systems, budgeting systems, tax preparation programs, and more. These programs, are typically called **canned programs,** meaning that you must conform to their techniques. This may not seem desirable, but in reality it may be cheaper than programming a system on your own.

Application Tools. An alternative popularized in recent years by Lotus Development Corporation is one of using the major productivity tools—data base, spreadsheet, word processing, graphics, and communications—to develop the **application** (such as payroll processing or budgeting). Development time can be reduced by using a general language, meaning that someone at a high position in an organization, not a programmer, can write the application.

WHAT IS A PERSONAL COMPUTER USED FOR?

The major difference between personal computers and the other tools of our electronic age is that a personal computer cannot merely be plugged in and immediately produce beneficial results. Most of the time it requires a great deal of effort in the form of research, study, practice, and upkeep to maximize its potential. These reasons have caused people to reexamine the use of personal computers to ensure that they are productive rather than counterproductive tools.[3]

[3] "Searching for the Perfect Computer," *Wall Street Journal,* June 16, 1986, pp. 1D–4D.

Figure 7A.5 BASIC PROGRAM LISTING

```
10 LPRINT CHR$(27)"1";
20 LPRINT CHR$(27)":"CHR$(0)CHR$(0)CHR$(0)CHR$(0);
30 LPRINT CHR$(27)"%"CHR$(1)CHR$(0);
40 READ L: PRINT CHR$(L)
50 FOR Y=0 TO 1: FOR Z=0 TO 1: A = L + 128*Y + 32*Z
60 LPRINT CHR$(27)"&"CHR$(0)CHR$(A)CHR$(A);
70 LPRINT CHR$(139);
80 FOR X=1 TO 11: READ N: LPRINT CHR$(N);: NEXT X
90 NEXT Z: NEXT Y
100 A$"": INPUT "ENTER A STRING";A$: IF A$="" THEN 180
110 INPUT "ENTER A MASTER PRINT MODE NUMBER";M
120 LPRINT CHR$(27)"!"CHR$(M);
130 FOR Y=0 TO 1: FOR X=1 TO LEN(A$)
140 A = ASC(MID$(A$,X,1)).+ 128*Y
150 LPRINT CHR$(A)CHR$(A+32);
160 NEXT X: LPRINT: NEXT Y
170 LPRINT: GOTO 100
180 LPRINT CHR$(27)"@": STOP
250 ' G
260 DATA 71
270 DATA 0,15,16,0,32,31,64,0,64,0,64
280 DATA 64,4,72,2,32,2,24,4,0,0,0-
290 DATA 0,120,4,0,2,124,1,0,1,0,1
300 DATA 1,64,0,124,2,68,8,120,0,64,0
```

SOURCE: Program on page 217 of the *FX-80 User's Manual,* reproduced with permission of Epson America, Inc., copyright 1983 by Epson America, Inc.

In Business

Business use of personal computers is addressed first because computers have been installed in and used by businesses for the longest period. Use of personal computers at home has often been to accomplish business duties or perform an application derived from business use.

More and more business managers are using the personal computer as a personal productivity tool. They store their own prospect lists, prepare their own memos, produce their own presentations, or communicate with other computers. The five major productivity tools used by business are described as follows.

Data Base. A **data base** is used to store similar information on a given subject. A customer data base is a good example: It might include each customer's account number, name, address, salesperson's name, products of interest, and so on. From that information the user can construct a query—for example, "List customer with salesman of 'Smith'." The techniques used by data base systems allow the user to store and retrieve the information without the help of a programmer.

Spreadsheet. A **spreadsheet** program, such as Lotus 1-2-3, is designed just like an accounting worksheet. It is a series of rows and columns. One simple use of a spreadsheet would be in the construction of an annual budget, as shown in Table 7A.1.

The benefit of a spreadsheet program is that once new numbers are entered the mathematical computations are performed automatically and correctly. Consider the benefit one corporation enjoyed after the building of a budgeting system. Previously, changes in the budget required 72 hours of effort to recalculate the results and correct any errors. Using the budget spreadsheets reduced the processing time to 15 minutes.

Word Processing. Perhaps the most widely used and understood use of personal computers is for **word processing.** Imagine the effort required to perfectly type—without one typeover—a term paper or a chapter in a book.

More and more word-processing programs now also incorporate a program to check spelling. This program not only checks your spelling but alerts you to typographical errors as well.

Graphics. Business **graphics** programs may be classified into two major groups, analytical and presentation. Lotus 1-2-3, which has a graphics capability and data base in addition to a spreadsheet, uses analytical graphics as shown in Figure 7A.6. When the spreadsheet is integrated with the graphics, a touch of a key can show changes via a graphic display immediately.

Although invaluable in helping to make decisions, analytical graphics may

Table 7A.1 FINANCIAL BUDGET

	Jan.	Feb.	Mar.	. . .	Dec.	Total
Salary						
Interest						
Total income						
Clothing						
Entertainment						
Food						
Utilities						
Total expenses						
Net income						

Figure 7A.6 ANALYTICAL GRAPHICS.

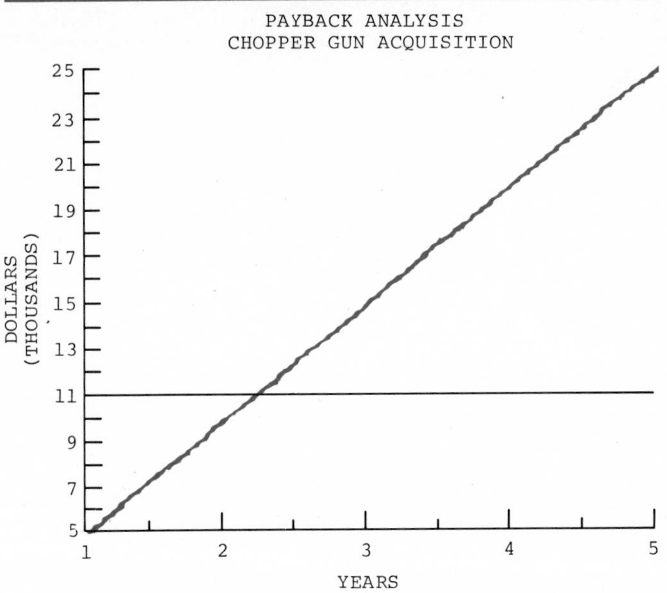

SOURCE: *Lotus Magazine,* July 1985, p. 61.

not be appropriate for boardroom presentations. Presentation graphics take over at this point to produce a more emphatic and desirable result. An example is presented in Figure 7A.7.

Communications. **Communicating** occurs when two different computers are able to talk to each other. Using a **modem,** a telephone device that connects two computers, you can connect to a corporate computer or another personal computer. On-line computer services, such as Dow Jones, permit you to obtain stock market information to stay abreast of a changing market.

Now that you know how a personal computer is used in business, we turn the discussion to computers in the home.

In the Home

To see how you might use a personal computer at home, consider research done by Link Resources Corporation, a market research firm. The information is presented in Table 7A.2. Let's briefly discuss a number of key items.

Personal Filing and Storing. Personal filing and storing encompasses much more than maintaining a recipe list. Personal lists might include an inventory of

Table 7A.2 PC USE IN THE HOME

	1984	1985	1986[a]
Applications by PC owners (in percent)			
Applications			
Entertainment	66%	64%	60%
Education	45	64	64
Filing/storing	49	59	66
Word processing	30	39	57
Electronic spreadsheet	N.A.	20	27
Personal finance	35	36	37
Office-related work at home	N.A.	N.A.	46
Frequency of use (in percent)			
Usage			
Every day	46	37	33
Every other day	21	19	21
Once or twice a week	22	30	29
Once or twice a month	5	7	8
Less than once a month	4	1	9

Note: Percentages may not total 100 due to no responses.
[a] Projected.
N.A. = Not available.

SOURCE: Reprinted by permission of *The Wall Street Journal,* © Dow Jones & Company, Inc., June 16, 1986, p. 30D.

your assets for insurance purposes, mailing lists, expense items, business and household files, current projects and their activities, and appointments. You can generate any of these filing and storing applications with a simple data base program.

Word Processing. Quite simply, word processing will assist you in creating documents, whether these be letters to family members, correspondence to your attorney or accountant, or social correspondence.

Financial Planning. One of the major uses of the personal computer for financial planning is investment analysis. Programs fall into three categories: portfolio management, technical analysis, and fundamental analysis. Portfolio management programs keep track of your investments, noting things like purchase prices, purchase volumes, current prices, yields, and gains/losses on the entirety of your portfolio. A technical analysis program will help you predict changes in the market as a result of price movements, volume, and trends.

Figure 7A.7 PRESENTATION-QUALITY GRAPHICS

SOURCE: Apple Computer Corporation.

Fundamental analysis relies on the principle of determining a company's real value in terms of assets and income relative to the price of the stock.

Many financial planning programs are canned programs, but using an integrated program such as Lotus 1-2-3, you can create your own application. One of the benefits of using a program such as Lotus 1-2-3 is that because it is so widely used, a number of supplemental books are available describing any number of applications.

In addition to programs that help you analyze the stock market or manage your portfolio, there are application programs that will create an overall financial plan. Consider the following examples, which could help in deciding whether to install a hot tub in your rental property (Figure 7A.8) or in determining the net present value of a time-share vacation condominium (Figure 7A.9).

HOW DO YOU DECIDE?

Purchasing a personal computer begins with a thorough evaluation of how you personally will use it. You have seen some potential business and home uses, but now you must consider several different factors:

Figure 7A.8 HOME INVESTMENT ANALYSIS

	A	B	C	D	E	F	G	H	I	J	K	L
1	STEP - 1 CALCULATE INITIAL COST OF INVESTMENT:											
2												
3	Cost of Hot Tub			$1,000								
4	Installation Costs			$200								
5	Water Conditioner Costs			$50								
6				-------								
7	Total Costs			$1,250								
8				=======								
9	STEP - 2											
10	FORECAST CASH FLOWS:			Month 1	Month 2	Month 3	Month 4	Month 5	Month 6	Month 7	Month 8	Month 9
11				-------	-------	-------	-------	-------	-------	-------	-------	-------
12	Beach House Rent Increase			$150	$150	$200	$200	$250	$250	$250	$250	$250
13	Apartment Rent Increase			$50	$50	$50	$50	$175	$175	$175	$175	$175
14				-------	-------	-------	-------	-------	-------	-------	-------	-------
15	Total Rent Increase			$200	$200	$250	$250	$425	$425	$425	$425	$425
16				=======	=======	=======	=======	=======	=======	=======	=======	=======
17												
18	STEP - 3 CALCULATE CUMULATIVE INVESTMENT, CUMULATIVE SAVINGS, AND NET POSITION:											
19												
20				Through	Through	Through	Through	Through	Through	Through	Through	Through
21				Month -	Month -	Month -	Month -	Month -	Month -	Month -	Month -	Month -
22				1	2	3	4	5	6	7	8	9
23				-------	-------	-------	-------	-------	-------	-------	-------	-------
24	Cumulative Investment			$1,250	$1,250	$1,250	$1,250	$1,250	$1,250	$1,250	$1,250	$1,250
25	Cumulative Savings			$200	$400	$650	$900	$1,325	$1,750	$2,175	$2,600	$3,025
26				-------	-------	-------	-------	-------	-------	-------	-------	-------
27	Net Position			($1,050)	($850)	($600)	($350)	$75	$500	$925	$1,350	$1,775

SOURCE: *Lotus Magazine,* July 1986, p. 62.

Figure 7A.9 NET PRESENT VALUE ANALYSIS

	A	B	C	D	E	F	G	H	I	J	K
1	NPV ANALYSIS OF TIME-SHARE VACATION CONDO										
2											
3						STEP 2: SELECT APPROPRIATE DISCOUNT RATE					
4	STEP 1: SUMMARIZE EXPECTED CASH FLOWS					Discount Rate:		10%			
5	A. Initial Costs										
6	- - - - - - - - - - - -	- - - - -									
7	Cost of unit	$10,500				STEP 3: CREATE NPV FORMULA					
8	Legal fees	$500				NPV=	($2,556)				
9	Excise tax	$158									
10		- - - - - - -									
11	Tot. Initial costs	$11,158									
12											
13	B. Cash Flow Stemming From Ownership										
14	- - - - - - - - - - - -	- - - - -									
15		Year 1	Year 2	Year 3	Year 4	Year 5	Year 6	Year 7	Year 8	Year 9	Year 10
16	Hotel Savings	$1,400	$1,400	$1,400	$1,400	$1,400	$1,400	$1,400	$1,400	$1,400	$1,400
17	Maintenance Fees	($500)	($500)	($500)	($500)	($500)	($500)	($500)	($500)	($500)	($500)
18	Income Tax Savings	$500	$500	$500	$500	$500	$500	$500	$500	$500	$500
19		- - - - -	- - - - -	- - - - -	- - - - -	- - - - -	- - - - -	- - - - -	- - - - -	- - - - -	- - - - -
20	Tot. ongoing savings	$1,400	$1,400	$1,400	$1,400	$1,400	$1,400	$1,400	$1,400	$1,400	$1,400

SOURCE: *Lotus Magazine*, March 1986, p. 68.

How will you use it?
Should you buy software or hardware first?
How important is it to buy a brand name?
Where do you buy?

How Will You Use It?

In addition to evaluating your intended uses, you might want to consider the compatibility of equipment between your home and your university. If you expect to spend a couple of hours at home each day working on university-related projects, it will be to your advantage to own a computer system that is compatible in hardware and in software with what you have at the university. Otherwise, you will be duplicating your work. Also, look to the future to determine if that mix of university/home use will change. On the other hand, if your use is restricted to the home, give consideration only to the home applications.

Consider the other applications discussed to determine if they might be of benefit sooner than you think. For instance, a middle-school child will be using the same college preparatory programs that you used before you know it.

Should You Buy Software or Hardware First?

The software refers to the programs, routines, and procedures that control the operations of a computer. The hardware is the actual computer equipment—monitor, CPU, disk drives, and printer. You should always evaluate the intended software first. It may seem peculiar that the purchase of a $300 software program will drive the purchase of a $2500 computer, but to do otherwise might result in your $2500 hardware purchase not running the computer software you selected.

As the price of hardware equipment declines, software is being developed to take advantage of the expanded memory. Most computers are also designed using what is known as **open architecture.** That means that the original manufacturer actually encourages others to manufacture products that can be added to the personal computer to enhance its performance. Once again, your software decision will ensure that you purchase a personal computer that has the capacity or can be expanded to execute your program. Even though you may consider purchasing an optical disk with storage capacities approaching 1 billion characters of information, a personal computer may not process the information within your time requirements. Assuming you already own one personal computer, these expansion devices just mentioned may be an alternative to purchasing a new computer to obtain more efficient processing.

How Important Is It to Buy a Brand Name?

Usually brand identification is established on the basis of certain quality and performance standards. The most predominant example in today's market is

IBM compatibility. You should consider two important issues in your brand decision. The first issue is whether or not you are buying a computer that is compatible with the brand name. You can achieve significant cost savings by purchasing a product that is compatible.

This issue leads to the second consideration, which is the strength and viability of the compatible manufacturers. What are their quality control standards? Have they built a reputation of reliability? When faced with problems, how do they respond to other users? And will they be in existence tomorrow should your computer break?

When deciding on brand, you might also consider the compatibility of your equipment with that of your peers. Your neighbor may have an extensive library of software programs that you would like to use. It is not our purpose to discuss valid licensing agreements or copyright laws, but should you decide to use your neighbor's programs, you can only do so if you have compatible equipment.

Where Do You Buy?

Four important points can help you decide where to buy your personal computer: support, service, training, and price. If you are fairly knowledgeable about personal computers, you will probably require relatively little support. On the other hand, if you are a first-time buyer, you should not be misled by computer stores' claims of offering full service. Upon questioning the salesperson, you will probably discover that you know almost as much as he or she.

Whether you are buying a brand name or a compatible clone (imitation), your computer may need service. Just as you should question the financial strength and viability of the manufacturer, you should also ask it of the retailer.

Any new purchase may require training. In addition to the training you can obtain from your purchase outlet or college or university, look to tutorial programs. A **tutorial** is a computer program that will guide you through the use of your computer or software programs.

You might at first proclaim that price is the most important factor. Price should not be considered first, though, but last. It does you very little good to have saved money on the purchase of your hardware and/or software by buying from a discounter or mail-order business if the products remain unused because you failed to consider the previous factors.

ARE YOU STILL CONFUSED?

Assuming that you now have a grasp of basic computer terms and some ideas on what you want to do with your personal computer, you are prepared to begin your search. Do not be concerned that you still have questions. Ask computer science professors at your university. Take introductory computer courses to reinforce what you have already learned. But don't stop there. Talk to friends who have personal computers. Visit several computer stores and research selected books and periodicals.

The following list of selected periodicals should help you in gathering information:

Popular Computing—Published monthly by BYTE/McGraw-Hill, P.O. Box 307, Martinsville, N.J. 08836; single issue, $2.50; annual subscription, $12.97.

Byte—Published monthly by BYTE/McGraw-Hill, P.O. Box 590, Martinsville, N.J. 08836; single issue, $3.50; annual subscription, $21.

Compute—Published monthly by Compute! Publications, Inc., P.O. Box 5406, Greensboro, N.C. 27403; single issue, $2.95; annual subscription, $24.

Creative Computing—Published monthly by Ahl Computing, Inc., a subsidiary of Ziff-Davis Publishing Co., P.O. Box 5214, Boulder, Co. 80322; single issue, $2.95; annual subscription, $24.97.

Infoworld—Published weekly by Computerworld Communications Inc., 375 Cochituate Rd., Box 880, Framingham, Mass. 01701; single issue, $1.50; annual subscription, $22.95.

PC Magazine—Published 26 times a year by Ziff-Davis Publishing Co., 1 Park Ave., New York, N.Y. 10016; single issue, $2.95; annual subscription, $27.97.

PC World—Published monthly (with 2 additional issues) by PC World Communications, Inc., P.O. Box 6700, Bergenfield, N.J. 07621; single issue, $3; annual subscription, $24.

Personal Computing—Published monthly by Hayden Publishing Co., P.O. Box 2941, Boulder, Co. 80321; single issue, $2.50; annual subscription, $11.97.

Personal Software—Published monthly by Hayden Publishing Company, Inc., 10 Mulholland Drive, Hasbrouck Heights, N.J. 07604; single issue, $2.50; annual subscription, $24.

KEY TERMS

application
byte
canned programs
communicating
CPU
data base
disk drive
dot matrix
floppy disk
graphics
hard disk
hardware
K
keyboard
laser
letter quality
Meg
modem

monochrome
open architecture
operating system
personal computer
program
RAM
ROM
software
spreadsheet
tutorial
word processing

Buying insurance does not carry the same psychic pleasure as purchasing a new car or investing in stocks and bonds, but it is every bit as important—perhaps even more important. While you may be able to accept the fact that you bought a lemon for an automobile or a home with a cracked foundation, your family may not be able to exist properly if you have not provided adequate life insurance protection. Also, if you are in an automobile accident, it may be imperative that you have sufficient insurance to cover liability claims.

Of course, the cost to completely insure yourself against everything that could possibly happen to you would be so high that you would have little left over to enjoy the simple pleasures of life. To go to an extreme, you could have millions of dollars of coverage against someone falling down in your house or apartment, a similar protection for meals served to guests in your home, and so on. Thus, a key message presented

PROTECTING YOUR PERSONAL AND PROPERTY RESOURCES

in the next three chapters is that it is extremely important to determine which risks you want to insure and which you want to retain for possible exposure to out-of-pocket costs or lawsuits. We do *not* recommend that you try to cover all exposure to liability, or even most, but that you spend your insurance dollars wisely. Generally, you should protect against the catastrophic and the highly damaging, and then do a more careful assessment of lesser risks to see if the coverage is worth the cost. Of course, state laws dictate a minimum amount of insurance for motor vehicles, and lenders will want adequate insurance coverage for collateral on a loan.

In Chapter 8, you will study insurance coverage for property (auto, home, jewelry, and so on). If you drive a car, you may want to compare your coverage to the various policies discussed in the chapter. In Chapter 9, the emphasis shifts to health care and disability coverage. Because of ever-increasing health care costs associated with hospital stays and doctors' fees, this has become an increasingly important area.

Finally, life insurance protection is discussed in Chapter 10. Here there is a whole package of products from which to choose, and you will be given a thorough grounding on the key differences and features of the traditional (term, whole life, and so forth) and the nontraditional policies (such as variable life and universal life) that are now in the marketplace. ■

8

Property and Liability Insurance

After studying this chapter, you should:

- Understand how insurance finances losses and reduces uncertainty
- Appreciate the differences among property risks, liability risks, and life and health risks
- Understand retention and loss control
- Be able to analyze and explain the major coverages in the personal automobile policy
- Be able to analyze and explain the major coverages in the HO-3 (homeowner's special form) policy
- Appreciate the costs and benefits of the umbrella liability policy
- Understand how deductibles, coinsurance, the definition of loss, and variations in limits affect coverage and the cost of that coverage

What would you do if your home burned down or if you were involved in a serious automobile accident? How would you handle these losses? In Part One, we discussed budgeting and taxes, but we assumed that you did not incur any catastrophic losses. Further, the banking and credit tools you studied in Part Two will not allow you to cover these losses. Now, you will learn how to deal with major risks, both through insurance and in other ways.

We will discuss (1) property risks, (2) liability risks, and (3) life and health risks. The three basic types of risks are portrayed in Figure 8.1. **Property risks** include possible damage to or loss of your property, plus indirect losses arising from damage to property, such as your inconvenience and income lost as a result of damage to your car. To help you visualize some property risks, look at

Figure 8.1 DIFFERENT CATEGORIES FOR RISK CLASSIFICATION

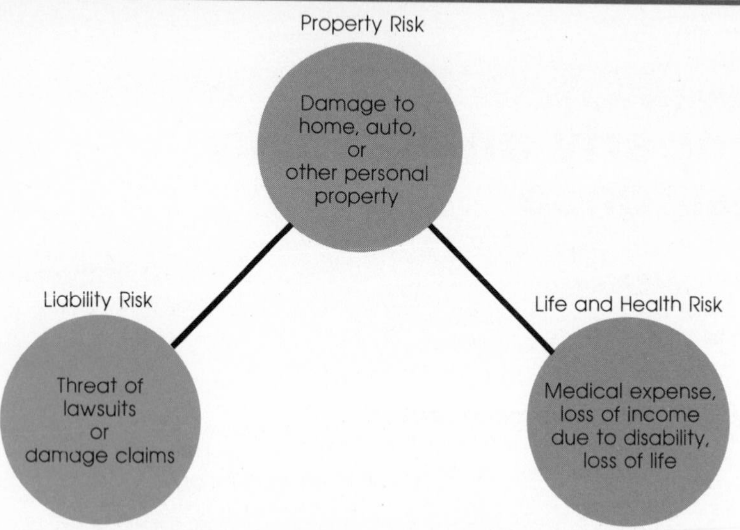

Potential Solutions to Risk Exposure

- Insurance–transferring the risk to an insurance company
- Retention–taking a chance on covering the loss yourself
- Loss control–attempting to reduce the possibility of the loss (driving carefully, dieting, etc.)

Tables 8.1 and 8.2. Table 8.1, on pages 264–265, shows parts of a checklist for a home's contents and Table 8.2, on page 266, shows a simple checklist that you might use for the actual home. You can obtain such forms from an insurance agent.

Liability risks are situations that could force you to defend yourself in court and to pay large sums to others. The increasing number and size of lawsuits make liability insurance more important each year.

Life and health risks involve the financial impact of death and loss of health, including taxes, medical and funeral expenses, and income loss. Chapters 9 and 10 examine life and health risks.

In this chapter, we explore some concepts important to the insurance process, explain how insurance works, and analyze key insurance policies that can help you protect yourself against property and liability losses. Finally, we discuss factors affecting insurance coverages and their costs, talk about shopping for insurance, and describe the claims process.

INSURANCE PROTECTION

Insurance is a device for transferring risk: your insurer accepts part or all of your risk in exchange for your payment of a premium. If you suffer an insured loss, the insurer then pays for that loss as the insurance policy stipulates. Insurance reduces your uncertainty regarding the risk situation, freeing you to pursue other goals while secure in the knowledge that your insured losses will be paid.

Noninsurance Risk Treatments

Although insurance transfers the financial burden of loss to the insurer, you can treat some risks by using other tools or by combining those tools with insurance in order to make the best use of your money. Among these alternatives are (1) retention and (2) loss control.

Retention means bearing the loss yourself rather than transferring it. Retention makes sense when the severity of loss is so small that it will not cause a major financial impact, even if losses occur fairly often. For example, you can easily retain the risk of loss of your pen or pencil, since the cost to replace it is minimal. You can combine retention with insurance by using deductibles, which allow you to absorb small losses while transferring large losses to your insurer.

Loss control entails efforts to reduce either the frequency or the amount of loss, or both. If you can save money or lessen possible injuries, loss control makes good sense. You can use it along with insurance and retention. The three techniques just discussed for handling risk are shown at the bottom of Figure 8.1. By relating them to the three circles in the figure, you can see how risk exposure can be managed in three different ways.

AUTOMOBILE INSURANCE

Your major sources of property and liability losses usually are your auto and your home. Because your car may represent your biggest immediate liability exposure, we will discuss automobile insurance first.

You can cut the risks associated with operating your car by using good driving habits and carefully maintaining your car. This loss control approach should save money, and it is a wise way to preserve your health, but it doesn't eliminate your need for auto insurance. Few of us can afford to pay the losses an auto can generate. In addition, many states require liability insurance for you to operate a motor vehicle, and lenders usually require property insurance to protect their collateral. Consequently, you probably will buy auto insurance if you own a car.

Traditional Versus No-Fault Automobile Insurance

The development of auto insurance in the United States was shaped by refinements in the legal liability system. As a result, most traditional coverages fell into one of two primary groupings, first-party coverages and third-party coverages. Further evolution brought about a third category, reverse third-party coverages. **First-party coverages** pay you if you suffer a loss, without concern as

Table 8.1 A PARTIAL CHECKLIST FOR THE PERSONAL PROPERTY RISK EXPOSURES IN YOUR HOME[a]

Living Room

No. of items	Description	Date of purchase	Original cost	Present value
	Books			
	Bookcases			
	Cabinets			
	Cabinet contents			
	Chairs			
	Clocks			
	. . .			
	Piano			
	Pictures			
	Rugs			
	. . .			
	Window curtains			
	Total			

Dining Room

No. of items	Description	Date of purchase	Original cost	Present value
	Buffet			
	Cabinets			
	Cabinet contents			
	Chairs			
	China			
	Crystal			
	. . .			
	Silverplate			
	Silverware			
	. . .			
	Table(s)			
	Table linen			
	Total			

[a] A complete form similar to this is available free from most insurers' local representatives.

Kitchen

No. of items	Description	Date of purchase	Original cost	Present value
	Blender			
	Cabinets			
	Cabinet contents			
	. . .			
	Food processor			
	Freezer			
	. . .			
	Refrigerator			
	Stove			
	Total			

Master Bedroom

No. of items	Description	Date of purchase	Original cost	Present value
	Bedding			
	Beds			
	Books			
	Dressers and contents			
	Dressing table			
	Lamps			
	Mattresses			
	Total			

continued

Table 8.1 continued

Breakfast Room

No. of items	Description	Date of purchase	Original cost	Present value
	Cabinets			
	Cabinet contents			
	Chairs			
	⋮			
	Rugs			
	Table			
	Total			

Summary

	Original cost	Present value
Living room	$	$
Dining room		
Den		
⋮		
Hallways		
Master bedroom		
⋮		
Garage		
Workshop		
Storage shed		
⋮		
Other (list)		
Total	$	$

to who caused that loss. You are the first party, and the insurer is the second party. **Third-party** or **liability coverages** pay another party (the third party) if you are responsible for that person's loss. **Reverse third-party coverages** are insurance policies that protect you if another party is responsible for your loss but is unable to pay. This type of coverage then acts as though it were that third party's liability coverage, and it pays your loss.

By the early 1960s, problems affecting the traditional insurance system caused many people to urge changes in our legal system as it applied to auto accidents. Lengthy court delays, uncertainty about judgments (which could be far too small or much larger than reasonable), and the economic drain of having to pay large lawyers' fees out of insurance premiums and judgments all were cited as problems. The idea proposed to correct the problem was called **no-fault insurance.** Under the no-fault concept, auto accidents are removed from the legal liability system and each driver is made responsible for his or her own loss. Thus, if you are insured, you can collect from your insurer no matter who causes the accident. If you are uninsured, you absorb your own loss. The other party collects from his or her own insurer, or absorbs his or her own loss.

Table 8.2 A SIMPLE CHECKLIST FOR RISK EXPOSURES IN YOUR ACTUAL HOME

Property	Original cost	Cost to replace	Actual cash value
Home	______	______	______
Detached garage	______	______	______
Detached greenhouse	______	______	______
Detached workshop	______	______	______
Detached tool shed	______	______	______
Swimming pool	______	______	______
Pool house or cabana	______	______	______
Barn or stable	______	______	______
Other structure	______	______	______
Total values	______	______	______

In its purest sense, this coverage would totally remove your right to sue another driver for your loss; however, every state that has passed a no-fault law has established a **threshold** of loss beyond which you regain the right to sue the other party. This threshold may be a set number of dollars of economic loss (usually in the form of medical expenses), or it may involve death or specified bodily injuries. It is designed to limit litigation of auto accidents to only the largest losses, but many states have set their thresholds so low that settlement of a large proportion of auto accidents is returned to the courts. Table 8.3 lists states with no-fault laws in effect today.

The Personal Automobile Insurance Policy

In a traditional insurance policy sold in states that have not passed no-fault legislation to limit your right to sue, the personal automobile policy's protection can be grouped into the previously mentioned categories of first-party coverages, third-party coverages, and reverse third-party coverages.

First-Party Coverages. First-party coverages include (1) collision, (2) other than collision, and (3) medical payments. Each will pay you without question as to who caused the loss, if the loss is covered under the policy. **Collision** pays for damage to your car if you collide with another object or roll the car over. This coverage usually is sold with a **deductible,** which means that you will retain (absorb) the first dollars of loss in each collision and that the insurer will pay losses after you have absorbed the prescribed dollar deductible. Lenders usually require collision coverage.

Other than collision is often called *comprehensive*. This property coverage pays for damage to your car caused by something besides collision or rolling

Table 8.3
NO-FAULT AUTOMOBILE INSURANCE STATES

Colorado	Massachusetts
Connecticut	Michigan
District of Columbia	Minnesota
Florida	New Jersey
Georgia	New York
Hawaii	North Dakota
Kansas	Utah
Kentucky	

Note: Nevada repealed its no-fault law in 1979, and Pennsylvania followed in 1984.

SOURCE: State Farm Insurance Companies. *No Fault Press Reference Manual* (as revised June 1986), pp. E-101–E-106.

it over. Its deductible typically is smaller than the collision deductible, and most lenders require you to purchase it. Major covered items include fire, theft, water, flood, windstorm, hail, vandalism and malicious mischief, riot and civil commotion, and collision with a bird or animal.

Medical payments coverage obligates the insurer to pay your medical expenses, up to the policy limit, if you are injured in an auto accident. It covers you and anyone riding in your car, and you and members of your household when riding in someone else's car. There usually is a low maximum benefit for each person per accident, but no limit on the number of persons covered.

Third-Party Coverages. Third-party coverage protects you when you are responsible for, or stand accused of, injury to others or damage to their property resulting from your use or ownership of an insured vehicle. It covers you and members of your family living with you while driving your car or someone else's car with their permission, whether that permission is express or implied. It also covers other persons driving your car with your permission. The insurer will defend you when you are sued, or it must settle the suit or pay its policy limit under the coverage. If it defends you and you lose the suit, it still must pay in your behalf, up to its policy limit. The cost of legal defense does not reduce the amount it will pay if you are found liable in court.

Third-party coverage may be in the form of bodily injury liability (BIL) and property damage liability (PDL). **Bodily injury liability** insurance coverage applies when you cause bodily injury to someone else, such as persons riding in other cars, pedestrians, or passengers in your own car. **Property damage liability** insurance coverage deals with your liability when you damage the property of others. While this property often is someone else's car, it includes other property as well.

Usually, bodily injury liability has two limits: (1) a limit *per person per*

Table 8.4 MINIMUM AUTO LIABILITY INSURANCE LIMITS IN THE UNITED STATES

State	Limits	State	Limits	State	Limits
Ala.	20/40/10	Ky.	25/50/10	N.Dak.	25/50/25
Alaska	50/100/25	La.	10/20/10	Ohio	12.5/25/7.5
Ariz.	15/30/10	Maine	20/40/10	Okla.	10/20/10
Ark.	25/50/15	Md.	20/40/10	Oreg.	25/50/10
Calif.	15/30/5	Mass.	10/20/5	Pa.	15/30/5
Colo.	25/50/15	Mich.	20/40/10	R.I.	25/50/10
Conn.	20/40/10	Minn.	30/60/10	S.C.	15/30/5
De.	15/30/10	Miss.	10/20/5	S.Dak.	25/50/25
D.C.	25/50/10	Mo.	25/50/10	Tenn.	20/40/10
Fla.	10/20/5	Mont.	25/50/5	Tex.	20/40/15
Ga.	15/30/10	Nebr.	25/50/25	Utah	20/40/10
Hawaii	25/unlimited/10	Nev.	15/30/10	Vt.	20/40/10
Idaho	25/50/15	N.H.	25/50/25	Va.	25/50/10
Ill.	15/30/10	N.J.	15/30/5	Wash.	25/50/10
Ind.	25/50/10	N.Mex.	25/50/10	W.Va.	20/40/10
Iowa	20/40/15	N.Y.	10/20/5[a]	Wis.	25/50/10
Kans.	25/50/10	N.C.	25/50/10	Wyo.	25/50/20

[a] 50/100 BIL when wrongful death occurs.

SOURCE: *Insurance Facts: 1986–87 Property/Casualty Fact Book,* New York: Insurance Information Institute, 1985, p. 104.

accident, and (2) a limit *for all persons injured per accident;* and property damage liability has its own aggregate limit *for all property you damage in one accident.* Your state will require some minimum limits of liability coverage. These minimum limits typically are shown as three numbers, such as 15/30/15. This would mean that you must have at least $15,000 in bodily injury liability (BIL) insurance per person per accident, and $30,000 for all persons per accident, plus another $15,000 of property damage liability (PDL) insurance per accident. Look at Table 8.4 to find your state's minimum auto liability insurance limits.

It is possible to merge these three limits into one *combined single limit* (CSL), within which it does not matter whether the loss is bodily injury or property damage, or if the bodily injury is to one or more persons. Combined single limit is a bit more expensive, but it can mean broader coverage that will pay more in certain cases.

Example. Fred Williams has 15/30/15 coverage. He runs a red light and broadsides Jane McDonald's new Corvette. The force of the collision propels Fred's 1987 van into a light pole, toppling the traffic light at the intersection before it comes to rest in the plate glass display window of J.B.'s Grocery Store. Jane's two sons, Jacob and Jonah, are injured in the collision, and Jane is hospitalized with facial injuries. The following damages are awarded by the court:

Damage to Jane's Corvette	$ 9,200
Repairs to traffic light	1,850
Replacement of light pole	900
J.B.'s display window	1,350
J.B.'s loss of sales	3,300
J.B.'s damage to grocery baskets and miscellaneous property	2,480
Jane's medical care	8,300
Jane's loss of income while in hospital	2,000
Jane's mental anguish	30,000
Jane's projected income loss due to facial scarring	5,000
Jacob's medical care	300
Jonah's medical care	1,200
Daycare for Jacob and Jonah while Jane is in hospital	2,300
Compensation to Jacob and Jonah for loss of maternal companionship	5,000
Total	$73,180

To see how much Fred's third-party coverages will pay, we should first break down the loss into items covered by bodily injury liability (BIL) and those covered by property damage liability (PDL). Since the bodily injury liability (BIL) covers only $15,000 per person, it will pay only $15,000 of Jane's awards, so Fred has no coverage for the other $30,300 in awards which the court has ordered him to pay to Jane. He must pay this part of the loss out of his own pocket. The analysis is as follows:

Jane's medical care	$ 8,300
Jane's loss of income while in the hospital	2,000
Jane's mental anguish	30,000
Jane's projected income loss due to facial scarring	5,000
Total awards to Jane	$45,300
Less:	
Fred's bodily injury liability (BIL) limit per person	−15,000
Fred's uninsured losses for Jane	$30,300

What about the court awards for Jacob and Jonah? They total $8,800 as indicated below.

Jacob's medical care	$ 300
Jonah's medical care	1,200
Daycare for Jacob and Jonah while Jane is in hospital	2,300
Compensation to Jacob and Jonah for loss of maternal companionship	5,000
Total awards to Jacob and Jonah	$8,800

Since Fred's bodily injury liability (BIL) insurance has a $30,000 limit for *all* persons injured in the accident and $15,000 has been allocated to Jane, $15,000 is still available to cover the awards to Jacob and Jonah. Fred is fully covered for the boys' claims, as the $15,000 exceeds their $8,800 in claims.

The total paid by Fred's bodily injury liability (BIL) insurance is $23,800

($15,000 + $8,800). Of course, Fred must pay for Jane's uninsured losses of $30,300.

So far we have examined only the bodily injury liability (BIL) portion of the accident. What about the property damage? Fred has $15,000 in property damage liability (PDL) insurance. The property damage from the accident is $19,080.

Damage to Jane's Corvette	$9,200
Repairs to traffic light	1,850
Replacement of light pole	900
J.B.'s display window	1,350
J.B.'s loss of sales	3,300
J.B.'s damage to grocery baskets and miscellaneous property	2,480
Total awards for property damage	$19,080

Since $19,080 exceeds the $15,000 limit of the property damage liability (PDL) coverage, Fred must bear an additional loss of $4,080 ($19,080 − $15,000).

In summary, the total losses and payments are as follows:

Losses	Value	Insurance pays	Fred pays
Total claims by Jane	$45,300	$15,000	$30,300
Total claims by Jacob and Jonah	8,800	8,800	0
Property damage	19,080	15,000	4,080
Totals	$73,180	$38,800	$34,380

If Fred had been covered under a combined single limit (CSL) liability coverage of $75,000, the insurer would have paid the full loss; and if the CSL coverage had been $60,000, Fred would have absorbed $73,180 − $60,000, or $13,180 of the loss.

Reverse Third-Party Coverages. Known as **uninsured/underinsured motorists insurance** (UMI), reverse third-party coverages are necessary because irresponsible drivers do not carry adequate liability insurance. UMI coverages turn the liability insurance concept around. That is, UMI coverages pay you if you (the person who bought them) or your car is hit by a hit-and-run driver or a motorist who is found liable for your loss, but who owns no liability insurance and cannot pay you. In many states, this coverage also applies if the other driver has liability insurance but the insurer becomes insolvent and cannot pay.

In states with *underinsured* motorists coverage, UMI will pay when your loss for which the other driver is liable exceeds that person's liability insurance limit, *if* your UMI limit is higher than that liability limit. For example, assume that another person's bodily injury liability insurance limit per accident is 15/30, and your UMI bodily injury liability limit is 50/100. The other person collides with you, and your $35,000 in medical expenses are caused by that driver's carelessness. You will recover $15,000 from his or her liability insurance, and then you will be paid the difference of $35,000 − $15,000, or $20,000, from your UMI coverage. If your UMI coverage were only 15/30 for bodily injury, it would not pay you anything in this case.

Premiums

The higher your insurance coverage, the larger your insurance costs or premiums will be. Also, a number of factors discussed later in this chapter help to determine the cost of auto insurance. For now, however, observe in Figure 8.2 how age, marital status, and gender affect the general cost of auto insurance protection. In all four graphics in the figure, as age goes up for young drivers, rates go down. Also note that rates are lower for married male drivers than for unmarried male drivers. Furthermore, unmarried female drivers enjoy slightly lower rates than married male drivers, but significantly lower rates than unmarried male drivers under age 30.

INSURING YOUR HOME

A home exposes you to many risks, whether you own or rent. Children and pets add to your possibilities for loss, as do swimming pools, power tools, and lawn mowers. Because home-related losses can be so large, insurance is a wise choice for much of your property and a necessity for the liability exposure arising from your use and maintenance of a home. In addition, you also should use loss control in many circumstances. Simple loss control efforts for the fire risk include installing and maintaining smoke alarms and fire extinguishers, planning and practicing fire drills, and removing or carefully storing flammables. Basic loss control for injury to children includes putting "child-proof" locks on cabinets where you store cleaners and other chemicals, storing medications under lock and key, unplugging and safely storing power tools, and limiting access to swimming pools, wells, or ponds.

Homeowner's Insurance

Most homeowner's insurance policies contain two major sections, each of which provides a distinct grouping of protection: (1) coverage for damage to, destruction of, or loss of your own property, and (2) coverage for liability for injury to others and for damage to their property, plus coverage for medical expenses of guests without concern about who is at fault. There is a variety of homeowner's insurance policies available to you. Table 8.5 summarizes property coverages in some popular forms used in most states. We will study the special form (HO-3) because it is very popular. If you rent, broad form (HO-4) will provide similar coverage for your personal property.

Form HO-3: The Special Form

The **HO-3 policy**—special form—is divided into two sections. Section I insures your property, and section II provides your personal liability and medical payments coverage. The primary coverages are arranged as follows:

Figure 8.2 PERSONAL CHARACTERISTICS AFFECTING THE COST OF AUTO INSURANCE PROTECTION

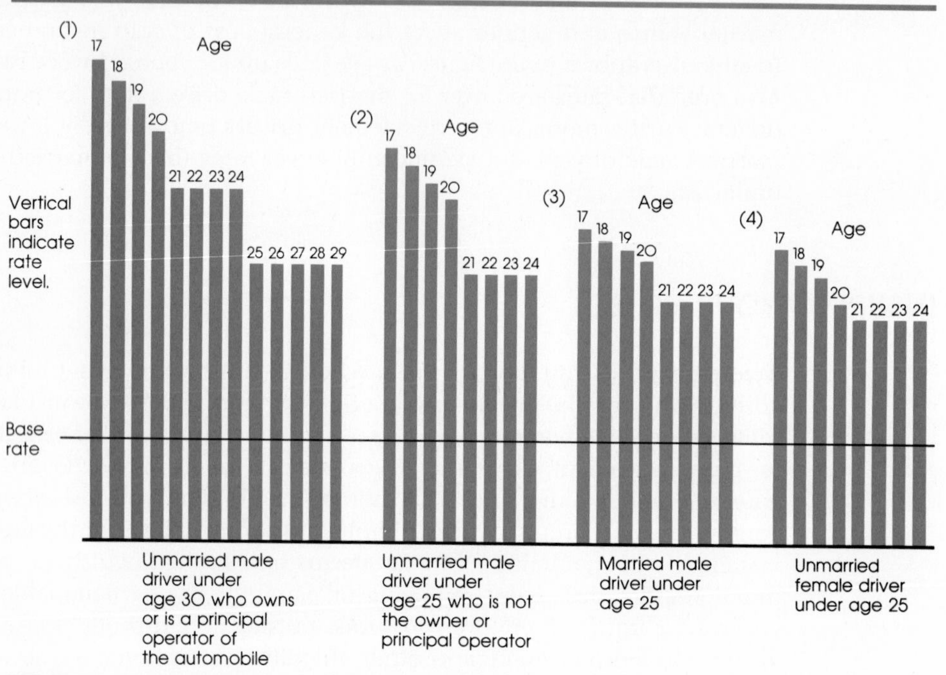

SOURCE: "A Family Guide to Auto and Home Insurance," Insurance Information Institute, 1978, p. 10.

Section I

Coverage	Name of coverage
A	Dwelling
B	Other structures
C	Personal property
D	Loss of use

Section II

Coverage	Name of coverage
E	Personal liability
F	Medical payments to others

A. Dwelling. Coverage A insures the **dwelling**—the residence itself—against all perils except those specifically excluded. If you have a workshop, garage, or other structure *attached* to the house, these items are covered. Among the major acts excluded from this coverage are war, nuclear contamination, losses that you intentionally cause, flood, and earth movement.

Table 8.5 SUMMARY OF THE PROPERTY COVERAGES[a] OF THE MOST POPULAR HOMEOWNERS POLICY FORMS USED IN MOST STATES

	Form name	Property coverage summary
HO-1	Basic form	Covers a short list of perils for both the home and its contents
HO-2	Broad form	Covers a long list of perils for both the home and its contents
HO-3	Special form	Covers a long list of perils for the contents of the home; covers all perils not specifically excluded for the home itself
HO-4	Contents–broad form	Covers a long list of perils for the contents of a rented home or apartment
HO-5	Comprehensive form	Covers all perils not specifically excluded for both the home and its contents

[a] The typical coverage limit under each form for personal liability is $100,000, and the usual medical payments limit is $1000 per person. Since the liability section is essentially the same from one policy to another, only property coverages are described in detail.

B. Other Structures. If there is another structure—such as a garage, workshop, or greenhouse—that is *separated* from your house by a clear gap, it is insured under coverage B. The limit of coverage is 10 percent of the dwelling coverage unless you specify a different limit by amending (endorsing) the policy. For example, if your house is insured for $100,000 under coverage A, your limit for other structures will be 0.10 × $100,000, or $10,000.

C. Personal Property. Coverage C, **personal property,** insures your clothing, furniture, appliances, and other personal property that you own, use, or wear. It covers them against a broad range of perils, including fire, lightning, hail, windstorm, freezing, riot and civil commotion, vandalism and malicious mischief, aircraft, vehicles, and collapse. Unless you specify otherwise, your limit of coverage for personal property is 50 percent of the limit stated for the dwelling under coverage A. Thus, if you insure your dwelling for $100,000, coverage C provides another $50,000 of insurance. You may reduce this to as low as 40 percent by amending the policy, and it may be changed to any higher amount agreed to by you and the insurer. In addition, you have coverage for up to 10 percent of the limit under coverage C for your personal property *anywhere in the world,* except at a second residence. So, if your coverage C limit is $50,000, you have $5000 in personal property insurance protection while traveling.

Coverage C contains several limitations that can be important to you. It pays only $200 for any one loss of money, gold, silver, platinum, coins, and

Box 8.1 COMPARING HOMEOWNERS' COSTS FOR INSURANCE, TAXES, UTILITIES, AND MORTGAGES

The cost of insurance represents less than 3 percent of the monthly housing expenses faced by home purchasers in the United States. A countrywide study by the U.S. League of Savings Institutions reflected an 8.6 percent increase from 1983 to 1985 in the median monthly housing expense after a 13 percent drop over the preceding two-year period. The cost of insurance represented 2.9 percent of the total in 1985, up fractionally from the 2.8 percent reported in 1983.

	1985		1983		1981	
Item	Cost	% of cost	Cost	% of cost	Cost	% of cost
Mortgage payment	$573	74.4	$524	73.9	$624	76.5
Real estate taxes	75	9.7	65	9.2	72	8.8
Utilities	100	13.0	100	14.1	100	12.3
Hazard insurance	22	2.9	20	2.8	20	2.5
Total	$770		$709		$816	

SOURCE: Insurance Information Institute, *Insurance Facts: 1986–87 Property/Casualty Fact Book*, New York: 1986, p. 61.

medals. It covers only $1000 for any one loss in each of a series of groups, including theft of jewelry, precious stones, semiprecious stones, watches, and furs; outboard motors and equipment, boats and boat trailers; and nonboat trailers. *Any one loss* really means any one burglary, fire, and so on. Thus, if a burglar takes $3000 in jewelry, $1500 in precious stones, and $5000 in furs, the any one loss provision would mean that you could only recover a total of $1000 in this category. Other categories have similar limitations. The coverage is limited to $2000 in any one loss by theft of firearms and to $2500 for any one loss in each of the following two groups: property at the home used for business purposes; and theft of silverware and silverplate, goldware and goldplate, and pewterware. Your total potential insurance under coverage C is $5700 ($200 + $1000 + $2000 + $2500).

Because these limits are so low—especially those dealing with jewelry, furs, silver and gold—you may want to add an endorsement to your policy that schedules, or lists, these items at their true values and insures them for those values. This means a higher premium, but it also means added protection against a potentially severe loss. Many families find that the jewelry limitation alone can cause a major loss. You should list your exposed properties and their values, price added coverage, and then decide just which properties you want to insure using a schedule.

D. Loss of Use. If your home were badly damaged in a windstorm, where would you live while it was being repaired? How would you pay your rent? Coverage D, **loss of use,** pays living expenses that are *in addition to* your normal living expenses, in housing similar to your own, during the time it takes to restore your home to a livable condition. The maximum benefit is 20 percent of the limit under coverage A. Thus, if you insure your dwelling for \$100,000, loss of use will pay up to 0.20 × \$100,000, or \$20,000. If your family's prewindstorm normal monthly living expenses of \$1200 were increased to \$2100 while you had to live elsewhere during repairs, the insurer would pay \$2100 − \$1200, or \$900, per month. This coverage allows you to retain your normal standard of living, but it does not pay for expenses above that standard.

E. Personal Liability. Coverage E, **personal liability,** is the first coverage in section II, liability coverages. It insures you against liability arising from bodily injury to others and damage to their property, when this liability is created by your use, ownership, or occupancy of your home. The coverage has an aggregate single limit of \$100,000 unless you choose to buy a higher amount. It will pay your legal defense cost, unless your insurer chooses to settle with the plaintiff or to pay its full maximum limit under the coverage.

F. Medical Payments to Others. Coverage F, **medical payments to others,** will pay up to \$1000 of the medical expenses for each person (other than you or a member of your family living in your home) injured on your property. It also covers other persons' injuries when you or your pet cause those injuries while away from your home. This is not a liability coverage, so there is no delay to determine if you are at fault before the insurer pays.

Conditions. In order to be protected when any insured loss occurs under your policy, you must satisfy the **conditions** stated in the policy. Some major conditions are as follows:

1 Promptly notify the insurer when a loss occurs.
2 Promptly notify the police if a theft occurs.
3 Promptly send to the insurer all legal process documents relating to an insured occurrence.
4 Protect property from further damage.
5 Show the insurer the damaged property.
6 Assist the insurer in claim settlement, at hearings and trials, and in conducting lawsuits.

THE UMBRELLA LIABILITY POLICY

Because your liability risk exposes you to potentially severe losses, you may want to consider adding more liability protection to that afforded by your

Box 8.2 A SUGGESTION FROM ESQUIRE: CONSIDER PACKAGING YOUR AUTO AND HOMEOWNER'S INSURANCE

Until recently, intense competition among insurers has insulated us from the premium shock experienced by commercial casualty customers, where hikes of as much as several hundred percent, and more, have become commonplace. While no one is predicting such increases for so-called personal lines, indications are that the good old days are over for drivers and, to a lesser extent, for homeowners and renters. Aetna expected its auto premiums to rise about 10 percent in 1985, with a similar increase in store for 1986. State Farm's auto rates are up an average of 7.9 percent, compared with a 1.6-percent average increase in 1984; and there are predictions of industry-wide increases in auto premiums of about 10 percent, with smaller increases for homeowners. Still, anyone buying both homeowner's *and* auto coverage can save money, possibly increase coverage, and cut down paper work to boot. The answer lies in what is known in the industry as a personal package policy.

At its simplest, a package is akin to a company's stapling together an auto and a homeowner's policy so that you have the same coverage, but only one policy and one bill. For this, many companies offer a discount. Sometimes called the portfolio approach, these are not true packages, but they have, until recently, been the most common version. Now, though, a number of companies have taken the idea a step further and devised true packages: hybrid policies that often combine auto and homeowner's coverage, floaters, and a personal-liability umbrella—and offer improved coverage as well.

The most common improvement is *blanket property and liability protection.* With a standard homeowner's policy, when you insure a home for its replacement value, you automatically receive

automobile and homeowner's insurance. With typical limits ranging from $1 million to $10 million, the **umbrella liability policy** can offer you that extra protection. It is especially valuable if you are locally prominent, believed to be affluent, or employed in a profession commonly regarded as being very highly paid.

This policy fits over your homeowner's and automobile liability coverages like an umbrella of added coverage and pays when the other coverages are exhausted. You will be required to have certain minimum limits of liability

protection of 50 percent of this amount for unscheduled personal possessions, and usually 10 percent of the total is the coverage for other structures on your property. With blanket coverage, however, your *total* coverage is available for either your personal belongings, your home, other structures, or any combination of these.

For many years, the leaders in the package field have been Continental Insurance, which has been offering packages since 1973, and St. Paul Fire and Marine, with package policies since 1977. Continental's PCP (Personal Comprehensive Protection) is a good example of a true package, with coverage for one or more homes, personal property, cars, and recreational vehicles and boats. It offers blanket replacement-cost coverage, as well as floaters, all with discounts of between 2 and 15 percent, depending on the state.

St. Paul's Pak II policy is similar in scope. Additional features include a provision for increasing your liability protection from the standard $100,000 up to $5 million, and for higher than standard limits for unscheduled valuables such as furs and jewelry ($2,000 instead of the more common $1,000). Overall discounts range from 5 to 15 percent.

Neither St. Paul nor Continental offers its packages to renters. St. Paul includes co-op owners; Continental does not. But at least one company, Atlantic Mutual, offers packages to renters and co-op owners, and with interest in the field heating up, others, including the Kemper Group, may follow suit.

Atlantic Mutual also has the most comprehensive extra coverage I know of. Its Atlantic Master Plan, introduced in 1983, is now offered in ten states, including California, Connecticut, Florida, Illinois, and New York. Like other true packages, Atlantic's offers blanket personal-property coverage, but other more unusual features include a clause that will cover the replacement cost of your residence even if it runs *more* than your coverage limits; and a special reserve so that even if you must use up most of your coverage to replace a residence, 50 percent will still always be available for personal property. Moreover, if your home is totally destroyed and your bank (as is usually the case) requires you to renegotiate the mortgage, a special mortgage-renegotiation-cost clause makes up any difference in monthly payments. And it offers valued contract floaters for furs, jewelry, and other scheduled items, all of this at discounts of 5 to 17 percent off Atlantic's normal premiums.

Are there any drawbacks to a package policy? Well, you could run into problems if you subsequently rack up a bad auto-claims record. This could result in the involuntary splitup of your policy—that is, the cancellation of your auto portion and the issuance of a separate homeowner's policy.

SOURCE: Peter D. Lawrence, "Insurance: Saving on a Package Deal," *Esquire,* January 1986, p. 46.

coverage under those other policies in order to buy an umbrella liability policy. For instance, the insurer might require $250,000 of homeowner's liability coverage, and $250,000/$500,000/$100,000 in automobile liability coverages. In this instance, a $5 million umbrella liability policy would pay $200,000 of a $450,000 automobile bodily injury claim involving one injured claimant, as the umbrella liability payment would start after the automobile insurer's $250,000 limit of payment was reached.

In addition to providing excess coverage over the auto and homeowner's liability coverages, the umbrella liability policy also broadens your coverage to include some exposures not previously covered. Although there is little standardization of umbrella policies, it likely will fill a few gaps between your auto and homeowner's liability coverages. Here, the umbrella liability policy will pay after a deductible. The deductible varies in size, ranging from $250 to as high as $10,000. As an example, if you lose a $25,000 defamation of character suit, the loss might be excluded from your homeowner's policy but be covered under the umbrella policy. If the umbrella policy has a $500 deductible, you pay $500 of the loss, and the umbrella liability policy pays $24,500, or $25,000 − $500.

Professional liability, aircraft liability, and some watercraft liability are excluded under the umbrella liability policy, but they can be covered by an amendment to the policy. The cost of an umbrella liability policy has been remarkably reasonable, and may be as low as $100 to $200 a year, although the insurance marketplace has undergone a rapid escalation in overall liability premiums since 1984. You may be able to save money by buying from the insurer that covers your car and home. Before you buy, consider the cost of increasing your auto and homeowner's coverages, if that is required. This is a hidden cost of the umbrella liability policy, but it is quite real.

FACTORS AFFECTING COST AND COVERAGE

Before deciding on your insurance purchase, you should understand a few major items that can strongly influence the premiums you will pay. These factors include (1) deductibles, (2) coinsurance, (3) the manner in which the insurer defines loss, and (4) variations in limits.

Deductibles

A **deductible** is a requirement that you retain, or absorb, the first dollars of an insured loss before the insurer begins to pay. It is designed to remove minor, frequent losses from the insurance process, and it saves you money by eliminating small claims. An insurer might absorb $100 in expenses to handle a $50 claim, while its cost to manage a $1000 claim might not be much greater.

Table 8.6 contains examples of deductibles and their impacts on premiums. Although the relative costs shown may not always match those for deductibles available to you, they do illustrate some important points. First, *as deductibles increase, premiums usually decrease.*

In reading Table 8.6, observe the size of the deductible in column 1; then note what happens to the premiums in the other three columns as the deductible changes. For example, in column 2, we see that the premium is 100 percent of the normal amount at a $200 deductible level. With a $250 deductible, it is only 95 percent of the normal premium; with a $500 deductible, it drops to 74 percent of the regular premium. If the normal premium for a $200 deductible was $240, you could buy the same insurance with a $500 deductible for only

Table 8.6 INSURANCE PREMIUMS FOR VARIOUS COVERAGES WITH COMMON DEDUCTIBLES

(1) Deductible ($)	(2) Auto collision ($200 deductible = 100%)	(3) Auto other than collision ($50 deductible = 100%)	(4) Homeowner's property damage, $100,000 home ($1,000 deductible = 100%)
0	[a]	118%	[a]
50	[a]	100%	[a]
100	[a]	95%	114%
200	100%	[a]	[a]
250	95%	[a]	105%
500	74%	[a]	104%
1000	[a]	[a]	100%

[a] Rates for this coverage and deductible were not published.

SOURCE: Texas State Board of Insurance, published rates, various dates.

$177.60 ($240 × 0.74). Column 2 applies to auto collision insurance. In columns 3 and 4, the same principle applies to other forms of insurance. As you can see in columns 3 and 4, if you choose a very low deductible, you will pay more than the normal premium. If the insurer does not decrease your premium in exchange for your accepting a higher deductible, you should choose the lower deductible.

The second point to remember is that *as deductibles increase, the rate of decrease in premiums declines.* This decline occurs because, for most risks, large losses are less frequent than small losses. Thus, the same dollar increase in deductible starting from a higher dollar base does not eliminate as many dollars in losses as it would if it started at a lower dollar base.

Coinsurance

Coinsurance can be confusing, because it can mean two different things, depending on the type of insurance policy you have. The coinsurance clause in property insurance requires you to insure your property for at least some stated minimum percentage (often 80 percent) of its full value if you are to recover the full amount of a loss from the insurer. If you insure for less than the required figure, you will recover only a portion of your actual loss. Thus, when you insure for less than the required amount, you must absorb a part of a loss.

In health insurance, the coinsurance provision causes you to bear part of the cost of a covered expense above the deductible. Usually, this percentage sharing is an 80–20 arrangement, with the insurer paying 80 percent of the covered expense and you absorbing 20 percent. If you had a $2200 loss and a $200 deductible, you and the insurer would share the $2000 balance of the loss. Your insurer would pay $1600 (80 percent × $2000), and you would absorb the remaining $400 (20 percent × $2000) out of your own pocket. In both types of coinsurance, both you and the insurer bear a part of the loss.

If there is no coinsurance provision, or if it is very generous (such as 90–10 in health insurance), your premium likely will be higher. In some cases you have no choice on coinsurance, but if you do, you must decide on the trade-off between a higher insurance premium and a more generous coinsurance clause. Often, it is better to accept some degree of coinsurance.

The Manner in Which the Insurer Defines Loss

The amount your insurer pays you for a loss depends strongly on how your policy defines a loss. You can buy replacement cost coverage for your home and much of your property. **Replacement cost** is the cost to replace or repair your property with materials, workmanship, and design of a quality like that it possessed before the loss, at today's prices. This does *not* consider depreciation, and it can put you in a better financial position after the loss than before it, since you can replace old with new.

Actual cash value usually is defined as replacement cost minus depreciation. Thus, if your roof is 40 percent depreciated and costs $5000 to replace using similar materials and workmanship, its actual cash value is $5000 × (1.00 − 0.40) = $5000 (0.60), or $3000. An insurance policy that agrees to pay replacement cost will probably cost you more than one that limits your recovery to actual cash value, but it usually will pay you more when a loss occurs.

Variations in Limits

As the maximum limit the insurer will pay for a loss rises, the premiums also rise. However, these premiums will rise *at a decreasing rate of increase,* because larger losses occur less frequently than smaller losses.

Consider the relative premiums for automobile liability insurance shown in Table 8.7. Based on those figures, if your premium for 10/20 (10,000/20,000) bodily injury liability (BIL) coverage were $100, you could buy ten times those limits, or 100/200 (100,000/200,000), for only 1.9 times your original premium, or a total of $190; or, you could purchase *50 times* the 10/20 limit, or 500/1,000 (500,000/1,000,000), for 2.33 times the original premium, or $233.

FINDING COVERAGE

When you buy auto, homeowner's, or umbrella liability insurance for the first time, or when you move to a new community, you should shop for an insurer. Some insurers (for example, GEICO, USAA, and AMICA Mutual) sell through the

Table 8.7 ONE STATE'S RELATIVE PREMIUMS FOR AUTOMOBILE LIABILITY INSURANCE (LIMITS IN $000s)

BODILY INJURY 10/20 = 100%		PROPERTY DAMAGE 5 = 100%	
Limits	%	Limits	%
10/20	100	5	100
15/30	121	10	110
20/40	134	15	115
25/50	146	20	118
50/100	170	25	120
100/200	190	50	125
200/400	209	100	130
300/600	219	200	137
500/1,000	233	500	145
1,000/2,000	258	1,000	155
5,000/10,000	338	5,000	189

SOURCE: Texas State Board of Insurance, published rates, effective February 1, 1986.

mail, and some sell through local representatives. Most local representatives are *agents.* An agent is a legal representative of the insurer. Some agents represent only one insurer or group of insurers (for example, State Farm, Nationwide, and Allstate agents located in Sears stores) and are called *exclusive agents* or *captive agents.* Other agents may represent several insurers. Known as *independent agents* or *American agents,* they will place you with one of the insurers they represent. Some insurers selling through these agents are Travelers, Kemper, CNA, Fireman's Fund, INA, Hartford, St. Paul, and Ohio Casualty. Finally, some local representatives, called *direct writers,* work as salaried employees of insurers (for example, Liberty Mutual, Employers of Wausau).

Which is best for you? The specific nature of the marketing system is less important than finding an insurer with services fitted to your needs, low prices, a solid financial base, and competent representatives with whom you feel comfortable.

First, learn about the financial solvency and operations of the insurers that interest you. For a factual overview, go to a major library and look up each insurer in *Best's Insurance Reports, Property-Liability,* for the most recent year available. A guide printed in the front of the volume will help you understand its ratings. Also, read *Consumer Reports,* which periodically analyzes the services of insurers selling auto and homeowner's insurance.

Second, ask people you respect to recommend solid, professional insurer representatives in your community. You may wish to check with the Better

Business Bureau for information about possible problems. Good representatives should have professional training. They also should be updating their skills regularly by attending seminars and through professional association activities. Ask them for references, and ask those references about the service they have received. Be sure that you are comfortable with them *now.* After all, if you are uncomfortable communicating with an agent before a sale, think how awkward things might be later if you need help on a claim or other problem.

Decide on the coverages that interest you and set up a worksheet to compare prices. During your interviews, ask representatives of various companies to price the coverages in the form you prescribe, so you can objectively compare those prices. Be sure to ask about varying deductibles and limits of coverage, and include any special features that interest you. Finally, ask the representative to suggest any needed coverages or modifications in coverage, to explain them, and to price them. Do not hesitate to call back and get more information if you need it.

With all of this information in hand, make your choice. Remember that price is important, but that you may be better off paying a bit more to have the specific coverages, insurer, and representative you want.

IF YOU HAVE A CLAIM

Should you suffer a loss, you will need to notify your insurer and file a claim. Be prepared to work with the insurer's claims representative to arrive at the best possible settlement. The insurer may require you to meet a number of conditions like those we discussed for the homeowner's special form (HO-3). The claims representative, called an **adjuster,** may be a salaried employee of the insurer (a *staff adjuster*) or an adjuster hired by the insurer to settle claims (an *independent adjuster*).

Some of the major questions an adjuster must consider are the following:

1 Did a verifiable loss occur?
2 Is the loss covered?
3 If the loss is covered, how much is the insurer obligated to pay?

The more accurately you organize and present information answering these questions, the quicker and fairer your settlement should be. It is also important to take certain actions at the time of an accident or loss. With an auto accident, for example, it is generally best to call the police immediately and to remain at the scene of the accident until proper documentation is established.

Organize all of your information about the claim, make copies of all documents, save one set of copies, and give one set to the adjuster. Clearly explain anything that may not be obvious, and answer all questions. Ask the adjuster if there is anything else you need to do or if other information is needed. Be reasonable and be cooperative. This approach usually results in an equitable and timely settlement.

However, if you are not satisfied with your treatment, ask for the name of the adjuster's superior and discuss your problem with that person. If the insurer remains uncooperative about your claim, write or call your state insurance regulator and ask for help. State the facts clearly, so the regulator can effectively support your claim. To assist you, the appendix at the end of this chapter lists the addresses and telephone numbers of insurance regulators in the United States.

If you still have a problem, you may be able to submit a property loss to a *binding appraisal,* in which you and the insurer each select your own appraiser, and the two appraisers then select an umpire. If necessary, the umpire will work with the appraisers on any differences, and the joint decision of any two is binding on you and the insurer. Another alternative is for you to hire a *public adjuster,* who will represent you for a fee (usually about 10 percent of the settlement). Since this takes part of your settlement, you should carefully weigh your likely net from the hoped-for greater total recovery against the settlement already offered by the insurer.

SUMMARY

You are faced with many risk situations in which a loss can occur. These risks can be classified as (1) property risks, (2) liability risks, and (3) life and health risks.

Insurance transfers part or all of your loss to an insurer. It is a logical tool for many of the risks created by your auto, your home, and a host of other activities. Other risk treatments are (1) retention, where you bear your own losses; (2) loss control, which reduces either loss frequency or loss severity, or both; and (3) various combinations of insurance, retention, and loss control.

Traditional auto insurance involves third-party (liability) coverages for bodily injury and property damage to others. You may want to have higher coverage limits than the minimums your state requires. First-party coverages pay you if you are injured or if your own auto is damaged. No-fault auto insurance limits your right to sue when an auto accident occurs and stresses first-party coverages.

Homeowner's insurance is divided into property coverages and liability coverages. There may be severe constraints on the property coverage for the contents of your home or apartment, and you should carefully evaluate that coverage and your need for additional coverages. Also, you may want more than the typical limit of liability coverage.

The umbrella liability policy can provide an added layer of protection against lawsuits that might cripple your finances. It is relatively inexpensive for the amount of coverage it provides, because the underlying liability coverages from your auto and homeowner's policies will cover most losses.

Deductibles, coinsurance, the manner in which the insurer defines loss, and variations in policy limits all affect the price you pay for insurance and the coverage it affords you. Shop carefully to find the right combination of coverage and price, and to find the right insurer and local representative.

In most cases, you can facilitate the claims process by being properly prepared and cooperating with the insurer. If this does not work, you can request assistance from the adjuster's supervisor or your state insurance regulator, consider binding appraisal on a property loss, and even use a public adjuster.

KEY TERMS

actual cash value
adjuster
bodily injury liability
coinsurance
collision
conditions
deductible
dwelling
first-party coverages
HO-3 policy
insurance
liability risk
life and health risk
loss control
loss of use
medical payments
medical payments to others
no-fault insurance
other than collision
personal liability
personal property
property damage liability
property risk
replacement cost
retention
reverse third-party coverages
third-party coverages
threshold
umbrella liability policy
uninsured/underinsured motorists insurance

SELECTED READINGS

Church, George C. "Sorry, Your Policy Is Canceled." *Time*, March 24, 1986, pp. 16–20, 23–26.

Dunn, Donald H., ed. "Now's the Time to Ask: 'Am I Covered?' " *Business Week*, October 21, 1985, pp. 141–142.

Farrell, Mary H. J. "Car Insurance: Where the Discounts Are." *Good Housekeeping*, July 1985, p. 165.

"Homeowners Insurance: Understanding Your Policy." *Consumer Reports*, August 1985, pp. 478–482.

Lynch, Richard A. "The Best Auto Policies." *Money*, December 1985, pp. 163, 165, 167, 169.

"Renters Need Insurance, Too." *Changing Times*, November 1985, p. 98.

QUESTIONS

1 Define insurance, and explain how it reduces uncertainty.
2 Explain retention, and discuss when you might want to use it to treat risk.

3 What is loss control? When might you consider using it along with insurance? Along with retention?

4 Contrast first-party automobile insurance coverages with third-party coverages.

5 Explain how reverse third-party coverages differ from third-party coverages in automobile insurance.

6 Discuss the reasons for no-fault automobile insurance, and describe how no-fault works.

7 Explain what a threshold in no-fault auto insurance is, and discuss how a low threshold would affect the treatment of auto accidents.

8 Compare collision coverage and comprehensive (other than collision) coverage in the personal automobile insurance policy.

9 Mrs. Jones lives across town. She is driving her car, and you are driving yours. She collides with you. Is she covered under the medical payments coverage of your personal automobile policy? Whose injuries are covered?

10 Mrs. Jones sues you for her injuries and for the damage to her auto that resulted from the collision in question 9. What coverage(s) will pay the cost to defend this suit? How do defense costs affect the coverage available to pay a judgment against you by the courts?

11 Compare the use of a combined single limit for liability coverage with the more common limits used for bodily injury liability coverage and property damage liability coverage under the personal automobile policy.

12 What is uninsured motorists insurance?

13 For the homeowner's special form (HO-3), briefly summarize what is covered under (a) dwelling coverage, (b) other structures, and (c) personal property.

14 Discuss why you might want to add an endorsement to your homeowner's insurance that lists certain items and insures them at the values stated.

15 Explain the loss-of-use coverage under a homeowner's insurance policy.

16 What are the major differences between the medical payments coverage in homeowner's insurance and the medical payments coverage in automobile insurance?

17 How does the umbrella liability policy fit together with your auto and homeowner's insurance?

18 Explain the likely costs of an umbrella liability policy.

19 Describe what happens to your insurance premiums as your deductible increases.

20 Compare replacement cost and actual cash value as definitions of loss in property insurance. Which would pay you more? Which would cost you more to buy?

21 Describe what happens to your premium as the maximum limit the insurer will pay for a loss rises.

22 What are some of the major questions a claims adjuster must answer?

23 If your bodily injury liability limits under your automobile insurance policy were \$15,000/\$30,000, how much would your policy pay if you were at fault in an accident, and the court awarded \$28,000 in damages to the other driver?

24 Suppose you have $25,000/$50,000 bodily injury liability limits under your automobile insurance, and you are judged to be at fault in an accident.
  a Mr. Klinski's court award is $22,000. How much will the policy pay if he is the only person you injure?
  b Mr. Klonski, a passenger in Mr. Klinski's car, is awarded $20,000 in damages. How much will the policy pay to Klonski? To Klinski?

25 The Smalls' homeowner's insurance (special form HO-3) provides $100,000 of coverage on their dwelling. If they travel out of state for a vacation and their personal property is lost in a fire at the resort where they are staying, what is the most they can hope to recover? Assume that they have not added any coverages by amending the policy.

26 The Lanes' homeowner's insurance (special form HO-3) provides $150,000 of coverage on their dwelling. A fire severely damages their home, making it uninhabitable. They incur living expenses of $5000 a month for the six months that they must live in rental housing while their home is repaired. Their normal monthly living expenses are $3000. Determine the recovery from their insurer for living expenses. What is the most the insurer would pay if their claim justified it?

27 Mrs. Brown owns a $2 million umbrella liability policy and an auto policy with $250,000/$500,000/$100,000 limits. She is at fault in an accident that occurs as she pulls out of her driveway. The other driver is Mr. White, who had no passengers in his car. He is permanently paralyzed, and the court awards him a total settlement of $1.5 million. Calculate how Mrs. Brown's insurance coverages would pay for Mr. White's injury. Show your calculations, and explain them.

CASE PROBLEMS

8.1 Phil and Jill Kelly's home is insured for $100,000 under their HO-3 (special form), and the other property coverages bear their normal percentage relationships to the dwelling coverage. The house itself is properly insured for its full value. Burglars break in by picking a lock. They do no damage to the house but steal some valuable items, as follows:

Matched pair of French dueling pistols	$ 2,600
Jill's diamond ring	7,400
Jill's diamond watch	2,300
Other jewelry (Jill's)	1,500
Gold coins	1,250
Jill's mink coat	6,875
Sterling silver flatware (settings for 16 plus serving pieces)	3,500
Silverplate trays, coffee and tea service	1,350
Total	$26,775

a Calculate what will be paid by the Kellys' homeowner's insurance and how much they must absorb out of their own resources. Use the personal property coverage (C) under the HO-3 homeowner's policy. Show your calculations, and explain them.

b Discuss how adding an endorsement that schedules (lists) certain personal property might have increased the Kellys' recovery from their insurance policy.

8.2 Fran Harris has 25/50/20 auto liability coverage limits. She is at fault in an accident in which she loses control of her car while exiting the expressway, sideswipes Tom Diaz's Mercedes, strikes Joan Burke's sports car (injuring Joan's right leg so that Joan will walk with a slight limp for the rest of her life), caroms into Bill Weaver (a pedestrian), plows through Jake Kobler's fence and yard, clips the corner of Jake's house, and crash lands in his empty swimming pool. Joan's two passengers, Ann and Jan Zane, also are injured. The court awards the following damages:

Damage to Tom's Mercedes	$ 8,500
Tom's medical expenses	800
Tom's income loss	200
Damage to Joan's sports car	6,700
Joan's medical expenses	14,000
Joan's income loss	17,500
Joan's mental anguish	25,000
Bill's medical expenses	3,200
Bill's income loss	1,100
Jake's fence	750
Jake's yard	250
Jake's house	2,400
Jake's swimming pool	5,500
Ann's medical expenses	350
Jan's medical expenses	1,650
Jan's mental anguish	600
Total	$88,500

a Calculate what will be paid by Fran's bodily injury liability (BIL) insurance and by her property damage liability (PDL) insurance, and calculate how much she must pay out of her own pocket. Show your calculations, and explain them.

b What would have been paid if Fran's policy had provided a combined single limit of liability of $75,000?

Appendix 8A

Insurance Regulators, Their Addresses, and Their Telephone Numbers

Jurisdiction	Address	Telephone
Alabama	Commissioner of Insurance, 135 S. Union St., Montgomery, Ala. 36130-3401	205/269-3550
Alaska	Director of Insurance, Pouch "D," Juneau, Alaska 99811	907/465-2515
Arizona	Director of Insurance, 801 E. Jefferson, Phoenix, Ariz. 85007	602/255-5440
Arkansas	Insurance Commissioner, 400 University Tower Building, 12th and University Sts., Little Rock, Ark. 72204	501/371-1325
California	Insurance Commissioner, 600 S. Commonwealth, 14th Floor, Los Angeles, Calif. 90005	213/736-2551
Colorado	Commissioner of Insurance, 303 W. Colfax Ave., 5th Floor, Denver, Colo. 80204	303/866-3201
Connecticut	Insurance Commissioner, State Office Building, 165 Capital Ave., Hartford, Conn. 06106	203/566-5275
Delaware	Insurance Commissioner, 21 The Green, Dover, Del. 19901	302/736-4251
District of Columbia	Superintendent of Insurance, 614 H St., N.W., Ste. 512, Washington, D.C. 20001	202/727-7419
Florida	Insurance Commissioner, State Capitol, Plaza Level 11, Tallahassee, Fla. 32301	904/488-3440
Georgia	Insurance Commissioner, Floyd Memorial Building, 704 W. Tower, 2 Martin L. King, Jr., Dr., Atlanta, Ga. 30334	404/656-2056
Hawaii	Insurance Commissioner, P.O. Box 3614, Honolulu, Hawaii 96811	808/548-5450

SOURCE: *Insurance Facts: 1986–87 Property/Casualty Fact Book,* New York: Insurance Information Institute, 1986, pp. 106–108.

Jurisdiction	Address	Telephone
Idaho	Director of Insurance, 700 W. State St., Boise, Idaho 83720	208/334-2250
Illinois	Director of Insurance, 320 W. Washington St., 4th Floor, Springfield, Ill. 62767	217/782-4515
Indiana	Commissioner of Insurance, 509 State Office Building, Indianapolis, Ind. 46204	317/232-2386
Iowa	Commissioner of Insurance, Lucas State Office Building, G23, Des Moines, Iowa 50319	515/281-5705
Kansas	Commissioner of Insurance, 420 S.W. Ninth St., Topeka, Kans. 66612	913/296-3071
Kentucky	Insurance Commissioner, 229 W. Main St., Frankfort, Ky. 40602	502/564-3630
Louisiana	Commissioner of Insurance, 950 N. 5th St., Baton Rouge, La. 70801	504/342-5328
Maine	Superintendent of Insurance, State Office Building, State House Station 34, Augusta, Maine 04333	207/289-3101
Maryland	Insurance Commissioner, 501 St. Paul Pl., 7th Floor S., Baltimore, Md. 21202	301/659-2520
Massachusetts	Commissioner of Insurance, 100 Cambridge St., Boston, Mass. 02202	617/727-3333
Michigan	Insurance Commissioner, 611 W. Ottawa St., Lansing, Mich. 48933	517/373-9273
Minnesota	Commissioner of Commerce, 500 Metro Square Building, 5th Floor, St. Paul, Minn. 55101	612/296-6907
Mississippi	Commissioner of Insurance, 1804 Walter Sillers Building, Jackson, Miss. 39205	601/359-3569
Missouri	Director of Insurance, 301 West High St., 6 North, P.O. Box 690, Jefferson City, Mo. 65102	314/751-2451
Montana	Commissioner of Insurance, Mitchell Building, 126 N. Sanders, P.O. Box 4009, Helena, Mont. 59601	406/444-2040
Nebraska	Director of Insurance, State Capitol Building, 301 Centennial Mall S., P.O. Box 94699, Lincoln, Nebr. 68509	402/471-2201
Nevada	Commissioner of Insurance, Nye Building, 210 S. Fall St., Carson City, Nev. 89710	702/885-4270
New Hampshire	Insurance Commissioner, 169 Manchester St., P.O. Box 2005, Concord, N.H. 03301	603/271-2261
New Jersey	Commissioner of Insurance, 201 East State Street, Trenton, N.J. 08625	609/292-5363
New Mexico	Superintendent of Insurance, PERA Building, Drawer 1269, Santa Fe, N.M. 87501	505/827-4535

Jurisdiction	Address	Telephone
New York	Superintendent of Insurance, 160 W. Broadway, New York, N.Y. 10013	212/602-0429
North Carolina	Commissioner of Insurance, Dobbs Building, P.O. Box 26387, Raleigh, N.C. 27611	919/733-7343
North Dakota	Commissioner of Insurance, Capitol Building, 5th Floor, Bismark, N.Dak. 58505	701/224-2440
Ohio	Director of Insurance, 2100 Stella Ct., Columbus, Ohio 43215	614/466-3584
Oklahoma	Insurance Commissioner, 408 Will Rogers Memorial Building, Oklahoma City, Okla. 73105	405/521-2828
Oregon	Insurance Commissioner, 158 12th St., N.E., Salem, Oreg. 97310	503/378-4271
Pennsylvania	Insurance Commissioner, Strawberry Square, 13th Floor, Harrisburg, Pa. 17120	717/787-5173
Rhode Island	Insurance Commissioner, 100 N. Main St., Providence, R.I. 02903	401/277-2246
South Carolina	Chief Insurance Commissioner, 2711 Middleburg Dr., P.O. Box 4067, Columbia, S.C. 29204	803/758-3266
South Dakota	Director of Insurance, Capitol Building, Pierre, S. Dak. 57501	605/773-3563
Tennessee	Commissioner of Insurance, 1808 West End Ave., 14th Floor, Nashville, Tenn. 37219	615/741-2241
Texas	Commissioner of Insurance, 1110 San Jacinto Blvd., Austin, Tex. 78701-1998	512/463-6464
Utah	Commissioner of Insurance, P.O. Box 45803, Salt Lake City, Utah 84145	801/530-6400
Vermont	Commissioner of Insurance, State Office Building, 120 State St., Montpelier, Vt. 05602	802/828-3301
Virginia	Commissioner of Insurance, 700 Jefferson Building, Richmond, Va. 23209	804/786-3741
Washington	Insurance Commissioner, Insurance Building AQ21, Olympia, Wash. 98504	206/753-7301
West Virginia	Insurance Commissioner, 2100 Washington St., E., Charleston, W. Va. 25305	304/348-3394
Wisconsin	Commissioner of Insurance, 123 W. Washington Ave., Madison, Wis. 53702	608/266-0102
Wyoming	Insurance Commissioner, Herschler Building, 122 W. 25th St., Cheyenne, Wyo. 82002	307/777-7401

Heavy on Test

9

Financing Health Care and Disability

After studying this chapter, you should:

- Understand the ways that loss of health can cause a financial loss
- Appreciate the potential financial severity of a total and permanent disability
- Be able to determine the amount of disability income insurance a person needs
- Be aware of medical expense insurance's methods of benefit payments
- Understand the different medical expense insurance policies and know how they differ
- Appreciate how Medicare works and understand the use of privately sold medigap insurance
- Be aware of how to buy health insurance and appreciate the need to avoid dollar swapping while obtaining catastrophic loss protection

Your good health is vitally important, yet many people take their health for granted. Your physician may be able to suggest many ways to improve your chances of staying healthy, but despite everything, you cannot avoid the possibility of being injured or falling ill in the future. In this chapter, we explore logical ways to meet the financial problems caused if you suffer loss of health.

If you are injured or fall ill, you can incur a financial loss in two ways:

1 You can *lose income* that you would have been able to earn if you had stayed healthy.
2 You can *incur additional expenses* beyond those you would experience if you were well.

Table 9.1
AVERAGE COST PER PATIENT DAY IN THE HOSPITAL

Calendar year	Total
1946	$ 9.39
1950	15.62
1955	23.12
1960	32.23
1961	34.98
1962	36.83
1963	38.91
1964	41.58
1965	44.48
1966	48.15
1967	54.08
1968	61.38
1969	70.03
1970	81.01
1971	92.31
1972	105.30
1973	102.30
1974	113.50
1975	133.70
1976	152.10
1977	173.90
1978	194.30
1979	217.10
1980	245.60
1981	271.30
1982	299.60
1983	328.15
1984	362.14
1985	398.20
1986	430.15

SOURCE: Various government documents.

An example of the importance of the second factor can be seen in Table 9.1. Note that the average cost of a day in the hospital has gone from $9.39 in 1946 to approximately $430 in 1986. A two-week stay would cost $6020 in hospital bills alone. Because of the two factors previously mentioned, the major divisions of health insurance policies are (1) *disability income insurance,* and (2) *medical expense insurance.*

DISABILITY INCOME INSURANCE

Assume that you have completed school and are working. What will happen to your income if you are injured or sick, and unable to work? Some employers provide sick leave programs that continue income for a short time, but many do not. What if your disability lasts a long time? Because sick leave benefits quickly run out in most cases, you can face a grim picture. From a financial point of view, if you are totally and permanently disabled, your family's loss will be greater than if you had died at the time your disability began. Your own expenses will continue (and even increase), while your income will stop just as it would if you had died.

Since your loss from disability can be so great, you probably should not attempt to cover the financial part of this risk. You might try to reduce its frequency (possibly by taking reasonable steps to stay healthy) and its severity (possibly by undergoing physical rehabilitation if you are disabled). Also, you can transfer most of your loss to an insurer through disability income insurance.

Disability income insurance provides monthly or weekly payments that are intended to replace part of the income you lose when you are disabled and cannot work. There are many sources of disability income insurance, including Social Security, workers' compensation, group insurance provided through your employer, and individual policies that you may buy directly from an insurer. In many cases, a person who is injured at work will be eligible for disability income insurance benefits from more than one of these sources.

Maximum Benefit Periods

The maximum time period over which most group and individual disability income insurance policies pay benefits ranges from paying up to 13 weeks to paying until you are age 65. Some policies even promise to pay for the rest of your life. If all other aspects of coverage are identical, you should expect to pay more to buy a policy with a longer benefit period.

Amount of Benefits

The monthly or weekly benefit paid by a disability income insurance policy usually is limited to the lesser of (1) a fraction or percentage of your income prior to disability, or (2) some set maximum periodic benefit. For example, a policy might pay two-thirds of your average monthly gross pay during the 12 months just before you were disabled or $2000 a month, whichever is less. If your average earnings exceed $3000 a month, the $2000 limit will apply. Insurers are cautious about selling benefit amounts that approximate full income. Because income tax, Social Security, and other items are deducted from paychecks but not from disability benefits, insurers fear that some people might be tempted to improve their financial position by pretending to become disabled.

Table 9.2
POTENTIAL DISABILITY PAYOUT BASED ON AGE

Age when disability begins	Payout
20	$1,080,000
25	960,000
30	840,000
35	720,000
40	600,000
45	480,000
50	360,000
55	240,000
60	120,000
65	0

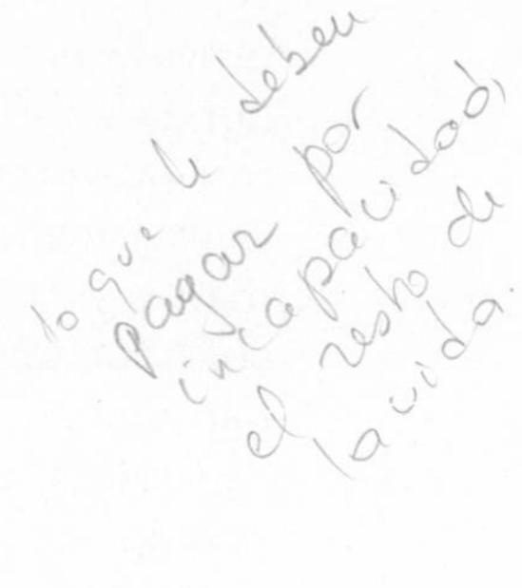

Note, in Table 9.2, the total amount of exposure an insurance company has as a result of guaranteeing $2000 a month in disability coverage to an individual at varying ages. The assumption is that the person would have worked to age 65.

Waiting Periods

The **waiting period** in disability income insurance is a deductible. It eliminates small losses just as the deductible in automobile insurance does, and it also lessens the amount the insurer has to pay on large losses. It is a period of time, starting when your disability begins, during which the insurer does not pay benefits. When it ends, if you are still disabled, the insurer begins benefit payments. If all other aspects of coverage are identical, you can expect to pay more to buy a policy with a shorter waiting period, because it will pay in cases where a policy with a longer waiting period will not pay and it will pay you sooner (and more total dollars) in the case of a disability that lasts a long time.

Definitions of Disability

Because disability is the factor that causes benefits to be payable, its definition is important. Usually, for the first one or two years after a disability begins, the definition will be your total inability to meet any and all duties of the regular job that you held before the disability. Then, if the benefit period continues, *disability* may be given a less generous definition: your total inability to meet any and all of the duties of *any job* for which you are reasonably suited by education, training, or experience. If you can hold a productive job other than the one you held prior to disability, you may be encouraged to reenter the work force, even if the new job pays less or is less prestigious.

A growing number of disability insurers will help pay for rehabilitation, especially if its cost is less than the cost of continuing to pay disability benefits. Some insurers offer rehabilitation coupled with only a partial reduction in benefits if you then are able to go back to work, but can work only at an occupation with low pay. Such a policy might reduce its monthly benefits by two-thirds of each dollar you earned, on earnings up to 50 percent of your predisability earnings level. Then, it might reduce its benefits dollar-for-dollar for your earnings above that level.

How Much Disability Income Insurance Should You Buy?

If you want to know how much privately purchased disability income insurance you need to protect yourself against a loss of your take-home income, here are some steps to consider using.

Step 1: Determine your monthly or weekly take-home pay. This is what is left of your gross pay after income tax, Social Security, and other payroll deductions. Estimate how much of this take-home pay you really need in order to sustain a satisfactory standard of living. If this is less than your take-home pay, it becomes your target figure. If it exceeds your take-home pay, the take-home pay must be the target figure, because insurers are unlikely to insure you for more.

Step 2: Estimate your current disability income available from other sources. This includes Social Security, workers' compensation, group insurance, and preretirement disability benefits from pension, thrift, profit-sharing, or other employer plans.[1]

Step 3: Subtract your current disability income benefit total from your target figure. The result is your needed disability income insurance.

Following the steps just mentioned, you can use the worksheet in Table 9.3 to determine how much disability income insurance you need.

[1] Under 1986 federal income tax law, disability income insurance benefits from a policy you pay for are not taxed. Benefits from a plan paid for by your employer are subject to income taxes but may have a tax credit to offset them if your total income is low. You may want to adjust the expected benefits provided by your group insurance or other employer program downward because of their possible taxability. Also, workers' compensation will not pay for disabilities caused off the job, so check to see if any other benefits pay in that event. And learn what privately provided benefits will pay if the disability is job-related. They probably will pay less than their full amount when workers' compensation does pay. The benefit amounts you are eligible for might differ depending on whether the cause of your disability is occupational or nonoccupational.

Table 9.3 WORKSHEET FOR DETERMINING THE AMOUNT OF DISABILITY INCOME INSURANCE YOU NEED

1. Monthly or weekly target pay		$______
2. Current disability income available		
a. Social Security	$______	
b. Workers' compensation	______	
c. Group disability plan	______	
d. Other employer plan(s)	______	
		$______
3. 1 minus 2 equals your additional disability income insurance needed.		$______

MEDICAL EXPENSE INSURANCE

Most of us experience some medical expenses each year, and we have few problems coping with them. But imagine the trouble you might have paying your bills if you were to need hospitalization, extensive testing, emergency treatment, surgery, or intensive care. The bills could be staggering, even if you had considerable savings and investments to cushion the blow. Medical expense insurance is designed to provide financial protection when you need medical care because of an illness or an injury.

Rising Cost of Medical Care

Medical expense coverage becomes especially important when you consider what has happened to medical care costs. The consumer price index (CPI) for urban consumers rose from a 1967 base of 100.0 to 328.4 in January 1986. If you break the CPI into two of its component parts, you will see that the medical care price index (which deals with the cost of medical care) rose to 418.2 in January 1986, while the "all other items" price index (which includes the cost of all parts of the CPI except medical care) rose to only 323.4. These two parts of the CPI are highlighted in Figure 9.1. If you were to look still further, you would find that the medical care index can be separated into a number of parts, including hospital room charges and physicians' services. In January 1986, the price index for hospital room charges had reached 732.1, while the index for physicians' services approximated the medical care price index at 412.4. Figure 9.2 contrasts these two components of the medical care index. By studying Figures 9.1 and 9.2, you can see how dramatically hospital room charges have accelerated the overall rise in medical expenses, and how much the rising cost of medical care has outpaced the cost of other items in the consumer price index. This high-

Figure 9.1 **COMPARISON OF THE MEDICAL CARE COST INDEX WITH THE INDEX FOR "ALL OTHER ITEMS" FROM THE CONSUMER PRICE INDEX SINCE 1967**

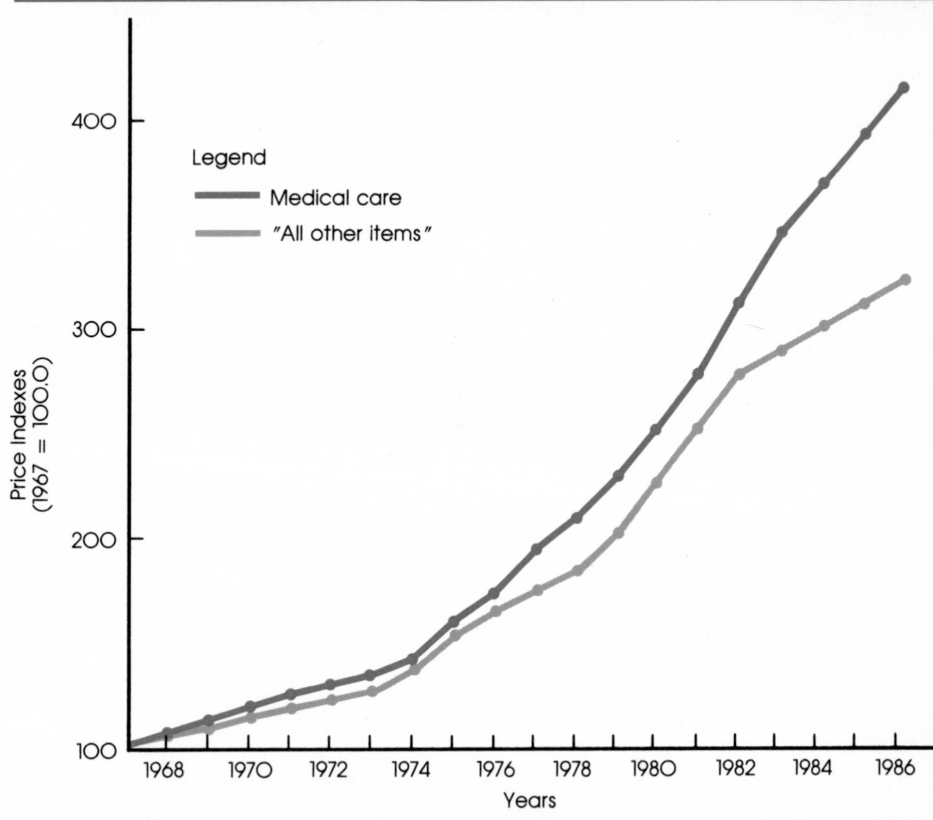

SOURCE: U.S. Department of Labor, Bureau of Labor Statistics, *CPI Detailed Report*, Washington, D.C.: various years, for January of each year.

cost medical care environment makes adequate medical expense insurance a necessity, but it also makes coverage more expensive because insurers expect to pay out more benefits each year. Consequently, it also leads to a complex situation in which medical providers, employers, insurers, consumers, and other parties all are trying to find ways to assure the delivery of good medical care while managing to control the cost of that care. Many experts are concerned that the availability of medical expense insurance to pay our medical bills removes price considerations from the medical services marketplace, because we no longer are sensitive to prices in deciding what medical services to purchase.

Figure 9.2 **COMPARISON OF PHYSICIANS' SERVICES COST INDEX WITH THE HOSPITAL ROOM CHARGE INDEX FROM THE MEDICAL CARE COST INDEX SINCE 1967**

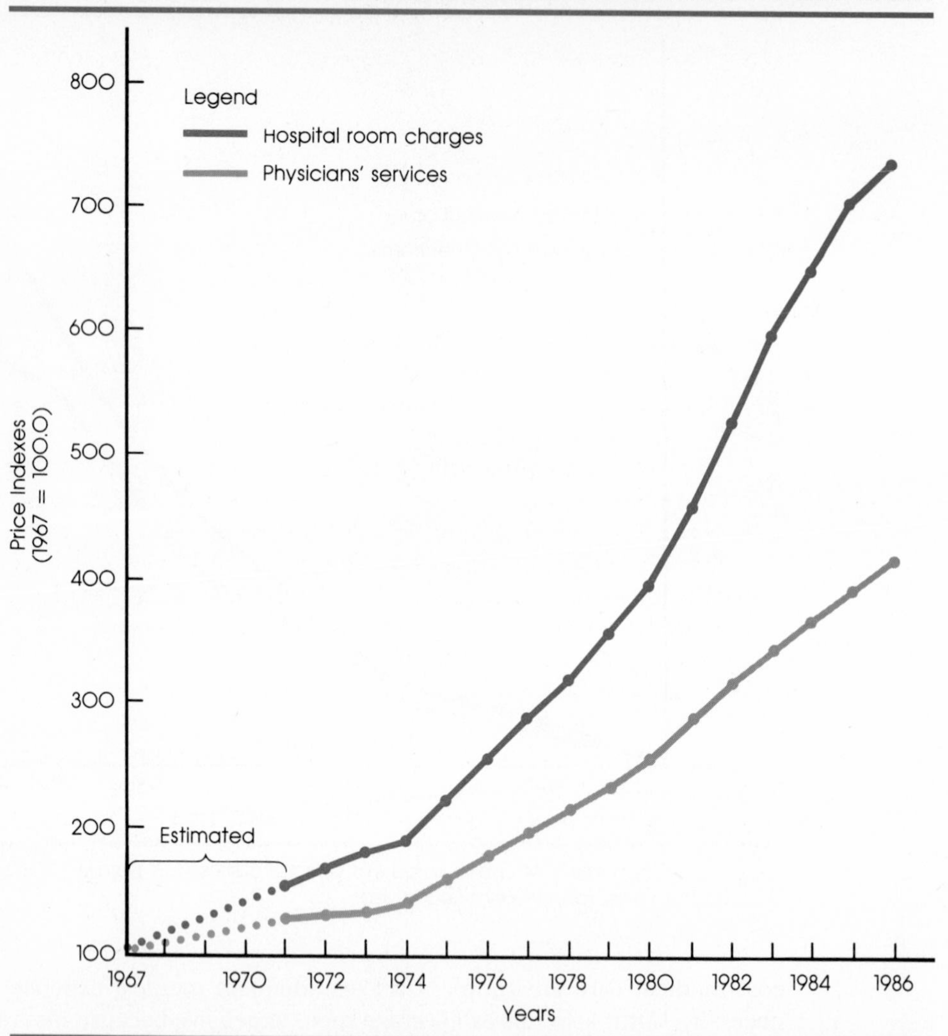

SOURCE: U.S. Department of Labor, Bureau of Labor Statistics, *CPI Detailed Report,* Washington, D.C.: various years, for January of each year.

- indemnity
- service benefit
- Value benefits

Basis of Benefit Payment

Your medical expense insurance can provide benefits in three different ways, and it can combine those payment forms.

Indemnity or Reimbursement. The majority of medical expense policies will pay benefits on an indemnity basis. With an **indemnity benefit,** you pay the doctor or other provider of medical care, then submit a claim to your insurer along with proof of the medical care and of your payment for it. In turn, the insurer reimburses you for its share of medical care costs.

Services. With another popular approach, the **services benefit,** the insurer contracts to pay the medical providers (such as doctors and hospitals) directly for their services to you. Thus, you do not have to pay for services and then wait for the insurer to reimburse you. The various Blue Cross and Blue Shield organizations across the United States use this system. Such insurers also may contract with providers in advance, securing discounts for medical services and thereby lowering the cost of medical care for the people they insure.

Valued. The **valued benefit** approach is used primarily in small, individual policies, whether disability income or medical expense. It seldom is used in health policies sold on a group basis and seldom in policies with high benefit levels. In this benefit payment plan, the insurer will pay you an agreed amount of dollars if a particular occurrence stated in the policy takes place. For example, a medical expense policy of this type might agree to pay you $125 per day, for each day you are confined to a hospital, for up to 50 consecutive days. These policies usually pay you without regard to the presence of other insurance.

Combination and Change. Both services and indemnity policies often act as though they were the other type. For example, if you are insured under an indemnity medical expense policy and are admitted to the hospital, you likely will give the hospital staff your insurance data, which they will record on a form. They then will ask you to sign the form. When this happens, you allow them to convert the policy into a form of services contract in which they will bill your insurer directly for its share of your bill. On the other hand, what if you have a services-type policy, and the doctor requires cash payment? If you pay, you then may file with the services insurer for reimbursement, effectively converting the services contract into an indemnity contract.

Some Important Policy Provisions

There are many policy provisions which are common to most medical expense insurance policies. Among the most important are provisions concerning (1) preexisting conditions, (2) continuation, and (3) the grace period.

Preexisting Conditions. Usually, if you are suffering from a medical condition when your coverage starts, that **preexisting condition** will be handled differently than if it begins after your coverage is in effect. This is done to lessen the insurer's cost of claims, and it is preferable to being excluded from any coverage at all. The preexisting condition may be covered at a lower coinsurance level, such as 50–50 (you pay 50 percent and the insurance company pays 50 percent); or it may be excluded from coverage until you go without treatment for it for some time period, such as 60 or 90 days; or it may be excluded for a stated period of time, such as one or two years, no matter what treatment you receive for it.

Continuation. Continuation provisions dictate your right to continue your coverage. The most desirable is the **noncancellable** provision, which allows you to renew the policy annually until you reach a stated maximum age. The insurer cannot increase its premiums. This is the most expensive continuation provision, but it assures you of constant coverage and cost.

Under a **guaranteed renewable** policy, you can renew annually until the stated maximum age, but the insurer can raise your premium if it raises the premiums of all other insureds in your policyholder class. This provision gives you constancy of coverage and some assurance of moderation in price changes. It should cost less than the noncancellable provision.

A **conditionally renewable** policy allows the insurer to refuse renewal at the anniversary date if a specified condition, such as unemployment or attaining age 70, exists at that date. It provides less security than the noncancellable or guaranteed renewable forms, and it should cost less.

Under a policy that is **renewable at the insurer's option,** the insurer may refuse to renew your policy at the anniversary date. There is little security in this coverage, and you should be cautious about buying such a plan, even though it probably will cost considerably less than the other forms discussed so far. It has largely replaced the **cancellable** policy, which most states have outlawed, in which the insurer can cancel at any time by giving you the proper written notice. Such a policy is of minimal value.

Grace Period. The **grace period** begins on the premium due date and usually continues for 31 days. It may be less than 31 days if your premiums are not paid on an annual basis. If you pay the premium before the grace period expires, your coverage will continue without interruption and you will not have to prove your insurability. This helps many persons retain their coverage when they neglect to pay their premiums on the due dates, and it also helps insurers limit renewal costs and earn customer goodwill.

IMPORTANT MEDICAL EXPENSE POLICIES

There are three significant types of medical expense policy classifications: (1) limited policies, (2) basic medical expense insurance, and (3) major medical and comprehensive medical expense insurance.

Limited Policies

A **limited policy** provides very narrow coverage, paying only if special events occur or in carefully defined circumstances. These policies tend to pay less often than do most other coverages and usually are a poor expenditure of your dollars. Two examples of limited policies are described below.

Dread Disease Policies. **Dread disease insurance** includes polio, leukemia, and cancer policies. This type of insurance plan will pay for certain medical expenses associated with the described dread disease or diseases but is limited to that disease or diseases. Since there are many other serious illnesses—plus the possibility of accidental injury—that also should be covered, you are wiser to spend your money on broader coverages.

Hospital Expense. Limited **hospital expense insurance** will pay a set number of dollars per day while you are in the hospital or will pay a set number of dollars if some other covered event occurs. Such plans tend to be overpriced relative to the maximum benefits they pay, and you probably should use your dollars elsewhere.

Basic Medical Expense Insurance

The **basic medical expense insurance** policy includes three distinct and separate coverages: hospital, surgical, and physician-related expenses. It often pays 100 percent of covered expenses after a very small deductible or none at all, but it has a fairly low maximum benefit level. Hospital and surgical coverages sometimes are sold alone and thus can work without each other. The physician expenses, however, normally will only be paid if incurred in combination with hospital or surgical expenses.

Hospital. Hospital coverage is for costs of care by the hospital. It does not include doctors' services. Covered costs include room and board (usually in a semiprivate room) for up to a set number of days, with a limit on the dollars per day. Other covered items usually include operating and recovery room rental, intensive care, some lab tests, basic nursing care, and basic medication and supplies.

Surgical. Surgical coverage pays for the services of surgeons and anesthesiologists or anesthetists. This coverage uses a schedule, or list, of covered surgical procedures to determine its maximum benefit for each covered surgery. Thus, it sometimes is called a surgical-schedule policy. It will pay the scheduled maximum for the surgery or the surgeon's actual charge, whichever is less. The limit of payment for the services of the anesthesiologist or anesthetist usually is a percentage of the limit for the surgeon. In order to control costs and discourage unnecessary surgeries, the surgical policy typically pays for only the most expensive surgical procedure performed during the same operative process; however, many policies will cover multiple procedures in the event of accidental injury.

Figure 9.3 EXAMPLE OF A BASIC MEDICAL EXPENSE OR A HOSPITAL-SURGICAL-MEDICAL INSURANCE POLICY

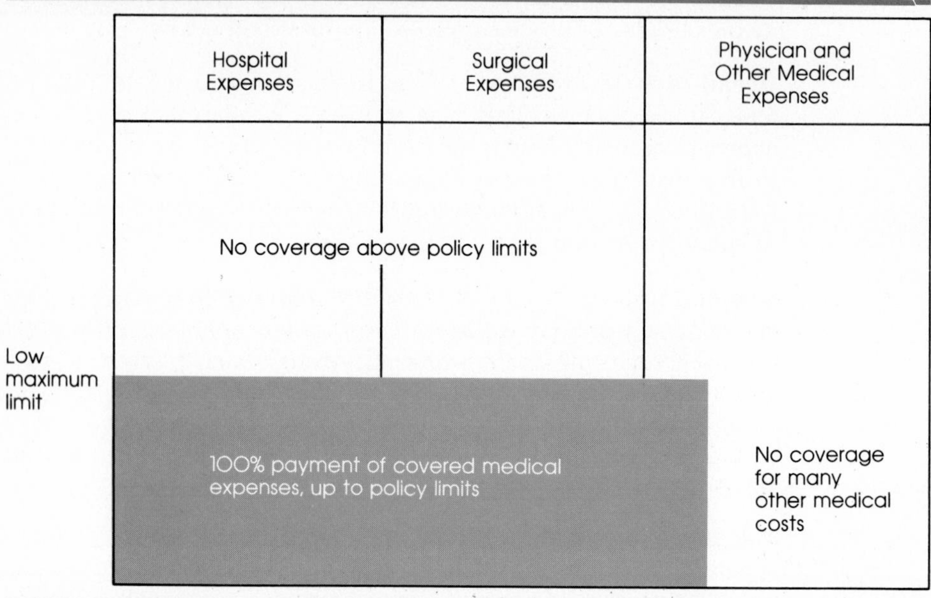

Medical. Medical coverage pays for doctors' visits. It almost always is combined with hospital and/or surgical coverage, and it usually is limited to doctors' visits while you are in the hospital and visits resulting from a stay in the hospital.

In Figure 9.3, you can see how hospital, surgical, and physician expense coverages are combined into one basic medical expense policy. Note that there is 100 percent payment for covered expenses, no deductible, a low maximum limit, and no coverage for a number of medical costs other than hospital and surgical expenses.

Major Medical and Comprehensive

Major medical expense insurance and **comprehensive medical expense insurance** policies have four basic characteristics that distinguish them from the other basic coverages:

1. A deductible before benefits are paid
2. Percentage coinsurance
3. High maximum benefits
4. Broad coverage with few internal limitations

Deductible. The deductible commonly used is an **aggregate annual deductible,** which allows you to count all medical expenses covered under the policy during the plan year toward the deductible. Once you have met the deductible, the policy will pay benefits for covered medical expenses during the remainder of the year. This 12-month year can start at any time during the calendar year, but it most commonly coincides with the January 1–December 31 calendar year. Most group major medical and comprehensive plans have annual deductibles of $100, $200, $250, or $500. A few plans use a $1000 annual deductible. The deductible is supposed to be large enough to keep most of the usual medical bills of normal, healthy people from becoming paid claims. Many plans, however, will pay some bills for most insureds during a year, because most consumers think insurance that doesn't pay quickly is a "bad deal." Unfortunately, this dollar swapping means higher premiums, because you pay the insurer $1.00 in premiums for every 70¢ to 90¢ it pays in claims. To get the most for your premium dollar, try to find the largest deductible that yields a significant premium reduction over the next-smallest deductible. Under group plans, usually only two or three family members have to satisfy deductibles in a given plan year. Then the other family members' covered medical expenses are paid from the first dollar. This kind of plan can save you quite a bit of money if your family is large, and especially if several members are injured or ill during a plan year.

Percentage Coinsurance. Under **percentage coinsurance,** you must bear part of the cost of covered medical expenses above the deductible. As described in Chapter 8, this percentage sharing is usually an 80–20 arrangement, with the insurer paying 80 percent of the covered medical expense and you paying 20 percent. The reason for the name is that you are said to "coinsure" your percentage share of the covered expenses. Coinsurance serves two purposes. First, it is intended to remove any likelihood of your profiting by receiving more for a loss than the loss actually costs you. Second, it is intended to motivate you to question the need for each possible medical service, since a portion of each dollar billed will come out of your own pocket. For example, assume that you have been in the hospital and that the total medical expenses covered under your major medical policy are $8200. The policy contains a $200 annual deductible and an 80–20 coinsurance clause. Here is what the policy will pay and what your out-of-pocket cost will be:

(1)	Total covered medical expenses during the year	$8200
	Less: annual deductible	200
	Equals: covered medical expenses subject to coinsurance	$8000
	Times: insurer's share under an 80–20 coinsurance clause	0.80
	Equals: insurer's payment to you (your recovery)	$6400
(2)	Total covered medical expenses during the year	$8200
	Less: your recovery	6400
	Equals: your out-of-pocket cost for the year on covered medical expenses	$1800

It is important to remember that you are likely to incur some expenses that are not covered under even the most generous medical expense policies. Because of this, your actual out-of-pocket expenses for the year probably will be higher than our example shows. You should not depend on having *all* of your medical expenses covered.

Another problem that can occur is that the covered medical expenses above your deductible might grow so large that you could suffer a major financial loss because of the coinsurance clause. In the example just shown, your coinsurance on the covered medical expenses above the deductible is (0.20) ($8000), or $1600. Imagine how devastating this could be if your covered medical expenses rose to $80,000! Because of this problem, comprehensive and group major medical expense insurance policies often contain a security, or stop-loss, provision. Under the **security provision,** your insurer will begin to pay 100 percent of all covered medical expenses after the total dollars you have absorbed from covered medical expenses equal a set amount.

To illustrate how a security provision works, let's return to the example we just used, where the total covered medical expenses under your major medical policy are $8200, there is a $200 annual deductible, and your policy has an 80–20 coinsurance clause. Add the assumption that your policy has a security provision with a $1000 annual out-of-pocket limit. Here is how you can compute your out-of-pocket cost and what the policy will pay:

(1) Annual deductible	$ 200
Plus: your maximum annual coinsurance to be paid (0.20)($4000)	800
Equals: your maximum annual out-of-pocket cost from covered medical expenses	$1000
(2) Total covered medical expenses during the year	$8200
Less: annual deductible	(200)
Equals: covered medical expenses subject to coinsurance	$8000
Less: your maximum coinsurance share (limited by the security provision less the deductible)	(800)
Equals: insurer's payment to you (your recovery)	$7200

As you can see, the security provision sharply reduces your out-of-pocket expenses. In this case, it cuts them from $1800 to $1000.

High Maximum Benefits. High maximum benefits protect you in the event of really large medical bills. After all, you can budget for a few doctors' visits and prescriptions, but a major illness or injury can result in a financial catastrophe. If you participate in a group insurance plan at work, the maximum lifetime limits on benefits paid under your major medical or comprehensive coverage may be as high as $250,000 or $1 million. Some group plans even have an unlimited lifetime benefit. If you don't have your employer's help in paying the premiums, however, you can afford only a much lower maximum benefit; thus, most individual policies have annual or lifetime maximum benefit limits of $25,000 to $100,000.

Broad Coverage with Few Internal Limitations. Most major medical and comprehensive insurance policies have very broad coverages. This means that they are likely to cover a wide array of medical costs, including such diverse items as ambulance service, emergency room treatment, allergy serum, and prescription drugs. Psychiatric and psychological care, along with alcoholism and drug dependency, often are covered as well, although at a much lower coinsurance percentage, such as 60–40 or 50–50. These expenses may have specific, lower absolute dollar limits as well, such as $50 per session with a psychiatrist, up to a maximum of 40 visits per year.

Lower coinsurance figures and dollar limits are examples of internal limitations that may be contained within a policy. If these limitations are extreme, they can severely restrict the effectiveness of your coverage. Imagine a $25 per day room and board limit, or a limit of 20 covered days in the hospital, or a 50–50 coinsurance clause applying to room and board and all in-hospital treatment and testing.

Remember that buying insurance involves a cost-benefit trade-off, and that the greater the likelihood of benefit payments, the higher the insurer's premium. You need to select a large enough deductible and accept enough of the coinsurance burden to keep premiums down. This approach will allow you to have higher maximum benefits with broader coverages and fewer restrictive internal limits. Figure 9.4 illustrates a typical comprehensive medical expense policy that is designed to be your only medical expense insurance. Note its deductible, coinsurance with a security provision limit, broad coverage, and high maximum benefit.

OTHER IMPORTANT MEDICAL EXPENSE INSURANCE CONCEPTS

There are three important factors that can affect your policy's effectiveness: (1) the coverage's cost containment features, (2) its use of reasonable and customary limitations, and (3) its provision for coordination of benefits.

Cost Containment

Cost containment is a relatively new term in the medical expense insurance area. It is a direct result of the soaring medical expense costs discussed earlier in this chapter. The benefits paid under (and the premiums charged for) medical expense have surged upward since the early 1970s, so insurers are attempting to reduce their claims costs. Sometimes cost containment adversely affects the quality of care, and other times it simply shifts the cost of care to you. Ideally, it would actually reduce the cost of care without negatively affecting the quality of that care.

Some effective cost containment features you are likely to encounter include (1) preadmission authorization, (2) concurrent review, and (3) second surgical opinions.

Figure 9.4 COMPREHENSIVE MAJOR MEDICAL EXPENSE INSURANCE POLICY WRITTEN WITHOUT OTHER INSURANCE

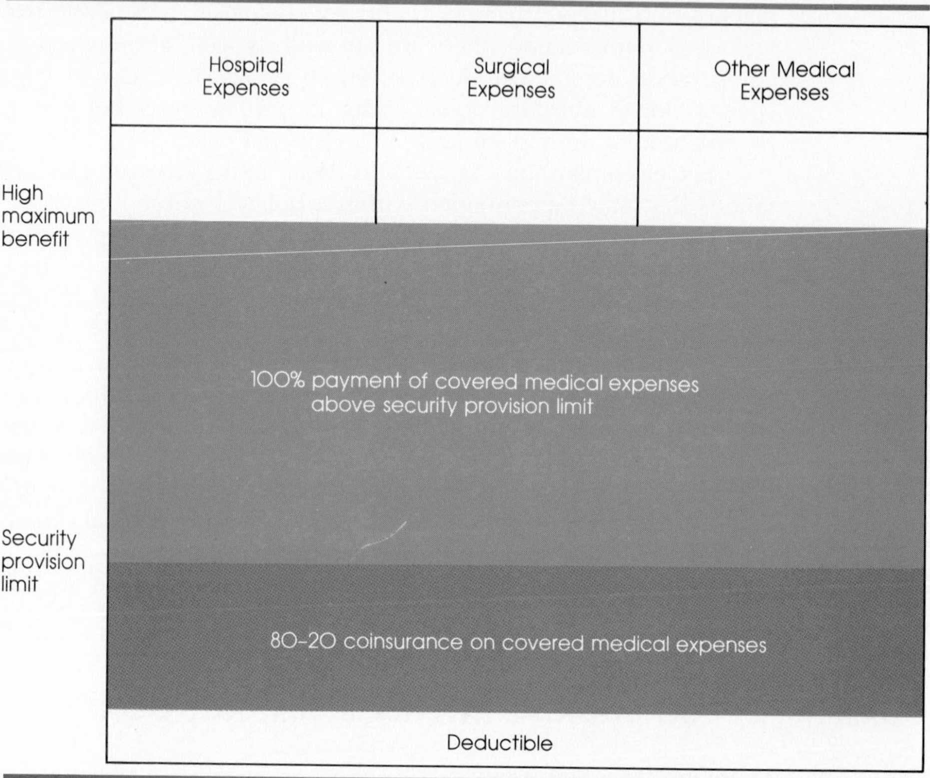

Preadmission authorization involves a deductible or coinsurance penalty if you are admitted to a hospital for routine (noncritical, nonemergency) treatment without that admission being approved by a designated third party *before* it occurs. This feature limits unnecessary admissions and thus controls a major cost area—hospital expenses.

With **concurrent review,** a third party reads your hospital chart and reports on your progress and care while you are undergoing treatment in the hospital. Unneeded courses of treatment and medication can be changed and improper billings quickly corrected.

A **second surgical opinion** provision helps to eliminate unnecessary elective surgeries, thus preventing considerable pain and cost. If the provision is *voluntary,* there is no penalty for not having a second opinion. If it is *mandatory,* you must get a second opinion before surgery or suffer a coinsurance or deductible penalty. In either case, the insurance typically pays 100 percent of the cost of a second surgical opinion without any deductible, and even pays for a third, or "tie breaker," opinion if the second opinion differs from the first and if you then want one more opinion before you make up your mind.

Reasonable and Customary

A major medical or comprehensive medical expense policy usually bases its payments on **reasonable and customary**—or "usual, customary, and reasonable"—limitations. These limitations are based on the typical charges for medical services in a given area of the country. The insurer will base its allowable limit for a covered medical expense on the charges made by medical providers in each respective area. It will array those charges from a recent time period for a specific service, and then determine a dollar limit based upon a preset percentile ranking of the charges in the array.

For instance, consider these two cases: Joanne, a divorced mother who has one child, works in Pittsburgh, lives in Wilkinsburg, Pennsylvania; and Frank, who works in San Francisco and lives with his wife and two children in Pacifica, California. Both have major medical policies provided by their employers. Each policy has a $200 annual deductible, 80–20 coinsurance on the first $4000 of covered medical expenses per year with 100 percent coverage of covered medical expenses beyond that point, few internal limitations and broad coverage, and a lifetime limit of $1 million per person.

The same medical services, however, cost Frank more than they cost Joanne. For example, a visit to her family practice doctor costs Joanne $28.00, while Frank's doctor charges $35.00. For identical office procedures, surgeries, and other services, his doctors generally charge more; but on a few services, Joanne's doctors are more expensive. Will the insurers pay the charges the doctors bill Joanne and Frank? If not, what will they pay, and how is it determined?

In Table 9.4, you can see a partial array of theoretical charges for medical visits during the most recent month for Joanne's and Frank's areas. If their insurers pay at the ninetieth percentile, both will be covered for the charge for a doctor visit (although coinsurance may cause them not to receive full payment). In fact, Joanne's doctor charges her $2.00 per visit less than the ninetieth percentile. If the insurers' reasonable and customary limitations are at the eightieth percentile, however, Joanne's insurer will cover only $25.00, and Frank's only $27.00. If Joanne and Frank have satisfied their deductibles but are still in the 80–20 coinsurance phase of coverage, their claims will be paid as follows.

	At the 90th percentile	At the 80th percentile
Joanne	($28.00)(0.80) = $22.40	($25.00)(0.80) = $20.00
Frank	($35.00)(0.80) = $28.00	($27.00)(0.80) = $21.60

Thus, when the reasonable and customary limitation is set at the ninetieth percentile, each will pay only the 20 percent coinsurance as a final cost. If the reasonable and customary limitation is set at the eightieth percentile, however,

Table 9.4 LAST MONTH'S THEORETICAL ARRAY OF DOCTORS' VISIT CHARGES IN JOANNE'S AND FRANK'S AREAS

Percentile[a]	Joanne (Wilkinsburg, Pa.)	Frank (Pacifica, Calif.)
99	$50.00	$65.00
.	.	.
.	.	.
.	.	.
90	$30.00	$35.00
.	.	.
.	.	.
.	.	.
80	$25.00	$27.00
.	.	.
.	.	.
.	.	.
70	$25.00	$25.00
.	.	.
.	.	.
.	.	.
50	$25.00	$25.00
.	.	.
.	.	.
.	.	.
20	$22.00	$23.50
.	.	.
.	.	.
.	.	.
10	$18.00	$20.00
.	.	.
.	.	.
.	.	.
0	$12.00	$15.00

[a] Percentiles are in 100 equal increments, ranging from 0 to 99.

Joanne will personally pay $28.00 − $20.00, or $8.00 per doctor visit, while Frank will absorb $35.00 − $21.60, or $13.40 per visit. Charges above the reasonable and customary limitation are not considered covered medical expenses under the contracts. Generally, the higher the percentile basis of the reasonable and customary limitation, the greater the benefits paid to you and the higher the premium you must pay for your major medical insurance.

Reasonable and customary arrays are updated periodically based on medical services in areas defined by zip codes of the medical providers. Some insurers update them monthly, and many do so quarterly. Assuming a constant percentile for the reasonable and customary limit, if you live in a part of the country with high costs, you will have a higher limit for covered medical expenses than a person residing in a lower-cost area. Since insurers typically adjust their premiums to take this into account, you are likely to pay a higher premium if you live in the higher-cost area. Also, your premiums may be higher if you live close to a major population center—especially one that is growing rapidly and experiencing a high demand for medical services.

Coordination of Benefits

A medical expense insurance policy contains a provision that tells you what it will and will not pay if there is another policy covering the same medical expense. This part of the policy is the **coordination of benefits** provision. Historically, it has been very simple in major medical expense policies providing coverage on a group basis, but this may change soon.

To see how coordination of benefits has worked, consider the following family. The husband, Wayne Mitchell (a landscape designer), has covered himself, his wife, and their two daughters under his employer's group major medical plan. His wife, Marcia Staff (an attorney who retains her maiden name for professional reasons), is insured under her employer's plan, which is identical to Wayne's plan. The children and Wayne are covered under Marcia's plan as well. Each plan has a \$200 annual deductible with 80–20 coinsurance until a \$1000 out-of-pocket security limit is reached, and then it pays 100 percent of an insured's covered medical expenses for the remainder of the year. Marcia is injured driving her sports car to work and incurs covered medical expenses of \$4200.

Under her policy, Marcia pays the \$200 deductible plus \$800 (0.20 × \$4000) in coinsurance, with her insurance paying \$3200. Wayne's would pay the same if Marcia were not covered under her own employer's plan. However, since her plan defines her own coverage as primary and Wayne's as secondary, hers pays as though his did not exist. His policy defines her coverage under it as secondary. The principle of indemnity would be violated if his policy paid another \$3200, so it will limit its payment to the lesser of (1) what it would have paid if it had been primary and (2) the difference between covered medical expenses and the amount that her insurer paid. Thus, it pays only \$4200 − \$3200, or \$1000.

In the end, Marcia recovers all of her covered medical expenses, absorbing none of the loss. To accomplish this, however, Marcia and Wayne have paid two premiums. If your employers do not cover your dependents without cost to you, think twice about covering them under both policies. You must pay a full premium on the second policy, and the most you can gain in return is the difference between covered medical expenses and the amount the primary insurer would pay.

Some new coordination of benefit rules went into effect in 1987. These rules may allow the second insurer to pay less than the difference just shown. This may occur through the use of coinsurance on the difference between the total covered medical expenses and the amount paid by the primary insurer. In that case, Wayne's policy would pay Marcia (0.80) ($1000), or $800, instead of the full $1000 difference.

You may wonder what happens when dependent children are covered under both parents' group medical insurance policies. For example, if Wayne and Marcia's two daughters, Kinsey and Lauren, incur medical bills, which policy will be primary and which will pay the difference? Under most group coverage prior to 1987, the husband's policy was primary and the wife's was secondary. But this male/female rule clearly involves sex discrimination and perhaps discrimination based on age as well, since the husband more often is older than the wife.

The "birthday rule" has been proposed by insurance regulators to cope with these problems. It is now being implemented in many plans. Under this new rule, the insurance of the parent whose birthday occurs first in the year would be primary, with the coverage of the other parent being secondary. The year of birth does not matter, only the day and month. Thus, since Wayne was born on March 2, 1948, and Marcia was born on October 20, 1946, his policy would provide the children's primary coverage. If both parents were born on the same day of the year, the plan of the parent covered the longest would be primary. So, if both Wayne and Marcia were born on June 12, but Marcia has been covered for eleven years under her plan while Wayne has been covered for five years under his plan, Marcia's plan would be primary and Wayne's would be secondary.

If parents are separated or divorced, the plan of the parent with custody is primary, the plan of the spouse of the parent with custody is secondary, and the plan of the parent not having custody is third (there may be multiple parents after a remarriage). When a court has decreed that a parent is responsible for the health care costs of a child, however, the court's instructions take precedence.

OTHER HEALTH CARE DELIVERY ALTERNATIVES

Until fairly recently, almost all Americans received their primary medical care in the private offices of doctors who charged individually set fees for their services as those services were rendered. But the past few years have seen dramatic changes in our health care delivery system. Because medical care costs have risen so sharply in recent years, government, employers, employees, insurers, and medical care providers all are involved in extensive efforts to limit cost while enhancing the quality of care. In addition, there is considerable social pressure to assure all citizens full access to quality medical care, no matter what they are able to pay. Many clinics and hospitals are changing their services and pricing, and several alternative approaches to health care delivery have evolved. Among the alternative approaches now in use are health maintenance organizations, preferred provider organizations, independent physicians' associations, hospices, and home health care.

Health Maintenance Organizations

Since the federal government began to support its development in 1973, a form of prepaid group medical practice called the **health maintenance organization (HMO)** has grown dramatically. In Figure 9.5, you can see that there were only 72 HMOs in the United States in June 1973, compared to 595 in June 1986, and that membership grew from 4.4 million to 23.7 million enrollees during that same time period. You may consider an HMO as an alternative to the traditional "fee-for-services plus insurance" approach discussed so far. Most HMOs are found in urban areas, and you are more likely to be able to join one if your employer offers it as an alternative to a group medical insurance plan.

HMO Characteristics. HMOs provide comprehensive health care services to their members in exchange for a set prepaid fee. Members live near HMO service locations, and they pay little or nothing for their medical care at the time of service. By stressing preventive medicine, an HMO makes it easy and inexpensive for you to visit the doctor while at the same time it tries to save money by limiting the number of days its members spend in the hospital. If an average doctor visit costs $25.00 and an average day's care in a hospital costs $400.00, a person can have $400/$25, or 16, doctor visits before the cost of those visits will equal the cost of just one day in the hospital. Because there is little or no out-of-pocket cost for visiting the doctor as an HMO member, you are encouraged to get care as early and as often as needed, thus stopping many problems before they become more serious.

Types of HMOs. There are two major kinds of health maintenance organizations. The *staff plan*, also known as a group practice or closed-panel plan, usually involves an organization that employs physicians and pays them a salary. The doctors share clinic or hospital space, which helps to coordinate their support staff, record keeping, and supplies.

This form of HMO often offers extended hours of service, although not all physicians will be available during all hours of service. As a member, you use the HMO physicians for your primary care, and if you need a specialist, the physician treating you can refer you to either a specialist employed by the HMO or one outside that organization. If you use an outside specialist to whom the HMO physician refers you, the HMO pays for that specialist's care. Unless you are away from home, your primary-care physician must be an HMO employee for your treatment to be covered. Normally, you do not choose your specialist unless multiple specialists are employed by the HMO and the referring physician is indifferent as to the specialist used.

Under the *individual practice association* (IPA) plan, also called an open-panel plan, independent physicians who have regular practices contract to treat

Figure 9.5 GROWTH OF HEALTH MAINTENANCE ORGANIZATIONS IN THE UNITED STATES SINCE 1973

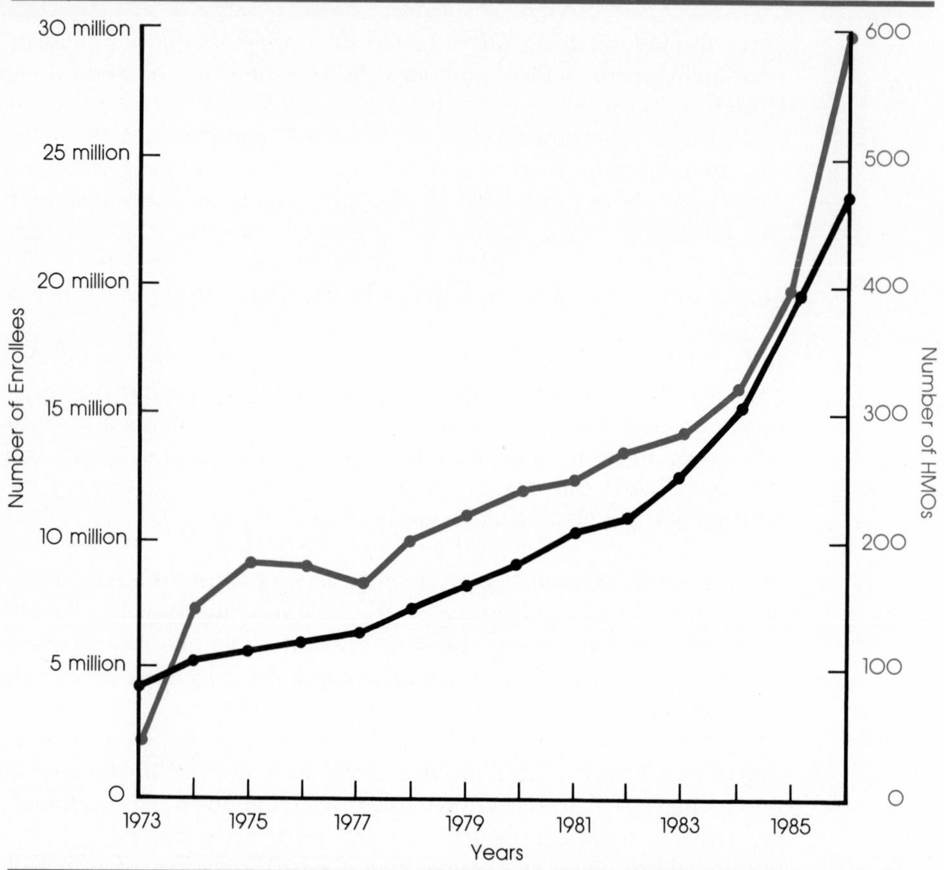

SOURCE: U.S. Public Health Service, *Annual Report to Congress*, Washington, D.C.: various years; and InterStudy, *National HMO Census*, Excelsior, Minn.: various years.

Note: Plot points are for June of each year, except for 1983 (December) and second 1985 point (December).

HMO patients for set fees which are paid them by the HMO. These physicians continue their regular practices in addition to treating HMO members, and they seldom have offices together in a single facility. There tends to be less supervision and less economy of operation in open-panel plans, resulting in less savings than might be the case in staff plans. Open-panel HMOs have not gained widespread popular support—about 16.8 million persons, or four-fifths of HMO enrollees, are members of staff plans in the United States today.

Advantages and Disadvantages of HMOs. There are many arguments made both for and against HMOs. Among the *advantages* you might encounter are the following:

- Extended service hours
- Little or no out-of-pocket cost at time of care
- Comprehensive services
- Little paperwork and no insurance claims to file
- Peer review of your care by physicians other than the one(s) treating you
- Preventive medical care, including an unlimited number of doctor visits
- Multiple physicians, all with access to your medical records if you need immediate care

Among the *disadvantages*, you might experience some or all of the following:

- Loss of freedom of choice of primary-care and/or specialist-care physicians and facilities
- Slowness of referral if the specialized care requested is not critical care
- Geographical inconvenience if you live some distance from the HMO service site(s)
- A sizable deductible (called a copayment) if you are out of town and need medical care before you return
- The need for approval by an HMO physician before you receive medical treatment when you are away from home

Not all HMOs are alike. Their management will vary, as will their doctors, support personnel, size, facilities, and other important features. Some will provide a more personal level of services than others; some will seem to be "production line" medicine with less interest in your problems than you might wish. If you are interested in a particular HMO, you should compare its features to those of competing HMOs and major medical health insurance plans. Ask for references, and talk to current members about their services with the HMO.

If an HMO and an insurance plan both cover the identical medical care, the HMO prepayment might be higher than the insurance premium, despite the cost efficiences that an HMO offers; however, you may want to weigh this against the lesser out-of-pocket cost of the HMO at the time of care. It is possible that an HMO can deliver quality medical care to you at a lower long-run cost than traditional fee-for-services medicine plus insurance, but this is not a certainty.

Preferred Provider Organizations

A recent response to the inroads of HMOs into traditional health care delivery and group medical insurance plans, **preferred provider organizations (PPOs)**

Box 9.1 AN EXPERT DISCUSSES HMOs AND THE QUALITY OF CARE ISSUE

Quality of care issues generally have not loomed large among the public. Most Americans trust their physicians, and the medical profession historically has had a very favorable image. Organized medicine has on occasion forcefully argued that health maintenance organizations (HMOs) have incentives to underserve, but those cries have become muted in recent years as more and more physicians, including American Medical Association members, have affiliated with HMOs.

Also worthy of mention is that available empirical research consistently has found quality of care in HMOs to equal or exceed that provided in the fee-for-service system.

These studies, however, are becoming obsolete. They mostly were performed in the late 1950s to 1970s when HMOs were an infant industry gasping for breath in the face of external threats and lack of employer and public understanding. The studies were performed almost entirely in nonprofit organizations with potentially different philosophies and operating procedures than many of their newer competitors, which more often are for-profit plans. Physicians in these plans may have felt the need to act in a medically conservative manner in light of the external threats.

In addition, the HMOs in those years tended not to transfer much of the financial risk to providers as many of the newer organizations are doing, although the medical group may have been capitated for physicians services. As a practical matter, it was inevitable and reasonable that many HMOs wanted their participating providers to operate under the same incentives as those faced by the plan as a whole. However, the distinction between how the HMO

entity is paid and how providers, particularly physicians, within the plan are paid is a critical one that has not had the attention it deserves in the research community.

As competition among plans intensifies, as it is now doing,

are health care providers that contract with an employer or insurer to provide medical services to the employees/insureds. These services usually are discounted, and PPOs also may impose controls to limit overuse of the services. In return, the PPO hopes to gain a larger volume of business because the employer or insurer encourages participants to use its services. Usually, this is done by reducing the deductible and/or the coinsurance which insureds must pay when they receive medical care from the PPO.

You don't lose freedom of choice with a PPO. Instead, you are encouraged to use the PPO, but if you are willing to absorb more of your own medical costs, you may use any other qualified medical provider you choose. Doctors still are paid on a fee-for-services basis, which many prefer; but they are encouraged to

HMOs and their providers will face tougher revenue constraints, and some underservice seems inevitable, potentially leading to scandals and exposes that will heighten public concerns.

This will occur at a time of increasing public awareness of the impact of the Medicare hospital prospective payment system (PPS), which was enacted in 1982. Medicare traditionally paid hospitals their costs, subject to some limits. In contrast, PPS, once fully implemented, entails paying on the basis of a per stay price that varies with diagnosis and other patient characteristics. This fundamental change leads, in the view of some, to creating incentives to discharge "quicker and sicker." Again, given the strength of the incentives, it seems inevitable that both real and perceived quality problems will arise periodically. Thus, the quality concerns are not limited to HMOs, and, ironically, the problems with PPS can be expected to heighten public concern with quality in HMOs.

This is not to argue that quality necessarily will suffer under the heightened competition and the new reimbursement schemes. No one knows the answer to this. Furthermore, quality is influenced by factors other than financial incentives, including how providers are selected, organized and supervised (not a term physicians like, but that is the reality).

Given these factors, it is likely that some HMOs will underserve and otherwise provide poor quality care, and that quality issues will become increasingly the subject of public (and employer) attention. There is a crying need for more research on both HMO and fee-for-service performance regarding quality, the effectiveness of alternative approaches within HMOs to quality assurance, and how employers and potential enrollees can assess quality.

If the new health care financing and delivery environment entails competition on the basis of cost only, then it must be considered a failure. Rather, one would hope for competition on the basis of quality and service as well, just like any other economic good. A critical test of whether the procompetitive strategy works is whether consumers can discern quality differences, albeit imperfectly, and vote with their feet. Fortunately, most HMOs worry that enrollees will do so if quality slips. It should be noted that this does not require that each enrollee obtain medical training any more than automobile purchasers need to become mechanics before buying a car.

SOURCE: Peter D. Fox, "HMO Qualilty of Care Concerns Predicted to Increase," *Business and Health,* December 1985, pp. 8–9.

control costs because their negotiated charges are lower than their regular charges.

PPOs can include hospitals, groups of independent physicians who are willing to work to control costs but who prefer the fee-for-services method of payment, pharmacies, medical equipment suppliers, and other providers. A relatively recent type of PPO is one providing prescription drugs by mail. It can be useful if you need long-term medication(s) that you must take for more than 30 days. To lessen costs, the PPO stresses generic drugs instead of brand-name drugs, and after your first month's prescription, the medication is mailed to you. The lower overhead involved in such a service by mail can save money. A typical program of this type would use a \$1.00 to \$5.00 copayment per prescription, with the insurer paying 100 percent of the prescription cost above that deductible and waiving any annual deductible that might otherwise apply. Thus, if your January renewal medication is priced at $15.25 and there is a copayment of $2.00 per prescription, you pay $2.00 and the insurer pays $13.25, despite the policy's deductible and coinsurance provisions.

Independent Physicians' Associations

To compete with HMOs, some physicians who prefer fee-for-services payment and the independence of controlling their own practices have formed **independent physicians' associations (IPAs).** IPAs encourage their members to keep their own charges competitive, to order only necessary tests, to use less expensive substitute treatments if available, and to take other steps to make their practices more competitive with HMOs. IPAs do not have any pricing authority, but some use peer review of members' treatment. Furthermore, member physicians are more aware of the need to be sensitive to price and service than was the case in the past. All of these factors combine to help make IPAs a positive development for you as a medical care consumer.

Hospices

Often, terminally ill patients can be kept alive in a hospital through the use of advanced medical equipment, drugs, and intensive care. Where there is no realistic chance of recovery, however, some persons feel that this use of "heroic measures" merely prolongs life and even suffering, robbing the patient of dignity through the constant intrusion of needles, tubes, and equipment. In addition, this technical continuation of life can be traumatic for the patient's family, both emotionally and financially.

One response to this problem is the use of the **hospice,** an organization designed to help the patient and family when a terminal illness strikes. The primary function of the hospice is to help the patient and family to understand and accept the dying process, and to provide psychological support. Some hospices provide bed space and others do not. By making the decision not to use heroic measures to prolong life in a hospital, the patient also gains the ability to live his or her final days at home with family and familiar surroundings, or in a homelike atmosphere at a hospice if bed space is available. Further, the high costs of intensive life support in a hospital are eliminated.

Home Health Care

As an alternative to staying in the hospital to complete your recovery after you no longer need critical care, you may want to explore the concept of **home health care.** Under this concept, you are released from the hospital and go home to complete your recuperation. This requires that someone be at home to help care for you. You remain under the doctor's care while at home, and a nurse with instructions from the doctor visits you at prescribed intervals to monitor your progress, administer medication, and sometimes provide physical therapy. Home health care can free needed beds in the hospital, save you money, and allow you to recover in a more cheerful setting.

MEDICARE

Social Security insurance includes **Medicare,** which provides medical insurance benefits to you if you are 65 or older, or if you are disabled for 24 months before age 65, or if you need long-term kidney dialysis. Medicare benefits come in two major parts: Part A—Hospital Insurance, and Part B—Supplementary Medical Insurance.

Part A—Hospital Insurance

Hospital Insurance is divided into three major benefits: (1) hospital inpatient care, (2) skilled nursing facility inpatient care, and (3) home health care/hospice care.

Hospital Inpatient Care. Covering up to 90 days per "spell of illness," hospital inpatient care requires a deductible and then pays for the first 60 days in the hospital without coinsurance. For days 61 through 90, a daily coinsurance charge applies, and after the ninetieth day you may use a *lifetime reserve* of 60 more days, during which your daily coinsurance charge is double that of days 61 through 90. A spell of illness begins when you have been discharged from a hospital or extended-care facility for at least 60 days since your last spell of illness. The deductible and coinsurance figures vary each year, based on changes in hospital charges.

Skilled Nursing Facility Inpatient Care. If you are confined to a hospital for medical reasons for three or more days, and then are confined in a skilled nursing facility, you will be covered for up to 100 days per spell of illness. You do not pay a deductible, and you pay no coinsurance for the first 20 days; however, there is a daily coinsurance charge for days 21 through 100. This charge changes each year and is about one-half the daily coinsurance charge for hospital inpatient care during days 61 through 90.

Home Health Care/Hospice Care. Under home health care, if you remain under a physician's plan of treatment, you are covered for an unlimited number of home visits by visiting nurses, speech and physical therapists, and other health care professionals. With hospice care coverage, if Medicare-certified hospital bed space is available, there is coverage for up to two 90-day periods and one 30-day period. Both home health care and hospice care have no deductible or coinsurance, but hospice care does require a small copayment per prescription while you are an outpatient.

Part B—Supplementary Medical Insurance

Supplementary Medical Insurance (SMI) is a *voluntary* coverage available for a modest monthly charge that changes each year. It pays for many services not covered under Hospital Insurance, including doctors' visits whether in a hospital, at home, or in the office. SMI also pays for hospital diagnostic services and X rays or tests that you receive as an outpatient, as well as services of the doctor's office nurse, drugs administered by the doctor, and supplies provided by the doctor. After you pay an annual deductible, it covers 80 percent of Medicare-approved charges for covered medical services. Mental illness outpatient treatment is covered, but includes 50–50 coinsurance.

Medigap Coverages and Other Private Benefits

If you are fortunate enough to have group medical expense insurance available after you retire, your plan probably will dictate that Medicare coverage is primary and that the group plan's coverage is secondary. However, many group plans provide coverage only for a short time after retirement, and you may want to buy individual coverage to supplement Medicare. This coverage, often called **medigap insurance,** can be very valuable, because Medicare does not pay for many of the medical care expenses of the elderly, especially custodial care. However, you should carefully price medigap coverage and scrutinize sample policies in order to be certain that they provide the coverage you need. Unfortunately, some unscrupulous insurers sell inferior coverages which pay for few expenses, so you must use care to obtain one of the many quality plans available.

BUYING HEALTH INSURANCE

You can buy health insurance from a number of sources, and at a variety of prices. This brief section is designed to help you understand some of your major options.

Where to Buy Health Insurance

There is little choice involved in Medicare. You must buy Part A, and Part B is a bargain that the federal government supplements with about $3.00 for every dollar of premium you pay. The other two major sources of health insurance, (1) group insurance and (2) individual insurance, are available in the private marketplace.

Group Health Insurance. Because they usually are supported by your employer's premium contribution and because they offer the insurer cost efficiency, most group health insurance plans make more coverage per dollar available to you than do individual health insurance policies. Often, you can join as long as you are a full-time employee, and you don't have to furnish evidence of your insurability. As a rule, the disability benefits are generous in amount and maximum benefit period.

Group major medical contracts often have very high maximum benefits with few internal limits to coverage, and these plans today tend to limit your annual out-of-pocket costs on covered medical expenses to a reasonable amount. Group medical expense plans must treat pregnancy as they treat any other covered medical expense, whereas individual plans often exclude the costs of a normal pregnancy and delivery. Overall, group plans should be your first consideration for health insurance other than Medicare if you are eligible to participate.

Individual Health Insurance. To buy an individual policy, you must furnish evidence of insurability. Because you pay all of your own premiums, these policies may not be as desirable as group insurance from a cost standpoint, and individual medical expense plans tend to offer less liberal benefits than group plans. However, there are many good plans available to supplement your group coverages if those coverages are inadequate; and if you do not have a group plan, you definitely should consider seeking individual coverages. If you are seeking medigap coverage for a relative or friend, an excellent source of information (and possibly of insurance) is the American Association of Retired Persons (AARP) in Washington, D.C.

Pricing and Benefits

Some pricing ideas have been discussed throughout this chapter, but we repeat two basic price-benefit ideas here. You should keep them in mind when considering your health insurance options. They are (1) avoid dollar swapping and (2) purchasing catastrophic loss protection.

Avoid Dollar Swapping. You pay a premium for insurance that includes many costs other than the claim payments actually returned to you and other insureds. The insurer compensates its employees; it pays legal fees and taxes; and it bears costs of office space, utilities, telephone, and transportation. Thus, if you and the insurer know that you will have $100 on claims this year, the insurer will charge you $100 *plus* your share of its other costs as your premium. This might mean a premium of $120 to $150 for that $100 in anticipated claims. In effect, for a predicted loss or claim, you pay the insurer a fee in advance so that it will budget your loss for you. This *dollar swapping* on small, easily absorbed losses is a poor economic choice. If you are reasonably sure that you will have some small losses that you can absorb, you should try to design your insurance to omit coverage for them, instead of swapping dollars with the insurer. This is best done through the use of deductibles, *if* the insurer will adequately reduce your premium. On the other hand, if the insurer doesn't give you a reasonable price decrease for an increased deductible, you may want to buy the coverage with the lower deductible.

Catastrophic Loss Protection. The most logical use of insurance is to protect against losses that are financially catastrophic. Although you want to limit dollar swapping, you do not also want to be penny wise and pound foolish. Do not try to save a few dollars in premiums if those dollars would provide a large volume of protection against an infrequent but quite possible event that could be financially devastating to you. Try to balance your savings from deductibles (and even coinsurance) against your need to buy adequate limits of coverage.

By avoiding dollar swapping and purchasing adequate protection against large losses, you will maximize the financial benefits from your health insurance expenditures.

SUMMARY

If your good health is impaired, you can lose income and suffer added expenses. Disability income insurance helps to replace lost income, while medical expense insurance can pay part or all of your added expenses.

You need enough disability income insurance to replace a target pay figure that usually is less than or equal to your take-home pay. Insurers probably won't sell you more than two-thirds of your gross pay as the maximum benefit. Waiting periods are deductibles, and they can help you control your premiums; however, the longer the waiting period, the longer you must go without benefits if you are disabled. Definitions of disability vary, and you should be certain that they fit your needs.

Medical expenses have soared in recent years, and medical expense insurance costs have kept pace. The rise in medical expenses, however, means a greater loss if you are injured or fall ill, so you probably have little choice but to transfer your risks of large medical expenses to insurers or to HMOs. Most likely you will use your employers' group plan for protection, but you may need to seek individual coverage.

The basic medical expense policy is a combination of hospital, surgical, and doctors' visit coverages. It is relatively expensive because it has low maximum benefits and it encourages too much dollar swapping. A better choice may be a major medical or comprehensive major medical plan. Such a plan has high maximum benefits, a high deductible, few internal limits as to what is covered, and coinsurance up to a security limit. These features encourage the most economic use of your premium dollars.

Cost containment is a major concern of insurers and employers, and you will encounter features designed to decrease insured medical expenses in most medical expense insurance plans. Reasonable and customary limitations can mean that you will pay part of your medical bills if the charges exceed your insurer's limit, and provisions for coordination of benefits will dictate your benefits when there are two or more insurance policies providing coverage.

Health maintenance organizations are group prepaid medical practices that may give you an alternative to "fee-for-services plus insurance" to finance your medical care. These organizations had almost 24 million members in 1986. Preferred provider organizations and independent physicians' associations also are attempting to control medical care cost increases, while hospices and home health care offer lower-cost alternatives to hospital stays in some circumstances.

Qualified persons will find Medicare benefits to be extensive. These include Hospital Insurance (Part A), plus Supplementary Medical Insurance (Part B). Part B is voluntary, and it is a bargain because it is heavily subsidized by tax revenues. Private insurers sell medigap coverages to supplement Medicare, but you should carefully choose these coverages and be sure to read the complete contract before buying.

In all your insurance purchases, be sure to try to use your dollars wisely. Avoid dollar swapping with insurers on small, relatively certain losses, and try to protect yourself against the very large but less frequent losses that may be financially serious. In this way, you will get the most for your insurance premiums.

KEY TERMS

aggregate annual deductible
basic medical expense insurance
cancellable
comprehensive medical expense insurance
concurrent review
conditionally renewable
coordination of benefits
cost containment
disability income insurance
dread disease insurance
grace period
guaranteed renewable
health maintenance organization (HMO)
home health care
hospice
hospital expense insurance
indemnity benefit
independent physicians' association (IPA)
limited policy
major medical expense insurance
Medicare
medigap insurance
noncancellable
percentage coinsurance
preadmission authorization
preexisting conditions
preferred provider organization (PPO)
reasonable and customary
renewable at the insurer's option
second surgical opinion
security provision
services benefit
valued benefit
waiting period

SELECTED READINGS

Hitchings, Bradley. "Why You Should Get a Second Opinion." *Business Week,* April 15, 1985, pp. 162–163.

"Keep Income Coming If You Can't Work." *Changing Times,* March 1986, pp. 53–55.

Leff, Laurel. "Companies Crack Down (Gently) on Remaining Medical Costs." *Working Woman,* January 1985, p. 18.

Michili, Robin. "Shopping for Health Insurance." *Parents,* October 1985, pp. 62–74.

"Ways to Protect What Medicare Won't." *Changing Times,* October 1985, pp. 85–88.

"Your Social Security Records: Be Sure They're Right." *Changing Times,* February 1985, pp. 77–79.

QUESTIONS

1 Name and explain the two major ways you can incur a financial loss if you are injured or fall ill.

2 Explain why disability income insurance may be a good way to treat the risk of loss of income.

3 Why are insurers cautious about selling disability income benefit amounts that approximate your full income?

4 Discuss the role of the waiting period in disability income insurance.

5 Describe the major types of definitions of disability found in disability income insurance policies.

6 Using Figures 9.1 and 9.2 and the text, describe the role of hospital room charges in the rising cost of medical care.

7 Explain how an indemnity basis of benefit payment works in a medical expense insurance policy.

8 Describe how a services basis of benefit payment works in a medical expense insurance policy.

9 Discuss how both services and indemnity basis medical expense insurance contracts sometimes act as though they were the other type.

10 What is a preexisting condition? How is it treated under a medical expense insurance contract?

11 Name and describe the two health insurance policy provisions affecting your right to continue coverage that give you the most security.

12 Explain what a limited health insurance policy is. Is buying such a policy likely to be a wise expenditure?

13 How do dread disease insurance policies work? What are the major types of dread disease policies today?

14 Describe the basic medical expense policy.

15 What are the four basic characteristics that distinguish major and comprehensive medical expense insurance?

16 What is the major medical expense policy deductible designed to do? How can you use it to maximize what you buy for your premium dollar?
17 Explain how the security provision in a comprehensive medical expense policy can help you avoid a large loss that the coinsurance clause might otherwise make you pay.
18 Describe how preadmission authorization and concurrent review could be effective cost containment features in medical expense insurance.
19 Explain the role of the coordination of benefits provision in a medical expense insurance policy.
20 Describe how a health maintenance organization (HMO) works. What is the HMO's role in medical care delivery?
21 Discuss some major advantages and disadvantages that you think HMOs provide.
22 Explain how a preferred provider organization (PPO) works.
23 Describe hospices, and explain how they work.
24 Briefly describe Medicare and its major parts.
25 Seth is insured under a major medical expense insurance policy with an 80–20 coinsurance provision. This means his insurer will pay 80 percent and he must pay the remaining 20 percent. He has satisfied the policy deductible and now incurs $500 in covered medical expenses. Calculate his recovery from the insurance, and discuss the financial impact of the coinsurance provision if his medical expenses are much higher.
26 Susan earns $2100 a month. She is covered under a group disability income policy that her employer provides. The policy will pay two-thirds of her income, up to a maximum of $1200 per month, after a one-month waiting period. She is disabled for four months. How much will the policy pay?
27 Terry Tubbs is insured under a comprehensive medical expense insurance policy with a $200 annual deductible, 80–20 coinsurance, and a security provision that provides a $1000 annual out-of-pocket limitation on what Terry must pay. Determine his total payment from the insurer (its payment to him) if he has (a) $8200 and (b) $18,200 in covered medical expenses this year. Discuss your answers.
28 Using the data shown in Table 9.4, assume that Joanne and Frank both have satisfied their annual deductibles under their major medical expense insurance policies. Both policies have 80–20 coinsurance provisions, and both use a reasonable and customary provision to contain costs. Joanne's doctor charges $36 per visit, and Frank's charges the same. How much will each recover from his or her insurer (a) at the ninetieth percentile and (b) at the eightieth percentile?

CASE PROBLEMS

9.1 Arnold Richardson, a mechanical engineer with 20 years' work experience, has a monthly income of $4200. His disability policy will pay the lesser of two-thirds of his salary or $2400 a month. The policy has a three-month waiting period.

Arnold is injured and is totally out of work for two years. In the third year he is able to partially work and earns $15,000. His policy reduces his disability payments in the third year by 60 percent of the amount earned in that year.

How much in total disability payments will Arnold receive over the three-year period? Compute each year separately and total the results.

9.2 Betty and Hunter Greer are married, and they are employed by different firms. She was born on July 13, and his birthday is October 2. They have identical group comprehensive medical expense insurance policies, with $300 annual deductibles, 80–20 coinsurance, and $1500 out-of-pocket limits under their security provisions. Their daughter Hope has $6300 of medical expenses during the year.

a Determine their recovery from each policy and their total recovery if Hunter's policy is primary for the dependents.
b Determine the same recoveries if the birthday rule is used.

10

Life Insurance

After studying this chapter, you should:

- Understand why life insurance may be needed
- Appreciate how income multiples and needs programming are sometimes used to help determine the amount of life insurance needed
- Be able to explain traditional term, endowment, and whole life insurance
- Understand how death rates affect life insurance premiums
- Understand how variable life and universal life insurance differ from traditional life insurance and from each other
- Be able to explain how life annuities create life incomes
- Understand many important life insurance policy provisions and riders

In Chapters 8 and 9 we discussed the financial treatment of property, liability, and health losses. Now we consider the financial treatment of another important loss exposure: the death of a human being.

WHY HAVE LIFE INSURANCE?

Assume you are the income earner for a family of four: a mother, a father, and two young children. How would your spouse and children cope financially if you died today? Would they be forced to drastically reduce their living standard, to sell important assets in order to pay debts, or even to rely on relatives or charity? Would there be enough money to educate the children and to allow your spouse to be home with the children while they are young? Could your spouse expect a reasonable living standard after retirement?

These are a few of the questions people must ask themselves. Because life insurance is the only major financial device that creates assets upon the death of an individual, it can help answer many of those questions. You can measure the difference between the dollars needed to support your dependents when you die and the dollars already available to those dependents. If you then purchase an equivalent amount of life insurance, at least the *financial* impact of your premature death would be lessened. An important function of life insurance is the creation of assets for survivors if the insured dies.

Life insurance also conserves existing assets by creating the cash needed by survivors to pay taxes and other debts. This function becomes more important as you build up investments and savings. With life insurance providing immediate dollars, your home can be passed to your spouse and children, and other properties are left as you intended. Your heirs can retain the assets you accumulated for them. If those assets had to be sold to pay debts, they might bring a much lower price than their true value.

A third and less vital use for life insurance arises when you use life insurance products as savings or investment tools.

Sometimes it is stressed that single people and young children do not have a substantial need for life insurance, and this point is probably valid. The key test is whether others will suffer a loss of income or standard of living should you pass away.

In any event, when you assess your needs for life insurance, it is helpful to keep in mind the life cycle of income needs that most families go through. One such example is presented in Figure 10.1. The numbers in the figure are not nearly as important as the pattern that evolves. Also, it is readily apparent that individuals or families may have different needs or priorities and this will influence the requirement for income.

In this chapter, we stress life insurance's primary function: *financial protection by creating assets that otherwise would not be there to help your dependents if you die.* The issue then becomes the amount of insurance that is necessary.

How Much Life Insurance Do You Need?

Two popular approaches for determining the amount of life insurance you might need are (1) income multiples and (2) needs programming.

Income Multiples. The simplest approach is income multiples. You select an appropriate multiple, determine your annual income, and multiply the two figures. The result is your life insurance requirement.

An example of the use of the income multiples approach is presented in Table 10.1, which is for a married couple. Basically, you multiply your present gross earnings by the factor shown in the table. Thus, if you are the primary earner and have an income of $30,000, and your spouse is 35 years old, you need an income multiplier of eight to maintain your spouse's living standard at 75

Figure 10.1 HYPOTHETICAL EXAMPLE OF INCOME NEEDS DURING A CHANGING LIFE CYCLE

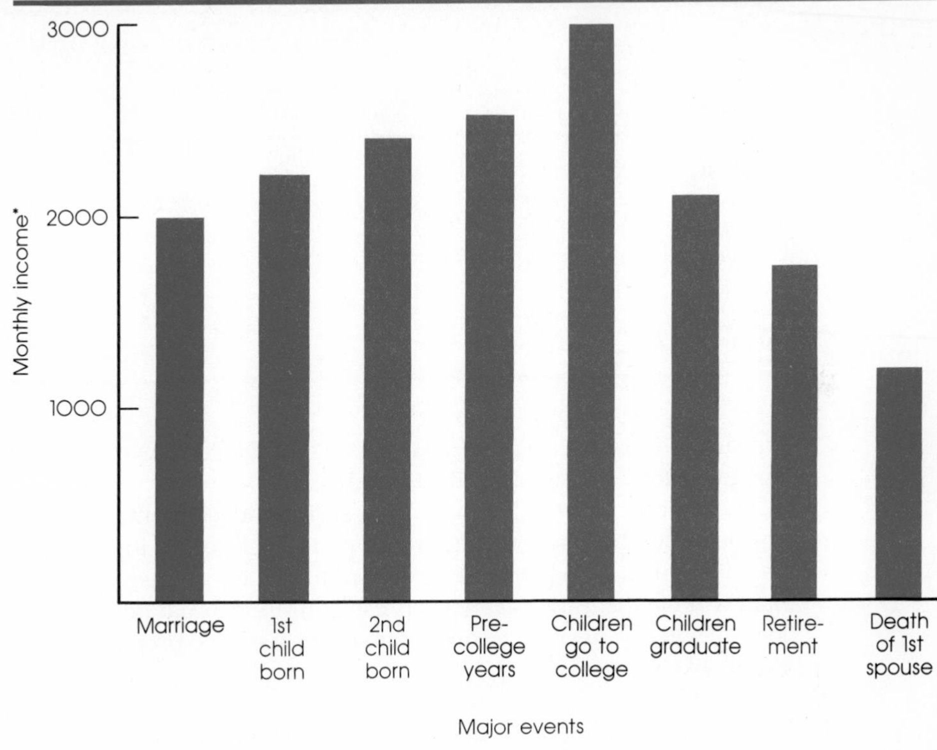

percent of the level prior to your death. A multiplier of six would be necessary to provide a standard of living equal to 60 percent of that before death.

Although this approach is easy to use, its result may not be accurate for you. Furthermore, any such table must accurately cover your family situation. There may be unequal wage earners, children of various ages, and so forth. A potentially more useful approach is needs programming.

Needs Programming. **Needs programming** compares the assets available to, and the needs of, your dependents if you die today. It converts future income (assets) and needs into dollars today. If needs exceed assets, the difference is the amount of new life insurance recommended. For example, if the funds needed were $240,000 and assets available were $100,000, the new life insurance needed would be $240,000 − $100,000, or $140,000.

Needs programming involves many assumptions regarding needs, such as

Table 10.1 HYPOTHETICAL MULTIPLES OF INCOME NEEDED IN LIFE INSURANCE AT VARIOUS AGES AND INCOME LEVELS

Your current gross annual income	YOUR SPOUSE'S CURRENT AGE					
	25		35		45	
	60%	75%	60%	75%	60%	75%
$ 10,000	3.1	4.1	4.1	5.7	5.7	7.6
20,000	4.0	5.9	5.0	7.3	6.2	8.2
30,000	5.0	7.5	6.0	8.0	6.5	8.5
40,000	5.0	7.5	6.0	8.0	6.0	8.0
50,000	5.3	7.5	6.0	7.7	6.0	7.7
75,000	5.5	7.5	6.0	7.5	6.0	7.5
100,000	6.0	7.5	6.0	7.5	6.0	7.5

housing, education, clearing your estate of debt, regular monthly expenses, and a reserve for emergencies. It also takes into account existing assets, such as Social Security, current life insurance, savings, investments, mortgage equity, and any accumulation in your retirement plan. Each future income or expense must be adjusted to its equivalent in dollars today. Fortunately, many financial planners and life insurance agents can use computer programs to run a free analysis for you. Do not hesitate to use their services, but be prepared for the sales pitch that is likely to follow.

Table 10.2 gives an example of needs programming for a single working mother. In Case 10.1 at the end of the chapter you will have an excellent opportunity to try out your skills at needs programming in a relatively simple framework for a young, married couple with a number of financial obligations.

TYPES OF LIFE INSURANCE POLICIES

Until the 1970s, there were only three basic types of life insurance policies in the United States. Rising interest rates and sharp competition among insurance companies, however, have spawned a new group of life insurance policies that vary distinctly from the older ones. The older policies are known as *traditional policies,* and the newer ones are called *nontraditional policies.*

Traditional Life Insurance Policies

Traditional life insurance policies fall into three groups: (1) term, (2) endowment, and (3) whole life. Another set of products sold for many years by life insurers is life annuities. Life annuities, however, are not life *insurance,* and we will discuss them separately.

Table 10.2 A SIMPLE EXAMPLE OF THE NEEDS PROGRAMMING APPROACH

Name: Catherine Williams | Marital status: single
Age: 35 | Number of dependents: 1 child

Dollars needed			
Immediate needs			
Federal estate tax	$ 0		
State inheritance tax	0		
Probate expenses	0		
Funeral expenses	5,000		
Debt retirement	6,500		
Medical expenses from final illness	1,500		
Total immediate needs		$ 13,000	
Future needs (in dollars today)			
Monthly living expenses	$ 140,000		
Emergency reserve fund	10,000		
Education fund	80,000		
Shelter (rent or mortgage)	60,000		
Total future needs		290,000	
Total dollars needed			$ 303,000
Dollars (assets) available			
Immediate assets			
Cash	$ 2,000		
Savings	8,000		
Stocks	20,000		
Bonds	15,000		
Employer pension plan	42,000		
Employer-supported savings plan	4,500		
Personal life insurance	30,000		
Group life insurance	40,000		
Other assets (list)	0		
Total immediate assets		$ 161,500	
Future assets			
Social Security benefits	$ 37,200		
Other future assets (list)	0		
Total future assets		$ 37,200	
Total dollars (assets) available			$ 198,700
Total dollars needed less total dollars available equals additional life insurance needed			$ 104,300

Term Life Insurance

Term life insurance pays its *face amount* (the amount you are insured for under the policy) if you die during the period, or term, of the policy. It will *not* pay if you live. Thus, payment of benefits is contingent on only one event: *death of the insured during the term of the policy.*

Term builds up no savings to be paid at the end of the policy, and the insurance company earns your premium even if you live. Your premium is pooled with the premiums of many other insureds, and the premiums of the fortunate many who live are used to provide benefits to the beneficiaries of the unfortunate few who die prematurely. Term life's face amount usually stays level for the entire policy period, but it may decrease in some cases.

Level Term

Level term life insurance pays a constant face amount if you die during the term of the policy. It can vary according to its period of coverage, the nature of its premiums, and your right to renew it.

One-Year Term. Because it is not automatically renewable at your option, you are unlikely to encounter the one-year term policy; understanding it, however, will help you understand other policies we will discuss. Figure 10.2 shows a $50,000, one-year term policy issued at age 25. It will pay $50,000 if the insured dies before reaching age 26. If the insured survives and wants insurance for another year, he or she must apply for a new policy and may be refused coverage if unhealthy.

Annually Renewable Term (ART). Also called *yearly renewable term,* the popular **annually renewable term (ART)** policy is illustrated in Figure 10.3. It

Figure 10.2 A $50,000, ONE-YEAR TERM LIFE INSURANCE POLICY ISSUED AT AGE 25

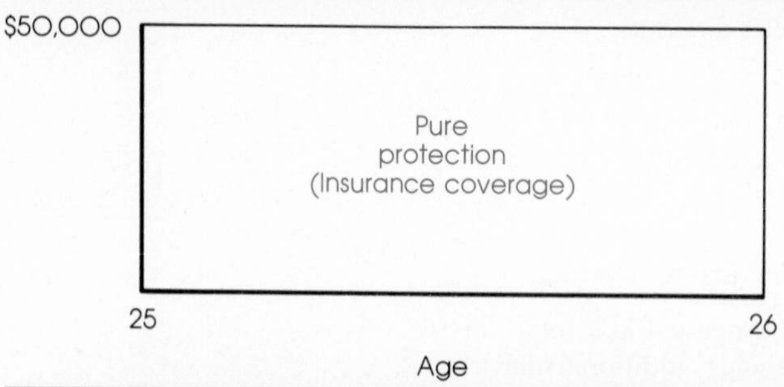

Figure 10.3 A $50,000, ANNUALLY RENEWABLE TERM LIFE INSURANCE POLICY ISSUED AT AGE 25 AND RENEWABLE TO AGE 70

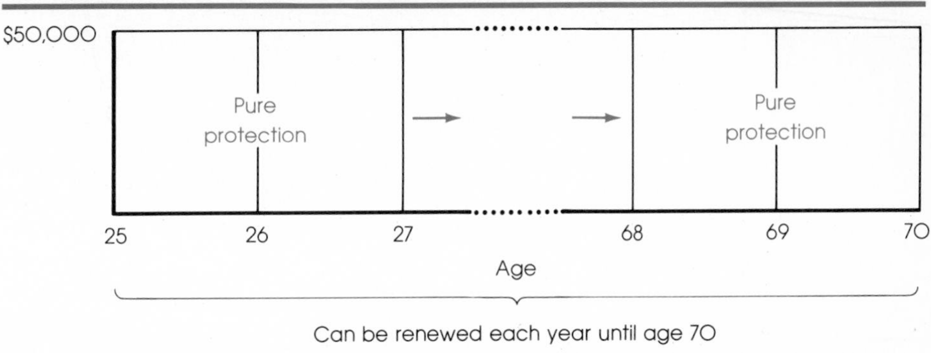

gives the owner the option of renewing the policy without having to prove insurability each year, up to some maximum age limit. Assume you are 25 today, and your insurer sells you a $50,000 ART policy that is renewable until you are 70. At age 26, you may renew the policy, even if you are in poor health. As long as you continually renew it each year, you can continue coverage until age 70. Your premiums will rise each year, however, because *your probability of dying rises, at an increasing rate of change, during every year* after you reach about age 10. Figure 10.4 illustrates this dramatic change. Note that the death rate declines at first, gradually begins to slope upward, and then sharply accelerates as you pass middle age. Your premium is based on frequency of death and severity (the amount the insurer must pay). Because the face amount stays the same, severity of loss is a constant. There is no partial loss; you either live or you die. Thus, your new annual premium each year is directly tied to the estimated frequency of death at your new age.

To see an estimated **mortality rate** for your own age, look at the 1980 Commissioners Standard Ordinary Mortality Table shown in Table 10.3 on pages 334 and 335. This table says that, if you are a member of a group of one thousand 35-year-old females, 1.65 of you are expected to die this year. Expressed another way, it says that your probability of dying this year is (1.65/1000), or 0.00165. Next year, this probability rises to 1.76/1000, an increase of 1.76 − 1.65, or 0.11/1000; the following year's change in deaths per thousand is 1.89 − 1.76, or 0.13/1000. Thus, your annual pure premium for $50,000 of ART life insurance at age 35 is ($50,000)(0.00165), or $82.50; and at 36 it is ($50,000)(0.00176), or $88.00. The insurer will add charges for its operational expenses to this number, making your actual premium higher.

Level Premium Level Term for a Multiyear Period. Because of the ART's annual change in premium, you may prefer level term life insurance that prom-

Figure 10.4 THE BASIC SHAPE OF THE MORTALITY CURVE

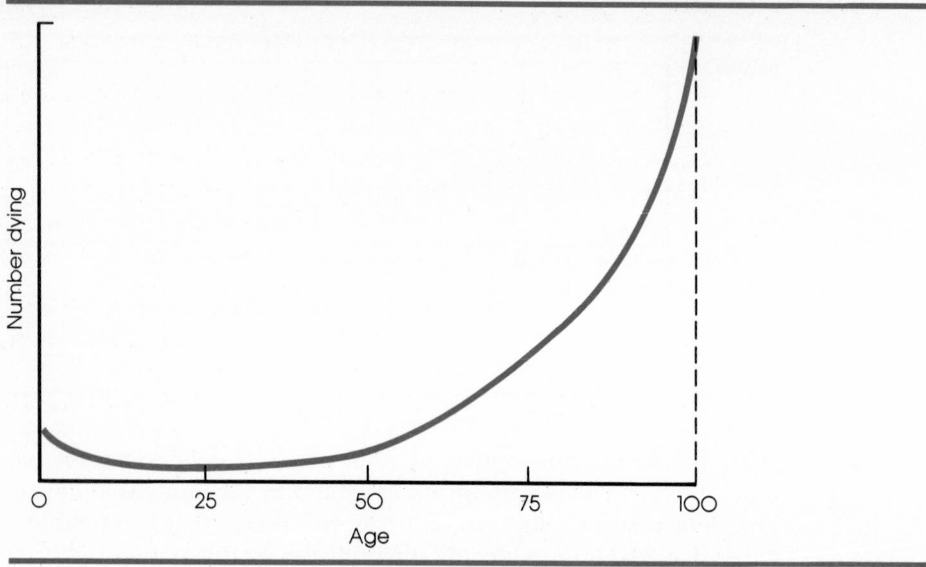

ises more than one year of protection, with premiums that stay the same each year. For example, consider the level term policy shown in Figure 10.5. Issued at age 25, it will pay $50,000 if the insured dies before reaching age 70. Its face amount and maximum period of protection are identical to the ART policy shown in Figure 10.3. The major difference between the two policies is that the one shown in Figure 10.5 has level annual premiums, while the ART policy's annual premiums start out very low and increase each year.

Level premiums are a result of the insurer charging more than the ART

Figure 10.5 A $50,000 LEVEL-PREMIUM LEVEL TERM LIFE INSURANCE POLICY ISSUED AT AGE 25 AND EXPIRING AT AGE 70

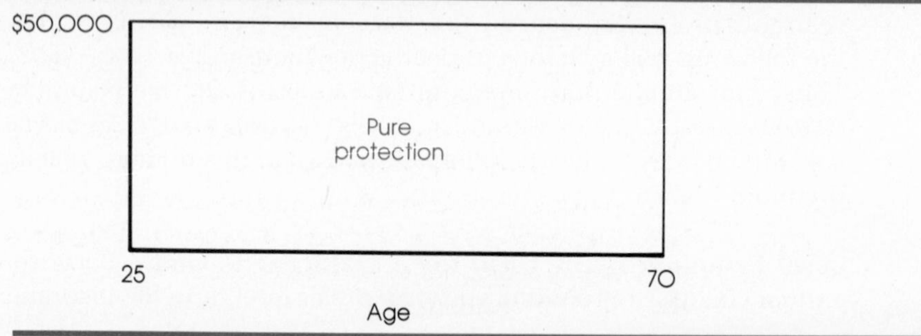

pure premium during the early years of coverage, investing the overcharge, and then using the resulting fund to offset the later years when the level premium is less than ART's increasing pure premium. Figure 10.6 contrasts annual premiums for the two policies shown in Figures 10.3 and 10.5. Note how the level-premium policy's overcharge is smaller than its later undercharge. This is because the undercharge equals the overcharge plus interest.

There are many combinations of level-premium term and the idea of automatic renewability. One popular example is five-year level term with level premiums, renewable until age 65. This product offers level premiums for five years, with premiums going up to another plateau each five years as the policy is renewed.

Decreasing Term

The face amount of a **decreasing term policy** decreases steadily throughout the period of protection. This means that if the insured dies soon after the policy is issued, it will pay close to the original face amount; if death occurs later in

Figure 10.6 COMPARISON OF LEVEL-PREMIUM LEVEL TERM LIFE INSURANCE PREMIUMS AND ANNUALLY RENEWABLE TERM LIFE INSURANCE PREMIUMS BETWEEN AGE 25 AND AGE 70

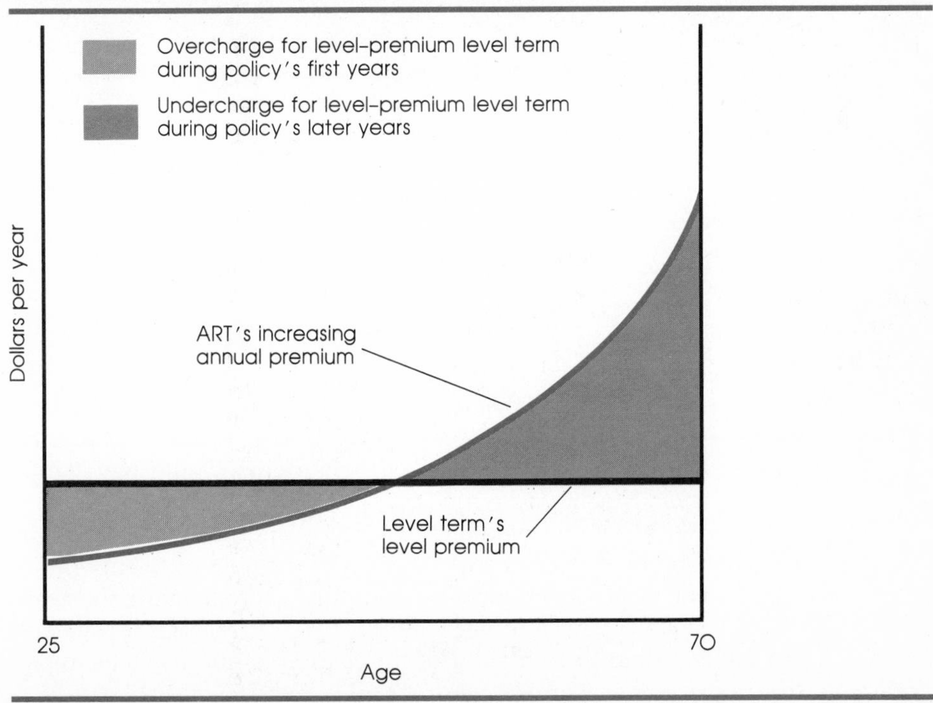

Table 10.3 1980 COMMISSIONERS STANDARD ORDINARY (CSO) MORTALITY TABLE

Age at first of year	DEATHS DURING YEAR PER 1000 LIVES AT FIRST OF YEAR		Age at first of year	DEATHS DURING YEAR PER 1000 LIVES AT FIRST OF YEAR	
	Male	Female		Male	Female
0	4.18	2.89	25	1.77	1.16
1	1.97	.87	26	1.73	1.19
2	.99	.81	27	1.71	1.22
3	.98	.79	28	1.70	1.26
4	.95	.77	29	1.71	1.30
5	.90	.76	30	1.73	1.35
6	.86	.73	31	1.78	1.40
7	.80	.72	32	1.83	1.45
8	.76	.70	33	1.91	1.50
9	.74	.69	34	2.00	1.58
10	.73	.68	35	2.11	1.65
11	.77	.69	36	2.24	1.76
12	.85	.72	37	2.40	1.89
13	.99	.75	38	2.58	2.04
14	1.15	.80	39	2.79	2.22
15	1.33	.85	40	3.02	2.42
16	1.51	.90	41	3.29	2.64
17	1.67	.95	42	3.56	2.87
18	1.78	.98	43	3.87	3.09
19	1.86	1.02	44	4.19	3.32
20	1.90	1.05	45	4.55	3.56
21	1.91	1.07	46	4.92	3.80
22	1.89	1.09	47	5.32	4.05
23	1.86	1.11	48	5.74	4.33
24	1.82	1.14	49	6.21	4.63

continued

the policy, a lesser amount will be paid. It is useful if you have a predictable, declining need for life insurance over time. Figure 10.7 shows how this might work if you were 25 today and wanted to use term life insurance as collateral on a 30-year, $50,000 mortgage loan. The policy would pay $50,000 if you died immediately after it was issued, $43,000 if you died at age 35 (10 years into the policy), $27,000 if you died at age 45 (20 years into the policy), and very little if you died between ages 54 and 55 (between the policy's twenty-ninth and thirtieth years). The death benefit declines monthly, approximating the remaining unpaid loan balance of your mortgage. Because your early loan repayments apply more to interest than to reduction of the loan amount, and later repayments apply

Table 10.3 continued

Age at first of year	DEATHS DURING YEAR PER 1000 LIVES AT FIRST OF YEAR		Age at first of year	DEATHS DURING YEAR PER 1000 LIVES AT FIRST OF YEAR	
	Male	Female		Male	Female
50	6.71	4.96	75	64.19	38.24
51	7.30	5.31	76	70.53	42.97
52	7.96	5.70	77	77.12	48.08
53	8.71	6.15	78	83.90	53.45
54	9.56	6.61	79	91.05	59.35
55	10.47	7.09	80	98.84	65.99
56	11.46	7.57	81	107.48	73.60
57	12.49	8.03	82	117.25	82.40
58	13.59	8.47	83	128.26	92.53
59	14.77	8.94	84	140.25	103.81
60	16.08	9.47	85	152.95	116.10
61	17.54	10.13	86	166.09	129.29
62	19.19	10.96	87	179.55	143.32
63	21.06	12.02	88	193.27	158.18
64	23.14	13.25	89	207.29	173.94
65	25.42	14.59	90	221.77	190.75
66	27.85	16.00	91	236.98	208.87
67	30.44	17.43	92	253.45	228.81
68	33.19	18.84	93	272.11	251.51
69	36.17	20.36	94	295.90	279.31
70	39.51	22.11	95	329.96	317.32
71	43.30	24.23	96	384.55	375.74
72	47.65	26.87	97	480.20	474.97
73	52.64	30.11	98	657.98	655.85
74	58.19	33.93	99	1000.00	1000.00

mostly to reduction of the loan, the decreasing term policy will decrease its face amount slowly at first and speed up the rate of decrease throughout the term of the policy. These policies usually have *level* premiums.

Endowment Life Insurance

Whereas term life insurance offers one promise to pay, endowment life insurance adds a second promise to pay. Its promises are that it will pay the policy face amount (1) if you die during the term of the policy (just as with term life insurance), *or* (2) if you live until the term of the policy expires. This means that

Figure 10.7 A $50,000, 30-YEAR MORTGAGE LIFE (DECREASING TERM LIFE) POLICY ISSUED AT AGE 25

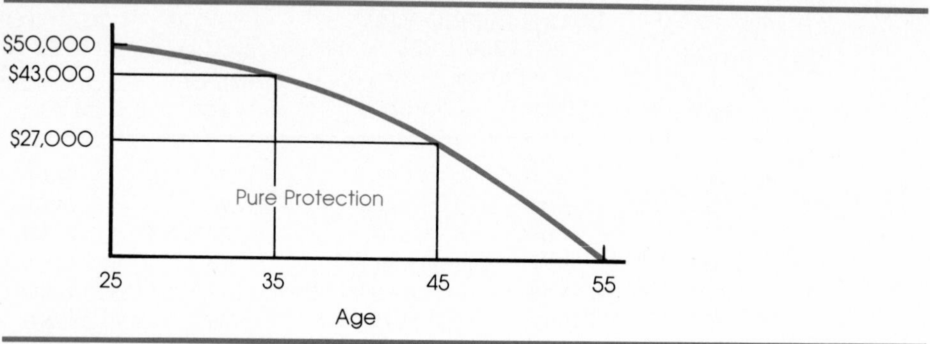

it *will* pay, as long as you keep the policy in force. The only question is the *timing of payment;* the face amount *will* be paid.

Whole Life Insurance

Whole life insurance promises to pay whenever you (the insured) die. It is called permanent life insurance, because the assumption is that you will not outlive its coverage, which lasts to age 100. You can see a whole-life policy in Figure 10.8. Note how the savings, or cash value, builds up over the term of the policy. The premium for whole life insurance is higher than that for level term, creating increasing savings that belong to you as the policyholder. These funds represent the **cash value** of the policy and equal the face amount of the policy by age 100. You may borrow from this cash value at a relatively low rate of interest. Should you borrow, no credit check is necessary and you may repay the loan at your convenience. Should you die before the loan is repaid, the loan balance will be subtracted from the proceeds of the policy. On the other hand, if you decide to terminate the policy, you may take any unborrowed cash value with you or use it in other ways.

When you buy whole life insurance, you may pay premiums for the entire period of coverage (your anticipated life span), or you may choose to make your premium payments over a shorter period. As you lessen the time period for premium payment, the size of the premium will grow.

Clearly, an advantage of whole life compared to term is that you build up cash value that you can borrow against or can take out in cash should you choose to terminate the policy. But keep in mind that because of this advantage, the premiums are higher for whole life than for term. This means you will be able to afford less whole-life coverage than term coverage for a given amount of insurance dollars. Many young people who wish to maximize the insurance coverage for an emerging family may choose term insurance for this reason.

Figure 10.8 A $50,000 WHOLE LIFE INSURANCE POLICY ISSUED AT AGE 25

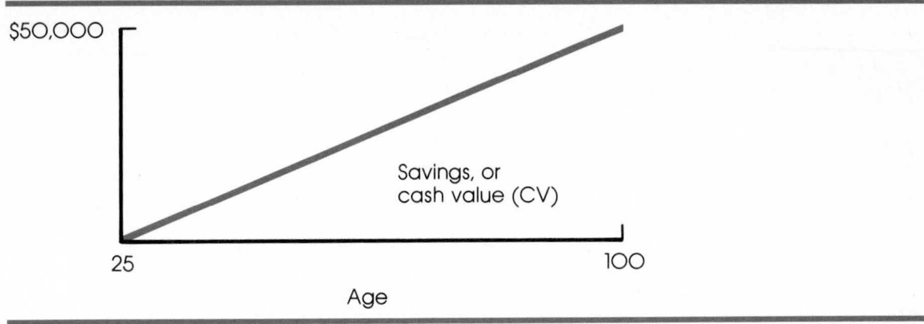

Regardless of the type of policy, you may want to consider the issue of group versus individual life insurance policies. Group policies cover entire groups of people, such as employees of a company or union members. Group policies tend to carry lower premiums than individual policies and may be an important fringe benefit to consider as part of a job offer.

The drawback to group insurance is that you can lose your coverage when you leave the group. This can be particularly damaging if you are no longer insurable. Most group policies do allow you to convert to individual coverage when you depart, but you must convert within 31 days after ending your employment.

PACKAGE POLICIES

Package policies are combinations of the types of life insurance we have already discussed. Some of the more popular package policies are discussed here. Each is designed to meet a specific life insurance need that is common to a large number of prospective buyers. Although a given package may meet your specific needs, it may contain some insurance you do not need or omit a feature that you want. Unless it is *exactly* what you need, you may be better off designing your own combination with the help of your agent.

Joint Life Policy

Joint life insurance insures the lives of two persons and pays its death benefit when the first of the two dies. It can be either term or whole life. After it pays its death benefit, coverage ends; the policy does not continue coverage on the life of the survivor. One use of this policy is to provide mortgage collateral when the lender bases its approval of the mortgage loan on the combined incomes of a wife and husband; if either dies, the other may not be able to meet the mortgage payments without such protection. A two-income family may feel the same need to provide protection for dependent children. A joint life policy is cheaper than two separate, individual policies, but it costs more than either of the two separate policies alone.

Family Income Policy

If you die within a specified period of time after your **family income policy** is issued (usually 10 to 20 years), this contract pays your beneficiary a monthly benefit of 1 percent of the face amount during the remainder of that specified period. Then it pays the death benefit.

Adjustable Life

As a response to consumers' needs to vary the amount of life insurance, the premiums, and/or the type of life insurance purchased, some insurers offer **adjustable life insurance.** As your protection and savings needs change, this plan allows you to change the face amount, the premium, and the type of plan without providing evidence to the insurance company that you are insurable. There are limitations on the maximum amount of life insurance you can elect and the ages at which changes may be made. Because this policy allows you to elect more insurance at a time when you are unhealthy, the insurer charges a higher premium than it might otherwise.

Nontraditional Life Insurance

During the latter 1970s and early 1980s, inflation led to very high interest rates in the United States. As a result, traditional endowment and whole-life policies became less attractive because their cash values earned lower rates of interest than investors could earn elsewhere. Inflation also eroded the purchasing power of these policies. Many policies were cancelled or their cash values withdrawn, and the sale of new policies suffered. To counteract these problems, life insurers developed and marketed some innovative new life insurance policies.

Variable Life. **Variable life insurance** is designed to provide a face amount that will give your beneficiary a relatively constant purchasing power. It does not offer the level amount of dollars provided by traditional level-term, endowment, and whole-life policies. As inflation occurs, the face amount of a variable-life policy should increase. The greater number of dollars payable should buy about the same group of goods and services that the original face amount would have purchased when the policy was issued.

Universal Life. **Universal life insurance** is a modified form of endowment or whole life insurance. The policy provides both death protection, in the form of term insurance, and an investment component or cash value. What is unique is that the pure insurance and cash value are identified separately. The cash value is based on an investment consisting of high-grade, short-term government or corporate bonds or notes. After a part of your premium is deducted to pay an administrative charge, the remainder is placed in the cash value. Each month, the price of one month's term insurance is withdrawn from the cash value. Interest is credited on the remainder. As long as enough savings exist to pay for the term insurance, the policy stays in force. If the cash value grows to a very high percentage of the face amount, universal-life policies then will increase the face amount. Thus, your policy's face amount *may* vary, but this is not a certainty. The major emphasis is your ability to earn *competitive* returns on your cash value. The popularity of universal life insurance has grown explosively in recent years.

Comparing Life Insurance Policy Types

We have discussed a number of types of insurance policy coverage. To better appreciate how many of these factors interact, please see Table 10.4. Here you see the period of coverage, the annual premium at a given age, the type of protection afforded, and other general factors. Perhaps you can identify the type of policy that best suits you.

LIFE ANNUITIES

An annuity provides a steady stream of payments (income) for a specified period of time. These payments consist of principal and interest, and use up all of the principal by the end of the payment period. A **life annuity** is a special form of annuity where the specified payment period is at least your remaining lifetime.

Although life annuities are sold by life insurers, they are not life insurance. Nevertheless, they are important to the financial planning process. From the time benefit payments begin, their income stream will continue for the rest of your life. This income comes from three sources: (1) dollars you pay to buy the annuity, (2) interest earned while the insurer holds your money, and (3) the averaging of your life span with those of others who buy life annuities. Life annuities can be either single-life or multiple-life. If they are *single-life,* their benefit payments depend on the continued life of one annuitant (the person on whose life the annuity is based). If they are *multiple-life,* benefit payments depend on the continued lives of two or more people.

Most multiple-life annuities are based on two lives: wife and husband. These annuities usually will pay benefits until the last of the two people die. They may pay the same full monthly benefit to the survivor after the first person dies, or they may pay some fraction (for example, one-half or two-thirds) to the survivor. Assume that you and your spouse retire, using a multiple-life annuity that will pay $1500 a month while you both live. If its survivor benefit is a full benefit, it will pay your spouse $1500 a month after your death; if two-thirds, it will pay ($1500) (⅔), or $1000 a month; if one-half, it will pay ($1500) (½), or $750.

Table 10.4 COMPARING TYPES OF $100,000 LIFE INSURANCE POLICIES

Policy type	Period of coverage	Sex	Hypothetical premiums for policies issued at age[a] 25	35	45	Emphasis	Other information
Annually renewable term	Most often up to age 70 or 75; sometimes to age 100	M F	$180 165	$195 175	$350 350	Pure protection	Constant coverage; premiums increase each year at an increasing rate of change
Decreasing term to age 70	To age 70	M F	$240 220	$280 245	$525 480	Decreasing pure protection	Constant annual premiums; coverage declines to zero at age 70
Whole life (traditional)	To age 100	M F	$575 500	$900 625	$1560 1285	Protection + increased savings	Constant coverage; savings equal face amount at age 100
Whole life paid up at 65	To age 100	M F	$990 945	$1625 1555	$2840 2645	Protection + increased savings	Constant coverage; savings increase rapidly up to age 65, then grow slowly, based only on interest
Universal (whole) life	To age 100	M F	Annual premiums for the same universal-life policy can vary widely, allowing the owner flexibility.			Protection + increased savings	Coverage, premiums, and savings all can vary; interest, mortality loadings, and management fees are factors

[a] Assumes policies issued to healthy nonsmokers.

Buyers should decide how much one person would need each month if the other died first and then choose the appropriate form.

MAJOR TYPES OF LIFE INSURANCE COMPANIES

There are two major types of life insurers: (1) stocks and (2) mutuals. Stock insurers are owned by stockholders and are operated for a profit. Mutuals are owned by their policyholders and are operated on a not-for-profit basis. Most life insurance sold by stock insurers is nonparticipating (or "nonpar"). The premium in this type of policy is set in advance and will not decrease or increase. Mutuals sell participating (or "par") life policies. These policies return a portion of the premium to their policyholders if the insurer performs well. The returned premium is called a policyholder dividend. It varies, and it cannot be guaranteed.

IMPORTANT LIFE INSURANCE POLICY PROVISIONS

If you consider buying a life insurance policy, you should read it carefully. There are many clauses and options in such contracts, and each is important. We will discuss some of the common provisions.

Beneficiary Designation

The **beneficiary** you designate will receive the life insurance policy proceeds if you die. You can retain the right to change that designation as you wish in the future, which makes the designation *revocable.* If you give up your right to make future changes without the permission of the beneficiary already named, the designation is *irrevocable.* Usually, it is wise to maximize your future flexibility in using the policy and make the designation revocable.

A beneficiary can be a person or another legal entity, such as a corporation. You can name multiple beneficiaries, designating how they are to share the policy proceeds. Also, you can name one or more *primary* beneficiaries who will receive the policy proceeds if living when you die, and one or more *secondary* beneficiaries who will receive the proceeds if the primary beneficiary(ies) is (are) not alive at the time of your death. Be sure to ask your insurance agent for help wording the designation so that it will distribute the proceeds exactly the way you wish. Insurers have lists of suggested wordings that have been upheld in courts of law, and the agent can help you use them.

A closely related issue is the ownership of the policy. The owner of the policy is typically the person who pays the premium. This person is normally different from the beneficiary. It is the owner of the policy who has control over the policy and may borrow against the cash value of the policy. In some cases, however, ownership of the policy is transferred to the beneficiary to diminish potential estate and inheritance taxes.

Grace Period

The **grace period** provision gives you one month from the premium due date to pay your premium before the policy lapses for premium nonpayment. If you pay the premium before the month is up, you owe no interest. If you die during the grace period, the insurer will deduct the premium owed from the policy face amount and pay the rest to your beneficiary.

Policy Loan Provision

If you buy a life insurance policy that builds up cash value, under a **policy loan provision** you will be able to borrow from that cash value at an interest rate set forth in the policy. If you die while a loan remains unpaid, the insurer will deduct the loan and interest from the policy face amount and pay the remainder to your beneficiary. An important provision to request is the **automatic policy loan provision.** Adding it costs you nothing. By authorizing the insurer to borrow an unpaid premium from the policy cash value, it protects your policy against cancellation if you forget to pay your premium by the end of the grace period. You pay a cost only if you use the provisions, and that cost (the interest on the premium loaned) is a small price to pay.

Incontestable Clause

The insurer can challenge, or contest, your policy if you give false information to the agent in your application. However, under the **incontestable clause,** the insurer gives up its right to contest the validity of the policy. Incontestability normally begins two years after the policy is issued, and with a few insurers it starts after only one year.

Suicide Clause

Under the **suicide clause,** the insurer states that it will not pay the policy face amount if you die by committing suicide within one or two years after the policy is issued. Until that time has passed, it will return your premiums (usually plus interest) to your beneficiary. After that time, it will treat suicide as an insured cause of death.

Surrender Options

Your **surrender option** is a choice you have if you own a policy with a cash value and do not want to keep the life insurance in force any longer. You can surrender the policy to the insurer and take the money in *cash.* Although this is the most popular choice, there are two other options that the insurer must offer you.

Under the *extended-term* option, your cash value is applied as a one-time premium to buy level term life insurance with a face amount equal to that of the policy surrendered. The period of protection provided depends on your age and the amount of cash value. Under the *paid-up life* option, you can use the cash value as a one-time premium to buy as much life insurance as can be purchased at your age. It is called paid-up because you will never have to pay another premium. The new insurance will be the same type as your original policy.

Dividend Options

If your endowment or whole-life policy returns part of your premium as a policyholder dividend, your **dividend option** allows you to choose how to use that dividend. The most popular choice is to take it in *cash,* but you will get the same net effect by having the insurer use the dividend to *reduce the next premium due.* Another option is to use the dividends to create *savings* that the insurer will hold and credit with interest. Be sure that the insurer is paying a competitive interest rate before choosing this option. In addition, you can choose to buy *single-premium paid-up units of life insurance* of the same type as the policy generating the dividend. Thus, a whole-life policy's dividends can be used each year to buy small, paid-up units of whole life insurance. You do not pay any more premiums on these units, and they also generate dividends, enabling you to receive larger dividends in future years. Also, some mutual insurers offer a *term option.* This option lets you buy limited amounts of one-year term life with the dividend each year, without proving your insurability.

Settlement Options

If you live until the endowment life insurance policy on your life matures, or if you are the beneficiary of a life insurance policy when the insured dies, you will have a number of choices for using the proceeds. These choices are called **settlement options.** The most popular choice is to take the proceeds in *cash* (lump sum). There are, however, some other choices that might be better suited to your needs. You can use an *interest accumulation* option, where you leave part or all of the proceeds with the insurer as a savings account earning interest. You can retain the right to withdraw the interest and to withdraw the principal. Further, you can use any of several *annuity* options. These can supply you a monthly income for a definite number of years, or you can opt for one of a number of life annuities. The life annuity can be for you alone, or it can cover you and another person.

You should discuss your options with a life insurance agent or other financial adviser. Notice at the bottom of Table 10.5 (on page 345) that the method of paying proceeds (settlement) tends to be a cash lump sum in over 95 percent of the cases.

Table 10.5 ANALYSIS OF LIFE INSURANCE PAYMENTS TO BENEFICIARIES IN THE UNITED STATES, APRIL 1981

	PERCENT OF POLICIES			PERCENT OF AMOUNT		
	Ordinary[a]	Group	Industrial	Ordinary[a]	Group	Industrial
Sex of insured						
Male	73.2	80.9	41.8	87.8	87.1	44.9
Female	26.8	19.1	58.2	12.2	12.9	55.1
Total	100.0	100.0	100.0	100.0	100.0	100.00
Age of insured at death						
Under 25	2.3	4.4	0.9	2.7	3.4	1.7
25–34	2.3	5.2	1.1	5.5	6.9	1.7
35–44	3.5	6.8	2.1	9.3	10.2	2.7
45–54	8.8	16.0	5.3	17.2	22.9	7.2
55–64	19.9	27.9	14.2	24.7	37.6	16.0
65–74	28.1	21.0	27.4	20.8	12.4	26.3
75 or older	35.1	18.7	49.0	19.8	6.6	44.4
Total	100.0	100.0	100.0	100.0	100.0	100.00
Relationship of beneficiary to insured						
Husband	9.6	7.0	12.9	4.6	6.1	13.2
Wife	47.2	52.9	24.1	53.6	59.9	26.2
Child or children	16.8	16.2	37.9	9.6	11.1	37.0
Other relatives	13.0	11.1	18.6	8.2	9.7	17.8
Estate or trust	4.8	6.2	3.2	7.6	6.7	2.9
Institution	0.6	3.2	0.6	1.7	2.9	0.5
All other	8.0	3.4	2.7	14.7	3.6	2.4
Total	100.0	100.0	100.0	100.0	100.0	100.00

continued

SOME POPULAR LIFE INSURANCE POLICY RIDERS

A rider or endorsement is an added provision attached to your policy. It either adds or deletes coverage. If it adds coverage, there usually is an additional premium charged. Some popular riders that add coverage include (1) accidental death benefit (ADB), or double indemnity, (2) waiver of premium, and (3) guaranteed insurability.

Accidental Death Benefit (ADB), or Double Indemnity

The **accidental death benefit (ADB)**, or **double indemnity,** is a coverage that pays an added benefit only if you die because of an accident. It will not pay if

Table 10.5 continued

	PERCENT OF POLICIES			PERCENT OF AMOUNT		
	Ordinary[a]	Group	Industrial	Ordinary[a]	Group	Industrial
Duration of policy when it became a claim						
Less than 1 year	1.7	—	0.6	5.1	—	1.0
1–5 years	5.6	—	4.3	16.9	—	6.5
5–10 years	7.5	—	5.6	15.2	—	7.1
10–20 years	19.1	—	11.3	22.5	—	12.7
20–30 years	17.6	—	19.0	15.6	—	20.5
30 years or more	48.5	—	59.2	24.7	—	52.2
Total	100.0	—	100.0	100.0	—	100.00
Sex of beneficiary						
Male	20.4	18.8	34.5	11.0	14.1	34.9
Female	62.0	67.4	58.4	62.6	69.0	58.0
Both sexes represented	5.9	5.7	1.8	5.6	4.6	2.5
All other	11.7	8.1	5.3	20.8	12.3	4.6
Total	100.0	100.0	100.0	100.0	100.0	100.00
Method of paying proceeds						
→ Lump sum	97.9	98.3	100.0	96.0	96.2	100.0
Life income	0.5	0.4	—	0.8	0.9	—
Annuity certain	0.8	0.7	—	1.2	1.8	—
Held at interest	0.7	0.4	—	1.7	0.8	—
All other	0.1	0.2	—	0.3	0.3	—
Total	100.0	100.0	100.0	100.0	100.0	100.00

[a] Figures exclude individual credit life insurance on loans of 10 years' or less duration.
[b] Less than 0.05%.
SOURCE: American Council of Life Insurance, *1983 Life Insurance Fact Book*, Washington, D.C., p. 42.

you die of natural causes. For example, if you were killed in an auto crash, it would pay; but if you died of a heart attack while driving, and the car then crashed, it would not pay. Because it insures against a limited cause of death, it is cheaper than regular term life. It often is sold in an amount equal to the face amount of the life insurance policy it is endorsed to, thus earning its other name, "double indemnity." If you bought a $50,000 policy with a $50,000 ADB rider and subsequently died in a car crash, the payment to your beneficiary would be $50,000 + $50,000, or $100,000, which is double the $50,000 face amount of the whole-life policy. You may, however, buy more or less than a multiple of one, and you should select the amount (if any) of ADB that is best for you. Remember that you cannot depend on an ADB as a certain asset for your

Box 10.1 YOUR MONEY AND YOUR LIFE

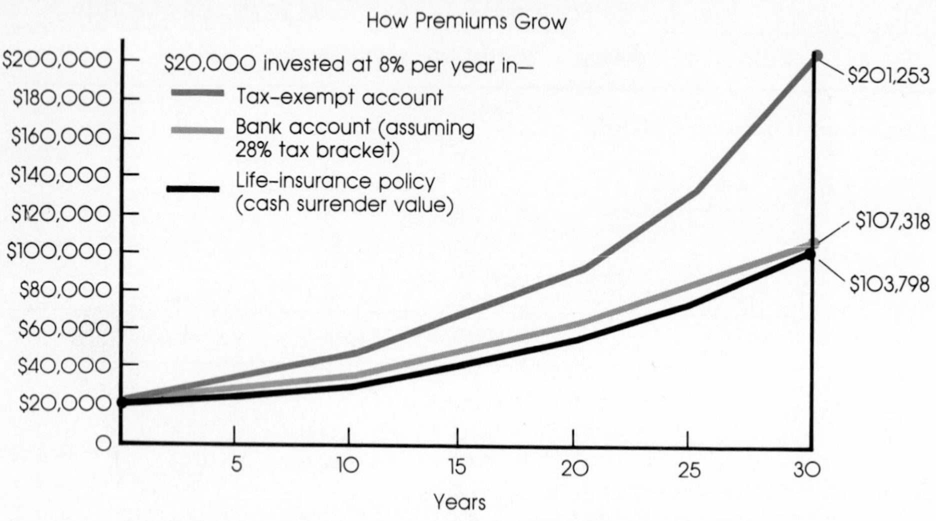

Note: Life-insurance policy is single-premium, variable-life coverage for a 35-year-old male. Assumes interest on other accounts is reinvested.

USN&WR—Basic data: Pruco Life Insurance Co. Calculations by *USN&WR* Economic Unit.

With billions of dollars about to be unshackled, thanks to the elimination of most shelters under tax reform, life insurers are eagerly pushing products that retain tax benefits. "Single-premium and variable-universal life policies are going to be major hitters in 1987," predicts Michael Rosenberg, director of personal-insurance marketing at Aetna Life & Casualty.

The drumbeat is already intense. "A lifetime of tax-free cash," proclaims one ad. "Tax advantages and investment flexibility," boasts the brochure from another firm.

What's being trumpeted is not new. Investment income on paid-in premiums has always been allowed to grow tax-free. But that feature stands out, now that other breaks are about to be scotched. If you surrender your policy before death, you will owe income tax on the earnings. Otherwise, you may withdraw income tax-free by borrowing against the policy. Should you die, the proceeds pass to your beneficiaries free of income tax.

Lucrative Options

The new generation of policies offers some potentially attractive returns, making it possible for more money to compound rapidly, sheltered from yearly taxes. Metropolitan Life's new single-premium policy, for example, is now paying a 7.6 percent rate. Hartford Life's variable-life policyholders can put their money into mutual funds investing in stocks, bonds, Ginnie Maes and zero-coupon bonds. Over the past 12 months, the return on the Hartford funds has ranged between 7 and

27 percent. The elimination of special treatment for long-term capital gains also makes tax-deferred insurance funds more attractive relative to traditional mutual funds.

Those intrigued by life insurance's post-tax-reform allure should scrutinize advertised claims. The insurance component can be very costly, and cashing in a policy early will depress returns. "If a person doesn't need death protection, he shouldn't buy life insurance," says David Woods, president of the National Association of Life Underwriters. "This isn't like buying 20 shares of AT&T. You have to hold on to it for a long time."

For someone with $10,000 or more to set aside, a single-premium whole-life contract offers significant investment opportunity with its death benefit. The policy resembles a savings account, since the whole premium works on your behalf.

The insurer guarantees an interest rate for a specified period of time. After that, the rate is adjusted periodically to reflect prevailing market rates. The company invests its pooled funds at a higher rate. "The spread between the rate we earn and the rate we credit you with pays for expenses, death claims and our profit," says Herb Lister, president of Allstate Life Insurance, whose brand-new Harbor SPWL policy is being offered through Dean Witter.

The larger the initial premium, the more dramatic the buildup. A 50-year-old man who today puts $100,000 into a Harbor contract could expect a death benefit of $335,035. By the time he's 70, he will have accumulated $424,785, assuming rates average 7.5 percent. Should he die at age 70, his beneficiaries would be owed $492,751.

These policies can be "a super way to save for retirement income or the kids' education," says Benjamin Baldwin, a Northbrook, Ill., financial planner affiliated with Equitable Financial Services. The holder can borrow from the earnings without triggering taxes, and little or no interest is paid on the loan.

Another form of single-premium insurance—the variable-life policy—offers greater investment leeway. Prudential Insurance's Discovery Life Plus plan offers a choice of nine investments, including stock, bond and zero-coupon-bond mutual funds. A fixed-rate account currently pays 7 percent and eliminates any risk to principal.

Administrative and advisory fees and the cost of the death benefit come out of a variable policy's cash value. With Prudential, about 2.25 percent goes toward expenses each year. So someone who doesn't need life insurance could likely do much better elsewhere. Unless you can consistently earn more than 8 percent a year in Prudential's investment options, tax-exempt municipal bonds or no-load mutual funds may be a better choice.

"I may be swimming upriver, but my view is that you should approach life insurance as insurance and not base your purchase on tax considerations," says Joseph Belth, an insurance professor at Indiana University.

Single-premium policies have other drawbacks. If you have to get your principal back, you could be in for a financial shock. Surrender penalties in the early years are substantial, and income-tax liabilities are severe.

People without a lump sum to invest might consider variable-universal life, which lets you pay periodically and select your own investments.

Given the marketing blitz that lies ahead, you should think twice before purchasing one of these policies. Whether the tax-deferral and income characteristics are a good deal will depend on your need for life insurance and your ability to make successful investment decisions within the framework of one of these policies.

dependents if you die; unlike regular term life insurance, it will not pay if you die from natural causes.

Waiver of Premium (WP)

The **waiver of premium** is an inexpensive rider that you should strongly consider adding to every individual life insurance policy that you buy. It assures you that, if you are disabled and cannot earn the money to pay your life insurance premium, the insurer will waive its premium requirement and keep the policy in force. If you recover, you do not have to repay the back premium(s) paid for you, but you must pay future premiums when they are due.

Guaranteed Insurability Option (GIO)

The **guaranteed insurability option** protects your ability to buy more life insurance in the future, even if your health deteriorates. You are able to buy more insurance on designated policy anniversaries, up to limits set in the rider. This option usually ends after the policy anniversary nearest to your fortieth birthday.

HOW LIFE INSURANCE IS SOLD

Stock and mutual life insurers can sell their policies in any of three ways: (1) individual policies, (2) group policies, and (3) industrial policies.

Individual or *ordinary* life insurance policies usually are sold to one person, and the insurer carefully determines whether or not that person is insurable. You are responsible for sending your premiums to the insurer, and you may pay them annually, semiannually, or monthly. In applying for insurance, you will be required to furnish the insurer information it needs to decide if it will issue you a policy.

Group life policies have one master policy (usually held by an employer) and many certificates of insurance (usually on the employees who want to be insured). They typically do not require individual proof of insurability. The policyholder (employer) is responsible for forwarding the monthly premium to the insurer. If you pay a part of the premium, it is deducted from your paycheck.

Industrial or *debit* life insurance is sold in small amounts, based on the weekly or monthly premium the buyer can afford. Because an agent calls at the insured's home to collect the small premium each week or month, this type of contract has a high labor cost built into its premium. Thus, it usually costs far more per $1000 of protection than a policy of the same type sold in the individual-insurance marketplace. Individual and group life insurance sales are growing, but industrial life insurance is declining in importance.

Choosing an Agent and an Insurer

Select an agent who gives you a comfortable feeling of professional competence. The agent should be well informed about new products and their uses. Two of the best known professional designations for life insurance agents are Chartered Life Underwriter (CLU) and Chartered Financial Consultant (ChFC). To receive these designations, an agent must pass multiple national examinations. An agent who has one or more of these designations, or who is currently working toward one, is more likely to be up-to-date than an agent who has not tried to earn one. You should also ask other people about an agent's professionalism and service. The agent should answer any questions you have and elicit a great deal of information about you in order to fit life insurance products to your specific needs.

A professional agent usually will represent a low-cost insurance company that stresses solid service and sound financial management. You can learn about the insurer's financial strength, general management, and overall cost to its insureds by going to your local library and looking that insurer up in the most recent year's *Best's Insurance Reports: Life-Health.* An excellent source of comparative policy costs is *Consumer Reports.* This magazine often publishes cost comparisons for selected life insurance policies issued at specific ages and having specific face amounts.

Inflation as a Factor

Inflation erodes the buying power of a dollar, so from time to time your life insurance program should be reevaluated. If you do not use products that adjust their face amount (such as variable life), you may need to buy more life insurance. Because the need for life insurance as an asset in your estate usually declines with age, however, this change may offset the effects of inflation. The only way to be sure is to periodically reevaluate your needs and assets. Ask your life insurance agent to perform this service for you.

SUMMARY

The primary function of life insurance is to create assets for your dependents if you die. This money can provide for your family's income needs if you die while young, or it may help to keep your accumulated assets intact by paying estate taxes if you are older and have built up investments and savings. Also, some types of life insurance can be used to build up savings.

Needs programming is the most accurate way to decide how much life insurance to buy. It compares the current and future needs of your dependents if you die with the assets already available to meet those needs. If there are not enough assets, the difference between assets and needs is a good measure of additional life insurance to consider buying.

The major types of traditional life insurance are (1) term, (2) endowment, and (3) whole life. Term pays its face amount if you die during the policy period; it pays nothing if you live. It has no savings at the end of the period and is the least expensive product per $1000 per year. Endowment pays its face amount if you die during the period covered or if you live until the end of that period. The payment if you live is based on a savings accumulation (cash value) that equals the face amount of the policy by the end of the period. This type of insurance requires higher premiums per $1000 per year than term. Whole life pays its face amount whenever you die, up to age 100. At age 100, it pays even if you are alive, and coverage ends. The policy accumulates a cash value that equals its face amount at that time. Because with whole life, savings do not build up as rapidly as the savings under policies endowing at younger ages, its premiums per $1000 per year are lower than premiums for those endowments. Its premiums are larger than those for term, however.

Package policies combine traditional life insurance and riders in a variety of ways. If such packages exactly fit your needs, consider them. Otherwise, work with your agent and create a policy plus riders that better fits your needs.

Universal life insurance is a new (nontraditional) life insurance policy stressing the rate of return on its cash value element. The premium you pay is flexible, and the policy's term element is purchased monthly by deducting its cost from the cash value. Variable life is nontraditional life insurance that changes its face amount to help compensate for the effect of inflation.

Life annuities are sold by life insurers, but they are not life insurance. They guarantee you (the life annuitant) a stream of benefit payments that will last as long as you live. They vary in several ways, including the number of lives covered, the number of premiums you pay, and the insurer's guarantee to pay a minimum amount of benefits if you die after you begin receiving benefits.

There are many important life insurance policy provisions. The beneficiary designation spells out who receives the policy proceeds if you die. The grace period allows you an extra month to pay premiums without losing coverage, and the policy loan provision lets you borrow from a policy's cash value. You can include an automatic policy loan feature that borrows from a cash value policy to pay an unpaid premium at the end of the grace period.

If you surrender a policy with a cash value, you can take that amount in cash or use it to buy either extended term life insurance or paid-up life insurance. If the policy is participating, its dividends can be taken in cash or used to reduce the next premium due. They also may be used to create savings that earn interest, to buy paid-up life insurance units with cash values, or (with some insurers) to buy one-year term. When the policy's face amount is paid, it can be taken in cash, left as savings at interest, or used to buy annuities.

You should choose a life insurance agent who makes you feel comfortable and who is professional and up-to-date. Your insurer should be financially sound and well managed. Inflation can adversely affect your life insurance program, so you should update that program regularly.

KEY TERMS

accidental death benefit (ADB)
adjustable life insurance
annually renewable term (ART)
automatic policy loan provision
beneficiary
cash value
decreasing term life insurance
dividend option
double indemnity
endowment life insurance
family income policy
grace period
guaranteed insurability option
incontestable clause
joint life insurance
level term life insurance
life annuity
mortality rate
needs programming
package policies
policy loan provision
settlement option
suicide clause
surrender option
term life insurance
universal life insurance
variable life insurance
waiver of premium
whole life insurance

SELECTED READINGS

"Four-Star Insurance Policy." *Money,* February 1985, p. 11.

"Insurance and an Investment, Too." *Changing Times,* May 1986, pp. 73–76, 78–79.

"Is Your Coverage Up to Date?" *Changing Times,* January 1985, pp. 57–58, 60.

"Life Insurance with Options Galore." *Fortune,* November 11, 1985, p. 155.

Quinn, Jane Bryant. "The New Investment Policies." *Newsweek,* January 20, 1986, p. 49.

"Should You Switch Policies?" *Changing Times,* May 1985, pp. 36–38.

QUESTIONS

1 Explain the primary function of life insurance.
2 Why is the income multiples approach likely to arrive at a life insurance figure that is not the amount you might need?
3 What is the basic concept used in the needs programming approach in order to determine the amount of life insurance you might need?
4 Briefly explain how term life insurance works.
5 Compare one-year term and annually renewable term life insurance.

6 Compare annually renewable term and level-premium level term for a multiyear period.
7 Explain how multiyear life insurance policies can have level annual premiums.
8 Describe how decreasing term life insurance works.
9 Briefly describe endowment life insurance's two promises to pay.
10 Describe whole life insurance.
11 Why might term insurance sometimes be preferable to whole life for a young, emerging family?
12 Describe the family income policy.
13 Describe adjustable life insurance.
14 What problems led to the development of nontraditional life insurance policies?
15 What is the purpose of variable life insurance? How does it accomplish that purpose?
16 What is universal life insurance?
17 For how long will a life annuity's benefit payments last? What are the sources of these income (benefit) payments?
18 Compare single-life and multiple-life life annuities, and explain when most multiple-life life annuities are used.
19 Describe the two major types of life insurance companies and explain the differences between most of their policies.
20 What does the beneficiary designation clause in a life insurance policy do?
21 Explain the grace period of a life insurance policy.
22 Describe the surrender options under a cash value life insurance policy, and note when they may be used.
23 When may life insurance settlement options be used? What are the major options?
24 Explain the accidental death benefit (ADB) rider.
25 Describe the waiver of premium (WP) rider.
26 Nicole Timmons is the owner of a participating whole life insurance contract. Her annual premiums each year are $300, due on the policy anniversary date of July 1. This year, her policyholder dividend, payable on June 30, is $75. Determine her new premium for next year if she takes this year's dividend in cash. What will the new premium be if she uses the dividend to reduce the premium due? Explain which of these dividend options leaves Nicole financially better off.
27 Art Adams owns a $100,000 whole life insurance policy with a $100,000 accidental death benefit (ADB) rider. Determine what this insurance will pay if Art:
  a Dies as a result of injuries from an auto accident
  b Dies from a stroke while driving, and his car crashes into a bridge abutment
  c Dies when his parachute fails to open while he is skydiving, and he plummets to earth

28 Using data from the 1980 Commissioners Standard Ordinary Mortality Table (Table 10.3), determine the annual pure premium for

a $100,000 of term life insurance for a male age 25

b $50,000 of term life insurance for a male age 65

c $250,000 of term life insurance for a female age 20

d $100,000 of term life insurance for a female age 50

29 Lou and Joyce Bennett, both 65, are comparing multiple-life life annuities that pay different amounts of monthly benefits. Determine what Joyce will receive monthly from each annuity, if Lou dies first.

a An annuity providing a full benefit for the survivor and paying $2000 a month while Lou and Joyce both live.

b An annuity paying $2250 a month to both Lou and Joyce, and two-thirds to the survivor.

c An annuity paying $2500 to Lou and Joyce, and one-half to the survivor.

CASE PROBLEMS

10.1 Bobbi Barnes, age 27, does not know how much life insurance she needs. She is the primary wage earner for her family. Her husband, Bill, age 28, is an artist whose income potential is very unpredictable. They have two children, Betty, 8, and Bruce, 5. Using the information given below, employ the needs programming approach to determine how much life insurance Bobbi might need to buy. Assume that all dollar figures given are in dollars today.

Make two columns. The first column should represent the needs that the family will have if Bobbi dies. This should include all debts, expenses, loss of income, cost of college, and so on.

The second column should include all assets or resources that the family might have to meet these needs. Every item mentioned in this case should fall into one column or the other, so make your best judgment.

Take the difference between the first and second column to determine how much added life insurance for Bobbi is necessary.

The current value of Bobbi's monthly Social Security benefits to be received by Bill while Betty and/or Bruce are 18 or younger is $68,000. The best estimate of Bill's future earnings, in today's dollars, is $110,000. This is considered an asset. They have accumulated $7000 in savings and own stock valued at $3500. Bobbi's group life insurance will pay $30,000, and she has no individual life insurance. Her retirement plan at work will pay a death benefit of $17,000. Funeral costs would be $3000, and the balance owed on their mortgage is $60,000. They owe another $2800 on furniture, $6500 on a car, and $1200 in installment debt. Bobbi and Bill estimate that Betty's and Bruce's college educations will cost $20,000 each in current dollars and that Bill and the children will need an emergency fund of $3000. Their best single estimate of the current value of Bobbi's future earnings potential that would be lost in the event of death is $150,000. They would need this sum to replace her future earnings if she died.

10.2 You are the owner of a $20,000 whole life insurance policy purchased when you are 20. Your surrender options are contained in the table shown below.

Using the table of surrender options provided, determine for your respective ages:

a 30
b 40
c 65

Surrender Options

End of[a] policy year	Cash or loan value	Paid-up insurance	EXTENDED-TERM[b] INSURANCE	
			Years	Days
1	$ 40	$ 160	1	20
2	160	650	3	5
3	290	1,350	4	206
4	460	2,160	7	198
5	650	2,980	11	165
6	870	3,760	15	101
7	1,110	4,510	18	15
8	1,360	5,250	20	177
9	1,620	5,980	21	344
10	1,890	6,690	23	154
11	2,160	7,370	24	182
12	2,320	8,040	25	213
13	2,480	8,700	26	228
14	2,640	9,350	26	304
15	2,790	9,990	27	15
16	2,940	10,610	27	80
17	3,090	11,220	27	136
18	3,230	11,820	27	63
19	3,470	12,410	26	202
20	3,610	13,000	25	199
Age 60	9,980	16,890	18	309
Age 65	11,370	17,840	16	228

[a] Number of years the policy has been owned.
[b] Time period beyond the purchase date of the policy to which extended term coverage protection could be provided.

1 The cash you will receive if you choose to surrender the policy for its cash value.
2 The amount of paid-up whole life insurance you will receive if you choose that option.
3 The maximum age to which your extended term protection will provide coverage (assuming that you purchased the policy on your twentieth birthday).

Nowhere are successes or failures more apparent than in the investments area. If you buy the wrong personal computer or stereo, it may take a few months to realize the foolishness of your ways. But if you own a stock or bond that is a "dog," you will receive daily reminders in the form of newspaper quotes each morning.

Of course, there is no reason to take a negative attitude. There are ample and exciting opportunities to make money in the stock market, the bond market, options, commodities, real estate, and other investment outlets. We strongly recommend a deliberate and well-thought-out approach. You may have luck with a hot tip from time to time, but long-term success in investments requires hard work and time.

The first step is to determine what factors are important to you in an investment: How much risk are you willing to take? How important to you is current income versus the potential for long-term gain? How

MANAGING YOUR INVESTMENT ASSETS

critical are tax considerations to the investment? and so on. You might want to take the personal profile test in Box 11.1, which helps determine what types of investments you or your family should undertake.

In Chapter 11, you will be introduced to overall investment strategy in general and fixed-income investments in particular. The latter include such items as certificates of deposit (CDs), money market funds, and bonds.

We then shift to stock market investments in Chapter 12, where you will develop a good background in analyzing basic information about companies. We suggest many important sources of investment data so that you can seriously consider actually participating in the market. We also talk about the different types of brokers you can use to execute transactions and the costs involved.

Many investors prefer the ease of investment through mutual funds (professionally managed portfolios of stocks and bonds) rather than individual investments. In Chapter 13, we present extensive data that should make it easier to select the mutual fund that best fits your needs. We also issue a warning about paying excessive commissions to some mutual fund sponsors. This expense can generally be avoided by the knowledgeable mutual fund investor.

For the more venturesome, we consider options, commodities and real assets in Chapter 14. If you want "more excitement for your money," read this chapter carefully. ■

11

Investment Strategy and Fixed-Income Securities

After studying this chapter, you should:

- Understand the key roles that risk and return play in investment decisions
- Be able to use present-value tables
- Appreciate the historical evidence on return for various forms of investments
- Understand the effect of inflation and disinflation on investment performance
- Appreciate the factors that should be considered in setting goals and objectives for an investor—return and safety of principal, liquidity, and so on
- Be able to differentiate between market risk, purchasing power risk, and credit risk
- Understand the key attributes of fixed income securities in terms of maturity, yield, and risk

In this chapter, we first discuss investment strategy in a general sense, and then consider fixed-income investments.

OVERALL STRATEGY

When you make an **investment,** you commit current funds in the hope of receiving an increased return in the future. In setting your investment strategy, you should be aware of the wide array of investments from which to choose. All too often an investor is lured by a hot stock tip or a savings account promotion and fails to consider the full spectrum of investments that are available. Only after becoming familiar with the various investments, and with the potential risk and return of each, should you commit your funds. You also need to consider the current and future economic environment. An investment that was an outstanding performer in the past may not hold up well in the future because of the changing dynamics in the economy.

Investments may be broken down into financial assets and real assets. This distinction was briefly covered in Chapter 2. **Financial assets** are cash, near-cash items, or financial documents that represent a claim to assets (such as stocks or bonds). **Real assets** are physical assets (such as real estate or gold). A list of potential investments, broken down into financial and real assets, follows.

A Financial assets
- **1** Short-term
  - Savings account
  - Certificate of deposit
  - Money market fund
  - Money market account
  - Treasury bill
  - Federal agency securities
  - Commercial paper
- **2** Intermediate
  - GNMA certificate
  - Treasury notes
  - Tax-deferred annuities
- **3** Long-term
  - Bond
  - Preferred stock
  - Common stock (also options, warrants)

B Real assets
- **1** Real estate (apartment, office building)
- **2** Collectibles
  - Art
  - Antiques
  - Coins
  - Stamps
  - Rare books
- **3** Precious metals
  - Gold
  - Silver
  - Platinum
- **4** Precious gems
  - Diamonds
  - Rubies
- **5** Other
  - Common metals
  - Oil

You can see in this list that financial assets can be separated into short-term, intermediate, and long-term assets. As you will find out later in this chapter, the length to maturity (life) of an investment affects potential returns, risk exposure, and a number of other factors.

Real assets are typically broken down by category rather than maturity, because most real assets, unlike most financial assets, do not end with the passage of time. The five key categories of real assets are real estate, collectibles, precious metals, precious gems, and other.

ECONOMIC ENVIRONMENT FOR INVESTMENTS

As we mentioned earlier, the economic environment is a strong influence in selecting the right investment. Almost any investment will work (or fail) depending on the economic climate. When inflation is moderating (as in the mid-1980s), stocks and bonds tend to perform best. When consumer prices are increasing rapidly and there is much uncertainty about the future, real assets such as real estate or gold tend to do well (as in the late 1970s). Generally, when financial assets are doing well, real assets are doing poorly and vice versa.

A 15-year analysis of outcomes from various forms of investments is presented in Table 11.1.

Table 11.1 COMPARATIVE RETURNS FROM ALTERNATIVE INVESTMENTS: COMPOUNDED ANNUAL RATES OF RETURN

	15 Years	Rank	10 Years	Rank	5 Years	Rank	1 Year	Rank
Oil	19.7%	1	8.0%	9	(5.4)%	12	(4.5)%	10
U.S. coins	17.7	2	20.4	1	0.1	9	11.5	4
Gold	15.5	3	6.9	13	(11.0)	14	(20.3)	14
Chinese ceramics	14.3	4	17.1	2	1.0	8	5.9	6
Stamps	14.1	5	14.5	3	0.1	10	(9.6)	11
Diamonds	10.4	6	9.5	7	1.2	7	0.0	9
Old masters	9.1	7	10.7	4	1.5	6	13.6	3
Treasury bills	9.1	8	10.0	6	12.0	3	9.5	5
Bonds	8.7	9	9.3	8	13.2	2	42.9	1
Silver	8.7	10	3.5	14	(15.9)	15	(34.3)	15
Stocks	8.5	11	10.4	5	15.2	1	28.7	2
U.S. farmland	8.5	12	6.9	12	(1.7)	11	(10.0)	12
Housing	8.2	13	7.9	10	4.3	5	2.5	8
CPI[a]	**7.1**	**14**	**7.3**	**11**	**5.7**	**4**	**3.7**	**7**
Foreign exchange	2.0	15	(0.6)	15	(7.9)	13	(11.3)	13

[a] CPI represents the consumer price index, a popular measure of inflation.

SOURCE: Salomon Brothers, June 6, 1985.

Note that over the 15-year period, real assets tend to show a strong performance. This showing relates back to the highly inflationary period of the prior decade. But, as the focus moves to the last five years, particularly the last year, financial assets, such as stocks and bonds, dominate in terms of performance.

Although it is helpful to have some historical perspective, the key issue is not what has worked well in the past, but what will work well in the future. Investors and investment advisers tend to be overly influenced by their most recent experiences. Stockbrokers who have made 20 to 30 percent a year for their clients in the last two or three years tend to assume that they will go on doing so. They will present the investor with fancy data and charts showing what a continuation of 20 to 30 percent growth could mean to the investor. It is at times like these that the unsuspecting get drawn into the process.

When silver went from $5 to $55 an ounce in 1980, people felt they had to act immediately or miss a chance to ride the price of silver up to $100. In fact, silver retraced its path down to $6. During that same period of high inflation, the stock market was thought to have taken its last gasp. Since then, with moderating inflation, both stocks and bonds have enjoyed the most dramatic rally since the depression.

The point to remember is that investors, like generals, tend to refight their last battles rather than their next one. They tend to be overly influenced by what is currently working well (or has worked well in the last investment cycle) and blind to new investment possibilities. The economic environment is extremely important, but focus on the future, not the past.

TAILORING INVESTMENTS TO YOUR NEEDS

The most recognizable attribute of a professional investment manager is that he or she will first insist upon knowing more about you before making a recommendation. Even the best adviser can pick a stock that goes down or a dry oil well, but there is no acceptable excuse for mismatching an investment with an investor's needs. To put an elderly widow on a restricted fixed income in a risky growth stock is a bad investment even if the stock doubles in price in the first month. It may be equally poor planning for a $300,000-a-year surgeon to place his or her funds in a highly conservative taxable money market fund.

In assessing your needs and setting your investment objectives, you should evaluate the following factors: return and safety of principal, current income versus capital appreciation, the need for liquidity, tax factors, and management considerations. We now discuss each of these factors in turn.

Return and Safety of Principal

The first decision an investor must make is how much risk he or she is willing to take. In most cases, high returns correlate with high risk and vice versa. That is not to say that you cannot make a shrewd investment in which you get a very high return for taking a small risk, but such investment opportunities are infrequent. Generally, if you are trying to make a 20 to 25 percent return, you are also taking a commensurately high risk.

You must ask yourself how much risk you are willing to take. If you are uncomfortable with taking risks or simply cannot afford to lose the funds, it is obviously unwise to make bold, aggressive moves. Don't allow yourself to be talked into an investment position that is not a good fit for you. On the other hand, if you are willing to take higher risks in search of higher returns, don't hesitate to make your move when circumstances dictate.

Clearly, a person's current financial position helps to determine what degree of risk taking is feasible. If you have a car or house payment staring you in the face, a conservative investment (such as a money market fund or certificate of deposit) is dictated. If you earn more than you spend or have just received a big bonus, you may wish to go for superior returns at a higher risk level.

Generally, investments that provide the going rate of return based on normal risk are referred to as being of investment quality. Most risky investments, which often promise very high returns, may be thought of as being speculative in nature.

Current Income Versus Capital Appreciation

Even if you decide to go with higher-risk investments, you must consider whether your primary orientation will be toward generating returns in the form of current income or **capital appreciation** (an increase in value).

For example, if you decide to buy common stocks, you can choose either high-yielding issues with somewhat limited capital appreciation potential (public utilities, apparel) or growth stocks that provide little in the way of current return (high-technology firms, health care). In real estate, a similar distinction can be made between high-income-producing property (an apartment complex) and undeveloped land that has good long-term potential.

Liquidity Considerations

The need for liquidity will also influence your investment decisions. The **liquidity** of an investment is measured by the ability to convert the investment into cash in a relatively short time. Financial assets tend to provide a high degree of liquidity. Stocks and bonds can generally be sold within a matter of minutes at a value very close to the latest quote.[1]

Real assets generally lack liquidity. It may take you weeks or even months to sell a house, a stamp collection, or a valuable painting. Furthermore, there may be a large commission involved in selling real assets. For a house, this may

[1] An exception to this rule for financial assets would be certificates of deposit (which are purchased at a bank or savings and loan). These have a stipulated holding period, and a penalty must be paid for early withdrawal.

be 6 percent; for a collectible item, the dealer (merchant) may operate on a 10 to 25 percent spread. The spread is the difference in price at which the dealer is willing to buy and sell the item. For financial assets, the commission charge is usually only 1 to 2 percent.

This difference in liquidity does not necessarily mean that real assets are inferior to financial assets. Over the longer term, transactions costs tend to be absorbed in large price swings. You can afford to pay a realtor a 6 percent commission if your house has doubled in value over the years. Nevertheless, in the short run, the illiquidity of most real assets must be considered along with many other items.

Tax Factors

Investors must also evaluate the tax implications of their investments. Those in high tax brackets will normally seek investments with favorable tax treatment. For example, a high-tax-bracket investor may place his or her funds in municipal bonds (because the interest is nontaxable). This same investment may not be wise for someone who is in a low tax bracket because part of the return to the investor is in the form of advantageous tax treatment.

Although tax considerations are important to investors, the prudent investor should not be overly influenced by the tax code. In the past decade, many investments have been put together that have tax advantages but very limited economic merit. It does little good to save part of your tax obligation but lose most of your investment in the process.

When considering any investment, look very hard at potential tax advantages, but make sure the deductions are legitimate and meet the requirements of the tax law, particularly the Tax Reform Act of 1986. A properly structured deal should generally have a favorable tax opinion from the IRS or a tax attorney.

Management Considerations

The amount of time and energy that you are able to put into your investments will also determine the nature of your holdings. For example, if you enjoy evaluating stocks on your own, you will probably buy and sell for your own account (through a stockbroker). On the other hand, if you do not have the time or the interest to follow such a process, you may invest in mutual fund shares (professionally managed stock funds).

The same principle applies to real estate. If you have a talent for picking out a good piece of property and fixing it up, you will probably handle your own transactions. Others will choose to invest in real estate through a limited partnership, in which perhaps 10 to 20 limited partners put up the funds and a general partner (professional real estate manager) manages the property.

Whichever route you go, there is an irreducible amount of time that you must spend in evaluating results. Even if you invest in a mutual fund or real estate limited partnership, you must still monitor the performance of those who are handling your funds.

Table 11.2 EVALUATION OF INVESTMENTS

	Savings account	Growth stock	Rental house
Safety of principal	+	0	0
High return potential	−	+	0
Inflation hedge	−	−	+
Current income	+	−	+
Liquidity	+	+	−
Tax advantages	0	0	+
Ease of management	+	0	−

In Table 11.2, we see a comparative evaluation of three different types of investments based on many of the factors we have just discussed. You should learn to trace potential investments through a similar analysis (either formally or informally). A plus means above average, a zero means average, and a minus means below average. You may also wish to do the exercise in Box 11.1 as it applies to you or your family (perhaps you will wish to do this after you complete the chapter).

RISK AND RETURN

We stated earlier that risk and return tend to go together. If you want exceptionally high returns, often you have to take greater than normal risks.

Risks may take many different forms. The most common risk you face as an investor is simply the potential loss in market value due to changing economic conditions. This is called **market risk.** Even if you invest in a seemingly safe common stock, such as IBM or General Motors, you may still suffer a loss in value of 20 to 30 percent in a declining stock market. The same can also apply to bond prices when interest rates go up. As you will see later, some investments are more subject to market risks than others.

There is also a **business risk** associated with most investments. This is the risk that the firm will not do well because of adverse business conditions (though it has nothing directly to do with the stock or bond market). It is the risk to airlines that fuel prices will go up, the risk to retailers that new products will replace their wares, and so on. If you want to avoid business risk, you may invest in U.S. government securities; if you are willing to take high business risk, you can invest in new companies, airline stocks, oil wells, and similar businesses.

Another significant risk is called the **purchasing-power risk.** This is simply the risk of loss of purchasing power due to inflation. If you invest $1000 today and there is a total of 60 percent inflation over the next 10 years (about 5 percent per year), your $1000 will only buy $400 worth of goods when it is

Box 11.1 WHAT SHOULD YOU OR YOUR FAMILY CONSIDER FOR INVESTMENTS?

Directions: Circle the answer that most nearly applies to you. Write that number in the space at right. Then add up the numbers and divide by 9 to get a median score.

AGE—My age is closest to:

(9) 30	(7) 40	(5) 50	(3) 60	(1) 70	_______

INCOME—My present annual income from all sources is nearest to (in thousands):

(2) 10	(4) 20	(5) 30	(6) 40	(8) 50	_______

ANNUAL EXPENSES—In relation to income, my annual expenses approximate:

(1) 100%	(3) 90%	(5) 80%	(7) 70%	(9) 50%	_______

NUMBER OF DEPENDENTS—I presently have these dependents:

(0) 0	(8) 1	(6) 2–3	(4) 4–5	(1) 6 or more	_______

ESTIMATED VALUE OF ASSETS—My house, insurance, savings, and investments total (in thousands):

(1) 50	(3) 100	(5) 250	(7) 350	(9) 500 or more	_______

LIABILITIES—My bills, mortgages, installment payments, and debts in relation to assets approximate (in thousands):

(9) 30%	(7) 50%	(5) 75%	(3) 90%	(1) 100%	_______

SAVINGS—I have cash on hand in savings or other liquid assets to equal this amount of expenses:

(1) 1 month	(3) 2 months	(5) 3 months	(7) 4 months	(9) 6+ months	_______

LIFE INSURANCE—My life insurance coverage equals (in thousands):

(9) 250	(7) 150	(5) 100	(3) 50	(1) 25 or less	_______

HEALTH INSURANCE—My health insurance coverage includes:

(9) Basic, major medical, catastrophic	(5) Major medical plus basic	(1) Basic	_______

returned to you. Thus, there is clearly a purchasing-power risk in some investments. Those wishing to avoid purchasing-power risks will invest in short-time financial assets (where they are not committed for extended periods of time) or real assets (such as real estate), which go up with inflation. In the economic environment of the middle to late 1980s, the purchasing-power risk has been much less important than in earlier time periods. Investors thus have gained from investing in items that benefit from low to moderate inflation (stocks and bonds) instead of high inflation. Of course, this may once again change.

Many investment advisers show their clients an array of investments that range from the low-risk, low-return category to the upper end of the scale in terms of risk and return. Figure 11.1 illustrates this point. Generally speaking, you must extend yourself further out along the horizontal axis to enjoy the higher returns on the vertical axis. Investors looking for higher returns will go with corporate bonds, stocks and possibly real assets; those seeking safer, lower-

Add up your scores and divide by 9 to get the average. Then consider the investment strategies that follow.

The investment strategy numbers below correlate with the average score you got from the profile analysis. The investment strategy ratings indicate investment categories ranging from (1) ultraconservative to (9) highly speculative. By matching the profile score with the nearest investment strategy numbers, you get some feel for investments that may be appropriate for you. You would probably choose from two or three categories.

1 Insured savings accounts.

2 High-grade government securities.

3 High-quality corporate and municipal bonds, preferred stocks, investment trusts, and annuity income.

4 Lower-rated corporate and municipal bonds, preferred stocks, investment trusts, convertible bonds and preferred stocks, and variable insurance.

5 Higher-rated common stocks and investment trusts, and investment annuities.

6 Lower-rated common stocks and investment trusts.

7 Speculative bonds, stocks, and investment trusts.

8 Gold and silver-related investments, and foreign investment trusts.

9 Rare and exotic investments: stamps, rare coins, art, antiques, gems and jewelry, rare books, autographs, prints, and lithographs.

SOURCE: "Profile Analysis: What Should You Invest in Now?" (pp. 16–17) from *How to Make Money During Inflation/Recession* by the editors of *Consumer Guide* with Peter A. Dickinson. Copyright © 1980 by Publications, Limited. Reprinted by permission of Harper & Row, Publishers, Inc.

return assets will want savings accounts, certificates of deposit, and similar instruments. Of course, during certain short-term phases of the business cycle, relationships may change and the only positive return may be from a savings account or other similar investment. This is considered the exception rather than the norm. Regardless of what you invest in, the timing must still be right. Long-term relationships mean very little if you buy stocks or real estate two weeks before a major downtrend begins.

FIXED-INCOME INVESTMENTS

Now that you have learned the general concepts of investment, you are ready to move into specifics. In the remainder of this chapter, we discuss fixed-income

Figure 11.1 POTENTIAL LEVELS OF RISK AND RETURN ON DIFFERENT INVESTMENTS

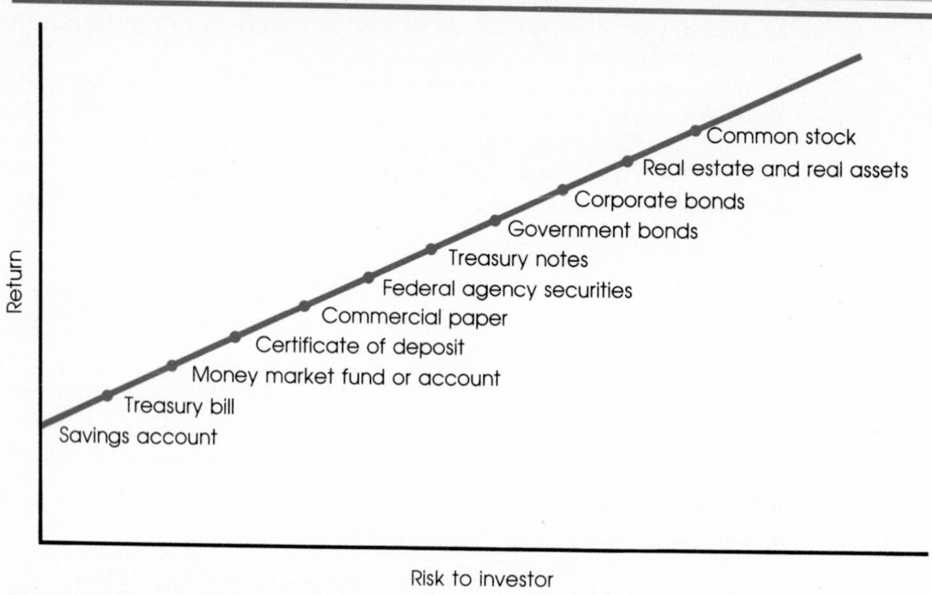

securities: investments that pay interest. Fixed income securities are measured by their **yield,** or the return they provide to investors.

Short-Term Fixed-Income Investments

Short-term fixed-income investments are a convenient place to "park" your funds. There is a virtual supermarket of securities from which to choose. All the investment outlets share the common characteristics of being highly liquid while paying you interest over a relatively short period of time. They also have very limited market risk; that is, they are not likely to experience wide swings in market value over the life of your investment (most do not change at all). In Table 11.3, we show a representative list of short-term investments, the typical maturity of each, the minimum required investment, and the yield on April 14, 1987. We now briefly discuss each type of investment.

Savings Account. A **savings account** is the lowest-yielding investment you will find. Before 1986, the federal government specified the maximum interest rate that could be paid on savings accounts. This is no longer true. Financial institutions still try to keep the rates as low as possible, however, particularly in smaller communities where there is less competition for funds. Before you place your savings anywhere, you should call around for three or four quotes to

Table 11.3 CHARACTERISTICS OF SHORT-TERM FIXED-INCOME INVESTMENTS

Investment	Maturity	Minimum amount	Yield April 14, 1987 (%)
Savings account	open	$ 0–$100	5.50
Certificate of deposit	3 months to 8 years	500	6.80
Money market account	open	1,000	6.48
Money market fund	open	1,000	6.50
Treasury bill	91 days to 1 year	10,000	6.01
Commercial paper	up to 6 months	25,000	6.90

determine what different banks and savings and loans are paying and where the best deal is.

Certificates of Deposit. Certificates of deposit are offered by banks, savings and loans, and other financial institutions. With a **certificate of deposit (CD),** you place your funds on deposit at a specified rate over a given time period. The transaction is evidenced by a certificate. A typical CD might represent a $1000 deposit for one year at 6.80 percent interest (or whatever the going rate of interest is at the time of deposit). An advantage (or disadvantage) is that you typically lock in the interest rate over the term of the CD. If interest rates go down by one percent during the year, you look smart because you have locked in a higher rate. Conversely, if interest rates go up, you will be trapped at a lower rate. If this feature bothers you, you can inquire about variable-rate CDs, which change with market conditions. Also, if you are going to invest a relatively large amount in a CD (perhaps over $10,000), you should look for a financial institution that pays a higher yield for larger deposits.

One clear disadvantage of a CD is that there is a penalty for early withdrawal of funds. Generally, for a CD of one year or less, the penalty is the loss of one month's interest. For a CD of over one year, you normally lose a whole quarter (three months) worth of interest if you take the funds out early. This is a very undesirable feature of CDs and may make them less attractive than other forms of short-term instruments, which we will soon discuss.

A final point is worthy of note. Savings and loans generally pay a slightly higher rate on CDs than commercial banks (perhaps ¼ percent). This difference was at one time actually mandated by law (Regulation Q), but this is no longer the case. Many people will accept a slightly lower yield on bank CDs than on savings and loan CDs because they perceive them to be less risky. This is a debatable point in that CDs in both kinds of institutions are generally insured by federal government agencies for up to $100,000. However, you should normally make sure your bank has Federal Deposit Insurance Corporation (FDIC) coverage or your savings and loan has Federal Savings and Loan Insurance Corporation (FSLIC) coverage. A few state-chartered institutions may not.

Money Market Account. If you find the early-withdrawal penalty associated with the certificate of deposit to be undesirable, you may want to open a **money market account.** Money market accounts came into existence in the early 1980s. A money market account generally pays a higher yield than a savings account and only a slightly lower yield than a certificate of deposit (perhaps 0.25 to 0.35 percent less). The advantage of a money market account is that you may put in funds and withdraw them as you wish without an early-withdrawal penalty. Actually, money market accounts generally allow you to write three checks or make three withdrawals a month without penalty.[2] This certainly gives you more flexibility than you get with a CD. Money market accounts, however, normally have a slightly higher minimum-deposit requirement than a CD ($1000 versus $500).

A special form of money market account, generally called a **money market checking account,** allows extensive check-writing privileges (typically 25 per month) and thus lets you combine your savings and check-writing functions. A money market checking account generally pays a 1 to 1.2 percent lower yield than the money market savings account. Keep in mind, however, that you are receiving extensive free check-writing privileges.

You should keep one other point in mind. With the total deregulation of savings programs at financial institutions, which began in 1986, more and more new attractively wrapped packages are likely to come on the market. Some carry higher interest rates, others carry special privileges, and a few even offer color TV sets for larger, long-term deposits. The financial institutions are literally challenging you to pick up the phone and find the best deal. Do not assume that everyone has the same product.

Money Market Fund. A **money market fund** is a special type of mutual fund in which investors pool relatively small amounts of funds to create large pools of money for investment in high-yielding securities. Money market funds became particularly popular in the late 1970s, when small investors were receiving 5 to 5½ percent on their savings accounts and large investors were receiving 18 percent on $100,000 CDs and other large investments. Creators of money market funds put together the savings of thousands of small investors to allow them to participate in high-yielding investments. Now that interest rates have come down substantially, the advantages of money market funds are not so apparent. A typical money market fund requires a minimum balance of $1000. You are generally allowed to write checks against your fund; but some funds require that the checks be for at least $250 or $500.

[2] Some funds require a minimum amount for each transaction, such as $250 or $500.

The yield on money market funds tends to be very close to the yield on money market accounts at any point in time—for example, see the quotes given in Table 11.3. Financial institutions often advertise that funds in money market *accounts* are federally insured and therefore safer. Practically speaking, investments in money market funds are also extremely safe. The money market fund pools the cash investments of small investors and places them in short-term U.S. government securities, larger bank CDs, and other similar high-quality instruments. Nevertheless, money market funds are not directly backed by federal insurance. A partial listing of money market mutual funds is shown in Figure 11.2 (because the date of the figure is different from the date of Table 11.3, the yields are different). Note that in the last column of Figure 11.2, an annual expense per $100 of funds is shown. This is the cost of managing the funds and is subtracted out before showing return from income dividends in column three. Funds are able to pay the expenses and still remain competitive with money market accounts. There is no sales commission in buying a money market fund.

There are also money market funds that specialize in nontaxable investments. Their yield is generally 2 to 3 percent lower than a normal taxable money market fund, but for high-income taxpayers, the differential may be justified. For a listing of all money market mutual funds (all mutual funds, for that matter), see the annual September *Forbes* issue on mutual funds. The mailing addresses of these funds are also included in the issue.

Treasury Bill. A **Treasury bill** (T-bill) represents a short-term obligation of the U.S. government. T-bills are issued by the U.S. Treasury, generally for 91 days, 182 days, or one year. They are sold in minimum units of $10,000 and are popular among some investors because of their low risk and very active resale (secondary) market. If you buy a 91-day Treasury bill and decide to sell it two days later, you will find a very liquid, active market in which to conduct the transaction.

Treasury bills can be bought on original distribution from a Federal Reserve bank at no commission. It is much more likely, however, that if you or members of your family were to buy a Treasury bill, you would purchase a previously issued T-bill from a bank or brokerage house and pay a $35 commission.

Treasury bills are different from many securities in that they trade on a discount basis rather than paying direct interest. This means that the return you receive is based on the difference between the price you pay and the face value of the instrument. A $10,000 one-year Treasury bill quoted at 8 percent sells for $9200, so you receive $800 in increased value over the life of the instrument. Although $800 represents 8 percent of the face value of the $10,000 Treasury bill, the effective yield is slightly higher: Because you are investing only $9200 to receive a return of $800, the effective yield is 8.70 percent.

$$\frac{\text{Gain in value}}{\text{Purchase price}} = \frac{\$800}{\$9200} = 8.70\% \text{ effective yield}$$

Suppose you buy a 182-day T-bill. To simplify, let's say the time period is six months. If the quoted rate is 8 percent, the discount is $400 and the price of the Treasury bill is $9600. These calculations follow (on page 373).

Figure 11.2 EXAMPLES OF MONEY MARKET FUNDS

Portfolio average maturity (days)	Fund/distributor	Date started	Investment results Latest 12 months total return	return from income dividends	Total assets 6/30/85 (millions)	% change '85 vs '84	Minimum initial investment	Annual expenses per $100
	FORBES government money fund companies			8.6%				
	FORBES tax-free money fund composite			5.3%				
	FORBES general money fund composite			8.9%				
General money market funds								
44	Delaware Cash Reserve/Delaware	6/78	—	9.2%	$1,424	−1%	$ 1,000	$0.81
1	Dreyfus Dollar International Fund/Dreyfus	8/83	—	9.4	578	−59	50,000	0.78‡
60	Dreyfus Liquid Assets/Dreyfus	1/74	—	9.3	8,297	6	2,500	0.69
63	Dreyfus MM Instruments Money Market/Dreyfus	4/75	—	9.3	766	−8	50,000	0.63
30	Eaton Vance Cash Mgmt Fund/Eaton Vance	1/75	—	8.9	193	1	1,000	0.71
47	EGT Money Market Trust/Eppler Guerin	4/81	—	8.6	77	0	1,000	1.20
54	Equitable MM Account-General Purpose/Bullock	10/80	—	9.0	238	−7	1,000	0.95‡
49	Fahnestock Daily Income Fund/Reich & Tang	6/81	—	8.9	145	21	1,000	0.86‡
49	FBL Money Market Fund/PFS Management	3/81	—	8.3	28	−14	500	1.34‡
45	Fidelity Cash Reserves/Fidelity	5/79	—	9.0	4,031	−1	1,000	0.86
40	Fidelity Daily Income Trust/Fidelity	5/74	—	9.0	2,499	−7	10,000	0.62
30	Fidelity MM Trust-Domestic/Fidelity	5/79	—	9.2	2,023	51	100,000	0.42
20	Financial Daily Income Shares/Financial Prog	3/76	—	9.1	220	−11	1,000	0.59
34	First American Money Fund/Dougherty	4/82	—	9.0	62	13	1,000	0.52‡
20	First Investors Cash Mgmt Fund/First Investors	10/78	—	8.8	359	0	1,000	0.93‡
36	First Trust MM Fund-General Purpose/First Trust	1/83	—	8.9	26	−8	none†	0.96‡
6	Flex-fund-MM Fund/Flex	3/85	—	—*	118	—	2,500	NA‡
17	Founders Money Market Fund/Founders	7/81	—	8.6	24	−61	1,000	0.90
28	Franklin Money Fund/Franklin	1/76	—	8.8	1,001	8	500	0.93
84	General MM Fund/Dreyfus	2/82	—	9.1	430	102	2,500	1.08‡
20	GIT Cash Trust-Regular MM/GIT	12/82	—	8.4	5	−7	1,000	1.26‡
39	Gradison Cash Reserves Trust/Gradison	5/76	—	8.9	445	7	1,000	0.77‡
27	Guardian Cash Management Trust/Guardian	9/82	—	8.8	20	74	1,000	0.50
41	John Hancock Cash Management Trust/Hancock	10/79	—	8.8	384	0	1,000	1.00
27	Home Life Money Mgmt Fund/Home Life	5/82	—	7.6	7	−5	1,000	0.75
22	Wayne Hummer Money Fund Trust/Hummer	4/82	—	8.6	69	20	1,000	1.00
60	Hutton AMA Cash Fund/Hutton	3/82	—	9.4	1,882	110	10,000	0.61‡
45	Hutton Investment-Short Term Invest/Hutton	1/82	—	9.0	107	−16	500	1.91‡
44	IDS Cash Management Fund/IDS	10/75	—	9.1	897	−4	2,000	0.67‡
42	IDS Strategy Fund-Money Market/IDS	5/84	—	7.5	10	547	2,000	1.32‡
34	Investment Portfolio-MM/Kemper	2/84	—	NA	11	24	250	NA‡
41	ED Jones Daily Passport Cash Trust/Jones & Co	5/80	—	8.8	611	18	1,000	1.03
37	Kemper Money Market Fund/Kemper	11/74	—	9.4	4,768	17	1,000	0.52
31	Keystone Liquid Trust/Keystone	7/75	—	8.6	216	−31	1,000	1.00‡
35	Kidder Peabody Premium Account/Kidder	5/82	—	9.1	418	66	25,000	0.63

Funds are added to this guide when they exceed $5 million in net assets and deleted when they drop below $2 million. *Fund not in operation for full period. †Most funds are no load. Some funds are offered as part of an integrated financial service account which has a minimum initial investment. ‡Fund has 12b-1 plan pending or in force *(see story, p. 82).* NA: Not available.

SOURCE: Reprinted by permission of *Forbes* magazine, September 16, 1985, p. 148. © Forbes Inc., 1985.

$$\begin{aligned}\text{Discount on Treasury bill} &= \text{quoted rate} \times \$10{,}000 \times \text{fraction of a year} \\ &= 8\% \times \$10{,}000 \times \tfrac{1}{2} = \$400\end{aligned} \tag{11.1}$$

$$\begin{aligned}\text{Price of Treasury bill} &= \text{face value} - \text{discount} \\ &= \$10{,}000 - \$400 = \$9600\end{aligned} \tag{11.2}$$

The effective yield on this Treasury bill can be computed using equation 11.3;

$$\begin{aligned}\text{Effective yield} &= \frac{\text{gain in value}}{\text{purchase price}} \times \frac{\text{1 year}}{\text{remaining life of T-bill}} \\ &= \frac{\$400}{\$9600} \times \frac{\text{1 year}}{\tfrac{1}{2}\text{ year}} \\ &= 4.17\% \times 2 = 8.34\%\end{aligned} \tag{11.3}$$

In working with Treasury bills, you can always use the quoted rate to help you determine the effective yield.

Commercial Paper. **Commercial paper** represents short-term notes issued to the public by corporations. Only the larger, more prestigious corporations participate in the market. Examples of issuers include Ford Motor Credit Corporation and General Electric Credit Corporation. Commercial paper normally has a maturity up to six months and trades at a minimum value of $25,000. Generally, it is purchased through a special broker or dealer for these instruments, and it typically pays a slightly higher yield than other short-term instruments. You probably will not consider purchasing commercial paper until you have been out of school for many years, but it is a popular investment outlet for some money market funds. Thus, if you are considering investing in a money market fund and you see that it has 10 to 15 percent of its assets in commercial paper (as well as government securities and bank CDs), this will have some meaning to you.

Intermediate-Term Fixed-Income Securities

Intermediate-term fixed-income securities generally have a maturity of one to ten years. They bridge the gap between the short-term investments we have just discussed and long-term, more permanent investments.

Federally Sponsored Agency Securities. Federally sponsored agency securities are issued by agencies of the government rather than directly by the U.S. Treasury. Examples of issuing agencies include the Federal Home Loan Bank, the Federal National Mortgage Association (FNMA), and the Federal Farm Credit Bureau. Though lacking the direct backing of the Treasury, they are guaranteed by the issuing agency and provide all the safety that one would normally need. No federal agency has defaulted on a security to date. These securities, which can be purchased through a securities broker, generally have maturities of one to ten years (or longer) and pay a slightly higher yield than direct issues from the U.S. Treasury. Federal agency issues generally trade in $5000 units.

Pass-Throughs. A special form of federally sponsored agency issues are the Government National Mortgage Association (GNMA) pass-through certificates, sometimes referred to as *Ginny Maes.* The Government National Mortgage Association buys a pool of mortgages from lenders (such as savings and loans) and then issues securities to the public based on these mortgages. As homeowners pay off the interest and principal on their loans, the funds pass through from GNMA to the investors. Each month, holders of GNMA pass-through certificates receive not only the interest on their investment, but also part of the principal they initially invested. The advantage is a large, steady monthly cash flow to investors, but the disadvantage is there is no longer an investment at the end of the life of the security (it has all been paid back). A direct purchase of GNMAs is only for wealthy investors as the minimum unit is $25,000. Nevertheless, you may purchase them indirectly through mutual funds with a small investment.

Long-Term Fixed-Income Securities

Long-term fixed-income securities are referred to as bonds and may be issued by the federal government, by state or local governments (municipal bonds), or by corporations. Because bonds normally pay stipulated interest rates, some investors think of them as representing a conservative investment. This is not necessarily the case. For example, in 1985, U.S. government bonds provided an average total return to investors of 31.75 percent, corporate bonds provided a return of 29.10 percent, and municipal bonds 20.02 percent. In some years (particularly in the 1970s), bonds actually showed a negative total return for investors.

How can this be? How can a bond that pays 10 percent annual interest provide such phenomenally high returns during certain time periods and negative returns during other time periods? The answer lies in the **market risk** associated with changing interest rates. Some investors also call this the interest rate risk. Just as common stock goes up and down in value due to changing economic conditions, so do bonds.

Let's use a numerical example to illustrate this point. Suppose you buy a 25-year government bond that pays 10 percent annual interest on $1000. This represents $100 per year in interest. Clearly, there is no business or credit risk in this case. The government is going to make the payments no matter what. But what happens if interest rates in the market go up to 12 percent shortly after you purchase the bond? Keep in mind that your bond has a fixed, contractual rate of 10 percent. Will your bond still retain its $1000 value after interest rates go up? If you wish to sell the bond, will another investor pay you your original purchase price of $1000?

The answer is no. Your bond only pays 10 percent, or $100 a year, in interest, while the going market rate is 12 percent, or $120 a year. In order to sell your bond, it is going to have to provide as good a yield as the current market rate of 12 percent. How can this be accomplished? What must change is the price of your bond. It must go low enough to give the investor a 12 percent return. As a first approximation,[3] you could say the new price of the bond must be:

$$\text{New bond price} = \frac{\text{annual dollar interest on the old bond}}{\text{current yield in the market}} \qquad (11.4)$$

Plugging \$100 into the numerator and 12 percent into the denominator, we arrive at a value of \$833.33.

$$\text{New bond price} = \frac{\$100}{0.12} = \$833.33$$

The value of your bond should fall to approximately \$833.33. At that price it will be fully competitive with new bonds that pay 12 percent interest.

	Your Old Bond	New Bond
$\frac{\text{Annual interest}}{\text{Price}}$	$\frac{\$100}{\$833.33} = 12\%$ yield	$\frac{\$120}{\$1000} = 12\%$ yield

Investors would be indifferent between buying your old bond from you at \$833.33 (which pays only \$100 a year in interest) or buying a new bond for \$1000 (which pays \$120 a year). In either event, the investor would get the desired 12 percent return.

Note the consequences of this price change on your total return from the bond. You received \$100 in annual interest, but your bond value declined by \$166.67 (\$1000 − \$833.33). This gives you a negative total return of \$66.67.

Interest payment	\$100.00
Loss in value	− 166.67
Negative total return	\$ 66.67

On a \$1000 investment, you lose 6.67 percent (\$66.67/\$1000). You started out in a supposedly conservative bond investment to make 10 percent and you've ended up with less than your beginning investment. Of course, if you hold on to the bond for the full 25 years, you will get your original \$1000 face value back, but this is a very small consolation to the investor who sees a dramatic change in market value over a short time period. It is difficult to console yourself with what might be true in 25 years.

We've only been talking about the bad news, that is, interest rates going up after you bought your bond. Now it's time for some good news. What happens if interest rates go down after your bond purchase? Let's once again use equation 11.4, but assume the current rate (yield) in the market goes down to 8 percent after you've bought your 10 percent bond.

[3] We will also look at a more exacting approach in this section.

$$\text{New bond price} = \frac{\text{annual dollar interest on the old bond}}{\text{current yield in the market}}$$

$$\text{New bond price} = \frac{\$100}{0.08} = \$1250$$

Your 10 percent bond now pays a rate far superior to the current yield in the market of 8 percent and will sell for about \$1250. At this price, your bond matches the new required yield on the market of 8 percent.

	Your Old Bond	New Bond
$\frac{\text{Annual interest}}{\text{Price}}$	$\frac{\$100}{\$1250} = 8\%$	$\frac{\$80}{\$1000} = 8\%$

At a price of \$1250, you not only have \$100 in annual interest but a gain in value of \$250, for a total return of \$350. On a \$1000 investment, this represents 35 percent. Clearly, you should buy long-term bonds in anticipation of interest rate declines and not when interest rates are going up. In Table 11.4, you see the annual gain or loss on long-term government bonds from 1965 through 1986. In 14 of the years investors made money, and in 8 of the years they lost money. The average gain in the 14 up years was 13.26 percent, and the average loss in the down years was 2.83 percent.

A More Exacting Calculation

In determining the new price of a bond as a result of changes in interest rates, we used equation 11.4. This was only an approximation that is correct for a bond that has a perpetual life. Nevertheless, equation 11.4 was very helpful in introducing the concept of bond valuation. For a more exacting approach, we

Table 11.4 TOTAL ANNUAL RETURNS ON LONG-TERM GOVERNMENT BONDS, 1965–1986 (INTEREST INCOME COMBINED WITH GAIN OR LOSS IN MARKET VALUE)

1965	+ 7.10%	1976	+16.75%
1966	+ 3.65	1977	− 0.67
1967	− 9.19	1978	− 1.16
1968	− 0.26	1979	− 1.22
1969	− 5.08	1980	− 3.95
1970	+12.10	1981	+ 1.85
1971	+13.23	1982	+40.35
1972	+ 5.68	1983	+ 0.68
1973	− 1.11	1984	+14.79
1974	+ 4.35	1985	+31.75
1975	+ 9.19	1986	+24.20

Table 11.5 PRESENT VALUE OF $1 IN THE FUTURE

Number of periods	INTEREST RATE 6%	8%	10%	12%	14%
1	.943	.926	.909	.893	.877
2	.890	.857	.826	.797	.769
3	.840	.794	.751	.712	.675
4	.792	.735	.683	.636	.592
5	.747	.681	.621	.567	.519
10	.558	.463	.386	.322	.270
20	.312	.215	.149	.104	.073
25	.233	.146	.092	.059	.038
30	.174	.099	.057	.033	.020
40	.097	.046	.022	.011	.005
50	.054	.021	.009	.003	.001

can use present-value tables. We are going to illustrate that these tables are extremely easy to use, and will dispense with algebraic statements and proofs and simply demonstrate how they work.

In Table 11.5 you see a numerical exhibit that shows the present value of a dollar to be received in the future. Along the side of the table, you see the number of periods in the future when the dollar might be received (running from 1 through 50). Along the top of the table, you see the interest or discount rate (ranging from 6 to 14 percent). The table merely tells you what a dollar in the future is worth today at a given interest rate. Let's look at the 12 percent column for three years. The value in the table is .712. This means that a dollar after three years is equivalent to only $.712 (71.2¢) today. You would be indifferent between someone offering you a dollar three years from now or $.712 today if you could earn 12 percent on your investment over that time period.

Table 11.6 is another present-value table, but it applies to the present value of a dollar received for a series of consecutive periods (sometimes referred to as an annuity). For example, the present value of a dollar received at the end of each period for three periods at a 12 percent interest rate is $2.402 as indicated in the table. You would be indifferent between receiving a dollar a year for three years or $2.402 today if you could earn 12 percent on your investment over that time period.

Let's apply these present-value tables to the bond investments we examined earlier. You will recall that your 25-year government bond pays $100 per year in interest. Since it has a face value of $1000, you can expect to receive $1000 back after 25 years in addition to the annual interest. If the yield in the market goes up to 12 percent, the value of your bond is going to go down. Earlier, we used an approximation approach to show that it would fall to $833.33. Using a more

Table 11.6 PRESENT VALUE OF $1 PER PERIOD IN THE FUTURE (ANNUITY)

Number of periods	INTEREST RATE 6%	8%	10%	12%	14%
1	0.943	0.926	0.909	0.893	0.877
2	1.833	1.783	1.736	1.690	1.647
3	2.673	2.577	2.487	2.402	2.322
4	3.465	3.312	3.170	3.037	2.914
5	4.212	3.993	3.791	3.605	3.433
10	7.360	6.710	6.145	5.650	5.216
20	11.470	9.818	7.606	7.469	6.623
25	12.783	10.675	9.077	7.843	6.873
30	13.763	11.258	9.427	8.055	7.003
40	15.046	11.925	9.779	8.244	7.105
50	15.762	12.233	9.915	8.304	7.133

exacting approach based on present-value analysis, we will actually show a decline to $843.30. We follow a three-step procedure, as follows.

Three-Step Procedure to Determining a More Exact Bond Price

Step One—Present Value of Final Payment. Find the present value of the final payment of $1000 at maturity. The final payment represents the face value (also termed par value) of the bond. The appropriate table is Table 11.5.

The face value is $1000.
The amount will come after 25 years.
The yield in the market is 12 percent.

The value in Table 11.5 of .059 represents the present value of $1 for 25 periods at 12 percent. To apply the value to $1000, we multiply $1000 × .059. Thus the present value of the $1000 payment at maturity is $59.

Step Two—Present Value of Annual Payments. Find the present value of the annual payments of $100 in interest. The appropriate source is Table 11.6.

The annual payments are $100 per year.
The payments will take place over 25 years.
The yield in the market is 12 percent.

The value in Table 11.6 of 7.843 represents the present value of $1 per period for 25 periods at 12 percent. To apply the value to $100, we multiply $100 × 7.843 to arrive at $784.30. Thus, $784.30 is the present value of the 25, $100 interest payments.

Step Three—Sum of Payments. Add together the answers to step one and step two to determine the current market value of the bond.

Step one—present value of the payment at maturity	$ 59.00
Step two—present value of the annual interest payments	784.30
Current market value of the bond	$843.30

The more exacting approach, using present-value tables, gives us an answer of $843.30.[4] Earlier, when we used an approximation (equation 11.4), we arrived at an answer of $833.33. If you understand the more exacting approach based on present-value analysis, your knowledge of bond pricing has taken a step forward. If you do not, there is no reason to be discouraged. You can continue to read the rest of the chapter without difficulty. Just remember that increasing interest rates decrease current bond prices and decreasing interest rates increase current bond prices. Furthermore, the longer the life of the bond, the greater the impact of interest rate changes.

Our discussion up to now has dealt with *general* principles of bond valuation. We now take a more specific look at special characteristics of three major types of long-term bonds; U.S. government bonds, state and local bonds (municipal bonds), and corporate bonds.

U.S. GOVERNMENT BONDS

Because there is no business (credit) risk associated with U.S. government bonds, the only factor that influences the price is the level of interest rates. To better understand the nature and pricing of U.S. government bonds, look at Figure 11.3. This is an excerpt from a published table in the *Wall Street Journal.* There are actually U.S. government bonds outstanding that mature anywhere from 1 year to 30 years in the future (so we are only looking at part of the issues).

The far left-hand column (1) in Figure 11.3 shows the actual interest rate the bonds are paying. For example, the first bond listed is providing an interest payment (coupon rate) of 10⅜ percent. We see in the next two columns (2) that it is due in May 1995. Its current price is next shown (3). The bid price is the price at which you can sell the bonds and the asked price is the price at which you can buy the bonds. The difference between the two quotes represents the

[4] We could get an even more exacting answer using semiannual analysis. We wish only to highlight the basic points, however, without adding complications.

Figure 11.3 QUOTES ON U.S. GOVERNMENT BONDS

Rate	Mat. Date	Bid	Asked	Bid Chg.	Yld.
10⅜s,	1995 May	114.24	115	+ .9	8.03
11¼s,	1995 May p	120.6	120.14	+ .11	8.06
12⅝s,	1995 May	128.20	128.28	+ .6	8.11
10½s,	1995 Aug p	115.23	115.31	+ .11	8.05
9½s,	1995 Nov p	109.19	109.27	+ .11	8.02
11½s,	1995 Nov	122.16	122.24	+ .14	8.07
8⅞s,	1996 Feb p	106.8	106.12	+ .19	7.94
7s,	1993-98 May	91.31	92.15	+ 1.1	7.98
3½s,	1998 Nov	89	90	+ .4	4.55
8½s,	1994-99 May	102.16	103	+ .2	7.99
7⅞s,	1995-00 Feb	97.15	97.31	+ .6	8.12
8⅜s,	1995-00 Aug	101.12	101.20	+ .3	8.13
11¾s,	2001 Feb	127.26	128.2	+ .4	8.41
13⅛s,	2001 May	139.9	139.17	+ .5	8.45
8s,	1996-01 Aug	98.11	98.27	....	8.13
13⅜s,	2001 Aug	141.17	141.25	+ .7	8.47
15¾s,	2001 Nov	161.1	161.9	+ .2	8.57
14¼s,	2002 Feb	149.8	149.16	+ .9	8.52
11⅝s,	2002 Nov	126.30	127.6	+ .6	8.54
10¾s,	2003 Feb	119.21	119.29	− .4	8,51
10¾s,	2003 May	119.26	120.2	+ .2	8.51
11⅛s,	2003 Aug	123	123.8	+ .8	8.54
11⅞s,	2003 Nov	129.24	130	+ .7	8.55
12⅜s,	2004 May	134.21	134.29	− .4	8.56
13¾s,	2004 Aug	147.8	147.16	+ .6	8.58
11⅝s,	2004 Nov k	128.24	129	+ .3	8.50
8¼s,	2000-05 May	99.13	99.29	− .5	8.26
12s,	2005 May k	132.16	132.24	− .1	8.51
10¾s,	2005 Aug k	120.31	121.7	− .3	8.50
9⅜s,	2006 Feb k	110.3	110.7	+ .23	8.32
7⅝s,	2002-07 Feb	93.19	94.3	− .3	8.22
7⅞s,	2002-07 Nov	96.17	97.1	+ .6	8.17
8⅜s,	2003-08 Aug	101.4	101.12	+ .1	8.23
8¾s,	2003-08 Nov	103.24	104	− .9	8.31
9⅛s,	2004-09 May	106.26	107.2	− .5	8.36
10⅜s,	2004-09 Nov	117.25	118.1	− .8	8.44
11¾s,	2005-10 Feb	129.30	130.6	+ .2	8.51
10s,	2005-10 May	114.10	114.18	− .8	8.45
12¾s,	2005-10 Nov	138.24	139	− .13	8.60
13⅞s,	2006-11 May	149.20	149.28	− .18	8.62
14s,	2006-11 Nov	151.14	151.23	− .17	8.60
10⅜s,	2007-12 Nov	118.2	118.10	− .4	8.51
12s,	2008-13 Aug	133.30	134.6	− .14	8.55
13¼s,	2009-14 May	146.24	147	− .4	8.56
12½s,	2009-14 Aug k	139.20	139.28	− .11	8.54
11¾s,	2009-14 Nov k	132.19	132.27	− .5	8.51
11¼s,	2015 Feb k	129.22	129.26	− .4	8.47
10⅝s,	2015 Aug k	122.29	123.1	− .12	8.49
9⅞s,	2015 Nov	115.31	116.3	− .3	8.40
9¼s,	2016 Feb k	112.10	112.14	+ .19	8.14

SOURCE: Reprinted by permission of the *Wall Street Journal*,

profit that a dealer in the bonds hopes to make. Each bond represents $1000 and the quotes are based on 100 percent of value. Thus, the asked price on the first bond of 115 represents $1000 × 115 percent, or $1150. The bid price of 114.24 is stated in terms of thirty-seconds to the right of the decimal point, so 114.24 represents $114\frac{24}{32}$. The actual bid price is $1000 × 114.75 percent, or $1147.50.

The next column (Bid Chg.) shows the change in the bid from the previous day. The last column (Yld.) lists the current yield on government bonds of a given maturity date (in this case May 1995). Note that the bonds are paying 10⅜ percent interest (the first column), but the going market rate (the yield in the last column) is only 8.03 percent. Therefore the bonds are trading well above their initial issue price of $1000 at approximately $1150. The highest-priced bonds in the table are the 15¾ percent interest rate bonds that mature in November 2001. They are trading at over $1600.

Zero-Coupon Government Bonds

Some brokerage houses have repackaged government bonds so that one part of the package contains only interest payments and the other part contains only the payment of $1000 at maturity. It is the second part of the package that is the subject of our discussion. Because these bonds contain no interest payments but only pay $1000 at maturity, they are called **zero-coupon bonds.** If you invest in these bonds and receive no interest, how do you generate a return on your investment? The answer is simple. You pay much less than $1000 to start with, and all your return comes from increase in value. For example, a 10-year zero-coupon bond priced to allow the investor a 9 percent annual yield will sell for $422. Sometimes zero-coupon bonds have very long lives. A 30-year $1000 zero-coupon bond, allowing a 9 percent yield, would be priced at $75 (7½¢ on the dollar). If you are ever interested in purchasing zero-coupon bonds, call a broker and ask for a quote. The broker will know exactly what you are talking about, because zero-coupon bonds are very popular. They all have funny names, like Merrill Lynch's TGRs, E. F. Hutton's TBRs, and Salomon Brothers' CATS. If you decide to buy zero-coupon bonds, you should consider their tax implications before you make your purchase.[5]

MUNICIPAL BONDS

Bonds that are issued by state and local governments are referred to as **municipal bonds.** Their most important feature is that the interest income is normally nontaxable for federal income tax purposes. Also, income from municipal bonds is exempt from state and local taxes if you buy them from the locality in which you reside.

Let's concentrate briefly on the exemption from federal income taxes. Suppose that you were to buy a long-term municipal bond paying 7 percent annual interest and that you were in a 28 percent tax bracket. How much would you have to receive on a taxable investment to get the equivalent after-tax return on the municipal bond? The procedure, as demonstrated in equation 11.5, is to take the annual interest rate on the municipal bond and divide by one minus the tax bracket of the investor.

[5] Generally, the annual increase in value is taxable as ordinary income. To avoid this problem, zero coupons should be purchased through nontaxable vehicles, such as an IRA, or by low-tax-bracket investors.

$$\text{Equivalent taxable yield} = \frac{\text{annual interest rate on the municipal bond}}{(1 - \text{the investor's tax bracket})}$$

$$= \frac{7\%}{(1 - 0.28)} = \frac{7\%}{(0.72)} = 9.72\% \tag{11.5}$$

In this case, we would say you must receive an **equivalent taxable yield** of 9.72 percent on a taxable investment to be as well off as you would be with a municipal bond. Municipal bonds usually pay a lower stated interest than taxable obligations, so this type of comparison is important.

Municipal bonds may be either general obligation bonds or revenue bonds. A general obligation (GO) bond is backed by the full faith, credit, and *taxing power* of the issuing unit (such as the state of New York or the city of Denver). A revenue bond is not backed by taxing power, but by the specific revenue-generating capacity from a given project, such as a toll road bridge or public housing project. Because of the taxing power behind general obligation issues, they tend to be of high quality. Revenue bonds are more uneven in quality, and each project must be carefully evaluated.

As will be pointed out in Chapter 13, the average investor is probably better off buying municipal bonds through a mutual fund than trying to go it alone. Individual purchases of municipal bonds usually require $5,000 to $10,000 or more, whereas one can get into a mutual fund for as little as $1000.

CORPORATE BONDS

The term *corporate bonds* generally covers all bonds that are issued in the private (nongovernmental) sector of the economy by individual firms, banks, or public utilities. They are issued in units of $1000. An excerpt from *Standard & Poor's Bond Guide* in Figure 11.4 illustrates key features associated with a number of corporate bonds.

Though it is beyond our scope and intent in this chapter to go through the details of this rather complicated table, one item is of particular interest and that is the Standard & Poor's (S&P) Quality Rating. If you read under that column, you will see that General Electric has an AAA rating and General Felt Indus. has a B− rating. These **bond ratings** imply that General Electric is of the highest quality and General Felt is definitely more speculative. Table 11.7 provides a clearer meaning of what letter evaluations by the two major bond-rating houses mean. Pluses and minuses (or other modifiers) may also be added to the various letters.

If you buy a bond of exceptionally high quality, you will not have to worry about receiving your interest payments at maturity, but you will have to accept a lower return. The lower return is because investors like to be compensated for risk and there is not much credit risk with highly rated bonds. If you buy a B- to C-rated bond, you will have a much higher promised return, but you may have a little difficulty sleeping at night. These are referred to as **junk bonds.** A D-rated bond would mean no sleep at all.

Figure 11.4 BOND GUIDE INFORMATION

64 Gel-Gen

STANDARD & POOR'S CORPORATION

Title-Industry Code & Co. Finances (In Italics)	Ind	Chgs. 1982	Times Earn. 1983	1984 Yr. End	Cash &Eqv (Million $)	Current Assets	Liabs Date	L. Term Debt (Mil $)	Debt % Prop		Interim Times Earn. Period		1983	1984					
Individual Issue Statistics Exchange	**Interest Dates**	**S&P Quality rating**	**Eligible**	**Bond Form**	**Legality M N N / a H Y**	**Redemption Provisions: Refund Earliest/ Other**	**Call Price: For S.F.**	**Call Price: Regular**	**Out-st'd'g (Mil $)**	**Underwriter Firm**	**Year**	**Price Range 1972-83 High**	**1972-83 Low**	**1984 High**	**1984 Low**	**1985 High**	**1985 Low**	**Mo. End Price Sale(s) or Bid**	**Curr Yield**	**Yield to Mat.**
Gelco Corp	26d	1.11	0.89		1.05 Jl	50.9		1-85	2127			6 Mo Jan'85		1.05	1.09					
• V/R[1]Nts 11.18s '90	[2]QFb15	BB-	Y	R	- - -	....	....	[3]103	100	D7	'83	101	98	No Sale		No Sale		104¼	10.72	....
• Sub SF Deb 14⅝s '99	jD	BB-	Y	R	- - -	....	[4]100	±106[15/16]	85.0	D7	'79	108¼	70	105	87	105½	97⅛	s104¼	13.96	13.85
• Sub Nts[5] 14¼s '87	jD15	BB-	Y	R	- - -	[6]	....	[7]±105	25.0	D7	'82	105¼	98¼	104	97½	104½	101½	s102½	13.90	13.05
GenCorp Inc[3]	60a	2.04	3.70		1.41 Nv	109	894	524 2-85	279	40.5		3 Mo Feb'85		1.31	1.92					
• Sub Deb 12⅝s 2003	Mn	BB-	Y	R	- - -	[9]105[15/16]	[10]100	±109½	75.0	K1	'83	99½	93	No Sale		92½	91½	91½	13.52	13.65
• Sub Nts 11⅞s '93	mS15	BB-	Y	R	- - -	[11]100	....	105	[12]60.0	K1	'83	95	92	93½	93⅛	93½	92	95	12.50	12.87
General Amer. Trans.[13]	55b	1.64	0.73		1.67 Dc	43.2		12-84	654	53.1										
Eq Tr 4.60s '85	mN15	A	X	CR	- √ -	....	100	100	3.98	K2	'65	93½	66½	94¾	89⅞	97¾	94	97¾	4.71	9.83
Eq Tr 5.45s '86	jD	A	X	R	- √ -	....	100	100	5.99	K2	'66	91	67¼	90	84⅞	92¾	89½	92¾	5.88	10.81
Eq Tr 6¼s '87	fA	A	X	R	- √ -	....	100	100.30	4.92	K2	'67	94	67¼	88⅛	81½	91¾	88	91¾	6.81	10.62
Eq Tr 6.95s '89	Jj15	A	X	R	- √ -	....	100	±100.60	12.4	K2	'68	97¼	64⅜	85⅛	78¾	88¼	84	88¼	7.88	10.97
Eq Tr 9s '90	fA15	A	X	R	- √ -	....	100	±101½	15.4	K2	'70	109⅝	70	88⅛	79⅛	93	87⅛	93	9.68	10.79
Eq Tr 8.60s '91	Jd	A	X	R	- √ -	....	100	±101¾	22.8	K2	'70	106⅞	68⅝	84⅛	77¼	87¼	82	87¼	9.86	11.60
Eq Tr 8.10s '92	Ms15	A	X	R	- √ -	....	100	±101½	21.3	K2	'71	104	64½	80½	73½	85¼	78⅛	85¼	9.50	11.26
Eq Tr 9¾s '95	Jd	A	X	R	- √ -	....	100	±104	32.6	K2	'74	108½	67¼	85	73⅛	88½	83	88½	11.02	11.73
Eq Tr 9½s '96	Mn	A	X	R	- √ -	....	100	[14]±103¾	35.7	K2	'75	109⅛	65⅛	82	72⅞	85¾	80¼	85¾	11.08	11.86
Eq Tr 8.15s '97	Jd	A	X	R	- √ -	....	[15]100	[16]103	30.0	K2	'76	100½	57⅛	72⅞	63⅞	76⅝	70	76⅝	10.64	11.84
Eq Tr 9s '98	mN15	A	X	R	- √ -	....	100	[17]103½	45.0	L4	'78	99¾	61½	76⅝	67¼	82½	75⅛	82½	10.91	11.60
Eq Tr 13⅞s 2001	mS15	A	X	R	- √ -	....	[18]100	[19]105.95	75.0	M8	'81	107¾	82¼	105¾	88½	109	102¼	109	12.73	12.56
Eq Tr 15⅞s 2003	Fa	A	X	R	- √ -	....	[20]100	[21]107.06	50.0	M8	'82	116½	100	116½	101¾	117	107¾	115⅝	13.73	13.52
[22]*General Aniline & Film*	17a	1.61	d0.79		5.49 Dc	69.6	255	114 12-84	72.5	45.6		3 Mo Mar'85		3.67	7.67					
SF Deb 5⅞s '91	jD	BB+	Y	R	- - -	....	100	±101.06	4.67	B9	'66	88	42	63⅝	51	69⅛	63	69⅛	8.47	12.99
General Cigar	69b	Now Culbro Corp,see																		
• Cm Inc Sub Deb 5½s '87	Jd	NR	Y	CR	- : -	....	100	100	[23]0.53	Exch	'57	90	61	96⅞	83⅛	97½	95⅝	93¾	5.87	8.98
General Defense[24]	6	18.42	3.40		2.92 Ja	19.3	85.4	52.3 1-85	★183	351										
◆Sr Sub Deb 14½s 2003	Fa	B-	Y	R	- - -	[25]106	[26]100	[27]114	30.0	D7	'83	99⅛	99⅛	No Sale		No Sale		100⅞	14.37	14.36
◆Sr Sub Deb 13s '95	Ao15	B-	Y	R	- - -	....	....	[28]100	[12]500	D7	'85	....	....	....	....	94½	89⅞	93¼	13.94	14.29
General Electric Co.	24a	6.39	6.56		7.88 Dc	1702	10983	8517 3-85	770	10.0		3 Mo Mar'85		6.51	7.81					
• SF Deb 5.30s '92	Mn	AAA	X	R	√ √ √	....	100	±100.48	34.0	M8	'67	89¼	51	71⅞	63¼	76⅞	70½	78¼	6.77	9.69
• SF Deb 7½s '96	Ms15	AAA	X	R	√ √ -	....	100	±102¼	95.0	M8	'71	106	55½	75½	64⅛	81¾	72⅝	82⅛	9.13	10.28
• SF Deb 8½s 2004	Mn	AAA	X	R	√ √ -	....	100	±104.76	217	M8	'74	111	56½	77⅝	64½	84	73½	s84	10.12	10.45
General Electric Credit	26	1.20	1.32		.... Dc	1898		9-84	★4270			9 Mo Sep		1.34	1.32					
• Nts 8¼s '86	Fa15	AAA	X	R	√ √ -	....	....	100	200	M8	'76	106⅛	73	98¼	92	100	98	s100	8.25	8.25
• Nts 9¾s '87	fA	AAA	X	R	√ √ -	....	....	100	200	M8	'79	102¾	75	98⅝	90	101	97	s100½	9.70	9.48
• Nts 7⅝s '88	Fa	AAA	X	R	√ √ -	....	....	100	150	M8	'77	101¼	64	92½	82⅛	95⅞	90¼	s95¾	7.96	9.46
• Nts 11½s '90	Ao15	AAA	X	R	√ √ -	....	....	[29]100	125	M8	'80	106½	78	102¾	90½	104¾	99⅛	s104	11.06	10.43
• Nts 13⅝s '91	mS15	AAA	X	R	√ √ -	....	....	[30]100	150	M8	'81	111¾	87¾	107½	97¾	110¾	104½	s109⅞	12.40	11.38
Deb 5½s 2001	mN	AAA	X	R	- √ -	....	....	100	[12]500	M8	'81	58	37⅞	55	45½	58⅝	52⅞	58⅝	9.38	11.00
• Deb 11¾s 2005	Jd	AAA	X	R	√ √ -	z±102	....	[31]102	200	M8	'80	106	72	99⅞	83⅞	104	93	104	11.30	11.24
• Sub Deb 8¼s '97	fA	AAA	X	R	- √ -	[32]z102½	....	[32]102½	50.0	M8	'77	101½	54	80½	65	83⅞	72	84½	9.76	10.54
• Sub Nts 11¾s '88	Ao15	AAA	X	R	√ √ -	....	....	[33]100	75.0	M8	'80	105⅞	80⅞	102⅝	94⅞	105	100½	103½	11.35	10.31
• Sub Nts 14s '90	Ms15	AAA	X	R	- √ -	....	....	[34]100	100	M8	'81	111⅞	91¼	108¼	100	108½	104¾	107	13.08	12.03
General Felt Indus.	32	1.27	3.43		.... Dc	74.2	201	63.3 12-83	142	183										
[35]VR[36]SrSbDeb 10.489s 2001	QF 15	B-	Y	R	- - -	....	[37]100	100	[12]70.0	D7	'81	76	64½	83	70	83	77	82	12.79	....
General Foods Corp.[38]	27f	3.32	3.19		3.28 Mr	288	2378	1403 3-85	725	41.4										
• SF Deb 8⅞s '90	jJ	AA	X	R	√ √ -	....	100	100.523	17.4	G2	'70	113½	70⅝	98¾	90⅛	100	91	98¼	9.03	9.31
Deb 6s 2001	Jd15	AA	X	R	- √ -	....	....	100	[12]150	G2	'81	99⅝	42¾	58⅞	47⅞	62⅛	56½	62⅛	9.62	11.06
Deb 7s 2011	Jd15	AA	X	R	- √ -	....	....	100	[12]200	G2	'81	67	45	61½	51	65¼	59	65¼	10.73	11.10

Uniform Footnote Explanations—See Page 1. Other: [1]Thru 8-14-85,adj qtrly aft for Treas rate. [2]. [3]Fr 2-15-88. [4]Fr 12-1-89. [5]Int incr fr 14%,6-15-83. [6]Red rest'n(14%)to maturity. [7]Fr 12-15-85. [8]Was Gen'l Tire&Rubber. [9]Red rest'n(12.443%)to 5-1-88. [10]Fr 5-1-93. [11]Red rest'n(13%)to 3-15-88. [12]Incl disc. [13]Subsid of GATX Corp. [14]Fr 11-1-85. [15]Fr 6-1-88. [16]Fr 12-1-86. [17]Fr 5-15-88. [18]Fr 9-15-85. [19]Fr 3-15-91. [20]Fr 2-1-87. [21]Fr 8-1-92. [22]Now GAF Corp. [23]SF call $0.21M 6-1-85. [24]See Hamilton Technology. [25]Red rest'n(14.625%)to 2-1-90. [26]Fr 2-1-93. [27]Fr 2-1-88. [28]Fr 4-15-89. [29]Fr 1-15-87. [30]Fr 3-15-88. [31]Fr 6-1-90. [32]Fr 8-1-87. [33]Fr 7-15-85. [34]Fr 3-15-87. [35]Thru 8-14-85,adj aft for T-Bill rates,etc. [36]Int:Min 8.012%,Max 15.297%. [37]Fr 1-15-91. [38]See Mayer(Oscar) & Co.

SOURCE: *Standard & Poor's Bond Guide,* June 1985, p. 64.

Other Characteristics of Corporate Bonds

Secured Versus Unsecured. **Secured bonds** are backed by the pledge of specific corporate assets as collateral; **unsecured bonds** are not. An unsecured bond is called a debenture. All things equal, investors prefer secured issues.

Convertible. Conversion works to the investor's advantage. You may convert your **convertible bonds** to the common stock of the corporation at a specified exchange rate over the life of the bonds. The advantage is that if the common

Table 11.7 EXPLANATION OF BOND RATINGS

Quality	Moody's	Standard & Poor's	Description
High-grade	Aaa	AAA	Bonds that are judged to be of the best quality. They carry the smallest degree of investment risk and are generally referred to as "gilt edge." Interest payments are protected by a large or exceptionally stable margin, and principal is secure.
	Aa	AA	Bonds that are judged to be of high quality by all standards. Together with the first group, they comprise what are generally known as high-grade bonds. They are rated lower than the best bonds because margins of protection may not be as large.
Medium-grade	A	A	Bonds that possess many favorable investment attributes and are to be considered as upper medium-grade obligations. Factors giving security to principal and interest are considered adequate.
	Baa	BBB	Bonds that are considered as medium-grade obligations; that is, they are neither highly protected nor poorly secured.

continued

stock price really goes up, you can convert from bonds to stock.[6] If the common stock price does not go up or goes down, you can forget about your conversion feature and concentrate on receiving interest payments. Because the conversion privilege is a clear advantage to the bond purchaser, the interest rate on convertible bonds is usually two or three percentage points lower than on nonconvertible corporate bonds.

Put Privilege. The **put privilege** allows the bondholder to sell a long-term bond back to the corporation at its face value after a relatively short period of time, regardless of the current market price. Perhaps you buy a 25-year, $1000 bond that drops in price to $740 after five years because of higher market interest

[6] You do not actually have to go through the formal process of conversion. Your convertible bonds will move closely up in value with the common stock because of the conversion privilege.

Table 11.7 continued

Quality	Moody's	Standard & Poor's	Description
Speculative	Ba	BB	Bonds that are judged to have speculative elements; their future cannot be considered as well assured. Often the protection of interest and principal payments may be very moderate.
	B	B	Bonds that generally lack characteristics of the desirable investment. Assurance of interest and principal payments or of maintenance of other terms of the contract over any long period of time may be small.
Default	Caa	CCC	Bonds that are of poor standing. Such issues may be in default, or there may be elements of danger present with respect to principal or interest.
	Ca	CC	Bonds that represent obligations which are speculative to a high degree. Such issues are often in default or have other marked shortcomings.
	C		The lowest-rated class in Moody's designation. These bonds can be regarded as having extremely poor prospects of attaining any real investment standing.
		C	Rating given to income bonds on which interest is not currently being paid.
		D	Issues in default with arrears in interest and/or principal payments.

SOURCES: *Moody's Bond Record* (published by Moody's Investors Service, Inc., New York, N.Y.) and *Bond Guide* (Standard & Poor's).

rates or deteriorating business prospects for the corporation. If you have a put privilege after five years, you can sell the bond back to the corporation at the $1000 face value. (Of course, if the bond price went up, you would not use the put privilege.) This is a very advantageous feature for the bondholder, and generally one must accept a lower initial rate on the bond for this privilege. Only a small percentage of bonds carry a put feature, but you can always ask your broker to suggest such issues.

Floating-Rate Bonds. **Floating-rate bonds** are an innovation of the 1980s. Instead of the annual payment on the bond being fixed, it goes up and down with market conditions. For this reason, the price of the bond remains at face

Box 11.2 JUNK BONDS AND YIELD

Financiers are doing land-office business in junk bonds, the ones with high coupons and low rating quality. Bereft of those fat money market yields of recent memory, unsophisticated investors are stretching their quality standards to maintain their yields. This, like any boom, gives pause to James Rogers, one of the sharpest investors around. Talking of the flood of such issues that has hit the market in the past few years Rogers told a Columbia Business School seminar in May, "It's a nightmare just waiting to happen. It is a financial excess that sometime in the next year or two or three is going to cave in."

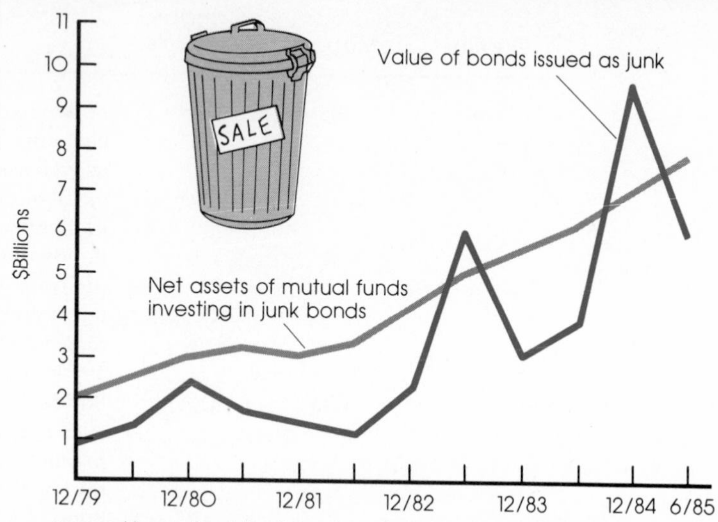

SOURCE: Lipper Analytical Services, Inc.; Securities Data Co.

If it caves, a lot of mutual fund investors will end up in a hole. The number of funds offering junk bonds has grown from 7 at the end of 1974 to 39 today. With $7.24 billion in assets at the end of 1984, according to Lipper Analytical Services, Inc., junk bond funds accounted for nearly 40% of all mutual fund assets invested in taxable bonds.

The reason for this massive flow of capital to low-rated bonds is simple. Junk bonds yield 3% and more over Treasury bonds. Investors got addicted to high yields back when they could get 15% on their money market funds. But with money market yields down to 7%, investors are showing withdrawal symptoms. Junk bonds are the methadone.

But junk bond funds, unlike money market funds, bear substantial credit risks. The real question is, what will be your total return—coupon interest minus any

value because the bond is always adjusting to paying the going market rate of interest. Though this product is relatively new, a good place to start looking would be in the floating-rate issues of Citicorp bank of New York.

Corporate securities have many other features as well. We have merely highlighted the most important items here.

SUMMARY

In setting your overall investment strategy, you should first consider your needs in terms of such factors as return and safety of principal, current income, liquidity, tax factors, and desire for management control. Within this framework you should try to allocate your assets to short-, intermediate-, and long-term

losses from defaults? It will do you very little good to receive 15% in yield if your principal deteriorates 12%.

Junk dealers know all about total return. History, they declare, shows that junk bonds provide a higher total return than timid investments in Treasurys or high-grade corporate bonds. The classic study, done by W. Braddock Hickman in 1958, showed that from 1900 to 1943 bonds below investment grade had an annual total return over 3% higher than that of more respectable bonds. What you lost in defaults, you more than made up for in yield. Convincing?

Not if the nature of junk bond issuers has changed. In the past, junk bonds were fallen angels, issued by companies that once had been considered strong credits but had come on hard times. Investors panicked out of the bonds, leaving behind terrific buys for contrarians.

Today, through the offices of Drexel Burnham Lambert and other investment houses, highly leveraged and relatively untested corporations are raising money through original issue junk bonds. These are not companies whose debt became high yielding when they stumbled. Instead, the bonds are high coupon and risky from day one. Since 1982, when the last recession ended, $31 billion in junk bonds has been issued. In 1984 alone, according to Securities Data Co., about 20% of all straight corporate debt issues were of marginal quality. Many of these will turn out to be excellent investments, but it is a good bet that many will default in the next serious recession.

Investor Warren Buffett, speaking at the same Columbia forum as James Rogers, reiterated that today's junk bonds are different from yesterday's. "A statistical study that shows the historical experience of junk bonds is a lot of nonsense in terms of determining the way the world is going to work in the future," Buffett declared. "[Today's bonds] are an entirely different species."

Rogers' fear is that in the next recession a few big junk bond defaults might lead the regulators to force savings and loans or insurance companies to sell their low-quality bonds. This could cause a crash in the junk market, and perhaps liquidity problems for insurers and thrifts. If the Fed tried to bail them out with easy money, the currency would turn into what Rogers calls "confetti."

For those who are willing to take the risks, mutual funds investing in low-quality bonds do offer high yields. But remember: You are certainly not buying Treasury bonds or money market instruments.

SOURCE: Reprinted by permission of *Forbes* magazine, September 16, 1985, pp. 91, 92.

investments, and decide on the appropriate mix between financial and real assets. Clearly, the near- and long-term outlook for the economy will influence your decision-making process. Some investments perform well in an inflationary economy, whereas others do their best in an environment of very small price increases. Bear in mind that the worst type of investment decision is one that is based on impulse, usually in an emotional environment where everything appears to be going up or going down. Also, remember that high returns are normally associated with taking some degree of risk. The 20 or 25 percent return, without commensurate risk, is difficult to achieve.

When you move to the long-term side of the fixed-income security market, you must be particularly sensitive to the outlook for interest rates. If you buy a 20- or 30-year bond at 10 percent interest and rates in the market go up to 12 percent, you will suffer a large paper loss. Your bond is simply not meeting market rates of interest. Of course, if interest rates go down after you purchase a long-term bond, you will enjoy an increase in value. In the last two decades, investors have experienced both losses and substantial gains in the bond market.

You may choose to invest in U.S. government bonds, tax-free municipal bonds, or corporate bonds. Whereas U.S. governments are free of credit risk, such is not the case for municipal and corporate bonds. Municipal bonds may be broken down into general obligation and revenue bonds, with the latter generally carrying greater risk.

In evaluating a corporate bond, you should consider such factors as the bond's rating, its security provisions, and the potential conversion privilege. These factors, along with lesser ones, will have a strong influence on how attractive the issue is.

KEY TERMS

bond ratings
business risk
capital appreciation
certificate of deposit (CD)
commercial paper
convertible bonds
equivalent taxable yield
federal agency securities
financial assets
floating rate bonds
GNMA certificates
investment
junk bonds
liquidity
market risk
money market account
money market checking account
money market fund
municipal bonds
purchasing-power risk
put privilege
real assets
savings account
secured bonds
Treasury bill
unsecured bonds
yield
zero-coupon bonds

SELECTED READINGS

Fabozzi, Frank J. *Readings in Investment Management*. Homewood, Ill.: Irwin, 1983.

Hirt, Geoffrey, Stanley Block, and Fred Jury. *The Investor's Desktop Portfolio Planner*. Chicago: Probus Publishing Company, 1986.

Nichols, Donald R. *Life Cycle Investing: Investing for the Times of Your Life*. Homewood, Ill.: Dow Jones–Irwin, 1986.

Salomon Brothers, Inc. Annual research data on returns on investments for 1, 5, and 15 years. Salomon Brothers, Inc., One New York Plaza, New York, N.Y. 10004.

"Twenty Winning Strategies for Your Investments." *Money,* October 1985, pp. 49–58.

Willis, Clint. "Investing and Saving for the Long Term." *Money Guide,* 1985, pp. 59–62.

QUESTIONS

1 Give two examples of financial assets that are short-term, intermediate-term, and long-term.

2 In what type of economic environment do financial assets perform best? What type of economic environment is best for real assets?

3 In advising an investor, what action should a professional investment money manager take first?

4 Generally describe the relationship between risk and return in making investments.

5 How is the liquidity of an investment measured? Do financial or real assets generally provide greater liquidity?

6 Why is there an irreducible amount of time that must be spent with your investments even if you use professional managers (through a mutual fund or real estate limited partnership)?

7 What is the difference between the concepts of market risk and business risk?

8 What types of investments would you purchase to reduce your exposure to purchasing-power risk?

9 Place the following investments in rank order, going from low-risk return to high-risk return.

    Corporate bonds
    Commercial paper
    Savings account
    Government bonds
    Certificate of deposit
    Common stock

10 What penalty feature is often associated with certificates of deposit? Can you overcome this feature with a money market account?

11 What is a money market checking account? What advantage and disadvantage does it have in comparison to a normal money market account?

12 What is a money market fund? How do money market funds compare to money market accounts in terms of safety?

13 What do we mean when we say that Treasury bills trade on a discount basis rather than paying direct interest?

14 What is commercial paper? Can any business firm normally expect to be able to issue commercial paper?

15 Why does the purchaser of a Government National Mortgage Association (GNMA) pass-through certificate have no investment left in the security when it reaches maturity?

16 Explain why changing interest rates cause existing bond prices to go up or down.

17 Should you buy long-term or short-term bonds in anticipation of interest rate declines? Explain.

18 Why are bonds issued by the U.S. government more price sensitive to interest rate changes than bonds issued by corporations?

19 What is the difference between the meaning of the bid and the asked price on a bond?

20 How does an investor in a zero-coupon bond receive his or her return?

21 What is a municipal bond? What is the most important feature associated with this type of security?

22 What is the difference between a general obligation and a revenue bond in evaluating municipal bonds?

23 Briefly discuss the relationship between a bond's quality rating (such as A or C) and its yield.

24 What is the advantage and disadvantage of owning a convertible bond?

25 If you own a floating-rate bond, are you likely to be subject to large changes in the market value of the bond?

26 A $10,000, one-year Treasury bill is quoted at a yield of 7 percent.
- **a** At what price will the Treasury bill sell?
- **b** What is the effective yield on this instrument?

27 Assume a $10,000, six-month Treasury bill is quoted at a 12 percent yield.
- **a** Use equation 11.1 to determine the discount on the Treasury bill.
- **b** Use equation 11.2 to determine the price of the Treasury bill.
- **c** Use equation 11.3 to determine the effective yield.

28 A top athlete at State University has just signed a pro basketball contract with the Los Angeles Lakers. He will receive an immediate signing bonus of $100,000. Furthermore, he will receive $200,000 a year for the next ten years. Also he will receive $400,000 after ten years. The interest or discount rate to be applied is 10 percent. What is the present value of all the benefits from this contract? Follow the procedure below.
- **a** Write down the signing bonus.
- **b** Take the present value of the annual payments. (Use Table 11.6.)
- **c** Take the present value of the single payment to be received after ten years. (Use Table 11.5.)
- **d** Add together the values in a, b, and c to get your answer.

29 Completely rework problem 28 based on all the same facts and procedures, but with a discount rate of 6 percent.

30 A 30-year bond pays $120 (12 percent) per year in interest for 30 years and $1000 after 30 years. Use a 10 percent interest rate (discount rate) to determine the current price of the bond. Follow the three-step procedure suggested in the chapter. That is:

a Determine the present value of $1000 after 30 years at a 10 percent interest rate by using Table 11.5.

b Determine the present value of $120 per year for the next 30 years by using Table 11.6. Once again, apply a 10 percent interest rate.

c Add together the answers to part a and part b to get your final answer.

d Explain why your answer is above or below $1000.

31 Rework problem 30 with a 14 percent interest rate (discount rate). All other values are the same.

32 Referring to Figure 11.3, translate the bid and asked price for the second bond in the table into dollars and cents. It is a $1000 bond. Make sure to follow the procedures suggested in the chapter.

33 You are going to choose between a municipal bond paying 8.1 percent interest and a taxable instrument paying 10.9 percent. You are in a 33 percent tax bracket.

a Using equation 11.5, determine the equivalent taxable yield on the municipal bond.

b Which instrument should you select?

CASE PROBLEMS

11.1 Grandma Ethel turned 75 years old today. It's been five years since Grandpa Sam passed away. They enjoyed 52 years of marriage together.

Grandma Ethel took the money she was left in Grandpa's estate and invested it in a $50,000 certificate of deposit (CD). The CD comes due next week. She can renew it for one year at 8 percent interest. She intends to use the income from the CD plus her monthly social security check to meet her living expenses.

At her recent annual physical exam, the doctor announced that Grandma Ethel was in excellent condition for her age. It would surprise no one if Grandma Ethel continued to live well into her eighties.

One of the guests at her 75th birthday party was her 20-year-old nephew, Lance Hamilton. Lance fancies himself an expert in investments and has suggested to Grandma Ethel that she can get a 1 percent higher yield by investing the $50,000 in 30-year U.S. government bonds. Please answer the following questions.

a Comment on whether there is business risk or market risk involved with investing in U.S. government bonds.

b Indicate how much extra income Grandma Ethel will receive a year if she follows Lance's suggestion.

c Assume that Grandma Ethel follows Lance's suggestion and buys $50,000 worth of U.S. government bonds (50 bonds at $1000 each). Further assume that each bond pays $90 a year in interest. Also assume that shortly after Grandma buys the bonds, the interest rate in the market (discount rate) goes up to 12 percent. Use the three-step procedure described in the chapter to find the new price of these 30-year bonds. *Note:* Find the price of one bond and then multiply this value by 50 to get the price of all 50 bonds.

d Rework part c based on an assumption that the interest rate in the market (discount rate) goes down to 6 percent rather than up to 12 percent. Once again, assume each bond pays $90 a year in interest and has 30 years remaining to maturity. Use the three-step procedure described in the chapter to get the value for one bond and multiply this by 50 to get the value for all 50 bonds.

e Given the information you have determined in parts b, c, and d, do you think the 30-year government bonds are generally a good investment for Grandma Ethel? Briefly comment.

f If Grandma Ethel decides to buy the $50,000 CD instead of the bonds, and needs to withdraw her funds after eight months, what type of penalty is she likely to incur?

g What other type of similar short-term investment might she consider where there would not be a penalty for early withdrawal?

11.2 Josh and Melissa Clayton have now accumulated $10,000 in savings. Josh sells BMWs for the largest dealership in the state, and Melissa is a registered nurse. They are both in their late twenties. They have one son, who is 3 years old. Their combined income is $44,000 per year.

a Josh has suggested that they buy a six-month $10,000 Treasury bill that has a quoted rate of 8.1 percent interest. Using equations 11.1, 11.2, and 11.3, determine the effective yield on the Treasury bill.

b One of the doctors that works at the same hospital as Melissa suggests that she and Josh look into the possibility of purchasing short- to intermediate-term municipal bonds. The bonds are currently paying 6.7 percent as an annual interest rate. Melissa recalls from last year's tax return that she and Josh are in a 28 percent tax bracket. Compute the equivalent taxable yield on the municipal bonds.

All things being equal, should Josh and Melissa purchase the Treasury bill or the municipal bonds?

c A third alternative that their stockbroker has suggested is that they purchase corporate bonds. He particularly recommends that they buy lower-rated bonds. Josh is a little shocked by the suggestion and wants to know what the advantage and disadvantage of buying lower-rated (B or C) bonds is. Explain the implications to him.

d Melissa generally likes the idea of buying corporate bonds (though not necessarily low-rated ones). She also thinks, however, that the stock market may be going up rapidly in the near future. Explain to her how she might be able to purchase corporate bonds and also participate in the potential upward movement in the stock market.

e Josh's fourth cousin, who is an assistant delivery boy on Wall Street, boldly predicts that interest rates are going to go up sharply in the next year. Explain why floating-rate bonds might be a good investment under this circumstance. Also, explain why bonds with a put privilege might be advantageous if Josh's fourth cousin is correct.

Appendix 11A

Preferred Stock as an Alternative to Debt

Some investors choose to invest in **preferred stock** as an alternative to debt-oriented fixed income securities. Because most of the advantage of preferred stock accrues to corporate owners rather than individual stockholders, we have decided to cover this topic briefly in an appendix. Preferred stock is simply not a very important investment outlet for the typical small investor.

Preferred stock has the attribute of a fixed-income security in that it pays a fixed dividend. Although the dividend yield is quoted on an annual basis, it is distributed quarterly to stockholders. For example, a $100 preferred stock, paying $8 annually in dividends, would provide an 8 percent yield to investors. The investor would actually receive $2 per quarter.

The dividend on preferred stock is not a contractual obligation of the corporation as is true of the interest on debt. If a corporation fails to pay the interest on its debt, it can be forced into bankruptcy by the bondholders. There is no similar remedy for preferred stockholders. Preferred stock, however, is normally cumulative. This means that all dividends that are not paid on preferred stock accumulate and must be paid before any dividends are paid to common stockholders. For example, in the case of the $8 annual dividend preferred stock described above, if the firm did not pay preferred stock dividends for three years, $24 in prior dividend obligations would accumulate and we would say the firm is $24 in arrears. The firm is not compelled to pay the $24 in the future to the preferred stockholders, but it cannot distribute any funds to common stockholders until it does.

As is true of corporate bonds, some preferred stock issues may be convertible to the common stock of the firm. There are also a limited number of preferred stock issues that have floating-rate dividend payments. That is, the annual (or quarterly) dividend payment goes up or down with interest rates in the market.

Unlike debt, preferred stock is perpetual in nature. It has no maturity date and can only be extinguished by the corporation deciding to call it in (buy it back), generally at a price slightly above par or stated value.

The most notable feature about preferred stock is the treatment of the dividend for tax purposes. To the corporate recipient, it is 80 percent tax-exempt.[1] For an \$8.00 a year preferred stock issue, only \$1.60 (20 percent × \$8.00) would be taxable. This, of course, makes the \$8.00 look more attractive. For this tax reason, preferred stock generally pays a slightly lower yield than comparable debt issues. Because the individual investor does *not* receive the same tax exemption benefit, the attraction of preferred stock is somewhat less.

[1] This same feature applies to all forms of dividends received by corporations, but is particularly valuable in the case of preferred stock because normally the entire return is in the form of dividends.

12

Investing in Common Stocks

After studying this chapter, you should:

- Understand the basic nature of common stock ownership in terms of claims to earnings, dividends, and voting rights
- Know how to compute earnings per share and dividend yield
- Be able to read and understand basic stock market data in the *Wall Street Journal*
- Understand the difference between investing and trading
- Distinguish between the concepts of fundamental and technical analysis
- Appreciate the differences in service and cost between traditional and discount brokers
- Understand the types of orders that can be placed and the use of margin and short selling

Having examined general investment strategy and fixed-income securities in Chapter 11, we turn our attention to common stock investments in this chapter. Over 40 million people in the United States own common stock, so this topic is worthy of careful examination.

Common stocks can be an exciting form of investment. Once you have invested your funds, you often become emotionally involved with the firm. There is a tendency to watch carefully for the new products the firm is introducing, to listen closely for its ads on television, to become familiar with the competitive products, and so on. When you make your first common stock investment, don't be surprised if you wake up 15 minutes earlier the next morning to race out for the newspaper to check the stock quote section.

Common stock represents the ownership interest in a firm. Whether the shareholder owns one share of General Motors or 1000 shares of a small family corporation, the rights and privileges of ownership reside with the common stockholder. This means, first of all, that any funds left over after the firm pays all its bills from operations (and the fixed return to other suppliers of capital) belong to the common stockholders. Their return is not limited to a specified amount, as is true of lenders. If the firm has a highly profitable year, the earnings of the common stockholders may be two or three times greater than the prior year. These earnings may be paid out to the stockholders in the form of dividends or reinvested in new projects for the benefit of stockholders. Of course, if the firm is not profitable, the stockholder must also live with the consequences. As was indicated in Figure 11.1 of the previous chapter, the common stockholders generally have the highest return potential as well as the highest risk exposure of any class of security holder. They are guaranteed nothing, but the upside potential is theoretically unlimited.

The common stockholder also is the only security classification that has the voting privilege. That is, the common stockholders elect the board of directors and vote on major proposals that affect the corporation, such as an offer by another firm to participate in a merger. The only time that bond or preferred stockholders are allowed to vote is when the corporation has failed to live up to its financial obligations, and their rights and privileges are accelerated as a result. Some would suggest that the voting right is not very important. A corporation may have hundreds of thousands of stockholders spread across the country or even the world. Furthermore, it is difficult for the average stockholder to be sufficiently informed to make intelligent voting decisions. It often appears that the operating officers of the firm are powerful enough to disregard the wishes and desires of stockholders. The lesson of the 1980s, however, is that management cannot afford to be unresponsive to the concerns of stockholders. In many cases, insensitive management has been replaced by new ownership as a result of a merger or acquisition.

KEY CHARACTERISTICS OF COMMON STOCK

In order to better explain the general nature of common stock, we present some material from the 1985 annual report of Pitney Bowes. The firm is the world's largest producer of postage and mailing equipment. It also manufactures and markets office copiers and dictating machines. A graphic display of some of its products is shown in Figure 12.1, and a statement of selected financial data for the firm is presented in Figure 12.2.

In evaluating the financial data for the firm, the investor normally asks, How much did it earn? Observe in Figure 12.2 that "income from continuing operations applicable to common stock" is $144,485,000 (this is the circled value under the 1985 column). This translates into net income per common share of

Figure 12.1 EXAMPLES OF THE PITNEY BOWES PRODUCT LINE

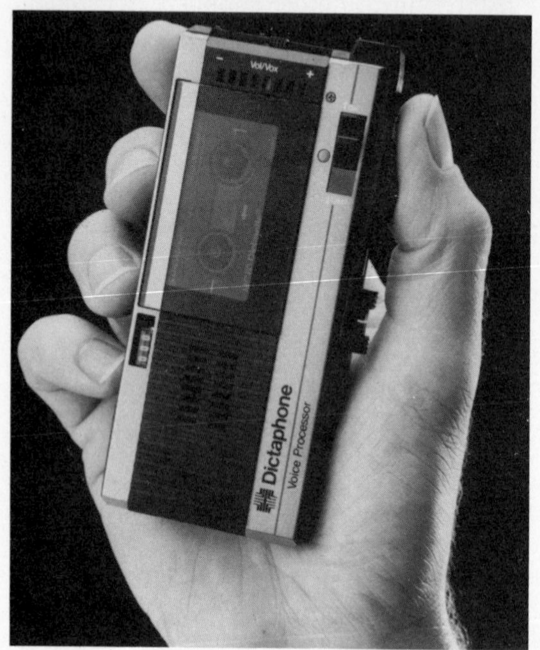

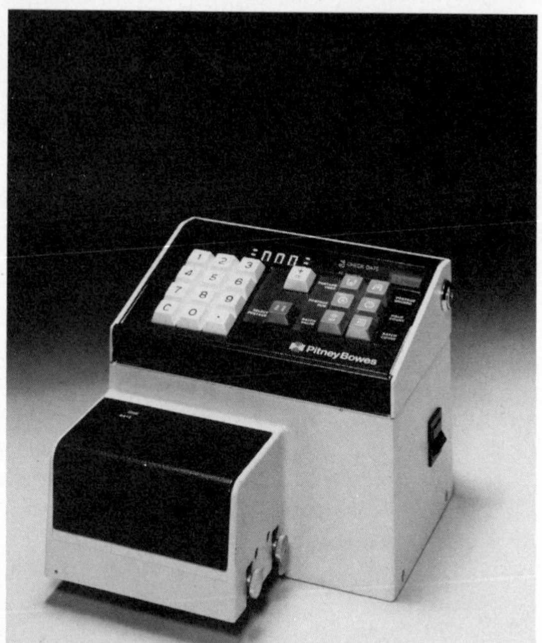

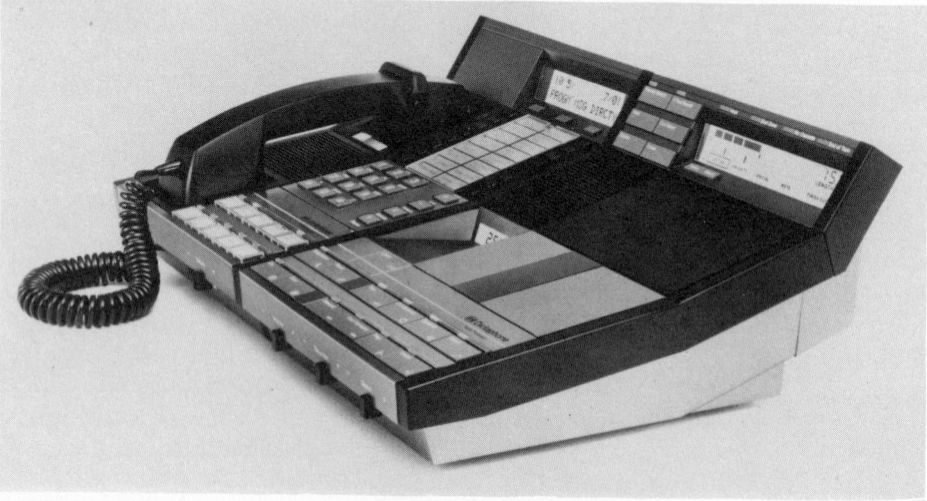

Figure 12.2 PITNEY BOWES FINANCIAL STATEMENT

Summary of Selected Financial Data

Pitney Bowes Inc. and subsidiaries

(Dollars in thousands except per share data)

Years ended December 31	1985	1984	1983	1982	1981
Total revenue	$1,831,804	$1,732,095	$1,606,454	$1,421,432	$1,391,076
Costs and expenses	1,663,956	1,538,192	1,427,372	1,285,859	1,265,491
Income from continuing operations before taxes and equity income	167,848	193,903	179,082	135,573	125,585
Provision for income taxes	73,413	88,737	88,108	61,330	61,400
Income from continuing operations before equity income	94,435	105,166	90,974	74,243	64,185
Equity in net income of finance subsidiaries	50,072	33,005	26,685	19,448	12,259
Income from continuing operations	144,507	138,171	117,659	93,691	76,444
Preferred stock dividend requirements	22	26	49	73	120
Income from continuing operations applicable to common stock	$ 144,485	$ 138,145	$ 117,610	$ 93,618	$ 76,324
Income per common and common equivalent share:					
Continuing operations	$3.65	$3.51	$3.01	$2.43	$2.08
Net income	$3.80	$3.51	$2.23	$2.16	$1.89
Total dividends on common, preference, and preferred stock	$46,904	$40,535	$35,065	$31,935	$30,827
Dividends per share of common stock	$1.20	$1.04	$.89	$.80	$.80
Average common and common equivalent shares outstanding	39,563,520	39,366,421	39,105,312	38,510,116	36,808,464
Balance sheet at December 31					
Total assets	$1,762,768	$1,613,572	$1,473,017	$1,338,044	$1,214,722
Long-term debt	107,182	100,920	100,240	112,352	113,587
Capital lease obligations	47,550	46,276	44,777	46,624	46,340
Stockholders' equity	802,847	694,465	600,331	547,353	503,459
Book value per common share	$20.70	$18.09	$15.72	$14.38	$13.10
Ratios					
Profit margin–continuing operations:					
Before tax and equity earnings	9.2%	11.2%	11.1%	9.5%	9.0%
After taxes and equity earnings	7.9%	8.0%	7.3%	6.6%	5.5%
Current ratio	1.24:1	1.32:1	1.32:1	1.45:1	1.45:1
Return on invested capital–continuing operations	12.8%	14.1%	13.6%	12.3%	11.1%
Return on stockholders' equity–continuing operations	18.0%	19.9%	19.6%	17.1%	15.2%
Debt to total capital	21.0%	21.2%	23.2%	25.6%	27.4%
Other					
Common stockholders	21,126	18,427	17,964	16,973	20,014
Total employees	28,995	27,976	26,468	26,475	26,791
Postage meters in service, U.S., U.K., Canada	1,150,998	1,103,690	1,057,597	1,025,135	1,010,763

SOURCE: Pitney Bowes Annual Report, 1985, p. 30.

\$3.65.[1] This translation is the result of dividing the \$144,485,000 in earnings by the 39,563,520 shares outstanding. The next question might be, How much did the firm pay out to stockholders in the way of dividends? If we read three rows down from the \$3.65 income (or earnings) per share figure, we observe that Pitney Bowes paid out \$1.20 in dividends per share in 1985. This indicates that Pitney Bowes distributed 32.9 percent of its earnings in the form of dividends (\$1.20/\$3.65). The rest of the earnings (67.1 percent) was retained for reinvestment to generate future earnings and dividends.

Our interest in Pitney Bowes is not so much as an individual company, but rather to illustrate many of the features associated with common stock. The next question might be, How are investors evaluating the firm in the marketplace? An excerpt from the March 17, 1986, issue of the *Wall Street Journal* in Figure 12.3 gives us additional insight. Read down the quotes until you arrive at Pitney Bowes (shown as Pitney B.)

First, you can see that the high and low price for Pitney Bowes over the last 52 weeks was 55⅞ and 36⅜, respectively. You can further see that the closing price of 55½ in the next to last column is very close to the 52-week high of 55⅞.

The column after the company name indicates that annual dividends of \$1.32 per share are to be paid. You may recall that the dividend figure shown in Figure 12.2 was \$1.20 per share. That value, however, was for year-end 1985 and Pitney Bowes has since increased the dividend by 12 cents per share (remember that the *Wall Street Journal* excerpt is for March 17, 1986). The next column, labeled Yield %, gives you the dividend yield on the stock. It represents the annual dividend of \$1.32 divided by the current price of 55½ and carries a value of 2.4 percent. Most stockholders anticipate two forms of return on their holdings: the dividend yield plus an increase in the value of the stock. For example, if Pitney Bowes increases by 10 percent in value over the next 12 months, the investor will have a total return of 12.4 percent.

Dividend yield	2.4%
Capital appreciation	10.0
Total return	12.4%

The next column shows the P-E ratio for the firm. This is an extremely important topic that we shall briefly examine now and cover in more depth later in the chapter. The **price-earnings (P-E) ratio** is the current stock price divided by the latest 12 months of earnings per share. It, in effect, tells us how many times earnings investors are willing to pay in valuing a stock. In the case of Pitney Bowes, the P-E is 15 and is arrived at as follows:[2]

[1] The \$3.80 for net income is after other special adjustments and is considered of lesser importance. The \$3.65 figure is the one reported in the financial press.

[2] Note that even though it is mid-March, the latest earnings report is still as of December 31, 1985. Dividends have changed, but earnings per share have not. The next earnings reporting date will be March 31, 1986. Earnings figures come out quarterly.

Figure 12.3 STOCK MARKET QUOTES FROM THE *WALL STREET JOURNAL*

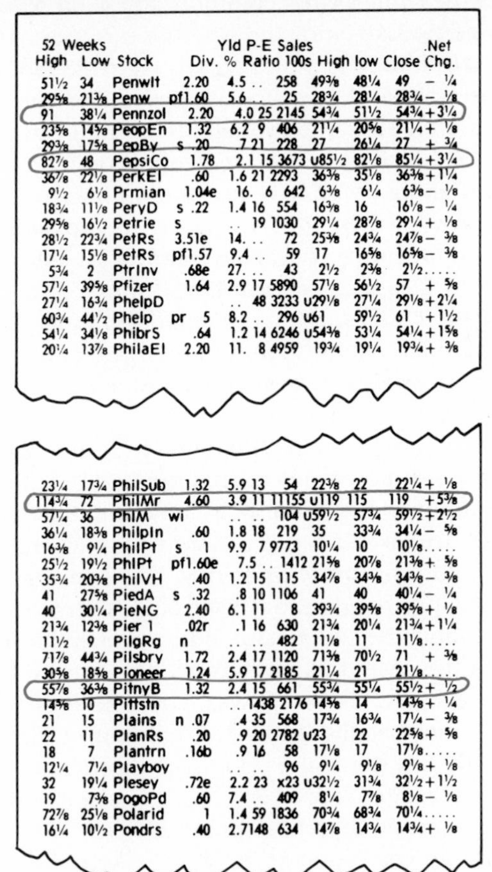

NEW YORK STOCK EXCHANGE COMPOSITE TRANSACTIONS

52 Weeks High	Low	Stock	Div.	Yld %	P-E Ratio	Sales 100s	High	low	Close	Net Chg.
51½	34	Penwlt	2.20	4.5	..	258	49⅜	48¼	49	− ¼
29⅝	21⅜	Penw	pf1.60	5.6	..	25	28¾	28¼	28¾	− ⅛
91	38¼	Pennzol	2.20	4.0	25	2145	54¾	51½	54¾	+ 3¼
23⅝	14⅝	PeopEn	1.32	6.2	9	406	21¼	20⅝	21¼	+ ⅛
29⅜	17⅝	PepBy	s .20	.7	21	228	27	26¼	27	+ ¾
82⅞	48	PepsiCo	1.78	2.1	15	3673	u85½	82⅛	85¼	+ 3¼
36⅞	22⅛	PerkEl	.60	1.6	21	2293	36⅜	35⅛	36⅜	+ 1¼
9½	6⅛	Prmian	1.04e	16.	6	642	6⅜	6¼	6⅜	− ⅛
18¾	11⅛	PeryD	s .22	1.4	16	554	16⅜	16	16⅛	− ¼
29⅝	16½	Petrie	s	..	19	1030	29¼	28⅞	29¼	+ ⅛
28½	22¾	PetRs	3.51e	14.	..	72	25⅜	24¾	24⅞	− ⅜
17¼	15⅛	PetRs	pf1.57	9.4	..	59	17	16⅝	16⅝	− ⅜
5¾	2	PtrInv	.68e	27.	..	43	2½	2⅜	2½	.....
57¼	39⅝	Pfizer	1.64	2.9	17	5890	57⅛	56½	57	+ ⅝
27¼	16¾	PhelpD		..	48	3233	u29⅛	27¼	29⅛	+ 2¼
60¾	44½	Phelp	pr 5	8.2	..	296	u61	59½	61	+ 1½
54¼	34⅛	PhibrS	.64	1.2	14	6246	u54⅜	53¼	54¼	+ 1⅝
20¼	13⅞	PhilaEl	2.20	11.	8	4959	19¾	19¼	19¾	+ ⅜
23¼	17¾	PhilSub	1.32	5.9	13	54	22⅜	22	22¼	+ ⅛
114¾	72	PhilMr	4.60	3.9	11	11155	u119	115	119	+ 5⅜
57¼	36	PhlM	wi	..	..	104	u59½	57¾	59½	+ 2½
36¼	18⅜	PhilpIn	.60	1.8	18	219	35	33¾	34¼	− ⅝
16⅜	9¼	PhilPt	s 1	9.9	7	9773	10¼	10	10⅛	.....
25½	19½	PhlPt	pf1.60e	7.5	..	1412	21⅝	20⅞	21⅜	+ ⅝
35¾	20⅜	PhilVH	.40	1.2	15	115	34⅞	34⅜	34⅜	− ⅜
41	27⅝	PiedA	s .32	.8	10	1106	41	40	40¼	− ¼
40	30¼	PieNG	2.40	6.1	11	8	39¾	39⅝	39⅝	+ ⅛
21¾	12⅜	Pier 1	.02r	.1	16	630	21¾	20¼	21¾	+ 1¼
11½	9	PilgRg	n	..	..	482	11⅛	11	11⅛	.....
71⅞	44¾	Pilsbry	1.72	2.4	17	1120	71⅜	70½	71	+ ⅜
30⅝	18⅝	Pioneer	1.24	5.9	17	2185	21¼	21	21⅛	.....
55⅞	36⅜	PitnyB	1.32	2.4	15	661	55¾	55¼	55½	+ ½
14⅝	10	Pittstn		..	1438	2176	14⅝	14	14⅜	+ ¼
21	15	Plains	n .07	.4	35	568	17¾	16¾	17¼	− ⅜
22	11	PlanRs	.20	.9	20	2782	u23	22	22⅝	+ ⅝
18	7	Plantrn	.16b	.9	16	58	17⅛	17	17⅛	.....
12¼	7¼	Playboy		..	..	96	9¼	9⅛	9⅛	+ ⅛
32	19¼	Plesey	.72e	2.2	23	x23	u32½	31¾	32½	+ 1½
19	7⅜	PogoPd	.60	7.4	..	409	8¼	7⅞	8⅛	− ⅛
72⅞	25⅛	Polarid	1	1.4	59	1836	70¾	68¾	70¼	.....
16¼	10½	Pondrs	.40	2.7	148	634	14⅞	14¾	14¾	+ ⅛

SOURCE: Reprinted by permission of the *Wall Street Journal*, © Dow Jones & Company, Inc., March 17, 1986, p. 37. All rights reserved.

$$\frac{\text{Current price}}{\text{Latest 12 months' earnings}} = \frac{\$55.50}{\$3.65} = 15.21$$

The value is rounded to 15 in the presentation in the *Wall Street Journal.* The P-E ratio actually represents the value that investors assign to a company's earnings. If a company's performance (past and anticipated in the future) is strong, a high P-E ratio will be used, and for weak performance, investors will tend to assign a lower collective valuation in the marketplace. You undoubtedly would follow the same procedure for your own assets. If you had a business that was doing quite poorly, you may be more than willing for someone to take it off your hands for three to five times last year's earnings. On the other hand, if it was a real winner, you might demand 20 to 25 times earnings.

Quite likely, the first time you call a stockbroker and have a serious discussion about the value of some firm's common stock, he or she will discuss the P-E ratio with you and perhaps indicate whether it is thought to be too high, too low, or just right. The P-E ratio is a particularly valuable tool in that it allows us to compare firms with widely diverse stock prices and earnings on a common measurement basis. In March 1986, the average P-E ratio on the New York Stock Exchange was 14.8. In the fall of 1987, the average P-E ratio was 20.

In the next column of Figure 12.3 we see the number of shares that were traded during the day. You always add two zeros to the value, so for Pitney Bowes the volume was 66,100. After you begin following a stock for a while, the volume figure can take on meaning for you. For example, if Pitney Bowes normally trades in a 50,000 to 100,000 volume range and one morning you pick up the paper and see that a million shares were traded, you can assume that a big development is in the works. Perhaps the firm is about to get a major government contract or another company is considering a merger tender offer for the firm's shares. You can often tell whether the high volume indicates good or bad news by watching the stock market movement during the day.

The next three columns indicate the high, low, and closing stock price for the day. Since the quotes are taken from the March 17, 1986 *Wall Street Journal*, they actually represent values from the prior day. This is much like reading the baseball box scores. If you pick up Tuesday morning's newspaper, you will find out who won or lost on Monday. The final column shows the net change from the prior day's quote. In the case of Pitney Bowes, the stock advanced ½ point (50¢). If you owned 100 shares of Pitney Bowes, you would be $50 wealthier. In looking at other firms' performances in the last column of Figure 12.3, we see that the market apparently was generally up for the day. There are considerably more pluses than minuses. Pennzoil (Pennzol), Pepsico, and Phillip Morris (PhilMr) all had gains of between 3 and 5½ points.

Prices for all stocks are determined by the marketplace (which we shall discuss shortly). If more investors want to buy the stock than sell it, the stock price will go up. Similarly, if the number of investors who want to unload the stock exceeds the number of buyers, the stock will decline in value. Once a firm begins trading its stock in the public marketplace, it has no control in determining day-to-day stock value. Investors, by "voting their dollars" for or against a security, are the ultimate determiners of value.

Now that we have discussed some of the fundamentals associated with a given stock, we'll show you how and where stocks are traded. After we have considered this issue, we will explain how you go about picking stocks for your portfolio.

MAJOR MARKETS FOR STOCK TRADING

Stocks trade either on organized exchanges or in the over-the-counter market. The organized exchanges have a central trading location where securities are bought and sold in an auction market. The best known of the organized exchanges is the **New York Stock Exchange** (NYSE). The exchange is on the corner of Wall and Broad Streets in New York City. The trading floor, where transactions take place, looks like an armory with a high ceiling and is about half the size of a football field. On the floor of the exchange there is an unbelievable amount of activity as market participants scurry around to transact their business. In most cases, you call your local broker and he or she transmits the order to the floor of the exchange for execution.

Approximately 1550 firms have their stocks listed for trading on the New York Stock Exchange, or *big board* as it is known. Generally, the largest and most prestigious companies such as IBM, AT&T, and Exxon trade on the New York Stock Exchange. To be listed on the exchange, a firm must initially meet such requirements as a minimum of 1.1 million shares publicly held, 2000 shareholders with 100 shares or more, $2.5 million in pretax earnings, and $16 million in tangible assets.[3] Most listed firms greatly exceed the minimum listing requirements. However, if a firm falls below the minimum standards for a number of years, it can be delisted.

The second largest organized exchange is the **American Stock Exchange,** also in New York City. The number of firms listed is approximately half of that on the New York Stock Exchange, and the listing requirements are generally less. The American Stock Exchange is populated by smaller, more aggressive firms such as Chilton Corp., Foodarama Supermarkets, and Forest Labs.

There are also 14 regional stock exchanges such as the Pacific Stock Exchange, the Midwest Stock Exchange, the Boston Stock Exchange, and the Cincinnati Stock Exchange. Most of the regional exchanges came into existence as a vehicle for trading local, lesser known firms. Many of these firms, however, eventually achieved listing on the American Stock Exchange and then the New York Stock Exchange. Also, some firms on the New York Stock Exchange simply choose to dually list their stocks on regional exchanges to increase trading volume. The Pacific Stock Exchange is used by some investors and brokers because it stays open later than the New York Stock Exchange due to the time differential between the west and east coasts.

Over-the-Counter Trading

Up until now, we have been talking about organized exchanges that have a central location for transacting orders. The **over-the-counter** (OTC) market does

[3] For a more complete listing of requirements, see the *NYSE Fact Book* published by the New York Stock Exchange.

not have a specific location but is a national network of telephone and computer devices that can be used to transact orders. The over-the-counter market is linked together by the National Association of Security Dealers Automated Quotation System, or **NASDAQ.** NASDAQ provides up-to-the-minute quotes on over 4000 of the OTC stocks.

The OTC market is considered to be a competitive dealer market in which multiple firms make a ready market in a security. That is, they stand ready to buy and sell the security. These dealers transact with hundreds of other brokers who represent clients. On the organized exchanges (such as the New York Stock Exchange), there is not a competitive multiple dealer system for each stock, but rather only one "specialist" who has exclusive responsibility for making a ready market in a security.

The OTC market has greatly increased in importance in the last decade. Generally, when a firm sells its stock to the public for the first time it will trade in the over-the-counter market.[4] Because the OTC market has no minimal listing requirements as to size or number of shareholders, it is a particularly popular market for smaller firms. If you are of a speculative nature, you may wish to do some of your investing in firms that are trading over the counter.

It would be a mistake, however, to think that all stocks that trade in the over-the-counter market are small or speculative in nature. Some firms prefer to trade in the over-the-counter market because of the previously mentioned competitive dealer system. Also, many banks and insurance companies trade over-the-counter out of tradition. The National Association of Security Dealers estimates that of the many thousands of firms that trade over the counter as many as 600 could qualify for listing on the New York Stock Exchange and many more on the American Stock Exchange. Examples of prestigious companies that have chosen to remain with over-the-counter trading are MCI Communications, Apple Computer, and Intel Corp.

In order to get a better feel for the various markets, look at the excerpt from the April 10, 1986, issue of the *Wall Street Journal* in Figure 12.4. The quotes are for the previous day's trading. The Stock Market Data Bank always appears on the next to last page of the *Journal.* At the top of the table are various market averages. We will discuss these in more detail later in the chapter, but for now observe that the New York Stock Exchange has its own indexes of performance as does the over-the-counter market in the form of NASDAQ values. The American Stock Exchange is represented under "others" as the AMEX. For now, it is enough to see that most of the indexes were up on April 9, 1986. (You may wish to note a few exceptions; for example, it was not a particularly good day for transportation stocks.)

In the bottom half of Figure 12.4 is a listing of the most active issues on the New York Stock Exchange (NYSE), the over-the-counter market (NASDAQ), and the American Stock Exchange (AMEX). The "close" column gives the ending

[4] Very large firms may go directly to the New York Stock Exchange. A recent example is Morgan Stanley in 1986.

Figure 12.4 MARKET AND INDEX DATA FROM THE *WALL STREET JOURNAL*

STOCK MARKET DATA BANK — April 9, 1986

Major Indexes

HIGH	LOW	(12 MOS)	CLOSE	NET CH	% CH	12 MO CH	%	FROM 12/31	%
DOW JONES AVERAGES									
1821.72	1242.05	30 Industrials	1778.62	+ 8.86	+ 0.50	+ 518.68	+41.17	+ 231.95	+15.00
830.84	571.08	20 Transportations	786.80	− 1.60	− 0.20	+ 193.69	+32.66	+ 78.59	+11.10
193.73	150.08	15 Utilities	x188.60	+ 0.97	+ 0.52	+ 33.70	+21.76	+ 13.79	+ 7.89
718.16	501.79	65 Composite	x696.04	+ 2.23	+ 0.32	+ 183.95	+35.92	+ 79.51	+12.90
NEW YORK STOCK EXCHANGE									
137.71	103.35	Composite	135.03	+ 0.30	+ 0.22	+ 31.04	+29.85	+ 13.45	+11.06
157.43	118.16	Industrials	154.33	+ 0.31	+ 0.20	+ 15.06	+10.81	+ 0.17	+ 0.25
69.66	54.53	Utilities	68.64	+ 0.17	+ 0.25	+ 13.57	+24.64	+ 5.56	+ 8.80
132.54	93.62	Transportation	125.29	− 0.01	− 0.01	+ 28.58	+29.55	+ 11.32	+ 9.93
157.74	107.17	Finance	153.87	+ 0.58	+ 0.38	+ 45.72	+42.27	+ 22.58	+17.20
STANDARD & POOR'S INDEXES									
238.97	178.37	500 Index	233.75	+ 0.23	+ 0.10	+ 54.33	+30.28	+ 22.47	+10.64
263.87	198.32	400 Industrials	258.44	+ 0.22	+ 0.09	+ 58.49	+29.25	+ 23.88	+10.18
217.28	147.43	20 Transportations	205.15	− 0.52	− 0.25	+ 52.55	+34.44	+ 16.43	+ 8.71
105.27	81.46	40 Utilities	102.81	+ 0.12	+ 0.12	+ 22.32	+27.73	+ 9.64	+10.35
31.13	20.45	40 Financials	30.09	+ 0.10	+ 0.33	+ 9.41	+45.50	+ 4.37	+16.99
NASDAQ									
374.72	276.95	OTC Composite	374.16	+ 1.07	+ 0.29	+ 95.40	+34.22	+ 49.23	+15.15
376.10	278.04	Industrials	376.10	+ 1.64	+ 0.44	+ 81.58	+27.70	+ 45.93	+13.91
467.05	323.18	Insurance	439.43	+ 0.36	+ 0.08	+ 116.25	+35.97	+ 57.36	+15.01
404.85	257.00	Banks	403.29	+ 1.20	+ 0.30	+ 146.29	+56.92	+ 53.93	+15.44
159.11	117.06	Nat. Mkt. Comp.	158.81	+ 0.40	+ 0.25	+ 41.38	+35.24	+ 20.55	+14.86
140.67	103.47	Nat. Mkt. Indus.	140.67	+ 0.53	+ 0.38	+ 31.31	+28.63	+ 16.54	+13.32
OTHERS									
270.95	220.70	AMEX	267.85	+ 0.35	+ 0.13	+ 38.18	+16.62	+ 21.72	+ 8.82
1425.9	911.0	Fin. Times Indus.	1376.5	− 11.6	− 0.84	+ 416.2	+43.34	+ 245.1	+21.66
15859.75	12052.82	Nikkei Stock Avg.	15110.18	+96.12	+ 0.64	+2508.25	+19.90	+1996.86	+15.23
242.28	188.61	Value-Line	237.43	+ 0.43	+ 0.18	+ 43.87	+22.66	+ 22.57	+10.50
2455.23	1839.12	Wilshire 5000	2413.59	+ 5.59	+ 0.23	+ 563.77	+30.48	+ 248.90	+11.50

Most Active Issues

NYSE	VOLUME	CLOSE		CH
WlkrHRes	5,399,100	26⅛	+	⅛
ReynldInd	2,314,200	44⅜	+	3⅝
JohnsJn	2,288,600	58⅜	+	2¾
Genstar	2,216,700	40	+	1¼
Amer T&T	2,135,700	22⅛	−	⅛
Disney	1,906,600	39¾	+	1¾
NatGypsum	1,895,000	57¼	+	2¼
IBM	1,654,400	149¼	−	2¾
PhilipMorr	1,586,900	124	+	9
USWest	1,474,000	99¼	−	¼
K mart	1,422,600	44⅞	−	¼
Mobil	1,226,300	29⅛	−	½
PanAm	1,225,500	7	−	¼
EastKodk	1,202,400	59¼	−	⅛
DetEdison	1,161,600	18⅞	+	½

NASDAQ	VOLUME	CLOSE		CH
GlaxoHold	1,889,100	15¼	+	¼
Quotron	1,291,200	19	+	⅛
Jaguar	1,144,500	$6\frac{23}{32}$	−	$\frac{11}{32}$
MCI Comm	1,091,700	11	−	⅜
SafgdHlth	905,900	7¾	−	2
Diasonic	868,400	4⅝	−	$\frac{1}{16}$
ApldComm	748,000	26¼	+	8¼

AMEX	VOLUME	CLOSE		CH
Wickes	8,480,400	6½	−	¼
BAT Ind	4,051,900	$5\frac{15}{16}$	+	½
TurnrBdcst pf	821,000	7⅜	+	¼
SFN pfA	638,900	7⅞	−	⅛
Wickes pf	526,400	40¼	+	1¼
JohnstwnAm	480,100	6⅞	+	⅝
WangLabB	463,300	17⅞	−	⅜

Diaries

NYSE	WED	TUE	WK AGO
Issues traded	2,066	2,048	2,046
Advances	990	1,392	748
Declines	688	330	899
Unchanged	388	326	399
New highs	137	88	99
New lows	7	4	13
Adv Vol (000)	83,365	113,673	68,655
Decl Vol (000)	56,983	22,029	58,143
Total Vol (000)	156,250	146,290	145,300
Block trades	2,927	2,811	2,785
NASDAQ			
Issues traded	4,186	4,185	4,179
Advances	1,095	1,270	933
Declines	897	735	1,093
Unchanged	2,194	2,180	2,153
New highs	191	150	186
New lows	53	71	95
Adv Vol (000)	52,949	64,417	44,095
Decl Vol (000)	40,611	18,467	34,531
Total Vol (000)	130,963	117,945	119,918
Block trades	1,753	1,722	1,521
AMEX			
Issues traded	853	856	841
Advances	324	422	299
Declines	293	217	322
Unchanged	236	217	220
New highs	45	47	43
New lows	6	7	13
Adv Vol (000)	12,863	9,739	4,036
Decl Vol (000)	4,860	3,306	4,117
Total Vol (000)	19,270	15,650	10,630
CompVol (000)	26,521	18,664	12,141
Block trades	241	203	165

price on April 9, 1986. As you can see, firms on the NASDAQ and AMEX generally trade in lower dollar values than NYSE firms. The "diaries" section (lower right-hand side) also shows how many stocks advanced or declined or made new highs or lows on that market for the day.[5] For example, on the AMEX, of the 853 issues traded on Wednesday, 324 stocks advanced, 293 declined, and 236 were unchanged. There were 45 new highs and 6 new lows.

In Figure 12.5, you see additional market data on gainers and losers for individual stocks on each of the markets. Look at the OTC market listing. If you owned ApldComm (Applied Communications), which specializes in electronic funds transfer for the banking industry, you enjoyed a *one-day* gain in value of 8¼ points, or 45.8 percent. If your money were invested in a 7 percent savings account, it would take you 5½ years of compounded growth to match that one-day return. Keep in mind, however, that stock investments can be a two-edged sword, and you can lose your money just as quickly as you made it.

In discussing the various security markets in this section, we have primarily directed our attention to common stock. Many other securities, such as bonds, preferred stock, options, and warrants also trade in these markets. For example, U.S. government bonds are far and away the largest dollar volume producer in the over-the-counter market.

MAKING AN INVESTMENT DECISION

When making an investment decision related to common stocks, you must first of all consider your financial goals or objectives. This, of course, is true of all investment decisions. Once the objectives are determined, then the investment mix can be tailored to meet them.

Fundamental Analysis

In selecting common stocks, you normally will go through a three-step decision process called **fundamental analysis.** First, you must make an overall assessment of the economy. This would include a consideration of the outlook for inflation, interest rates, and a number of other variables. For the sophisticated investor, an in-depth analysis based on Department of Commerce or Federal Reserve data might be appropriate. For the typical investor, a daily reading of the business section of the local paper or the *Wall Street Journal* normally will suffice.

Once you have established some assumptions about the economy, the next step is to determine an appropriate industry for investment. Some industries do better in different phases of the business cycle than others. In the early stages of recovery from a recession, interest rates tend to be low and interest-sensitive

[5] The number of issues on the NYSE is greater than 1550 because many firms have preferred stock as well as common stock trading on the NYSE.

Figure 12.5 ADDITIONAL MARKET DATA ON GAINERS AND LOSERS

Percentage Gainers . . . and Losers

NYSE	CLOSE	CH	% CH		CLOSE	CH	% CH
RdgBat adj pf	11½	+ 2¼	+ 24.3	GalvstHou	2¼	− ¼	− 10.0
SauveShoe	7¾	+ ⅞	+ 12.7	vjGlobMr pf	3⅜	− ¼	− 6.9
KoreaFd	25⅜	+ 2⅜	+ 10.2	FtCityInd	7½	− ½	− 6.3
GoldnNug wt	2¾	+ ¼	+ 10.0	KanebSvc	3¾	− ¼	− 6.3
ReynldInd	44⅜	+ 3⅝	+ 8.9	Quanex	7½	− ½	− 6.3
GenlDevl wt	8⅝	+ ⅝	+ 7.8	UnivarCp	11¾	− ¾	− 6.0
PhilipMorr	124	+ 9	+ 7.8	UnitDrill	2	− ⅛	− 5.9
PublickInd	3½	+ ¼	+ 7.7	ArmcoInc	9⅜	− ½	− 5.1
RLC	10½	+ ¾	+ 7.7	Comdisco	20¾	− 1⅛	− 5.1
EntexInc	19⅜	+ 1⅜	+ 7.6	TranscnInc	9⅜	− ½	− 5.1
CannonGp	41¼	+ 2⅞	+ 7.5	McLean wt	2⅜	− ⅛	− 5.0
ClairesStr	10⅞	+ ¾	+ 7.4	Harsco	24¼	− 1¼	− 4.9
NatEduc	29½	+ 2	+ 7.3	GtAtlPac	22¼	− 1⅛	− 4.8
PhilipMor wi	61¾	+ 4⅛	+ 7.2	Coleco	17¾	− ⅞	− 4.7
GenRefrac	13¾	+ ⅞	+ 6.8	SunChem	47⅞	− 2⅜	− 4.7
OhEd adj pf	41	+ 2⅝	+ 6.8	SagaCp	28½	− 1⅜	− 4.6
MB Ltd	21⅞	+ 1⅜	+ 6.7	Paradyne	7⅞	− ⅜	− 4.5
OTC							
MacroChm wt	3½	+ 1¼	+ 55.6	SafgdHlth	7¾	− 2	− 20.5
ApldComm	26¼	+ 8¼	+ 45.8	StrikerPtrl	2	− ½	− 20.0
AdvNmr wt	5	+ 1⅜	+ 37.9	MagellnPetrol	2	− 7/16	− 17.9
MacroChem	6	+ 1⅝	+ 37.1	Compusve pf	2½	− ½	− 16.7
AllyGargan	12¼	+ 3	+ 32.4	IndBnchInc	4	− ¾	− 15.8
MacroChm un	14½	+ 3½	+ 31.8	RadiatnDisp	9	− 1⅜	− 13.3
LaserMedic	2⅝	+ ⅝	+ 31.3	FstComlBcp	5⅞	− ⅞	− 13.0
HstnOil pf	3	+ ⅝	+ 26.3	Comptek	6¾	− 1	− 12.9
SpartanMot	3⅜	+ ⅝	+ 22.7	Copytele	7¾	− 1⅛	− 12.7
LasrMd un	2⅞	+ ½	+ 21.1	Bluerid un	14½	− 2	− 12.1
NmrCenters	3⅝	+ ⅝	+ 20.8	PaternProc	4¾	− ⅝	− 11.6
LeisureConcpt	17¾	+ 3	+ 20.3	CongresVd wt	2	− ¼	− 11.1
AMEX							
Vicon	5½	+ ⅝	+ 12.8	Halmi wt	2½	− ⅜	− 13.0
SwiftEngy	2¼	+ ¼	+ 12.5	ConsEnPart	2⅝	− ⅜	− 12.5
ActonCp	2⅜	+ ¼	+ 11.8	PicoProd	2⅝	− ⅜	− 12.5
JohnstwnAm	6⅞	+ ⅝	+ 10.0	Enstar pf	2	− ¼	− 11.1
SCI Lsg	15½	+ 1¼	+ 8.8	GrahamMccor	2⅜	− ¼	− 9.5
DeroseInd	5	+ ⅜	+ 8.1	ArmelInc	6⅛	− ⅝	− 9.3
BatInd	5⅞	+ 7/16	+ 8.0	Fidata	6¼	− ⅝	− 9.1
PopeEvan	3½	+ ¼	+ 7.7	CMI Corp	7	− ⅝	− 8.2
WienerEntr	12¾	+ ⅞	+ 7.4	PetLew pfC	4½	− ⅜	− 7.7
HealthChm	11⅛	+ ¾	+ 7.2	Vertipile	4⅞	− ⅜	− 7.1
HeritEntmnt	11⅛	+ ¾	+ 7.2	Courtaulds	4⅛	− 5/16	− 7.0
MtgeRty wt	3⅞	+ ¼	+ 6.9	NuclrData	5⅛	− ⅜	− 6.8

SOURCE: Reprinted by permission of the *Wall Street Journal*, © Dow Jones & Company, Inc., April 10, 1986, p. 49. All rights reserved.

stocks should perform well. Examples of such stocks are savings and loans, public utilities, and home-building firms. In the intermediate stages of the business cycle, consumer-oriented firms often exhibit strength, so the investor may look to clothing, travel, publishing, and so on. In the later stages of the business cycle, firms involved in capital investment activities might do well. Such firms

Figure 12.6 **RELATING INDUSTRIES TO VARIOUS PHASES OF THE BUSINESS CYCLE FOR INVESTMENT**

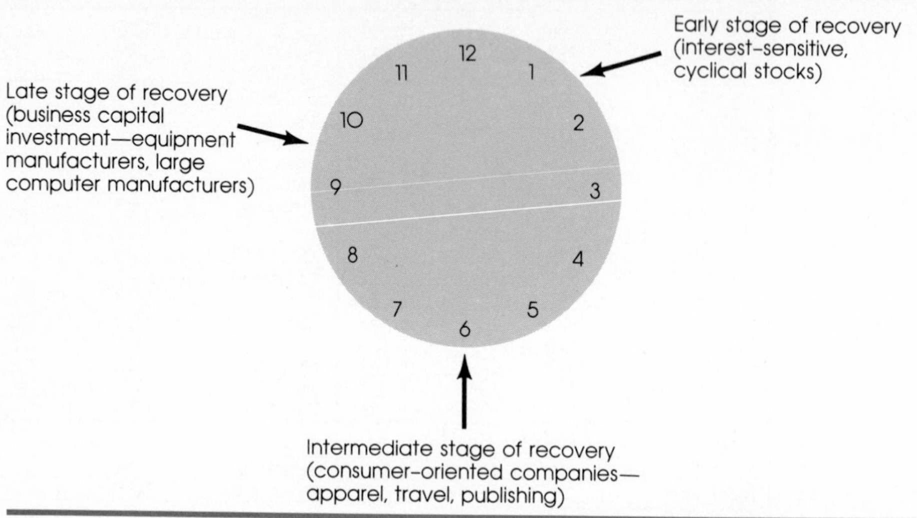

include manufacturers of heavy equipment, computers, and other large-ticket items. The astute investor tries to read the changes in the business cycle (and related investments) like hands on a clock, as indicated in Figure 12.6.

Of course, Figure 12.6 merely represents an indication of general patterns. Every business cycle has its own unique features. You may also wish to look at such publications as the ***Value Line Investment Survey*** to determine what industries are in favor or disfavor. *Value Line* ranks 91 different industries for probable performance over the next 12 months. *Value Line* is one of the most widely distributed business advisory services and can be found in most public libraries and in many university libraries. An illustration of the May 16, 1986, *Value Line* industry rankings is presented in Figure 12.7. The rankings directly follow the industry classification and are enclosed in parentheses. A new ranking comes out weekly, so you may wish to consult a more recent *Value Line*.

The Standard & Poor's Corporation also does an excellent job of providing in-depth industry data through a publication called *Standard & Poor's Industry Surveys*. In this material, you will find a 10 to 15 page write-up on major industries, such as computers and automobiles, with more data than you could possibly hope to absorb. There is a description of major trends in the industry, with historical financial data, as well as information on key firms in the industry. Many public and university libraries carry Standard & Poor's data. It may be worth your while to ask your librarian about the nearest source.

We must point out that some industries are attractive because they are *not* subject to the whims of the business cycle. Their products are sufficiently necessary or accepted so as not to be influenced by changing business condi-

Figure 12.7 *VALUE LINE* INDUSTRY RANKINGS

ANALYSES OF INDUSTRIES IN ALPHABETICAL ORDER WITH PAGE NUMBER

Numeral in parenthesis after the industry is rank for probable performance (next 12 months).

	PAGE		PAGE		PAGE		PAGE
Advertising (62)	1821	Computer Software & Serv.(3)	2108	*Insurance-Life (7)	1196	Petroleum-Producing (92)	1830
Aerospace/Defense (64)	551	*Copper (52)	1216	Insurance-Prop./Cas. (56)	635	Precision Instrument (65)	151
Agric. Equip./Diversified (85)	1432	Distilling/Tobacco (24)	336	Investment Company (47)	2006	Publishing (20)	1786
Air Transport (86)	251	*Drug Industry (4)	1250	Japanese Diversified (16)	1563	Railroad/Resources (75)	305
*Aluminum (22)	1216	Drugstore (60)	784	Machinery (53)	1301	Real Estate (50)	673
Apparel (9)	1601	Electrical Equipment (46)	1001	Machinery-Const. (69)	1356	*REIT (80)	1169
Auto & Truck (33)	101	Electric Utility-Cent. (54)	1140,701	Machine Tool (57)	1345	Recreation (27)	1751
Auto Parts-OEM (10)	801	Electric Utility-East (45)	178	Manu.Housing/Rec.Veh. (13)	1551	Restaurant (72)	316
Auto Parts-Replacement (74)	113	Electric Utility-West (67)	1718	Maritime (73)	294	Retail-Special Lines (41)	1688
Bank (6)	2001	Electronics (79)	1029	*Medical Services (68)	1272	Retail Store (37)	1634
Bank (Midwest) (15)	650	European Diversified (17)	826	Medical Supplies (5)	214	*Savings & Loan (1)	1907, 1151
Bank (Southwest) (91)	666	Financial Services (8)	2049	Metal Fabricating (58)	588	*Securities Brokerage (2)	1184
Brewing/Soft Drink (11)	1540	Food Processing (26)	1451	*Metals & Mining-Gen'l (48)	1216	Semiconductor (82)	1069
Broadcasting/Cable TV (77)	373	Food Wholesalers (23)	1530	Metals & Mining-Ind'l (71)	622	Shoe (61)	1674
Building (32)	851	Furn./Home Furnishings(43)	913	Multiform (66)	1376	*Silver (89)	1216
Building Supplies (25)	895	*Gold/Diamond (S.A.) (—)	1208	Natural Gas (Diversified)(88)	448	Steel-General (29)	609
Canadian Energy (87)	431	*Gold (No. American) (84)	1216	Natural Gas (Utility)(76)	469	Steel-Integrated (70)	1420
Cement (78)	903	Grocery (39)	1505	Newspaper (36)	1809	Steel-Specialty (83)	2102
*Chemical-Basic (12)	1240	Home Appliance (14)	139	Office Equip. & Supplies(49)	1121	Telecommunications (59)	751
Chemical-Diversified (40)	1889	Hotel/Gaming (30)	1771	Oilfield Services (90)	1850	Textile (19)	1622
Chemical-Specialty (31)	503	Household Products (28)	974	Packaging & Cont. (34)	953	Tire & Rubber (63)	127
Coal/Uran./Geothermal (42)	1879	Industrial Services (18)	347	Paper & Forest Prods. (55)	925	Toiletries/Cosmetics (21)	813
Computer & Peripherals (44)	1082	Insurance-Diversified (38)	2067	Petroleum-Integrated (81)	401	Toys & School Supplies (51)	793
						Trucking/Trans Lease (35)	277

*Reviewed in this week's edition.

SOURCE: *The Value Line Investment Survey,* May 16, 1986, p. 1. © 1986 Value Line, Inc.

tions. Can you think of any such industries? Examples might be health care products, food, and soft drinks.

After you have considered information about the economy and industry, you will take the third step of fundamental analysis: evaluating data on individual companies. Let's assume your interest is in the apparel industry. You could go to a source such as *Value Line* and identify the 10 leading firms in the industry. If one of your choices was Liz Claiborne, a maker of women's sportswear and dresses, you would see financial data such as those shown in Figure 12.8. Although the financial data are much more detailed than the typical reader would need, there is also general information that is useful to any investor. Note that in the box about one inch below the upper right-hand margin, there is information on timeliness and safety. A firm can score anywhere from 1 to 5; the lower the score, the stronger the evaluation. With a timeliness ranking of 2 on March 7, 1986, Liz Claiborne was thought to have above-average prospects for market performance over the next 12 months. The safety rating of 3 indicates that there is average risk associated with the firm.[6] *Value Line* has similar information on 1700 other companies.

Another, more broad-based source of information on over 10,000 companies

[6] The more sophisticated reader may observe that the firm has a beta of 1.30. This means that the returns on the firm's stock are 30 percent more volatile than the market.

Figure 12.8 *VALUE LINE* ANALYSIS OF AN INDIVIDUAL FIRM

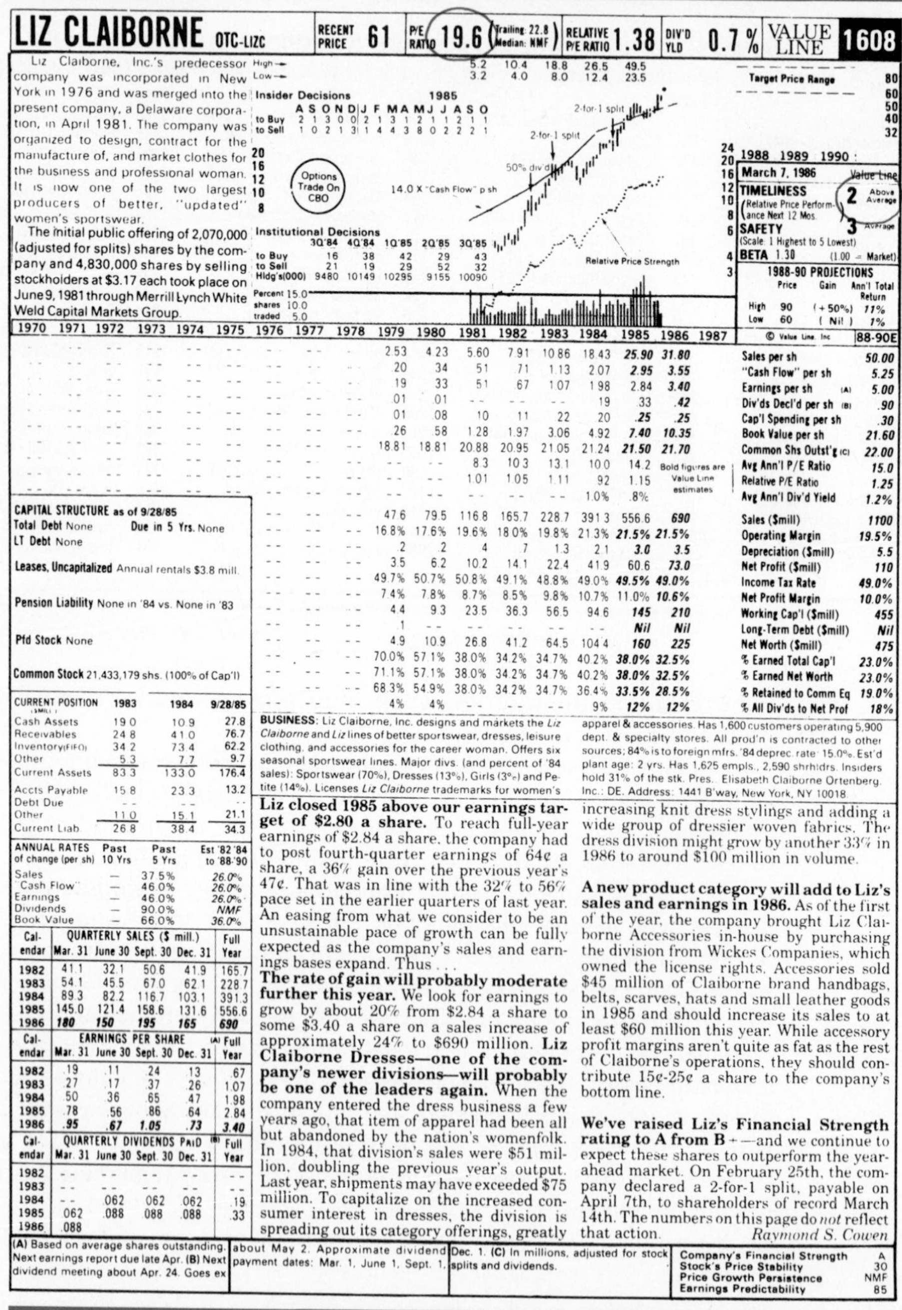

LIZ CLAIBORNE OTC-LIZC | RECENT PRICE 61 | P/E RATIO 19.6 (Trailing: 22.8 / Median: NMF) | RELATIVE P/E RATIO 1.38 | DIV'D YLD 0.7% | VALUE LINE 1608

Liz Claiborne, Inc.'s predecessor company was incorporated in New York in 1976 and was merged into the present company, a Delaware corporation, in April 1981. The company was organized to design, contract for the manufacture of, and market clothes for the business and professional woman. It is now one of the two largest producers of better, "updated" women's sportswear.

The initial public offering of 2,070,000 (adjusted for splits) shares by the company and 4,830,000 shares by selling stockholders at $3.17 each took place on June 9, 1981 through Merrill Lynch White Weld Capital Markets Group.

	1981	1982	1983	1984	1985
High	5.2	10.4	18.8	26.5	49.5
Low	3.2	4.0	8.0	12.4	23.5

Insider Decisions

	A	S	O	N	D	J	F	M	A	M	J	J	A	S	O
						1985									
to Buy	2	1	3	0	0	2	1	3	1	2	1	1	2	1	1
to Sell	1	0	2	1	3	1	4	4	3	8	0	2	2	2	1

Institutional Decisions

	3Q'84	4Q'84	1Q'85	2Q'85	3Q'85
to Buy	16	38	42	29	43
to Sell	21	19	29	52	32
Hldg's(000)	9480	10149	10295	9155	10090

March 7, 1986 — Value Line

TIMELINESS (Relative Price Performance Next 12 Mos.) 2 Above Average

SAFETY (Scale: 1 Highest to 5 Lowest) 3 Average

BETA 1.30 (1.00 = Market)

1988-90 PROJECTIONS

	Price	Gain	Ann'l Total Return
High	90	(+50%)	11%
Low	60	(Nil)	1%

1970	1971	1972	1973	1974	1975	1976	1977	1978	1979	1980	1981	1982	1983	1984	1985	1986	1987	© Value Line, Inc.	88-90E
--	--	--	--	--	--	--	--	--	2.53	4.23	5.60	7.91	10.86	18.43	**25.90**	**31.80**		Sales per sh	50.00
--	--	--	--	--	--	--	--	--	.20	.34	.51	.71	1.13	2.07	**2.95**	**3.55**		"Cash Flow" per sh	5.25
--	--	--	--	--	--	--	--	--	.19	.33	.51	.67	1.07	1.98	2.84	**3.40**		Earnings per sh (A)	5.00
--	--	--	--	--	--	--	--	--	.01	.01	--	--	--	.19	.33	**.42**		Div'ds Decl'd per sh (B)	.90
--	--	--	--	--	--	--	--	--	.01	.08	.10	.11	.22	.20	**.25**	**.25**		Cap'l Spending per sh	.30
--	--	--	--	--	--	--	--	--	.26	.58	1.28	1.97	3.06	4.92	**7.40**	**10.35**		Book Value per sh	21.60
--	--	--	--	--	--	--	--	--	18.81	18.81	20.88	20.95	21.05	21.24	**21.50**	**21.70**		Common Shs Outst'g (C)	22.00
--	--	--	--	--	--	--	--	--	--	--	8.3	10.3	13.1	10.0	14.2	Bold figures are Value Line estimates		Avg Ann'l P/E Ratio	15.0
--	--	--	--	--	--	--	--	--	--	--	1.01	1.05	1.11	.92	1.15			Relative P/E Ratio	1.25
--	--	--	--	--	--	--	--	--	--	--	--	--	--	1.0%	.8%			Avg Ann'l Div'd Yield	1.2%
						--	--	--	47.6	79.5	116.8	165.7	228.7	391.3	556.6	**690**		Sales ($mill)	1100
						--	--	--	16.8%	17.6%	19.6%	18.0%	19.8%	21.3%	**21.5%**	**21.5%**		Operating Margin	19.5%
						--	--	--	.2	.2	.4	.7	1.3	2.1	**3.0**	**3.5**		Depreciation ($mill)	5.5
						--	--	--	3.5	6.2	10.2	14.1	22.4	41.9	60.6	**73.0**		Net Profit ($mill)	110
						--	--	--	49.7%	50.7%	50.8%	49.1%	48.8%	49.0%	**49.5%**	**49.0%**		Income Tax Rate	49.0%
						--	--	--	7.4%	7.8%	8.7%	8.5%	9.8%	10.7%	11.0%	**10.6%**		Net Profit Margin	10.0%
						--	--	--	4.4	9.3	23.5	36.3	56.5	94.6	**145**	**210**		Working Cap'l ($mill)	455
						--	--	--	.1	--	--	--	--	--	**Nil**	**Nil**		Long-Term Debt ($mill)	Nil
						--	--	--	4.9	10.9	26.8	41.2	64.5	104.4	**160**	**225**		Net Worth ($mill)	475
						--	--	--	70.0%	57.1%	38.0%	34.2%	34.7%	40.2%	**38.0%**	**32.5%**		% Earned Total Cap'l	23.0%
						--	--	--	71.1%	57.1%	38.0%	34.2%	34.7%	40.2%	**38.0%**	**32.5%**		% Earned Net Worth	23.0%
						--	--	--	68.3%	54.9%	38.0%	34.2%	34.7%	36.4%	**33.5%**	**28.5%**		% Retained to Comm Eq	19.0%
						--	--	--	4%	4%	--	--	--	9%	**12%**	**12%**		% All Div'ds to Net Prof	18%

CAPITAL STRUCTURE as of 9/28/85

Total Debt None **Due in 5 Yrs.** None

LT Debt None

Leases, Uncapitalized Annual rentals $3.8 mill.

Pension Liability None in '84 vs. None in '83

Pfd Stock None

Common Stock 21,433,179 shs. (100% of Cap'l)

CURRENT POSITION ($MILL.)	1983	1984	9/28/85
Cash Assets	19.0	10.9	27.8
Receivables	24.8	41.0	76.7
Inventory(FIFO)	34.2	73.4	62.2
Other	5.3	7.7	9.7
Current Assets	83.3	133.0	176.4
Accts Payable	15.8	23.3	13.2
Debt Due	--	--	--
Other	11.0	15.1	21.1
Current Liab.	26.8	38.4	34.3

ANNUAL RATES of change (per sh)	Past 10 Yrs	Past 5 Yrs	Est '82-'84 to '88-'90
Sales	—	37.5%	26.0%
"Cash Flow"	—	46.0%	26.0%
Earnings	—	46.0%	26.0%
Dividends	—	90.0%	NMF
Book Value	—	66.0%	36.0%

Calendar	QUARTERLY SALES ($ mill.) Mar. 31	June 30	Sept. 30	Dec. 31	Full Year
1982	41.1	32.1	50.6	41.9	165.7
1983	54.1	45.5	67.0	62.1	228.7
1984	89.3	82.2	116.7	103.1	391.3
1985	145.0	121.4	158.6	131.6	556.6
1986	**180**	**150**	**195**	**165**	**690**

Calendar	EARNINGS PER SHARE (A) Mar. 31	June 30	Sept. 30	Dec. 31	Full Year
1982	.19	.11	.24	.13	.67
1983	.27	.17	.37	.26	1.07
1984	.50	.36	.65	.47	1.98
1985	.78	.56	.86	.64	2.84
1986	**.95**	**.67**	**1.05**	**.73**	**3.40**

Calendar	QUARTERLY DIVIDENDS PAID (B) Mar. 31	June 30	Sept. 30	Dec. 31	Full Year
1982	--	--	--	--	--
1983	--	--	--	--	--
1984	--	.062	.062	.062	.19
1985	.062	.088	.088	.088	.33
1986	.088				

BUSINESS: Liz Claiborne, Inc. designs and markets the *Liz Claiborne* and *Liz* lines of better sportswear, dresses, leisure clothing, and accessories for the career woman. Offers six seasonal sportswear lines. Major divs. (and percent of '84 sales): Sportswear (70%), Dresses (13%), Girls (3%) and Petite (14%). Licenses *Liz Claiborne* trademarks for women's apparel & accessories. Has 1,600 customers operating 5,900 dept. & specialty stores. All prod'n is contracted to other sources; 84% is to foreign mfrs. '84 deprec. rate: 15.0%. Est'd plant age: 2 yrs. Has 1,625 empls., 2,590 shrhldrs. Insiders hold 31% of the stk. Pres.: Elisabeth Claiborne Ortenberg. Inc.: DE. Address: 1441 B'way, New York, NY 10018.

Liz closed 1985 above our earnings target of $2.80 a share. To reach full-year earnings of $2.84 a share, the company had to post fourth-quarter earnings of 64¢ a share, a 36% gain over the previous year's 47¢. That was in line with the 32% to 56% pace set in the earlier quarters of last year. An easing from what we consider to be an unsustainable pace of growth can be fully expected as the company's sales and earnings bases expand. Thus . . .

The rate of gain will probably moderate further this year. We look for earnings to grow by about 20% from $2.84 a share to some $3.40 a share on a sales increase of approximately 24% to $690 million. **Liz Claiborne Dresses—one of the company's newer divisions—will probably be one of the leaders again.** When the company entered the dress business a few years ago, that item of apparel had been all but abandoned by the nation's womenfolk. In 1984, that division's sales were $51 million, doubling the previous year's output. Last year, shipments may have exceeded $75 million. To capitalize on the increased consumer interest in dresses, the division is spreading out its category offerings, greatly increasing knit dress stylings and adding a wide group of dressier woven fabrics. The dress division might grow by another 33% in 1986 to around $100 million in volume.

A new product category will add to Liz's sales and earnings in 1986. As of the first of the year, the company brought Liz Claiborne Accessories in-house by purchasing the division from Wickes Companies, which owned the license rights. Accessories sold $45 million of Claiborne brand handbags, belts, scarves, hats and small leather goods in 1985 and should increase its sales to at least $60 million this year. While accessory profit margins aren't quite as fat as the rest of Claiborne's operations, they should contribute 15¢-25¢ a share to the company's bottom line.

We've raised Liz's Financial Strength rating to A from B+—and we continue to expect these shares to outperform the year-ahead market. On February 25th, the company declared a 2-for-1 split, payable on April 7th, to shareholders of record March 14th. The numbers on this page do *not* reflect that action.

Raymond S. Cowen

(A) Based on average shares outstanding. Next earnings report due late Apr. (B) Next dividend meeting about Apr. 24. Goes ex about May 2. Approximate dividend payment dates: Mar. 1, June 1, Sept. 1, Dec. 1. (C) In millions, adjusted for stock splits and dividends.

Company's Financial Strength	A
Stock's Price Stability	30
Price Growth Persistence	NMF
Earnings Predictability	85

SOURCE: *The Value Line Investment Survey*, March 7, 1986, p. 1608. © 1986 Value Line, Inc.

Figure 12.9 EXCERPT FROM *STANDARD & POOR'S STOCK GUIDE*

140 **Mar-McG** Standard & Poor's Corporation

¶S&P 500 •Options Index	Ticker Symbol	Name of Issue (Call Price of Pfd. Stocks)	Market	Com. Rank. & Pfd. Rating	Par Val.	Inst. Hold Cos	Inst. Hold Shs. (000)	Principal Business	Price Range 1971-84 High	1971-84 Low	1985 High	1985 Low	1986 High	1986 Low	Mar. Sales in 100s	March, 1986 Last Sale Or Bid High	Low	Last	%Div. Yield	P-E Ratio
1	MDNT	**Maryland National**	OTC	A	2½	125	10207	Bank hldg:Maryland	22⅛	5¼	37¼	21½	46⅝	34¾	10509	46⅝	41⅞	45⅛B	2.2	11
¶2	MAS	**Masco Corp**	NY,B,M	A	1	287	29366	Bldg & home improv't prod	37	4¾	42⅜	26	60½	39	34506	60½	50⅝	57⅞	1.1	23
3	MASX	**Masco Industries**	OTC	NR	1	39	1456	Mfr oil field/ind'l prod	9⅝	5⅞	26½	9⅛	30¼	17¾	7262	30¼	24	30B	...	..
4	MLD	**Masland (CH)& Sons**	AS	B—	1⅔	8	296	Carpeting for home/auto	20⅝	3¾	24⅜	10½	32½	23¾	585	32½	29⅜	32½	†1.2	9
5	MSCP	**Massachusetts Computer**	OTC	NR	1¢	27	3329	Computers for science/eng'g	16⅞	7½	12½	4⅜	8¼	5⅛	9694	8¼	5¾	8B	...	d
¶6	MSE	**Massey-Ferguson Ltd**	[1]NY,B,M,P,Ph	C	No	40	27607	Farm & ind'l mchy:engines	32¼	1⅝	3½	1⅞	2½	1¾	140172	2½	1¾	1⅞	...	d
7	MCI	**MassMutual Corp Inv**	NY,M	NR	1	12	795	Closed-end mgmt invest co	25⅜	11¼	31	24⅞	36¼	30½	997	36¼	33¼	34⅛	8.8	..
8	MIV	**MassMutual Inc Inv**	NY,M	NR	1	10	72	Closed-end mgmt invest co	15	8⅜	13	10⅞	13⅛	12⅜	1624	13⅛	12½	12⅞	†9.8	..
9	MSCO	**MASSTOR Systems**	OTC	NR	No	34	2245	Mkts on-line data strge sys	30¼	2⅛	6¾	1¼	2½	1⅜	15530	2⅛	1⅜	1½B	...	d
10	MXC	**MATEC Corp**	AS	B—	5¢	6	199	Mfr electronic comp/systems	8⅞	⅝	7⅝	5	6⅝	4¾	929	6⅝	5⅝	5⅞	...	d
11	MSC	**Material Sciences**	AS,M	NR	2¢	34	1750	Steel coil protective coat'gs	12⅜	8¾	20	9⅝	21⅞	14½	3884	21⅞	17½	21½	...	10
12	MTL	**Materials Research**	AS,P	B—	1	30	1409	Sputtering, zone refining eq	39	⅝	22½	9⅝	14⅝	11⅝	1827	14	11⅝	11⅞	1.0	..
13	MAX	**Matrix Corp**	AS,P	NR	1	68	5635	Imaging instrumentation	20¾	⅛	23⅞	15½	26⅝	19¾	14865	25⅛	19¾	21⅛	...	22
14	MTRX	**Matrix Science**	OTC	B+	1¢	47	2358	Electrical connectors-defense	38¾	13¼	34½	24¼	35½	32⅞	2964	35½	33¾	35¼B	0.3	18
15	MC	**Matsushita El Ind [59]ADR**	NY,B,M,P,Ph	NR	[59]	74	7172	Japan mfr consumer elec eq	80⅝	6½	67½	48½	80⅞	60	22827	80⅞	66	80¼	0.5	12
¶16	MAT	**Mattel, Inc**	NY,B,M,P,Ph	C	1	100	15286	Major mfr of toys	52¼	4¾	17⅛	9⅞	14⅛	10¾	84462	14⅛	10⅞	13⅞	...	14
17	WS	**Wrrt(Purch 1 com at $4)**	NY,Ph,P	...	...	7	702		27⅜	2⅜	13¼	6⅝	9¾	6¾	6707	9¾	6¾	9⅝	..	..
18	MAUI	**Maui Land & Pineapple**	OTC	B—	No	8	434	Canned pineapple: resort	49	5	77½	40	87½	74	38	87½	74	87B	0.6	29
19	MAXC	**Maxco Inc**	OTC	C	1	.3	63	Material handl'g eq: dstr	6⅜	⅜	3¾	2⅛	3½	2⅝	2214	3½	3	3B	...	5
20	MAXI	**Maxicare Health Plans**	OTC	NR	No	141	28162	Health maintenance programs	19⅜	7¾	24¾	13½	22⅞	17⅝	67358	22½	19⅝	22¼B	...	30
21	MXTR	**Maxtor Corp**	OTC	NR	No	27	1850	Mfrs winchester disk drives	...	...	15½	10⅞	20⅜	14⅜	11520	20¼	17⅝	19⅞B	...	20
22	MXM	**MAXXAM Group**	NY,B,M,P,Ph	NR	8⅓¢	36	3132	Real estate mtge loans	58⅞	6⅛	15⅝	10½	20¼	11	7792	20¼	14⅜	18	...	9
23	MXWL	**Maxwell Labs**	OTC	NR	1	13	600	Defense/comm'l electr sys	29¼	6½	15½	8¾	15½	12	1549	14¼	12¾	13½B	...	16
¶24	MA	**May Dept Stores**	NY,B,C,M,P,Ph	A+	1⅔	267	22331	Large department store chain	43⅛	7⅛	65	38⅛	78¼	60	14861	78¼	66	77	2.7	14
25	MEP	**May Energy Partners Ltd[69]**	AS	NR	No	9	18	O&G expl/dev:Okla,La,Tex	24¾	12⅛	16⅜	7	8½	4	2071	5	4	4⅛	9.7	d
26	MAYP	**May Petroleum**	OTC	B—	5¢	22	1847	Oil & gas explor & devel	44	1½	6⅛	2⅜	3⅝	1⅞	15608	2¾	1⅞	2B	...	d
27	MYFRA	**Mayfair Super Mkts Cl'A'**	OTC	B—	1	3	134	'Foodtown'supermkts,N.J	10⅜	⅛	26	6	31	23¼	598	29¾	26½	27⅝B	0.3	11
28	MFL	**Mayflower Corp**	AS	B+	No	47	2504	Moving/storage:transp eq	17	2	26⅞	15⅞	27⅜	19⅝	2964	27⅜	23⅞	27⅛	2.9	14
29	MOIL	**Maynard Oil**	OTC	C	10¢	18	927	Drill'g:oil/gas explor/dev	24¼	1¼	6¼	3½	4¾	3¾	1550	4¼	3¾	3⅞B	...	d
¶30	MYG	**Maytag Co**	NY,B,M,P	A	1.25	172	11984	Home laundry eq:dishwasher	28⅜	8	39⅞	21¾	47¾	36⅞	18148	47¾	40	46½	†3.8	18
31	MBOX	**MBI Business Centers**	OTC	NR	1¢	20	1195	Sells microcomputer sys/prod	12½	8⅜	14¾	6¾	13¾	7½	17448	13¾	10½	13B	...	17
32	MCCRK	**McCormick[71] & Co**	OTC	A—	No	76	5166	Spices. flavoring, tea, mixes	35⅞	10⅜	38⅛	30¾	43⅜	33¾	6479	43⅜	37⅝	41⅝B	2.1	18
¶33•[2]	MDR	**McDermott Int'l**	NY,B,C,M,P,Ph	B—	1	155	22776	Offshore oil & gas constr	46⅝	7⅜	30⅛	16⅜	19⅛	13⅝	111328	19⅛	14½	16⅝	10.8	d
34	WS	**Wrrt(purch 1 com at $25)**	NY,Ph	...	...	15	805	steam gen eqp:tubular goods	12	4⅞	9⅞	2⅜	2¾	1½	7358	2¼	1⅝	1⅝		..
35	MDEPrA	**$2.20cmCvA Pfd([75]32.35)½vtg**	[3]NY	BBB+	1	23	565		47½	17½	31½	21	24	20⅛	1636	24	20⅞	22⅞	9.6	..
36	Pr B	**$2.60 cm B Pfd([76]31.75)½vtg**	[4]NY,M	BBB+	1	3	192		32⅛	16¾	26⅜	20⅝	24	19⅞	953	22½	20⅜	21¾	12.0	..
37	MDD	**McDonald & Co Invest**	NY	NR	1	10	130	Investm't bank'g/brokerage	18⅞	6½	13	7⅛	14½	11¾	2685	14½	12½	14¼	1.4	16
¶38•[1]	MCD	**McDonald's Corp**	NY,B,C,M,P,Ph,To	A+	No	575	55670	Fast food restaurant:franch'g	55⅞	6⅝	81¾	51⅛	98⅜	73	53560	98⅜	88	96⅝	0.9	19
¶39•[1]	MD	**McDonnell Douglas**	NY,B,C,M,P,Ph	†A+	1	237	14158	Jet aircraft: space: missiles	73¾	7⅝	87	64¼	88	72⅛	21430	88	77¾	87⅝	2.4	10
40	ME	**McDowell Enterprises**	AS	C	No	6	150	Asphalt paving:construction	17¾	3½	6⅜	3¼	5⅞	3⅝	214	5½	4½	4¾	...	d
41	MV	**McFaddin Ventures**	AS	NR	10¢	10	656	Operates entertainment clubs	12½	9⅝	12	6	7	4⅜	4896	5¾	4⅝	5	...	8
42	MCFE	**McFarland Energy**	OTC	B	No	25	1274	Oil & gas expl & prod'r	28¾	1½	14⅛	10¼	12¼	8½	1937	10¾	8½	9¾B	...	11
43	MGLL	**McGill Mfg**	OTC	B	No	10	205	Bearings & electrical pr	47	8¾	36	28	35	32	126	34	32	32B	4.4	20
44	MGRC	**McGrath RentCorp**	OTC	NR	No	7	216	Rents/sells modular offices	6½	5½	14¼	5¾	15	11	1382	15	12¾	13¾B	...	17
¶45•[2]	MHP	**McGraw-Hill**	NY,B,M,P,Ph	★	1	316	26441	Books:educ/info svs:publ:TV	53⅞	2¹¹⁄₁₆	52	39¾	62	46½	26038	62	53⅜	59¾	2.5	20
46	Pr	**$1.20 cm Cv Pref (40)vtg**	NY	★	10	1	4	fin'l svs:magazines:film	155	12¾	139¾	126¾	181½	181½	1	181½	181½	197⅛B	0.6	..

Uniform Footnote Explanations—See Page 1. Other: [1]Mo,To. [2]Ph:Cycle 2. [3]M,Ph. [4]Ph. [5]CBOE:Cycle 3. [6]P:Cycle 2. [51]®$3.86,'86. [52]△$0.28,'82. [53]□$1.12,'81. [54]11 Mo Jun,'82. [55]Accum on Pfd. [56]Fiscal Oct'81 & prior. [57]12 Mo Jan'83:Fiscal Oct'82,d$8.95. [58]Fiscal Aug'85 & prior:12 Mo Jul'85 earned $0.80. [59]Each ADR equal 10 com yen 50 par. [60]®$6.63,'85. [61]Fiscal Jan'84 & prior. [62]△$1.05,'81. [63]△$0.04,'83. [64]△$0.04,'84. [65]Fiscal Jan 82 & prior. [66]®$0.71,'85. [67]□$0.09,'82. [68]△$0.03,'83. [69]Units Ltd Partnership int. [70]Return of capital. [71]Non-vtg. [72]△$0.30,'81. [73]△$0.18,'82. [74]Subsid Pfd in M$. [75]To 3-30-87,scale to $31¼ in'89. [76]To 3-30-86,scale to $31¼ in'87. [77]□$0.21,'82. [78]□$0.03,'84. [79]®$0.63,'84.
★S&P is a sub. of McGraw-Hill; common not ranked, pfd not rated.

SOURCE: *Standard & Poor's Stock Guide*, April 1986, p. 140.

is the *Standard & Poor's Stock Guide*. The guide can be found at most public libraries. An excerpt from the stock guide is presented in Figure 12.9.

After you have identified a company in which you have an interest, you may wish to write or call the company to request a copy of their annual report or other corporate information. You may also look up the firm in the *Wall Street Journal Index* to find out what stories about the firm have appeared in prior *Journals*. Many libraries keep old *Wall Street Journals* on microfilm. Also, you may call a local stockbroker to see if his or her firm has done a report on the company or if he or she has an opinion on the company.

As we pointed out earlier, most investors are quite interested in the firm's price-earnings (P-E) ratio. The average P-E ratio for firms trading on the New York Stock Exchange was 14.8 in March 1986. How would a firm such as Liz Claiborne, which was presented in Figure 12.8, stack up against this norm? If you look across the top of Figure 12.8, you see that Liz Claiborne had a P-E ratio of 19.6. This means that investors were willing to pay more for this firm's earnings than for a typical company's earnings. Why? First of all, Liz Claiborne was considered to be one of the stronger companies in the women's fashionwear industry. It was also thought to have strong management, and the prospects for a 20 percent growth in earnings per share (on top of a 43 percent growth in the prior year). Whether a company lives up to the expectations indicated by a high P-E ratio can only be determined over time. Some firms with high P-E ratios justify investors' expectations, while others do not. It is interesting to note that a number of other firms in the apparel industry have lower P-E ratios (and probably more modest expectations), as indicated in Table 12.1.

As an exercise at the end of the chapter, you will be asked to compare the price performance of high and low P-E ratio stocks in the apparel industry from the date in Table 12.1 until now.

Technical Analysis

Another form of analysis that is quite different from the three-stage fundamental analysis in the previous section is called **technical analysis.** Technical analysts choose to ignore basic fundamental data related to a company's actual operating performance (earnings, growth, new products, quality of management), and concentrate on charts and graphs related to the firm's stock market performance. Technical analysts examine prior price and volume data, as well as other market-related indicators, in the hope of projecting past trends into the future.

An example of the use of technical analysis can be seen in Figure 12.10.

Figure 12.10 AN EXAMPLE OF TECHNICAL ANALYSIS

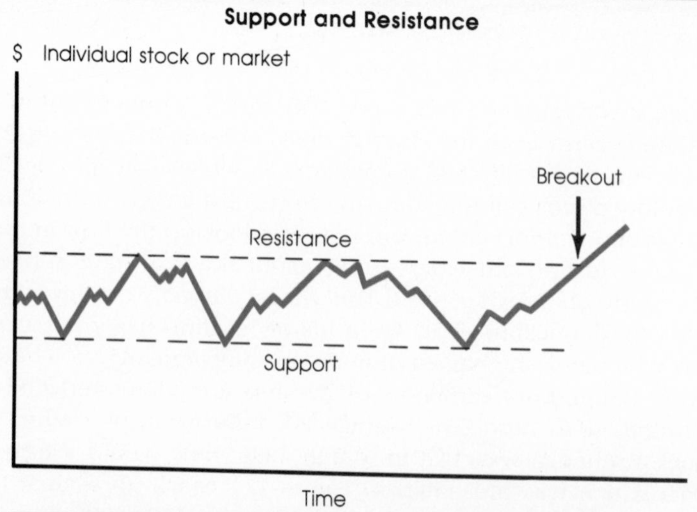

Table 12.1
SELECTED P-E RATIOS IN THE APPAREL INDUSTRY, MARCH 1986

Firm	P-E Ratio	Price
Russ Togs	9.6	$24
Phillips-Van H.	10.5	32
Adams-Mills	11.5	25
Farah Mfg. Co.	13.3	24
Tultex Corp.	13.8	22
Manhattan	16.3	13
Oxford Inds.	18.9	17
Liz Claiborne	19.6	61
Munsinger	22.4	19

Here the analyst is using past market data to determine where there is support and resistance for the stock in terms of its price and where there is a potential breakout in the stock price. Although not too many investors use technical analysis, and some hold it to be highly suspect, proponents of the approach claim it is valuable and rewarding to them. If you are interested in technical analysis, you may want to read such books as Edwards and Magee, *Technical Analysis of Stock Trends* and Zweig, *Understanding Technical Forecasting* (full citations are given in the Selected Readings at the end of the chapter).

CLASSIFYING STOCKS FOR INVESTMENTS

If you are going to invest in common stock, you must have some feel for the way brokers and analysts classify securities. As you are examining economic, industry, and company data, you must also consider whether you are evaluating growth stocks, high-dividend-yield stocks, and so forth. Let's look at some of the more common categories.

Growth Stocks

A **growth stock** is one that is assumed to have greater than average growth potential for the future. Historically, corporate earnings have increased by 4 to 6 percent per year, and a firm that is categorized as a growth stock should be able to demonstrate growth in earnings of 10 to 15 percent annually or more.

Because growth stocks place a high emphasis on internal growth opportunities, they usually try to reinvest the major portion of their earnings in the company rather than pay them out as dividends. A typical growth stock distributes 0 to 25 percent of earnings in the form of dividends. Its **dividend yield** (annual dividends/price) is normally 2 percent or less. Because of the low dividend yield, more of the **total return** to investors must come in the form of capital appreciation (increased stock value).

Growth stocks are often found in the more exciting areas of the market such as medical services and supplies, sophisticated office equipment, computer software, and telecommunications. The best opportunities for achieving big gains are often found in early-stage growth companies. Classic examples of accumulated fortunes can be found in the early history of IBM, Xerox, and Polaroid. But the investor also needs to be cautious. Growth stocks usually carry high P-E ratios and a substantial downside exposure, or risk of going down, if they do not deliver on their promises. You have to do your homework to make sure that a company masquerading as a growth stock is not actually yesterday's tired favorite rather than tomorrow's leader. Look for evidence of continued research and development, unique products or superior methods of marketing existing products, progressive management, and other factors that will produce continued high growth rates. An example of a rapid-growth company is presented in Table 12.2. Automatic Data Processing is a leading supplier of computer data systems for business. Note the rapid growth in earnings (per share), the high P-E ratio over the years, and small dividends relative to earnings.

High-Yield Stocks

An opposite approach to investing in growth stocks is to invest in a high-dividend-yielding security, or **high-yield stock.** The average dividend yield in

Table 12.2 INFORMATION ON AUTOMATIC DATA PROCESSING—A GROWTH STOCK

Per share data ($) yr. end June 30	1985	1984[a]	1983[a]	1982	1981	1980[a]	1979	1978	1977[a]	1976
Book value	**12.21**	10.81	9.93	8.30	7.23	5.12	4.52	3.73	3.35	2.65
Earnings[b]	**2.47**	2.14	1.86	1.71	1.51	1.31	1.11	0.92	0.79	0.63[a]
Dividends	**0.63½**	0.57½	0.51½	0.45½	0.39½	0.33½	0.27½	0.21½	0.14	0.10½
Payout ratio	**26%**	27%	28%	27%	28%	26%	25%	23%	18%	17%
Prices[c]—high	**54¾**	40¼	44½	38	31¾	26½	20½	18¼	15⅜	17⅞
low	**35¼**	29½	32⅞	20⅝	23⅜	16⅜	14⅜	11½	10⅞	12½
P/E ratio—	**22–14**	19–14	24–18	22–12	21–15	20–12	19–13	20–13	19–14	28–20

Data as orig. reptd. Adj. for stk. div(s). of 100% May 1981, 100% Jul. 1976.

[a] Reflects merger or acquisition.

[b] Bef. results of disc. opers. of −0.06 in 1980 and spec. item(s) of +0.06 in 1981, +0.06 in 1980.

[c] Cal. yr.

SOURCE: *Standard & Poor's Stock Reports*, April 1986, p. 256.

the U.S. economy has been around 3 to 4 percent. Therefore, a high-yielding stock should provide a dividend return twice this value or more. Keep in mind that you should always be looking at total return potential. If you want a total return of 12 percent and the first 6 or 8 percent comes in the form of dividend yield, then you are much closer to achieving this goal from the start. Furthermore, with the changes in the tax laws in 1986, dividend income is now given the same tax treatment as capital gains. Historically, long-term capital gains were taxed at a much lower rate than dividends or other forms of income. Thus, dividend income has become more acceptable to wealthy taxpayers.

High-dividend-paying stocks also tend to be somewhat defensive in nature during market declines. That is, they are less susceptible to declines. Let's use an example to show why. If a $50 stock is paying a $4 annual cash dividend, that represents an 8 percent dividend yield. If the overall market begins declining rapidly, the stock may not go below $40, because at that level the stock is providing a 10 percent yield ($4/$40) and investors may be attracted to the issue. Of course, if a high-yielding stock reduces its cash dividend, all bets are off and the stock price may plummet.

As you might anticipate, high-yielding stocks may have limited growth or capital appreciation potential. The reason is that a large portion of earnings is being paid out to stockholders in the form of dividends rather than being reinvested in new company projects. A typical high-yielding stock may pay out 50 percent or more of earnings to stockholders. High-yielding stocks are often found in older, more mature industries such as public utilities, banking, international oil, and real estate (particularly real estate investment trusts). Look at Table 12.3, which gives information on Southern California Edison, a public utility company. The payout ratio is in the range of 60 to 70 percent. The dividend yield, based on an annual dividend payment of $2.13 in 1985 and an average stock price of approximately 25¼, is 8.44 percent.[7] Also note the low P-E ratio, which is a characteristic of most income-oriented stocks.[8]

Cyclical Stocks

As we indicated earlier, a **cyclical stock** tends to be heavily influenced by the current state of the economy. In our prior discussion of fundamental analysis, we referred to the hands on the clock and industries that did well at different stages of economic recovery. In a sense, all these industries possess cyclical characteristics (that is, housing, capital investment, and so on). Other cyclical industries besides those shown on the clock in Figure 12.6 include autos, steel, chemicals, metals, and paper products. You may be able to name others. A major

[7] For purposes of this particular calculation, we use an average of the 1985 high-low price. Normally, the current stock price is used to compute the dividend yield.

[8] Don't automatically assume that low P-E stocks provide inadequate opportunities for high total returns over time. The opposite is often true. If you have an interest in this area, you may wish to read John W. Peavy III and David A. Goodman, "The Significance of P/Es for Portfolio Returns," *Journal of Portfolio Management,* Winter 1983, pp. 43–47.

Table 12.3 DATA ON SOUTHERN CALIFORNIA EDISON—A HIGH-YIELD STOCK

Per share data ($) yr. end Dec. 31	1985	1984	1983	1982	1981	1980	1979	1978	1977	1976
Book value[a]	**NA**	19.89	18.76	17.48	16.87	16.60	17.11	16.29	16.80	15.95
Earnings[b]	**3.26**	3.18	3.11	2.57	2.47	1.75	2.28	1.76	1.94	1.85
Dividends[c]	**2.13**	2.00½	1.83	1.69	1.55	1.42	1.30	1.15	1.03	0.84
Payout ratio	**65%**	63%	59%	66%	61%	81%	57%	65%	53%	45%
Prices—high	**28½**	24⅜	21½	18⅝	15⅜	13⅞	13¾	13½	13⅝	11⅞
low	**22⅛**	17⅛	17¼	14	11½	10	11⅞	11½	10⅝	9¼
P/E ratio—	**9–7**	8–5	7–6	7–5	6–5	8–6	6–5	8–6	7–5	6–5

Data as orig. reptd. Adj. for stk. div(s). of 100% Aug. 1984.
[a] As reptd. by co. NA-Not Available. E-Estimated.
[b] Giving effect to the 1976 rate refund affirmed by Calif. Supreme Court in 1978, primary sh. earns. for 1977, 1976 were restated as follows: 1.90 in 1977, 1.90 in 1976.
[c] Declared.

SOURCE: *Standard & Poor's Stock Reports*, April 1986, p. 2064.

characteristic of a cyclical stock is that earnings tend to be highly volatile, soaring during certain time periods and rapidly declining during others. Cyclical stocks, more so than growth or high-yielding stocks, tend to be two-decision stocks. You need to know when to buy and when to *sell*. They are either in or out of vogue, but seldom in between. A classic example of a cyclical stock is General Motors. Selected information on the firm is presented in Table 12.4.

Note the roller coaster ride that the investor takes in earnings (per share) and dividends (per share). Furthermore, you can observe that the P-E ratio has been as low as 4 and as high as 54.

Some investors like to emphasize countercyclical stocks as well as cyclical stocks. As the name implies, a **countercyclical stock** moves in the opposite direction of the business cycle rather than with it. Countercyclical stocks are generally appealing when the economy is moving into a recession. Can you think of any firms or industries that do well when the economy is faltering? Classic examples are used auto parts, fast-food restaurants, low-rental housing, and home movies.

We have been discussing three general categories of stocks. No doubt we could add additional classifications. Many stocks fit neatly into these categories, but others do not. Some firms have attributes of two or more categories. For example, a firm that is growing at a rate of 6 percent per year, pays a dividend yield of 5 percent, and is somewhat influenced by booms and recessions falls into the gray area between all three categories.

Table 12.4 DATA ON GENERAL MOTORS—A CYCLICAL STOCK

Per share data ($) yr. end Dec. 31	1985	1984	1983	1982	1981	1980	1979	1978	1977	1976
Book value	**NA**	69.80	65.05	57.75	57.43	59.22	65.30	60.56	54.16	49.18
Earnings	**12.28**	14.22	11.84	3.09	1.07	d2.65	10.04	12.24	11.62	10.08
Dividends	**5.00**	4.75[a]	2.80	2.40	2.40	2.95	5.30	6.00	6.80	5.55
Payout ratio	**41%**	33%	24%	79%	224%	NM	53%	49%	58%	55%
Prices—high	**85**	82¾	80	64½	58	58⅞	65⅞	66⅞	78½	78⅞
low	**64¼**	61	56	34	33⅞	39½	49⅜	53¾	61⅛	57¾
P/E ratio—	**7–5**	6–4	7–5	21–11	54–32	NM	7–5	5–4	7–5	8–6

Data as orig. reptd.; pertains to $1.66⅔ par common stk. NA—not available, NM—not meaningful, d—deficit.

[a] Plus 0.05 sh. Class E com. stk.

SOURCE: *Standard & Poor's Stock Reports*, April 1986, p. 978.

SPECIAL SITUATIONS

A special situation is not a category of stock but a unique form of investment opportunity. Special situations have become very important in the 1980s. Two forms of special situations will be briefly discussed: the merger tender offer and the new public issue.

Merger Tender Offer

Time and again in the 1980s, the volume leader and most rapidly advancing stock was a merger candidate. The reason is that firms to be acquired in a merger are frequently offered a premium well in excess of their current market value. The typical premium in the 1980s is of the magnitude of 50 to 60 percent. That is, the tender offer price is approximately one-and-a-half times the value of the stock before the effect of the merger offer (researchers often observe a value many months before the actual announcement of the merger to establish the premerger value). A select list of merger premiums paid in the 1980s is presented in Table 12.5.

Similar premiums were paid in major mergers between U.S. Steel and Marathon Oil, Phillip Morris and General Foods, Chevron and Gulf Oil, and many other cases.

If you are fortunate enough to own a stock many months before the annual announcement and eventual completion of a merger, your expected return is the 50 to 60 percent premium. Even if you wait until the announcement of the merger to invest, your anticipated gain may be 20 percent or more. Of course, if the merger is called off, you may suffer large losses on your investment in the

Table 12.5 PREMIUMS PAID IN MERGERS

Acquiring firm	Acquired firm	Price paid in cash for acquired company's stock	Value of acquired firm three months before announcement	Premium paid (percent)
Pepsico, Inc.	Pizza Hut	$38.00	$23.375	69.83
Time, Inc.	Inland Containers	35.00	20.75	66.67
Allis Chalmers Corp.	American Air Filter	34.00	19.50	74.36
Colt Industries	Menaso Man.	26.00	15.00	77.33
Dana Corporation	Weatherford Co.	14.00	9.375	49.33
Walter Kidde & Co.	Victor Comptometer	11.75	7.375	59.32

acquisition candidate. Incidentally, there is almost no advantage in investing in the stock of the acquiring firm; it, on average, only does about as well as the stock market in general.

New Public Issue

A stock is classified as a **new public issue** when it is distributed in the securities markets for the first time. New public issues often represent hot stocks in that they may have strong stock market performances immediately after issue. Classic examples of 50 percent gainers are Apple Computer and Genentech, a health care firm involved in gene splicing. A more normal gain may be 10 to 15 percent in the first month after issue. Of course, not all issues equal the norm and in a down market, you can get burned. Even if you latch on to a hot new issue (they are often in short supply) and make a nice profit, researchers indicate you are usually wise to bail out and take your profits a month or so after the public offering.[9]

SELECTING A BROKER FOR YOUR ACCOUNT

Once you are prepared to begin your investment program, you must select a stockbroker for your account. You really have two choices: traditional brokers and discount brokers.

Traditional Brokers

The traditional brokerage house is a full-service operation. **Traditional brokers** not only buy and sell stocks for you on a commission basis, but they provide

[9] Frank K. Reilly, "New Issues Revisited," *Financial Management*, Winter 1977, pp. 28–42.

Box 12.1 TAKEOVER STRATEGY FOR A SMALL INVESTOR

Wall Street's merger mania is raising the chances that a company in which you own shares will become a takeover target. What should you do then? Sell? Wait? Or what?

Ask yourself these questions:

Is the Offer Friendly or Hostile?

If two companies disclose plans to merge, you have no choice but to turn in your shares.

However, if an unwanted buyer is involved, wait. Within a few days after a tender is announced, both the bidder and your board will send you documents trying to win you over.

What Are the Terms of the Deal?

Frequently, the buyer will take only a certain percentage of the shares outstanding at a specified price. In such a case, circle the proration and expiration dates on your calendar. All who tender by the proration date will be able to sell an equal portion of their shares. If you're late and the offer is oversubscribed, the buyer may not take your shares.

The withdrawal date is a deadline for rescinding your promise to sell. If you do so before the deadline, you can cash in on any richer offer that comes later.

It may help to consult your broker to assess the value of the company to the bidder and the value of your shares if the company succeeds in resisting the takeover. Weigh, too, whether the offer is for cash or for securities whose value must be determined in the future.

Is Your Company's Management Taking Defensive Measures?

If so, the result could be a later, higher bid for your shares.

Who Owns Most of the Stock?

If a founding family or one investor holds a huge chunk of stock, it can dampen the likelihood of a hostile takeover or seal the success of a friendly offer.

The rule of thumb is that the market knows more than you do.

If the market price remains below the takeover bid price, it is time to tender your shares. If the price soars above the bid, hold on. Another offer may be coming.

If the price of the buyer's stock rises, he's getting either a steal or a deal that makes a lot of sense.

SOURCE: Copyright, 1985, *U.S. News & World Report.* Reprinted from issue of June 10, 1985.

you with advice, supply you with literature on companies, and share the findings of their research analysts on companies and the economy. You deal with a broker who represents the brokerage house on a very personal basis.

A representative list of the better-known national brokerage houses is presented below:

Merrill Lynch Pierce Finner & Smith
Shearson Lehman American Express
E. F. Hutton & Co.
Prudential-Bache
Dean Witter Reynolds Inc.
Paine Webber
Smith Barney Harris Upham

If you live in a large metropolitan area, most of the firms can be found in the yellow pages of a telephone directory. If you live in a small community, only one or two of the national firms may be represented. There are also smaller, regional brokerage houses that perform many of the same functions as the larger national houses.

Although brokerage commissions have been legally negotiable since 1975, they tend to be fixed for smaller trades. For small trades, they usually run 2 to 4 percent of the amount involved. On larger trades, the commission may be 1 percent or less.

An example of a fee schedule for a national brokerage house is presented in Table 12.6.

Using Table 12.6, for a trade of $801, the fee would be 1.875 percent of $801 plus $16. This adds up to $15.02 + $16, or $31.02. Based on a trade of $801, the commission is 3.873 percent. Table 12.6 is based on round-lot (100 shares or multiple of 100 shares) trades. If you are trading in less than 100 shares, there is also a small odd-lot fee that typically amounts to 12½¢ per share. For example, if you are buying 20 shares, you may have to pay an extra $2.50. There are also very small stock transfer fees on all trades.

Most traditional brokerage houses simply tell you what the commission is without giving you an in-house schedule. A quick glance at the last column of Table 12.6 indicates that there are some real economics of scale in trading stocks. Realistically, you need at least $1000 to $2000 to consider opening a brokerage account. Larger accounts will also tend to get better service (though a broker may view a small account as having the potential to become a larger account).

The fee schedule discussed in this section only applies to stocks. If you are buying or selling bonds or other securities, you will find a different commission structure. In any event, always ask about the commission before you initiate a transaction.

Discount Brokers

Discount brokers are an innovation of the late 1970s and 1980s. They offer only one service, the buying and selling of securities. But they can do it cheaply because they do not provide you with advice, research reports, or other information developed by security analysts.

Each investor must decide on the importance of the items mentioned above. If you value a broker's advice and the firm's research, you will want to go with a full-service traditional broker. If you already know the stock you wish to buy or sell and the price at which you plan to execute your transaction, you may prefer to use a discount broker.

A discount broker can normally execute a transaction at 30 to 75 percent less than a full-service retail broker. The bigger the transaction, the bigger the discount. The largest discount broker in the country is Charles Schwab and Co. To get a quote on the commission for a trade, you can call them from anywhere in the country with a toll-free number (listed in your phone book). Many banks in local communities may also have subsidiaries that offer discount brokerage service, so you may wish to check with your local financial institution.

Table 12.6 ROUND-LOT COMMISSION SCHEDULE

Size of transaction	Commission	Total commission as a percentage of the lower bracket amount
$0–$800	2.500% + $11	at least 3.875%
$801–$2,500	1.875% + $16	at least 3.873%
$2,501–$5,000	1.395% + $28	at least 2.515%
$5,001–$20,000	1.255% + $35	at least 1.955%
$20,001–$30,000	0.910% + $104	at least 1.430%
Over $30,000	fully negotiable	under 1%

Types of Orders

After you have decided what type of broker to use, you still have other decisions to make. For example, what type of order do you place? You may wish to place a market order, a limit order, or a stop-loss order.

Market Order. A **market order** simply means to execute the order at the current market price. If you call your broker and ask to purchase 100 shares of Mobil, he or she will transmit your order to the floor of the New York Stock Exchange and your order will be executed at the going market rate.

Limit Order. A **limit order** allows you to specify the price at which you wish to transact. Assume that Mobil (oil) Corporation stock is currently trading at $42, but you wish to purchase at $40 or less if the stock reaches that level. You can place a limit order at $40 with your broker, and the order will be transmitted to the specialist in Mobil on the floor of the New York Stock Exchange. He or she will record your limit order in the specialist's book, and when the stock price reaches your specified level, a transaction will take place (unless many others are also in front of you at that price). You can also use a limit order to sell. Once again assume that Mobil is at $42 and you wish to sell at $45 or higher. You can use a limit order to attempt to achieve this objective. A limit order may be good for a day or perhaps longer, or simply be good 'til canceled (GTC). The choice is yours.

The advantage of a limit order is that it lets you fine-tune your transactions. Maybe you think that Mobil is a good buy at $40 and a good sell at $45. The danger is that the stock can get away from you before it hits your limit points. Mobil may go down from $42 to $40½ but never make it to $40. If Mobil hits a major oil discovery, you may not get your order in before the stock runs up. The same is true on the sell side. The stock may only make it up to $43 or $44 but fall short of your limit sell point of $45. If Mobil receives an adverse ruling in a

Box 12.2 WALL STREET'S ANALYSTS: ARE THEY ANY HELP?

Who can tell you how much money IBM will make this year? Or the risks in Coca-Cola's new formula? Or the effects of a possible restructuring at Allied Corporation?

The answer: Wall Street analysts.

Sometimes they are right and sometimes wrong. Either way, they almost always have an opinion of interest to investors.

Each year, Dean Witter Reynolds sends out more than 2,000 research reports on corporations, the stock market and the economy. At Prudential-Bache Securities, 20 percent of the analysts are on the road each week interviewing corporate chieftains, talking to clients and looking at new factories. E. F. Hutton often prints 50,000 to 60,000 copies of an individual research report.

Prudential-Bache Securities

Research Weekly

Research

May 18, 1987

This Week In Research — Page

Brownout—Electric Utility Prospects Dim As Rate Fears Persist. *We expect utility stocks to be under selling pressure as long as there are concerns about higher inflation and rising interest rates. The only exceptions, in our view, are those electric utility common stocks which have above-average yields, regardless of their long-term growth prospects. Our favorites—Southern California Edison and Consolidated Edison.* Barry M. Abramson, CFA 1

Changes In Opinion

Gottschalks Inc.—Looking Better	Elizabeth Shamir	3
Applied Biosystems—Revenues Up, Earnings Down	Stuart Weisbrod, Ph.D.	3
Atlantic Richfield—Crude Leverage	Frank Knuettel, CFA	4

Tables

Upward		**Downward (Cont'd)**	
Gottschalks Inc.	5	Atlantic Richfield	5
Varian Associates	5	Florida Progress	5
		Watkins-Johnson	5
Downward			
Applied Biosystems	5		

Changes In Earnings Estimates

Computer Associates Int'l—Outstanding Results	Charles Taylor, CFA	6
Republic American Corp.—Momentum Builds	Herbert E. Goodfriend	6
McDonnell Douglas—Lower Margins, Higher Taxes	Paul Nisbet	7

Tables

Upward		**Downward**		**Downward (Cont'd)**	
Atlantic Richfield	8	Applied Biosystems	8	Loral Corp.	8
Chevron Corp.	8	Florida Progress	8	McDonnell Douglas	9
Computer Associates Int'l	8	GCA Corporation	8	Transco Energy	9
Republic American Corp.	8	KLA Instruments	8	Watkins-Johnson	9
Varian Associates	8				

Initiating Coverage

L. Luria & Son, Inc.—Reformats Catalog Showroom	Linda Baker	10
Himont, Inc.—Patience Should Pay Off	Leonard Bogner	10
Bankers Trust Corp.—Long-Term Valuation Breakout	Douglas Stone	11
Emerald Homes L.P.—Exception Yield	Barbara Allen	11

Prudential-Bache Research Department's Recommended List Of Buys And Sells 16

The Goal

Research is big business on Wall Street. Every week, securities analysts put corporate earnings, products and management under a microscope and translate their research into buy and sell recommendations. This advice is transmitted to stockbrokers, who try to interest their customers in taking action based on this knowledge of corporate health.

"Our basic aim," says Lawrence Adelman, director of research at Dean Witter Reynolds, "is to find undervalued stocks and to maximize money on our clients' investment."

Adds Thomas Stiles, director of research at Hutton: "Our mission is to present a broad investment framework—how we see the world working—and presenting that view to institutions as well as individuals. From this, we derive specific investment strategy and recommendations." To get its views to individuals and institutions, Hutton uses a telephone system that reaches all its 400 U.S. offices at once.

Prudential-Bache's director of research, Greg Smith, says the goal is "to try to know the companies we follow as well as or better than anyone else."

To understand companies, brokerage-house analysts often go to great lengths. Mark Manson of Donaldson, Lufkin & Jenrette Securities Corporation recently did some financial detective work in estimating the April, May and June sales at Tandy Corporation. This entailed studying Tandy's past computer and noncomputer sales and factoring in historical monthly sales swings. Even the company had no idea how sales were doing at all of its stores.

As a result of his compilations, Manson suggested his clients buy Tandy stock, since he estimated that the company would have a good spring—contrary to what many other analysts were saying.

Often, analysts talk to a company's customers and competitors to get a feel for sales. However, William Trainer of Merrill Lynch went one step further several years ago when he started examining monthly catalogs sent out by Simplicity Pattern Company.

"By monitoring the catalog," he says, "you could make a determination on the composition of sales. You could tell how much was reorder or changes in inventory forced by the company." As a result of his detective work, he decided Simplicity would be a bad investment, keeping his clients out of a stock that fell from $50 to $10 per share.

Sometimes, the scrutiny is far off the mark. A year ago, Montgomery Securities, which has been very successful at picking restaurant stocks, recommended that its clients buy Diversifoods, Inc., a large fast-food franchiser. Montgomery reasoned that new management at Diversifoods would turn the operation around. The new executives failed, however, and the stock fell steeply from $16 per share when Montgomery recommended it. Fortunately, a run-up in the stock late last year permitted Montgomery's clients to bail out at close to their purchase price.

Such occurrences are not rare. But Stanley Levine, a vice president of Lynch, Ryan & Jones, says that analysts are "trying to forecast something which is uncertain—the future. Some are more accurate than others; some companies are easier to forecast."

For example, Lynch, Ryan & Jones has a service called Institutional Brokers Estimate System (IBES) that tracks analysts' earnings estimates and compares them with actual numbers.

Moving Target

In January, 1984, the analysts' consensus estimate on the Standard & Poor's 500 index was 18.95. The preliminary S&P earnings were 16.80. This January, analysts predicted S&P 500 earnings of 20.61 but are now dropping their estimates.

How can an individual know when to rely on an adviser? "The key to evaluating a research product," says Stiles of E. F. Hutton, "is looking to see if it's consistent. Do the recommendations jibe with the overall perspective of the company?"

Smith, director of research at Prudential-Bache Securities, adds that an individual should follow analysts through both up and down market cycles. "It's a good idea to know how conservative or optimistic an analyst is."

Monte Gordon, director of research at the Dreyfus Corporation, a mutual-fund organization, advises investors to focus only on the company reports that meet their investment objectives. "Otherwise, an investor will be swamped by information." In addition, Gordon advises investors to look for the negatives in the reports. "You have to know what can go wrong."

lawsuit, it may plummet before you can get out. Clearly, limit orders have advantages as well as disadvantages. The former normally outweigh the latter.

Stop-Loss Order. A **stop-loss order** enables you to protect your downside exposure in a falling market. It normally runs in the opposite direction from a limit order. Suppose you bought Mobil at $42 and you fear that it could go down by 10 or more points (dollars) under truly adverse circumstances. You can enter a stop-loss order at $38 or $40. When the stock's price hits that point, the stop-loss order, which is placed with a specialist on the floor of the exchange, becomes a market order and the sale will be consummated in the first transaction possible. Some investors like to enter stop-loss orders when they are going to be out of town for extended periods of time.

The Use of Street Name

Regardless of the type of broker you use or the nature of the order you place, chances are the actual stock certificate involved in a purchase will be held for safekeeping by the brokerage firm. The stocks are said to be kept in *street name.* This facilitates the trading of securities in that you do not have to endorse the certificate when you want to sell the stock. This is a common practice, so do not be surprised when you buy a stock and do not actually receive the stock certificate (as people did a generation or two ago). You will still receive a monthly statement listing all your holdings. If this procedure is unacceptable to you, you can specifically request that the stock be registered in your name and take possession of the stock certificate. This is infrequently done and causes extra paperwork for everyone.

The Use of Margin

A common option that you have with a broker is to buy a stock on **margin.** This means that part of the purchase price is provided through funds borrowed from your broker. The margin requirement is set by the Federal Reserve and is currently 50 percent, which indicates that the investor may put up 50 percent in cash and borrow the balance from the broker. If the margin requirement were 60 percent, the investor could borrow 40 percent. The interest rate on the borrowed funds is usually 1 to 1½ percent above the prime interest rate (the rate that commercial banks charge their most creditworthy customers).

The use of margin is appealing to investors who are very confident in their purchases and want to control a larger portfolio than their current funds dictate (the same objective can be accomplished by trading in options, which we discuss in Chapter 14). The danger of trading on margin is that your losses can be magnified in a down market as a result of owning more stock than you have invested in cash. Also, your broker may ask for additional cash to provide an adequate equity position if your stock declines rapidly. You may be forced to either supply additional cash or sell your stock at a large loss. Trading on margin clearly has its advantages and disadvantages.

Short-Sale Transactions

A **short sale** allows you to sell stock you do not own with the intention of repurchasing it in the future. Actually, you borrow the stock from your broker and sell it, and then replace the stock when you later buy it. A short sale reverses the normal process in that you sell now and buy later. Investors sell short when they believe the stock's price is going to go down. Assume a stock is currently selling for $40 and your third cousin assures you that the stock is going to go down to $30 because the firm has a lousy product or is about to lose a major government contract. You may engage in a short sale, perhaps selling 100 shares now for $4000 with the hope of buying them back in the future for $3000.[10]

It takes a special breed of investor to engage in a short-sale transaction. You have to hope and pray for bad news. Of course, if the stock goes up instead of down, you may absorb large losses. You could be forced to buy back a stock that you sold for $40 at $50 or $60 per share. Short selling is not suited for the inexperienced investor. Also, many of the potential advantages of short selling can be gained through trading in options, as you will see in Chapter 14.

MARKET AVERAGES

Now that you have learned how to select a stock and how to buy and sell securities, you may want to improve your market knowledge by following daily barometers of how the stock market is doing.

In Figure 12.11, you can see major market indexes in mid-April 1986. We referred to some of the averages earlier in the chapter (though for a different date). The most popular market measure is the **Dow Jones Industrial Average.** This is shown under the Dow Jones averages under "30 industrials." This average of large industrial firms is considered a blue chip measure (of stocks of high quality). Examples of firms in the Dow Jones Industrial Average (DJIA) are DuPont, Eastman Kodak, Exxon, General Motors, IBM, Procter & Gamble, and Westinghouse Electric.

The closing value on April 15, 1986, of 1809.65 is obviously not an average of the current prices of the 30 stocks. The average has been computed since the late nineteenth century, and the current value adjusts for all the stock splits and stock dividends that have taken place over the years.[11] For example, a stock may have a current value of $60, but if the stock has been split 2 for 1 five different times in its history, that is really the equivalent of $1920 ($60 × 2 × 2 × 2 × 2 × 2). The same principle would apply to the other 29 stocks in the average.

If you don't fully understand the explanation above, don't worry. Even

[10] There is also a 50 percent initial margin requirement associated with a short sale. You would have to put up $2000 in cash in this instance.

[11] A stock split means that you get a multiple of shares for each share you currently hold. For example, in a 2 for 1 stock split, the holder of 100 shares would now have 200 shares. Of course, the earnings and dividends are adjusted downward to compensate for the greater number of shares.

Figure 12.11 MAJOR MARKET INDEXES, APRIL 15, 1986

Major Indexes

HIGH	LOW (12 MOS)		CLOSE	NET CH	% CH	12 MO CH	%	FROM 12/31	%
DOW JONES AVERAGES									
1821.72	1242.05	30 Industrials	1809.65	+ 4.34	+ 0.24	+ 540.10	+42.54	+ 262.98	+17.00
830.84	571.08	20 Transportations	789.13	+ 0.86	+ 0.11	+ 190.92	+31.92	+ 81.06	+11.45
193.73	150.08	15 Utilities	189.73	+ 0.56	+ 0.30	+ 33.95	+21.79	+ 14.92	+ 8.53
718.16	501.79	65 Composite	704.50	+ 1.51	+ 0.21	+ 188.53	+36.54	+ 87.97	+14.27
NEW YORK STOCK EXCHANGE									
137.71	103.35	Composite	137.15	+ 0.22	+ 0.16	+ 32.13	+30.59	+ 15.47	+12.72
157.43	118.16	Industrials	157.26	+ 0.39	+ 0.25	+ 36.88	+30.64	+ 17.99	+12.92
69.66	54.53	Utilities	69.12	+ 0.13	+ 0.19	+ 13.44	+24.14	+ 5.93	+ 9.38
132.54	93.62	Transportation	124.43	− 0.57	− 0.46	+ 27.33	+28.12	+ 10.46	+ 9.18
157.74	107.17	Finance	155.59	− 0.61	− 0.39	+ 46.20	+42.23	+ 24.30	+18.51
STANDARD & POOR'S INDEXES									
238.97	178.37	500 Index	237.73	+ 0.45	+ 0.19	+ 56.53	+31.20	+ 26.45	+12.52
263.87	198.32	400 Industrials	263.67	+ 0.70	+ 0.27	+ 61.81	+30.62	+ 29.11	+12.41
217.28	147.43	20 Transportations	206.22	+ 0.08	+ 0.04	+ 53.47	+35.00	+ 17.50	+ 9.27
105.27	81.46	40 Utilities	103.42	+ 0.31	+ 0.30	+ 21.86	+26.80	+ 10.25	+11.00
31.13	20.45	40 Financials	30.26	− 0.21	− 0.69	+ 9.34	+44.65	+ 4.54	+17.65
NASDAQ									
381.71	276.95	OTC Composite	381.71	+ 0.87	+ 0.23	+ 99.43	+35.22	+ 56.78	+17.47
386.67	278.04	Industrials	386.67	+ 1.45	+ 0.38	+ 89.06	+29.93	+ 56.50	+17.11
467.05	326.64	Insurance	445.91	− 0.70	− 0.16	+ 116.84	+35.51	+ 63.84	+16.71
406.05	265.07	Banks	406.05	+ 1.18	+ 0.29	+ 140.98	+53.19	+ 56.69	+16.23
162.18	117.06	Nat. Mkt. Comp.	162.18	+ 0.40	+ 0.25	+ 43.12	+36.22	+ 23.92	+17.30
144.99	103.47	Nat. Mkt. Indus.	144.99	+ 0.61	+ 0.42	+ 34.29	+30.98	+ 20.86	+16.80
OTHERS									
272.26	220.70	AMEX	272.26	+ 0.78	+ 0.29	+ 41.33	+47.90	+ 26.13	+10.62
1425.9	911.0	Fin. Times Indus.	1370.8	− 28.5	− 2.04	+ 391.3	+39.95	+ 239.4	+21.16
15859.75	12052.82	Nikkei Stock Avg.	15352.33	−44.43	− 0.29	+3145.05	+25.76	+2239.01	+17.07
242.28	188.61	Value-Line	240.42			+ 45.87	+23.58	+ 25.56	+11.90
2455.23	1839.12	Wilshire 5000	2453.54	+ 5.42	+ 0.22	+ 585.21	+31.32	+ 288.85	+13.34

SOURCE: Reprinted by permission of the *Wall Street Journal*, © Dow Jones & Company, Inc., April 16, 1986, p. 50. All rights reserved.

professional investors aren't concerned with the precise computations. The really important factor to observe is the change in the average on a daily, weekly, or annual basis. For example, you can see in Figure 12.11 that the Dow Jones Industrial Average was up 4.34 points on April 15, 1986. That represents a 0.24 percent increase from the prior day. More importantly, observe that the average was up 540.10 points over the last 12 months, a gain of 42.54 percent. The performance of the DJIA over that time period was one of the best in history. Also, note that the DJIA was up 262.98 points, or 17 percent, since the end of the prior year (12/31).

Table 12.7 HISTORICAL DATA ON THE DOW JONES INDUSTRIAL AVERAGE

Year	High	Low	Year	High	Low
1987 (Oct.)	2722.42	1730.28	1963	767.21	646.69
1986	1967.84	1605.00	1962	726.01	535.76
1985	1570.00	1177.00	1961	734.91	610.25
1984	1286.62	1086.58	1960	685.47	566.05
1983	1287.20	1027.04	1959	679.36	574.46
1982	1070.55	776.92	1958	583.65	436.89
1981	1024.05	824.01	1957	520.77	419.79
1980	1000.17	759.13	1956	521.05	462.35
1979	897.61	796.67	1955	488.40	388.20
1978	907.74	742.12	1954	404.39	279.87
1977	999.75	800.85	1953	293.79	255.49
1976	1014.79	858.71	1952	292.00	256.35
1975	881.81	632.04	1951	276.37	238.99
1974	891.66	577.60	1950	235.47	196.81
1973	1051.70	788.31	1949	200.52	161.60
1972	1036.27	889.15	1948	193.16	165.39
1971	950.82	797.97	1947	186.85	163.21
1970	842.00	631.16	1946	212.50	163.12
1969	968.85	769.93	1945	195.82	151.35
1968	985.21	825.13	1944	152.53	134.22
1967	943.08	786.41	1943	145.82	119.26
1966	995.15	744.32	1942	119.71	92.92
1965	969.26	840.59	1941	133.59	106.34
1964	891.71	766.08			

Normally, the Dow Jones Industrial Average moves up or down 8 to 10 points during the day. Investors tend to take note when the move is in double or triple digits, such as 50 or 100 points or more. If you listen to the appropriate radio station in many communities, you can get quotes on the DJIA on almost an hourly basis. In any event, it is published daily in most newspapers. In order to get a historical feel for the Down Jones Industrial Average, look at the data in Table 12.7.

The other market indexes in Figure 12.11 tend to be more broad-based than the Dow Jones Industrial Average. For example, the New York Stock Exchange Indexes cover 1550 stocks, the Standard & Poor's Indexes cover up to 500 stocks, the NASDAQ Averages track over 4000 stocks, the Value-Line Average 1700 stocks, and the Wilshire Index 5000 stocks. The investment textbooks cited as references at the end of the chapter give you an opportunity to study the meanings, weightings, systems, and nuances of the various indexes if you so desire. But for now, keep in mind that the DJIA is the one you are going to hear the most about, even if it is limited in scope to 30 stocks.

BRINGING INDIVIDUAL STOCKS TOGETHER—THE PORTFOLIO

Managing your stocks calls for more than merely trying to pick individual winners. You must also consider the composition of your total portfolio of stocks. Most investors attempt to achieve a measure of diversification in their portfolio in order to reduce risk. If you have stocks in six or seven industries rather than just one or two, you are not as likely to be hurt by a single adverse development such as a labor strike or new industry regulations. Of course, if you have limited funds, it may be difficult to diversify into many different stocks. For some investors desiring diversification, the only feasible approach may be to invest in a mutual fund, a topic that is covered in Chapter 13. Of course, if you enjoy taking risks and truly wish to go with one or two stocks that you strongly believe in, diversification may not be an appropriate strategy for you.

Another consideration in your portfolio management is the time perspective for your transactions. Some investors are oriented to the short term, continually moving in and out of stocks at small profits (or even large ones) or losses. They are called *traders,* or **short-term traders.** Others have a longer time horizon in buying stocks, perhaps one to five years. They are normally termed *investors.* Most researchers and investment counselors support the longer-term approach, that is, to buy a stock you believe in and stay with it until it has a reasonable opportunity to perform. A longer-term orientation also saves on commissions. Most short-term traders do not come out ahead, but there is no denying that some are successful at this game. The truly successful short-term trader must be very perceptive, unemotional, and often willing to go against the grain. In summary, he or she must be good enough to compensate for all the extra commissions that must be paid.

Throughout the chapter, we have talked about the need to do thorough analysis in an investment decision. This applies with equal force to short-term or long-term market participants. However, in some instances you will be called by a broker or other party with a hot tip and the need to act quickly and decisively. While this may prove fruitful in some cases, the best rule is not to make impulsive decisions, but rather to carefully match your decisions with your goals and objectives.

As a final consideration in portfolio management, there are a number of computer software packages that can be of potential value to an investor who has such an inclination.[12]

1 Value/Screen (Value Line Inc., 711 Third Avenue, New York, N.Y. 10017).
Phone number 212/687-3965.
$495 per year (1986 price).

You receive monthly data relating to 32 variables for over 1650 companies. You can screen the data to select certain companies that

[12] An excellent source of information on this topic is "Computerline: Fundamental Analysis Software," *Personal Investor,* November 1985, pp. 73–74.

meet specified criteria such as high dividend yield, strong earnings growth, and low P-E ratios.

2 Stockpak II (Standard & Poor's Corp., 25 Broadway, New York, N.Y. 10004). Phone number 212/208-8581.
$275 per year (1986 price for NYSE disk).
A data base of financial information on widely held companies. If you wish to include the American Stock Exchange disk, the fee is an additional $275, and for 4000 OTC firms, the cost is $520. Stockpak II allows you to look up more than 100 items of information and to screen data for specific criteria.

3 Dow Jones Market Microscope (Dow Jones and Co.), P.O. Box 300, Princeton, N.J. 08540. Phone number 800/257-5411.
$349.
Unlike Value/Screen and Stockpak II, you get the information necessary for stock screening via telephone hookup with Dow Jones News Retrieval, a leading news development organization. Information can be obtained on 4300 companies divided up into 180 industry classifications. The disadvantage is that you have to pay a telephone connection fee for the time it takes to retrieve the data.

SUMMARY

Common stockholders are the actual owners of the firm; as a result they have a legal claim to undistributed earnings, which may be paid out as dividends or reinvested for their benefit in the firm. Common stockholders also have voting rights that are used to elect the directors of the corporation and to express approval or disapproval on major corporate issues.

The common stockholder is particularly interested in the earnings per share of the corporation and how these earnings per share are evaluated in the market in terms of the firm's price-earnings ratio. The P-E ratio represents the multiple that investors are willing to assign to the last 12 months earnings in determining valuation. Normally, the higher the P-E ratio, the more optimistic investors are about the firm's outlook and vice versa. Of course, if expectations are not met, the P-E ratio and stock price may sharply decline.

Stocks are normally traded on organized exchanges (the New York Stock Exchange, the American Stock Exchange, or 14 regional exchanges) or in the over-the-counter market. The OTC market has multiple dealers making a market in securities and is particularly popular for smaller emerging firms.

Investors who follow a fundamental approach usually use a three-step approach to investment analysis in which they evaluate the economy, the industry, and the firm. They hope to determine stocks that are attractively priced based on the financial and operating fundamentals of the firm. Those who follow a technical approach are not really so interested in the operating performance of the firm, but rather in the charts and graphs related to the firm's stock market performance. Technical analysts examine prior price and volume data, as well as other market-related indicators, in the hope of projecting past trends into the future.

Investors sometimes classify stocks into categories such as growth stocks, high-yielding stocks, or cyclical stocks. Other categories are possible as well. Although the definitions are less than precise and some stocks may overlap into many classifications, categorizing stocks in some fashion allows you and your investment adviser to concentrate on certain types of stocks that are of particular interest to you.

In selecting a broker, you may decide to go with a traditional full-service broker that provides advice and guidance or a discount broker that offers much lower commissions. Once again, the decision comes back to your needs, desires, and objectives.

Throughout the investment process you must make essential decisions about your portfolio. An important decision relates to the degree of diversification that you desire. Diversification reduces risk but requires more capital. You must also decide whether you wish to participate as a short-term trader or a long-term investor.

KEY TERMS

American Stock Exchange
common stock
countercyclical stock
cyclical stock
discount brokers
dividend yield
Dow Jones Industrial Average
fundamental analysis
growth stock
high-yield stock
limit order
margin
market order
NASDAQ
new public issue
New York Stock Exchange
over-the-counter market
price-earnings (P-E) ratio
short sale
short-term traders
stop-loss order
technical analysis
total return
traditional brokers
Value Line Investment Survey

SELECTED READINGS

Edwards, R. D., and John Magee, Jr. *Technical Analysis of Stock Trends,* 5th ed. Springfield, Mass: Stock Trends Service, 1966. (Although the book is old, it is a classic on technical analysis.)

Gitman, Lawrence J., and Michael E. Joehnk. *Fundamentals of Investing,* 3rd ed. New York: Harper & Row, 1988.

Goodman, David A., and John W. Peavy III. *Hyperprofits,* Garden City, N.Y.: Doubleday, 1985.

Hirt, Geoffrey A., and Stanley B. Block. *Fundamentals of Investment Management,* 2nd ed. Homewood, Ill.: Irwin, 1986.

Reilly, Frank K. *Investments,* 2nd ed. New York: Dryden Press, 1986.

Zweig, Martin E. *Understanding Technical Forecasting.* Homewood, Ill.: Dow Jones, 1978.

QUESTIONS

1 What is the advantage to common stockholders of not having their return specified, as is true of lenders? What is the disadvantage?

2 What might happen to management if it is unresponsive to the needs of common stockholders?

3 What are the two forms of return that investors anticipate receiving from their stock investment?

4 What does the P-E ratio mean? What does a high P-E ratio generally indicate?

5 What is an organized exchange? What is the best-known organized exchange?

6 Given that the over-the-counter market does not have a specific location, how does it operate?

7 What is a competitive dealer market? How does this process differ from the use of specialists?

8 Why is the over-the counter market a particularly popular market for smaller firms?

9 What is the three-step decision-making process in selecting common stocks?

10 Match the following industries with the stages in the business cycle at which they are likely to perform best.

Industry	**Stage of Business Cycle**
Clothing or travel	Early stage
Manufacturer of heavy equipment	Intermediate stage
Savings and loan	Late stage

11 Suggest two industries that are generally not subject to the effects of the business cycle.

12 What does a timeliness classification of 1 in *Value Line* suggest about a company?

13 Generally describe the emphasis in the use of technical analysis.

14 What rate of growth does a firm normally need to achieve to be classified as a growth stock? Describe the typical dividend-paying policy of a growth stock.

15 Why does an investor need to be cautious in investing in growth stocks? What evidence should an investor look for in true growth stocks?

16 Why has the 1986 tax legislation made high-yield stocks more attractive?

Why are these stocks said to be somewhat defensive in nature? Why are they somewhat limited in growth potential?

17 What is meant by the statement, "Cyclical stocks tend to be two-decision stocks"?

18 What is a countercyclical stock? Give examples of four industries that might fall into the category of being countercyclical.

19 If you are going to invest in a merger situation, should you generally invest in the stock of the acquiring firm or the firm to be acquired?

20 What is the basic difference between a discount broker and a traditional broker in terms of services offered? How much of a savings can you normally anticipate with a discount broker?

21 Explain the difference between a market order and a limit order.

22 What does the process of buying stock on margin mean? What is the advantage and what is the disadvantage?

23 What is a short sale? When do you normally use a short sale?

24 What is the most popular stock market average or index? What are some stocks that are included in this index?

25 What is the advantage of diversification? How may an investor with limited funds achieve diversification?

26 When we refer to someone as a market trader, what does that mean?

27 The Bentson Corporation has $9.8 million in total earnings and 3.5 million shares outstanding.

a Compute earnings per share.

b If the firm pays dividends of $.70 per share, what is the dividend distribution (or payout) ratio?

c If the firm has a stock price of $44.80, what is the price-earnings ratio?

d What is the dividend yield? (Round to two places to the right of the decimal point.)

28 You are an investor in the Hedges Corporation. The firm pays a $1.25 annual dividend and its stock is priced at $25.

a If the stock goes up to $29 over the course of the year, what is the *total* return to the investor?

b If the stock goes down by one point from $25 to $24, what is the total return to the investor? Use the same dividend information as in the first part of the problem.

29 Go to a recent edition of the *Wall Street Journal* or any other newspaper that has stock quotes and update the stock quotes for the nine apparel firms in Table 12.1. Did the high or low P-E firms perform best?

30 Using the same newspaper source as in Problem 29, update the closing market quotes in Figure 12.11 for the Dow Jones Industrial Average and Standard & Poor's 500 Stock Index. What is the percentage increase or decrease in both of these measures from the values in Figure 12.11?

31 Using the commission schedule in Table 12.6:

a Compute the commission on an $8600 stock purchase. (Use the second column in the table). Apply the percentage to the amount involved and add in the dollar amount ($35) also.

b If a discount broker offered a 45 percent discount from the commission computed in part a, what would the commission be?

32 You sell 250 shares of Dismal Corporation short at $40 per share.

a If the stock goes down to $31, what will be your gain or loss on your short-sale transaction?

b If the stock goes up to $46 from $40, what will be your gain or loss on your short-sale position?

CASE PROBLEMS

12.1 Barbara and Jim Collins own 300 shares of High Fly Corporation. The firm has $152 million in total earnings and has 40 million shares outstanding. The stock has a price of $76. It pays an annual dividend of $.50 a share. The firm has had a growth rate in earnings of 15 percent per year.

a Compute the firm's earnings per share.

b What is the firm's P-E ratio?

c What is the firm's dividend yield? (Round to two places to the right of the decimal point.)

d Would you classify the firm as a high-yield or growth stock? Comment.

e The Collinses are planning a ten-day trip to Europe and will be leaving next week. They have a large profit in the stock of High Fly Corporation and fear the stock may go down sharply in value during their departure. What type of order might they want to place during their trip?

f Jim recently heard a rumor that the Allied International Corporation may be making a tender offer to try to acquire High Fly. Should the Collinses sell their stock in High Fly now to avoid any future hassle in the event there is a potential future offer for their stock? Should they consider buying stock in Allied International?

g Assume the Collinses hold on to their stock in High Fly. Also, no merger is to take place. Barbara notices that the firm's timeliness rating in *Value Line* has been changed from 2 to 5. What advice might you offer the Collinses?

12.2 Ruth Simon, Ph.D., has been out of college for five years. Although she has already established an outstanding reputation as a biologist at Western University, she has no previous experience in investing in the stock market.

a Comment on any advantages and disadvantages to her of using a traditional, full-service broker versus a discount broker.

b Assume she is considering buying 200 shares of Dissect Corporation at $24 per share. Using the commission schedule in Table 12.6, compute her anticipated commission. (Use the second column in the table). Apply the percentage to the amount involved and add in the dollar amount ($28) also.

c If she uses a discount broker that charges 35 percent less than the values computed in the table for this transaction, what will her commission be?

d Assume her shares had a P-E ratio of 10 when she bought them. Twelve months later the earnings per share of $2.40 for the Dissect Corporation have not changed, but the P-E ratio is now 14 (the corporation is about to announce an exciting new product). What is the new stock price?

e If Ruth Simon is in a 28 percent tax bracket and she sells her stock, what will be her after-tax return (in dollars) on her investment given the new stock price computed in part d?

f A colleague of Ruth's at Western University has heard that another firm in the same industry as the Dissect Corporation will be severely hurt by an announcement that Dissect has developed a new competitive product that will cut into its market share. The other firm's name is Lab Science Unlimited. If Ruth wants to take an aggressive position in regard to Lab Science Unlimited, what course of action might she take? What is the danger in taking such action?

13

Investing Through Mutual Funds

After studying this chapter, you should:

- Appreciate the diversification potential of mutual funds, but realize they do not outperform the market on average
- Understand the difference between an open-end and closed-end fund
- Know the difference between a load and no-load fund, and have a questioning attitude about paying a commission
- Be aware of the different classification of funds—stock funds, bond funds, balanced funds, municipal security funds, money market funds, and so on
- Know what sources to go to for further information on mutual funds
- Appreciate the many special features offered by mutual funds such as automatic reinvestment plans and fund switching
- Be able to compute net asset value for a fund and total return on an investment

Mutual funds pool the funds of a large number of individual investors and redeploy those funds in stocks and bonds. Typically, a mutual fund specializing in stocks or bonds may own 50 to 100 securities and have thousands of investors.

Of the over 40 million common stockholders in the United States, about one-third choose to participate through the purchase of mutual funds rather than through direct ownership. This percentage is steadily increasing. At one point in time, there was a stigma associated with purchasing mutual fund shares. It meant you were taking the remedial or slow track to common stock investments. You presumably didn't know how to buy stocks yourself, so you called in others to help you. If you were at a cocktail party, you stood quietly by as others bragged about the latest hot tip they had just gotten from their broker or how they were buying stocks on margin. This is no longer the case. The mutual fund investor can now drop names like Fidelity Magellan Fund or the Alliance International Fund and sound like the best-informed investor around, particularly when he or she can cite performance data and also indicate how the funds are ranked by various publications and services.

ADVANTAGES AND DRAWBACKS

Mutual funds are an efficient way to diversify your investments. One mutual fund can expose you to every sector of the economy if you so desire. Furthermore, you can select a fund in which you do not have to pay a commission to participate and thus greatly reduce your transactions costs.

When you purchase a mutual fund, you are also buying the expertise of the fund managers. In many cases, they have been in the business for a long time and may be specialists in certain areas such as international securities, natural resources, or precious metals.

Today you can select from a wide range of funds. You have not only general-purpose funds from which to choose, but those with specific purposes or missions. You can buy common stock funds that specialize in high growth or income, or that are keyed in to one particular industry or sector of the world. You also may select funds that specialize in bond investments, and you may specifically choose a bond fund that provides taxable or nontaxable income. Also, money market funds, which were discussed in Chapter 11, are a special form of mutual funds.

It is little wonder that mutual funds have enjoyed tremendous growth in the 1980s. In 1986, there were over 1200 mutual funds, four times the number of only a decade before. Mutual fund net sales exceeded $100 billion in 1985. This figure is particularly impressive when you consider that between 1940 and 1981, the best year for mutual fund net sales was a mere $3 billion (net sales equal new sales minus repurchase of existing shares).

Having just read about the many virtues of mutual funds, you should be aware that there are drawbacks as well. First of all, mutual funds, on average, do not normally outperform the market. On balance, they do no better than the popular market averages such as the Dow Jones Industrial Average or the Standard & Poor's 500 Stock Index. Nevertheless, they provide a very efficient means for diversifying your portfolio. Also, a few funds have exceptional performance over time.

Furthermore, the purchase of mutual fund shares can be expensive if you are not careful. Some funds charge high commissions while others do not. By the time you finish this chapter, you will be well informed on this topic.

Another problem in buying mutual funds is the selection process. Mutual funds are supposed to take most of the difficulty out of the decision-making process, but this is hardly the case when there are over 1200 funds from which to choose. Selecting a mutual fund can be almost as difficult as selecting a stock for the uninformed investor. We will help you overcome part of the selection problems as you become better informed and more sophisticated after reading this chapter.

Finally, a mutual fund investor must be sensitive to the excessive claims that are made in advertisements for mutual funds. The most abusive are bond fund advertisements that tell you their fund is investing in fixed-income securities that pay 10 to 12 percent in interest per year, so you would be foolish to invest in a 7 percent certificate of deposit. What they fail to tell you is that their securities have a 20- or 30-year life, and if interest rates go up, the value of your fund may go down by 10 to 20 percent. Also some funds take one year's spectacular gain and extrapolate it 20 years into the future, claiming phenomenal potential for growth. Although the Securities and Exchange Commission is constantly monitoring and regulating advertising practices, many opportunities for abuse remain.

Now that we have briefly considered the advantages and drawbacks of mutual funds, let's go down to the actual mechanics. In the remainder of the chapter, we will discuss the following topics: the open-end versus the closed-end investment company, the commission structure for mutual funds (load versus no-load funds), the different types of specialized mutual funds (stocks versus bonds, and so on), the services that funds provide, the measurement of performance, and tax features related to mutual funds.

OPEN-END VERSUS CLOSED-END FUNDS

An **investment company** (fund) may be either open-end or closed-end. An **open-end fund** is one in which the number of shares is unlimited. Thus, if the fund has 10 million shares outstanding and investors wish to purchase another million shares, then one million new shares are issued and the proceeds are invested in additional securities in the market. Actually the term *mutual fund* applies specifically to open-end investment companies. We shall later describe closed-end investment companies, which technically are not mutual funds. The financial press, however, calls both types of investment companies mutual funds, and we shall, too.

Open-end funds not only agree to sell an unlimited amount of new shares, but they also agree to buy back (redeem) any and all shares as requested by shareholders. In buying and selling the shares of open-end funds, you do not deal on the organized exchanges or in the over-the-counter market but directly with the fund, the fund distributor, or a representative of the fund. For example, if you want to buy or sell shares in the Fidelity Puritan Fund, you will deal directly with the fund or its distributor, Fidelity Distributors Corporation, or a broker that distributes shares of the fund.

Transactions in a fund are priced at the fund's net asset value (there may or may not also be a commission, as we shall discuss in the next section). The

Figure 13.1 QUOTATIONS OF A MUTUAL FUND GROUP, MAY 19, 1986

	NAV	Offer Price	NAV Chg.
Vanguard Group:			
Explor	37.40	N.L.	– .16
Explr II	22.94	N.L.	– .05
Gemini	73.69	N.L.	+ .29
Morgan	14.15	N.L.	– .01
Naess T	48.28	N.L.	– .15
Prmcp	40.88	N.L.	– .02
QualDv 1	19.42	N.L.	+ .12
QualDv 2	9.42	N.L.	– .05
QualDv 3	23.35	N.L.	– .07
Star Fnd	11.43	N.L.	+ .01
TCF Int	38.63	N.L.	+ .17
TCF usa	33.75	N.L.	+ .09
GNMA	9.88	N.L.	...
HiY Bnd	9.22	N.L.	– .01
IG Bond	8.55	N.L.	+ .01
ST Portf	10.65	N.L.	...
Index Tr	25.50	N.L.	+ .05
Mun HiY	10.48	N.L.	– .04
Mun Insr	11.49	N.L.	– .06
Mun Intr	11.76	N.L.	– .04
Mun Lng	10.71	N.L.	– .05
Mun Shrt	15.40	N.L.	...
Vsp Gold	7.03	N.L.	...
VSP Hlth	18.16	N.L.	– .10
VSP Svc	18.95	N.L.	...
VSP Tec	13.22	N.L.	– .04
Welsley	16.16	N.L.	+ .01
Wellgtn	15.61	N.L.	+ .03
Windsr	15.98	N.L.	+ .04
Wndsr II	12.16	N.L.	+ .02
WF US	13.16	N.L.	+ .10
WF Intl	10.08	N.L.	+ .02

SOURCE: Reprinted by permission of the *Wall Street Journal*, © Dow Jones & Company, Inc., May 20, 1986, p. 52. All rights reserved.

net asset value is equal to the total value of the securities owned by the fund less any liabilities, divided by the number of shares outstanding.

$$\text{Net asset value (NAV)} = \frac{\text{total value of securities} - \text{liabilities}}{\text{share outstanding}} \tag{13.1}$$

If a firm has securities worth \$120 million, with \$1 million in liabilities and 10 million shares outstanding, the net asset value is \$11.90.

$$\frac{\$120 \text{ million} - \$1 \text{ million}}{10 \text{ million}} = \frac{\$119 \text{ million}}{10 \text{ million}} = \$11.90$$

If one million new shares are sold at \$11.90,[1] the proceeds of \$11.9 million are immediately reinvested so that the net asset value does not change as a result of the sale (normally daily sales might take place in much smaller amounts).

Net asset value is recomputed daily and goes up or down as a result of changes in the value of the portfolio. An example of changes in net asset value can be seen for the Vanguard Group of funds in Figure 13.1. Clearly some of

[1] If there were a commission associated with the sale, the gross sales price would be higher than \$11.90, but the net proceeds to the fund would still be \$11.90.

their funds went up while others went down on May 19, 1986. The largest absolute gainer was the Gemini fund (+$.29) and the largest loser was the Explorer fund (−$.16). The middle column, labeled "offer price," with NL symbols under it, can be ignored for now. We will consider this designation later in the chapter. As you can see, the Vanguard Group sponsors over 30 funds. A listing of the primary purpose of many of the Vanguard funds is presented in Figure 13.2. Later in the chapter, you will also see the offerings of other fund sponsors.

Figure 13.2 DESCRIPTION OF VANGUARD FUNDS

Allows switching from one fund to another without charge

Fund distributor	Type of fund
Vanguard Group Vanguard Financial Center Valley Forge, PA 19482 800-362-0530 (local) 800-662-7447 (out of state) Exchange privilege: Yes	
Explorer Fund	stock
Gemini Fund	stock
Ivest Fund	stock
WL Morgan Growth Fund	stock
Naess & Thomas Special Fund	stock
PrimeCap Fund	stock
Trustees' Commingled-International Equity	stock
Trustees' Commingled-US Equity	stock
Vanguard Fixed Income Secs-GNMA	bond & preferred
Vanguard Fixed Income Secs-High Yield	bond & preferred
Vanguard Fixed Income Secs-Invest Grade	bond & preferred
Vanguard Fixed Income Secs-Short Term	bond & preferred
Vanguard Index Trust	stock
Vanguard MM Trust-Federal	money market
Vanguard MM Trust-Insured	money market
Vanguard MM Trust-Prime	money market
Vanguard Muni Bond-Intermediate-Term	municipal bond
Vanguard Muni Bond-Long-Term	municipal bond
Vanguard Muni Bond-Short-Term	money market
Vanguard Muni Bond-High Yield	municipal bond
Vanguard Muni Bond-Insured Long-Term	municipal bond
Vanguard Muni Bond-MM	money market
Vanguard Qualified Dividend I	stock
Vanguard Qualified Dividend II	bond & preferred
Vanguard Qualified Dividend III	bond & preferred
Vanguard Specialized-Gold & Prec Metals	stock
Vanguard Specialized-Health Care	stock
Vanguard Specialized-Service Economy	stock
Vanguard Specialized-Technology	stock
Vanguard Star Fund	balanced
Wellesley Income Fund	balanced
Wellington Fund	balanced
Windsor Fund	stock
Windsor II	stock

SOURCE: Reprinted by permission of *Forbes* magazine, September 16, 1985, p. 174. © Forbes Inc., 1985.

Closed-End Funds

The open-end type of fund that we have been discussing represents approximately 95 percent of the funds outstanding. You should, however, also be familiar with closed-end funds. A **closed-end fund** has a specified number of shares outstanding, and this number does not change with each purchase or sale. The only way you can buy the shares of a closed-end fund is when someone else is selling. Actually, a closed-end fund is similar to any stock that is trading on an organized exchange or in the over-the-counter market. Instead of the firm being involved in the manufacturing of automobiles or the design of computers, a closed-end fund is engaged in the investment and management of a security portfolio. Perhaps two million shares are initially sold at $20 per share. The $40 million is then redeployed in investments in securities. If you later wish to buy 100 shares of the fund, you must purchase them from a willing seller, and you must go through a stockbroker, just as you would with any stock, and pay the normal commission. You do not deal directly with the fund because they have "closed out" the number of shares in which they deal.

One of the justifications for sponsors organizing a closed-end fund is that there are only limited opportunities for redeployment of funds in accordance with the objectives or investment philosophy of the fund. For example, the fund may specialize in emerging companies in the electronics industry or in stocks of a small foreign country.

An example of a closed-end investment company trading on an organized exchange can be seen in Figure 13.3. Note that the Korea fund is quoted on the New York Stock Exchange just as any other stock, such as the Kroger store chain directly below it.[2]

You may recall that in our earlier discussion of open-end funds we said that they always trade at their net asset value. Such is not the case for closed-end funds. They may trade above (premium) or below (discount) their NAV depending upon investor enthusiasm. A fund may trade at a premium because it has holdings in a "hot" industry or country or simply because the demand exceeds the supply for the limited (closed) number of fund shares. Another reason for a premium might be that the fund has, as part of its portfolio, non-publicly traded stocks that investors believe are carried at too low an asset value on the fund's books.[3]

Closed-end funds trade at a discount from their net asset value because they have had a prior record of poor performance or are heavily invested in an unpopular industry. Many investors actually choose to invest in funds trading at a discount on the premise that they are irrationally priced — that is, they should be worth at least their net asset value.

[2] The .83e after the Korea fund means that this is the total dividends per share paid over the last 12 months. The value may or may not remain the same in the future.

[3] A non-publicly traded stock is one that is in private hands, and therefore there is no market quote available. The non-publicly traded stock may simply be carried at book value or some other arbitrary measure.

Figure 13.3 A CLOSED-END FUND QUOTE ON THE NEW YORK STOCK EXCHANGE

NYSE COMPOSITE TRANSACTIONS

52 Weeks High	Low	Stock	Div.	Yld %	P-E Ratio	Sales 100s	High	low	Close	Net Chg.
36	25	KerrMc	1.10	3.8	11	380	29	28¾	28¾	– ¼
30⅝	16¾	Keycp s	1.00	3.9	10	82	25⅞	25⅝	25⅞	...
5	2⅝	KeysCo		...	...	10	3¾	3¾	3¾	+ ⅛
19⅝	12¾	KeyInt		...	21	288	18⅝	18⅜	18½	– ⅛
38½	30⅜	Kidde	1.20	3.6	11	472	33⅞	32¾	33	– 1
89	53⅜	KimbCl	2.48	3.1	13	407	79¾	78⅝	78⅞	+ ¼
53¾	33⅛	KnghtRd	.88	1.7	23	1018	51¼	51	51⅛	+ ⅛
28⅜	13⅛	Knogo		...	23	154	27⅜	27¼	27¼	– ¼
30¾	25¼	Koger	2.50	8.8	51	67	28⅝	28½	28½	...
19½	12½	Kolmor	.32	1.9	...	x292	17	16½	16½	– ⅜
30⅜	15⅜	Kopers	.80	2.8	...	323	29	28⅛	28½	– ¾
114	95	Koppr pf	10.00	9.5	...	3	106½	105½	105½	– 1
34¾	12¾	Korea	.83e	2.5	...	816	33⅜	32¼	33	+ 1½
53¼	41¼	Kroger	2.00	3.9	12	927	51½	51	51	– ⅜
24⅜	14¾	Kuhlm	.40	2.2	17	65	18¼	18⅛	18⅛	– ¼
56¼	28½	Kyocer	.40e	.7	...	27	54¼	53½	54	+ 1
27	17¼	Kysor	.88	3.5	9	93	25½	25⅜	25⅜	– ¼
		– L–L–L –								
29⅞	12½	LAC n	.30	1.9	...	x45	15⅝	15⅜	15⅝	+ ¼
34⅜	26¼	LN Ho	2.98e	9.5	11	63	31⅜	30¾	31⅜	+ 1
15¾	7⅞	LLE Ry	2.35e	21.9	...	401	10¾	10½	10¾	+ ⅛
3	1	LLCCp		...	...	1499	2½	2¼	2½	+ ⅛
9⅞	5¼	LTV		...	...	1101	7¼	7⅛	7¼	...
20¾	8½	LTV pfB	2.29i	...	...	32	13⅝	13½	13⅝	– ⅛
53¾	31	LTV pfC		...	...	1	43½	43½	43½	...
14	8¼	LTV pfD		...	...	110	11	11	11	...
16¾	11½	LQuint		...	29	41	14¼	14	14¼	+ ⅛
38⅛	21½	LaclGs	1.90	5.2	9	35	37	36¾	36¾	+ ¼
12⅛	6¾	Lafarge	.20	1.8	24	3	11⅛	11⅛	11⅛	...
30½	21¼	Lafrg pf	2.44	8.7	...	25	28⅛	28	28	– ¼
13⅜	7¼	Lamaur	.24	2.0	23	56	12	11¾	12	...
4⅞	3⅛	LamSes		...	15	20	4	3¾	3⅞	...
14¼	10⅜	Lawtint	.56	4.0	...	281	14⅛	13¾	14⅛	+ ¼
17⅝	5¼	LearPt	.05i	...	...	334	6⅜	6¼	6⅜	...
24¾	13⅝	LearP pf	.72i	...	...	154	14⅝	14⅜	14½	– ⅛
62¼	45¾	LearSg	2.00	3.6	13	34	54⅞	54⅜	54⅞	+ ¾
20⅝	14¾	LeaRnl s	.40	2.1	20	253	19¾	19½	19½	– ¼

SOURCE: Reprinted by permission of the *Wall Street Journal*, © Dow Jones & Company, Inc., May 20, 1986, p. 60.

An example of closed-end funds trading at premiums and discounts is presented in Figure 13.4. Note how far some funds can get away from their net asset value.

One of the hopes of an investor in a closed-end fund trading at a discount from net asset value is that the fund may decide to liquidate its holdings and distribute the proceeds from the sale of its securities (at net asset value) to its investors. Another way to achieve basically the same objective is for the fund to convert from a closed-end fund to an open-end fund. After this conversion, the fund will then be bought and sold at net asset value. The Growth Fund of Florida followed precisely this route in 1986, providing investors with an extra 15 percent return as assets were effectively brought up to net asset value.

Figure 13.4 PREMIUMS OR DISCOUNTS FROM NET ASSET VALUE

Fund	% premium (+) or discount (–)[1]	Fund	% premium (+) or discount (–)[1]
Adams Express Co	–7.6%	Equity Strategies Fund	–15.1
American Capital Conv Sec[2]	+10.1	General American Investors	–5.9
ASA Ltd	+4.2	Japan Fund	–4.3
Baker, Fentress & Co	–15.5	Korea Fund	+28.3
Bancroft Convertible Fund[2]	–7.2	Lehman Corp	–5.9
Castle Convertible Fund[2]	+0.3	Mexico Fund	–25.4
Central Securities	–5.3	Niagara Share Corp	–4.0
CL Assets	–11.3	Petroleum & Resources Corp	–3.1
Claremont Capital	+5.8	Source Capital	+6.9
Combined Penny Stock Fund	–38.0	Spectra Fund	–46.2
Emerging Medical Technology Fund	–9.8	Tri-Continental Corp	–0.7
Engex	–34.5	Z-Seven	–10.7

[1]As of June 30, 1985. [2]Balanced fund.

Sells at a premium because the investment is in a "hot" country

SOURCE: Excerpted by permission of *Forbes* magazine, September 16, 1985, p. 96 © Forbes Inc., 1985.

Unit Investment Trusts

A variation of the closed-end fund is the unit investment trust. We briefly mention this topic because sometimes investors are asked to choose between an open- or closed-end fund and a unit investment trust. We have only given you two-thirds of the picture.

A **unit investment trust** is an unmanaged pool of securities. The securities usually are bonds, and may represent federal government, corporate, or municipal issues. Once the securities in the unit investment trust are purchased, they remain in place until they mature. The sponsor of a unit investment trust does not try to actively manage the assets. A trust has a prescribed life, such as 10 or 15 years, that matches the anticipated life of the securities in the trust.

The advantage of a unit investment trust is that you get a diversified portfolio of securities (as is true of closed- and open-end investment companies). You also have the advantage of knowing you will get your initial investment back at the end of the life of the trust (unless there are defaults). In the meantime, you will draw a set rate of interest that is specified at the outset based on the securities in the trust. Even if interest rates go up and bond prices go down during the life of the trust, you know you will get your investment back in the end.

With an open- or closed-end fund you do not have a similar assurance. The value of your fund may go up or down and not return to the original purchase price because there is no set life to an open- or closed-end fund. Of course, with a fund you have active management, which may provide you with superior returns (we also know that active management can take you in the opposite direction).

The normal commission for buying a unit investment trust is 3 percent and it may be subtracted from the first few years of interest payments rather than from the initial contribution. This, of course, will slightly lower the yield on the trust.

Having examined the general nature of open-end and closed-end funds as well as unit investment trusts, we now sharpen our focus on open-end funds. As you may recall, we stated earlier that they represent 95 percent of the funds outstanding.

LOAD VERSUS NO-LOAD FUNDS

One of the most important features of an open-end fund is whether it is a load or no-load fund. The term **load** stands for commission, and it may range up to 8.5 percent of the purchase price. Thus, if you invested \$2000 in a mutual fund and paid an 8.5 percent load, you would be allocating \$170 (8.5 percent × \$2000) of your funds to commissions. You would only have \$1830 in actual mutual fund shares. Your \$1830 would have to go up by 9.29 percent, or \$170, just for you to be up to your original investment of \$2000.

Mutual fund investment	\$1830
Return	×9.29%
Gain	\$170

Even if the commission was prorated over a number of years, you would still have to climb out of a hole to cover it.

Because of the heavy burden that a commission can place on a mutual fund investment, we suggest that you generally concentrate your attention on funds that do not require commissions. These are termed **no-load funds.** Researchers over many decades have concluded that no-load funds perform as well as load funds, so normally there is no reason to buy a load fund. Because of the commission available to load fund salespersons, however, these funds are often marketed much more aggressively than no-load funds. The typical small investor may buy a load fund without realizing that he or she could have accomplished precisely the same objective with a no-load fund. No-load funds make their return through the annual management fee that is charged to investors. It is normally a modest ½ to 1½ percent of the amount involved. Load funds have a similar management fee, so this fee is not really an extra cost of buying a no-load fund.

Note in Figure 13.5 the declining importance of load funds. They have gone from managing 96 percent of all open-end mutual fund assets in 1965 to 62 percent in 1986. Although not reflected in the figure, approximately half of all

Figure 13.5 PERCENTAGE OF MUTUAL FUND ASSETS MANAGED BY LOAD FUNDS

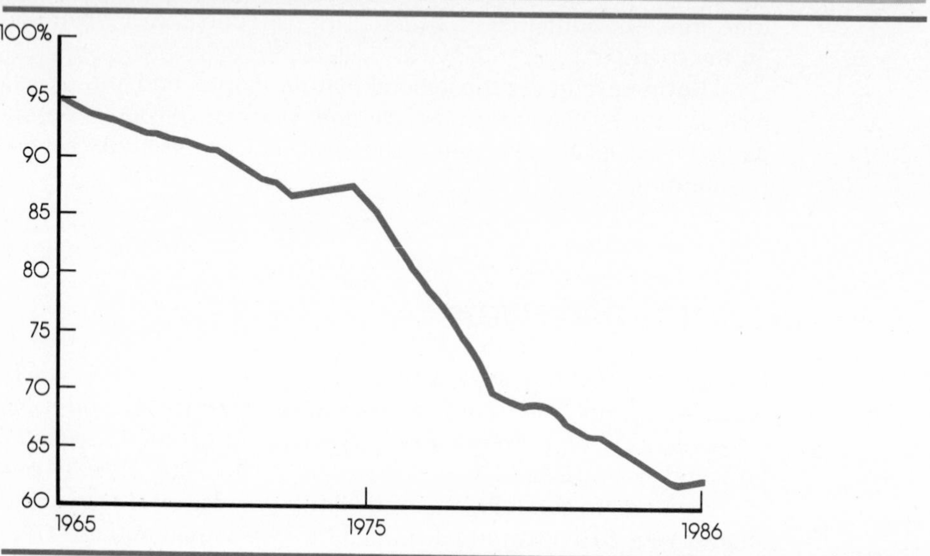

new funds are no-loads. **Low-load funds**—those that have small loads, such as 2 to 3 percent—are much more acceptable as an investment outlet than full-load funds. They fall somewhere between the 8.5 percent load funds and the no-loads.

In order to see how you determine whether an individual fund is a load or no-load fund, look at the quotes from the *Wall Street Journal* in Figure 13.6. After each fund's name, there are three items of information given (see the top of each column). The first item is the NAV (the net asset value), the second is the offer price, and the third is the change in the net asset value. You will recall that the net asset value represents the total value of the firm's securities minus liabilities divided by the shares outstanding. It indicates the fund's value on a per share basis.

By looking under the offer price column, you can tell if the fund is a load or no-load fund. If it is a no-load, you will see the letters N.L. If it is a load, you will see an actual dollar value. Let's go to the ABT Midwest funds listed in the first column. Note that part of their funds are no-loads (N.L.s) and part are not. For example, their Int. Govt. (intermediate government bond fund) is a no-load (N.L.). This means that you can buy or sell it at its NAV of $10.66. The Emgr. Gr. (emerging growth fund), however, is a load fund. The net asset value is $9.41 and the offer price is $10.28. This means the actual value per mutual fund share is $9.41, but the purchase price is $10.28. The difference between the two is the load or commission. In this case, you are paying a commission of $.87.

Figure 13.6 *WALL STREET JOURNAL* **MUTUAL FUND DATA**

Load fund

No-load fund

MUTUAL FUND QUOTATIONS

Wednesday, May 14, 1986

Price ranges for investment companies, as quoted by the National Association of Securities Dealers. NAV stands for net asset value per share; the offering includes net asset value plus maximum sales charge, if any.

	NAV	Offer Price	NAV Chg.
AARP Invest Program:			
Cap Grw	22.35	N.L.+	.05
Gen Bnd	16.04	N.L.+	.01
Ginnie M	16.01	N.L.+	.03
Gro Inc	21.35	N.L.+	.10
TxFr Bd	(z)	(z)	...
TxF Shrt	15.53	N.L.–	.01
ABT Midwest Funds:			
Emrg Gr	9.41	10.28	...
Growth I	13.73	15.01+	.01
Int Govt	10.66	N.L.	...
LG Govt	10.72	11.17+	.02
Sec Inc	11.06	12.09	...
Util Inc	14.53	15.88+	.10
Acorn Fnd	41.36	N.L.+	.03
Adtek Fd	12.13	N.L.+	.04
Advest Advantage:			
Govt	9.97	N.L.–	.02
Growth	10.65	N.L.+	.01
Income	10.33	N.L.–	.04
Specl	10.11	N.L.–	.11
Afuture Fd	14.97	N.L.+	.05
AIM Funds:			
Charter	7.93	N.L.+	.04
Constel	27.98	N.L.+	.17
Conv Yld	12.88	13.78	...
Grnway	10.58	11.32+	.04
HiYld Sc	10.15	10.86+	.01
Summit	(z)	(z)	...
Weingr	(z)	(z)	...
Alliance Capital:			
Alli Conv	9.82	10.39	...
Alli Gov	9.29	9.83	...
Alli HiY	10.52	11.13–	.11
Alli Intl	21.74	23.76–	.17
Alli Mtge	9.72	10.29+	.01
Alli Tech	24.50	26.78–	.06
Chem Fd	9.16	10.01+	.01
Surveyr	(z)	(z)	...
Alpha Fd	8.05	8.80+	.05
American Capital Group:			
Comstk	16.05	17.54+	.01
Corp Bd	7.58	8.28+	.01
Enterpr	14.81	16.19–	.03
Exch Fd	56.41	(z) +	.17
Fd Amer	12.39	13.54+	.04
Govt Sec	11.76	12.61	...
Growth	27.08	(z) +	.17
Harbor	14.77	16.14+	.02
High Yld	10.95	11.74+	.02
Muni Bd	21.44	22.51+	.04
O T C	12.23	13.37+	.06
Pace Fd	23.87	26.09+	.01
Prov Inc	5.02	5.41+	.02
TxE HY	12.29	12.90+	.02
Venture	16.62	18.16+	.02
Mass Tx	16.22	N.L.–	.01
New Ldr	22.89	N.L.+	.08
NYT Ex	15.30	N.L.+	.01
Spl Incm	9.88	N.L.+	.05
Tax ExB	12.46	N.L.	...
Third Cn	7.96	N.L.–	.02
Eagle Gth	8.21	8.97–	.03
Eaton Vance Funds:			
Cal Mn r	10.29	N.L.–	.01
EH Stk	14.24	15.35+	.04
Gov Obli	12.42	13.32	...
Growth	7.92	8.66	...
Hi Mun r	10.31	N.L.+	.01
High Yld	5.23	5.61–	.01
Inc Bost	10.21	10.95	...
Invests	8.26	9.03+	.01
Muni Bd	8.86	9.21+	.01
Naut Fd	14.21	15.53+	.07
Spc Eqty	21.24	22.90+	.14
Tax Mge	20.77	22.70+	.11
VS Specl	13.93	15.22+	.02
Empir Bld	16.81	17.65–	.01
ES Tot rt	13.60	N.L.+	.02
Evergrn	14.15	N.L.+	.04
Evrgrn TR	18.91	N.L.+	.03
Fairmnt	231.90	N.L.+	.24
Farm B Gr	16.34	N.L.+	.05
Federated Group:			
Fed StkB	15.53	N.L.	...
Cash Tr	11.18	N.L.	...
Exch Fd	49.09	N.L.+	.05
FT Intl	20.30	N.L.+	.03
GNMA	11.38	N.L.	...
Grow Tr	15.30	N.L.+	.03
Govt Tr	10.45	N.L.+	.01
Hi Incm	12.66	13.54	...
Hi Yld	11.02	N.L.	...
Incm Tr	10.78	N.L.–	.01
Intrmd	10.12	N.L.–	.01
SIMT	10.28	N.L.+	.01
Stock Tr	21.97	N.L.+	.01
Fidelity Investments:			
Aggr TF	11.26	N.L.–	.02
Cal HYld	11.41	N.L.–	.01
Congr St	78.74	N.L.+	.73
Contra	12.62	N.L.+	.05
CT ARP	10.69	N.L.	...
Discovr	25.53	N.L.–	.08
Eq Incm	29.03	29.62–	.04
Exch Fd	63.07	N.L.+	.62
Fidel Fd	18.65	N.L.+	.01
Flex B	7.35	N.L.–	.01
Freedm	17.14	N.L.–	.03
GNMA	10.62	N.L.	...
Govt Sec	10.15	N.L.	...
Gro Inc	13.14	N.L.+	.01
Janus Funds:			
Jan Fnd	14.94	N.L.	...
Janus VI	13.63	N.L.–	.01
Jans Vn	29.58	N.L.+	.14
John Hancock Funds:			
Bond Fd	16.27	17.78–	.05
Globl Tr	14.16	15.48+	.02
Growth	16.59	18.13+	.07
Spcl Eqt	6.99	7.64+	.02
US GvSc	9.52	10.40–	.01
Tax Ex	10.72	11.72–	.01
USGG	10.77	11.77–	.02
Kauf Fund	1.12	N.L.+	.03
Kemper Funds:			
Cal Tax	14.05	14.71+	.02
Income	9.08	9.61–	.01
Growth	13.35	14.59+	.04
High Yld	11.44	12.11	...
Int'l Fd	22.42	24.50–	.18
Muni Bd	9.40	9.84+	.01
Optn Inc	10.91	11.92–	.01
Summit	6.10	6.67	...
Technol	13.61	14.87–	.01
Total R	17.00	18.58+	.04
US GvSc	9.86	10.32–	.02
KY Tax Fr	6.80	N.L.	...
Keystone Mass Group:			
Cust B1 r	17.74	N.L.–	.06
Cust B2 r	20.33	N.L.–	.02
Cust B4 r	8.43	N.L.	...
CustK1 r	10.01	N.L.+	.01
CustK2 r	8.86	N.L.+	.03
Cust S1 r	24.03	N.L.+	.07
Cust S3 r	9.99	N.L.+	.01
Cust S4 r	7.35	N.L.+	.01
Intl Fd r	6.96	N.L.–	.01
PrecM r	11.16	N.L.–	.08
TaxEx r	10.77	N.L.–	.03
Tax Fr r	8.68	N.L.–	.02
Kidder Group:			
KPEQI	17.38	N.L.+	[illegible]
Govt Inc	15.33	N.L.–	.01
Spcl Grw	15.26	N.L.+	.07
TFI Ntl	15.33	15.97+	.01
TFI NY	15.14	15.77–	.02
Legg Mason Funds			
Sp Invst	11.52	N.L.–	.01
Totl Ret	10.77	N.L.	...
Pil Ginn	15.41	15.64+	.01
Pil HiYd	8.26	8.39–	.01
Pil Mag	10.24	11.04+	.01
Pil Pfd	25.74	26.13+	.01
Pioneer Funds:			
Bond Fd	9.65	10.10–	.01
Pionr Fd	23.44	25.62+	.05
Pionr II	19.15	20.93+	.01
Pionr III	17.09	18.68–	.01
Price Rowe:			
Eqty In	12.31	N.L.+	.04
GNMA	10.09	N.L.	...
Growth	19.47	N.L.+	.04
Grw Inc	14.37	N.L.+	.03
High Yld	11.15	N.L.–	.01
Income	9.09	N.L.–	.01
Intl Fd	23.45	N.L.+	.02
New Am	14.04	N.L.+	.06
New Era	19.34	N.L.–	.01
Nw Horz	16.73	N.L.–	.01
S-T Bond	5.20	N.L.	...
TxFr Inc	9.58	N.L.–	.01
TxFr HY	11.36	N.L.–	.01
TxFr SI	5.18	N.L.	...
Principal Preserv:			
S&P 100	10.34	11.06+	.06
TX EX	8.67	9.08+	.01
GOVT PI	9.83	10.29	...
Pro Services Funds:			
Med Tec	14.79	N.L.+	.09
Pro Fnd	12.99	N.L.+	.03
Pro Inco	9.21	N.L.+	.01
Prudential Bache:			
Adjust R	24.62	N.L.–	.01
CalMn r	11.47	N.L.–	.01
Equity r	9.79	N.L.+	.01
Global r	20.00	N.L.–	.15
GNMA	15.88	N.L.+	.05
GovtPI r	10.70	N.L.+	.02
Govt Sec	10.75	N.L.	...
Grwth r	15.33	N.L.–	.05
HiYld r	10.81	N.L.+	.01
HY Mn r	15.91	N.L.–	.01
InVer r	11.21	N.L.–	.01
MnNY r	11.61	N.L.–	.01
OptnGr r	8.85	N.L.+	.01
Resrch r	12.64	N.L.+	.04
Util Fd r	14.12	N.L.+	.04

SOURCE: Reprinted by permission of the *Wall Street Journal*, © Dow Jones & Company, Inc., May 15, 1986, p. 44. All rights reserved.

Offer (purchase price)	$10.28
Net asset value	9.41
Commission or load	$ .87

To determine what percent the commission represents, the normal procedure is to divide the commission by the offer price. In this instance the commission is 8.46 percent.[4]

[4] You could make a strong case for dividing the commission by net asset value. However, we are following industry practice.

$$\frac{\text{Commission}}{\text{Offer price}} = \frac{\$\ .87}{\$10.28} = 8.46 \text{ percent}$$

In the case of the load fund, if you buy it today for $10.28 and want to sell it immediately, you will only receive $9.41. Another way to examine the effect of the load is to assume that the load fund shares you bought go up immediately by $.10 in net asset value. Your $10.28 purchase will still be worth only $9.51 (the original net asset value of $9.41 plus $.10). With a no-load fund, none of these problems exists. If a no-load fund goes up by $.10 immediately after you buy it, you are clearly $.10 ahead.

In perusing Figure 13.6, note the array of load and no-load funds. Most groups are purely load or no-load funds, so the ABT Midwest funds are somewhat of an exception in this regard. The important point is that there is an ample supply of no-load funds from which to choose.

Another way of studying funds is through the *Forbes Annual Mutual Fund Survey. Forbes* compiles data on over 1000 funds and rates them on performance. This is an excellent source that comes out in September of each year. Your library, in all likelihood, has a copy of the September *Forbes* mutual fund issue. The *Forbes* issue is a very good data source for the new investor who does not know where to begin. An excerpt from the issue is presented in Figure 13.7.

Some of the information in the table will be discussed later in the chapter, but note for now that you get a rating on performance in up and down markets (left margin), average annual return data for ten years (1976–1985), returns for the latest 12 months, size of total assets, maximum sales charges, and annual expenses per $100. Although not specifically listed, most of these funds have an initial minimum investment of $1000, but the amount may vary from fund to fund (later additional contributions may be smaller).

Our primary interest in this section of the chapter is the maximum sales charge column (second column from the right). These data tell you whether a fund is a no-load or a load, and if it is a load, what the percentage commission is. The first fund listed, Nicholas Fund/Nicholas is clearly a no-load. The first load fund shown in the table is the Old Dominion Investors' Trust, with an 8.5 percent commission. You can also casually observe that no-loads generally do at least as well as loads in terms of performance ratings or investment results. Furthermore, the annual expenses per $100 (last column) are generally not any higher for the no-load funds than the load funds. The clear message, then, is to look for no-load funds first.

Let's assume that you see a few mutual funds in the annual *Forbes* issue (or some other source) that interest you. Because no-loads are not aggressively sold by salespersons because there are no commissions, you may need to make the first move. What you generally do is contact the fund through their telephone numbers (often toll-free) or by mail and ask for information. They will respond quickly with data about the fund. You will get a detailed sales prospectus as well as summary literature that allows you to easily understand the objectives and strategy of the fund. You will also get detailed data on the fund's performance record.

Figure 13.7 *FORBES* MUTUAL FUND DATA

1985 Fund Ratings

Stock funds

Performance in UP markets	Performance in DOWN markets	Fund/distributor	Investment results: Average annual total return 1976-85	Latest 12 months: total return	Latest 12 months: return from income dividends	Total assets 6/30/85 (millions)	Total assets % change '85 vs '84	Maximum sales charge	Annual expenses per $100
		Standard & Poor's 500 stock average	12.5%	30.9%	4.2%				
		FORBES stock fund composite	15.2%	22.3%	2.7%				
B	A+	Nicholas Fund/Nicholas	25.4%	39.0%	1.9%	$462	194%	none	$0.82
		Nicholas II/Nicholas	—*	42.3	0.6	78	NM	none	1.59
		North Star Apollo/North Star	—*	10.0	2.4	20	35	none	1.00
•B	•C	North Star Regional Fund/North Star	—*	31.2	1.3	64	45	none	0.80
C	B	North Star Stock Fund/North Star	14.5	25.2	2.9	59	28	none	0.70
•C	•C	Northeast Investors Growth/Northeast Inv	—*	33.8	0.8	5	42	none	2.02
•C	•C	Nova Fund/Nova	—*	21.6	1.3	28	−1	none	1.50
D	B	Old Dominion Investors' Trust/Investors Secs	12.2	24.9	7.4	5	21	8.50%	1.17
B	D	Omega Fund/Omega	12.3	36.1	0.9	29	26	none	1.53
B	D	One Hundred Fund/Berger	11.7	12.5	2.1	10	1	none	1.90‡
		PaineWebber Olympus Fund/PaineWebber	—*	—*	—*	34	—	8.50	NA
C	A	Partners Fund/Neuberger	20.6	32.6	4.1	222	52	none	0.91
•D	•C	Pax World Fund/Pax World	—*	29.6	4.3	25	80	none	1.50‡
D	C	Penn Square Mutual Fund/Penn Square	12.5	22.5	4.6	183	13	none	0.65
B	A	Pennsylvania Mutual Fund/Penn Mutual	22.6	23.1	1.3	292	97	†	1.18
A	D	Petroleum & Resources Corp/closed end	14.0	12.9	5.0	231	−9	NA	0.59
C	C	Philadelphia Fund/Universal	14.0	17.9	2.7	108	7	8.50	0.91
		Phoenix Growth Fund/Phoenix	—*	32.8	2.7	105	52	8.50	0.88
		Phoenix Stock Fund/Phoenix	—*	32.0	2.3	65	39	8.50	1.01
D	A	Pilgrim MagnaCap Fund[19]/Pilgrim	14.7	37.1	3.3	66	803	7.25	1.60
B	D	Pilot Fund/Criterion	14.1	25.1	3.6	70	12	8.50	1.25
C	C	Pine Street Fund/Alliance	12.9	36.7	4.3	52	32	none	1.09‡
C	C	Pioneer Fund/Pioneer	14.2	24.9	3.8	1,443	21	8.50	0.69
B	A	Pioneer II/Pioneer	20.7	27.7	3.3	1,834	49	8.50	0.71

Total return is for 9/30/76 to 6/30/85. Funds are added to this guide when they exceed $5 million in net assets and deleted when they drop below $2 million. Stock and balanced funds are rated only if in operation since 11/30/80. *Fund not in operation for full period. •Fund rated for two periods only; maximum allowable grade A. †Fund not currently selling new shares. ‡Fund has 12b-1 plan pending or in force *(see story, p. 82)*. [19]Formerly MagnaCap Fund. NA: Not applicable or not available. NM: Not meaningful.

Table of distributors, showing addresses and phone numbers, begins on p. 150.

SOURCE: Reprinted by permission of *Forbes* magazine, September 16, 1985, p. 110.

The same *Forbes* issue that gave us the financial data in Figure 13.7 also supplies the phone numbers and mailing addresses for over 1000 funds. A second excerpt is presented in Figure 13.8. There you can see mailing information on the Nicholas fund, distributed by the Nicholas Company, which we alluded to in Figure 13.7. Although this fund does not have a toll-free 800 number, many other funds shown in the table do.

The two pages shown in this chapter as Figure 13.7 and Figure 13.8 from the *Forbes* annual mutual fund issue are part of a 52-page survey, so you may want to consider a trip to the library. *Business Week, Financial World, Consumer*

Figure 13.8 ADDRESSES OF MUTUAL FUNDS

Fund distributor	Type of fund
NEL Equity Services 501 Boylston Street Boston, MA 02117 617-267-6000 (local) 800-343-7104 (out of state) Exchange privilege: Yes	
Loomis-Sayles Capital Development Fund	stock
Loomis-Sayles Mutual Fund	balanced
NEL Cash Management Trust-MM	money market
NEL Cash Management Trust-US Govt	money market
NEL Equity Fund	stock
NEL Growth Fund	stock
NEL Income Fund	bond & preferred
NEL Retirement Equity Fund	stock
NEL Tax Exempt Bond Fund	municipal bond
NEL Tax Exempt MM Fund	money market
Neuberger & Berman Management 342 Madison Avenue New York, NY 10173 212-850-8300* (local) 800-367-0770 (out of state) Exchange privilege: Yes	
Energy Fund	stock
Guardian Mutual Fund	stock
Hemisphere Fund	stock
Liberty Fund	bond & preferred
Manhattan Fund	stock
Neuberger & Berman Government Money	money market
Neuberger & Berman Tax-Free Money	money market
Partners Fund	stock
Newton Fund PO Box 1348 Milwaukee, WI 53201 800-242-7229 (local) 800-247-7039 (out of state) Exchange privilege: Yes	
Newton Growth Fund	stock
Newton Income Fund	balanced
Newton Money Fund	money market
Nicholas Company 312 East Wisconsin Avenue Milwaukee, WI 53202 414-272-6133 (local) Exchange privilege: Yes	
Nicholas Fund	stock
Nicholas II	stock
Nicholas Income Fund	balanced
North Star Funds PO Box 1160 Minneapolis, MN 55440 612-371-7780 (local) Exchange privilege: Yes	
North Star Apollo	stock
North Star Bond Fund	bond & preferred
North Star Regional Fund	stock
North Star Stock Fund	stock
Northeast Investors Trust 50 Congress Street Boston, MA 02109 617-523-3588 (local) 800-225-6704 (out of state) Exchange privilege: Yes	
Northeast Investors Growth Fund	stock
Northeast Investors Trust	bond & preferred

SOURCE: Excerpted by permission of *Forbes* magazine, September 16, 1985, p. 165. © Forbes Inc., 1985.

Reports, and *Money* magazine also have annual evaluations and ratings of funds. If you are interested in mutual funds, you may also wish to consult the Wiesenberger Financial Services *Investment Company Guide* (published by Warren, Gorham and Lamont, Boston). This oversized, hardback book has a full page of information on most funds and is carried in many libraries.

A Final Comment on Commissions and Charges

A few funds have a **back-end sales charge** that may apply when you sell the fund. They normally are 2 to 3 percent and can be part of either a load or no-load fund. Only about 1 in 20 funds has this feature, but you should check the literature to see if a given fund has the charge.

Another factor to be aware of is a 12b-1 plan that a fund may have.[5] A **12b-1 plan** is a way in which the fund may recover part of its selling and promotional expenses in the form of annual operating and management fees on the fund's shares. If you are a shareholder, you normally do not consider this a desirable feature because it cuts down on your annual yield. If you refer back to Figure 13.7, you can identify funds that have 12b-1 plans by the symbol (‡) in the last column of annual expenses per $100.[6] The three funds in the figure that show 12b-1 plans have fairly high operating expenses, though not prohibitively so. A firm's sales literature should indicate whether it has a 12b-1 plan.

SPECIAL FEATURES OFFERED BY MUTUAL FUNDS

Mutual funds offer a number of special features. We shall examine some of the most important.

Automatic Reinvestment Plans

Most funds continually generate dividend and interest income. The income can be paid out to you on a regular basis or, with an **automatic reinvestment plan,** be reinvested in new fund shares with no commissions.[7] This choice to receive or reinvest this income will be among the first you have to make when you fill out the initial form for the fund. Also, when the fund realizes capital gains from the profitable sales of securities, these funds can also be paid out to you or automatically reinvested in new fund shares. Once again, the option is yours.

[5] The 12b-1 designation refers to the ruling number of the Securities and Exchange Commission allowing for these plans.

[6] In rare cases, the firm may deduct 12b-1 expenses directly from capital.

[7] The procedure generally applies to both load and no-load funds.

Box 13.1 REVENUE ENHANCEMENT

When it comes to marketing fees, here's our candidate for the worst deal in town: The Keystone family of funds, which has the dubious distinction of prompting an SEC proposal to crack down on fund accounting. As a third of funds do, the Keystone funds pay their sponsor a so-called 12b-1 charge to cover selling expenses—in Keystone's case, up to 1.25% of net assets annually, one of the highest charges in the industry. The funds have a back-end redemption fee as high as 4%. To top off the cake, Keystone has devised a novel accounting method for 12b-1 expenses that buries them.

Take the B-2 corporate bond fund. The reported expense ratio was 1.06% for 1984. Not bad, except that it excludes most of the 12b-1 charges, which hit 1.25% last year. Add them in, and expenses top 2%. Because Keystone deducts the charges from capital rather than from income, they don't show up in the expense ratio as they do for other funds.

The SEC proposal would force funds to show 12b-1 costs as expenses rather than charges to capital. "So it's not comparable," concedes Roger T. Wickers, senior vice president at Keystone Massachusetts Group and architect of the 12b-1 plan. "I think more important than forced comparability are alternatives. Alternative pricing, alternative distribution methods."

The picture gets even bleaker for those souls who have stuck with Keystone since it was a load fund charging the maximum 8.5%. Not only did they pay an upfront fee to get in, but they're also carrying the yearly 12b-1 costs. But Keystone hasn't forgotten them. For them, there's "redemption value group life insurance," which guarantees that the faithful who continue to hang in won't have less in their account on the day they die than when the fund converted.

Wickers complains that the proposed SEC rule stifles creativity. "Who knows what new kinds of plans will be developed by marketing people," he says. "We have some further innovative thoughts on the drawing board right now." Buyer beware.

SOURCE: Reprinted by permission of *Forbes* magazine, September 16, 1985, p. 83. © Forbes Inc., 1985.

Maintenance of Tax Records

Almost all mutual funds qualify as a regulated investment company under the provisions of the Investment Company Act of 1940. This means that profits are only subject to single taxation; that is, the fund shareholder pays the tax on profits, but the fund does not. This is in contrast to the normal double taxation of a corporation in which the corporation first pays taxes on earnings and then the stockholder must pay a second tax on earnings that are distributed in the form of dividends.

Thus, whenever interest or dividends are credited to your account or the fund sells securities and has a capital gain or loss, you are responsible for the tax consequences. This is true whether you choose to have the funds paid out to you or reinvested in new shares.

At the end of each year, you will receive a 1099 form in which the fund indicates the taxable consequences of your account for the prior year. You can then combine this tax documentation with your other tax records in filing with the IRS. Also, the fund's tax records only cover the tax consequences of the *fund's* actions. If you are trading in the fund by buying and selling its shares, you must keep separate tax records on how much *you* gained or lost on these transactions.

Payment of Regular Income

Most funds will allow you to specify a regular income figure that you wish to receive. For example, if you have $10,000 invested in a fund and you want to receive x dollars a month in regular payments, normally funds will accommodate you. Typically, the distribution comes from the fund's dividends or interest as well as its realized capital gains. If there is not adequate income to cover the distribution, however, part of your original investment may be returned to you in the form of regular payments. The payment of regular income is particularly well suited for the investor who is using his or her mutual fund income to cover living expenses. Although many mutual funds can be purchased for as little as $1000 as an initial investment, the payment of regular income provision normally requires an investment of $5000 or more.

Fund-Switching Privileges

Many mutual fund sponsors or distributors have multiple mutual funds under their supervision. You can see this if you look back at Figure 13.2. The Vanguard Group has over 30 funds under its control. Examples of other large fund distributors include Dreyfus Service Corporation, Fidelity Corporation, Massachusetts Financial Services, and Seligman Marketing. Most of these sponsors control between 20 and 40 funds. Even small fund distributors control from two to ten funds.

Almost all such funds give their investors a **fund-switching privilege;** that is, they will allow you to switch among funds under their control at no expense or at a very limited expense. Thus, if you invest in the Vanguard family of funds, you may decide from time to time to reallocate your resources among different stock funds (some are aggressive while others are conservative), or between stock, bond, or money market funds. This switching privilege gives you flexibility in establishing your investment strategy and allows you to alter your investment mix with changes in the economy.

There is one drawback to the switching privilege. Each time you switch funds, a taxable event takes place. Your profit or loss on the old fund shares must be determined and included in your tax return. To the IRS, it is exactly the same as if you had sold an old fund and bought a completely new one.

Check-Writing Privileges

Some funds allow you to write checks against your ownership position. They actually send you checks through the mail after you invest your money. This is a typical procedure for money market mutual funds (discussed in Chapter 11).

Some large bond funds also allow you a check-writing option. The use of checks is usually not available with stock-oriented funds, however.

When checks are written, they typically must be for a minimum amount of $250 to $500. When you write a check on a fund, it has the same effect as if you had sold off part of your fund shares.

Savings Plan

A savings plan may be voluntary or involuntary in nature. Under a **voluntary savings plan,** you simply agree to place a certain amount in the fund monthly, quarterly, or annually. There is nothing formally arranged. These plans work particularly well when you are using a mutual fund for your annual IRA contributions.

Under an **involuntary savings plan,** you contractually agree to make a regular payment. In a sense, it brings a certain degree of discipline to your investments, but watch out for such plans. They are usually associated with load funds and often involve substantial front-end loads, meaning that part or all of your early payments go toward commissions rather than the purchase of securities. Let's see how this works. Suppose you agree to participate in an involuntary savings plan in which you contribute $500 a year for the next ten years. That represents $5000. Further, assume that the fund has a load or commission equal to the legal maximum of 8.5 percent. This means your commission will be $425 (8.5 percent × $5000). With the front-end load, the commission comes off the top. That is, of your first payment of $500, $425 will go toward commissions and the remaining $75 will be applied toward purchasing mutual fund shares. Even if the front-end commission is spread over two or three years (perhaps $150 to $175 a year), the impact is still great.

The real problem comes into play if you decide to sell the mutual fund before the involuntary contribution period is over (perhaps you decide the fund is not well managed). According to Securities and Exchange Commission rules, if you sell (cancel) within 45 days, you are entitled to receive a refund of all prepaid commissions. If you cancel within 18 months, you are still entitled to receive 85 percent of your prepaid commissions. After that time frame, however, you normally do not receive any reimbursement. In the example above, if you had signed up to participate in the involuntary plan and decided to drop out after two years, you would have contributed $1000 over two years, with $425 going to nonrefundable commissions. The fund would close out your account by returning $575 in cash (this amount could be larger or smaller depending upon whether the fund had gone up or down in value). The front-end load only becomes reasonably tolerable if you stay in for the total life of the contract. Some consumer-oriented states (such as California and Ohio) specifically forbit the use of involuntary, front-end load funds. In most cases, the plan can hardly be called a stockholder service. It will be very obvious to you if you are being asked to participate in an involuntary savings plan with a front-end load.

CHOOSING A FUND TO MEET YOUR OBJECTIVES

There is a vast array of funds from which to choose in attempting to meet your investment objectives. We shall consider common stock funds, balanced funds, bond funds, municipal securities funds, and taxable money market funds.

Stock Funds

Common stock funds may emphasize growth or high yield, or have a special industry emphasis. Examples of the last might include health care, natural resources, science and technology, or precious metals. Also, some funds are international in nature. With a strong stock performance around the world in the 1980s, some of the best-performing funds have had an international orientation. Of course, with international funds you are influenced not only by stock performance but by the strength or weakness of the foreign currency. If West German stocks are going up while the mark is appreciating relative to the dollar, you get a double payoff. Of course, a declining mark relative to the dollar reduces part of the gains or causes losses.

The following list of mutual funds will give you an idea of some of the alternative types of funds available to you. The symbol N.L. stands for no-load; L. represents load.

Columbia Growth Fund	N.L.
Energy Fund	N.L.
Fidelity Overseas	L.
Fidelity Select–Health Care	L.
ISI Income Fund	L.
Lexington Growth Fund	N.L.
National Aviation and Technology Fund	L.
Over-the-Counter Securities Fund/Review	L.
Scudder International	N.L.
Steadman Oceanographic Technology and Growth Fund	N.L.
Vanguard Qualified Dividend I	N.L.

Money magazine (usually the October issue) does a particularly good job of breaking down funds by the following categories: maximum capital gains, long-term growth, and growth and income. The funds are conveniently ranked by performance, with the best-performing funds shown first. An excerpt of the rankings of maximum-capital gains-oriented funds is shown in Figure 13.9. As previously mentioned, the September *Forbes* issue also has information on virtually every mutual fund.

Balanced Funds

The **balanced fund** has a balanced portfolio of stocks and bonds. The intent is to give the investor the upside potential associated with a common stock port-

Figure 13.9 EXCERPT FROM THE *MONEY* MAGAZINE CLASSIFICATION SYSTEM

MAXIMUM-CAPITAL-GAINS FUNDS

	% gain (or loss) to Sept. 1, 1985 One year	Five years	Ten years	Risk/ reward rating*	Total assets (in millions of dollars)	% sales charge	Expenses per $100	IRA start-up/ annual fees	Phone switch
Average for the group	**6.7**	**82.7**	**631.1**		**236.4**				
1 Babson Enterprise 800-821-5591; 816-471-5200	26.2	—	—	—	27	None	$1.67	None $10	Yes
2 Quasar Associates **800-221-5672; 800-522-2323 (N.Y.)**	**26.1**	**124.2**	**891.1**	**—**	**78.9**	**None**	**$1.18**	**$5 $10**	**No**
3 Evergreen Fund 800-635-0003; 914-698-5711	24.1	116.5	948.2	2	336	None†	$1.10	$10 $10	Yes
4 Neuberger & Berman Manhattan **800-367-0770; 212-850-8300**	**23.4**	**125.2**	**249.1**	**1**	**98.1**	**None**	**$1.50**	**None $3**	**Yes**
5 Acorn Fund 312-621-0630	22.9	98.5	657.5	2	282.9	None†	$.85	$5 $2.50	Yes
6 Stein Roe Discovery **800-621-0320; 312-368-7826**	**22.8**	**—**	**—**	**—**	**96.3**	**None**	**$1.49**	**None $10**	**Yes**
7 Neuberger & Berman Partners 800-367-0770; 212-850-8300	21.6	125.3	544.2	1	218.1	None	$.91	None $3	Yes
8 Neuwirth Fund **800-221-5672; 800-522-2323 (N.Y.)**	**21.6**	**76.9**	**249.2**	**4**	**22**	**None**	**$1.64**	**$5 $10**	**No**
9 Omega Fund 800-343-0529; 617-357-8480	21.4	26.4	246.6	4	29.1	None	$1.78	**	No
10 Tudor Fund **800-223-3332; 212-908-9582**	**20.4**	**179.9**	**568.2**	**3**	**138.5**	**None**	**$1.01**	**$10 $10**	**Yes**
11 Quest for Value 800-221-5833; 212-825-4497	18.9	228.5	—	—	31.3	None	$2.34	None $7.50	No
12 Stein Roe Special **800-621-0320; 312-368-7826**	**18.0**	**123.0**	**546.3**	**2**	**268.9**	**None**	**$.96**	**None $10**	**Yes**
13 Value Line Leveraged Growth 800-223-0818; 212-687-3965	17.6	88.5	613.4	5	221	None	$.86	None $10	Yes
14 Weingarten Equity **212-986-1370**	**17.2**	**108.5**	**640.7**	**3**	**149**	**None**	**$1.10**	**$10 $10**	**Yes**
15 Lexington Growth 800-526-7443; 800-522-4503 (N.J.)	16.1	20.2	268.9	5	26.8	None	$1.50	None $5	Yes
16 New York Venture **800-545-2098; 505-983-4335**	**15.2**	**109.9**	**468.3**	**1**	**121.1**	**8½**	**$1.05**	**None $10**	**Yes**
17 Hutton Growth Series 800-821-7770	14.2	—	—	—	844.5	None†	$1.92	None $15	Yes
18 Janus Fund **800-525-3713; 303-333-3863**	**14.0**	**152.5**	**501.8**	**2**	**413.8**	**None**	**$1.51**	**$10 $10**	**Yes**
19 Dreyfus Leverage 800-645-6561; 718-895-1206	14.0	68.9	337.3	1	417.3	8½	$.99	$5 $5	Yes
20 Sigma Capital Shares **800-441-9490; 302-652-3091**	**13.8**	**134.1**	**462.4**	**2**	**55**	**8½**	**$1.17**	**None $10**	**Yes**
21 Leverage Fund of Boston 800-225-6265; 617-482-8260	12.3	—	—	5	31.3	None	$3.47	None $10	No
22 Financial Dynamics **800-525-8085; 303-779-1233**	**10.7**	**72.1**	**284.6**	**5**	**76.9**	**None**	**$.78**	**$5 None**	**Yes**

**Does not accept Individual Retirement Accounts
†Fund may impose a back-end load or exit fee

*Indicator of risk exposure in terms of magnitude of price movement relative to potential return. The lower the better.

SOURCE: *Money,* October 1985, p. 175.

folio and the higher income associated with a bond portfolio. Historically, the investor has received a stable but unspectacular return in balanced funds. In an up market, the fund does well, but not as well as a pure stock portfolio. In a down market, the fund is not as vulnerable to a decline as a straight common stock fund. Many balanced funds also take heavy positions in convertible bonds, that is, bonds that may be converted to common stock at the option of the holder.

Historically, balanced funds have been conservative in nature, but they have been subjected to wider market swings in the mid-to-late 1980s. The reason is that bond prices have become much more volatile with the wide swings in interest rates.

Bond Funds

Bond funds have become extremely popular in the 1980s. These fixed-income funds were offered at a ratio of about 5 to 1 to new stock funds in 1985–1986 (though there are still considerably more stock funds outstanding in total). Their popularity can be traced, in part, to the large gain in value in fixed-income securities as interest rates dropped in the mid-1980s. Also, lower interest has made money market funds and money market accounts less popular and encouraged investors to shift their funds to longer-term, higher-yielding fixed-income investments (which may or may not turn out to be wise).

There are bond funds of every conceivable size and shape. The average maturity of this portfolio may be short (three to five years), intermediate, or long (10 to 30 years). The quality of the portfolio may be very high (government securities) or of lower quality (perhaps B-rated corporate bonds). The latter may be packaged to achieve a considerably higher yield. Some bond funds also include preferred stock and other fixed-income securities in their portfolio. Once again, you are encouraged to look to *Forbes* or *Money* magazine or similar sources to identify bond (fixed-income) funds that may be of interest to you.

Municipal Securities Funds

Funds that specialize in municipal securities provide tax-free income to the investor. Of course, any capital gains involved in buying and selling the fund are taxable.

Municipal securities funds can be broken down into two categories: those that represent investments in municipal bonds and those that represent investments in tax-free money market funds. The former represents long-term investments (up to 30 years), while the latter generally invest in 30- to 60-day tax-free money market investments. Municipal bond funds normally offer the opportunity for higher yield and the possibility of capital appreciation or loss. Tax-free money market funds are thought of as a convenient place to park funds for a short time.

Municipal funds are only attractive to high-tax-bracket investors. With the decline in the maximum marginal tax rate, such funds are becoming less popular.

Taxable Money Market Funds

As discussed in Chapter 11, taxable money market funds are a competing outlet for the investor's short-term funds. Under normal circumstances, taxable money market funds pay a yield two to three percentage points higher than tax-free money market funds.

EVALUATING INVESTMENT PERFORMANCE

Throughout the chapter we have made references to fund performance. We now address the issue more directly by showing you how to compare a fund's performance to those of other funds and the market in general.

A good place to start the discussion is with the previously presented Figure 13.7, which presented mutual fund data from *Forbes* magazine. Under "investment results" in Figure 13.7 are three columns of data. The first column shows the average annual total return over a ten-year period (1976–1985). The **total return on a fund** is composed of capital appreciation and dividend or interest income. Notice that the Standard & Poor's 500 Stock Average (a measure of the stock market in general) had an average annual return of 12.5 percent, while the Forbes Stock Fund Composite (a measure of mutual funds) was up 15.2 percent. We see under total return for the latest 12 months, however, that the market in general had a gain of 30.9 percent while funds only provided 22.3 percent. Finally, we see that return from income dividends was also higher for the overall market than for the mutual funds (4.2 percent versus 2.7 percent).[8] As you can infer from the data, sometimes mutual funds do better than the market and sometimes they do not. If we were to look at many other ten-year and one-year periods over the decades, we would reach a similar conclusion.

Of course, you may want to identify individual funds in Figure 13.7 that have shown stronger than average performance. Examples might include Nicholas Fund/Nicholas and the Partners Fund/Neuberger. Underperformers would include One Hundred Fund/Berger and the Philadelphia Fund/Universal.

As we mentioned previously, funds are also assigned grades for how they performed in up and down markets for the last 10 years. The grades theoretically range from A+ to F (though there are no F's among the particular funds in this exhibit). Most investors like funds that do reasonably well in both types of markets. Of course, if you feel certain the market is about to move in one direction or the other, you may concern yourself less with one category than the other.

One caveat: Past performance in no way ensures future performance. In fact, a fund that did poorly in the past may do well in the future and vice versa.

[8] As indicated earlier, the income figure is already included in the total-return data.

Figure 13.10 BREAKDOWN OF FUND PERFORMANCE

LIPPER MUTUAL FUND INVESTMENT PERFORMANCE AVERAGES

Thursday, May 8, 1986

LIPPER FUND INDICES

	Close	Percentage Change Year to Date	Weekly
Growth Funds	323.42	+15.97	+ 1.05
Growth Income	486.96	+12.68	+ 1.03
Balanced Funds	409.46	+13.35	+ 0.63

OTHER MARKET INDICATORS

D. J. Industrial	1,786.21	+15.49	+ 0.47
S. & P. 500	237.13	+12.24	+ 0.83
S. & P. 400	265.04	+13.00	+ 1.06
N.Y.S.E. Comp.	136.75	+12.48	+ 0.94
Amex Index	272.53	+10.73	+ 1.34

AVERAGE FUND PERFORMANCES

No.	Type of Fund	Percentage Change Year to Date	Weekly
115	Capital Appreciation	+16.74	+ 0.98
206	Growth Funds	+15.51	+ 0.97
34	Small Co. Growth Fds	+16.85	+ 1.13
124	Growth & Income	+13.22	+ 0.82
36	Equity Income	+10.99	+ 1.18
515	Average Performance	+14.99	+ 0.96
6	Health Funds	+23.64	+ 3.29
11	Natural Resources	+ 0.06	+ 2.70
26	Science & Tech.	+15.66	+ 1.16
6	Utility Funds	+12.05	+ 1.36
23	Specialty Funds	+17.14	+ 0.88
19	Global Funds	+23.02	+ 1.46
26	International	+31.43	+ 2.47
21	Gold Oriented	+ 6.95	+ 0.61
4	Option Growth	+11.99	+ 0.80
19	Option Income	+ 5.57	+ 0.76
676	Average Performance	+15.21	+ 1.07
25	Balanced Funds	+11.99	+ 0.55
25	Income Funds	+ 8.95	+ 0.40
253	Fixed Income	+ 6.98	+ 0.00
979	Average Performance	+12.92	+ 0.76
979	Median Performance	+12.50	+ 0.63

Year to date and weekly percentage changes on Thursday for mutual funds include reinvestment of income dividends and capital gains distributions, other market indicators do not. Only funds in existence for the entire period covered are included. Total number of funds, by objective, may include funds with net asset values unavailable at compilation time. Source: Lipper Analytical Services Inc.

SOURCE: Reprinted by permission of *Barrons*, © Dow Jones & Company, Inc., May 12, 1986, p. 121.

Nevertheless, investors often choose to go with funds that have shown strong performances in the past. You don't know whether they can replicate the performance, but at least they have shown the capacity for accomplishment in the past. The same cannot be said for funds with past records of underperformance.

Lipper Mutual Fund Performance Measures

Each week Lipper Analytical Services Inc. tracks the performance of mutual funds and reports the information in *Barron's*. A sample of the data is shown in Figure 13.10. This type of information gives you a feel for what categories of funds are doing best.

Computing Total Return on Your Investment

Assume you own a fund for a year and you want to compute your total return on your investment. There are three potential sources of return:

Box 13.2 A NOBLE BEGINNING

In Only Its First Year, Fidelity Overseas Fund was 1985's Top Performer.

At 25, George Noble joined Peter Lynch's "SWAT" team at Boston-based Fidelity Investments. After three years as a foreign stock selector for Lynch's legendary Magellan Fund, Noble was tapped at the end of 1984 to manage his own fund—Fidelity Overseas. Now 29, the Yale and Wharton economics graduate debuted spectacularly, ending 1985 with a 78.6% total return. Here Noble tells FW's Robert Sonenclar why his fund is No. 1.

Q ***What's driving U.S. interest in overseas stock markets?***

A There are three main factors. One is the enormous improvement in global communications technology. Second, the high level of international trade is bringing markets together; everyone knows Sony and Honda. Before, if you wanted to buy an auto stock, you had to choose among three massive, highly cyclical companies. Today, if you want to buy a specialty automaker with noncyclical earnings growth, you'll look at BMW or Volvo—of which Fidelity, by the way, owns 5% as a firm. Third, people wish to diversify their portfolios, and relative valuations are more attractive abroad. You can buy world-class German chemical companies like Bayer, Hoechst and BASF at six or seven times earnings and two times cash flow. But DuPont sells at 12 times earnings and six times cash flow.

Change in net asset value (NAV) of the shares
Dividends distributed
Capital gains distributed[9]

Assume the following:

Beginning NAV	$12.00
Ending NAV	13.10
Change in NAV (+)	$ 1.10
Dividends distributed	$ .30
Capital gains distributed	.20
Total return	$ 1.60

[9] This represents net capital gains that the fund actually had as a result of selling securities. They are distributed to shareholders.

Q ***But what will you do if the U.S. economy takes off and leaves the rest of the world in the lurch?***

A The prospectus allows for up to 35% of our assets to be invested in U.S. securities, but we don't plan to buy any. There are countless funds that will do that. It doesn't worry me at all to have only foreign stocks because that $2 trillion universe is as big as the U.S. market. As for the "safe haven" issue, I'm not that keen on the U.S. economy.

A rising dollar and rising interest rates in the States mean lower stock markets everywhere. True, investors in foreign markets would have additional currency burdens, but domestic stocks wouldn't be much better. In any case, we can hedge the currency if we want, which removes a lot of risk. Bottom line, this fund is for people who want to diversify. It should not be someone's sole investment vehicle.

Q ***The falling dollar obviously helped, but you beat all the other funds that benefited. Was that luck, skill or both?***

A Well, my father always told me it's better to be lucky than smart. To put it in perspective, note that the foreign stock markets far and away outperformed the U.S. market for five years until December 1984. But you gave back all of your profits in the currency exchange.

In hindsight, our timing was perfect: We started the fund not long before the dollar peaked. I'd like to tell you we predicted it, but it was a case of right place, right time. Not that other funds didn't have the same advantage. About two-thirds of our 78.3% total return since we started the fund is in local stock markets, and the rest is in currency. Basically, we did so well because we were underinvested in Japan and overinvested in Europe. Most of the other foreign funds had a much higher percentage of assets riding on Japan.

SOURCE: *Financial World,* February 5–18, 1986, p. 17.

In this case there is a total return of $1.60 on an initial NAV of $12.00. The return is 13.33 percent.

$$\frac{\text{Total return}}{\text{Beginning NAV}} = \frac{\$\ 1.60}{\$12.00} = 13.33\%$$

An additional consideration may be that instead of taking dividend and capital gains income in cash, you decide to automatically reinvest the proceeds to purchase new shares. In order to compute the percentage return in this case, you must compare the total value of your beginning shares to the total value of your ending shares. Let's assume you had 100 shares to start with and you received a total of $50 in dividends and capital gains (see prior example). Furthermore, assume you bought (reinvested in) new shares at an average price of $12.50 per share. This would provide you with four new shares.[10]

[10] In this case, the number of new shares came out to be a whole number. It is also possible to buy fractional shares in a mutual fund.

$$\frac{\text{Dividends and capital gains allocated to account}}{\text{Average purchase price of new shares}} = \frac{\$50}{\$12.50} = 4 \text{ new shares}$$

In comparing the beginning and ending value of your investment based on the example presented in this section, you would show

$$\text{Total return} = \frac{\begin{pmatrix}\text{no. of ending shares} \\ \times \text{ ending price}\end{pmatrix} - \begin{pmatrix}\text{no. of beginning shares} \\ \times \text{ beginning price}\end{pmatrix}}{(\text{no. of beginning shares} \times \text{beginning price})} \tag{13.2}$$

$$= \frac{(104 \times \$13.10) - (100 \times \$12.00)}{(100 \times \$12.00)}$$

$$= \frac{\$1362.40 - \$1200}{\$1200} = \frac{\$162.40}{\$1200} = 13.53\%$$

In deciding whether the returns computed in this section are acceptable, you must compare your returns to the popular market averages and to the returns of other mutual funds. You must also consider the risks that the fund is taking. A highly aggressive growth fund should generally provide a higher return than an income fund over the long term to compensate for the potentially greater risk exposure.

SUMMARY

Mutual funds, through pooling the resources of a large number of investors and redeploying the funds in various forms of investment, are an efficient means for diversification. On average, though, they do not consistently outperform the market over long periods of time.

You may choose to invest in open-end or closed-end investment funds. An open-end fund is one in which the number of shares is unlimited. If investors want to purchase more shares, the fund simply distributes them and then immediately reinvests the money so that the investment position of prior stockholders is not diluted. Open-end funds not only agree to sell an unlimited amount of new shares, but they also agree to buy back (redeem) all shares as requested by stockholders. The transactions take place at net asset value (with a commission added on in some funds). Net assets value is equal to the total securities owned by the fund less any liabilities divided by the total number of shares outstanding.

A closed-end fund has a specified number of shares outstanding, and this number does not change with each purchase or sale. The only way you buy shares of a closed-end fund is when someone else is selling. Closed-end funds trade on an organized exchange (or over the counter) just as other stocks do. In that sense they are quite different from open-end funds.

Of the two types of funds discussed in this chapter, most of the attention is formally directed to open-end funds. The open-end fund may or may not have a commission associated with the purchase of the fund. Funds without commissions are called no-load funds, while those requiring a sales fee are termed load funds. This fee may be as large as 8.5 percent of the purchase price. In most cases, you are well advised to concentrate on no-load funds. The performance of load and no-load funds normally tends to be about equal over time, so it is somewhat difficult to justify the added sales charge.

You should also focus your attention on the various features offered by the funds. These include such items as automatic reinvestment plans, fund-switching privileges, check writing, and other such services.

Funds may be classified as stock funds, balanced funds, bond funds, municipal security funds, and taxable money market funds. There are also many subcategories. For example, with stock funds, you can go for growth or income or you can specialize in various industries.

Finally, you must carefully consider the total return on an investment in the fund. This calls for evaluating the change in net asset value as well as dividend and realized capital gains distributions.

KEY TERMS

automatic reinvestment plans
back-end sales charge
balanced fund
closed-end fund
fund-switching privilege
investment company
involuntary savings plan
load fund
low-load funds
municipal securities funds
mutual funds
net asset value
no-load funds
open-end fund
total return on a fund
12b-1 plan
unit investment trust
voluntary savings plan

SELECTED READINGS

"A Guide to Mutual Funds." *Consumer Reports,* July 1985, pp. 390–397. (Comes out annually.)

"The *Money* Rankings of Mutual Funds." *Money,* October 1985, pp. 173–218. (Comes out annually.)

"Mutual Funds: A Path for Everyone." *Money,* July 1984, p. 69.

"The 1985 Mutual Fund Survey." *Forbes,* September 16, 1985, pp. 76–174. (Comes out annually.)

Rugg, Donald D., and Norman B. Hale. *The Dow Jones–Irwin Guide to Mutual Funds,* rev. ed. Homewood, Ill.: Dow Jones, 1985.

"Tallying the Totals: Mutual Fund Scorecard." *Financial World,* February 5–18, 1986, pp. 30–34. (Comes out annually.)

Weisenberger Financial Services. *Investment Company Guide.* Boston: Warren, Gorham and Lamont, published annually.

QUESTIONS

1 What are three advantages of investing in mutual funds?
2 Approximately what percentage of common stockholders choose to buy stock through mutual funds?
3 Do mutual funds generally outperform the popular market averages? Comment.
4 What are some questionable claims to watch out for in mutual fund advertisements?
5 What is an open-end fund? How does it differ from a closed-end fund? Which is the most widely used form?
6 What is meant by net asset value (NAV)? Does an open-end fund always trade at net asset value? Why might a closed-end fund trade at a premium or discount from net asset value?
7 Describe how a unit investment trust operates. Indicate how such a trust may offer an advantage over a mutual fund in an environment of highly volatile interest rates.
8 What is the difference between a load fund and a no-load fund? Do researchers generally indicate that one type of fund (load) outperforms the other (no-load)?
9 How do no-loads provide income to the fund management?
10 Using information in Figure 13.7, answer the following questions about the Omega Fund/Omega.
  a Is it a load or no-load?
  b What was its total return for the last 12 months?
  c How much of that return came from dividend income?
  d How large is the fund in total assets?
  e What are its annual expenses per $100?
  f Does the fund generally do better in an up or down market?
  g Did the fund outperform the Standard & Poor's 500 Stock Average over the latest 12 months in terms of total return? What about the Forbes Stock Fund Composite over the latest 12 months?
11 Suggest five magazines that have annual evaluations of mutual funds.
12 What is a 12b-1 plan? Do mutual fund shareholders generally consider it a desirable feature?
13 Are mutual fund shareholders normally subject to a double tax?
14 What is the advantage of fund-switching privileges? Is there an expense involved? Does a switch in funds represent a taxable event?
15 Explain why an involuntary savings plan with a front-end load may be undesirable.
16 What is a balanced fund? How would you describe the nature of the return you are likely to get from a balanced fund?

17 What are the two categories for municipal securities funds?

18 A fund has $281.4 million in total securities, $1.3 million in liabilities, and 12.545 million shares outstanding. Compute the net asset value. (Round to two places to the right of the decimal point.)

19 A fund has a net asset value of $14.50. The offer (purchase) price is $15.65.
  a What is the dollar value of the load (commission)?
  b What is the percentage load? (Round to two places to the right of the decimal point.)
  c Suppose you buy 200 shares in the fund. After two weeks, the net asset value of your shares increases by $.25 per share. Because you need your funds, you sell your shares. What is your total dollar gain or loss?
  d If you bought a no-load fund instead of a load, would there be less chance of good overall market performance for the fund?

20 You are supposed to invest $1200 at the beginning of each year for ten years into an involuntary savings plan for a fund. The fund has a front-end load of 8.5 percent.
  a How much of your first payment will go toward commissions and how much will be applied directly to the purchase of shares?
  b If you decide to sell your shares after two $1200 contributions, how much will you receive back on your investment? Assume this takes place after 13 months and the shares have gone neither up nor down in value.

21 An investor pulls out his mutual fund file folder on December 31 and discovers the fund has a value of $17.37. During the year, he received dividends of $.83, and $.46 was distributed as capital gains. The beginning net asset value was $16.85. What is the percentage return on the beginning NAV? (Round to two places to the right of the decimal point.)

22 Jill Hopkins had 200 shares of the Super-Go Mutual Fund on January 1. The shares were valued at $22.20. During the course of the year, she received $460 in dividends and capital gains. She used the funds to purchase new shares at an average price of $23 per share. By the end of the year, the fund's value was up to $24.30. What is her percentage total return? Use equation 13.2 for your computation. (Round to two places to the right of the decimal point.)

CASE PROBLEMS

13.1 Samuel Walton, a clothing store owner, is a single parent with two young children. Whenever he makes an investment, he likes to be sure he understands all the ins and outs of the transaction.

The 21st Century High Technology Fund has securities valued at $950,475,000, liabilities of $1,274,000, and 31,162,000 shares outstanding. It is a no-load fund.

  a Compute the net asset value of the fund. (Round to two places to the right of the decimal point.)

b Assume that one year after he purchases the fund it increases to $34.60. Furthermore, $1.08 is distributed in dividends, and capital gains distributions are $.52. What is his percentage return on the beginning net asset value? (Round to two places to the right of the decimal point.)

c Assume the same facts as in part b and also that Samuel initially purchased 100 shares. Furthermore, he took his distributions, which totaled $160, and bought five new shares at an average price of $32 during the year. Use equation 13.2 to compute the percentage return on his investment. Use as the beginning price the net asset value computed in part a. Use as the ending price the value given in part b of $34.60. (Round to two places to the right of the decimal point.)

13.2 Ted Haily is a history teacher at Hamlin Junior High School. His wife, Phyllis, is also on the faculty and teaches English.

Ted recently walked into the faculty lounge and announced that he and Phyllis were drawing their $5000 in savings out of a local financial institution and investing the funds in the Far Horizon Mutual Fund. He was particularly impressed by the fact that the fund had increased in value by 15 percent per year for the last five years. He showed his colleague, Rick Turner, the literature on the fund. Rick was a math teacher and had been investing in mutual funds for the last four years.

The math teacher noticed the fund had a net asset value of $20 and a sales price of $21.80. He suggested to Ted that he was paying a pretty high commission (or load) to get into the fund. Ted quickly replied that the subject of the commission had come up with the mutual fund saleswoman, who had assured him that all the best funds charge a commission. The saleswoman had said, "There's no such thing as a free lunch. If you buy a fund without a commission, chances are you are buying a loser that nobody feels they can sell."

a Comment on the statement by the mutual fund saleswoman.

b How large is the percentage commission or load in this case? (Round to two places to the right of the decimal point.)

c If the fund increases at its historical rate this year, how much will Ted and Phyllis be ahead on their investment (per share) in dollar terms? Remember to net out the commission from your answer.

d If Ted and Phyllis bought a no-load fund with a net asset value of $20 and it went up by 12 percent, how much would they be ahead on their investment (per share) in dollar terms?

e The math teacher actually suggests that the load fund would have to go up by 21 percent in net asset value to provide the same dollar return (per share) as the no-load fund described in part d. Do you agree? Do any calculations you consider to be necessary.

14

Broadening the Investment Horizon

After studying this chapter, you should:

- Understand how different economic environments influence investments
- Appreciate how a put or call option works
- Understand the use of high-leverage investments to increase returns (as well as percentage loss exposure)
- Appreciate the use of options as a protective device against downside risk exposure
- Understand how a commodities futures contract works
- Be able to distinguish between speculative and hedging positions in the commodities market
- Be able to determine the key categories of real assets that are available for investment

The array of investment alternatives available to the investor is expanding at a very rapid pace. Twenty years ago an investor was primarily confronted with stocks, bonds, and perhaps a few other alternatives. Today, a broker or financial planner can give you so many alternatives that you do not know where to turn or what questions to ask.

We will broaden your investment horizon somewhat in this chapter. Our intent is not only to prepare you for possible investments in the areas discussed, but to protect you from unrealistic claims by overzealous salespeople.

The topics for coverage in this chapter are put and call options, commodities futures, and various forms of real assets, including real estate, collectibles, precious metals, and precious gems. Where appropriate, we also point out how new tax laws affect particular forms of investments such as real estate.

Many of these investments tend to move from a position of investor favor to disfavor and back again over long periods of time. Sometimes it is best to accumulate your knowledge when there is a lack of market hysteria rather than when investors are trampling each other to get their money on the table (though none of us fully exercises this discipline). In this chapter, we consider the key characteristics of various forms of investments as well as their advantages and disadvantages.

As we have indicated throughout the book, you must choose the best mix of assets for your life-style and for your current and future needs. For those with limited income who are on a tight budget, a conservative strategy is recommended. Those who are aggressive in nature with some measure of financial flexibility may wish to consider innovative ways to increase their returns.

INVESTING THROUGH OPTIONS

An **option** is the right to buy or sell 100 shares of stock at a specified price over a given time period—until the **expiration date.** An option allows you to invest (or speculate) in a given stock with less cash than if you bought the stock directly.

Suppose you buy an option to purchase 100 shares of Fiction Corporation at $50 per share. The option is good for the next six months. The shares are currently selling in the market at $52, and the price of the option is $5. Since 100 shares are involved, the investment will be $500 (the option price of $5 times 100).

Important Terms

There are some important terms used with option transactions. We shall introduce some now and others in later discussions of options. The first term is **strike price.** The strike price is the value at which the option holder can purchase the stock. In the example we are using, it is $50. A second term is the *intrinsic value* of the option. The **intrinsic value** is equal to the current stock price ($52) minus the strike price ($50). In this example, the intrinsic value is equal to $2.

Current stock price	$52
Strike price	−50
Intrinsic value	$ 2

Because the option allows you to buy a $52 stock for only $50, we say it has a minimum or intrinsic value of $2. Actually, most options sell above their intrinsic value because they have many months to go before expiring and because they offer the opportunity for large speculative gains. In this example, the option was earlier stated to be trading for $5, so we could say it was trading at a $3 **speculative premium** over its intrinsic value of $2.

Option price	$5
Intrinsic value	−2
Speculative premium	$3

The relationships are shown in Figure 14.1.

Now that we have defined some of the important terms, let's get down to some actual examples of buying options and making or losing money.

Profit Potential

Suppose you bought the $5 option referred to above because you were **bullish** and thought the market would go up. The investment based on 100 shares would be $500. Now let's assume that the stock really takes off over the next few months and its price goes to $70. What will happen to the value of the option? Since it entitles the holder to buy the stock at $50 per share, it will have a value of at least $20.[1] Thus, your $5 investment per option will now have a $20 value. This represents a return of $15 per option, or 300 percent.

$$\frac{\text{Gain in option price}}{\text{Option purchase price}} = \frac{\$15}{\$5} = 300 \text{ percent return}$$

Figure 14.1 DETERMINATION OF THE SPECULATIVE PREMIUM

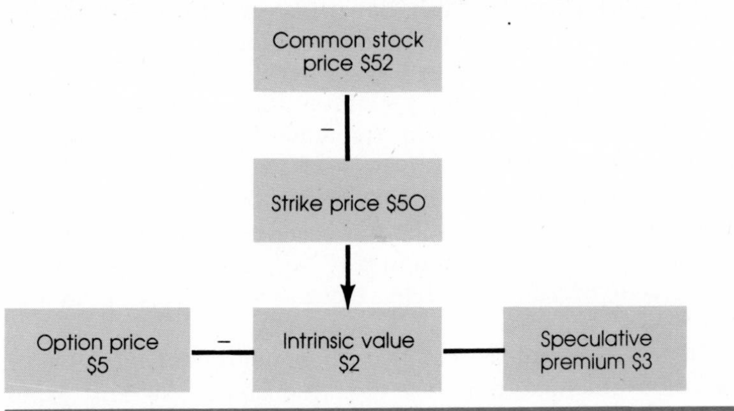

[1] If we add in a speculative premium, your return may be even higher. However, we are assuming we are closing in on the expiration date (end of the option), so the speculative premium may be very small or nonexistent.

Note that you can make your profit purely from investing in the option. Even though the option entitles you to purchase the stock, this really is not necessary. You can simply make your money by buying the option, and watching its value move with the stock value, and then selling it. The next purchaser of the option may also speculate in the option or actually use the option to purchase new shares.

Observe the tremendous profit potential from the option. While the stock value increased by 34.6 percent from $52 to $70, the option value increased by 300 percent. In this case, the profit potential was 8.7 times greater in the option than in the stock itself.

$$\frac{\text{300\% gain in option (\$5 to \$20)}}{\text{34.6\% gain in stock (\$52 to \$70)}} = 8.7\times \text{ greater profit in the option than the stock}$$

Another way to examine the same impact is to consider the dollar profit generated as a result of investing $500 in the options as opposed to investing $500 in the stock. As we showed earlier, the $500 option purchase provided a $1500 return (100-share option contract with a $15 profit). If the same $500 had been invested in stock, you would only have been able to buy 9.62 shares.

$$\frac{\text{Investment}}{\text{Stock price}} = \frac{\$500}{\$52} = 9.62 \text{ shares}$$

Because you cannot buy fractional shares of common stock, we will round up to 10 shares. If the stock price goes from $52 to $70 as previously indicated, you will make $180. This is a far cry from the $1500 profit in the options.

Loss Potential

What if the stock price goes way down instead of up? Let's assume the stock declines to $30 from $52. Furthermore, let's look at the consequences of buying an option for 100 shares at $5 or buying 100 shares at $52.

If the stock goes down to $30, the option, which entitles you to buy the stock at $50, cannot go below zero. The most you can lose is the amount of your initial investment of $500.

What would be your loss if you bought 100 shares of stock for $52 and the stock went down to $30? Clearly, in this case you have lost $2200. This is a much larger dollar loss than in the option play (although with the option you lost 100 percent of your investment, while your percentage loss is much less on the stock).

In general, we can say that investments in options not only provide much larger upside potential, but they limit the *dollar* loss and exposure on the downside. They give you the *maximum* potential for your money. If you feel a stock is about to really take off, you should seriously consider taking a position in the options for the stock rather than buying the stock directly. Although the option investment can be an attractive alternative to include in your financial planning package, few investments can claim advantages without disadvantages.

Other Considerations

In the case of this example, one of the drawbacks of the option is that the stock must go up to at least $55 to break even on the option play. Remember that you purchased an option with a $50 strike price (the price at which the stock can be bought). Only at a price of $55 or higher would you recover the $5 investment in the option. Since the stock was $52 at the time the option was purchased, the price must go up by 3 points for you to break even. A 3-point rise in a $52 stock represents a 5.77 percent gain ($3/$52). There may be less than a 50-50 chance that you will come out ahead—assuming that the stock has an equal chance of going up or down. Of course, if you come out ahead, you are likely to be way ahead. The profit or loss on the option play is shown in Figure 14.2.

Also, you should keep in mind that while an option play limits your dollar loss exposure, it tends to lead to large percentage gains or losses (as previously indicated). At a final stock price of $50 after six months, your option is worthless and you will lose 100 percent of your investment. If you had bought the stock at $52 instead, at an ending stock price of $50 you would only have a loss of $2, or 3.85 percent ($2/$52).

Actual Option Quotes

Having considered the basic features, advantages, and drawbacks of options, let's look at some actual option data from the May 28, 1986, *Wall Street Journal.* In Figure 14.3, we see option quotes in the *Journal* from the Chicago Board Options Exchange. For illustrative purposes, let's examine the Bristol-Myers (BrisMy) options. Under the firm's name, we see the price at which Bristol-Myers' common stock is selling (80⅞). We also see that there are options outstanding with strike prices ranging from 60 to 85. Furthermore, we can observe across the top of the table that the options expire (terminate) in June, September, and December.

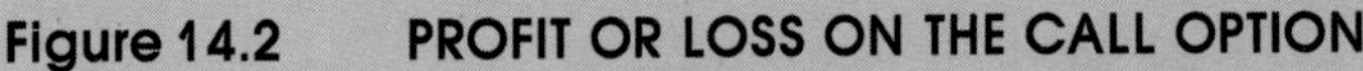

Figure 14.2 **PROFIT OR LOSS ON THE CALL OPTION**

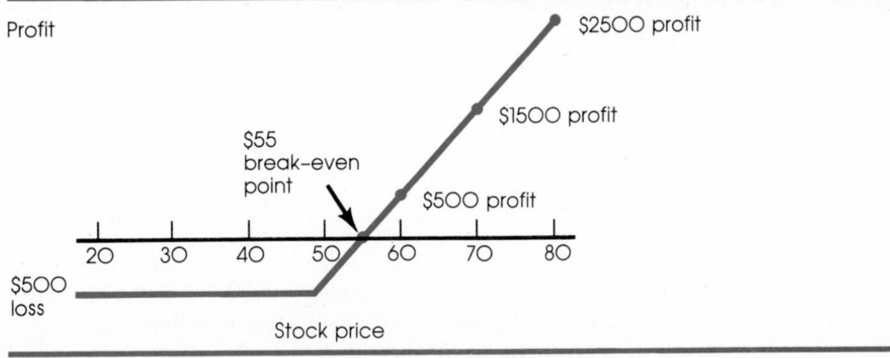

Figure 14.3 OPTION QUOTATIONS

CHICAGO BOARD

Option & NY Close	Strike Price	Calls—Last			Puts—Last		
		Jun	Sep	Dec	Jun	Sep	Dec
AlldSt	27 1/2	19	s	s	r	s	s
46 3/8	35	r	12	r	r	1/16	r
46 3/8	37 1/2	8 7/8	r	r	r	r	r
46 3/8	40	6 1/4	7 1/4	r	r	r	r
46 3/8	45	2	3 3/4	r	r	r	r
46 3/8	50	1/2	1 3/4	r	r	r	r
Apache	10	1/8	r	r	r	r	r
BrisMy	60	20	20 1/2	s	r	1/8	s
80 7/8	65	16 3/8	16 1/2	r	r	1/4	3/4
80 7/8	70	11 3/8	12 1/4	13 1/4	1/16	3/4	1 3/8
80 7/8	75	6 3/8	8 1/4	9	1/8	1 3/4	3 1/8
80 7/8	80	2 1/2	5 1/8	6 1/2	1 3/8	3 3/8	4 1/2
80 7/8	85	3/4	2 7/8	4 1/2	r	r	r
Bruns	25	r	10 7/8	r	r	r	r
35 1/8	30	5 3/8	6 1/8	r	1/16	1/2	1
35 1/8	35	1 3/8	3 1/4	3 1/2	1	r	r
35 1/8	40	1/4	1	r	r	r	r
Celan	130	83 7/8	s	s	1/16	s	s
214 3/4	140	74	r	s	1/16	r	s
214 3/4	175	r	r	s	1/16	1	s
214 3/4	185	r	r	s	1/8	2 1/2	s
214 3/4	190	25	r	r	1/4	2 1/2	r
214 3/4	195	r	r	r	7/16	r	r
214 3/4	200	r	r	29	9/16	r	8
214 3/4	210	8 3/4	18	25	r	9 1/2	r
214 3/4	220	4 1/8	13	r	r	r	r
ChamIn	22 1/2	4 1/4	4 3/4	r	r	r	r
26 7/8	25	1 3/4	2 3/4	4	3/16	7/8	r
26 7/8	30	1/8	5/8	1 1/16	r	3 3/8	r
Chryslr	35	3 1/2	5 1/4	6 1/4	1/4	1 5/8	2 1/4
38 3/8	40	11/16	2 1/2	3 5/8	2 1/2	3 7/8	5
38 3/8	45	1/8	1 3/16	2 3/8	7 1/2	8	r
38 3/8	50	r	1/2	r	r	r	r
Chrys o	30	8 5/8	9 1/2	s	r	5/8	s
38 3/8	33 3/8	5 1/8	5 1/2	s	1/8	r	s
38 3/8	36 5/8	2	r	s	7/8	r	s
38 3/8	40	r	r	s	r	4 1/4	s
CompSc	25	r	r	s	r	1/8	s
36 1/2	30	6 1/2	r	r	r	r	r
36 1/2	35	2 1/4	3 7/8	r	15/16	r	r
36 1/2	40	7/16	r	r	r	r	r
Dow Ch	35	21 1/2	r	s	r	r	s
55 7/8	40	15 7/8	15 5/8	s	r	r	s
55 7/8	45	10 3/4	10 1/2	r	r	r	r
55 7/8	50	5 7/8	7 1/4	8	1/16	7/8	1 7/8
55 7/8	55	2	4	5	1 1/2	2 1/2	3 3/4
55 7/8	60	5/16	2	2 3/4	5 1/8	6	r
FBost	45	13	r	s	r	r	s
57 7/8	50	7 3/4	9 1/2	r	r	15/16	r
57 7/8	55	3 7/8	6 1/2	r	5/8	2 1/8	r
57 7/8	60	1	3 3/4	5 1/2	2 3/4	r	r
57 7/8	65	5/16	2 1/4	3 7/8	r	r	r
Ford	45	33 1/2	s	s	r	s	s
79 1/4	55	23 7/8	r	s	r	r	s
79 1/4	60	18 1/2	r	s	r	r	s
79 1/4	65	13 7/8	r	s	r	1/2	s
79 1/4	70	9 5/8	11	13	1/4	1 1/2	r
79 1/4	75	5 1/8	8	9 3/4	3/4	2 7/8	r
79 1/4	80	2 1/8	5 1/2	6 1/4	2 3/4	4 3/4	7
79 1/4	85	9/16	3 1/4	4 1/2	6 1/4	r	9 3/4
79 1/4	90	1/8	1 3/4	r	r	r	r

SOURCE: Reprinted by permission of the *Wall Street Journal*, © Dow Jones & Company, Inc., May 28, 1986, p. 50.

At the top of the table, there are two categories of options: calls and puts. The term *last* after calls and puts merely indicates that it is the last quote of the day for all values throughout the table. A **call option** is an option to *buy* 100

shares at a specified price over a given time period. Basically, our discussion so far in this chapter has related to calls. A **put option** is an option to *sell* 100 shares at a specified price over a given time period. We discuss puts later in this section. The first three columns of quotes in the table deal with calls and the last three columns cover puts.

Returning to the Bristol-Myers' quotations, let's look at their call options with a strike price of \$80. If you buy short-term options, such as those expiring in June, you will pay \$2.50. Keep in mind that the stock is at 80⅞. This means the options have an intrinsic value of \$.875.

Current stock price	\$80.875
Strike price	− 80
Intrinsic value	\$ .875

In this instance, you are paying a speculative premium over the intrinsic value of \$1.625.

Option price	\$2.50
Intrinsic value	− .875
Speculative premium	\$1.625

Since the quotes are as of May 28 in this example, you may decide that you want to purchase an option with a longer expiration date than June (the options actually expire the third Friday of the designated month). If you decide to buy December options on Bristol-Myers with a strike price of \$80, the option price is \$6.50, as indicated in Figure 14.3. Because the December option has a longer time period to produce value for you, it carries a higher price. What is the speculative premium on the December \$80 option? If you say \$5.625, you are correct.

Option price	\$6.50
Intrinsic value	− .875
Speculative premium	\$5.625

A key feature of these options is that you are able to control a stock priced at 80⅞ with very little cash. For example, if you buy the June \$80 option at \$2.50, for \$250 you are able to participate in the performance of 100 shares of stock currently valued at \$8087.50 (100 × \$80.875). If you bought four such options for \$1000, you would be participating in the performance of \$32,350 worth of stock (4 × \$8087.50). Clearly, options offer the small investor an opportunity to participate on a larger scale and to make or lose a lot of money relative to the size of the investment.

You should also be aware that you do not need to hold your options to expiration. You may buy them and sell them a day or two later. Assume that Bristol-Myers goes from 80⅞ to 81⅞ over a two-day period. Your options will also go up in value, but it is difficult to say by exactly how much. The intrinsic value of the June \$80 options is now \$1.875 and the option price may go up to

$3.25.[2] This would allow you a ¾-point profit on your $2.50 investment. Option traders often take profits on such small amounts.

In- or Out-of-the-Money

The Bristol-Myers $80 options that we have been examining are said to be **in-the-money options.** This means that the current stock price of 80⅞ is above the strike price of $80. Almost all the Bristol-Myers options are in-the-money. With **out-of-the-money options,** the stock price is less than the strike price. For example, in the case of the Bristol-Myers $85 options, the options are out-of-the-money; the stock price is only at 80⅞ while the strike price is $85. Clearly, the options do not have any intrinsic value (it is said to be negative). Because of this, the prices of the $85 options in Figure 14.3 are relatively cheap, particularly for June. Buying out-of-the-money options is a little like betting on a long-shot at the race track. The price is low, the odds of winning are not very great; but if you do win, you will have a high return on your investment.

Gaining from a Downward Movement in a Stock

Options are not only used to profit from an anticipated upward movement in a stock. They also can be used in anticipation of a decline. This can be accomplished either by selling a call option or buying a put option.

Selling a Call Option. If you are able to buy a June $80 call option on Bristol-Myers' common stock for $2.50 or a December $80 call option for $6.50, someone must be willing to sell these options. Who are the parties willing to sell these options? Generally, they are **bearish** investors—market participants who believe the stock is more likely to go down than up.

The person who sells the December $80 call option for $6.50 immediately pockets $650 (100 × $6.50). Of course, that person is promising to deliver 100 shares of Bristol-Myers at $80 per share by December. If the stock ends up at $80 or less as the option seller (writer) anticipates, the seller will *not* have to provide the shares at $80 because no one will want them and he or she has a clear profit of $650. Of course, if the stock goes up instead of down, the option seller may absorb a large loss. Assume the stock goes up to $92 as the option expires. Now, the option seller will have to deliver 100 shares to be purchased by another party at $80 per share. Since the stock presently costs $92, the seller will be giving up $92 shares to another party at a generous purchase price of $80. This represents a $1200 difference. Another way the option seller can absorb

[2] The exact price of the option will depend on the speculative premium. The speculative premium is influenced by the amount of time to expiration, the volatility of the stock, whether the stock is in- or out-of-the-money, the general tone of the market, and a number of other factors. The option price does not move exactly with the stock price except when there is a positive intrinsic value and the options are approaching expiration. These factors go beyond the scope and intent of this chapter. The interested reader is encouraged to consult such texts as Geoffrey Hirt and Stanley Block, *Foundations of Financial Management,* 2nd ed., Homewood, Ill.: Irwin, 1986; and Frank K. Reilly, *Investments,* 2nd ed., New York: Dryden Press, 1986.

the same loss with less trouble is to simply buy back the $6.50 options for $12, which is the likely value for an $80 call option when the stock price is $92. Whichever route the option seller takes, he or she will be out $1200. Since the seller got $650 initially, the net loss is $550.

This discussion can get considerably more complicated, but that is not our intention. The main point is that if you are bearish on a stock, you might consider selling options rather than buying them. Actually, buyers and sellers of options do not interact directly with each other, but rather through the Options Clearing Corporation. Options trading is very easily accomplished; the tough part is to make sure you are moving in the right direction with your decision.

Some investors choose to sell options on stocks they currently own. This is called covered option writing and is a relatively conservative hedging strategy. If the stock price goes down, it is to be hoped that the money you make on your option sale will offset most of your loss on your stock. If the stock price goes up, you will make money on your stock and lose money on your option, but you hope to have a net gain.

Other investors choose to sell options on stocks they do not own. They are said to have a *naked* option position. This term is appropriate in that the investor can be exposed to large losses if the stock price goes up.

Buying a Put Option. For an investor who is bearish on a stock but wants less risk than that associated with selling a call option, buying a put option may be the solution. You may recall that a put option allows one to sell 100 shares of stock at a specified price over a given time period. If a stock is quoted at $48 a share, you may be able to purchase a put option with a strike price of $50 for $5. If the stock goes down to $30 at expiration, your put will be worth $20 and you will have a $15 profit. Multipled by 100, this value gives you a gain of $1500.

If you guess wrong and the stock goes up instead of down, your maximum loss is only the $5 purchase price of the put. The total loss potential is only $500 ($5 × 100). You can't lose more than your original investment on the put. Buying a put in anticipation of a fall in a stock price is clearly a much safer strategy than selling a call option (particularly a naked call option). With the purchase of a put option, if you guess wrong and the stock goes up instead of down, your loss is limited to the purchase price of the put. When you sell a call option, your loss is theoretically unlimited. The only drawback with buying a put option is that you normally need a larger decline in the price of the stock to make a profit than you do with selling a call.

To get actual quotes on puts, please refer back to Figure 14.3. For this example, we will look at Dow Chemical (Dow Ch) puts. Dow Chemical stock is selling for 55⅞, and a $60 September put has a value of $6. If Dow goes to $50, the put option will be worth at least $10. The put option holder will be able to sell a $50 stock for $60 under the terms of the option and thus the minimum value of $10.

Incidentally, the symbol *r* in Figure 14.3 indicates that a particular option did not trade the prior day. An *s* symbol indicates that there is no option contract available for the month and strike price indicated.

Box 14.1 CALL OPTIONS: WRITING OFF THE RISK

The investment management firm of Albarella, Moscovitz & Associates may never do as roaring a business as a Merrill Lynch. But that has something to do with its specialties—one of which is call-option writing. If the very words recall the terrors of college calculus, they shouldn't. Like buyers of common stocks, those who write call options are apt to get the handsomest returns when they outguess other investors. If they're wrong, however, they may still reap rewards. And if the firm calls the market correctly, conditions could not be better for conservative investors to play the call-writing game.

By way of "a perfect example," Scott Albarella, a partner in the firm, trots out recent takeover candidate Gulf & Western. From late March to early April, when Irwin Jacobs set his sights on acquiring the company, the stock climbed to 35¾ from about 32—and that set the stage for trading in G&W call options, or contracts to buy G&W shares at a set price for a set period of time. The buyer garners a profit only if the stock climbs a fair amount above the guaranteed option price, enabling him to exercise the option and then sell the shares at a higher price. But to the person "writing" the call option, or offering up his stock for possible sale, even a modest downturn in G&W's shares, as Albarella explains it, would bring a profit.

How does it work? The procedure, like the arithmetic, is simple. At the time G&W hit 35¾, an investor could have bought the stock at that price, and then sold an option, at a cost of $4 a share to the option buyer, to pick up the shares at 35. If the stock rises to above 39, the break-even level for the option buyer, who then "calls in" the shares, the option writer reaps a tidy $3.25 a share—or $4 a share, minus the 75¢ difference between what he paid for the stock and sold it for. In-

Overall Comments on Options

Options are traded on over 500 stocks. An entire page of the *Wall Street Journal* is normally devoted to option prices. Options not only trade on the Chicago Board Options Exchange (shown in Figure 14.3), but also on the American, Philadelphia, Pacific, and New York Stock Exchange (surprisingly, the New York Stock Exchange is a relatively late arrival among the exchanges trading options). Options may have a maximum expiration date up to nine months and trade on various cycles such as March/June/September/December for some stocks and other months for others.

You can buy a call or put option not only on an *individual* stock but on a large group of stocks as well. For example, you can buy a call option that covers all the stocks on the New York Stock Exchange or all the firms in the Standard & Poor's 500 Stock Index. These options are generally no more expensive than options on individual stocks. However, the stock index options tend to be for more sophisticated investors. Generally, an investor trades in options on individual stocks before attempting stock index options.

TRADING IN COMMODITIES

The 1983 movie *Trading Places* with Eddie Murphy showed the frenzy and excitement of trading in commodities. In the movie, Eddie Murphy's character was trying to make a killing in the orange juice futures market. Even if you didn't see *Trading Places,* however, you may have heard of people trying to amass fortunes in silver, pork bellies, or wheat.

deed, he doesn't lose unless the stock drops below 31¾. Remarks Albarella: "On a call option that runs through September, that works out to at least a 10% return if you include the dividends [the writer stands to receive]. On an annualized basis, the return is 23%."

Needless to say, writing call options makes little sense if a stock looks poised to skyrocket. Nor does it, of course, if a stock seems likely to nose-dive. However, for conservative investors sensing that a stock—or the market as a whole, for that matter—is fully valued and about to "move sideways or trend downward," call-option writing stacks up as a safe bet. And in the wake of the early-1985 rally, and with the Federal budget deficit "possibly putting pressure on interest rates and causing the market to break," now may well be an "optimum time" to write call options, says Albarella.*

Albarella concedes that these esoteric instruments are perhaps intimidating to the average investor. But he stands staunchly by their virtues, noting, "Sure, you're limiting your upside potential. But the returns can be good, and they're definitely less risky than buying common stocks." How much less? In 1984, Albarella reports, the firm averaged a 9% return for its clients, far outperforming a lackluster stock market. What's more, Value Line, the investment research firm, provides some independent evidence of its own. In an industrywide five-year survey, it found the risk of writing call options to be 65% that of playing common stocks.

*This part of the strategy did not prove to be correct.

SOURCE: *Financial World,* May 15–28, 1985, p. 24.

Commodities are an exciting and somewhat dangerous form of investment. Because commodity trading is such an important part of the broad spectrum of investments in the United States, you should have an introductory knowledge of these markets.

A **commodities futures contract** is one that provides for the delivery of a specific commodity at a designated time in the future at a given price. An example might be a contract to deliver 5000 bushels of wheat in December at $2.50 a bushel. The person selling the contract does not have to have possession of the commodity. Almost all commodity contracts are closed out before the actual transaction is to take place. For example, the seller of the contract for the 5000 bushels of wheat will eventually buy a similar contract for the purchase of 5000 bushels and close out the position. The buyer of the contract will also reverse his or her position by selling the contract. Only a minute percentage of contracts ever lead to physical delivery. There is a tremendous volume of activity but very little movement of goods. This is somewhat similar to the option markets previously described.

Types of Commodities Traded

Before we describe how a trader makes or loses money in the commodities markets, let's first consider the different types of commodities that are available for trading. Table 14.1 shows the five major categories of commodities and examples of commodities in each category. The last category, financial futures, has become extremely popular in the 1980s.

The commodities listed in Table 14.1 trade on major exchanges in the

Table 14.1 FIVE CATEGORIES OF ACTIVELY TRADED COMMODITIES

1. Grains and Oilseeds
   a. Corn
   b. Soybeans
   c. Wheat
   d. Barley
   e. Flaxseed
   f. Rye
2. Livestock and Meat
   a. Cattle—feeder
   b. Cattle—live
   c. Hogs
   d. Pork bellies
3. Food and Fiber
   a. Cocoa
   b. Coffee
   c. Cotton
   d. Orange juice
   e. Sugar—world
   f. Sugar—domestic
4. Metals and Petroleum
   a. Copper
   b. Gold
   c. Platinum
   d. Palladium
   e. Silver
   f. Crude oil
   g. Heating oil
5. Financial
   a. Foreign currency
      - British pound
      - Japanese yen
      - Swiss franc
   b. Interest rates
      - Treasury bond
      - Treasury bills
   c. Stock index
      - S&P 500 Index
      - NYSE Composite Index
      - KC Value Line Index

United States and Canada. The two most active exchanges are the Chicago Board of Trade and the Chicago Mercantile Exchange. An illustration of the highly active, crowded nature of buying and selling on the Chicago Board of Trade is shown in Figure 14.4.

Buying and Selling a Contract

Let's return to the wheat contract that we mentioned earlier. Suppose you buy a commodities contract for the future delivery of 5000 bushels of wheat at $2.50 per bushel. The contract has six months to expiration. The dollar value of the contract is $12,500 (5000 bushels × $2.50). One of the interesting features of commodity trading, however, is that you put up margin rather than the full purchase price. The **margin on a commodities contract** usually is 5 to 10 percent of the purchase price.[3] In this example, let's assume the margin requirement is $800, or 6.4 percent of $12,500.

[3] The concept of margin in a commodities contract is somewhat different from margin associated with stock purchases (Chapter 12). Not only is the percentage much smaller, but it is considered as good faith money or a deposit. This means you do not have to pay interest on the difference between the purchase price and the cash margin as you do with stocks or bonds.

Figure 14.4 FLOOR TRADING ON THE CHICAGO BOARD OF TRADE

With such a small dollar amount controlling a large investment, any price movement of significance will generate a large gain or loss on your investment. We say the investor has a *highly leveraged position* (the same is true of option contracts).

Let's assume that the price of wheat covered by your contract goes up by \$.10 a bushel in the first week after you purchase the contract. Since the price of wheat has traded as high as \$5.00 a bushel in the last decade, this is entirely plausible. Because you own a contract to buy 5000 bushels at \$2.50 and the price is now \$2.60, you have a \$.10 gain on each bushel, or \$500. With an initial investment of only \$800, your return is 62.5 percent.

$$\frac{\text{Gain in contract value}}{\text{Margin investment}} = \frac{\$500}{\$800} = 62.5 \text{ percent}$$

This gain took place in one week. If you were to annualize it by multiplying by 52 weeks, the return would be over 3000 percent. The main reason is the use of margin; after all, the price of wheat only changed by \$.10.

As you may have guessed, the use of margin is a two-way street. It can generate large percentage losses as well as large percentage gains. If the price of wheat goes down by $.10 instead of up, you will lose $500 of the $800 you invested. Actually, your broker is certain to give you a phone call well before you have lost the full $500. When you engage in a commodities contract, you not only have an initial margin requirement equal to 5 to 10 percent of the value of the contract, but you also have a margin maintenance requirement. The requirement says you must maintain the margin at 70 to 80 percent of its original value. For example, 70 percent of the original margin of $800 is $560. Thus, after you lose $240 of your original margin of $800 due to a price decline, you will be called upon to put up more margin.

On a 5000-bushel contract, a $240 loss occurs with a price decline of less than five cents a bushel. Your broker might be calling you for more margin an hour or two after you buy the contract if prices are moving against you. You must decide whether to put up more margin ($240 in this case) and brace yourself against another possible price decline or sell (close out) your position and take your $240 loss. The commodities market is not a place for the meek or indecisive investor. It is rather like playing no-pot-limit poker.

The seller of a commodities contract has exactly the opposite motivation. Because the seller has a contract to sell at $2.50 a bushel, he or she will make money if commodity prices go down and lose money if they go up. The seller also puts up margin and must meet margin maintenance requirements.

Commodity Market Quotes

In Figure 14.5, we see an excerpt from the *Wall Street Journal* that shows actual quotes on various grains and oilseeds (one of the five categories of commodities). Let's look at corn as an example. Looking across the top row for corn, we see that it trades on the Chicago Board of Trade (CBT). Furthermore, corn trades in 5000-bushel (bu) contracts and is quoted in cents per bushel.

As indicated in the excerpt, corn contracts can be traded for many different months in the future, including July, September, December, March, and May. The actual price quotes are in cents. For example, the first July contract opened at 233¼ cents per bushel. Most market participants insert a decimal point two places to the left of the whole number and read the quote in dollars. Thus 233¼ cents becomes $2.3325. In this instance, we can see the opening, high, low, and settle (closing) price for the July corn contract (and others as well). We observe that the contract was up 2 cents or $.02 for the day. The lifetime high and low indicate the trading range for this contract since it was issued (spanning a 12-month period). The last column gives the open interest, or the number of contracts still outstanding for that delivery month. Note that as we move further out into the future, the value of the corn contracts goes down. This indicates that investors were very bearish (negative) on corn during this time period.

Observe in Figure 14.5 that wheat also trades in 5000-bushel contracts and

Figure 14.5 COMMODITY QUOTES

	Open	High	Low	Settle	Change	Lifetime High	Lifetime Low	Open Interest
–GRAINS AND OILSEEDS–								
CORN (CBT) 5,000 bu.; cents per bu.								
July	233¼	236½	233¼	235¾	+ 2	286	215½	34,927
Sept	203½	203¾	202	202¼	– 1	270	197	13,434
Dec	196	196¾	195	195¼	– 1¼	235½	193	50,738
Mar87	205¾	206	204½	204¾	– 1¾	242½	202	6,562
May	211	211	209½	210	– 2	242	207	2,382
July	210½	211	210	210	– 2	227	207½	904
Est vol 20,000; vol Fri 23,776; open int 109,039, –405.								
SOYBEANS (CBT) 5,000 bu.; cents per bu.								
July	530¼	535	530	532½	+ ¼	658	497	25,024
Aug	526½	529	524¾	526½	....	609	498½	5,129
Sept	514½	518	514½	515¾	– 1	555½	496	3,820
Nov	511¾	515	511¼	512¾	– 2	556½	497¼	25,755
Jan87	521	523½	520¾	521¼	– 2½	565	506	2,671
Mar	530½	532½	529	530½	– 2½	576	515½	1,578
May	536	537½	535	535	– 3	574	522	459
Jly	537½	540	537½	537½	– 2½	577½	526	100
Est vol 20,000; vol Fri 14,141; open int 64,539, –69.								
SOYBEAN MEAL (CBT) 100 tons; $ per ton.								
July	147.10	148.60	146.80	147.60	....	167.00	134.00	21,313
Aug	147.20	148.40	146.70	147.20	– .30	163.50	135.50	6,614
Sept	146.60	147.00	146.10	146.50	– .10	160.50	137.50	3,220
Oct	145.50	146.00	144.80	145.20	– .80	162.10	136.00	4,751
Dec	146.60	146.90	145.50	146.20	– .70	162.10	136.00	10,729
Jan87	147.50	147.50	146.50	147.00	– .50	163.10	136.10	1,265
Mar	150.00	151.00	149.60	149.60	– .90	163.10	147.60	893
May	153.50	154.00	152.00	152.40	– 1.10	169.70	150.50	417
Est vol 11,000; vol Fri 11,277; open int 49,202, +21.								
SOYBEAN OIL (CBT) 60,000 lbs.; cents per lb.								
July	18.45	18.71	18.30	18.36	– .21	25.25	17.05	21,043
Aug	18.50	18.75	18.39	18.42	– .17	25.15	17.05	8,075
Sept	18.50	18.75	18.45	18.47	– .03	24.05	17.10	4,237
Oct	18.45	18.62	18.28	18.40	– .12	22.80	17.25	5,250
Dec	18.55	18.85	18.53	18.62	....	22.50	17.51	10,938
Jan87	18.80	18.90	18.75	18.75	+ .08	22.35	17.70	1,593
Mar	19.15	19.25	19.05	19.15	+ .25	20.25	18.20	1,028
May	19.30	19.40	19.27	19.37	+ .35	20.90	18.50	415
Est vol 12,000; vol Fri 18,225; open int 52,579, +174.								
WHEAT (CBT) 5,000 bu.; cents per bu.								
July	256	258¼	254½	255½	– ¼	310	241	16,761
Sept	257½	259½	255¾	256¾	– ¾	299	242	8,496
Dec	266	268¼	264½	265	– 2	309	251	6,323
Mar87	267½	268½	265¼	265¼	– 2½	308	251	1,255
May	262	262	257½	257½	– 4¼	300	244	141
Est vol 6,000; vol Fri 5,657; open int 33,037, +120.								
WHEAT (KC) 5,000 bu.; cents per bu.								
July	246	248	245¾	246½	+ 1¼	298½	237½	13,405
Sept	249¾	251¼	248¾	249	– ¾	291	239⅝	3,656
Dec	258	258¾	256½	257	– ½	298	247½	2,248
Mar87	259½	259¾	259	259½	+ ½	302½	249½	73
Est vol 3,813; vol Fri 5,813; open int 19,404, +307.								
WHEAT (MPLS) 5,000 bu.; cents per bu.								
July	289	289½	285½	286	– 5	328	247½	2,458
Sept	272	274	272	274	+ 1	350	268½	1,716
Dec	281	281¼	280¼	280¼	+ ¼	321½	275	726
Est vol 1,616; vol Fri 1,537; open int 5,025, –178.								
BARLEY (WPG) 20 metric tons; Can. $ per ton								
May	108.00	110.20	108.00	109.10	+ 3.90	130.00	84.60	455
July	98.70	103.80	98.70	101.70	+ 2.90	119.17	86.70	3,025
Oct	90.60	91.30	89.30	89.30	– 1.70	106.00	86.40	2,838
Dec	91.60	91.60	90.00	90.00	– 1.70	99.50	86.90	2,685
Est vol 1,585; vol Mon450; open int 9,003, –53.								
FLAXSEED (WPG) 20 metric tons; Can. $ per ton								
May	271.30	271.60	271.30	271.60	+ 1.40	352.50	270.10	38
July	274.50	275.80	274.50	275.50	+ 1.00	326.20	274.00	2,923
Oct	283.00	283.90	283.00	283.80	+ 1.60	333.80	281.00	1,682
Dec	....	....	....	287.80	+ 1.50	325.00	283.20	1,568
Est vol 340; vol Mon562; open int 6,211, –23.								
RAPESEED (WPG) 20 metric tons; Can. $ per ton								
June	286.50	287.80	286.10	287.00	+ .40	400.40	271.00	5,402
Sept	296.30	297.60	296.00	297.30	+ .80	351.00	281.20	11,802
Nov	299.70	301.30	299.70	301.10	+ 1.10	352.00	284.20	4,569
Jan87	305.00	305.90	305.00	305.70	+ 1.00	354.90	289.60	1,832
Mar	....	....	....	310.50	+ 1.40	318.50	294.90	312
Est vol 4,920; vol Mon3,272; open int 23,917, +500.								
RYE (WPG) 20 metric tons; Can. $ per ton								
May	....	....	....	108.50	+ 1.00	134.00	91.70	63
July	108.00	110.40	108.00	110.20	+ 1.70	130.00	95.50	978
Oct	....	....	....	112.10	+ 1.30	127.50	97.70	1,276
Dec	111.40	113.30	111.40	113.30	+ 1.30	127.40	99.00	636
Est vol 360; vol Mon62; open int 2,953, –4.								

SOURCE: Reprinted by permission of the *Wall Street Journal*, © Dow Jones & Company, Inc., May 28, 1986, p. 44.

cents per bushel. Soybean meal, however, trades in 100-ton contracts, soybean oil in 60,000-pound contracts, barley in 20 metric tons, and so on.[4] Although the dimensions of the contracts are different, the basic principles of commodity trading remain the same. The investor must put up margin equal to 5 to 10 percent of the value of the contract and gains or loses money depending on whether the contract moves in accordance with or against the investor's position.

Hedging Through the Commodity Markets

Participants in the commodity markets not only speculate on price movements in an attempt to capture large profits, they also use the markets to hedge vulnerable or exposed positions against losses. Suppose you own hundreds of thousands of bushels of wheat which you are going to physically deliver to the market and sell at the going market rate in a few months. A sharp fall in the price of wheat between now and then can wipe you out. One way to protect your position is to sell commodities futures contracts on wheat now. Perhaps you will sell the contracts at $2.50 a bushel. If the price of wheat goes down, you will be making a profit on your commodities contracts by buying them back at a lower price than you sold them. This profit will offset a similar decline in value on the wheat you plan to sell in the market in a few months.

Of course, if the price of wheat goes up instead of down, you will lose money on your commodity contracts (you will have to buy them back for more than you sold them); but this loss will be compensated for by the increased price you will receive for your actual wheat when it goes to market. **Hedging** through commodity futures contracts wipes away not only the potential for loss but the opportunity for gain as well. For this reason, those who hedge may only wish to partially cover or hedge their position.

The concept of hedging has become particularly popular in the area of financial futures (the fifth category we listed earlier in Table 14.1). Investors who hold large portfolios of bonds may use Treasury bond futures to hedge the risk of their portfolio going down. Similarly, investors with large, diversified common stock portfolios may use stock index futures to hedge the possible loss in their portfolio if they believe the market may decline (it's cheaper than selling off the portfolio and trying to buy it back after the anticipated market decline). For example, a bearish investor may sell a $70,000 NYSE Composite Index futures contract in anticipation of a market decline.[5] If the market goes down by 10 percent, the investor can buy back the contract for $63,000. The $7000 profit on the futures contract may help to offset actual losses on the investor's portfolio.

[4] For those commodities quoted in dollars rather than cents, a movement of the decimal point is not necessary. Soybean meal and barley are in this category.

[5] A small margin position of only a couple of thousand dollars or less may be necessary to set up this hedge. Margin requirements tend to lower when you are hedging rather than speculating. Also, they are lower for financial futures than for traditional commodities.

INVESTING IN REAL ASSETS

Real assets are physical assets (such as real estate or gold). They normally can be seen, felt, held, or collected. In Chapter 11 we presented a partial list of real assets, which we reproduce below:

1 Real estate (apartment, office building)

2 Collectibles
   Art
   Antiques
   Coins
   Stamps
   Rare books

3 Precious metals
   Gold
   Silver
   Platinum

4 Precious gems
   Diamonds
   Rubies

5 Other
   Common metals
   Oil

Real assets have attributes that are quite different from the financial assets (stock, bonds, mutual funds, options, and so on) that we have been discussing throughout this section of the book. We shall first consider the advantages and disadvantages of owning real assets.

Advantages of Real Assets

A primary advantage of real assets is that they offer a hedge against inflation. In the hyperinflation era of the late 1970s, the value of real assets increased annually at a double-digit rate. If you refer back to Table 11.1, which showed comparative returns on alternative investments, you will see that the best-performing investments over 15 years were real assets. This has certainly not been true for the 1980s, however.

Many people now believe that inflation is tamed or dead for the foreseeable future. We are not so sure. The important point is that the best time to buy real assets of any sort is when they are out of favor, and the era of the 1980s certainly qualifies for that definition. Of course, a high degree of patience is required. A rare gold coin or quality painting may take five years or more to strongly appreciate in value in an unenthusiastic investment environment for real assets.

Most investors go the opposite route. They wait until investment enthusiasm for real assets reaches a feverish pitch and then they buy gold, silver, or collectibles at the peak of the market. A good rule to follow is watch for the number of articles on real assets in such magazines as *Money, Personal Investor, Forbes,* or *Fortune.* If you are going to make an investment, consider doing it when the coverage is the lowest.

Another advantage of real assets, besides being an inflation hedge, is that they provide additional diversification for a portfolio. In most market environments, financial and real assets move in opposite directions. For this reason, even if you have little interest in real assets, you may consider putting 5 to 10 percent of your investments in this category. And keep in mind that if you own your own home, you have a major real asset investment that may represent a dominant percentage of your total asset holdings.

Real assets also provide psychic pleasure to the investor. One can hardly put a dollar value on the enjoyment received from a beautiful painting on the wall, a stunning diamond worn at a dinner party, or the childhood memories of a stamp collection. It is difficult to match these same pleasures through the receipt of a monthly statement of stock holdings from a brokerage house (that is, unless your stocks are going up like mad and you are rejoicing in your good fortune).

Disadvantages of Real Assets

There are many disadvantages associated with owning real assets. The first is the absence of large, liquid markets for trading. Whereas stocks and bonds almost instantly trade at prices very close to the latest quote, such is not the case with real assets. It may take many months to sell a piece of real estate, and the price is never certain until the deal is closed. Selling off a coin collection or valuable painting may also take time if market conditions are not right.

There is also the problem of dealer spread or middleman commissions. Whereas financial assets, such as stocks and bonds, can normally be sold at a 1 to 3 percent commission, dealer spreads on real assets may be as large as 20 to 25 percent or more. A **dealer spread** is the difference between the price at which a dealer is willing to buy and sell an asset. The dealer may be offering to sell it to you for $100, but only be willing to buy it back for $75. The dealer sets the spread based on operating costs and desired profit margin. Even if a diamond has an appraised value of $3000, it may only bring $2500 on a sale. On a truly valuable item, such as a rare stamp, the dealer spread may be quite small (perhaps 5 percent or less). On a common item, it will be as large as the market will allow.

The best way to avoid the high dealer spread on real assets is to try to sell them yourself directly to another investor. If you are sophisticated and well informed on market conditions, this is not difficult. If you are uninformed, it is almost impossible.

Another disadvantage of real assets, with the exception of real estate, is that they do not generate income. Furthermore, there may be additional costs for storage or insurance. This makes the required capital appreciation even greater if acceptable total returns are to be achieved.

In the remainder of the chapter, we discuss real estate as a real asset investment and then briefly look at collectibles, precious metals, and gems. We do not go into a lot of detail, so you may wish to consult the reference material at the end of the chapter for additional sources.

REAL ESTATE INVESTMENTS

Real estate has traditionally been one of the most popular forms of inflation hedges. With the passage of tax reform legislation in 1986, however, it has lost some of its tax-related advantages.

Tax Reform and Real Estate Investments

With tax reform, the life over which a real estate investor can write off his or her depreciation deduction for tax purposes was extended from 19 to 31½ years. This means you have to wait longer to take full advantage of tax deductions. Furthermore, the lowering of the marginal tax rate has reduced the incentive to invest in real estate as a tax shelter. When your maximum tax rate is 33 percent, there is much less incentive to go for tax write-offs than when it is 50 percent. Finally, passive investors (those not actively involved in the management of real estate) can no longer write off paper losses created through limited partnerships against other forms of income.

The effect of tax reform is to make real estate a less attractive investment, at least for the next few years. Because of the loss of some traditional tax benefits for real estate, existing properties will have less value and new construction will proceed at a slower pace. Over the long term, however, real estate may still be a good investment. Why? With fewer new properties being developed as a result of tax reform, the glut in office space and apartments in certain sections of the country (Houston, Atlanta, Denver, and other areas) will eventually disappear. Furthermore, with fewer new properties brought to the market, rents will eventually go up on existing properties. The increased rents will also be necessary to provide adequate cash returns to investors who previously received a large portion of their total return from tax shelter benefits but no longer do. The eventual impact of higher rents will be higher valuation, perhaps by the early 1990s.

The above comments about real estate apply primarily to commercial real estate (apartments, shopping centers, and so on) as opposed to homeownership as described in Chapter 6. All the benefits of homeownership basically remain in effect after tax reform. There is no depreciation deduction on your personal residence, so this is really not an issue. The only slight disadvantage to homeownership as a result of tax reform is that marginal tax rates are now lower so there is somewhat less benefit in taking tax deductions. Nevertheless, the overall tax advantages of owning your own home still remain firmly in place. Homeownership was simply too much a part of the American way of life to be attacked by tax reformers in Congress.

Types of Properties for Real Estate Investments

The most popular forms of real estate investments are listed below:

Your own home	Mini-warehouse
Duplex or fourplex	Industrial building
Apartment complex	Hotel or motel
Office building	Raw land
Shopping center	

The most obvious place to start for any real estate investment is your own home. Not only will you be able to borrow the money at a lower rate than if you were investing in other forms of real estate, but you are in control of your own destiny. You do not have to worry about vacancies, and the upkeep and maintenance of the property is clearly in your own hands.

Many of the other forms of real estate investment are beyond the capability of the individual investor, but real estate investments are often undertaken on the basis of investors pooling their funds in partnerships, trusts, and so on. More will be made of this point in the next section. Regardless of the type of real estate you are considering, you must have a feel for the demand-supply relationship for the property, the vacancy rate in the geographical area in which it is located, and the quality of the management involved if you are investing with others or allowing others to manage your property.

Most real estate advisers recommend apartments and shopping centers, with a diversified tenant base, as fairly conservative forms of real estate investment. Downtown office buildings tend to carry more risk because of competitive and economic pressures. Raw land is perhaps the most speculative type of investment, but it can provide the highest percentage returns if you guess right.

As we indicated in Chapter 6, real estate investment advisers talk about the importance of the three L's of real estate: location, location, and location. It is not only important that you are properly located within a given community but that your funds flow into a strong geographic area of the country if you are participating in a major investment program with other investors. In the mid- to late 1980s, the Boston and New York metropolitan areas were strong, whereas the major cities in the Southwest were not. This, of course, was a reversal of only a few years before. The smart real estate investor is able to assess not only the here and now, but also what might lie around the corner.

Forms of Real Estate Ownership

Investing as an *individual* or with two or three others in a *regular partnership* is the simplest way to get into real estate. You will have a major say in the decisions that are made and in the management of the property. Unlike the passive investor in the limited partnership, you will also be able to deduct a reasonable amount of paper losses against your other income should that become necessary. Individual or regular partnerships are best suited for small investments in your own community. For larger investments, a limited partnership may be more appropriate.

The **limited partnership** (normally synonymous with a real estate syndicate) works as follows: A general partner forms the limited partnership and assumes unlimited liabilities for the partnership obligations. The general partner then sells participation units ($5,000 to $10,000) to limited partners, whose liability is limited to the extent of their investment. Limited liability is one of the appealing features of a limited partnership because there is often a high degree of debt involved in real estate deals and limited partners are protected. In addition to having unlimited liability, the general partner is normally responsible for managing the property and making day-to-day decisions. The general partner receives a commission and annual management fee for putting the deal together.

The traditional advantages of a limited partnership to investors were the limited liability and the potential for large tax write-offs against other income. The losses were somewhat fictitious in nature due to the fact that the partnership was taking very large depreciation deductions for tax purposes. In many cases the property was actually going up in value.

As we mentioned at the beginning of this section, passive investors in a limited partnership can no longer take such deductions against other income. This means that limited partnerships must now prosper or fail based on the economics and cash-generating capacity of the project. Leading syndicators for limited partnerships now try to select projects based exclusively on their cash flow and capital appreciation potential rather than as a tax shelter. The limited partnership is still an effective vehicle for getting into such major real estate deals as regional shopping centers and 100-unit apartment complexes, but it will never fully regain the popularity it enjoyed prior to tax reform.

Finally, an investor may participate in real estate through a **real estate investment trust (REIT).** REITs invest in real estate or loan money to major real estate projects. You can participate in an REIT through purchasing their shares in the stock market. Buying the shares of an REIT is exactly like buying any other common stock. You get your return from the dividend yield as well as any appreciation in stock value.

OTHER FORMS OF REAL ASSETS—COLLECTIBLES, PRECIOUS METALS, AND PRECIOUS GEMS

The other real assets that we shall discuss all provide a high degree of psychic pleasure. That is, they are fun to own. Collectibles, precious metals, and precious gems are also effective for hedging against inflation. Furthermore, they do well when investors are apprehensive about the future because of economic turmoil or the threat of war.

Box 14.2 HOW A PRO PROBES FOR PROFITS IN BATTERED REAL ESTATE DEALS

Limited partnerships were bathed in sunshine when Paul T. Green started his investment advisory firm, Southport Advisors, in 1981. A former financial manager for Exxon, he now sets out to assess partnerships for individual investors seeking tax-sheltered income and capital gains. Both oil and gas and real estate deals were prospering then: sky-high energy prices and Saudi embargoes made domestic oil drilling and exploration partnerships seem patriotic as well as profitable. And raging inflation practically guaranteed gains in real estate.

Today, however, with a depression in oil prices, moribund inflation and the prospect of a drop in the maximum personal income tax bracket from 50% to 35%, energy programs have all but dried up, and some real estate operators have had trouble generating cash to meet mortgage payments. In recent months, two giant real estate syndicators—Balcor, an American Express subsidiary, and Hall Financial Group—have experienced foreclosures on some of their properties. One of Hall's programs and those of several smaller syndicators recently went bankrupt.

Surprisingly, Green is more optimistic about the now foundering oil drillers than he is about the future of some real estate deals. "I believe energy prices will rebound, but not for at least two years," he says. "So I'm coming around to the contrarian position that oil and gas partnerships could be attractive again soon." As for real estate, Green believes that "it's taken too long for many syndicators to realize that inflation is not going to increase their properties' values 10% each year. I'm afraid that we will continue to see problems in some real estate partnerships, especially in those deals that have borrowed heavily." He advises caution on leveraged proposals that provide much more than one-to-one write-offs.

Last year investors handed over some $18 billion to public and private partnerships. About 60% went into public deals—those usually offered to hundreds of small investors for as little as $2000 a unit. Private deals are smaller and generally cost $20,000 and up. Green expects 1986 sales to repeat 1985's.

If you buy into a partnership

The other side of the issue is that when inflation subsides or the world enjoys a fairly peaceful existence, the investment value of real assets may decline substantially. This is particularly true if they have been bid up all out of proportion to their historical value due to investor enthusiasm. This price reversal was quite evident in the case of gold and silver in the last decade. Gold went from $35 an ounce in the early 1970s to $850 an ounce in 1980, then fell to $200 an ounce in 1982. Silver followed a similar route, going from $2 an ounce in the early 1970s to $55 an ounce in 1980 and then tumbling to $6 an ounce two years later. By 1987, neither precious metal had made a serious run at returning to its previous high value.

A good rule to follow in investing in collectibles, precious metals, or precious gems is to decide how much money you want to invest (perhaps 5 to 10 percent of your personal portfolio) and then go for the highest quality possible. Whether it's a painting, rare coin, or diamond, normally the best price appre-

this year, Green suggests three essential questions to ask the broker or financial planner selling you the partnership:

- How much of my money in a real estate deal will go toward the purchase of property? From the total investment, a sponsor deducts commissions and other nonrecurring charges. "In a deal where the sponsor is not borrowing to finance his purchases, total charges should never exceed 20%," notes Green. "In a leveraged arrangement, because loan costs and large property purchases are involved, the fees can be higher, between 20% and 30%."
- How will the general partner and the limited partners share in the profits? First, says Green, the investors should get most of the current income generated by the partnership until they get back what they put in. After that, arrangements vary greatly. Says Green: "A deal that is generous to the investor might give the general partner 15% after the limited partner has received his investment back plus an extra 10%."
- How strong is the sponsor's financial position? A net worth equal to 10% of the total amount being raised is a bare minimum. Green likes to see contingency funds that are equal to 25% of the amount being raised.

After examining such critical questions, Green assigns each deal a rating similar to, but not as comprehensive as, a credit rating given to a public company by Standard & Poor's. A Columbia Ph.D. in economics and a father of three, Green publishes his updated ratings on all the public deals currently available for purchase each month in the Partnership Record, a newsletter available at many large brokerage offices or by subscription for $250 a year (P.O. Box 682, Southport, Conn. 06490). Green's firm also provides assessments of private partnerships for investors on an individual basis.

Real estate syndication and drilling partnerships are both such young industries, Green believes, that "nobody has the kind of lengthy performance record an investor might like to see." Still, certain syndicators consistently offer deals that he considers to be of sound quality. In the oil patch, he points to Dyco Petroleum, Minneapolis, Minn., 612-545-2828; Red Eagle Exploration, Oklahoma City, Okla., 405-755-2023; and Woods Petroleum, Oklahoma City, Okla., 405-947-7811. And in real estate he likes Equitec Financial Group in Oakland, Calif., 415-430-9900; and Krupp Corp. in Boston, 617-423-2233; Paine Webber Properties in Boston, 617-439-8150; Realty Income Corp., Escondido, Calif., 619-741-2111; and USAA Investment Management Co., San Antonio, Texas, 512-690-6916.

SOURCE: *Money,* May 1986, p. 241.

ciation goes with the highest-quality items. You are better off investing $500 or $1000 in one or two quality coins than accumulating a sack of 25 coins of marginal value.

We now briefly discuss collectibles, precious metals, and precious gems individually.

Collectibles

Collectibles include such items as art, antiques, coins, stamps, rare books, and all forms of memorabilia. The credibility of collecting art has been enhanced by the development of the Sotheby's Art Index, which is published in *Barron's* financial weekly. An example of the index is presented in Figure 14.6. Note how the change in value is carefully chronicled over time. Paintings represent one of

Figure 14.6 VALUE INDEX FOR SELECTED COLLECTIBLES

SOTHEBY'S ART INDEX ®

Category	Weight	May 12	May 5	May 1985	May 1984
Old Master Paintings	17	303	303	278	242
19th Century European Paintings	12	249	249	228	203
Impressionist & Post-Impressionist Paintings	18	380	380	356	317
Modern Paintings (1900-1950)	10	364	364	336	301
American Paintings (1800-pre-WW II)	3	667	667	589	556
Continental Ceramics	3	284	284	284	284
Chinese Ceramics	10	493	486	486	459
English Silver	5	314	314	277	237
Continental Silver	5	181	181	175	161
American Furniture	3	333	333	324	241
French & Continental Furniture	7	285	273	273	270
English Furniture	7	447	419	382	342
Weighted Aggregate		350	347	325	294

Sept. 1975=100.

The most important event recently was the sale in Amsterdam of "The Hatcher Collection" of Chinese export porcelain. Fears that the large number of items would overwhelm the market proved to be unfounded. The sale topped £10 million, more than three times the estimate; most lots sold.

Although the results had some effect on the Chinese ceramics' sector, it will have very little influence on the market overall. The so-called "glamour" factor means that examples from this sale will invariably get higher prices than identical pieces from more conventional sources.

Another highlight: A New York auction of French and Continental furniture drew high prices for rare, high-quality items; more average pieces didn't fare as well. The sale featured an item which brought more than $1 million, an auction record for furniture sold in the U.S.

Rare, high-quality works attracted new buyers and those who've been less active lately. Foreign buyers were encouraged by the weakening of the dollar.

The data reflected in the Sotheby's Art Index are based on results of auction sales by affiliated companies of Sotheby's and other information deemed relevant by Sotheby's. Sotheby's does not warrant the accuracy of the data reflected therein. Nothing in any commentary furnished by Sotheby's nor any of the Sotheby's Indexes is intended or should be relied upon as investment advice or as a prediction, warranty or guaranty as to future performance or otherwise. All individual prices quoted in this review are aggregate prices, inclusive of the buyer's premium.

SOURCE: Reprinted by permission of *Barron's* © Dow Jones & Company, Inc., May 12, 1986, p. 113.

the best opportunities to combine pleasure and investment. A $300 to $500 painting may decorate your living room as well as serve as a storehouse of value.

In buying collectibles, you must be particularly careful to find a reputable dealer. Look for a person who has been in business for a reasonable period of time and who has an established list of satisfied customers. Avoid the fast talker who is going to double your money overnight.

Figure 14.7 BASEBALL CARD PRICE GUIDE

Sports Collectors Digest PRICE GUIDE

(1950 Bowman, con't.)

46	Yogi Berra	30.00	13.50
56	*Del Crandall*	6.00	2.70
62	Ted Kluszewski	6.50	2.90
71	Red Schoendienst	6.50	2.90
75	Roy Campanella	35.00	15.75
77	Duke Snider	26.00	11.75
84	Richie Ashburn	5.50	2.45
94	Lou Boudreau	7.50	3.35
98	Ted Williams	65.00	29.00
101	Bobby Brown	3.50	1.55
112	Gil Hodges	12.00	5.50
139	Johnny Mize	11.00	5.00
148	Early Wynn	9.50	4.25
217	Casey Stengel	20.00	9.00
219	*Hank Bauer*	8.00	3.60
220	Leo Durocher	6.25	2.80
229	Frank Frisch	6.25	2.80
232	*Al Rosen*	8.00	3.60
234	*Bobby Shantz*	4.50	2.00

1951 BOWMAN

1951 Bowman (324)	Ex-Mt.	VG
Common 1-252	$2.50	1.10
Common 253-324	7.00	3.15
Complete Set	1875.	850.

1	*Whitey Ford*	85.00+	38.25
2	Yogi Berra	29.00	13.10
3	Robin Roberts	8.00	3.60
7	Gil Hodges	12.00	5.40
10	Red Schoendienst	4.00	1.80
26	Phil Rizzuto	12.00	5.40
30	Bob Feller	16.00	7.20
31	Roy Campanella	29.00	13.10
32	Duke Snider	22.00	9.90
46	George Kell	8.00	3.60
50	Johnny Mize	10.00	4.50
53	Bob Lemon	8.75	3.95
58	Enos Slaughter	8.00	3.60
62	Lou Boudreau	8.00	3.60
78	Early Wynn	8.75	3.95
80	Pee Wee Reese	15.00	6.75
110	Bobby Brown	3.25	1.45
122	Joe Garagiola	7.75	3.50
127	Sal Maglie	4.00	1.80
134	Warren Spahn	12.00	5.40
143	Ted Kluszewski	4.00	1.80
165	Ted Williams	60.00	27.00
181	Casey Stengel	16.00	7.20
186	Richie Ashburn	4.00	1.80
187	Al Rosen	4.00	1.80
198	Monte Irvin	7.25	3.25
232	Nellie Fox	7.00	3.15
233	Leo Durocher	5.50	2.45
253	*Mickey Mantle*	400.00+	180.00
254	*Jackie Jensen*	9.25	4.15
260	Carl Erskine	9.25	4.15
275	Bucky Harris	9.00	4.05
282	Frank Frisch	12.00	5.40
290	Bill Dickey	24.00	10.80
295	Al Lopez	11.00	4.95
305	*Willie Mays*	305.00	138.00
306	*Jim Piersall*	10.00	4.50
312	Gene Mauch	9.50	4.25

Player's name in *italic type* indicates a rookie card.

1952 BOWMAN

1952 Bowman (252)	Ex-Mt.	VG
Common 1-180	$2.25	1.00
Common 181-216	2.00	.90
Common 217-252	4.25	1.90
Complete Set	1175.	530.

1	Yogi Berra	60.00	27.00
2	Bobby Thomson	4.00	.80
4	Robin Roberts	9.25	4.15
8	Pee Wee Reese	13.75	6.25
11	Ralph Kiner	10.50	4.70
21	Nellie Fox	6.00	2.70
23	Bob Lemon	9.75	4.40
27	Joe Garagiola	8.00	3.60
30	Red Schoendienst	3.00	1.35
33	*Gil McDougald*	4.50	2.00
43	Bob Feller	16.00	7.20
44	Roy Campanella	30.00	13.50
52	Phil Rizzuto	13.00	5.85
53	Richie Ashburn	3.75	1.70
75	George Kell	7.00	3.15
80	Gil Hodges	12.00	5.50
101	Mickey Mantle	225.00	101.00
105	Bobby Brown	3.25	1.45
116	Duke Snider	20.00	9.00
142	Early Wynn	8.25	3.70
145	Johnny Mize	8.00	3.60
146	Leo Durocher	5.50	2.45
151	Al Rosen	3.50	1.55
156	Warren Spahn	12.25	5.50
158	Bucky Harris	4.00	1.80
162	Monte Irvin	8.00	3.60
196	Stan Musial	65.00	29.00
217	Casey Stengel	25.00	11.25
218	Willie Mays	180.00	81.00
232	Enos Slaughter	10.00	4.50
252	Frank Crosetti	19.50	8.75

1952 TOPPS

Topps' premiere set, and most difficult to complete. Cards 1-80 exist with red or black back printing. Cards 48 (Joe Page) and 49 (Johnny Sain) exist with each other's backs as well as with correct backs.

1952 Topps (407)	Ex-Mt.	VG
Common 1-80	$5.25+	$2.35
Common 81-250	4.00+	1.80
Common 251-310	11.00+	5.00
Common 311-407	52.00+	23.50
Complete Set	12100.+	5450.

All prices appearing in the SCD PRICE GUIDE are intended to serve only as an aid to evaluate your cards. The values quoted are not a solicitation to buy or sell cards on the part of the publisher or any other party.

1	Andy Pafko	125.00+	56.25
10	Al Rosen	7.00+	3.15
11	Phil Rizzuto	18.00	8.25
22	Dom DiMaggio	7.00+	3.15
26	Monte Irvin	8.00+	3.60
29	Ted Kluszewski	7.00+	3.15
33	Warren Spahn	18.00	8.10
36	Gil Hodges	18.00	8.10
37	Duke Snider	26.00	11.75
48	Joe Page (correct)	8.00+	3.60
48	Joe Page (error)	75.00+	33.75
49	J. Sain (correct)	12.00+	5.50
49	J. Sain (error)	75.00+	33.75
59	Robin Roberts	11.00	5.00
65	Enos Slaughter	11.00	5.00
88	Bob Feller	19.00	8.55
91	Red Schoendienst	6.50+	2.90
129	Johnny Mize	11.00	5.00
175	*Billy Martin*	27.00	12.15
191	Yogi Berra	36.00	16.25
200	Ralph Houk	7.00+	3.15
216	Richie Ashburn	7.00+	3.15
227	Joe Garagiola	10.00+	4.50
246	George Kell	8.00+	3.60
261	Willie Mays	325.00	145.00
268	Bob Lemon	45.00	20.25
277	Early Wynn	45.00	20.25
311	Mickey Mantle	2000.00+	900.00
312	Jackie Robinson	265.00	120.00
313	Bobby Thomson	75.00+	33.75
314	Roy Campanella	285.00	128.00
315	Leo Durocher	90.00+	40.50
333	Pee Wee Reese	210.00	95.00
369	*Dick Groat*	90.00+	40.50
372	*Gil McDougald*	90.00+	40.50
384	Frank Crosetti	75.00+	33.75
392	*Hoyt Wilhelm*	130.00+	58.50
394	Billy Herman	70.00+	31.50
396	*Dick Williams*	70.00+	31.50
400	Bill Dickey	210.00	95.00
407	*Eddie Mathews*	355.00	160.00

1953 BOWMAN

Bowman's most popular set, with fewer cards, a larger format ($2\frac{1}{2}$x$3\frac{3}{4}$") and full color photos.

1953 Bowman (160)	Ex-Mt.	VG
Common 1-112	$4.25	1.90
Common 113-128	10.50	4.70
Common 129-160	7.75	3.50
Complete Set	1725.	775.

1	Dave Williams	12.00	5.40
8	Al Rosen	6.25	2.80
9	Phil Rizzuto	18.00	8.10
10	Richie Ashburn	6.50	2.90
18	Nellie Fox	7.00	3.15
21	Joe Garagiola	9.50	4.25
32	Stan Musial	75.00	33.50
33	Pee Wee Reese	25.00	11.25
44	Bauer, Berra, Mantle	55.00	24.50
46	Roy Campanella	36.00	16.25
51	Monte Irvin	8.00	3.60
55	Leo Durocher	7.00	2.45
57	Lou Boudreau	9.00	4.10
59	Mickey Mantle	260.00	117.00
61	George Kell	8.00	3.60
62	Ted Kluszewski	6.50	2.90
65	Robin Roberts	13.75	6.20
80	Ralph Kiner	13.75	6.25
81	Enos Slaughter	12.00	5.40
92	Gil Hodges	16.75	7.55
93	Rizzuto & Martin	35.00	15.75
97	Eddie Mathews	17.00	7.65
99	Warren Spahn	16.75	7.55
101	Red Schoendienst	5.50	2.45
114	Bob Feller	54.00	24.50
117	Duke Snider	125.00	56.00
118	Billy Martin	36.00	16.25
121	Yogi Berra	115.00	51.50
143	Al Lopez	11.00	4.95
146	Early Wynn	25.00	11.25
153	Whitey Ford	60.00	27.00

1953 BOWMAN BLACK & WHITE

Identical in format to Bowman's color issue, this separate set featured black and white photos. Limited distribution and high demand make it especially challenging.

1953 Bowman B/W (64)	Ex-Mt.	VG
Common Player	$9.00	$4.05
Complete Set	825.00	375.00

1	Gus Bell	18.00	8.25
15	Johnny Mize	29.00	13.10
25	Johnny Sain	21.00	9.45
26	Preacher Roe	22.00	9.90
27	Bob Lemon	29.00	13.05
28	Hoyt Wilhelm	27.00	12.15
36	Jim Piersall	21.00	9.45
39	Casey Stengel	110.00	49.50
46	Bucky Harris	17.00	7.65

A + sign behind the Ex.-Mt. or Mint price indicates the value of that card has risen since its last listing in the PRICE GUIDE. A — sign indicates the value has dropped.

SOURCE: *Sports Collectors Digest,* May 23, 1986, p. 141.

For the young at heart, a fun form of collecting is in baseball cards, and they increase in value too. Note in Figure 14.7, the value in May 1986 of various one-cent baseball cards from the 1950s. The highest value shown is for the 1952 Mickey Mantle card, which is circled in the table. It carries a price tag of $2000.[6] Some cards from the 1960s and 1970s also have values in the hundreds of dollars. If you still have cards you collected as a child, hold on to them.

Precious Metals

The primary investments in precious metals are gold and silver. Ownership may take many forms such as bullion (bars or wafers), valuable coins, gold or silver stocks on the security exchanges, or commodity futures in gold and silver. Also, you may buy gold or silver to enhance a wardrobe (ring, watch, necklace). If you have physical possession of precious metals, insurance protection is important, as is secured storage. Some financial institutions and brokerage houses will buy gold or silver in your name and keep it in safe storage for you for a small fee.

Precious Gems

Precious gems include diamonds, rubies, sapphires, and emeralds. They are popular because of their beauty, small size, and durability. There are many unscrupulous dealers in the precious gem market, though, so you have to be especially careful. You may think your investment has doubled in value, but if it lacks the quality you thought you purchased or was vastly overpriced, you may not even be at the break-even point. The assessment of any stone should be certified by the Gemological Institute of America.

Before you invest in any form of real assets, you must do your homework as an investor. Prior to making an actual purchase, you should also talk to two or three different dealers to get a feel for price and quality.

SUMMARY

There are many alternative forms of investment that allow you to broaden your investment horizon beyond stocks and bonds. The list of these alternatives could be expanded well beyond those covered in this chapter.

Options are the right to buy or sell 100 shares of stock at a specified price over a given time period. An option to buy is termed a call and an option to sell is a put. Purchasing a call option gives the investor the opportunity for high returns on a very small investment, and if the stock price plummets, the loss is limited to the price of the option. The disadvantage is that the stock must normally go up a few points for the option buyer to break even (there are

[6] The first column indicates the value of the collectible in extremely good condition. The next column is for normal condition.

exceptions to this principle). Furthermore, although there is not generally a large *dollar* loss exposure with call options, a large *percentage* loss is quite possible.

The bearish investor may decide to sell (write) call options or buy put options. In either case, profits can be made from a declining stock price. Selling call options is riskier than buying put options and has the same type of risk exposure as selling short (described in Chapter 12).

Trading in commodities also allows the investor to greatly multiply the impact of price changes on return on invested capital. A commodity futures contract provides for the delivery of a specific commodity at a designated time in the future at a given price. Delivery almost never takes place because the investor/speculator reverses (closes out) the position before the transaction is finalized. An investor can normally control a large contract with investing only 5 to ten percent of actual dollar value of the contract through the use of margin. Commodity trading covers such items as grains, livestock, metals, petroleum, foreign currency, interest rate instruments, and stock market indexes.

The commodity markets are frequently used for hedging as well as for speculating. A hedger takes the opposite position in the commodities market that he or she has in terms of actual ownership. Then, if the price goes up or down, the performance in one investment or market will neutralize the other.

Real assets are physical assets that can be seen, felt, held, or collected. Major categories of real assets include real estate, collectibles, precious metals, and precious gems. These assets tend to move in the opposite direction of financial assets (stocks, bonds) in most market environments and therefore provide for effective diversification. They also serve as a hedge against inflation and may provide psychic pleasure to the investor through their beauty or rare quality.

Real assets also have disadvantages. The first is the absence of a large and liquid market. As a corollary to this point, there tend to be large commissions or dealer spreads. Also, with the exception of real estate, real assets do not generate interest income. The trick to investing in real assets is to try to take a position when they are in relative disfavor rather than when investors are in a state of euphoria and bidding prices up to unrealistic levels.

KEY TERMS

bearish
bullish
call option
commodities futures contract
dealer spread
expiration date
hedging
in-the-money options
intrinsic value
limited partnership
margin on a commodities contract
option
out-of-the-money options
put option
real assets
real estate investment trust (REIT)
speculative premium
strike price

SELECTED READINGS

Duthy, Robin. *Alternative Investment: A Guide to Opportunity in the Collectibles Market.* New York: New York Times Books, 1978.

Francis, Jack Clark. *Management of Investments.* New York: McGraw-Hill, 1983.

Gup, Benton. *The Basics of Investing,* 2nd ed. New York: Wiley, 1983.

Hirt, Geoffrey, Stanley Block, and Fred Jury. *The Investor's Desktop Portfolio Planner.* Chicago: Probus Publishing Company, 1986.

Periodicals—*American Arts and Antiques, Antique Monthly, Coin World, Collector/Investor, Linn's Stamp News,* and the *Sports Collectors Digest.*

Van Caspel, Venita. *Money Dynamics for the New Economy.* New York: Simon and Schuster, 1986.

"Will Gold Gleam Again?" *Personal Investor,* July 1985, pp. 66–71.

QUESTIONS

1 What is an option? What is meant by the term *strike price?*

2 What does the intrinsic value of an option mean? How does the speculative premium relate to the intrinsic value?

3 Even if an option entitles you to purchase stock, explain why you do not actually have to purchase the stock to take advantage of an upward stock movement if you own an option.

4 Is your *dollar* loss potential with an option generally as large as your dollar gain potential?

5 What is the difference between a call option and a put option?

6 Why do options with longer expiration dates tend to carry higher market values?

7 What is an in-the-money stock option? How does it differ from an out-of-the-money stock option? What is the intrinsic value for an out-of-the-money stock option?

8 Why does one who has sold a call option hope that the price will go down?

9 What is a covered-option-writing strategy? Why is this strategy considered to be conservative in nature?

10 If you are bearish on a stock and want to gain from the potential downward movement in the stock, why is buying a put option less risky than selling a naked call option?

11 What is a commodities futures contract? Does a person actually need to have physical possession of the commodity?

12 Why is it said that a commodities trader has a highly leveraged position?

13 In what area of the market has the concept of hedging become particularly popular?

14 List four different categories for real assets.

15 In what type of market environment do real assets tend to go up most in value?

16 Explain how real assets can bring diversification to a portfolio.

17 What are three disadvantages of investing in real assets?

18 In what ways does tax reform negatively impact investments in real estate?

19 Why might the impact of tax reform on real estate not really be bad over the long term?

20 Why might the most obvious and best investment in real estate be a person's own home?

21 How is a limited partnership normally set up? What is the traditional tax advantage to investors? Is that advantage still available?

22 Generally speaking, when investing in collectibles, precious metals, or precious gems, how should quality influence the nature of your decision?

23 Call options to buy shares in the Barker Corporation have a strike price of $30. The stock is currently selling for $33.25 per share. The option price is $5.50.

a Compute the intrinsic value.

b Compute the speculative premium.

24 Use Figure 14.3 to compute the intrinsic value and the speculative premium for the Ford December $75 call options.

25 Ed Able purchases a call option in the Denver Corporation with a strike price of $60. The stock has a value of $61 and the option sells for $3. Assume that after three months, as the expiration date approaches, the stock is selling for $76 and the option for $16.

a Compute the percentage return on the option.

b Compute the percentage return on the stock.

c How many times greater is the return on the option than the return on the stock?

d Further assume that Ed Able has $600 to invest. If he buys the options, how much total dollar profit will he make?

e Assuming he uses the same $600 to buy stock, how many shares can he buy? (Round to the nearest whole number.)

f If he buys the stock described in part e, how much will his total dollar profit be?

26 Lewis Archer can't decide whether to buy an option to purchase 100 shares of stock in the Wilkins Corporation or to buy 100 shares directly. The stock has a strike price of $40 and is currently selling for $41.50. The option is priced at $4.

a Assume that a disaster hits the corporation and the stock price ends up at $18. What is the dollar loss on the option? What is the percentage loss?

b If the stock is purchased instead, what will the dollar loss be? What will the percentage loss be?

27 Lucille Collins purchases a call option to buy 100 shares of the Mobile Transit Corporation. The strike price is $70. The stock is selling for $71.25 and the option for $4.50. Assume the stock ends up at $72.50.

a How much will Lucille make or lose (in total dollars) if she buys the option?

b How much would Lucille have made or lost (in total dollars) if she had bought 100 shares of the stock?

28 Virginia Willingham owns 100 shares of the Elite Products Corporation. The stock currently sells for $55. Her total portfolio value is $5500. She is considering selling a call option on the stock. The option has a strike price of $50 and sells for $8.

a How much will her total revenue be from selling the call option? (Remember to multiply by 100.)

b If the value of her stock falls to $49, will she have an overall gain or loss? In answering the question, add the profit on selling the option to the loss on the stock.

29 Randall Horton buys a put option that entitled him to sell 100 shares of the Trinity Corporation at $70 per share. The stock currently is selling for $68 and he pays $4 for the put option. If the stock ends up at $58,

a What will be the value of the put option?

b What will be his total dollar gain or loss?

30 Phil Goldman buys a commodities contract for 5000 bushels of corn at $2.00 per bushel. He puts up $500 in margin.

a What is the total value of the contract?

b What percentage of the total value of the contract does the margin represent?

c If the price of corn ends up at $2.08 per bushel, what will be the total dollar gain on the contract?

d What will be the percentage return on the margin investment?

e If the price of corn ends up at $1.95, what will be the total dollar loss on the contract?

CASE PROBLEMS

14.1 Mary Wilson has just talked to her stockbroker for the third time this morning. The broker assures her that it is very likely that Digital Tech Corporation is going to receive a very important government defense contract. Digital Tech stock is currently selling for $32 a share. Call options with a strike price of $30, which will expire in three months, are selling for $5.25.

a How much in total dollars will it cost Mary to buy four options, which will allow her to control 400 shares?

b If the stock has a value of $48 at expiration, how much will her total dollar profit or loss be? (Subtract out the initial investment in arriving at your answer.)

c If she had used the same investment as computed in part a to buy shares of stock instead of options, how many shares could she buy? (Round to the nearest whole number.) What would her total dollar profit or loss be if the ending stock value was $48?

d Suppose Mary decides to buy 100 shares at $32 and sell one option (representing 100 shares) for $5.25. As indicated above, the strike price is $30. If the stock price ends up at $52 and Mary buys back the option at its final value, how much will Mary's total combined profit or loss be from the stock and from the option? Do each calculation separately and add them together. Given Mary's information about the likely government contract, do you think she should sell the call option?

e Just as Mary is about to place an order with her broker, she hears a news bulletin that National Dynamics Inc. will probably get the big government contract instead of Digital Tech. Suggest two option strategies that Mary might follow to take advantage of the likely decline in Digital Tech stock.

14.2 Alfred Hartley is in charge of the hedging operations for his large family farm business. The family plans to sell 100,000 bushels of soybeans in three months. Assume it is now August, so they will be selling the soybeans in November. The members of the family are concerned that the price of soybeans might go down over this time period so they instruct Alfred to fully hedge their position. He turns to Figure 14.5 on page 479 and observes that soybeans are the second item listed.

a What was the closing (settle) price for the November soybean contract? (Insert a decimal point to convert total cents to dollars.)

b How many contracts should he sell in order to fully hedge the 100,000 bushels that the family anticipates selling in three months?

c If the price of soybeans ends up at $4.90 per bushel in November, what will be the total dollar gain from selling the futures contracts on the 100,000 bushels? Explain how this will offset the losses from actually selling the soybeans in three months.

d Assume another investor bought one November contract at the price determined in part a, and the price ended up at $5.3075 per bushel. The margin investment required is $1250. What is this investor's return on the investment?

You may think that a section on retirement and estate planning was especially written for a senior citizens group or people in retirement homes. Nothing could be further from the truth. The time to do lifelong retirement and estate planning is when you're young; it's too late when you're in your later years because most of your best options will have been closed out.

For example, much of your retirement income may come from corporate pension plans. If you are continually changing jobs throughout your career, you may fail to maximize your later benefits.

The use of individual retirement accounts (IRAs) is another example of the need to begin your retirement planning and nest egg building early in your career. As we point out in Chapter 15, if you put aside $2000 a year from age 20 to age 70 at a 10 percent annual rate of return, you will accumulate $2,327,817. If you wait until you are 50 to begin making contributions, your funds will only grow to $114,550 by age 70. The message is to start your retirement and estate planning

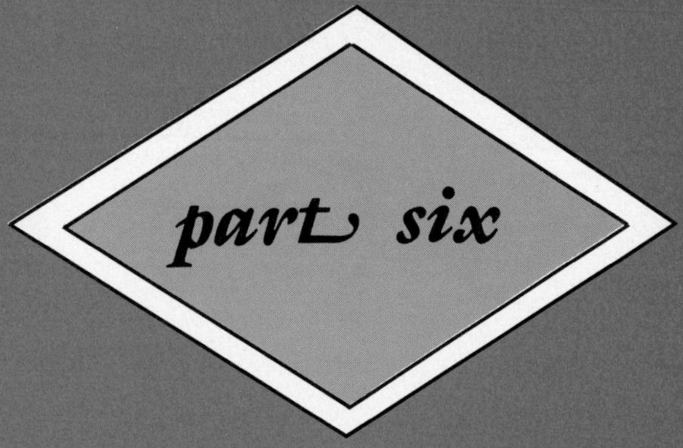

RETIREMENT AND ESTATE PLANNING

now. Because people are generally living longer, you need not only life insurance to protect against an untimely death but retirement planning to prepare for a long life.

Estate planning requires that your assets be properly managed and preserved during your lifetime and distributed in the desired manner when you die. Through the use of trusts and gifts to family members as described in Chapter 16, some of the ultimate tax burden at death may be diminished. It is very foolish to spend a lifetime creating wealth and then unnecessarily hand over more than is absolutely required at death. Chapter 16 also stresses the importance of a will. Even a young person with modest resources should make sure that assets are properly directed to the appropriate loved ones (whether it be a spouse, a sibling, or a child). If you do not state your intentions, your assets may be allocated in an inappropriate manner. ■

15

Retirement Planning

After studying this chapter, you should:

- Appreciate the importance of retirement planning
- Understand the role of Social Security and know how the Social Security system provides benefits
- Become familiar with the basic features and uses of employer pension and retirement plans
- Know how to use supplementary retirement plans, such as Keogh plans, IRAs, SEP/IRAs, salary reduction plans, profit-sharing plans, and thrift plans
- Understand how annuities work and be familiar with their key features
- Appreciate the wealth accumulation potential of steady, consistent savings

Retirement planning may currently rank as one of your lowest priorities. If you are like many young people, you are far more concerned with day-to-day activities and developing your career. Because retirement is a distant event, you may feel no urgency to consider it until later in your life. The fact remains, however, that most of us will live several years in retirement. With continued improvements in health and medical care, today's young person may live much longer than current expectations. You may have a retirement lifetime of 20 years or even longer.

In earlier chapters we discussed the importance of protecting your family against loss of income caused by your death or disability. These misfortunes can occur at any time to any person, so most people recognize the importance of providing financial protection against these possibilities. Your retirement, however, is another matter. You know that you will not retire for many more years. Therefore, you may decide to delay retirement planning. Unfortunately, many individuals who postpone retirement planning do not recognize the importance of this type of activity until it is too late. Once you near retirement age, the opportunity to build the financial foundation for a comfortable and enjoyable retirement may already be gone. As a result, you could face the dilemma of having enough time during retirement to enjoy those activities you always wanted to pursue, but being unable to afford them.

Everyone wants to have a financially secure retirement. You probably anticipate receiving retirement benefits from Social Security, your employer's retirement plan, and other forms of retirement plans. You may believe that these sources will provide sufficient retirement income. Most retirees, however, do not receive enough income from these kinds of payments to be financially secure. For these individuals, retirement can become a financial nightmare. Only by accumulating enough savings to supplement these traditional retirement benefits can these people be assured of a comfortable retirement. To make sure that you avoid financial problems at the time you retire, you should develop a regular savings program. The amount you must save each year depends on many factors. We will attempt to address these factors and provide a convenient approach for determining how much you should save for retirement.

SOCIAL SECURITY

During the Great Depression many Americans saw their life savings wiped out as the result of bank failures and the collapse of the stock market. The elderly were particularly hard hit. Government estimates at that time indicated that, without some form of governmental assistance, more than half the elderly would have had incomes below the poverty level. It was in this environment that Congress passed the Social Security Act of 1935. Today, as a result of that legislation, workers rely on the federal government to provide income for retirees, medical care for the elderly, disability insurance, and aid to the families of deceased workers. In 1940, when benefits began, only 106,000 people received payments. Today, about 37 million individuals receive payments totaling more than one-quarter trillion dollars a year. After national defense, Social Security comprises the largest expenditure of the federal government.

Social Security is administered through the **Old-Age, Survivors, Disability, and Health Insurance (OASDHI)** program. Since its beginning, Social Security has expanded considerably and now offers benefits beyond its original mandate. At first, Social Security provided only modest retirement payments. Only workers in commerce and industry were covered. Currently, however, Social Security also pays benefits to disabled individuals and families of deceased workers and provides health insurance through its Medicare program.

Funding

Social Security is supported by payroll taxes imposed on covered employees and their employers under the **Federal Insurance Contributions Act (FICA).** The

Figure 15.1 MAXIMUM SOCIAL SECURITY TAXES PER EMPLOYEE PER YEAR, EMPLOYER CONTRIBUTIONS ONLY

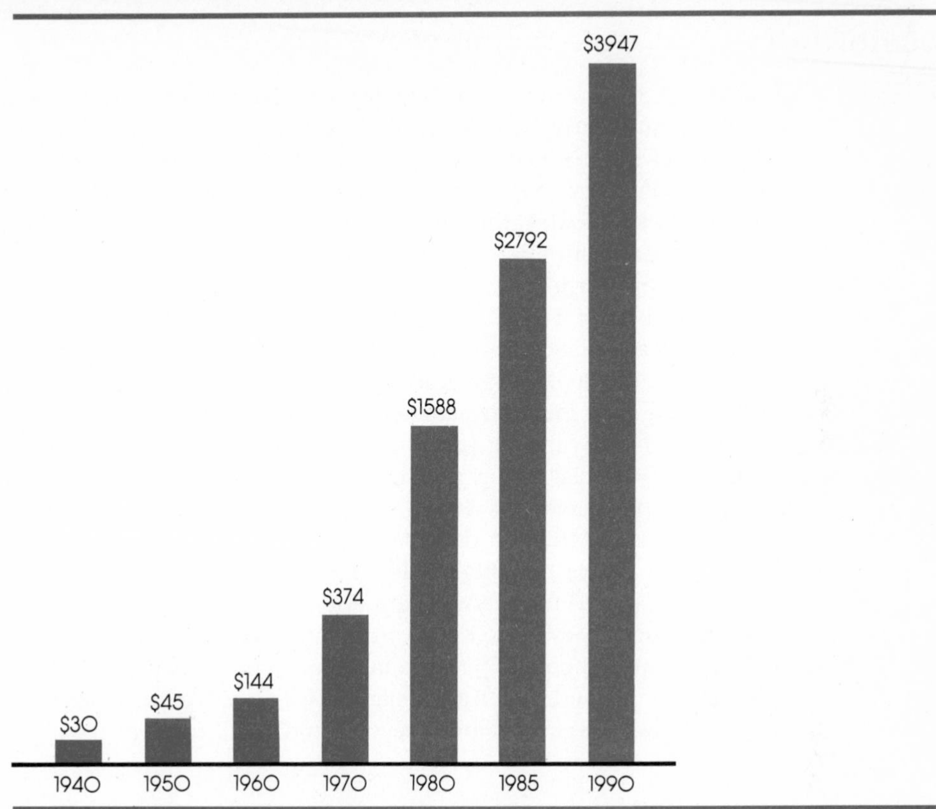

current (1987) tax rate is 14.3 percent, of which one-half, or 7.15 percent, is paid by the employee and the other half is paid by the employer. Self-employed persons pay FICA taxes at a total rate of 12.3 percent. These taxes are imposed on a maximum wage base of $43,700. Therefore, the maximum tax paid by each, the employer and the employee, is $3124.55[1]—a dramatic increase from the $30 maximum tax in 1937 when Social Security taxes were first collected. Figure 15.1 shows the trend of increasing maximum Social Security taxes.

Some people believe that their Social Security contributions are set aside in an investment fund to provide for their retirement benefits at a later time. This belief is incorrect. Rather, Social Security operates on a "pay-as-you-go" system where taxes collected today are soon paid out as benefits to current retirees. As such, it is an income transfer program under which those who are

[1] The maximum annual total Social Security tax for a self-employed individual is $5375.10.

currently employed transfer income to those who are retired or disabled. While you are working, you pay the Social Security benefits of others. When you retire, you hope to receive benefits paid by people who are working at that time.

Durability

A 1985 survey conducted by Civic Service, Inc., for *U.S. News & World Report* revealed that nearly two of every five Americans seriously doubted that they would receive the Social Security benefits they had been promised. The primary concern focuses on the growing proportion of retired persons in our population. As Table 15.1 indicates, the percentage of the population 65 and over continues to grow. Since retirement benefits are paid by taxes on current workers, an increasing proportion of retirees imposes a heavier financial burden on the current work force. Figure 15.2 shows that in 1945, a large group of active workers supported each eligible retiree. In 1985, only 3.3 workers carried each beneficiary. Estimates indicate that by the time current young workers retire, only two workers will exist for each beneficiary.

Does this dwindling proportion of workers to retirees increase the likelihood that the Social Security system will eventually fail? As long as workers are available to pay taxes, the system is likely to survive. As a result of the increasing number of retirees in the population, however, a financial crisis could emerge. In this case future benefits could be reduced for some beneficiaries, benefits could be subjected to income taxes, and/or payments could be delayed. In 1983, the Social Security system was revamped to prevent its insolvency. In the process, some retirement benefits became taxable for the first time, cost-of-living adjustments were delayed, and future eligibility ages were increased. Future revisions are also possible if tax receipts become too small to meet payment obligations.

Table 15.1 PERCENTAGE OF PERSONS AGE 65 AND OVER

Year	Percentage of persons 65 and over	Year	Percentage of persons 65 and over
1940	6.8	1990	12.1
1950	8.2	2000	12.1
1960	9.1	2010	12.6
1970	9.7	2020	15.5
1980	11.3	2030	18.4

SOURCE: Actual values (1940–1980) obtained from the *Economic Report of the President*, Washington, D.C.: U.S. Government Printing Office, 1986. Estimated values (1990–2030) based on population forecasts from the *1977 Annual Report of the Board of Trustees of the Federal Old-age and Survivors Insurance and Disability Trust Funds.*

Figure 15.2 NUMBER OF WORKERS FINANCING RETIREES

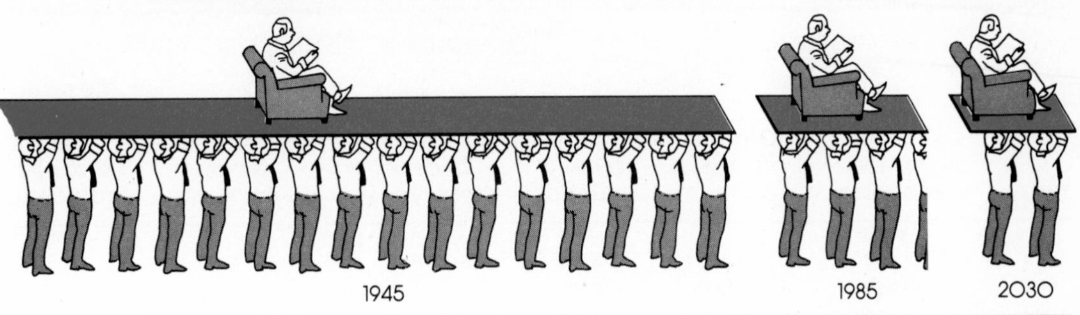

In 1945, each Social Security pensioner was supported by 50 active workers. Today each pensioner is supported by 3.3 workers, and in 2030, 2 workers will carry the burden.

Coverage

Social Security is an involuntary benefit program under which most workers are required to participate. As a result, more than 160 million Americans, about 95 percent of the work force, currently pay Social Security taxes. You may be surprised, however, to see that the assets and reserves of the Old-Age, Survivors, Disability and Health Insurance program (Social Security) are much less than those for private pension plans (see Table 15.2). Social Security coverage now includes persons on active duty in the armed forces and employees of nonprofit organizations—both groups were traditionally exempt from participation. The largest group of exempt workers is the employees of federal, state, and local governments. Most federal employees hired after December 31, 1983, however, must now participate in Social Security. Coverage is still optional for state and local government workers. Although all states have entered into agreements with the federal government making Social Security coverage available, not all state and local government employees have elected to participate in the program. Therefore, for example, a public school teacher may be covered in one town but not another. Some low-income workers are also excluded. If an employee receives less than $50 of cash wages from each employer in a given quarter, coverage is not required.

Eligibility of Participants

Only **fully insured** employees are eligible to collect Social Security benefits at retirement. To obtain fully insured status, you must have worked a required number of covered quarters (three-month periods). Since 1977, quarters of cov-

Table 15.2 ASSETS AND RESERVES OF MAJOR PENSION AND RETIREMENT PROGRAMS IN THE UNITED STATES (000,000 OMITTED)

	PRIVATE PLANS		GOVERNMENT-ADMINISTERED PLANS			
Year	With life insurance companies	Other private plans	Railroad retire-ment	Federal civilian employees[a]	State and local employees	Old-age, survivors and disability insurance[b]
1950	$ 5,600	N.A.	$2,553	$ 4,344	$ 5,154	
1960	18,850	$ 38,148	3,740	10,790	19,600	
1965	27,350	73,647	3,946	16,516	33,100	19,841
1966	29,425	75,781	4,074	17,619	36,900	22,308
1967	32,000	89,417	4,236	18,799	41,500	26,250
1968	34,975	101,456	4,245	20,224	46,300	28,729
1969	37,900	102,385	4,347	21,600	51,800	34,182
1970	41,175	110,394	4,398	23,922	58,200	38,068
1971	46,400	130,121	4,300	26,532	64,800	40,434
1972	52,300	160,359	4,100	29,978	73,400	42,775
1973	56,085	146,604	3,800	32,283	82,700	44,414
1974	60,810	138,609	3,600	35,366	92,400	45,886
1975	72,210	186,593	3,100	39,248	103,700	44,342
1976	88,990	211,609	3,065	44,089	117,300	41,133
1977	101,520	225,147	2,584	50,832	130,800	35,861
1978	119,110	257,374	2,787	57,677	142,573	31,746
1979	139,180	318,618	2,611	65,914	161,649	30,291
1980	165,845	412,659	2,086	75,802	185,226	26,453
1981	190,925	431,012	1,126	86,867	209,444	24,539
1982	225,195	518,071	460	99,462	245,252	24,778[c]
1983	264,575	607,777	601	114,219	289,731	24,867[c]
1984	309,080	623,348	3,712	129,550	323,455	31,075[c]
1985	361,748	639,779	3,802	147,221	360,998	38,833[c]

Note: Some data are revised. These data are as of various dates during the year, since the fiscal years of the plans are not necessarily the same. Trends from year to year are not affected.

[a] Includes members of the U.S. Civil Service Retirement System, the Tennessee Valley Retirement System, the Foreign Service Retirement System, and the Retirement System of the Federal Reserve Banks, which includes the Bank Plan and the Board of Governors' plan.

[b] Beginning in 1957, assets of Disability Insurance Trust Funds are included. Hospital and Supplementary Medical Insurance is not included.

[c] Includes funds borrowed from the Hospital Insurance Trust Fund.

Sources: Railroad Retirement Board; Social Security Administration, U.S. Department of Health and Human Services; Securities and Exchange Commission; Federal Reserve System; other administrative agencies; and the American Council of Life Insurance.

SOURCE: *Life Insurance Fact Book Update,* Washington, D.C.: American Council of Life Insurance, various issues.

erage are based on annual earnings in covered employment. In 1985, for example, you acquired one quarter of coverage for each $410 in annual covered earnings, up to a maximum of four quarters per year. The amount of earnings required to obtain a quarter of coverage will fluctuate in future years according to changes in average wages. The number of quarters required to be fully insured depends upon when you reach age 62. If your sixty-second birthday occurs in 1987, you need 36 quarters of coverage to be fully insured. Those who turn 62 in 1991 or later will need 40 quarters of coverage to attain fully insured status.

Benefits of Participants

The Social Security system provides four major types of benefits: (1) retirement income, (2) survivor's benefits, (3) disability income, and (4) health care benefits. Disability and health care benefits are discussed in Chapter 9. In this section we examine retirement income and survivor's benefits because these payments are important considerations for retirement income planning.

Retirement Income. You are entitled to monthly retirement benefits if you are fully insured and have reached age 62. As shown in Figure 15.3, in 1986 the average monthly Social Security retirement benefit paid was $520 and the average spouse's benefit was $260. Although these amounts represent substantial increases over the corresponding payments in prior years, they are still insufficient to provide a comfortable retirement without some other kind of retirement income. The amount you receive depends on two factors: (1) your average monthly earnings in the past and (2) the age at which you begin receiving benefits. Table 15.3 shows a recent retirement benefit schedule. Generally, the higher your average yearly earnings are, the greater will be your monthly retirement income. You cannot, however, receive your entire benefit amount unless you wait until age 65 to retire. If you choose to retire between the ages of 62 and 65, you will receive a reduced benefit. On the other hand, by waiting until you are older than age 65, your monthly benefits will increase for each month between the ages of 65 and 70 in which you do not receive payments. If you are married but only one of you worked for pay, Social Security will increase your monthly benefit to 1½ times a single worker's entitlement, assuming payments do not begin until the worker reaches age 65. After you begin to receive monthly benefits, the amount increases automatically by the percent amount of the annual consumer price index (or in some instances the average wage increase), if that amount is 3 percent or more.

This type of Social Security payment is often called retirement income, but, contrary to the implication, you do not have to stop working entirely to receive it. The amount you can earn without causing a reduction in your benefits is called your **exempt earnings.** In 1987, a person age 65 to 69 was entitled to $8160 of exempt earnings, whereas an individual under age 65 could earn $6000 without reducing benefits. The exempt earnings amount is increased automatically each year to compensate for increases in average wages. You forfeit $1 in

Figure 15.3 AVERAGE MONTHLY SOCIAL SECURITY BENEFITS, 1950–1985

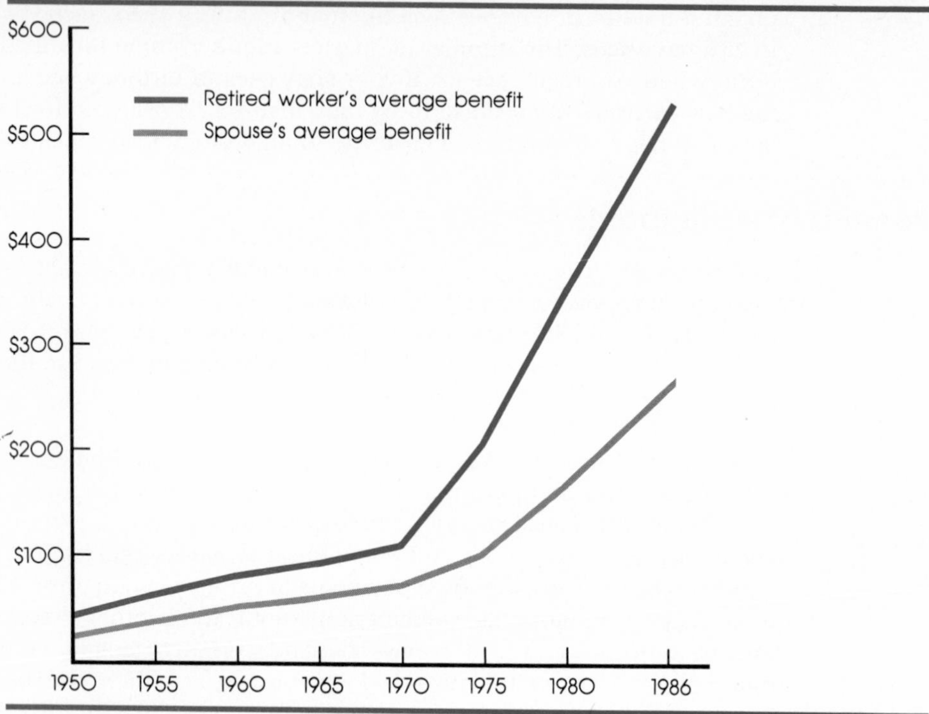

SOURCE: *Economic Report of the President,* 1986.

retirement benefits for each $2 earned over the exempt amount. When you reach age 70, however, you may earn any amount and still receive full benefits.

Survivor's Benefits. If a covered worker dies, his or her survivors may be eligible for Social Security benefits. These benefits may include a small lump-sum payment and monthly benefit checks. The lump-sum death benefit is typically paid to the surviving spouse or a child entitled to survivor's benefits. A monthly payment may be made to the widowed spouse in either of two instances: (1) if the spouse is at least age 60 or (2) if the spouse has an unmarried child of the deceased worker in his or her care. Benefits for those under age 65, however, are reduced and may be terminated if the surviving spouse remarries before age 60. Also, once a dependent child attains age 16, payments to the widowed spouse end. The child, however, may be eligible for monthly benefits until reaching age 19. Your dependents will receive 75 percent of your monthly retirement benefit in the event of your death, limited to a maximum amount that can be paid to a single family.

Table 15.3 MONTHLY RETIREMENT BENEFITS FOR WORKERS WHO REACH 62 IN 1979–1983

	FOR WORKERS				FOR DEPENDENTS[a]				
Average yearly earnings	Retire-ment at 65	at 64	at 63	at 62	Spouse at 65 or child	at 64	at 63	at 62	Family[b] benefits
$ 1,200	$156.70	$146.30	$135.90	$125.40	$ 78.40	$ 71.90	$ 65.40	$ 58.80	$235.10
2,600	230.10	214.80	199.50	184.10	115.10	105.50	95.90	86.40	345.20
3,000	251.80	235.10	218.30	201.50	125.90	115.40	104.90	94.50	384.90
3,400	270.00	252.00	234.00	216.00	135.00	123.80	112.50	101.30	434.90
4,000	296.20	276.50	256.80	237.00	148.10	135.70	123.40	111.10	506.20
4,400	317.30	296.20	275.00	253.90	158.70	145.40	132.20	119.10	562.50
4,800	336.00	313.60	291.20	268.80	168.00	153.90	140.00	126.00	612.70
5,200	353.20	329.70	306.20	282.60	176.60	161.80	147.20	132.50	662.70
5,600	370.60	345.90	321.20	296.50	185.30	169.80	154.40	139.00	687.10
6,000	388.20	362.40	336.50	310.60	194.10	177.80	161.70	145.60	712.10
6,400	405.60	378.60	351.60	324.50	202.80	185.80	169.00	152.10	737.10
6,800	424.10	395.90	367.60	339.30	212.10	194.30	176.70	159.10	762.30
7,200	446.00	416.30	386.60	356.80	223.00	204.30	185.80	167.30	788.90
7,600	465.60	434.60	403.60	372.50	232.80	213.30	194.00	174.60	814.70
8,000	482.60	450.50	418.30	386.10	241.30	221.10	201.10	181.00	844.50
8,400	492.90	460.10	427.20	394.40	246.50	225.80	205.40	184.90	862.60
8,800	505.10	471.50	437.80	404.10	252.60	231.40	210.50	189.50	883.80
9,200	516.00	481.60	447.20	412.80	258.00	236.40	215.00	193.50	903.00
9,400	520.40	485.80	451.10	416.40	260.20	238.40	216.80	195.20	910.40
9,600	524.60	489.70	454.70	419.70	262.30	240.30	218.50	196.80	918.00
9,800	530.40	495.10	459.70	424.40	265.20	243.00	221.00	198.90	928.00
10,000	534.70	499.10	463.50	427.80	267.40	245.00	222.80	200.60	935.70

[a] If a person is eligible for both a worker's benefit and a spouse's benefit, the check actually payable is limited to the larger of the two.

[b] The maximum amount payable to a family is generally reached when a worker and two family members are eligible.

SOURCE: "Estimating Your Social Security Retirement Check," U.S. Department of Health and Human Services, Social Security Administration, January 1986.

Taxation of Benefits

From the beginning of Social Security in 1937 until 1983, all benefits were exempt from federal, state, and local taxes. This is no longer the case. As the result of legislation passed in 1983, you may find that up to half your benefits are now subject to federal income taxes. If the sum of your adjusted gross income (you may want to refer to Chapter 3 for a description of this amount), tax-exempt interest, and half of your Social Security benefits exceeds $32,000 and you are married ($25,000 if single), you will be taxed on half the excess over that amount or half of your Social Security benefit, whichever is smaller. Say, for example, you are married and have a $28,000 adjusted gross income, $6,000 in tax-exempt interest, and $10,000 in Social Security benefits. Table 15.4 shows that in this situation $3500 of your benefits are subject to federal income taxes (half the amount exceeding $32,000).

Checking Your Social Security Record

Your earnings must be reported to the Social Security Administration. Benefits are based on these reported earnings. You should check at least once every three years to see if these amounts have been correctly credited to your account.[2] Unfortunately, mistakes sometimes occur. These mistakes may be difficult to correct if more than three years have elapsed since you received the earnings. The Social Security Administration provides a routine form (Form SSA 7004 PC) which you may use to request a statement of your earnings. The statement you receive gives the amount of earnings credited to your account, not the actual amount you were paid. If you detect an error, you should immediately notify the administration.

Claiming Your Social Security Benefits

You do not automatically receive Social Security benefits. You must apply for them at your local Social Security office. You should visit the office at least a few months before you reach retirement age or as soon as possible after a death or disability occurs. Otherwise, valuable benefits may be permanently forfeited. After you make application, the Social Security Administration will determine your eligibility for benefits.

The Role of Social Security in Retirement Planning

Contrary to popular belief, Social Security is not a form of unemployment insurance because you are not guaranteed a certain amount of benefits. Congress determines how much your retirement benefit will be. This amount does not fully depend on the amount you contributed during your working years. Because of this dependency on congressional mandate, you cannot determine the amount of Social Security benefits you will receive years from now. If future Congresses are less generous, you may receive smaller benefits than you expected. Therefore, if you rely entirely upon Social Security payments to provide for your retirement livelihood, you may eventually find that you have insufficient income to satisfy your basic living expenses. And the more you earn in excess

[2] Annual reported earnings are shown only for each of the most recent three years. Previous reported earnings are added together and reported as a single lump-sum amount.

Table 15.4 DETERMINING TAXABLE SOCIAL SECURITY BENEFITS

Step	Action	Item	Amount	Total
1		*Adjusted Gross Income*		$28,000
	plus	1. Tax-exempt interest	$6,000	
		2. One-half of Social Security Benefits	5,000	
	equals	Excess income before exemption		$39,000
2		*Excess Income Before Exemption*		$39,000
	minus	Statutory exemption	− $32,000	
	equals	Excess income		$ 7,000
3		*Excess Income*		$ 7,000
	minus	50% tax exclusion	− $3,500	
	equals	Amount taxable[a]		$ 3,500

[a] The amount taxable is added to taxable income for purposes of determining federal income tax liability. This amount is limited to a maximum of one-half of the total Social Security benefits.

of the wage base, the smaller will be the percentage of total preretirement earnings replaced by Social Security.

Congress never intended for Social Security benefits to provide for all of your retirement needs. These benefits, therefore, should be considered only as a foundation for your retirement income. You must plan for other retirement income sources in order to reasonably anticipate a financially sufficient retirement. In the next sections of this chapter we examine three additional sources of retirement income: employer retirement plans, other types of retirement plans, and annuities.

PRIVATE PENSION PLANS

We previously indicated that about 95 percent of the American work force is currently covered by Social Security. While this statistic may seem to suggest that nearly all workers are guaranteed a steady retirement income, you must remember the basic philosophy behind Social Security benefits. That philosophy is that Social Security is to provide only a floor amount of income. If you desire a comfortable retirement, you must obtain additional sources of retirement income. To supplement your Social Security benefits, you may rely on accumulated savings, financial assistance from family or friends, welfare payments, or private pension plans. If you are like most people, you abhor the idea of depending on others or on welfare for your retirement livelihood. You may not, however, have sufficient savings to support all your retirement needs. As a result, private pension plans become an important consideration in your retirement planning.

Box 15.1 TEN TOP COMPANY PLANS

A handful of employers in particular industries offer outstanding retirement packages. The best plans usually are found at oil companies, banks, insurers and drug manufacturers. The following list, compiled with the help of leading benefits consultants, represents a healthy sampling of such firms.

Bankers Trust, New York City
While many employers match 50¢ on the dollar for savings-plan contributions, Bankers Trust kicks in $2. Employees can receive an annual total equal to 12% of their pay.

Exxon, New York City
Pension benefits here are based on an employee's three highest-earning years. Most companies average out five years or longer. Exxon also has a fine savings plan and a salary-reduction plan that allows employees to make pretax contributions of up to 14% of pay.

Goldman, Sachs, New York City
Unlike most employers, this investment bank is committed to increasing for inflation the accrued pensions of its workers. In 1980, it raised benefits by as much as 100%, with the biggest boosts going to the lowest paid. Goldman Sachs also contributes about 15% of pay into each employee's profit-sharing account, compared with a standard 5% to 10%. Year-end bonuses averaging more than 20% of pay are standard operating procedure, and employees can put up to 15% of their bonus in a pretax investment account.

Mesa Petroleum, Amarillo, Texas
Maverick oilman T. Boone Pickens has no pension for his workers but offers one of the best profit-sharing and stock-purchase plans. Mesa puts an amount equal to 15% of each employee's pay into a profit-sharing account. Workers can also contribute up to 6% of pay into the stock plan and the company matches the investment dollar for dollar. Mesa figures a 30-year-old earning $30,000 can expect to get $2.9 million from the two plans if he stays on until age 65.

Morgan Guaranty, New York City
Most companies use a pension formula that multiplies 1% or so by your years of service and final salary. Morgan is one of the few us-

A **pension plan** is an investment medium established by an employer through which monetary contributions are made today in order to provide future retirement income for employees. Pension plans are currently the fastest-growing means for accumulating funds earmarked to provide future retirement benefits. Fewer than 10 percent of individuals age 65 and over received pension benefits 50 years ago. Today, however, over 40 percent of retirees receive pensions and 80 percent of full-time employees earning over $20,000 are covered by pension plans. Without a doubt, the pension system appears to be replacing Social Security as the cornerstone of retirement income.

Why Participate in a Pension Plan?

A pension plan may be the most convenient and effective way to provide for a meaningful retirement income. Most major employers provide attractive pension plans. If your employer satisfies certain Internal Revenue Code requirements, the plan is a **qualified pension plan** and thus receives important income tax

ing a 2% multiplier. For the past 18 years, the bank has also provided a profit-sharing largesse equal to 15% of annual pay.

Northwestern Mutual Life Insurance, Milwaukee

Some employers ladle out grand pensions only to workers who stick with them for 30 years or longer. Northwestern Mutual doesn't ask for a lifelong commitment. The pension formula uses a 2.5% multiplier for the first 20 years of employment. If you retire from a $60,000 salary after putting in two decades with Northwestern Mutual, you'll get a $30,000 annual pension; at most employers, you would get less than $20,000.

Pfizer, New York City

In a Bankers Trust survey of 240 companies, this drug company's pension ranked No. 1 for replacing the biggest chunk of preretirement salaries. Someone retiring from a $50,000 job at Pfizer after working there 35 years will get a pension of about $30,000 a year—60% of pay. A 40% rate is standard.

Shell Oil, Houston

Shell's savings plan is a gusher. After nine years, the company annually contributes an amount equal to 10% of your pay to the plan. And Shell is one of the best-paying companies too. A 30-year-old now starting out with a $40,000 salary could retire at 65 with a $1.6 million lump sum plus an excellent pension.

Tektronix, Beaverton, Ore.

This maker of oscilloscopes and other electronic devices funnels 35% of its annual pretax earnings into a profit-sharing plan. It's generally risky to count on your company's profit performance for your retirement, but even in the last recession, Tektronix workers got the equivalent of 15% of their pay in profit-sharing funds.

Tenneco, Houston

Pensions at this oil conglomerate provide about 47% of pre-retirement pay after 35 years of service, slightly less if you quit work at 61. The annual benefit is roughly 20% fatter than at most Fortune 500 companies. Tenneco matches all savings-plan contributions dollar for dollar.

SOURCE: *Money Guide/Retirement*, 1984, p. 31.

benefits. These tax benefits come in two forms: (1) employer contributions made on your behalf are not taxed until you actually receive the benefits, and (2) investment income and gains are untaxed until distributed. Therefore, pension contributions have a substantial tax deferral benefit. For young workers, income taxes may be postponed up to 50 years. Because of the importance of the tax benefits to qualified pension plans, we offer the following example which illustrates these tax savings.

The Situation. Chris Gaylord, a single male, is employed by the Ajax Machine Company. Ajax makes regular payments on behalf of its employees to a qualified pension plan. Chris estimates that in 1987 the company will contribute $5000 to the plan on his behalf. Having heard about the tax benefits of a qualified pension plan, Chris wants to see how he stands to benefit from this contribution as compared to the alternative of receiving the $5000 as additional salary. The following provides a comparison of the value of his retirement investment fund under these two alternatives.

The Comparison. We assume that Chris is in a 28 percent tax bracket and can earn a 10 percent pretax return this year on his investments. Table 15.5 shows the value of his investment account assuming the $5000 contribution is made to the pension plan. As you can see, under this alternative all $5000 of Chris' money is tax sheltered and thus the entire amount is available to invest. In the first year the $5000 principal amount earns a 10 percent return, or $500. Since this amount is also shielded from income tax by the pension plan, all of these earnings remain in the investment account. Therefore, after one year, Chris has the following investment accumulation in his pension fund:

Accumulation	=	Contribution	+	Interest
$5500	=	$5000	+	$500

If, on the other hand, Chris received the $5000 as additional salary, he would have to pay current income tax on that amount. Given his 28 percent tax bracket, only $3600 would remain for investment purposes. A 10 percent return on that after-tax amount yields a $360 return before taxes in the first year. After payment of income taxes of $101 ($360 × 28 percent), this amount falls to $259. Table 15.6 shows these calculations and indicates that Chris would accumulate the following by saving and investing $5000 of salary:

Accumulation	=	Contribution[a]	+	Interest[a]
$3859	=	$3600	+	$259

[a] After payment of income taxes

The final results are clear. After one year, the $5000 contributed to a pension plan totals $5500. After the payment of income taxes, however, the $5000 taken as additional salary amounts to only $3859 in one year. The difference is substantial; Chris has $1641 more after one year under the pension alternative. When compounded over several years, this difference becomes even more pronounced.

Table 15.5 $5000 CONTRIBUTED TO PENSION PLAN

Step	Action	Item	Amount	Total
1		*Pension Contribution*		$5000
	minus	Income taxes (28% rate)	none	
	equals	Net amount to invest		$5000
2		*Net Amount to Invest*		$5000
	times	Rate of return	× 10%	
	equals	Investment return		$ 500
3		*Investment Return*		$ 500
	minus	Income taxes (28% rate)	none	
	plus	Net amount to invest	$5000	
	equals	Fund value (after one year)		$5500

Table 15.6 $5000 RECEIVED AS ADDITIONAL SALARY

Step	Action	Item	Amount	Total
1		*Additional Salary*		$5000
	minus	Income taxes (28%)	−$1400	
	equals	Net amount to invest		$3600
2		*Net Amount to Invest*		$3600
	times	Rate of return	× 10%	
	equals	Investment return		$ 360
3		*Investment Return*		$ 360
	minus	Income taxes (27% rate)	−$ 101	$ 259
	plus	Net amount to invest	$3600	
	equals	Savings value (after one year)		$3859

IMPORTANT PENSION PLAN FEATURES

Pension plans come in many forms. Some employers offer only the most basic coverage, while others provide very generous benefits. Although pensions are an important component of retirement planning, most employees are not well versed in the mechanics of their pension plans. In order to obtain the greatest benefits from your pension, you should be familiar with the following important features: (1) employee eligibility, (2) benefit computations, (3) vesting, (4) employee contributions, (5) funding, and (6) payment options.

Employee Eligibility

Pension plans must satisfy stringent employee eligibility requirements to become qualified. The Internal Revenue Code, however, allows an organization to exclude from coverage some categories of workers. As a result, many plans impose certain minimum criteria that an employee must meet before becoming eligible for participation. These criteria generally relate to employment status, years of service, minimum age, and level of earnings.

Employment Status. Most pension plans exclude from coverage part-time or seasonal workers who work less than 1000 hours per year for the employer. This exemption helps reduce administrative expenses.

Years of Service. To avoid the high administrative costs associated with high-turnover employees, many pension plans do not cover employees during their first year of employment. This feature is based on the premise that a much greater turnover rate applies to newly hired employees.

Minimum Age. Younger employees often turn over rapidly. Some pension plans limit enrollment to employees 25 years of age or over in order to reduce administrative expenses associated with these persons.

Level of Income. Some pension plans allow participation only to employees who earn in excess of a stipulated amount. Most common are plans that integrate with Social Security and thus provide coverage only to employees earning more than the maximum wages covered by Social Security.

Benefit Computations

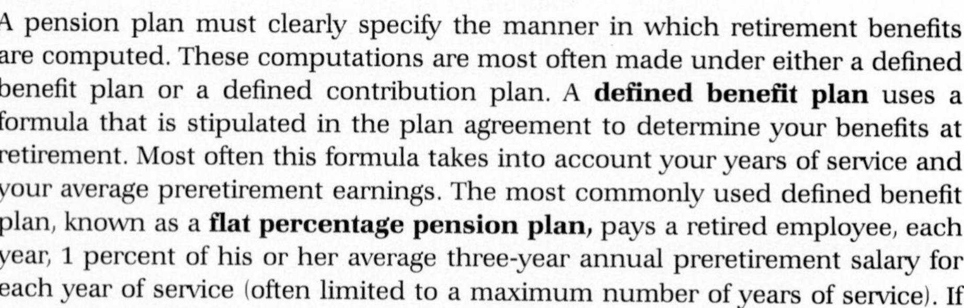

A pension plan must clearly specify the manner in which retirement benefits are computed. These computations are most often made under either a defined benefit plan or a defined contribution plan. A **defined benefit plan** uses a formula that is stipulated in the plan agreement to determine your benefits at retirement. Most often this formula takes into account your years of service and your average preretirement earnings. The most commonly used defined benefit plan, known as a **flat percentage pension plan,** pays a retired employee, each year, 1 percent of his or her average three-year annual preretirement salary for each year of service (often limited to a maximum number of years of service). If you retired after 25 years of service and had a $38,000 final three-year average salary, your annual retirement benefit under this plan would equal $9500, calculated as follows:

Annual Pension Benefit	=	Average Preretirement Salary	×	Replacement Percentage	×	Years of Service
$9500	=	$38,000	×	1%	×	25

A less commonly used defined benefit plan is the **flat amount pension plan,** under which all employees receive the same amount with no consideration given to either earnings or years of service. Another less common plan is the **unit benefit pension plan,** where employees receive benefits according to the number of units accumulated multiplied by a set dollar unit value. The units may relate to number of years worked, value of services performed, and so on.

Under a **defined contribution plan,** you make a fixed contribution to the pension plan—usually a percentage of your wages. Your retirement benefits depend entirely on the amount accumulated in your account. Thus, to a large extent your payouts are based on how well your investments perform. Younger workers usually prefer defined contribution plans because very sizable amounts can accumulate in these plans in the long run, so the employee will receive a larger benefit than would be available under a defined benefit plan. Alternatively, older workers, who do not have enough working years remaining to accumulate a large fund under a defined contribution plan, typically prefer the fixed retirement amount guaranteed by a defined benefit plan.

Vesting

Although your employer may make contributions on your behalf to a pension plan, you are not necessarily guaranteed the right to receive this money. You must go through a process of meeting certain criteria before you have a nonforfeitable right to these contributions. This process is called **vesting.** Depending upon how you satisfy these criteria, you may have a full or partial vested interest in a pension, or you may have no vested interest at all.

Once you become a participant in a pension plan, your portion of your employer's contributions vest according to a fixed schedule. Before 1974, vesting schedules often were very restrictive. In some instances an employee had to work full-time for 25 years or more to obtain any vested right to a pension. If for any reason the employee left the job before that period of employment was completed, he or she forfeited all rights to the pension. As a result, many employees who made job changes during their careers approached retirement age without the prospect of receiving pension benefits.

The restrictiveness of vesting rights was largely eliminated by the **Employee Retirement Income Security Act of 1974 (ERISA).** This legislation imposed minimum vesting schedules for employers in order to ensure that more employees become vested and thus qualify for regular benefits upon retirement. Currently most pensions vest in five years. You should check with your employer to find out how long it takes for pension contributions made on your behalf to vest.

Employee Contributions

Many plans permit employees to make supplementary contributions. This type of plan is known as a **contributory pension plan,** whereas a pension plan where all contributions are made by the employer is termed a **noncontributory pension plan.** Most corporate pension plans are noncontributory, but almost all federal, state, and local government plans are contributory. Contributory plans generally require the employee to contribute from 5 to 10 percent of wages. Employee contributions vest immediately. Therefore, if you terminate employment and have participated in a contributory plan, you are legally entitled to the amount you contributed and any accumulated earnings on that amount.

Funding

Prior to ERISA, employee retirement benefits were sometimes paid directly from general corporate funds. No funds were set aside on a regular basis to provide the retirement income. This type of plan, known as an **unfunded pension plan,** is risky for employees because the employer does not set aside assets to offset the accumulating retirement liabilities. As a result, some retirement plans were unable to pay the benefits promised to employees. Such failures can have devastating effects on retired employees who rely on these promised benefits for their retirement livelihood. To help eliminate this problem, ERISA requires that specific assets be accumulated in segregated accounts to meet pension obligations.

A **funded pension plan** makes current payments into a separate pension fund to offset pension liabilities as they accrue. Unfortunately, the amount of pension liability accruing each period cannot be determined precisely, so it is estimated based on several actuarial assumptions. These assumptions focus on factors such as normal retirement ages, mortality and disability rates, salary levels, employee turnover, and investment returns. Changes in these assumptions can dramatically affect the amount of money an employer must contribute to a pension fund to achieve fully funded status.

After funds are contributed to a pension fund, they must be prudently invested in order to earn a return sufficient to provide promised retirement benefits. To accomplish these objectives, pension plans are generally administered in one of three ways. Under an **insured pension plan,** an insurance company receives the periodic pension contributions and, in return, promises to pay agreed-upon benefits to retired employees. The trust department of a commercial bank may also receive and manage pension contributions. Under this arrangement, called a **trusteed plan,** the bank manager does not promise a specific retirement benefit; rather, the bank tries to earn a large enough investment return to ensure that the pension plan will have sufficient assets to meet payment obligations. Finally, the corporation may form a separate department to accept and manage segregated pension funds. This is referred to as a **self-administered plan.** These plans have become popular with large corporations in recent years.

Payment Options

Employment statistics indicate that the probability of your remaining with the same employer for all your working years is very low. More likely, you will work for several different employers during your career. When you leave a job, your former employer must inform you of any vested benefits that you have accumulated. The final disposition of these benefits depends on the portability of the pension plan. A **portable pension plan** allows you to take your vested pension accounts with you when you leave a job. In most cases, you will receive a lump-sum cash payment equal to your vested amount. You must pay income tax on the full amount of the lump sum in the year you receive it, unless you transfer or roll over the funds to another qualified retirement plan.

Some retirement plans do not provide for portability of benefits. In these instances the vested funds must be left in the employer's pension plan to be taken later as monthly retirement benefits. Usually the employer decides whether a plan is portable or not, but some employers allow terminating employees to make the selection.

OTHER TYPES OF RETIREMENT PLANS

Pension plans are only one of the means through which retirement benefits can be accumulated. Many alternatives are available. The most commonly used are Keogh Plans, individual retirement accounts (IRAs), IRA rollovers, SEP/IRAs, salary reduction plans, profit-sharing plans, and thrift plans. Each of these retirement alternatives can be structured to provide the mechanism to accumulate tax-advantaged retirement benefits. We now discuss each of these plans.

Keogh Plans

Self-employed persons and partnerships can establish a qualified retirement plan for themselves and their employees. This is referred to as a **Keogh (HR-10) plan.** If qualified, a Keogh plan receives the same tax deferral benefits as a corporate plan. Until recently, contributions into Keogh plans were more restricted than payments into corporate pension plans. At present, however, the lesser of $30,000 or 25 percent of annual income can be contributed to a Keogh plan for the account of an individual. Many professional workers, such as doctors, lawyers, and consultants, who are not eligible for corporate pension plans, use this plan.

Individual Retirement Accounts (IRAs)

The **individual retirement account (IRA)** allows many individuals to deposit and accumulate funds for retirement on the same tax-deferred basis available to regular corporate pension plans. Annual IRA contributions are limited to $2000 per employed person.[3]

If you are covered by a corporate pension, however, you can take a full IRA deduction only if your adjusted gross income is less than $25,000 ($40,000 if married). The deduction then begins to phase out, being reduced by 10 percent for every $1000 in added income, until it disappears at $35,000 ($50,000 for married individuals). If you are not covered by a pension plan, you can take a full IRA deduction regardless of your income level. (These matters were previously covered in Chapter 3.)

You cannot hold IRA funds yourself. Rather, a financial institution (typically a bank, insurance company, or mutual fund) must serve as your trustee. You may still direct the investment activities of your IRA by establishing a self-directed account which allows you to tell the trustee how to invest your IRA funds. If you withdraw IRA funds before attaining age 59½, you will incur a one-time 10 percent penalty. At age 59½ you can withdraw any amount without penalty, but you must pay income tax on the withdrawn amount. You do not have to begin

[3] An individual must earn at least $2000 in a year to make a maximum IRA contribution. Earnings less than $2000 mean a reduced IRA maximum contribution.

Table 15.7 VALUE OF IRA FUND AT AGE 70 ($2000 ANNUAL CONTRIBUTION)

Age contributions begin	COMPOUND ANNUAL RATE OF RETURN			
	8%	10%	12%	14%
20	$1,147,540	$2,327,817	$4,800,036	$9,989,043
25	773,011	1,437,810	2,716,460	5,181,130
30	518,113	885,185	1,534,183	2,684,050
35	344,634	542,049	863,327	1,387,145
40	226,566	328,988	482,665	713,574
45	146,212	196,694	266,668	363,742
50	91,524	114,550	144,105	182,050
55	54,304	63,545	74,559	87,685
60	28,973	31,875	35,097	38,675

withdrawals until age 70½. At that time you must withdraw a specified minimum amount each year based upon your life expectancy and the amount of funds in your IRA. For example, an unmarried woman must withdraw a minimum of 8.27 percent of the account's balance in the year she becomes age 70½.

You may think that you can't build up a meaningful retirement fund on only $2000 per year. If you hold that belief, you are mistaken. Table 15.7 shows how much you can accumulate in your IRA under various assumptions. The results are startling. If you begin contributions at age 20 and earn 14 percent annually, your IRA account will total nearly $10 million dollars at age 70 when you must begin withdrawals. Two important relationships are evident. First, the sooner you begin IRA contributions, the more you will have at retirement. For example, if you earn 10 percent on your IRA funds, at age 70 you will have $2,327,817 if you begin contributions at age 20, as compared to $328,988 if you wait until age 40 to begin your IRA. Second, the value of your IRA fund at your retirement is very sensitive to the compound rate of return you achieve. For the individual beginning contributions at age 20, for example, the accumulated IRA value at retirement (age 70) will total $1,147,540 at an 8 percent compound rate of return. On the other hand, if that compound return equals 14 percent, the IRA fund will total an awesome $9,989,043.

IRA Rollovers. You may take a lump-sum distribution from a qualified retirement plan and, as long as you deposit the funds in a special IRA within 60 days, still avoid taxation on this distribution. This special IRA is referred to as an **IRA rollover.** Funds in an IRA rollover enjoy the same tax benefits as deposits in a regular IRA, namely, deferral of income taxes until funds are actually received and tax deferral on the accumulated earnings on the deposited funds. IRA rollovers also have the same distribution requirements, trustee provisions, and penalties as ordinary IRAs.

SEP/IRAs

The **simplified employee pension (SEP/IRA)** is a retirement plan through which an employee can make supplemental deposits to an IRA. A SEP/IRA is most often offered by an employer who does not have an ordinary pension plan. Therefore, the SEP/IRA, in effect, acts as a substitute. Your employer can contribute an amount up to 15 percent of your earnings or $15,000, whichever is less, to this plan. In this manner a SEP plan substantially increases the amount that can be deposited to your IRA each year. SEP/IRAs have the same basic tax advantages, trustee requirements, distribution schedules, and penalties as regular IRAs.

Salary Reduction Plans

Employers may offer a special **salary reduction plan** that permits employees to deposit a portion of their salary to a qualified retirement plan. Two main types of salary reduction plans are available: (1) a 403(b) plan, which may be provided to educators and employees of some nonprofit organizations, and (2) 401(k) plans, which are available to employees of some profit-oriented companies.

403(b) Plan. Under a *403(b) plan,* a portion of your salary can be paid directly to a qualified retirement account. Because you do not receive this portion of your salary, you are not currently taxed on that amount. Furthermore, investment earnings on the funds deposited in your 403(b) account are tax deferred. Only upon withdrawal of funds does an income tax liability occur. Withdrawals before age 59½ also incur a 10 percent penalty. Contributions to a 403(b) plan are typically limited to 20 percent of your earnings, but may be reduced further if your employer also provides a pension plan.[4] Unlike with an IRA, your investment choices for a 403(b) plan are limited to those offered by your employer. These choices most often include life insurance companies and mutual funds.

401(k) Plan. A *401(k) plan* is a type of salary reduction plan available to the employees of many for-profit organizations. The portion of an employee's salary that is deposited to a 401(k) plan is not currently taxable, nor are the accumulated earnings on the invested funds. As with a 403(b) plan, your employer must deduct your contribution from your salary before you receive it. You cannot directly deposit funds in the plan yourself. These plans, first offered in 1982, became very popular because they enabled employees to tax-shelter sizable amounts of money. Until 1987, for example, a maximum of $30,000 could be

[4] This 20 percent annual limitation is cumulative. If you make less than the maximum contribution in a year, then you may be able to contribute more than 20 percent in a future year.

contributed to a 401(k) plan. Congress believed that this tax benefit was too generous, however, and reduced the maximum contribution to $7000 yearly beginning in 1987.

Profit-Sharing Plans

A **profit-sharing plan** enables you to participate in your employer's profits. A qualified profit-sharing plan receives the same tax deferral benefits as other types of qualified retirement plans. Employers like these plans because of the greater contribution flexibility than that available with a pension plan. Whereas a pension plan requires a specific contribution each year, a profit-sharing plan does not impose any fixed level of contribution. Therefore, in lean years the employer can make small (or zero) contributions. But when profits are high, the company can make larger payments and thus the employees benefit. Because employees receive proportionally higher contributions in high-profit years, many employers believe that profit-sharing plans encourage employees to work harder. Contributions to a profit-sharing plan are limited to 15 percent of an employee's salary. When combined with pension plan contributions, a maximum of 25 percent of an employee's annual earnings may be set aside in corporate retirement plans.

Thrift Plans

The **thrift plan** is a popular way to supplement employee pension plans. Under these plans, you make a voluntary contribution that is partially or wholly matched by your employer. Although employer matching rates vary, a common arrangement is for the employer to contribute 50 percent of the employee's payment, up to some maximum percent of salary (for example, 6 percent). If you contribute the maximum 6 percent of your $30,000 salary into a thrift plan, your $1800 contribution will be supplemented by a $900 payment from your employer.

Thrift plans generally have two important advantages: (1) Your employer's contribution and the earnings on the accumulated funds are not taxed until you withdraw these amounts, and (2) both employer and employee contributions typically vest immediately. Employee contributions, however, are treated as taxable income and, unlike some other types of retirement plans, do not provide immediate tax deductions. Because the salary reduction plans previously discussed generally provide for employer matching contributions but still generate tax deferral benefits for *all* contributions, you should usually use that alternative to the maximum before using a thrift plan.

ANNUITIES

Purchasing an annuity is one of the most effective ways to insure against the risk of outliving your savings (as previously discussed in Chapter 10 under life

Figure 15.4 AMOUNT OF ANNUITY BENEFIT PAYMENTS, 1950–1985 (IN MILLIONS)

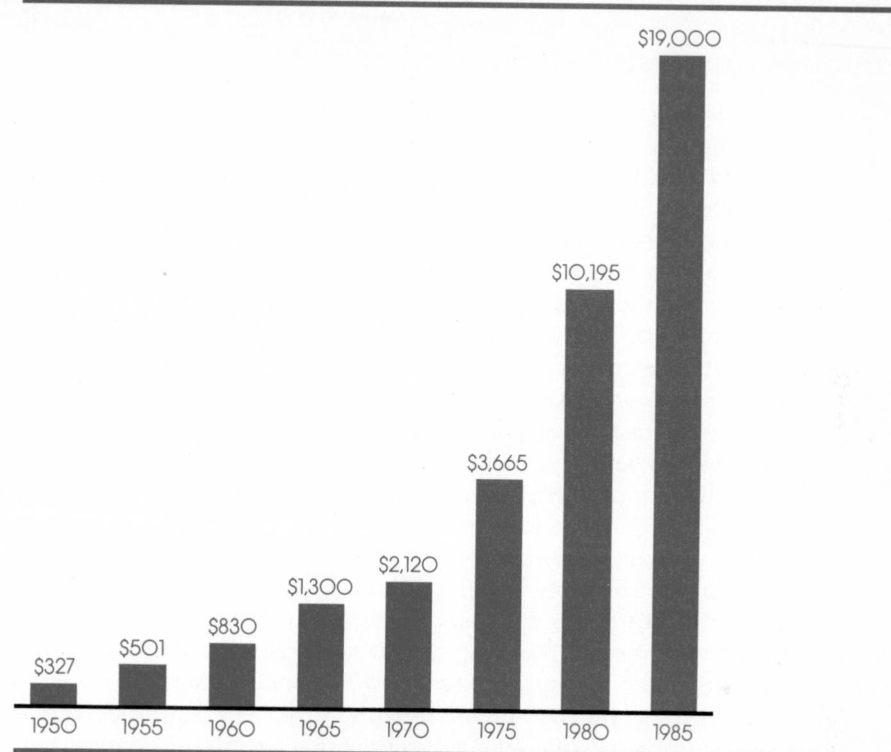

SOURCE: *Life Insurance Fact Book,* Washington, D.C.: American Council of Life Insurance, 1985.

insurance). An **annuity** is a contract that guarantees you income for an indicated period of time (normally your lifetime). In recent years annuities have become increasingly popular with individuals planning for retirement. In 1986, approximately 11.5 million annuity contracts were outstanding in the United States, compared to only 1 million 20 years earlier. Figure 15.4 shows the dramatic growth in annual annuity payments since 1950.

Most annuities are sold by life insurance companies. A person buying an annuity (the **annuitant**) pays premiums for a certain period of time, called the **accumulation period,** in return for a guarantee of receiving periodic payments over a set time period, known as the **distribution period.** An annuity operates on the principle of **risk sharing** through which annuitants living longer than expected continue to receive periodic payments at the expense of those who died prematurely. The amount of an annuity payment depends on three factors: principal, interest, and the payment option. The **principal** is the dollar amount the annuity purchaser invests through premium payments during the accumulation period. **Interest** is the amount earned on the principal from the time paid until it is distributed. The **payment option** is the method you select for receiving your annuity payments.

Advantages and Disadvantages of Annuities

The most important use of an annuity is to provide sufficient retirement income. As we have already seen, Social Security payments and retirement plan benefits are often insufficient to satisfy your retirement needs. By using savings to fund an annuity, you can ensure that there will be additional income during your retirement years. Generally, annuity payments last for your entire life; you cannot outlive them. The assurance of a lifetime income will give you peace of mind during your retirement years.

Annuities also offer an important tax advantage. Income taxes on the accumulated earnings from an annuity are postponed until payments begin. This delayed taxation feature allows the principal amount to grow more rapidly and therefore to make available a larger sum for benefit payments when you retire. However, unlike with tax-deferred retirement plans, the amount you contribute to buy the annuity receives no special tax advantage.

Annuities have several disadvantages. The total dollar amount returned can be very limited if you die soon after your annuity benefit payments begin. Therefore, the annuity issuer, and not your heirs, keeps the bulk of the money used to fund the annuity. Most annuity payments are "fixed" for the life of the annuity purchaser. This feature can be especially detrimental during times of high inflation because annuity benefits cannot increase to offset higher costs of living. During the high-inflation years of the late seventies and early eighties, many annuitants suffered a substantial deterioration in their living standards as inflation eroded the purchasing power of their annuity benefits. Finally, many annuities provide surprisingly low returns on your invested capital. Returns among the various issuers differ significantly, so it pays to shop for the most competitive return.

Characteristics of Annuities

Annuities exist in many different forms and, if used properly, can fulfill various objectives. Because of the wide variety of annuities available, we present a classification system to help you understand them. The diagram in Figure 15.5 categorizes annuities in five ways: type of contract, method of paying premiums, when benefits begin, method of paying benefits, and method of calculating benefits. This material is, by its very nature, quite detailed. It's probably best just to glance through the various options without trying to memorize them. If you or your family later decide to buy an annuity, you may use this material as a reference source.

Figure 15.5 TYPES OF ANNUITIES

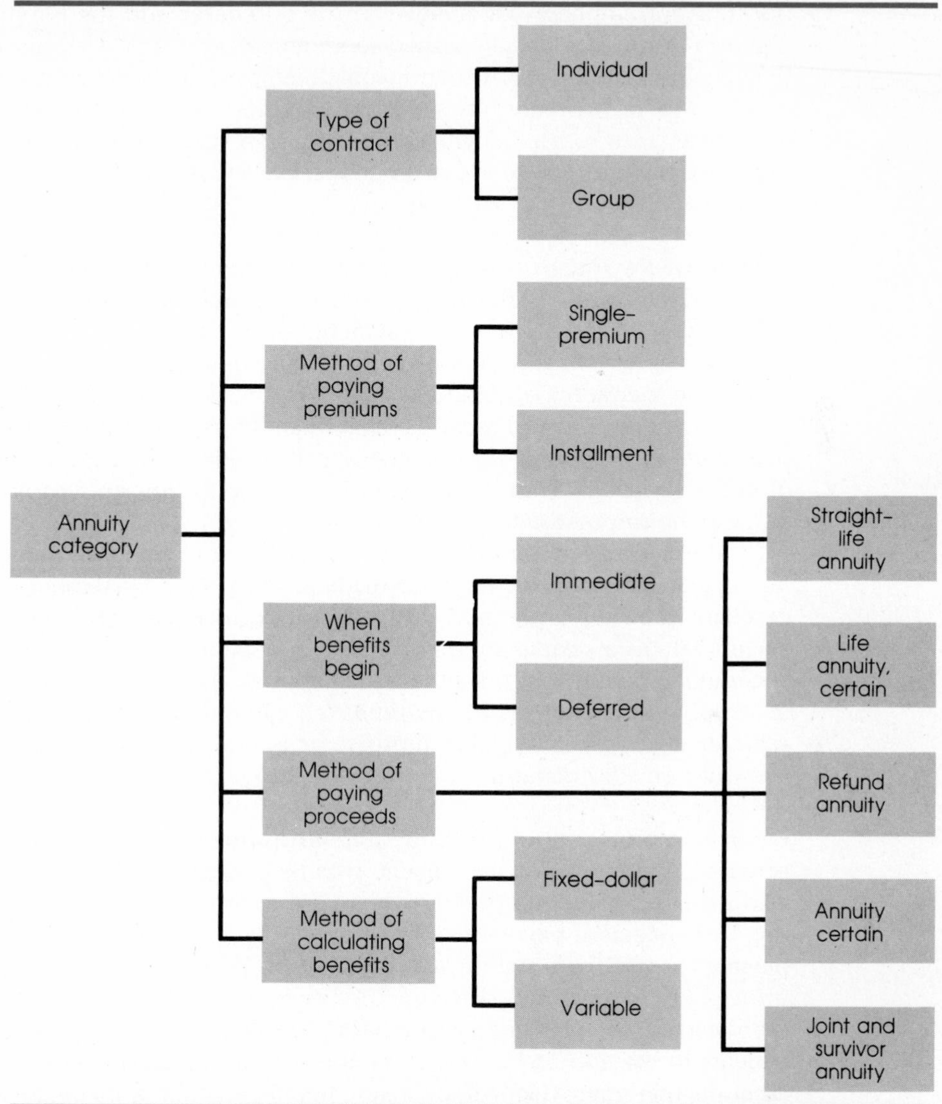

Type of Contract. Annuities may be issued either through an individual contract or a group contract. Under an **individual annuity,** a single person (or persons if it is a joint annuity) directly purchases an annuity from an issuer. The resulting annuity contract is between the purchaser and the issuing company. A **group annuity** is usually issued to an employer under a master contract for the benefit of employees. The individual members of the group hold certificates as evidence of their annuities. Group annuities are most often used to fund employees' retirement benefits under pension plans. In 1987, group annuity premium payments were approximately triple the premiums paid for individual annuities.

Method of Paying Premiums. You may purchase an annuity either with a single premium or installment premiums. A **single-premium annuity** is purchased with a single lump-sum payment. As you approach retirement age, you may want to use some portion of your life savings to purchase a single-premium annuity to guarantee a lifetime income stream. If you make a single-premium payment earlier, you will receive a larger benefit payment at retirement. Individuals often use the lump-sum proceeds from a retirement plan or the cash value of death proceeds from a life insurance policy to buy an annuity under the single-premium method.

Alternatively, you may acquire an **installment premium annuity** by making regular payments during your working years. The installment method is an excellent vehicle for planned savings. Your regular payments into the annuity accumulate as a savings fund and the insurance company pays interest on the accumulated amount. Under the installment method, you also have the option to terminate the contract at any time. You can either withdraw the entire cash value or use the accumulated funds to acquire a paid-up, single-premium annuity of a smaller amount.

When Benefits Begin. An **immediate annuity** is purchased under the single-premium method, and the benefit payments begin immediately. A **deferred annuity** is typically purchased several years before retirement, either by making regular installment payments over several years or by paying a single lump-sum payment some years before the distribution period is scheduled to begin. A principal advantage of a deferred annuity is that income taxes on its earnings are deferred. Income taxes are not due until those earnings are paid out as benefits to the annuitant. Therefore, the annuity continues to earn interest on amounts that otherwise would already have been paid in income taxes. This tax deferral allows the compounded value of the annuity to grow more rapidly. Annuities acquired under a group contract are generally immediate annuities, but most individually purchased annuities are installment-type deferred annuities.

Method of Paying Proceeds. The amount of monthly proceeds you or your beneficiary can expect to receive and the length of time you can anticipate receiving these payments depend largely on the payment option you choose. The five most commonly selected options for the distribution of annuity proceeds are the straight-life annuity, life annuity with period certain, refund annuity, annuity certain, and joint and survivor annuity.

Straight-Life Annuity. A **straight-life annuity** guarantees you a fixed amount of income for life. All payments cease when you die, however, whether you had received only one payment or 100 payments. If you die before your principal is fully refunded, the company providing the annuity retains the balance; your survivors receive nothing. This type of annuity makes the highest monthly payment of any distribution type because the issuer does not have to distribute any remaining principal to your heirs. Most people avoid this type of annuity for fear of sacrificing a large portion of their savings in the event of an untimely death soon after annuity payments begin.

Life Annuity, Period Certain. Under a **life annuity, period certain** you receive a specified amount of income for life. In addition, you are guaranteed payments for a certain time period (say, 10 or 20 years). If you die before the end of that period, your estate or beneficiaries continue to receive payments during the guaranteed period. As a result of this guarantee, your monthly payments are less under this payment option than under the straight-life option. The longer the guarantee period, the larger the benefit reduction.

Refund Annuity. A **refund annuity** again guarantees you payments for life. At your death your designated beneficiary receives an amount equal to the total premiums you paid less the total amount of annuity payments you received. There are two kinds of refund annuities. Under an **installment refund annuity,** your beneficiary receives installment payments (usually monthly) until the total purchase price of the annuity has been refunded. A **cash refund annuity** provides that, rather than in monthly payments, the refund is paid to your beneficiary in a lump sum.

Annuity Certain. An **annuity certain** provides monthly payments to you or your beneficiary for a specified time period. Annuity payments cease at the end of that period, regardless of whether you are still alive. This type of annuity is most often used by those who have a temporary need for monthly income. For example, someone retiring five years early might purchase a five-year annuity certain contract to provide monthly income until retirement benefits begin. This is one of the few annuities that does not consider the mortality table in determining the amount of benefit payments.

Joint and Survivor Annuity. Two or more individuals (often husband and wife) receive monthly annuity payments as long as either is living under the **joint and survivor annuity.** When the first annuitant dies, the survivor typically receives some reduced portion (often two-thirds) of the original amount for life. Because the annuity continues for two persons' lifetimes, the payments offered under this option are lower than those provided under other types of annuities.

Method of Calculating Benefits. Most annuity contracts are designed so that once an annuity payment is determined, the amount of that payment does not change. This is known as a **fixed-dollar annuity.** In 1986, about $22 billion of fixed-dollar payments were made to purchasers. Although fixed-dollar annuities offer the comfort of guaranteed and set payments, they are very vulnerable to the ravages of inflation. As living costs rise, those fixed-dollar payments become less and less attractive.

The **variable annuity** was designed to overcome the primary disadvantage of the fixed-dollar annuity. Under this type of contract the amount of each benefit payment may fluctuate. Although the fluctuation may be related to almost any variable factor, most variable-annuity payments are linked to the performance of the issuer's investments (typically common stocks). In this way a variable annuity is similar to a stock mutual fund.

Variable annuities are based on the belief that an equity-based portfolio should provide an attractive inflation hedge and thus allow annuity payments to increase during times of rising inflation. Unfortunately, however, this is not always the case. For example, Table 15.8 shows that an indexed variable annuity (that is, an annuity whose payments are tied to the performance of the Standard & Poor's Composite Stock Index) underperformed the annual rate of inflation, as measured by the consumer price index, for seven of the years from 1970 to 1986. Variable annuities performed especially poorly during 1973–1974 when inflation occurred at a 17.2 percent combined rate, but stock prices declined 48.6 percent. Over the long term, however, variable annuities, on average, have been attractive inflation hedges.

Shopping for an Annuity

You may believe that once you have determined the type of annuity that best suits your needs, all you need to do is contact a large insurance company to purchase the annuity. If this is your belief, you are most likely preparing to make an unfortunate financial mistake. Although most large insurers sell annuities, they typically offer widely varying terms and rates of return. You would never consider buying a new car without shopping around for the best deal. Therefore, it makes even more sense to shop for the best annuity. Whereas that new car will last you only a few years, the annuity you purchase is yours for life. Before buying, you should investigate an annuity's promised return, safety, and fees and penalties.

Promised Return. The rate of return earned on your annuity premiums largely determines the amount of benefit payments you will ultimately receive. Most annuity issuers offer a guaranteed rate of return for only a few months or a year. After that, the rate changes at the issuer's discretion, although it cannot fall below a stated minimum (typically 3.5 percent). Unfortunately, you cannot always determine how the issuer's rate will change in the future. You can, however, investigate to see which issuers provided the highest rates of return in the past. You will probably be surprised at your findings. For example, a 1982 National Education Association study of 45 companies offering fixed annuities to teachers

Table 15.8 COMPARISON OF VARIABLE ANNUITY PAYMENTS AND INFLATION, 1970–1986

Year	Percentage change in consumer price index	PERCENTAGE CHANGE IN INDEXED ANNUITY PAYMENT[a]	
		Actual	Real[b]
1970	5.9	−14.9	−20.8
1971	4.3	10.1	5.8
1972	3.3	18.4	15.1
1973	6.2	−19.4	−25.6
1974	11.0	−29.2	−40.2
1975	9.1	32.2	23.1
1976	5.8	18.0	12.2
1977	6.5	−10.4	−16.9
1978	7.7	2.5	−5.2
1979	11.3	12.2	0.9
1980	13.5	23.8	10.2
1981	10.4	−7.3	−17.7
1982	6.1	12.6	6.5
1983	3.2	17.9	14.7
1984	4.3	0.1	−4.2
1985	3.6	31.6	28.0
1986	1.4	18.6	17.2

[a] Assumes that the annuity fund is invested in a portfolio of common stocks that replicates the Standard & Poor's Composite Index.

[b] The annual real return is an inflation-adjusted return calculated as follows: actual percentage change in indexed annuity payment *minus* percentage change in the consumer price index.

SOURCE: *Federal Reserve Bulletin,* Washington, D.C.: Board of Governors of the Federal Reserve System, various issues, 1971–1986.

revealed average annual rates of return varying from less than ½ percent to more than 8 percent over the most recent 12 years. Usually, a company with a good track record can be expected to continue offering competitive returns.

Safety. Your annuity is only as safe as the underlying issuing company, and, of course, some issuers are safer than others. The recent backruptcy of Baldwin-United Corp. emphasizes the importance of acquiring an annuity from a sound issuer. Although the people who bought annuities from Baldwin-United eventually had their principal returned, they did not earn the returns initially promised and their funds were tied up for several years. The life and health edition of *Best's Insurance Reports,* which is available at most large public libraries, rates the financial quality of issuing companies. A good way to ensure safety is to buy only from an issuer rated A+.

Fees and Penalties. Many annuities are sold through insurance agents or stockbrokers. If you buy an annuity through these sources, you typically must pay a sales commission ranging up to 8½ percent. If you deal directly with the issuing company, you often can avoid the commission. Issuers also charge a yearly fee against your account balance for administrative expenses. These fees vary among issuers, but generally range from ½ to 1½ percent annually. Withdrawal fees can also differ. Most issuers allow you to take out up to 10 percent of your annuity account balance each year without charge. If you withdraw more than 10 percent, the issuer imposes a surrender charge that usually begins at 7 percent of your excess withdrawal during the annuity's first year and then gradually declines. Finally, any annuity withdrawals made before age 59½ incur a federal tax penalty, in addition to the income tax liability.

SUMMARY

Although your retirement may be many years from now, you should still consider saving for this event immediately. If you wait until you are approaching retirement age, it may be too late to accumulate sufficient funds to provide for a financially secure retirement. By starting a regular savings program while you are young, you can build the foundation for a comfortable retirement. You may believe that Social Security and your company's pension plan will provide sufficient retirement income, but more and more Americans are finding that these income sources are inadequate. You will probably need to rely on savings to supplement these sources.

The amount you must set aside each year depends on several factors. After deciding on your required annual retirement income, you must determine how much of this income is accounted for by Social Security, pension plans, and other retirement plans. The remaining amount must be provided from your savings. You may already have savings, but you should determine the additional savings you'll need to fund your retirement.

There are several important sources of retirement income. Social Security provides the foundation of a retirement program for most people. Benefits are designed to provide a floor level of retirement income. The amount of benefits depends upon the retiree's average monthly earnings in previous years and the age at retirement. Generally, the higher the average yearly earnings and the later the age at retirement, the larger will be the monthly Social Security payment. Social Security is funded on a pay-as-you-go basis, so current workers pay the benefits of retired persons.

Employer pension and retirement plans are another important source of retirement income. These plans have grown in importance during the last 40 years and now cover about 80 percent of all full-time workers earning $20,000 or more. When qualified, these plans provide important tax benefits that allow contributions to grow more rapidly than possible on a fully taxable basis. You should be familiar with the following important features of pension and retirement plans: eligibility requirements, benefit computations, vesting requirements, employee contributions, funding, and payment options.

You may also benefit from other types of retirement plans. You should consider the advantages and disadvantages of Keogh plans, IRAs, IRA rollovers, SEP/IRAs, salary reduction plans, profit-sharing plans, and thrift plans. Each of these plans is unique; the appropriateness of each plan depends largely on your individual situation. As a general rule, these plans are used to supplement retirement income from Social Security, pensions, and savings.

Annuities have become an increasingly popular retirement planning vehicle. An annuity provides for lifetime income and therefore protects the annuitant against outliving his or her income. The many types of annuities can be grouped in five ways: type of contract, method of paying premiums, when benefits begin, method of paying proceeds, and method of calculating benefits. The costs and quality of annuities vary considerably among issuers, so you should shop carefully before making your purchase.

KEY TERMS

accumulation period
annuitant
annuity
annuity certain
cash refund annuity
contributory pension plan
deferred annuity
defined benefit plan
defined contribution plan
distribution period
Employee Retirement Income Security Act (ERISA)
exempt earnings
Federal Insurance Contributions Act (FICA)
fixed-dollar annuity
flat amount pension plan
flat percentage pension plan
fully insured
funded pension plan
group annuity
immediate annuity
individual annuity
individual retirement account (IRA)
installment premium annuity
installment refund annuity
insured pension plan
interest
IRA rollover
joint and survivor annuity
Keogh (HR-10) plan
life annuity, period certain
noncontributory pension plan
Old-Age, Survivors, Disability, and Health Insurance (OASDHI)
payment option
pension plan
portable pension plan
principal
profit-sharing plan
qualified pension plan
refund annuity
risk sharing
salary reduction plan
self-administered plan
simplified employee pension (SEP/IRA)
single-premium annuity
straight-life annuity
thrift plan
trusteed plan
unfunded pension plan
unit benefit pension plan
variable annuity
vesting

SELECTED READINGS

Anrig, Greg. "Getting a Grip on Your Golden Years." *Money*, November 1985, pp. 191–200.

Dreyfus, Patricia A. "Annuities Can Be Forever." *Money*, March 1986, pp. 66–70.

Gould, Carole. "Pension Planning Gets Tougher." *New York Times Financial Planning Guide*, September 14, 1986, pp. 30–33.

"Packing It In Before 65." *Business Week*, June 24, 1985, pp. 134–136.

"Planning for Retirement." *Consumers Digest*, May 1986, pp. 76–79.

Schurenberg, Eric. "Get a Lead on a Retirement Plan." *Money*, August 1986, pp. 69–73.

"Social Security Faces New Crossroads." *U.S. News & World Report*, August 12, 1985, pp. 40–45.

QUESTIONS

1 Why is retirement planning important? Why do many people neglect to plan properly for retirement?

2 Briefly describe the main reason why Social Security was established.

3 Explain how Social Security is funded. Why is Social Security often referred to as a pay-as-you-go system?

4 How does the proportion of workers to retirees today compare to that proportion in 1945? Explain the effect on the Social Security system of any change in this proportion.

5 Are all American workers required to participate in Social Security? Explain.

6 What are the major types of benefits provided by Social Security?

7 Discuss the proper role of Social Security in your retirement planning. Should you rely on Social Security payments to provide for your retirement livelihood? Explain.

8 What is a pension plan? How does a pension plan differ from Social Security in terms of funding? That is, is it on a pay-as-you-go basis?

9 Identify and briefly describe the six important features of a pension plan with which the employee should be familiar.

10 Compare a defined-benefit pension plan with a defined-contribution pension plan. Which type of plan would you prefer? Explain.

11 Describe vesting. Explain the difference in vesting requirements for contributory and noncontributory pension plans.

12 Compare each of the following ways of administering a pension plan: (a) insured plan, (b) trusteed plan, and (c) self-administered plan.

13 Distinguish between an individual retirement account and a Keogh plan.

14 Compare a profit-sharing plan with a pension plan. Can an employee be covered by both of these plans simultaneously?

15 Define an annuity. Explain how an annuity is different from a life insurance policy.

16 Distinguish between a group annuity and an individual annuity.

17 Explain how an immediate annuity differs from a deferred annuity.

18 Identify and briefly describe the five basic ways in which annuity benefits may be paid.

19 Use Table 15.7 to answer the following questions about the future value of an IRA.

  a If $2000 annual contributions begin at age 20 and the compound annual rate of growth is 10 percent, how much will be accumulated at age 70?

  b If $2000 annual contributions begin at age 30 and the compound annual rate of growth is 8 percent, how much will be accumulated at age 70?

  c If two working spouses each contribute $2000 annually beginning at age 25, and the compound annual growth rate is 10 percent, how much will their combined total accumulation be at age 70?

20 Jim Feferberg, an unmarried retiree, received $9000 in Social Security benefits in 1987. For the year, Jim had an adjusted gross income of $22,000 and an additional $5,000 in interest from tax-exempt bonds. Calculate the amount of Jim's Social Security benefits that is subject to federal income taxes. Remember to use the $25,000 exemption because he is single.

CASE PROBLEMS

15.1 Betty Gimbel, a 25-year-old unmarried college graduate, is employed by Macy's department store. Although Betty is covered by Macy's pension plan, she wants to accumulate additional retirement savings. She estimates that she can save 10 percent (pretax) of her yearly $20,000 salary and wants to determine the best alternative for the purpose of building up these retirement savings. She currently is in a 15 percent income tax bracket.

a Assume that Betty invests $2000 savings for the year 1987 in an individual retirement account (IRA). How much of this amount is income tax deductible?

b Determine the dollar value of Betty's IRA after one year if these savings earn 8 percent yearly.

c Determine the dollar value of Betty's IRA at the time of her retirement at age 70 if she makes a $2000 contribution each year. Assume that the account continues to earn 8 percent annually (see Table 15.7). What dollar amount will Betty accumulate at retirement age if she waits until another ten years to begin her IRA contributions? Once again, use an 8 percent assumption.

d Assume that Betty does not choose to open an IRA, but rather elects to earmark $2000 (pretax) of her salary each year to invest in a personal savings account. Calculate the dollar value of her personal savings that will be available for investment after taxes are paid.

e Determine the dollar value of Betty's investment in part d after one year if these savings earn 8 percent. How does this amount compare to the value of an IRA at the end of one year? (See part b above.)

15.2 Lou Ferrara, age 66, recently retired after 28 years of employment as a personnel director for a firm in Cleveland, Ohio. Lou is covered by the firm's defined-benefit plan, which pays a retired employee 1½ percent of his average three year annual preretirement salary for each year of service with the firm. Lou's average earnings over his career were $25,000, but in the last three years he earned $37,000, $40,000, and $43,000, respectively. His wife, Carol, who is 65 years old, keeps all the couple's financial records. Although Carol is very active in volunteer work in the community, she does not have a direct dollar income. Carol is in the process of determining their annual retirement income. She thinks they need a retirement income at least equal to 75 percent of Lou's last year of preretirement salary.

a Determine the amount per year that Lou will receive from the defined benefit plan.
b How much will Social Security pay Lou and Carol each year? Go to Table 15.3 and read down to the $10,000 row (which is as far as such tables go). Then read across to the monthly benefits for the worker at age 65 (which applies to age 65 or older) and the spouse at age 65. Add these two benefits together and multiply by 12 to convert from a monthly to an annual basis.
c What is the amount of the Ferraras' total annual retirement income? Add a and b together (disregard taxes).
d How does your answer to part c compare to Carol's requirement that they have a retirement income at least equal to 75 percent of Lou's last year of preretirement salary?
e Assume that the Ferraras own a piece of land that they can sell for $80,000. It is Carol's intention to take the proceeds and reinvest them in an annual annuity that will cover the deficiency you computed in part d. What is the minimum rate of return that Carol must earn on the $80,000 to achieve this objective?

Appendix 15A

DETERMINING HOW MUCH TO SAVE FOR RETIREMENT

This is a fairly sophisticated appendix that may be of interest to some readers. You can determine how much you must save each year to meet your retirement income needs by using the following five steps.

Step 1: Determine your *required annual retirement income* in today's dollars. This amount should reflect the fact that you will have lower taxes and expenses after you retire. As a general rule, your retirement income needs may range from 60 to 80 percent of your preretirement requirements.

Step 2: Subtract your estimated annual income from Social Security, employer pension plans, and other retirement plans from your required annual retirement income to determine the *annual retirement income needed from savings.*

Step 3: Determine the *amount you must save by retirement* in today's dollars to have enough funds to provide the necessary yearly retirement income calculated in step 2. This is done by multiplying the amount calculated in step 2 by the appropriate multiplication factor in Table 15A.1. This factor assumes that your savings earn 2 percent annually after inflation and taxes.

Step 4: Multiply the amount of your current savings by the appropriate multiplication factor in Table 15A.2 to determine how much your current savings will be worth in today's dollars by the time you retire. This multiplication factor represents the compound value of a dollar over selected time periods. For example, the 2.000 factor corresponding to 35 years in Table 15A.2 means that after 35 years, a dollar compounded at 2 percent (the assumed rate of return after inflation and taxes) will be worth two dollars ($1.00 × 2.000). Subtract this amount from the amount computed in step 3 to calculate the *amount of savings still needed.*

Step 5: Compute the *amount of savings needed yearly* (today's dollars) by multiplying the appropriate discount factor in Table 15A.3 by the amount determined in step 4. This discount factor shows how much you must save each year to fund a desired savings amount. For example, the .020 factor corresponding to 35 years means that you must save 2¢ yearly to fund each

Table 15A.1 AMOUNT OF SAVINGS REQUIRED TO FUND RETIREMENT INCOME

Life expectancy after retirement	Multiplication factor[a]
10 years	9.2
15 years	13.1
20 years	16.7
25 years	19.9
30 years	22.8
35 years	25.5
40 years	27.9

[a] These factors provide built-in inflation and tax adjustments by assuming that your money earns 2% annually after inflation and taxes.

Table 15A.2 MULTIPLICATION FACTORS FOR RETIREMENT PLANNING

Years until retirement	Multiplication factor[a]
5 years	1.104
10 years	1.219
15 years	1.346
20 years	1.486
25 years	1.641
30 years	1.811
35 years	2.000
40 years	2.208

[a] These factors provide a built-in inflation adjustment by assuming that your savings will earn 2% after inflation and taxes.

dollar of savings desired in 35 years (assuming you earn 2 percent annually after inflation and taxes).

We now provide an example to illustrate the way to determine how much you should save each year to accumulate enough savings to provide a financially secure retirement.

Table 15A.3 DISCOUNT FACTORS FOR RETIREMENT PLANNING

Years until retirement	Discount factor[a]
5	.192
10	.091
15	.058
20	.041
25	.031
30	.025
35	.020
40	.017

[a] These factors provide built-in inflation and tax adjustments by assuming that your money earns 2% annually after inflation and taxes.

The Situation

Henry and Joan O'Connor want to determine how much they must save each year to ensure a sufficient level of retirement income. The O'Connors, both age 40, expect to retire in 25 years and estimate their combined preretirement income at $60,000 in today's (1987) dollars. They believe that a reduction in living expenses and taxes will enable them to live comfortably in retirement on 75 percent of their preretirement income. The O'Connors have already saved $75,000 toward retirement and estimate the following annual retirement income amounts upon retirement: Social Security payments equal $12,000, corporate pension payments equal $15,000, and other retirement plan payments equal $6,000.

We use the previously described five-step procedure to assist the O'Connors in determining their required annual savings. The findings, presented in Table 15A.4, indicate that the O'Connors, if their funds earn a 2 percent annual return after inflation and taxes, should save $3587 each year to provide for their retirement income needs. An explanation of this determination follows.

Explanation of Calculations in Table 15A.4

Step 1: The O'Connors' estimated required retirement income is 75 percent of their $60,000 (current dollars) preretirement income. Therefore, the O'Connors need a $45,000 yearly retirement income in today's dollars.

Step 2: To determine the annual retirement income needed from savings, we subtract from the estimated annual retirement income required

Table 15A.4 DETERMINING ANNUAL SAVINGS NEEDED TO FUND RETIREMENT (ALL AMOUNTS IN TODAY'S DOLLARS)

Step	Action	Item	Amount	Total
1		*Preretirement Annual Income*		$60,000
	minus	Expenses eliminated upon retirement	− $15,000	
	equals	Annual retirement income required		$45,000
2		*Annual Retirement Income Required*		$45,000
	minus	1. Social Security payments	− $12,000	
		2. Pension plan payments	− $15,000	
		3. Other retirement plan payments	− $6,000	
	equals	Annual retirement income needed from savings		$12,000
3		*Annual Retirement Income Needed from Savings*		$12,000
	times	Multiplication factor (Table 15A.1)	× 19.9	
	equals	Total additional savings required		$238,800
4		*Total Additional Savings Required*		$238,800
	minus	Value of current savings at time of retirement[a]	$123,075	
	equals	Amount of savings still needed		$115,725
5		*Amount of Savings Still Needed*		$115,725
	times	Discount factor (Table 15A.3)	× .031	
	equals	Amount of savings needed yearly		$3,587

[a] Determined by multiplying the current amount saved by the multiplication factor in Table 15A.2. In this example, the calculation is as follows: $75,000 (total current savings) × 1.641 (multiplication factor for 25 years) = $123,075.

the amount of anticipated Social Security, pension, and other retirement plan payments. The O'Connors estimate that these benefits will total approximately $33,000 a year in current dollars. Therefore, $12,000 ($45,000 annual retirement income required minus $33,000 yearly benefit payments) is the estimated annual retirement income needed from savings.

Step 3: Since the $12,000 must be provided each year during the O'Connors' retirement, we must determine the total amount of savings that the O'Connors have to accumulate in 25 years, when they plan to retire. By multiplying the appropriate 19.9 multiplication factor by the $12,000 estimated annual retirement need, we determine that the O'Connors must accumulate savings of $238,800 in today's dollars by the time of their retirement to provide sufficient retirement income.

Step 4: We determine the value of the O'Connors' present $75,000 savings fund at the time of their retirement. The appropriate 1.641 multiplication factor from Table 15A.2 times the $75,000 current savings yields a $123,075 value (today's dollars) of current savings at the time of retirement. This assumes the O'Connors earn 2 percent yearly after inflation and taxes on their savings. We subtract the resulting amount from the $238,800 total savings requirement to determine that $115,725 of savings is still required ($238,800 − $123,075 = $115,725).

Step 5: We multiply the .031 discount factor in Table 15A.2, corresponding to 25 years, by the amount of savings still required ($115,725) to arrive at the amount of savings needed yearly to accommodate the O'Connors' expected retirement income needs. Therefore, the O'Connors must save $3,587 (in 1987 dollars) yearly to build a retirement fund that is large enough to enable them to retire financially secure.

16

Estate Planning

After reading this chapter, you should:

- Understand the importance of estate planning
- Appreciate the basic steps involved in estate planning
- Be able to discuss the key features of a will
- Understand the reasons behind the use of a trust
- Know the basic considerations involved in making gifts and computing gift taxes
- Understand the fundamentals of state and federal estate taxes, their computations, and estate tax reduction strategies

You have heard the old saying that there are only two certainties in life: death and taxes. Although neither subject is particularly pleasant, you should carefully consider both if you want to provide the best ultimate distribution of your wealth to your heirs. Without proper planning, much or all of your accumulated wealth can be consumed by taxes, administrative expenses, court costs, and the like. As a result, your loved ones will receive less of your wealth to enjoy. Or, even worse, if you neglect to plan, state and federal laws may require that your property be given to family members of whom you disapprove while neglecting those for whom you care.

Your **estate** consists of all the property you own or have an interest in at the time of your death, including automobiles, collectibles, jewelry, household furnishings, securities, real estate, and cash. Your estate may also include assets that materialize as a result of your death, such as life insurance proceeds, lump-sum retirement benefits, and corporate death payments.

Through estate planning, you can assure that your wealth is properly managed and preserved during your lifetime and distributed in the desired manner when you die. **Estate planning** is a process that sets objectives and identifies the techniques best suited to accomplish those objectives in order to provide the greatest possible financial benefits and personal satisfaction for you and your heirs. Estate planning is a continuous process that requires the periodic review and revision of the various strategies.

THE PROCESS OF ESTATE PLANNING

No one likes to consider the thought of his or her own mortality. Although we all realize that death is inevitable, most of us see it as an event destined to occur in the distant future. Yet each year thousands of people die prematurely as a result of accidents or unexpected illnesses. Because death always looms as a possibility, you should have available an estate plan that recognizes that such an event may occur. A little time and effort devoted now to estate planning can avert serious financial and personal hardships for your loved ones when you die.

Estate planning should be an orderly and continuous process. Listed below is a six-step estate-planning process.

1 Establish objectives
   - **a** Identify your heirs
   - **b** Decide what each heir receives
   - **c** Determine who should control assets

2 Take inventory
   - **a** Identify your estate property
   - **b** Determine your estate's value

3 Identify estate liabilities
   - **a** Estimate estate tax liability
   - **b** Estimate other estate expenses
   - **c** Analyze asset liquidity

4 Select proper estate-planning tools
   - **a** Identify your team of professional planners
   - **b** Determine what tools are available
   - **c** Decide which tools are best for you

5 Implement the estate plan
   - **a** Execute relevant documents
   - **b** Communicate the plan to heirs

6 Review and revise the estate plan

These steps are not independent; rather, they interact to create a viable estate-planning process. In the following paragraphs we review each of the six steps in the estate-planning process.

Establishing Objectives

The first step in estate planning is to decide who will be the beneficiaries of your estate. Once you have identified your heirs, you must determine which specific assets (or portion of assets) each beneficiary should receive. This task can be most difficult, because the value of your estate fluctuates and your feelings toward individual heirs vary. Finally, you must determine the degree of control over property each beneficiary should be given. You may be concerned about your spouse's ability to manage assets after you are gone, or you may prefer that someone else manage assets you pass to your minor child or your financially reckless brother. In these instances, a properly selected professional can preserve and manage the assets so that your beneficiaries will be able to enjoy the benefits of your estate for a long time.

Taking Inventory of Possessions

The second step in the estate-planning process is to identify and value the property comprising your estate. You are probably aware of most assets in your estate. Cash, stocks, bonds, real estate, and business ownership are obvious examples of property ownership. But you must also include automobiles, furniture, art objects, and other personal effects in your estate. And you must also remember that your estate at the time of your death may include the proceeds from life insurance, lump-sum retirement benefits, and employer death payments. You need to consider all these death-related assets when determining the value of your estate.

Once you have identified the property comprising your estate, you must next determine the fair market value of that property. Your estate's fair market value may turn out to be higher than you expected. The market value of your home may have increased considerably, or your coin collection may have appreciated to many times what you paid for it. Also, life insurance proceeds or payments from a retirement plan can substantially increase your estate's value. All factors must be considered to accurately determine the fair market value of your estate.

Finally, you must remember that your estate's value may fluctuate over time. A sizable inheritance, for example, might cause a sudden change in your estate's value and thus considerably alter the estate-planning techniques which are best suited for you. As a result, you should always maintain complete and current information on your estate's composition and value. You should also be aware of any potential future occurrences such as gifts or inheritances that might affect the value of your estate.

Identifying Estate Liabilities

The third step in estate planning is the estimation of estate liabilities. An estate liability is any required payment that must be made from estate assets before the estate can be closed and funds distributed to your heirs. Estate liabilities may include any unpaid debts you owed at the time of your death, burial expenses, legal fees, and unpaid income taxes.

Estate taxes are computed on your gross estate less certain deductions. A carefully developed estate plan allows you to keep estate taxes as low as possible while still permitting you to achieve personal estate objectives. Without an estate plan, the cost of dying can be very high. Many estate planners recommend that you prepare a hypothetical estate tax analysis to determine how much estate taxes your estate would owe if you died today. In this process you must identify and determine the amount of all assets and liabilities that would be included in your estate. This lets you see what would happen to your estate if you died suddenly.

You should also consider other liabilities that may arise when you die. The administration of your estate can consume as much as 4 percent of the estate's value, and may be even higher if you do not have a viable estate plan. Funeral and burial expenses may also be higher than expected.

Another factor to consider is the availability of estate assets to meet expected liabilities. Many estates have been severely crippled because liquid assets were unavailable to meet estate obligations. You can imagine the frustration of heirs who find that a profitable family business must be sold at a low price in order to pay estate taxes. Such financial hardship is avoidable with proper estate planning—in this case, through a provision for life insurance or a business continuation agreement.

Selecting Estate-Planning Tools

You may be aware of most of the major estate-planning tools such as wills, trusts, gifts, and life insurance. Selecting among these many varied tools is the fourth estate-planning step. You probably don't understand the complexities of all these tools. Fortunately, attorneys, accountants, estate planners, financial advisers, and life insurance specialists are available to assist you.

Each specialist can advise you about the planning tool(s) that are best for you. By carefully choosing your estate-planning team, you incorporate the best advice from many experts into your estate plan. Proper planning is a very complex process—certainly beyond the capabilities of any lone individual—so you must be sure to select competent advisers.

Implementing the Estate Plan

Once you and your advisers have designed the estate plan, you are ready to engage in the fifth estate-planning step. Assuming you have properly completed the previous four steps, the implementation of your estate plan should be a relatively simple and straightforward task. You should already have contemplated and enumerated your objectives, identified the best estate-planning tools and techniques, and had your team of experts prepare the necessary documents to place your estate plan in action. After you and your advisers are satisfied that these documents are appropriate, you should act at once to execute them and put your estate plan in motion.

Reviewing and Revising the Plan

An estate plan should reflect your current situation and desires. Therefore, as changes occur in your family, financial, or personal life, you should update your estate plan to reflect these changes. This is the final step in the estate-planning process. An obsolete plan may be more detrimental to your heirs than no plan at all. There is almost an endless list of changes that may affect your estate plan. The following are among the most important:

A significant change in the value of your estate
A change in the tax laws
A change in your marital status
A change in the status of your children or other dependents
The death, disability, or other incapacitation of an executor, guardian, or trustee named in your will
A change in desired trust provisions
A move to another state or country

If any of these changes occur, then your estate plan should be reviewed and possibly revised. In any event, you should review your estate plan periodically with members of your professional team to ensure that it reflects your most current objectives.

PREPARING A WILL

A **will** is a legally enforceable declaration of a person's instructions about matters to be attended to after his or her death. A will is inoperative until the death of the person making the will (known as the **testator,** or **testatrix,** if female). This is why a will is said to be **ambulatory** (walking) until the death of the testator.

A properly executed will allows you to direct the final disposition of your estate. Without a will your property will be dispersed at your death according to state law. These laws vary considerably from state to state and may require your property to be distributed to individuals of whom you disapprove while neglecting those you favor. Also, if you die **intestate** (without a will), your estate may be subjected to a lengthy and expensive court process to select an administrator for your estate and require the court-appointed administrator to post a surety bond, which may cost as much as 4 percent of the total assets of the estate. A properly executed will allows you to select the administrator (referred to as the **executor,** or **executrix** if female) of your estate and enables this person to function without posting a costly surety bond.

Your will may be the most important document you execute because it offers you a rare opportunity to direct the disposition of your estate after your death. Its significance depends less on the size of your estate than the type of property you leave, the persons to whom you want to leave your property, and other details you want handled after your death. A will can not only specify how to distribute your assets, but also can address important family details such as naming a guardian for your minor children or a trustee to handle the financial affairs of your spouse.

Who Can Make a Will

The legal requirements for making a valid will vary from state to state. All states, however, require that you have the capacity to execute a valid will; that is, you must be of *proper age,* of *sound mind,* and *free from undue influence.*

In most states, *of proper age* means 18 years or older (19 in Alabama and Wyoming). Wills made by individuals under age 18 are accepted only by a few states, and then only in unusual situations.

In determining the sound mind, the court must be satisfied that at the time you made the will you knew what you were doing and intended to do it. Courts are often lenient in their interpretation of the sound-mind requirement. Unless overwhelming evidence of mental incompetence exists, the courts generally uphold a will. Therefore, for example, the courts often recognize a will of an elderly person of diminishing mental capacity or an individual with an unusually low IQ.

The courts also tend to be lenient in the interpretation of whether you were under undue influence when you signed your will. Obviously, a court is going to reject a will if you were forced to sign at gunpoint. But the mere fact that an elderly millionaire left most of his estate to the attractive new maid will not invalidate his will unless some evidence emerges to show that he was so helpless that the maid was able to direct his decision.

When to Make a Will

You should make your will at the earliest possible date. Your unexpected death can severely handicap your heirs if you die without a will. Not only is the settlement process delayed, but also your estate may be subjected to unnecessary expenses. Further, without a will your estate may be distributed against your desires. No one wants to think about his or her premature death; nonetheless, your will should be drawn as if you expect to die tomorrow.

Saying What You Mean

Furthermore, your will must be worded correctly to ensure the desired distribution of your property. Without proper wording, the law may require the courts or your executor to distribute your property in a way that you never intended.

A will is typically written in formal legal language that is often difficult to understand. But it is essential for you to understand what it means. The best procedure is to take each clause and see if you can state it briefly in simple words. If you do not understand a particular clause, ask your attorney to explain it to you. There should be no margin for error in the wording of a will. The following example illustrates this key point.

A father, disapproving of his daughter's choice of a mate, provided in his will for a substantial annual income to the daughter "for as long as she remains above ground." This seemingly harmless statement ultimately created significant problems when the daughter died and her husband had her entombed "above ground."

One of the most common construction problems, as they are called, concerns specific dollar bequests. For example, a man who was a millionaire when he made his will left $100,000 to a charity and the remainder to his children. Unfortunately, the father unintentionally cut off his children because when he died the value of his assets had fallen below $100,000. This problem could have been avoided by willing 10 percent of the assets to the charity and the remainder to the children. That way, the children would have been guaranteed a part of the estate.

When you go to your lawyer to discuss your will, you should bring with you the following information and documents:

- **a** A complete list of all your assets, including bank accounts, stock, bonds, business ownership and money owed to you, as well as your more valuable personal effects, such as jewelry, furs, art objects and the like.
- **b** An itemization of all of your real estate, together with its value and location, including property you own jointly with your spouse or others.
- **c** A list of your obligations, including mortgages on your house or business, leases and debts.
- **d** Any inheritances you expect to receive before your death.
- **e** A statement of any instruments, such as trusts or wills or others, under which you are given a **power to appoint**—that is, the power to designate to whom certain assets will go upon your death.
- **f** A statement of your approximate income and general standard of living for the past several years.
- **g** Records on insurance of all kinds, including numbers and face amounts of the policies, their premiums and any outstanding loans that have been made against them.
- **h** Family information, such as the ages and the state of health of its members, adopted children, marital problems, family feuds and black sheep, if any.[1]

Types of Wills

Three types of wills are recognized in this country—attested, holographic, and nuncupative. The individual state laws determine which of these wills are legally enforceable in a particular state.

[1] *You and the Law,* Pleasantville, N.Y.: Reader's Digest Association, Inc., 1985, p. 638.

Attested Will. An **attested will** must be written, signed, and witnessed. This is the most common type of will and is valid throughout the United States. It may be handwritten or typed on any kind of material that will take writing or typing. It must be signed by you and should bear the signatures of at least two adults who saw you sign the will and who agree to serve as witnesses. Beneficiaries of the estate do not qualify as witnesses. Because there have been many instances of attempted fraud against estates, the purpose of having witnesses is to enable the probate court to ensure that the will is legitimate.

Holographic Will. A **holographic will** must be entirely in your own handwriting and signed. If it is properly witnessed, it becomes an attested will. But, if unwitnessed, the problem of proving the legitimacy of the will becomes significant because no witness can come forward to testify that you intended the document to be your will. As a result, most states will not accept a holographic will. And even in states where they are legal, most probate courts are reluctant to accept them.

Nuncupative Will. A **nuncupative will** is your oral declaration of the desired distribution of your estate. An oral will is usually valid only in extreme circumstances, such as during combat. Even then, courts are reluctant to accept this kind of will because it is often made under the fear of death or extreme emotional stress.

Naming an Executor

The executor (or executrix, if female) is responsible for carrying out the instructions contained in your will. The executor's responsibility is considerable, so you should carefully deliberate your choice of executor(s). If you do not appoint an executor in your will, the court must select one for you.

In selecting your executor(s), you should choose someone you trust and who has the best interests of your heirs at heart. Most often, a spouse, close friend, or relative is appointed as executor. You may also want to name a co-executor to assist the executor in carrying out his or her duties. Your accountant, banker, lawyer, or business associate may be a desirable choice as co-executor. Banks, in particular, are popular choices because they are impartial, permanent (usually), and experienced in handling estates. You should also name a substitute executor(s) in case your original selection dies first, refuses to serve, or is otherwise incapacitated.

Maximum fees for executors are set by state law. Banks often charge the maximum, whereas friends and relatives typically charge little or nothing. Executors' fees apply to the **probate estate,** which is the total value of property passed by will. Property passing outside the will (joint property, life insurance proceeds, and so on) is not included in the probate estate. The following maximum fees, although possibly not applicable to your state, give you an idea of maximum executor fees:

Box 16.1 HEIRS GETTING THEIR MONEY LATER—AND WITH MORE STRINGS ATTACHED

Parental generosity is on the wane, or at least on hold.

Longer life spans and the two-income family mean that parents have more money to bestow upon their children than ever. But they are keeping it to themselves longer. Heirs are not only receiving their inheritances or trust funds later in life, but with more strings attached, attorneys and financial planners say.

Parents typically used to entrust money to their children when they reached 18 or 21 years of age, says Hank Madden, senior financial planner of IDS Financial Services Inc. Now, he sees more "staggered distributions at age 25, 30 and 35 or even later."

Parents concern that children will squander their inheritance or use it to fund an "objectionable" life style is nothing new, but the measures parents are taking to deal with it are. In the 12,000 wills that Fidelity Bank of Philadelphia handles, there has been a sharp increase in controversial provisions that "keep assets from an irresponsible child, or that attempt to cope with a problem, such as drug addiction, that the parents couldn't cope with while alive, or that get revenge from beyond the grave," says George Stolberg, head of trust and tax services for the bank.

Elaborate Wills

"Contingent benevolence" isn't just a rich man's phenomenon. Social and legislative changes are accelerating the trend at all income levels. The frequency of divorce and remarriage has made estate planning an intricate business, with the result that even middle-income parents are preparing elaborate wills. Furthermore, a 1982 change in tax law has cut the costs of bequeathing assets to a spouse. That has encouraged parents to leave their estate first to their spouse, who may attach more strings to the inheritance as he or she grows older and more frugal.

Common provisions now appearing . . . include clauses that withhold funds until a child is gainfully employed, is treated for alcoholism, is no longer a member of a "cult" or is divorced from an unapproved spouse. Also on the rise are provisions that leave money to grandchildren only if they are raised in the grandparents' faith or to step-grandchildren only if the child's biological parent remains married to the benefactor's child.

Lawyers note . . . that many of these clauses are of questionable legality. Parents often "try to govern all their childrens' actions by saying: 'you won't get the money if you do that,'" but that's "frowned upon by the courts," in many states, says William Shea, senior partner of the New York law firm of Shea & Gould.

The most common, and perfectly legal, method to shield assets from a child is to postpone the age at which the child receives funds or to leave the distribution of money to the discretion of a trustee. But children who are cooling their heels waiting for a trust or inheritance can attempt to borrow heavily against it, and banks are often quite obliging.

'Spendthrift Clause'

Some states allow a "spendthrift clause" to be inserted into a will or trust that would prohibit such borrowing, but others don't. And Mr. Madden cautions that parents who restrict a child's access to an estate until a certain age should provide for it to be tapped earlier for reasons of "health, maintenance, welfare and education."

As to whether children are truly irresponsible, or parents just reluctant to give up control of their money, estate experts say the truth often lies between. "In isolated cases, the child says, 'Here's a windfall!' and is imprudent," says William Goldberg, head of financial planning for Peat, Marwick, Mitchell & Co. One teenager who received $10,000 for college tuition spent it on a Cadillac, a stereo and a camera, he says. More often, there's an initial spending spree, but children "don't run right through the money," he says.

Estate experts say concern that a child will lose part of an inheritance in a divorce is well-founded. While most states don't treat an inheritance as marital property, such income as interest earned on it is. And children with trust funds tend to tap them for major purchases, such as houses or cars, that are treated as marital property. Worried parents can structure their will to give a child access to funds as needed in an open trust fund rather than an outright inheritance, thereby allowing the child exclusive access to the money and also an excuse for not commingling funds.

Parents concerned that unwise investments will erode the value of their estate can mandate that funds remain invested with certain advisors or be invested at the discretion of a trustee. They can also require heirs to take courses in money management as a condition of receiving funds. But one of the biggest errors parents make, estate experts say, is to allow the eldest child, or the one viewed as most responsible, to manage the money for other siblings. This situation often results in bad feelings and strained family relations.

Restricting Behavior

The trickiest issue for parents preparing wills may be whether to include a clause regulating their child's behavior after their death. The most popular restriction right now requires children to prove freedom from drug dependency before receiving funds. "These clauses are often tied to the particular phobia of the moment," says Ira Lustgarten, head partner of the trust and estate department of [the] law firm Willkie, Farr & Gallagher of New York. "Probably one day you'll see clauses, as ridiculous as it sounds, that say: 'He'll get the money if he doesn't have AIDS.' "

While parents can insert any conditions in their will that aren't considered to be either against public policy or infringing on human rights, state laws differ widely and there's no guarantee of how courts will interpret them. New York State judges . . . have generally held that gifts hinging on an heir's leaving a spouse aren't valid because they act as "an inducement to divorce."

However, provisions requiring an heir to remain married or to adhere to a particular religious faith and marry in that faith are frequently upheld. Clauses that require that a child refrain from certain conduct, such as drinking or drug use, have a spotty record in some states, with courts basing rulings on the specific situation and how the will was structured.

In one case, a will required that a daughter who had separated from her husband remain separated to receive her inheritance. A . . . court upheld the provision, reasoning that it didn't violate public policy because it hadn't acted as an inducement to the separation. But the daughter reconciled with her husband, opting to forfeit the inheritance.

Surprisingly, children often choose not to contest such clauses, either because court costs are prohibitive or because they treat the will as a parent's last wish. But, even if left uncontested, such provisions often backfire in bitterness and discord for the surviving members of a family, estate experts warn.

The moral of the story, says Mr. Shea of Shea & Gould, is "be nice to your parents."

Sample Executor Fees

4% of the first $25,000
3½% of the next $125,000
3% of the next $150,000
2% of everything above $300,000

The executor or executrix is responsible for the management of the property described in the will until disposition of the estate is completed. The executor serves in a **fiduciary capacity** to the beneficiaries of the estate and thus must adhere to high standards of integrity and responsibility in managing the estate's property and carrying out the provisions of the will. The executor must make periodic reports to the probate court and provide a final accounting before closing the estate.

The executor's responsibilities, shown in detail in Figure 16.1, are numerous and may include the following:

1 Assemble and inventory all estate assets
2 Obtain appraisal of all estate assets
3 File federal, state, and local tax returns for the estate
4 Settle all claims against the estate
5 Carry out all instructions in the will
6 Manage estate property
7 Maintain records of all transactions made on behalf of the estate
8 Distribute residual assets to beneficiaries
9 Make final accounting to the court and beneficiaries

Revising a Will

A will can be changed at any time before a person's death. Within a comparatively short time after making a will, you may find that your circumstances have changed substantially enough that the existing will is no longer appropriate. A change in your health or financial condition may necessitate a change in your will. Changes in family situations such as births, deaths, marriages, or divorces may also make it advisable to revise your will. Experience shows that for most people not many years pass without need for changing a will. When the time comes for revising the will, there are two alternatives available.

Codicil. A **codicil** is an addition to an existing will and, as such, does not invalidate the will. It must be executed in the same manner as a will and should be signed and witnessed. A codicil is appropriate if a will needs to be revised in only a minor way. This might be the case if the only change is the change of an executor or the addition of a specific gift.

New Will. If major changes are to be made to the will, a new will is preferable to a codicil. The new will will revoke all previously executed wills and codicils.

Figure 16.1 EXECUTOR'S DUTIES

SOURCE: Estate Research Institute, Vernon Publishing Co., 1979.

A new will should be executed carefully and completely because if it is not accepted by the probate court, a previous will may become operative.

Revoking a Previous Will

You may revoke a will by

1. Making a later will in which you declare that any previous wills are revoked.
2. Making a later will that is totally inconsistent with any previous will
3. Intentionally destroying the will

When you revoke a will and replace it with a new one, you must still have the legal capacity for the new will to be valid.

A Letter of Last Instruction

You may want to leave instructions that are to be carried out after your death but that are not suitable for inclusion in your will. These instructions should be contained in an informal **letter of last instruction.** This letter is not a legal document and thus cannot be used as a substitute for a will. The purpose of such a document is to assist the person administering your estate to do a better job.

A letter of last instruction should be opened at death and may contain some or all of the following information: (1) location of your will, (2) funeral instructions, (3) location of other relevant documents, (4) instructions about a business you may have been operating, (5) an explanation for not giving property to someone who ordinarily would receive it, (6) personal information which would be useful to the executor but which you prefer not to publicize through a will, and (7) recommendations regarding accounting and legal services (the executor is free to select an attorney but often would like to know the deceased's preference).

Safekeeping

You must make sure that your will is readily available. If it cannot be found at the time of your death, the court will rule that you died intestate, even if it knows that you made a will. Accordingly, the safekeeping of your will is of crucial importance. Your lawyer, executor, and/or a close family member should know where your will is kept. In most cases, it is advisable to leave your will with your lawyer so that the probate process can begin immediately after your death.

Probating a Will

After your death, your executor must submit your will to the probate court for **probate**—to be validated as your last will and testament. The court makes sure that the will is authentic and that it carries out your intent as closely as possible.

To begin probate, your executor must petition the court by submitting the document purporting to be your will and requesting a hearing to establish its authenticity. After receiving the petition, the court will notify all interested parties and set a date for the probate hearing. At the hearings, the witnesses to the will supply the necessary proof to satisfy the court that the will is genuine. If one or more of the witnesses is dead or otherwise unavailable, the court may still admit the will to probate assuming, of course, that no other doubts about the will's validity exist.

Probate is a relatively routine procedure to prove the validity of a will and should not be confused with challenges to a particular provision of the will. For example, if your spouse believes that your will is unfair, he or she may decide to **elect against the will.** This type of attack is not necessarily part of the probate process. Rather, the attack is on the will itself and should not delay the probate of the will.

Contesting a Will

Although a will exists at the time of death and is properly submitted to the probate court, someone may still appear to contest the validity of the will. The probate hearing is the first chance for anyone to contest the validity of the will. There are only six legally acceptable grounds for **contesting the will:**

1 The will was not properly executed; for example, it did not have enough witnesses.
2 The testator (person making the will) did not have capacity to make the will.
3 The testator was unduly influenced to make the will.
4 The testator was defrauded or misled into making the will.
5 The will is a forgery.
6 The will was revoked by the testator or by operation of the law.

Sometimes a person may be suspicious of one or more heirs. In this instance the person making the will may include a provision stating that any person who contests the will must forfeit any interest in the estate. If you intentionally omit a close relative as a beneficiary, you might specifically mention the omission in your will to prevent the disinherited individual from contesting the will.

ESTABLISHING TRUSTS

A **trust** is a legal arrangement whereby one party (the **grantor**) transfers property to a second party (the **trustee**) to be managed for the benefit of a third party (the **beneficiary**). The grantor specifies the provisions of the trust such as how income is to be distributed and how property is to be disposed at the trust's termination (all states limit the time that property can be held in trust). The trustee takes legal title to the property in the trust and manages it for the sole benefit of the trust beneficiary.

Types of Trusts

There are two main types of trusts: (1) the living trust and (2) the testamentary trust.

Living Trust. A **living trust,** also known as an **inter vivos trust,** is established during the lifetime of the grantor. It may be either a **revocable living trust,** one that you can change or terminate at any time, or an **irrevocable living trust,** one that you cannot legally change or terminate except in exceptional circumstances. A living trust can be made to expire after a limited time or can last for a considerable time after the death of the grantor.

Testamentary Trust. A **testamentary trust** is created by a deceased's will and can come into existence only after the will has been probated. Because the trust's grantor is deceased, a testamentary trust is always irrevocable.

The Trustee

The trustee can be an individual or a financial institution that has been granted trust powers. Each type of trustee may offer unique advantages to the trust. An individual may be selected because he or she is familiar with the grantor's property and may be aware of special problems or considerations. An institutional trustee (such as a bank), on the other hand, may possess special investment capabilities, will be more impartial and objective than an individual trustee, and will not be incapacitated by death or inability to serve. Because of these different advantages, a grantor may decide to select both an individual and a financial institution to serve as cotrustees. Regardless, a trustee should be trustworthy and capable of effectively managing the trust property in the beneficiary's best interests.

Why Create a Trust?

Trusts are commonly regarded as a device for the rich to protect their property from taxes. Recently, however, more people with moderate incomes are discovering how to use trusts. A trust can be designed to accomplish any of a number of goals. Parents can create a trust to provide for the financial security of children in the event of the parents' death. An older person can use a trust to provide property management during his or her lifetime and to direct property disposition after death. You can even use a trust to control your property after you die. Young families often use trusts to reduce the cost of providing a college education for their children, subject to the restrictions of the Tax Reform Act of 1986. And other people employ trusts to maximize their charitable gifts. Of course, another popular use of a trust is to minimize income and estate taxes.

Without a doubt, trusts have become very popular means of accomplishing various financial, tax, family, and charitable goals. In the next section, several prominent trust arrangements are outlined. The diversity of these special trusts illustrates the wide array of goals that can be pursued through trusts.

Special Kinds of Trusts

Although numerous types of trust exist, not all are commonly used. Among the most common trust plans are the following:

Q-tip trust. Assets passing from one spouse to another are free of estate or gift tax, whatever the amount. By using a so-called Q-tip, or qualified terminable-interest property trust, however, you can keep strings attached.

A Q-tip lets you provide income for your surviving spouse, but upon his or her death the assets can go to whomever you choose. That can let you block the assets from going to someone he or she later marries. It can also be used in a second marriage to provide for your second spouse, but later direct assets to go to children of your first marriage. In a normal marital trust, your spouse can direct the disposition of assets.

Exemption-equivalent trust. Although you can leave all assets to your spouse free of estate tax, that may not be the best idea in a big estate. Doing so can waste the tax exemption for assets left to others and hike the taxable value of your spouse's estate. A husband's will can thus provide that an amount equal to his exemption be put in a trust to pay income to his wife and after her death pass to their children. That way the $600,000 avoids tax in his estate and isn't counted in his wife's.

Sprinkling trust. This trust can be set up to cover a number of children—grandchildren, too—and gives a trustee the power to distribute income, and possibly principal, according to the needs of each child. One beneficiary, for example, might get a larger amount one year because of medical bills and another a larger payment in a different year to get started in a career.

Charitable remainder trust. This can lock in a fixed income to you for life and give you a current income-tax deduction for leaving the trust's assets to charity after you die. The annual income, fixed as a percentage of your donation, also can go to a survivor, such as your spouse, before the charity gets the assets. In one variation, tax-exempt bonds may provide extra kick. Take a 70-year-old who donates $100,000 in municipal bonds that pay 10 percent a year in interest. The donor gets $10,000 tax-free annually plus a current tax deduction, based on government tables, of $37,000 for the future charitable gift.

One strategy can hike your current return from an asset. Someone who holds property not yielding income, such as a piece of undeveloped land, can give it to a charity, which can then sell it and reinvest the cash in income earning assets that may grow in value. If all works out, the donor gets rising income from the charity and an income-tax deduction for a percentage of the gift—and also can escape capital-gains tax on the property given away.

Charitable lead trust. Unlike a remainder trust, a lead trust provides a charity with income over a number of years, but the principal then goes to the donor's heirs. Though there is no income-tax deduction, you can save on family gift and estate taxes. In a variation, you may regain the assets before

Box 16.2 WHO SHOULD YOU NAME AS TRUSTEE?

A well-designed trust agreement can accomplish just about anything you want, whether it's an *inter vivos* arrangement that will take effect while you're still alive or a testamentary trust designed to take effect after your death. But no matter how carefully the document is written, it takes people to make it work. Choosing a trustee, someone who will be responsible for seeing that the terms of your trust are carried out, is among the most important steps in the process of setting up a trust of any kind.

By law, a trustee has a duty to use a high degree of care and good faith in handling the trust. If this fiduciary duty is violated, the beneficiaries can go to court for help.

Before you're ready to consider possible candidates for the job, you have to decide exactly what you expect your trustee to do.

Do you want someone to just disburse income earned by the trust's assets to your beneficiaries? Will the person you choose be expected to manage assets as well? Do you need someone who can help guide your children or who will conduct financial supervision for someone unable to manage his or her own money? Choose your trustee on the basis of his or her ability to perform the job. You have several possible sources.

Friends and family members are one immediate source, since you already know about the character, compassion and integrity of people close to you. But don't make those traits your only criteria. Look also for someone who has dependable skills at mon-

10 years, in which case you get a current income-tax deduction but are taxed on the trust earnings.

Life-insurance trust. The only asset in this plan is an insurance policy on your life. When you die, the insurance goes to the trust, and if certain rules are met the funds aren't tallied in your estate.[2]

[2] Copyright, 1985, *U.S. News & World Report*. Reprinted from issue of January 21, 1985.

ey management, recordkeeping and general administration. Trustees may be required to post bonds unless the trust specifically states otherwise.

Attorneys, another obvious choice, are fine if you can find one who fills the bill. However, you might think twice about using the same one who did the estate plan. There's nothing unethical or illegal about an estate attorney serving as trustee. But Howard Zaritsky, adjunct professor at Georgetown University Law Center, cautions, "If the lawyer who makes up your trust instrument promotes himself for the job, drop him immediately."

Attorneys are not the only professionals who can serve as trustees. Accountants, financial planners and others can serve, too. Look for competence at the best price. Explore fee arrangements. And get the best fee arrangement in writing.

Also consider banks and trust companies. These institutions are staffed to do the tax accounting and other required paperwork. In many cases efficient management in these areas can offset the fees involved. . . . Shop around for the best arrangements at financial institutions in your area. Talk to trust officers and explain your trust needs. Ask to see how comparable trusts are being handled. Although they're obliged to maintain their clients' confidentiality, banks will often block off names from the account records and let you see portfolios.

If you want your trust handled in a more aggressive manner, have specific directions spelled out in the instrument or name a cotrustee. A common arrangement is to name an individual (usually a family member or a close friend) as cotrustee to manage specific investments and disbursements, while also naming an institution to handle routine investments, accounting, tax reporting and other paperwork matters.

If you plan to appoint an individual as either a trustee or cotrustee, it's a good idea to name a backup at the same time who can take over in case your primary choice dies or is unavailable for any other reason.

Be careful to avoid possible conflicts of interest. For example, someone who might later benefit from the trust could be reluctant to disburse funds that otherwise would eventually come to him or her. Another example: Appointing the broker who handles the family's investments to manage the trust's securities puts both the broker and the beneficiaries in a potentially difficult situation because the broker stands to profit from trading stocks. If he or she trades the stocks heavily, an accusation could arise that he or she is churning the account to earn extra commissions. If the broker trades very little, he or she may be accused of missing opportunities to enhance the trust's assets.

Your trustee selections have to be reviewed from time to time to take account of personal and financial changes. Your trustee may become infirm or move to another city. Your assets may reach a point where you need a professional cotrustee to help manage them. Or your relationship with the trustee might deteriorate.

To control legal costs, try to make any necessary changes at the same time you update other terms of your estate plan.

SOURCE: Reprinted with permission from *Changing Times* magazine, © 1985. Kiplinger Washington Editors, Inc., 1729 H Street, Northwest, Washington, D.C. 20006. This reprint is not to be altered in any way, except with permission from *Changing Times.*

AN OVERVIEW OF GIFT AND ESTATE TAXES

There are only two ways that you can legally transfer your assets to those you choose without formally receiving payment or property in exchange. The first method is through a lifetime gift and the second way is through your estate (via the instructions in your will, if you have one) at the time of your death. Recognizing that you can transfer property only in these two ways, the federal government devised a joint gift and estate tax schedule that imposes the same tax rate on both types of transfers. The intention of this schedule is to prevent an individual from avoiding taxation on one type of transfer by making the other kind of transfer. Before 1977, for example, gift taxes were imposed at only three-quarters of the estate tax rate and were computed separately from estate taxes. As a result, overall tax savings could be achieved in many instances by making gifts instead of waiting to have property transfer at the time of death, thus invoking the more expensive estate tax. Although lifetime gifts and estate transfers at death are now taxed at the same rate, there may still be some advantages to making lifetime gifts because of the limited annual exemption from taxation accorded to gifts.

GIFTS

One of the most common methods of transferring your assets to another person is by making a gift during your lifetime.

Why Make a Gift?

You may find one or more of the following to be a motivating tax-related reason(s) for making a lifetime gift.

Annual Exclusion. Any person can give to any number of individuals up to $10,000 per year without causing a gift tax obligation. Thus a person with five children can give each child $10,000 in a single year (a total of $50,000) entirely tax-free. And if the giver is married, the spouse can also make a tax-free $10,000 gift to each child. As a result, in this instance up to $100,000 of gifts are exempt from taxes. Further, because the $10,000 is an **annual exclusion,** the same gifting process can be repeated each year without invoking any gift tax obligations.

Gift Splitting. A married person can make a gift and, with the consent of his or her spouse, can elect to treat the gift as if it were made equally by each spouse. This option provides that a husband, for example, can give $20,000 to his child and, as long as the wife consents, view his gift as only $10,000 with the other $10,000 coming from his wife. Such **gift splitting** entirely exempts the gift from gift taxes because each spouse is entitled to a $10,000 annual exclusion. This tax reduction option applies even if one spouse makes all the gifts and the other spouse gives nothing.

Reducing Estate Taxes. Once property is given to another person, it no longer is included in the estate of the person who made the gifts. As a result, when the giver eventually dies, his or her estate tax liability will be less. For instance, if you give $10,000 each year to your only child, then you will have removed $50,000 from your estate after five years. Of course, these gifts fall within the $10,000 annual exclusion and thus are tax-free. If you had not made the gifts, the $50,000 would still be in your estate and subject to estate taxes when you die.

Appreciation in Value. Another way to reduce estate taxes is by giving property that is likely to appreciate in value. Suppose you give your child an attractive parcel of real estate valued at $10,000—a tax-free gift. If after five years the property has doubled in value to $20,000, you will have effectively removed $20,000 from your estate, thereby reducing potential estate taxes even further. If the gift were not made, then at your death the full fair market value of the property would be included in your estate—an occurrence that could substantially increase estate taxes.

College Fund. Until 1987, one of the most popular reasons for gifting was to provide for a college fund for children. By making a gift to a minor under the Uniform Gifts to Minors Act, you could transfer assets to an individual with a lower income tax bracket. The income earned on those assets would be taxed at the child's lower rate. Now, however, income over $1000 from assets given to the child will be taxed at the parent's rate until the child attains 14 years of age. From age 14 on, all income from those gifted assets will be taxed at the child's rate. Therefore, although the new tax law severely limited this gifting advantage, it still remains usable for older children. If properly structured, gifts can help reduce the cost of your child's college education.

Gift Taxes

The first federal **gift tax** was imposed in 1924. Since then, it has undergone numerous revisions, the most recent being in 1981. Gift taxes differ considerably from the more familiar annual income taxes. An understanding of the tax implications of a gift can enable you to enhance the value of your estate through favorable tax treatment.

Unified Tax Rate. Recent tax legislation brought together gift and estate taxes. Both of these taxes are imposed on the transfer of assets. A gift tax is imposed on lifetime gifts and an estate tax is imposed on a transfer at death. Both types of transfers are considered cumulatively and are subjected to the same progressive tax rate schedule. This **unified tax rate schedule** is shown in Table 16.1.

What Property Is Subject to the Gift Tax?

Virtually any transfer of property can invoke a gift tax. Obviously cash gifts are subject to the gift tax, as are gifts of both personal and real property. For example, a single parent's gift of a new $15,000 automobile to a child creates a gift tax liability. Indirect gifts also cause a potential tax liability. In the past, interest-free loans were a popular way to transfer assets tax-free. In such cases, a lender

Table 16.1 UNIFIED ESTATE AND GIFT TAX RATE SCHEDULE

TAXABLE ESTATE OR GIFT		ESTATE OR GIFT TAX[a]		
From	To	Tax is	Plus	Of amount over
$ 0	$ 10,000	$ 0	18%	$ 0
10,000	20,000	1,800	20	10,000
20,000	40,000	3,800	22	20,000
40,000	60,000	8,200	24	40,000
60,000	80,000	13,000	26	60,000
80,000	100,000	18,200	28	80,000
100,000	150,000	23,800	30	100,000
150,000	250,000	38,800	32	150,000
250,000	500,000	70,800	34	250,000
500,000	750,000	155,800	37	500,000
750,000	1,000,000	248,300	39	750,000
1,000,000	1,250,000	345,800	41	1,000,000
1,250,000	1,500,000	448,300	43	1,250,000
1,500,000	2,000,000	555,800	45	1,500,000
2,000,000	2,500,000	780,000	49	2,000,000
over 2,500,000		1,290,800	50	2,500,000

[a] The amount of estate or gift tax payable before subtracting any allowable credits.

would lend funds to another individual and charge no interest. The borrower, of course, could invest these funds at a competitive interest rate and then keep the interest income. As a result, these interest earnings could be effectively transferred from one individual to another, completely free of gift taxes. Now, however, a gift tax is imposed on the amount of interest that the lender could have earned on the loaned funds.

The timing of a gift is important because it determines when the gift tax, if any, is due. A gift becomes effective upon the occurrence of two events: (1) the person making the gift gives up the power to reclaim the property and (2) the giver forfeits the right to alter the manner in which the recipient uses or enjoys the gift. For example, if a parent buys a savings bond for a child and jointly registers the bond in his or her name along with the child, no gift has occurred. The reason is because the parent can still redeem the bond and retrieve the property. Only when the child (or if a minor, the child's custodian) redeems the bond will the gift become effective. For gift tax purposes, therefore, a gift is not taxable until it is effective.

Who Pays Gift Taxes?

The donor is liable for any gift taxes due on a gift. The recipient receives the property tax-free. Therefore, a gift may be more expensive to the donor than it appears. If a donor gives more than $10,000 to a person in a particular year, a gift tax results. The donor is obligated to pay the taxes in addition to the amount given. For example, suppose you gave $20,000 this year to your only child. The initial $10,000 of this gift would be tax-exempt, but the next $10,000 would be subject to a gift tax. As shown in Table 16.1, the gift tax payable on this gift would be $1800.

Loss of Control over Property

A gift is irrevocable. This means that once you make a gift, you completely forfeit control over the transferred property. Furthermore, the person receiving the gift may use the property in any way he or she desires. After you make a gift to someone, he or she may spend it in a manner you consider reckless, but there is nothing you can do about it. Thus, you should always consider the maturity and responsibility of a potential recipient before making an outright gift.

There are several kinds of special gift arrangements, including gifts to minors, marital gifts, and charitable gifts.

Gifts to Minors. You may make outright gifts to minors. For example, U.S. savings bonds may be purchased for and redeemed by minors. But difficulties may arise when other property is given to minors. Brokers are reluctant to deal in securities owned by a minor because in certain instances the minor can later back out of a transaction. A minor's signature on a real estate deal gives the buyer no assurance of permanent title. To avoid these problems, each state has passed a **Uniform Gift to Minors Act.** These acts allow an adult custodian to hold title to the minor's property. The custodian can legally transact business on the minor's behalf. When the minor attains majority, the property automatically transfers to the new adult.

Marital Gifts. A gift from one spouse to another is exempt from federal gift taxes. Therefore, an individual making a gift to his or her spouse would avoid federal gift taxes regardless of the amount or type of assets given.

Charitable Gifts. No gift tax is imposed on gifts from an individual to a qualified charity. You can give any amount of your assets to charity without invoking a gift tax liability. Further, you can claim a **charitable deduction** for income tax purposes for many charitable gifts.

Calculating Gift Taxes

Gift tax calculations are relatively simple and straightforward. The following example illustrates the manner in which gift taxes are calculated.

Betty Brown has two grandchildren: David, age 5, and Pamela, age 2. Betty gave $18,000 to a custodian for each child under the Uniform Gift to Minors Act.

Betty can exclude the first $10,000 of the gift to each child—a total exclusion of $20,000. The remaining $16,000 of gifts ($8,000 to each grandchild) is taxed as follows (see Table 16.1):

Gift tax = $1,800 plus 20% of the amount over $10,000
= $1,800 plus 20% × $6,000
= $3,000

Thus the total gift tax is $3,000. Actually, an individual has a $192,800 lifetime gift/estate tax unified credit and could apply $3,000 of this credit to eliminate this gift tax liability. Because this is a one-time credit amount to be applied to either gift or estate taxes, however, once any portion of the credit is used, it is no longer available for use to apply against future gift or estate taxes. Therefore, if Betty uses $3,000 of this credit to offset the current gift tax, then total credits available to offset future gift/estate taxes will be reduced by that same amount.

You already may have noticed that Betty did not take full advantage of her *annual* gift tax exclusions. Instead of making all gifts in one year, Betty could have spread the gifts over two years. By giving $10,000 to each child in one year and another $8,000 per child in the next year, Betty would not exceed her annual $10,000 gift exclusion per donee. This strategy would allow the same amount ($18,000) to be given to each child. Because the gifts are spread over two separate years, however, no gift tax would be due. Therefore, Betty would either reap a $3,000 gift tax savings or preserve $3,000 of her unified tax credit to eliminate future gift or estate taxes.

ESTATE TAXES

The **estate tax** is levied on all property in an estate at the time of the owner's death. The tax applies to the fair market value of the property or interests in property owned by the deceased. Certain deductions and credits, however, can be used to reduce estate tax liabilities. Deductions are allowed for property passed directly to a surviving spouse (the **marital deduction**), charitable gifts, and funeral and administrative expenses. A deduction reduces the amount of the estate that is subject to estate taxes. The higher an estate's tax bracket, the more valuable a deduction is.

Credits are given for state and foreign death taxes paid and taxes paid on prior transfers (gifts). A credit offsets dollar for dollar the estate tax liability and thus is more valuable than a deduction. Beginning in 1987, a unified tax credit of $192,800 is available to all estates (assuming, of course, that none of this unified credit had been used to offset lifetime gift taxes). At current estate tax rates, this credit is sufficient to offset the taxes on the first $600,000 of estate property value, determined as follows (see Table 16.1):

Estate tax on $600,000 = $155,800 plus 37% of amount over $500,000
= $155,800 plus 37% times $100,000
= $192,800

Estate planners estimate that due to the generous amount of this credit, over 95 percent of estates will not owe federal estate taxes.

There are five basic steps involved in the computation of the amount of estate taxes payable:

Step 1: The total value of the **gross estate** is reduced by any debts in the estate and by the amount of funeral and administrative expenses. The resulting amount is the *adjusted gross estate.*

Step 2: The adjusted gross estate is reduced by the amount of applicable deductions and exclusions to arrive at the **taxable estate.**

Step 3: The amount of previously taxed lifetime gifts (that is, the total amount of gifts made exceeding the annual $10,000 exclusions) made by the deceased is added to the taxable estate to obtain the *tentative tax base.*

Step 4: The *tentative estate tax* (that is, the tax owed *before* allowing for gift tax and death tax credits) is computed using the Unified Estate and Gift Tax Schedule (see Table 16.1).

Step 5: The **net estate tax payable** is determined by subtracting out various credits.

By following these five basic steps, you can calculate the net estate tax due for an estate. In the following section, we provide an estate tax computation example to illustrate the mechanics of this process.

Calculating Federal Estate Taxes: An Example

Charles R. Green died in 1988, after a lengthy illness, leaving a gross estate valued at $2 million. In his will, Charles directed that $1 million go to his surviving spouse, $100,000 to various charities, and the remainder (after the payment of debts, taxes, and expenses) to be divided evenly between his two children.

Other pertinent information about Charles and his estate includes the following:

1 Funeral expenses totaled $10,000.
2 Administrative (legal and executor) expenses amounted to $40,000.
3 At the time of his death, Charles owed $50,000 to the ABC State Bank.
4 Charles's income tax liability for 1988 amounted to $20,000.
5 Although Charles made several lifetime gifts to his children, no gift to a child exceeded the $10,000 tax-exempt amount in a single year.
6 State death taxes equal $12,200.

Following the five basic steps presented for tax calculation, we find that Charles's net federal estate tax payable amounts to $55,000. We show these estate tax calculations in Table 16.2 and explain these computations in the following section.

Table 16.2 CALCULATING THE NET FEDERAL ESTATE TAX: CHARLES R. GREEN EXAMPLE

Step	Action	Item	Amount	Total
1		*Gross Estate*		$2,000,000
	minus	1. funeral expenses	$ 10,000	
		2. administrative expenses	40,000	
		3. loan payable	50,000	
		4. income taxes payable	20,000	
		5. losses	None	
	equals	Adjusted gross estate		$1,880,000
2		*Adjusted Gross Estate*		$1,880,000
	minus	1. marital deduction	$1,000,000	
		2. charitable deduction	100,000	
	equals	Taxable estate		$ 780,000
3		*Taxable Estate Base*		$ 780,000
	add	Adjusted taxable gifts	None	
	equals	Tentative tax base		$ 780,000
4		*Tentative Estate Base*		$ 780,000
	compute	Tentative estate tax	$ 260,000[a]	
	minus	Gift taxes payable on post-1976 gifts	None	
	equals	Estate tax before credits	$ 260,000	
1		*Estate Tax Before Credits*	$ 260,000	
	minus	1. Unified credit	192,800	
		2. State death tax credit	12,200	
		3. Credit for foreign death taxes	None	
		4. Credit for tax on prior transfers	None	
	equals	Net federal estate tax payable		$ 55,000

[a] See the unified tax rate schedule presented in Table 16.1. The calculation for the tentative estate tax is made as follows: $248,300 + 0.39($780,000 − $750,000) = $248,300 + 0.39($30,000) = $248,300 + $11,700 = $260,000.

Explanation of Estate Tax Calculations

We calculate the amount of estate taxes payable by the estate of Charles R. Green using the five basic steps previously described. Table 16.2 contains a summary of these calculations.

Step 1: The $2 million total estate value is reduced by funeral expenses ($10,000), administrative expenses ($40,000), and debts, which include notes payable ($50,000) and income taxes payable ($20,000). The resulting adjusted gross estate equals $1,880,000.

Step 2: The adjusted gross estate is reduced by applicable deductions and exclusions, which in this case include the marital deduction ($1 million) and a charitable deduction ($100,000), to arrive at the taxable estate of $780,000.

Step 3: Because Charles did not make any taxable lifetime gifts, the taxable estate is not increased to obtain the tax base. Therefore, the tentative tax base equals $780,000.

Step 4: The tentative estate tax on the $780,000 tentative tax base using the unified estate and gift tax schedule in Table 16.1 is calculated as follows:

$248,300 plus 39% of the amount over $750,000
= $248,300 plus 39% times $30,000
= $260,000

Note that in this example, there are no gift taxes payable so the tentative estate tax is equal to the estate tax before credits.

Step 5: Charles did not use any of his unified estate/gift tax credit during his lifetime, and therefore the entire $192,800 of his one-time unified credit is intact. Also, the $12,200 of state death taxes paid by the estate can be used as a credit to be applied against federal estate taxes. After deducting these combined credits totaling $205,000 from the tentative estate tax of $260,000, the resulting net federal estate tax for the estate of Charles R. Green is $55,000. This amount must be paid to the federal government at the time the estate tax return is filed.

State Death Taxes

Many people carefully plan for federal estate taxes but ignore the consequences of state **death taxes.** Thirty states collect death taxes independently of the federal government, a few of them on estates as small as $100. Further, state death taxes vary significantly. For example, if a Massachusetts resident died leaving a $400,000 estate to his child, the child would owe $32,000 in state inheritance tax even though there would be no federal estate tax liability. If the parent lived in Florida, no state death tax would be due.

There is a much higher likelihood that you will owe state death taxes than federal estate taxes. The reasons for this include the following:

1 Certain deductions (such as the marital deduction) are allowed at the federal, but not the state, level.
2 Certain assets (such as death benefits under qualified corporate retirement plans) are exempted for federal, but not state, death tax purposes.
3 The federal estate tax unified credit exceeds the tax credit available, if any, from most states.

Box 16.3 EASING THE ESTATE-TAX BITE

Now that you have taken care of last year's taxes, it's a good time to think about a future matter—your estate.

The good news is that the threshold at which estates become subject to federal tax is rising. This year, those with a value of up to $500,000 escape taxation, up from $400,000 last year and just $175,625 in 1981. Next year, the exclusion tops out at $600,000. Amounts over the ceiling are taxed at rates of 37 to 55 percent, with the top rate set to drop to 50 percent in 1988.

Although the dollar thresholds may seem high, many are surprised at how big their estates are when the values of a home, life insurance and other assets are totaled.

Here are some suggestions from estate-planning experts on things to keep in mind.

Bequests to a Spouse

You can leave any amount to your spouse, and it won't be hit by the estate tax. In a big estate, however, that tack may mean that you get no benefit from the estate-tax exclusion. Moreover, all assets will be lumped in your spouse's estate, leading to a possibly bigger tax bite when he or she dies. One way you can use the exemption is to leave an amount equal to it—$500,000 this year—to your children, thus sheltering the funds from estate tax. The rest then can go to your spouse—also free of tax. To give your spouse the benefit of the assets left to your children, you can leave the money to them in an exemption-equivalent trust. That lets your spouse get lifetime income from the assets, with the principal going to the children later on.

Gifts

One way to trim the value of your estate is to make gifts while you are alive. You can give up to $10,000 a year to any number of recipients and not be subject to gift tax. You and your spouse can jointly give $20,000 to each recipient.' If the gift is a check, the Internal Revenue Service says it must be cashed and cleared by your bank in the year it is given in order to count against that year's exclusion. Though some courts have overruled the IRS on this, "it's

A state may impose either an estate tax or an inheritance tax but not both. A state *estate tax* is imposed on the net value of the property included in your estate when you die. An **inheritance tax,** which is the most common type of state death tax, is assessed on each beneficiary's share of your estate assets. Inheritance tax rates usually depend on the relationship of the beneficiary to the deceased. In most states, lower rates are charged to those beneficiaries most closely related to the deceased.

If you spend time in two or more states, you can provide savings for your beneficiaries by clearly establishing residency in only one state. Otherwise, two or more states may assess death taxes on your estate. This is especially true of intangible personal property such as stock, bonds, mortgages, and notes, which generally are taxed only by the state where the deceased resided at the time of death. Unfortunately, if the deceased did not clearly establish his or her state of residency, two or more states may impose taxes on these properties. While tests of residency vary, most states may consider you a resident if you vote, do your banking, obtain your driver's license, register your automobile, and maintain your primary residence there.

safest not to wait until the last minute," advised Philip Temple, a New York lawyer.

Family Businesses

The family of a deceased owner of a closely held firm often is hard pressed to pay the estate tax. One way to prevent a fire sale of the family firm is to defer the payment. If conditions involving matters such as the extent of family ownership are met, you can spread the payment over 14 years. Interest on at least part of the unpaid tax will be just 4 percent, and payments of principal don't have to begin until the fifth year, with only interest payable until then.

One rule for deferral is that the firm's stock held in the estate must exceed 35 percent of the total value of the estate. It may be wise to reduce the value of an estate beforehand by giving away assets other than the stock so the percentage test can be met, note tax experts at Panel Publishers, an advisory service for small businesses.

Life Insurance

The payoff from insurance on your life is generally included in your estate. To avoid tax on the payment, you can set up a trust to own the policy, with the proceeds going to your beneficiaries. You may, though, incur gift tax in this arrangement.

Warning: If you die within three years of transferring an existing policy to the trust, the payout will be included in your estate. To protect against that, you could buy a new policy for the trust and let the existing policy lapse, says New York accountant Edward Mendlowitz.

Trusts

Even if estate tax is not an immediate factor, trusts can be useful. In a qualified terminable-interest property—or Q-tip—trust, you can leave assets to your spouse but direct who receives them after his or her death. In a sprinkling trust, you can give a trustee the power to distribute cash according to the varying needs of each of your children.

SPECIAL ESTATE-PLANNING TECHNIQUES

The fact that most estates escape federal estate taxes lulls many people into the notion that estate planning is unnecessary. Nothing could be further from the truth. All too often the inclusion of an inheritance, life insurance proceeds, or the fair market value of a residence can balloon the value of an estate to a substantial amount. Without proper tax planning, you run the risk that your estate tax liability will be much larger than necessary. Further, even if your estate escapes estate taxes, your neglect to plan can still cause your property to be taxed unnecessarily in the future as it passes successively to your spouse, from your spouse to your child, and later on to your grandchild.

Minimizing Estate Taxes

Our federal tax code, although complex, does not require you to pay more taxes than the minimum amount for which you are legally liable. As Judge Learned Hand once stated: "Anyone may so arrange his affairs that taxes shall be as low as possible; he is not bound to choose that pattern which will best pay the treasury; it is not even a patriotic duty to increase one's taxes."

Only you can make sure that you pay no more than that minimum amount. Without a properly designed estate plan, you are virtually assured of subjecting your assets to higher taxes than necessary. Several estate tax reduction techniques are available, but only if you act to take advantage of them. Among these techniques are the following.

The Marital Deduction. The Economic Recovery Tax Act of 1981 permits an unlimited marital deduction for property passing outright tax-free. Therefore, any property willed to your spouse is exempt from federal estate taxes.

Dividing Property. Each person has a lifetime gift and estate tax credit sufficient to exempt $600,000 of assets from estate taxes (assuming none of the credit was used to offset gift taxes). Therefore, a husband and wife combined can pass $1.2 million of assets to their heirs without invoking an estate tax. By spreading family assets among several owners, no single family member accumulates such a sizable estate as to incur significant estate taxes.

Trusts. A properly designed trust can be used to postpone property distribution by as much as an entire generation. This delay can eliminate a second estate tax bite on the assets you leave at your death.

Life Insurance. If the proceeds from your life insurance policy are paid to your estate, they are subject to estate taxes. On the other hand, if you transfer ownership in the policy to someone other than yourself and make the policy payable to someone other than your estate or your executor, then the proceeds will not be taxable to your estate. You must make sure that at the time of your death you are not the owner of one or more incidents of ownership in the policy. *Incidents of ownership* include the power to change the beneficiary, to assign the policy, to borrow against it, to surrender it for cash, or to exercise any other contract right or privilege pertaining to the policy.

Gifts. If the gift is $10,000 or less per donee per year, you incur no gift tax liability. One caveat: Some gifts made in the three years immediately preceding your death may be deemed to have been made in contemplation of death and will be included in your gross estate for estate tax computations.

Flower Bonds. Certain U.S. Treasury bonds, called **flower bonds,** can be tendered at face amount in payment for federal estate taxes. Because these bonds can be purchased at less than face value, they offer the opportunity to discount the net estate tax payable. Although no longer issued by the Treasury, these bonds can still be purchased through your bank or stockbroker.

Stepped-up Basis. The property your beneficiaries receive from your estate does not assume your original cost basis. Rather, the property's new cost basis is the market value of the property at the time you die. Although this **stepped-up basis** does not lead to estate tax savings, it may produce sizable income tax savings when your beneficiaries sell the property. These tax savings may be especially large if your cost basis was very low compared to the value of the property at the time of your death.

SUMMARY

Only through proper estate planning can you be assured that your financial and personal goals will be fulfilled. The neglect of this important process can lead to unexpected hardships for your heirs when you die. Estate planning is a continuous process involving six interactive steps: (1) establishing objectives, (2) taking inventory, (3) identifying liabilities, (4) selecting proper estate-planning tools, (5) implementing the estate plan, and (6) periodically reviewing and revising the estate plan.

At the foundation of your estate plan is your will. A will allows you to direct your final property distribution. To die without a will means that your property will be dispersed according to state law, often in an undesired way. Because of its extreme importance, your will should be carefully worded, flexible enough to respond to changes in financial or personal situations, and reviewed periodically to ensure that your wishes continue to be satisfied. You can accommodate a change in your circumstances either by making a new will (thus automatically revoking all previous wills) or by executing a codicil to amend the existing will. A will can be made by any person having proper legal capacity, that is, of proper age, of sound mind, and free from undue influence.

You can establish a trust by transferring property to a second party (the trustee) to be managed for the benefit of a third party (the beneficiary). A trust may be living (inter vivos) or testamentary and may be established for any number of reasons. Most often, however, trusts are created for one or more of the following reasons: (1) to obtain tax advantages, (2) to receive professional asset management, and (3) to preserve trust property. Trusts are complex legal instruments, so you should seek the help of competent legal counsel if you want to create a trust.

The federal government imposes a gift tax on some lifetime property transfers and an estate tax on certain property transfers at the time of death. Both of these taxes are assessed on a graduated basis using the same unified tax rate schedule. The judicious use of deductions and credits often can significantly reduce the amount of taxes due. All states also impose death taxes, although these taxes usually can be used as a credit against federal estate taxes. Proper estate planning can often result in considerable gift and death tax savings.

KEY TERMS

- ambulatory
- annual exclusion
- attested will
- beneficiary
- charitable deduction
- charitable lead trust
- charitable remainder trust
- codicil
- contesting the will
- credits
- death taxes
- elect against the will
- estate
- estate planning
- estate tax
- estate tax deduction
- executor (executrix)
- exemption-equivalent trust
- fiduciary capacity
- flower bonds
- gift splitting
- gift tax
- grantor
- gross estate
- holographic will
- inheritance tax
- intestate
- irrevocable living trust
- letter of last instruction
- life insurance trust
- living (inter vivos) trust
- marital deduction
- net estate tax payable
- nuncupative will
- power to appoint
- probate
- probate estate
- Q-tip trust
- revocable living trust
- sprinkling trust
- stepped-up basis
- taxable estate
- testamentary trust
- testator (testatrix)
- trust
- trustee
- unified tax rate schedule
- Uniform Gift to Minors Act
- will

SELECTED READINGS

Gamble, Richard H. "Estate Planning for the Unmarried Person." *Trusts & Estates,* April 1986, pp. 25–28.

"Gifts That Give Back." *Changing Times,* June 1986, pp. 81–86.

McNatt, Robert. "When Someone Close Dies." *Money,* August 1986, pp. 101–108.

"Smart Ways to Plan Your Estate." *U.S. News & World Report,* June 2, 1986, pp. 46–47.

"Take Care of Your Heirs." *Changing Times,* September 1986, pp. 32–38.

Topolknicki, Denise M. "Trimming Your State Tax Man's Take." *Money,* June 1985, pp. 149–154.

QUESTIONS

1 What is estate planning, and why is it important?

2 List and briefly describe the six steps of the estate-planning process.

3 Why is it important to make an inventory of your estate? Identify what property comprises an estate.
4 Identify and explain reasons that might require a change in an estate plan.
5 What is a will? Should everyone have a will? Explain.
6 Identify the three requirements that all states impose for a person to make a valid will.
7 Compare and contrast the three types of wills. Which type of will is most appropriate for most people? Explain.
8 What is an executor or executrix? Why is it important for an executor or executrix to be selected in a will?
9 Explain the two ways in which the provisions of a will can be changed.
10 What is the purpose of probating a will? Can a will be contested after it has been probated? Explain.
11 What is a trust? How do living trusts and testamentary trusts differ? Distinguish between a revocable and an irrevocable living trust.
12 Describe the role of a trustee. Explain how a trustee is selected.
13 What is a gift? Describe reasons for which one person might make a gift to another person.
14 Answer the following questions as they pertain to federal gift taxes: (a) What property is subject to gift taxes? (b) When is a gift effective? (c) Who pays gift taxes?
15 Describe the basic steps involved in the computation of the amount of estate taxes payable.
16 Explain the difference between an estate tax and an inheritance tax.
17 Identify and explain techniques available to reduce estate taxes.
18 Larry Glazer makes a $40,000 gift to his son in 1988. After allowing for a $10,000 exclusion, compute the tax on this gift using Table 16.1.
19 In problem 18, if the gift were made by Mr. and Mrs. Glazer (gift splitting), how much would the tax on the gift be?
20 Compute the tax on a total estate (or gift) of the following values using Table 16.1.
   a $375,000
   b $618,000
   c $2,450,000

CASE PROBLEMS

16.1 Warren and Lisa Todd have decided to give $60,000 to each of their three children. The children are between ages 14 and 17. They believe the advantages of these gifts are twofold: (1) to start a fund to provide for their children's college educations and (2) to remove assets from their estates and thus to reduce the potential estate tax liabilities.

The Todds plan to give all or part of these amounts to their children at the end of the year. They are considering the following four alternatives:

1 Warren would give each child $60,000 in the current year.
2 Warren would give each child $30,000 this year and another $30,000 next year.
3 Warren would give each child $30,000 this year and Lisa would also give each child $30,000 this year.
4 Warren would give each child $15,000 this year and another $15,000 early next year. Lisa would give each child the identical amounts at the same time.

a After considering the $10,000 annual exclusion rules and the gift-splitting rules for husbands and wives, determine how much of the total gift will be taxable under each alternative. That is, determine the amount of the gift that is taxable each year and add up the total. You do not need to compute the actual tax.
b Which of the above gifting alternatives should the Todds use? Why?
c Can you recommend a gifting arrangement through which Warren and Lisa can give each of their children $60,000 without incurring any gift taxes?

16.2 June Collier, a 55-year-old widow with two grown children, recently met with her attorney to obtain estate-planning advice. The attorney recommended that June prepare a hypothetical estate tax analysis to determine how much estate taxes her estate would owe if she died today. June approved of this advice, and in preparation for this task accumulated the following information.

June estimates the fair market value of her gross estate at $1.4 million. Her only liabilities are the $75,000 outstanding balance on the mortgage loan on her home and an $8,000 automobile loan. Administrative expenses on an estate of this size are estimated at 2 percent of the gross estate. Funeral expenses would cost an estimated $10,000. June's tax accountant estimates income taxes on this year's income to date would be $16,000.

June's will directs that a charitable contribution of $200,000 go to her alma mater, Old Ivy University. The remainder of her estate (after the payment of expenses and taxes) is to be distributed equally between her two children. Using Table 16.2 as a guideline, answer each of the following questions:

a Calculate the value of June's adjusted gross estate, assuming she died today.
b Determine June's taxable estate.
c Because the taxable estate is equal to the tentative tax base (there are no gifts), use the value computed in part b to determine the tentative estate tax. That is, apply the tax rates in Table 16.1 to the answer in part b to determine the tentative estate tax.
d Subtract out the unified tax credit of $192,800, which is available on all estates, from the answer in part c to determine the net federal estate tax payable. Ignore other credits in the process.
e How much will each of her children receive? Subtract the answer in part d from the answer in part b and divide by 2.

Glossary

accidental death benefit (ADB) (10) Level term life insurance coverage that pays only if death is caused by an accident. Usually sold as a rider on another life insurance policy. Also called double indemnity.

account reconciliation (4) A procedure in which you verify that the dollar balance that the bank reports to you is the same as the amount you show in your checkbook ledger.

accumulation period (10, 15) The period of time over which a person buying an annuity pays premiums.

actual cash value (8) A measure of insured property value, usually equal to replacement cost minus depreciation.

add-on method (5) A method to determine finance charges in which the total finance charges are calculated by multiplying the original loan balance by the stated interest rate. The finance charges are added to the principal amount, and the total is divided by the number of payments to be made to obtain the amount of the monthly payment.

adjustable life insurance (10) Life insurance that lets you change the face amount, the premium, and the type of plan without evidence of insurability.

adjustable-rate mortgage (ARM) (6) A loan in which the interest rate goes up or down based on an index to which the loan is pegged. Accordingly, the amount of the monthly mortgage payment fluctuates in direct proportion to the interest rate.

adjusted gross income (3) Gross income minus certain specified deductions such as IRA contributions or alimony payments.

adjuster (8) A representative who helps settle insurance claims. Most represent an insurance company, and some may be hired to represent you.

aggregate annual deductible (9) A type of deductible commonly used in major and comprehensive medical expense policies, allowing you to count all covered medical expenses during the plan year to satisfy the deductible.

ambulatory (16) Adjective used to describe the state of a will until the death of the will writer.

American College (2) A certifying organization for financial planners. The American College is located in Bryn Mawr, Pennsylvania.

American Stock Exchange (12) The second largest organized exchange. The number of firms is approximately half that of the New York Stock Exchange, and the listing requirements are generally less. The American Stock Exchange is composed of smaller, more aggressive firms.

annual exclusion (16) The amount (currently $10,000) that any person can give to any number of donees without causing a gift tax obligation.

annual percentage rate (APR) (5, 7) The true rate of interest on a loan. It is the percentage rate of interest the borrower pays on the average loan balance outstanding.

annually renewable term (ART) (10) Level term life insurance that you can renew each year, up to some maximum specified age, without evidence of insurability.

annuitant (10, 15) A person buying an annuity.

annuity (10, 15) A contract that typically guarantees lifetime income. A person can buy an annuity to receive regular payments in the future.

annuity certain (15) An annuity that pays monthly payments to you or your beneficiary for a specified time period. Annuity payments cease at the end of that time period, regardless of whether you are still alive.

applications (7A) The uses to which a record-keeping system is put, for example, payroll applications or an accounts receivable application.

assessed value (6) The value assigned to property by an appraisal.

asset (2) An item that one owns. Assets may be financial or nonfinancial in nature.

attested will (16) The most common type of will. It must be handwritten or typed, signed by the maker of the will, and witnessed by at least two adults.

automatic policy loan provision (10) A life insurance policy provision you can request that will authorize the insurer to borrow an unpaid premium from the policy's cash value. This protects your policy against cancellation if you forget to pay the premium on time.

automatic reinvestment plans (13) Plans in which a mutual fund automatically reinvests the proceeds paid out to an account.

automatic teller machine (ATM) (4) A stand-alone computer terminal at which customers can make deposits, withdrawals, and other basic transactions.

average daily balance (4) A method of determining the minimum monthly balance of your checking account by calculating the average amount of money you maintained in the account each day.

back-end sales charge (13) A sales charge that is applied when you sell out of a mutual fund. It generally runs 2 to 3 percent and may be part of either a load or no-load fund. Only a small number of funds have this provision.

balanced fund (13) A mutual fund that has a balanced portfolio of stocks and bonds. Many balanced funds also take a heavy position in convertible bonds.

balloon loan (7) A loan in which the borrower borrows a fixed amount and pays interest on this full amount, but repayments of principal are figured on the difference between the loan's face amount and the expected resale value of the asset that is used as collateral.

balloon payment (6) A requirement of some fixed-rate mortgages in which a lump-sum cash payment typically pays off the remaining balance on the mortgage loan in full at a specified future time.

bank credit card (5) A credit card, such as MasterCard or Visa, that is issued by a group of affiliated financial institutions. The cardholder is assigned an upper credit limit. If you pay the entire balance within the specified 25- to 30-day grace period, no finance charge is imposed.

bargain and sell deed with convenant against grantor's acts (6) A deed in which the seller guarantees that he or she has done nothing to cause a defect in the title.

basic medical expense insurance (9) Health insurance composed of coverages for hospital, surgical and physician-related expenses; it usually pays 100 percent of covered expenses up to a low maximum limit and has a low deductible or none at all.

bearish (14) Having a negative outlook for an investment.

beneficiary (life insurance) (10) The person(s) designated to receive your life insurance policy's proceeds if you die.

beneficiary (trust) (16) A person or institution that receives the benefits from a trust.

blank endorsement (4) The least restrictive form of check endorsement, in which the payee signs the back of the check so it can be cashed by anyone who gets possession of it.

bodily injury liability (8) Third-party automobile insurance coverage that applies when you cause injury to someone else with your car.

bond ratings (11) Quality ratings of bonds produced by firms that evaluate bonds, such as Moody's and Standard & Poor's. Ratings may range from AAA to D; the higher the rating, the lower the yield and vice versa.

budget (2) A planning document used to forecast income, expenditures, and future surpluses and deficits. It helps in anticipating future problems and correcting them in advance.

budgetary controls (2) A system you may use to determine if you are over or under budget.

bullish (14) Having an optimistic outlook for an investment.

business risk (11) The risk that a firm will perform poorly because of adverse business conditions.

byte (7a) A measure of computer capacity. A byte is the equivalent of an alphabetic character or number.

call option (14) An option to buy 100 shares of stock at a specified price over a given time period.

canceled check truncation (4) The elimination of the service of returning customers' canceled checks to them each month.

cancellable (9) A type of provision in a health insurance policy that allows the insurer to cancel at any time by giving proper written notice.

canned programs (7A) Software programs in which the user must conform to the programs' particular techniques.

capital appreciation (11, 12, 13) The increase in value for an investment. Current income plus capital appreciation determines total return.

cash credit (5) Money obtained through an actual loan. Cash credit may be extended for many reasons and can be obtained from a wide variety of lenders.

cash refund annuity (15) A type of refund annuity that provides for a lump-sum payment to your beneficiaries.

cash value (10) The increasing savings in a whole life or endowment life insurance policy; the base from which you may borrow if you own such a policy.

cashier's check (4) A check that is made payable to a specific vendor and is backed by the issuing bank.

certificate of deposit (CD) (11) A type of investment offered by banks, savings and loans, and other financial institutions in which the investor places funds on deposit at a specified rate over a given time period. The transaction is evidenced by a certificate.

certified check (4) A personal check that is guaranteed by a bank.

charitable deduction (16) A deduction from income taxes that can be claimed for gifts from an individual to a qualified charity.

charitable lead trust (16) A trust that provides a charity with income over a number of years, but the principal then goes back to the donor's heirs.

charitable remainder trust (16) A trust plan that permits you to lock in a fixed income for life and gives you a current income tax deduction for leaving the trust's assets to charity after you die.

check (4) A standard preprinted form that permits you to make payments and obtain cash.

check clearance (4) The process by which a bank receives a check and makes payment for the face amount on it.

check hold (4) A restriction placed on a deposit that prevents the release of funds to the depositor's account for some amount of time.

checkbook ledger (4) A list of checks you have written; includes check number and amount.

checking account (4) An account at a financial institution that permits you to make deposits and withdrawals through writing checks. Regular checking accounts may charge service fees. NOW and super NOW accounts pay you interest on your deposits.

clearing fee (4) An amount that can be charged for each check written against an account.

closed-end fund (13) A fund with a specified number of shares outstanding that does not change with each purchase or sale. The only way you can buy the shares of a closed-end fund is when someone else is selling.

closed-end lease (7) A type of automobile lease that requires a fixed monthly payment, and at the end of the term the automobile is owned by the lessee (the one granted the lease).

closing costs (6) Expenses beyond the purchase price of a home such as expenditures for a title search, title insurance, appraisal fees, attorney's fees, termite inspection, and recording fees.

codicil (16) An addition to an existing will. It must be executed in the same manner as a will and should be signed and witnessed.

coinsurance (8) An insurance provision requiring you to insure your property to a minimum percentage of its full value in order to be able to recover the full amount of a loss. Also, your sharing of the potential burden for losses.

collateral (5) A specific asset that is pledged as security for a loan.

collision (8) Auto insurance coverage paying for damage to your car if you collide with another object or roll the car over.

commercial paper (11) Short-term notes issued to the public by the larger, more prestigious corporations. Commercial paper normally has a maturity up to six months and trades at a minimum value of $25,000.

commission-based compensation (1) Payment for a financial planner's services that is based on the commissions the planner generates for himself or herself.

commodities futures contract (14) A contract that provides for the delivery of a specific commodity at a designated time in the future at a given price. Almost all commodity contracts are closed out before the actual transaction is to take place.

common stock (12) A security that represents the ownership interest in the firm. It carries a voting privilege and a claim to earnings after all other forms of security holders have been compensated.

communications (**7A**) The interface allowing two computers to talk to one another. The connection is made by a device known as a modem.

compounding (**4**) The frequency with which your savings account is credited with the interest earned. Compounding permits you to earn interest on interest.

comprehensive medical expense insurance (**9**) A medical expense health insurance policy having a deductible, percentage coinsurance with a security provision, high maximum benefits, and broad coverage with few internal limits.

concurrent review (**9**) A health insurance cost containment feature limiting unnecessary treatment and correcting inaccurate billings by monitoring your care while you are in a hospital.

conditional endorsement (**4**) A check endorsement that has some condition placed on it. The intent is to prevent the check from being cashed prior to the condition being satisfied.

conditionally renewable (**9**) A type of provision in a health insurance policy that allows the insurer to refuse renewal at the anniversary date if a specified condition exists at that date.

conditions (**8**) The part of an insurance policy stating what you must do in order to be able to collect when an insured loss occurs.

condominium (**6**) An apartment unit, attached townhouse, or house among a cluster of houses for which the owner receives title to an individual unit in a group of units and shares possession of such common facilities as swimming pools, lakes, and tennis courts.

consumer durables (**7**) Items that are important to consumers, have long service periods, and are relatively high in cost. Examples include automobiles, furniture, appliances, and personal computers.

contesting the will (**16**) A legal proceeding in which someone tries to prove that a will is invalid.

contributory pension plan (**15**) A plan that permits employees to make supplementary contributions along with the employer contributions.

conventional mortgage (**6**) A loan made directly between the borrower and the lender in which there is no governmental participation in the form of loan insurance or loan guarantees.

convertible bonds (**11**) Corporate bonds that may be converted to common stock at a specified exchange rate over the life of the bonds.

cooperative apartment (**6**) An arrangement where people own shares in an entire dwelling complex. Typically, ownership interest is proportionate to the living space a person occupies in the complex.

coordination of benefits (**9**) An insurance policy provision that tells what the policy will pay if another policy covers the same loss.

cost containment (**9**) Insurer efforts to reduce claims payments in health insurance.

cost of acquisition (**7**) The immediate loss of value of an automobile when it is first driven and is therefore no longer a "new" car.

cost of living index (**2**) An index that measures a change in the cost of living over time. It normally has a base value of 100.

countercyclical stock (**12**) A stock that moves in the opposite direction of the business cycle.

CPU (**7A**) A computer's central processing unit, which performs all the computer's calculations and analysis.

credit card (**5**) A card offering a preapproved credit limit that can be used for purchases or borrowing.

credit limit (5) A specified limit on the amount that can be borrowed or purchased on credit.

credit line (4) An amount that can be automatically borrowed if you write a check for more than your account balance. This service is provided to cover overdrafts.

credit reporting agency (5) An agency that maintains files related to credit histories and makes this information available for members.

credit scoring (5) A technique used to determine an individual's creditworthiness. Points are assigned to various loan applicant characteristics, and the total number of points is compared to a predetermined target.

credits (16) Amounts subtracted from an estate for state and foreign death taxes paid and on prior transfers. They offset dollar for dollar the estate tax liability and thus are more valuable than deductions.

creditworthiness (5) The probability, as perceived by a lender, that you will be able to repay a loan.

cumulative deficit (2) The size which the deficit in a personal budget has accumulated to after a number of months.

cumulative preferred stock (11A) The most common kind of preferred stock. All dividends that are not paid on preferred stock accumulate and must be paid before any dividends are paid to common stockholders.

cumulative surplus (2) The size which the surplus in a budget has accumulated to after a number of months.

cyclical stock (12) A stock that is heavily influenced by the current state of the economy. It does well during business boom periods but poorly during recessions. Automotive and steel firms generally fall into this category.

data (7A) Information that is or can be stored in a computer.

data base (7A) A collection of data stored in a systematic and logical structure that will allow access to the data for more than one application.

day of deposit to day of withdrawal method (4) A method of computing interest in which interest is paid on funds from the day they are deposited until the day they are withdrawn.

dealer spread (14) The difference between the price at which a dealer is willing to buy and sell an asset.

death taxes (16) Taxes imposed by the state or federal government on a deceased person's assets.

debit card (4) A card that you can use at a special point-of-sale terminal in a store to automatically transfer money from your account to the store's account.

decreasing term life insurance (10) A term life insurance policy with a face amount payable at your death that decreases steadily throughout its period of protection.

deductible (8) A requirement that you absorb the first dollars of a loss before the insurer begins to pay.

deed (6) A legal document that transfers the ownership of a house from one person to another.

deferred annuity (15) An annuity that is typically purchased several years before retirement, either by making regular installment payments over several years or by making a single lump-sum payment some years before the distribution period.

defined benefit plan (15) A pension plan in which a formula stipulated in the plan agreement is used to determine retirement benefits.

defined contribution plan (15) A pension plan in which a fixed contribution, usually a percentage of an employee's wages, is made to the plan. Retirement benefits depend entirely on the amount accumulated in the employee's account.

dependent (3) One who qualifies as a personal exemption on another party's tax return. To be classified as a dependent one must pass the relative or member-of-household test, the support test, the income test, and the citizen/resident test.

deposit (4) Money or checks that you give to a financial institution to be credited to your account.

deposits in transit (4) Deposits you have made that have not yet been added to your account by the bank.

depreciation (7) The decline in the value of real estate or durable goods over time.

deregulation (1) The removal of government regulations from an industry or company.

disability income insurance (9) Health insurance providing monthly or weekly payments intended to replace part of the income you lose if you are disabled and cannot work.

discount brokers (12) Stockbrokers who buy and sell stocks at lower commissions than traditional brokers but do not provide advice, research reports, or other information developed by security analysts.

discount method (5) A method of calculating finance charges in which the amount of the finance charge is subtracted in advance from the amount of money lent.

disk drive (7A) The device on a computer into which disks are placed for use.

distribution period (15) A set period of time over which the owner of an annuity is to receive periodic payments.

dividend option (10) One of the choices you have for using your policyholder dividend if you own a participating endowment or whole life insurance policy.

dividend yield (12) The annual dividend divided by the current price of a stock. It is normally 3 to 4 percent.

dot matrix (7A) A type of printer in which the characters are composed of a series of dots.

double indemnity (10) See *accidental death benefit (ADB).*

Dow Jones Industrial Average (12) The most widely quoted stock market average. It is based on the stock price movements of 30 large industrial firms.

down payment (6) The initial amount of cash that must be invested to purchase a house.

dread disease insurance (9) Limited health insurance that pays only for certain medical expenses associated with the described dread disease(s).

dwelling (8) The residence covered against all nonexcluded perils under the homeowners special form (HO-3).

earned income (3) Income from wages and salary, as contrasted with investment income or other forms of income.

earned income credit (3) A tax credit of up to $800 that can be applied to the first $5714 of earned income for those low-income workers who qualify. In order to qualify, a low-income worker must maintain a household for dependents. The ability to use the credit is phased out if there is total income over $9000 and ceases altogether at $17,000.

effective rate of interest (4) The actual rate at which your money earns interest. This may differ from the stated rate of interest.

elect against the will (16) An attack by someone, such as a spouse, against the fairness of a will.

Employee Retirement Income Security Act (ERISA) (15) Legislation that imposes minimum vesting schedules for employees in order to ensure that more employees become vested and thus qualify for regular benefits upon retirement.

endorsement (4) A process by which you can designate another person to receive payment from a check made out to you.

endowment life insurance (10) A life insurance policy that promises to pay its face amount (1) if you die during the term of the policy, or (2) if you live until the term of the policy expires.

entrepreneur (1) One who starts his or her own business with some measure of success. Most entrepreneurs are thought to be risk takers as well as self-starters.

Equal Credit Opportunity Act (5) A law that requires the creditor, if requested, to provide the consumer with the specific reason for not extending credit. It also prevents a creditor from discriminating on the basis of sex, marital status, age, race, religion, or national origin when considering a credit application.

equity buildup (6) The increase in equity that results from the repayment of principal on a mortgage loan.

equivalent taxable yield (11) The yield that an investor must receive on a taxable investment to equal the lower yield on a tax-exempt investment such as a municipal bond.

estate (16) All the property an individual owns or has an interest in at time of death, including assets that materialize as a result of death, such as life insurance proceeds.

estate planning (16) A process that sets objectives and identifies the techniques best suited to accomplish those objectives in order to provide the greatest possible financial benefits and personal satisfaction for an individual and his or her heirs.

estate tax (16) A tax levied on all property in an estate at the time of the owner's death. The tax applies to the fair market value of the property or interests in property owned by the deceased.

estate tax deduction (16) A reduction in the amount of an estate that is subject to estate taxes.

executor (executrix) (16) The person who is selected by the testator to be responsible for carrying out the instructions of a will.

exempt earnings (15) The amount one can earn between the ages of 65 and 69 without causing a reduction in Social Security benefits.

exemption-equivalent trust (16) A trust plan in which an amount equal to the tax exemption for assets is put into a trust.

expiration date (14) The date on which an option or commodity contract is ended.

factory-built house (6) A house that is partially or totally built in a factory as opposed to on the homesite. It offers the advantages of faster construction and lower cost.

Fair Credit Billing Act (5) A law that gives consumers legal rights pertaining to credit disputes and protects them from creditors' actions while a bill is in dispute.

Fair Credit Reporting Act (5) A law that grants consumers access to their credit bureau records and entitles them to check the source of information and its accuracy. Denials of credit by banks on the basis of credit bureau information must be reported to consumers.

Fair Debt Collection Practices Act (5) A law that protects delinquent borrowers from abusive collection practices.

family income policy (10) A package life insurance policy. If you die within a specified period after its issuance, it pays your beneficiary 1 percent of its face amount per month during the remainder of that period. It then pays the face amount.

federal agency securities (11) Securities issued by agencies of the government rather than directly by the U.S. Treasury. Though lacking the direct backing of the Treasury, they are guaranteed by the issuing agency and provide all the safety that one would normally need. They pay a slightly higher yield than direct issues from the U.S. government.

Federal Deposit Insurance Corporation (FDIC) (4) A federal agency that provides insurance to protect the depositor's account against the failure of a commercial bank or mutual savings bank up to some maximum dollar limit (currently $100,000).

Federal Insurance Contributions Act (FICA) (15) An act that imposes payroll taxes on covered employed persons to support Social Security.

Federal Savings and Loan Insurance Corporation (FSLIC) (4) A federal agency that provides insurance to protect the depositor's account against the failure of a savings and loan association up to some maximum dollar limit (currently $100,000).

fee-based compensation (1) Direct payment for a financial planner's services. There are no commissions involved in this arrangement.

FHA mortgage insurance (6) Default insurance provided by the Federal Housing Administration. The borrower pays a premium and the FHA reimburses the lender for any resulting loss up to a specified maximum.

fiduciary capacity (16) Term used to describe the confidence or trust inherent in the position of the executor.

finance charge (5) The total dollar amount of the cost of credit. This fee is essentially a rental fee for the use of money.

financial assets (2, 11, 14) Cash, near-cash items, or financial documents that represent a claim to assets.

first-in, first-out method (4) A method of calculating savings account interest in which any withdrawals during the interest crediting period are deducted from the initial balance and then from later deposits in the order made.

first-party coverages (8) Insurance coverages that pay if you suffer a loss, without regard to who caused the loss.

fixed costs (7) Expenses that do not change with an increase in use.

fixed-dollar annuity (15) An annuity contract in which the annuity payment is determined and does not change.

fixed-rate mortgage (6) A form of financing under which both the interest rate and the monthly payment are fixed over the life of the mortgage.

flat amount pension plan (15) A type of defined benefit plan under which all employees receive the same amount with no consideration given to either earnings or years of service.

flat percentage pension plan (15) A type of defined benefit plan that pays a retired employee each year 1 percent of his or her average three-year annual preretirement salary for each year of service.

floating-rate bonds (11) Corporate bonds whose interest payments change with market conditions instead of being fixed. The bonds remain at face value (or very close to face value) because they are continually adjusting to the going market rate of interest.

floppy disk (7A) A removable, permanent storage device for computer information.

flower bonds (16) Specific U.S. Treasury bonds that can be tendered at face amount in payment for federal estate taxes. These bonds must be owned before your death.

fully insured retirement benefits (15) A status reached by an employee after working a required number of covered quarters. Only fully insured employees are eligible to collect Social Security benefits at retirement.

fundamental analysis (12) A three-step evaluation process to determine whether a stock is appropriately valued in the market or not. The analyst examines the economy, the industry, and the firm, emphasizing earnings performances and quality of management.

funded pension plan (15) A pension plan in which the employer makes current payments into a separate fund to offset pension liabilities as they accrue.

fund-switching privileges (13) The ability to switch among the many funds that a mutual fund sponsor has at no expense or at a very limited expense.

gift splitting (16) A situation in which a married donor can make a gift and, with the consent of his or her spouse, can elect to treat the gift as if it were made equally by each spouse.

gift tax (16) A tax imposed on the transfer of property during an individual's lifetime.

GNMA certificates (11) Pass-through certificates issued by the Government National Mortgage Association (GNMA), which buys a pool of mortgages from lenders (such as savings and loans) and then issues securities to the public based on these mortgages.

grace period (credit) (5) The period of time in which you can pay the full balance of your credit card bill and not incur any finance charges.

grace period (insurance) (9, 10) A provision of medical expense and life insurance policies granting 31 days or one month of coverage after the premium due date. Coverage does not lapse during this period, and if the premium is paid before the period ends, no interest is owed.

grace period (savings) (4) A specific number of days during which, if you deposit funds in a bank or other financial institution, you earn interest on the amount for the entire period. If your deposit arrives after the grace period, no interest is earned on it.

graduated-payment mortgage (GPM) (6) A loan for which the interest rate and maturity are fixed but the monthly payments are set to start out low and get larger later.

grantor (16) A person who sets up a trust with his or her assets.

graphics (7A) Visual representations of data.

gross estate (16) The total value of an estate before any debts or expenses are removed.

gross income (3) All of a person's sources of income, such as salary, interest, dividends, rent, royalties, and unemployment compensation.

group annuity (15) A type of contract usually issued to an employer under a master contract for the benefit of employees. The individual members of the group hold certificates as evidence of their annuities.

growing-equity mortgage (GEM) (6) A loan that offers a fixed interest rate over the life of the loan but has monthly payments that are scheduled to increase by a specified percentage each year. The growing payments repay the loan more rapidly than under the traditional fixed-rate mortgage.

growth stock (12) A stock that is assumed to have greater than average growth potential for the future. Historically, corporate earnings have increased 4 to 6 percent per year, and a firm that is categorized as a growth stock should be able to demonstrate growth in earnings of 10 to 15 percent annually or more.

guaranteed insurability option (10) A life insurance policy rider that protects your ability to buy more life insurance in the future, even if your health deteriorates.

guaranteed renewable (9) A type of provision in a health insurance policy that allows you to renew until a stated maximum age, with the insurer free to raise your premium only if it raises the premiums of all other insureds in your policyholder class.

hard disk (7A) An alternative method of computer data storage to the usual floppy disk, often containing more than 20 times the storage of a single floppy.

hardware (7A) the actual computer equipment—the monitor, CPU, disk drives, and printer.

health maintenance organization (HMO) (9) A form of prepaid group medical practice designed to provide comprehensive health care services to its members by stressing preventive medicine.

hedging (14) The process of taking a second position that will offset an initial exposed position. An example would be selling a commodities contract to offset possible losses on items you own. Hedging is used to reduce or eliminate risk.

high-yield stock (12) A stock that provides a high dividend yield. The yield may be twice the normal yield of 3 to 4 percent or more.

holographic will (16) A will that is entirely handwritten and signed but has not been witnessed.

home health care (9) A health care alternative in which a patient completes recovery at home instead of in the hospital, while remaining under a doctor's care and with a visiting nurse to monitor progress, administer medication, and provide physical therapy.

homeowner's insurance (6) An insurance policy to protect a home from damage.

hospice (9) An organization designed to help terminally ill patients and their families cope with the process of dying and to remove the patients from expensive, life-prolonging hospital treatment.

hospital expense insurance (9) A limited medical expense policy that pays a set number of dollars a day while you are in the hospital.

HO-3 policy (8) A popular form of homeowner's policy that covers the home, personal property, loss of use, personal liability, and medical payments.

immediate annuity (15) An annuity purchased under the single-premium method; its benefit payments begin immediately.

incontestable clause (10) A life insurance policy provision where the insurer gives up its right to contest the validity of the policy. Incontestability begins one or two years after the policy is issued.

indemnity benefit (9) An insurance benefit payment occurring when you pay for insured services and then file a claim with the insurer for reimbursement.

independent physicians' association (IPA) (9) An association of independent physicians formed to encourage member doctors to make their practices competitive with HMOs.

individual annuity (15) A type of contract in which a single person directly purchases an annuity from an issuer.

individual retirement account (IRA) (3, 15) A type of retirement plan in which an individual is allowed to deposit and accumulate funds for retirement on the same tax-deferred basis available to regular corporate pension plans.

information card (4) A card that you must complete when you open a checking account. On it you are asked to give your name, address, telephone number, occupation, employer, and other pertinent facts.

inheritance tax (16) The most common type of state death tax, assessed on each beneficiary's share of the estate assets.

installment loan (4, 7) A loan that is repaid through a series of equal monthly payments.

installment premium annuity (15) An annuity that is bought by making regular payments that accumulate as a savings fund.

installment refund annuity (15) A type of refund annuity in which the beneficiaries receive installment payments until the total purchase price of the annuity has been refunded.

Institute of Certified Financial Planners (ICFP) (2) One of the certifying organizations for financial planners. The ICFP is located in Denver, Colorado.

Institute of Chartered Financial Analysts (ICFA) (2) A certifying organization for financial analysts and portfolio managers. The ICFA is located in Charlottesville, Virginia.

insurance (8) A risk transfer device where the insurer accepts all or part of your risk in exchange for a premium.

insured pension plan (15) A method of pension plan administration in which an insurance company receives the periodic pension contributions and, in return, promises to pay agreed-upon benefits to retired employees.

interest (11, 15) The amount earned on the principal.

interest-crediting period (4) The amount of time funds were earning interest.

intermediate goals (1) Personal financial planning goals that have a medium-length focus, such as finding a permanent job, purchasing a home, and setting up comprehensive insurance coverage.

International Association of Financial Planners (IAFP) (2) One of the certifying organizations for financial planners. The IAFP is located in Atlanta, Georgia.

intestate (16) Having died without a will.

in-the-money options (14) Options for which the price of the stock is above the strike price.

intrinsic value (14) The market value of a stock minus its strike price.

investment (11) The commitment of current funds in anticipation of an increased return in the future.

investment company (13) A firm that organizes and sponsors an open-end (mutual) or closed-end fund.

individual retirement account (IRA) (3, 15) An account that allows a taxpayer to deduct $2000 from taxable income and invest the funds tax free at a bank, savings and loan, brokerage house, mutual fund, or other financial institution. There are limitations on the contributions those who participate in a company pension plan can make.

involuntary savings plan (13) A mutual fund provision in which the investor contractually agrees to make regular payments. It is usually associated with load funds and often involves substantial front-end loads, so all the payments go toward commissions rather than the purchase of securities.

IRA rollover (15) A special IRA into which you can place a lump-sum distribution from a qualified retirement plan and still avoid taxation if the money is deposited within 60 days.

irrevocable living trust (16) A trust that cannot legally be changed or terminated except in exceptional circumstances.

itemized deductions (3) Deductions that are specifically itemized on a tax return as an alternative to taking a standard deduction. Examples of itemized deductions include state and local taxes, mortgage interest, and charitable contributions.

joint account (4) An account opened in the name of two people that allows either person to withdraw funds or write a check on it.

joint life insurance (10) A life insurance policy covering the lives of two persons, paying when the first dies and then ending coverage.

joint return (3) A tax return that is filed jointly by a husband and wife.

junk bonds (11) Lower-rated bonds that carry high risk but compensate by paying very high yields.

K (7A) A measure of computer capacity; 1K equals 1024 bytes.

Keogh (HR-10) plan (15) A qualified retirement plan for self-employed persons and partnerships; it receives the same tax deferral benefits as a corporate pension plan.

keyboard (7A) Hardware, similar to a typewriter keyboard, which is used to type text and issue commands to a computer.

laser (7A) A type of printer that uses a copier technique to print a page at a time rather than a letter or character at a time.

last-in, first-out method (4) A method to calculate savings account interest in which any withdrawals during the interest-crediting period are deducted from the latest deposits before the withdrawals.

lease agreement (6) A written contract that sets forth the rights and obligations of both the landlord and the renter.

lessee (6) An individual who is renting property from a lessor.

lessor (6) An owner who is renting property to a lessee.

letter of commitment (6) A letter given by the lender to the borrower summarizing the provisions of a loan.

letter of last instruction (16) A document written to assist the person administering an estate. The letter should include information such as the location of a will, funeral instructions, and the location of other relevant documents.

letter quality (7A) A type of printer that produces documents with the same quality as that of a letter typed on a typewriter.

level term life insurance (10) Term life insurance that pays a constant face amount no matter when during the term of the policy you die.

liability (2) A form of debt or credit extension. Examples include auto loans, home mortgages, and charge accounts.

liability risk (8) A situation that could force you to defend yourself in court and to pay large sums to others.

life and health risk (8) A situation involving the financial impact of death and loss of health.

life annuity (10, 15) A product sold by life insurance companies, providing an income that will continue for the rest of your life.

life annuity, period certain (10, 15) An annuity under which you receive a specified amount of income for life. In addition, you are guaranteed payments for a certain time period. If you die before the end of the period, your beneficiaries continue to receive payments during the period.

life insurance trust (16) A trust plan in which the only asset is an insurance policy on your life.

limit order (12) An order that allows you to specify the price at which you wish to transact. There will be no attempt to execute your order until the stock gets to that price.

limited partnership (14) A real estate partnership in which a general partner, who assumes unlimited liabilities for the partnership obligations, sells participation units ($5,000 to $10,000) to limited partners, whose liability is limited to the extent of their investment.

limited policy (9) A medical expense health insurance policy that provides narrow coverage, paying only if special events occur or in carefully defined circumstances.

line of credit (5) The maximum amount of credit permitted at any point in time on a revolving charge account or other credit arrangement.

liquidity (11, 14) The ability to convert an investment into cash in a relatively short time.

living (inter vivos) trust (16) A trust that is established during the lifetime of the grantor.

load fund (13) A mutual fund that charges a commission that may range up to 8.5 percent of the purchase price.

loan consolidation (5) The combination of several different loans into a single loan in order to reduce the overall finance charges and eliminate cumbersome paperwork.

loan-to-value ratio (6) The percentage of a property's value that can be borrowed.

long-term goals (1) Personal financial planning goals that emphasize long-term objectives such as wealth accumulation and retirement.

loss control (8) Efforts to reduce either frequency or amount of loss, or both.

loss of use (8) Homeowner's insurance coverage paying living expenses that are in addition to normal living expenses, when insured damage to your dwelling forces you to live elsewhere.

low-balance method (4) A procedure to determine the necessary account balance to earn interest. Only the customer's lowest account balance during the month is considered.

lowest daily balance (4) A method used to determine the minimum monthly balance of a checking account by setting it equal to the lowest balance at any time during the month.

low-load funds (13) Mutual funds that charge a commission that is well below the maximum limit of 8.5 percent. A low load may be 2 to 3 percent.

major medical expense insurance (9) A medical expense health insurance policy with deductible, percentage coinsurance (sometimes with a security provision), high maximum benefits, and broad coverage with few internal limits.

manufacturer's suggested list price (7) The price shown on the sticker of a new car or other item for sale.

margin (on stock) (12) A type of stock purchase in which part of the purchase price is provided through funds borrowed from the broker. The margin requirement is set by the Federal Reserve and is currently 50 percent, which means that the investor may put up 50 percent in cash and borrow the balance.

margin on a commodities contract (14) Good faith money (deposit) that an investor in a commodities contract puts up. It is usually 5 to 10 percent of the value of the contract. Unlike margin on stocks or bonds, no actual borrowing takes place.

marginal tax rate (3) The tax rate that applies to the next dollar of income. Basically, the marginal tax rates under the Tax Reform Act of 1986 are 15, 28, and 33 percent.

marital deduction (16) A tax deduction permitted for property passed directly to a surviving spouse.

market order (12) An order that is to be executed at the current market price.

market risk (11) The potential loss in market value of an investment due to changing economic conditions.

medical payments (8) Auto insurance coverage that pays your medical expenses when you are hurt in an auto accident.

medical payments to others (8) Homeowner's insurance coverage that pays for the medical expenses of others injured on your property.

Medicare (9) Social Security medical insurance available at age 65; automatically provides Part A—Hospital Insurance to eligible persons, and allows individual purchase of Part B—Supplementary Medical Insurance.

medigap insurance (9) Individual medical expense health insurance designed to supplement Medicare.

Meg (7A) A measure of computer capacity; 1 Meg, or megabyte, equals 1 million bytes.

modem (7A) A telephone device that connects two computers.

money market account (11) An account at a financial institution that usually provides a higher yield than a traditional savings account and greater check withdrawal flexibility than a certificate of deposit.

money market checking account (11) A special form of money market account that allows you extensive check-writing privileges (typically 25 per month) and thus lets you combine your savings and check-writing functions.

money market fund (11) A special type of mutual fund in which investors pool relatively small amounts of funds to create large pools of money for investment in high-yielding securities. A typical money market fund requires a minimum balance of $1000.

monochrome (7A) Single color on a computer monitor (usually green or amber letters on a black background).

mortality rate (10) The expected death rate, usually expressed in terms of the number of persons expected to die per year for each 1000 alive at the beginning of the year.

mortgage (6) A separate document under a mortgage loan that provides the lender with a claim on the property as security for the loan.

mortgage loan (4, 6) Usually a long-term installment loan used to finance the purchase of real estate.

mortgage payment (6) The regular interest payments on a mortgage loan and the systematic repayment of the principal on that loan.

mortgage points (6) An up-front charge for borrowing money. A point is one percent of the amount of the mortgage loan.

municipal bonds (11) Bonds that are issued by state and local governments. Their interest income is nontaxable for federal income tax purposes and exempt from state and local taxes if bought from the locality in which the purchaser resides.

municipal securities funds (13) Mutual funds that specialize in tax-exempt municipal investments.

mutual funds (13) Organizations that pool the funds of a large number of individual investors and redeploy those funds in stocks and bonds. A typical mutual fund may own 50 to 100 securities and have thousands of investors.

NASDAQ (12) The National Association of Security Dealers Automated Quotation System. NASDAQ provides up-to-the-minute quotes on over 4000 of the over-the-counter stocks.

National Credit Union Association (NCUA) (4) A federal agency that provides insurance to protect the depositor's account against the failure of a credit union up to some maximum dollar limit (currently $100,000).

needs programming (10) An approach used to determine the amount of life insurance you might need to buy, by subtracting assets from needs.

negative amortization (6) A feature of some graduated-payment mortgages in which for some period of time the principal amount of the loan increases instead of diminishing.

negotiable order of withdrawal (NOW) account (4) A type of checking account on which banks pay interest.

net asset value (13) The value of a fund determined by taking the total value of the securities owned, subtracting the liabilities, and dividing by the shares outstanding.

net estate tax payable (16) The amount determined by subtracting any gift taxes paid and other death tax credits from the tentative tax.

net worth (2) The value of assets minus liabilities. It is the financing that is provided by the owners.

New York Stock Exchange (12) The largest and best known of the organized exchanges. Approximately 1550 firms have their stocks listed for trading there.

no-fault insurance (8) Auto insurance that makes each driver responsible for his or her own loss by removing auto accidents from the legal liability system.

no-load funds (13) Mutual funds that do not charge a commission.

no-minimum account (4) A checking account for which the bank charges a monthly service fee regardless of the balance in the account.

noncancellable (9) A type of provision in a health insurance policy that allows you to renew annually at a constant premium until you reach a stated maximum age.

noncontributory pension plan (15) A pension plan in which all contributions are made only by the employer.

nonfinancial asset (2, 14) A tangible asset that can be seen, held, or worn. Examples include real estate, books, jewelry, clothing, and collectibles. Nonfinancial assets are also referred to as real assets.

N-ratio method (5) A formula used to calculate an approximate APR on an installment loan using the add-on method.

nuncupative will (16) An oral declaration of the desired distribution of your estate. It is usually valid only in extreme circumstances.

Occupational Outlook Handbook (1) A book published by the U.S. Department of Labor, in which over 200 career paths are discussed under 20 different major headings. In each case, training, working conditions, job outlook, earning potential, and sources of information are covered.

Old-Age, Survivors, Disability, and Health Insurance (OASDHI) (15) The program through which Social Security is administered.

open architecture (7A) The computer-manufacturing process whereby competitors are given manufacturing specifications to allow them to create add-on or complementary products.

open-account credit (5) Preapproved credit, typically used for a specific consumer purchase.

open-end fund (13) A mutual fund in which the number of shares is unlimited. Actually, the term *mutual fund* applies specifically to open-end funds as opposed to closed-end funds.

open-end lease (7) A type of automobile lease that requires fixed monthly payments, but the final cost of the car depends on the car's resale value. At the end of the term, the lessee may receive a refund or pay an extra amount, depending on the value of the car.

operating system (7A) The underlying computer software that manages the hardware and supports the application program.

option (14) The right to buy or sell 100 shares of stock at a specified price over a given time period. The term more generally means the privilege to buy or sell an item at a set price in the future.

other than collision (8) First-party auto insurance coverage that pays when damage to your car is caused by something besides collision or rolling it over; also called comprehensive.

out-of-the-money options (14) Options for which the price of the stock is below the strike price.

outstanding check (4) A check you have written that has not been cashed by the bank.

overdraft (4) A check that is written for an amount greater than your current checking account balance.

over-the-counter (OTC) market (12) A national network of telephone and computer devices that can be used to transact stock market orders. It is considered to be a competitive dealer market in which many firms stand ready to buy and sell a security.

package plan (4) An account at a financial institution that provides a combination of services for a single fee.

package policies (10) Life insurance policies that are combinations of term, endowment, and whole-life policies and/or modifications of those three policies.

payment option (15) The method selected for receiving annuity payments.

pension plan (15) An investment medium established by an employer through which monetary contributions are made today in order to provide future retirement income for employees.

percentage coinsurance (9) A medical expense health insurance policy provision causing you to absorb a percentage share of covered expenses above the policy deductible.

personal balance sheet (2) A balance sheet that is constructed for an individual or family rather than for a business. Assets are shown at current market value rather than at historical cost, as is true of a business balance sheet. The assets must equal the liabilities and net worth.

personal computer (7A) An electronic device used by one person to assimilate information.

personal exemption (3) A tax deduction for yourself or a dependent that is $1950 in 1988 and $2000 in 1989. This is not directly related to a dollar expenditure.

personal financial planner (1) One who helps others plan their financial affairs.

personal liability (8) Third-party homeowner's insurance coverage for liability for bodily injury to others and damage to their property.

personal property (8) First-party homeowner's insurance coverage of clothing, furniture, appliances, and other personal property that you own, use, or wear against a broad range of perils.

planning horizon (2) The time period over which financial planning takes place. For a budget, it may be six months or a year. For retirement and estate planning, it may be a half century or, longer.

policy loan provision (10) A provision in an endowment or whole-life insurance policy allowing the owner of the policy to borrow from the policy's cash value.

portable pension plan (15) A pension plan that permits employees to take their vested pension accounts with them upon termination of employment.

power to appoint (16) The power to designate to whom certain assets will go upon your death.

preadmission authorization (9) A cost containment feature in medical expense health insurance that involves a deductible or coinsurance penalty if you are admitted to a hospital for routine treatment without preadmission approval by a designated third party.

preexisting conditions (9) A health insurance policy provision limiting coverage for a medical condition from which you suffer when coverage begins.

preferred provider organization (PPO) (9) A health care provider that contracts with an employer or insurer to provide discounted medical services to the employees or insureds.

preferred stock (11A) Stock that pays a fixed dividend which does not change over the life of the security. The dividend is not a contractual obligation of the corporation as would be true of a bond.

prepayment penalty (6) A feature of some mortgages carrying a prepayment provision in which an additional amount must be paid on any amount that is paid off early.

prepayment provision (6) A feature in some mortgages that allows the borrower to pay off part or all of the outstanding amount of the loan before the due date.

price-earnings (P-E) ratio (12) The current stock price divided by the latest 12 months of earnings per share. The ratio represents the value investors assign to a company's earnings; the stronger a company's performance, the higher the P-E ratio.

principal (15) The amount on which interest is paid. It also refers to the dollar amount that an annuity purchaser invests through premium payments.

probate (16) The judicial determination of the validity of a will.

probate estate (16) The total value of property that is passed by a will.

profit-sharing plan (15) A retirement plan that enables employees to participate in their employer's profits. The employer's contribution to the plan is tied to company profitability.

programs (7A) Logical sequences of precise instructions that direct a computer to solve specific problems or to manipulate data.

promissory note (6) A written agreement between a lender and borrower stating how much money is owed and how this amount is to be repaid.

property damage liability (8) Third-party auto insurance coverage that applies when you damage the property of others.

property risk (8) A situation involving possible damage to or loss of property.

property taxes (6) Taxes imposed on the appraised value of a home that are levied by local governments to support schools, police and fire departments, and other local services.

purchasing-power risk (11) The risk of loss of purchasing power due to inflation.

put option (14) An option to sell 100 shares at a specified price over a given time period.

put privilege (11) A special feature of some corporate bond issues that allows the bondholder to sell a long-term bond back to the corporation at its face value after a relatively short period of time, regardless of the current market price.

Q-tip trust (16) A qualified terminable-interest property trust allows you to provide income for a surviving spouse, but upon the spouse's death the assets can go to whomever you choose.

qualified pension plan (15) A pension plan that satisfies certain Internal Revenue Code requirements and thus receives important income tax benefits.

quitclaim deed (6) A deed in which the seller only maintains that he or she is transferring whatever title is owned. No guarantee is made about defects.

RAM (7A) Random access memory, the type of memory usually associated with a computer's processing capacity.

real assets (2, 11, 14) Physical assets such as real estate, gold, silver, or collectibles. They can actually be seen, felt, or held.

real estate agent (broker) (6) A person who provides aid and advice in the buying and selling of a home for a commission.

real estate investment trust (REIT) (14) A trust that invests in real estate or loans money to major real estate projects. Shares in REITs are traded in the stock market.

realtor (6) An agent employed by a home seller to sell a house.

reasonable and customary (9) A health insurance limit for covered medical expenses based on recent charges for a given medical service in a specific area.

refund annuity (15) An annuity that guarantees you payments for life. In addition, at your death your designated beneficiary receives an amount equal to the total premiums you paid less the total amount of annuity payments you received.

regular account (4) A checking account that offers unlimited checking services. Its cost depends on the number of transactions in a month and the minimum balance maintained during the month.

regular charge account (5) A charge account provided for customer convenience and not designed to offer credit for any extended period. Payment is usually due 10 to 30 days after the billing date, with no finance charge.

Regulation Z (5) Also called truth-in-lending, a rule requiring that consumers be given meaningful and consistent information on the cost of credit. Certain nonprice information must also be disclosed.

renewable at the insurer's option (9) A type of provision in a health insurance policy that allows the insurer to refuse to renew a policy at its anniversary date.

replacement cost (8) A measure of insured property value; the cost to replace or repair property with materials, workmanship, and design of the same quality it possessed before loss, at current prices.

restrictive endorsement (4) A type of endorsement in which the payee endorses the check to another party exclusively and prevents it from being endorsed over to anyone else.

retail store and oil company cards (5) Credit cards offered for use only in the retail outlets of the issuers.

retention (8) Bearing a loss yourself rather than transferring it.

reverse third-party coverages (8) Auto insurance protection against losses caused by another party who is unable to pay.

revocable living trust (16) A trust that can be changed or terminated at any time.

revolving (open-end) charge account (5) A charge account that allows you to purchase goods and services up to a specified credit limit and requires only a minimum payment instead of repayment of the full balance.

risk sharing (10, 15) An operational principle of annuities in which annuitants living longer than expected continue to receive periodic payments at the expense of those who died prematurely.

rollover mortgage loan (ROM) (6) A loan that offers a fixed interest rate and fixed monthly payments for a specified period of time. At the end of that period, the entire loan is renegotiated.

ROM (7A) Real-only memory, a computer's continuously accessible memory that stores frequently used software.

safe deposit box (4) A container in a bank's vault that can be used to store valuables.

salary reduction plan (15) A plan that permits employees to deposit a portion of their salary to a qualified retirement plan and therefore lets them avoid current taxation on this amount.

savings account (4, 11) An account that earns interest and permits easy access to your money.

second mortgage (6) An additional mortgage on a home. A second mortgage lender can receive payment only after the first mortgage lender's entire claim has been satisfied.

second surgical opinion (9) A medical expense health insurance provision encouraging or requiring a second medical opinion on elective surgery.

secured bonds (11) Bonds backed by the pledge of specific corporate assets as collateral.

security provision (9) A provision in comprehensive and major medical expense health insurance policies under which the insurer pays 100 percent of covered expenses after your expenses equal a set amount.

self-administered plan (15) A method of pension plan administration in which a corporation forms a separate department to accept and manage segregated pension funds.

service contract (7) A policy that can be purchased with most cars and appliances that is similar to an insurance policy. The buyer pays a premium as protection against expensive breakdowns.

service fee on a checking account (4) A monthly charge from a bank to cover the cost of servicing a checking account.

services benefit (9) A medical expense health insurance benefit whereby the insurer contracts to pay the providers for the services they render to you.

settlement option (10) One of your alternatives in using the life insurance policy proceeds if you are the beneficiary and the insured dies or if you are the owner and the policy endows.

share draft (4) An account that is essentially the same as a NOW account but is offered by credit unions instead of banks and savings and loans.

shared-appreciation mortgage (SAM) (6) A loan in which the lender charges a lower interest rate than for a traditional loan in exchange for a share in any appreciation in the property's value.

short sale (12) A means of selling stock you do not own with the intention of repurchasing it in the future. You borrow the stock from your broker, sell it, and then replace it when you later buy it.

short-term goals (1) Personal financial planning goals that have an immediate focus, such as maintaining a positive balance in your checking account, repaying a loan, or getting a summer job.

short-term traders (12) Those who continually move in and out of stocks rather than taking a long-term investment position.

signature card (4) A form signed by a consumer when opening an account so that the bank will have documentation to verify the authenticity of checks.

signature loan (4) An unsecured loan made only on the belief that the borrower will repay the bank. The bank does not have claim to specific collateral.

simple interest method (5) A method of calculating finance charges in which the charge is calculated on the average loan balance outstanding for the length of time the money is borrowed.

simplified employee pension (SEP/IRA) (15) A retirement plan through which an employee can make supplemental deposits to an IRA. This plan is most often offered by an employer who does not have an ordinary pension plan.

single account (4) An account opened by only one person. Only that person can withdraw funds from or write a check on the account.

single-payment loan (7) A loan that requires the repayment of the entire loan amount in one lump sum.

single-premium annuity (15) An annuity that is purchased with a single lump-sum payment.

software (7A) The programs, routines, and procedures that control the operations of a computer.

special endorsement (4) A payee's endorsement of a check to a specific person to whom the check is to be paid. The new person can then cash it or endorse it over to yet another party.

speculative premium (14) The difference between the price of an option and the intrinsic value related to the option. It is generally based on the outlook for the stock and the amount of time remaining until the expiration date on the option.

spreadsheet (7A) A series of rows and columns like an accounting worksheet.

sprinkling trust (16) A trust that can be set up to cover a number of children or grandchildren and gives the trustee the power to distribute income, and possibly principal, according to the needs of each child.

standard deduction (3) An alternative to actually listing out expenses on a tax return. You simply take a single lump-sum deduction that applies to the category in which you fall.

stated rate of interest (4) The interest rate quoted by a financial institution. This rate may vary from the effective interest rate depending on several factors.

stepped-up basis (16) The new cost basis of property received by your beneficiaries. It is the market value of the property at the time you die.

stop payment (4) An order given to your bank in which you tell them not to release the funds on a specific check you have already written.

stop-loss order (12) An order that enables you to protect your downside exposure in a falling market. You specify the price at which you want to bail out and if the stock gets to that low level, the stop-loss order becomes a market order and the sale will be consummated in the first possible transaction.

straight-life annuity (15) An annuity that guarantees you a fixed amount of income for life. All payments cease when you die, however, and the company providing the annuity retains any balance in your account.

strike price (14) The price at which an option holder can buy or sell a stock.

subordinated claim (6) The claim of a second mortgage lender to property. The lender can receive payment only after the first lender's entire claim has been satisfied.

suicide clause (10) A life insurance policy provision limiting insurance payment if the insured commits suicide within the first one or two years after the policy is issued.

super NOW account (4) A type of checking account similar to the NOW account, but on which financial institutions pay a higher interest rate if a large minimum balance is maintained.

surrender option (10) The option to give up an insurance policy with a cash value.

surtax (3) A special tax that is imposed in addition to the normally assessed tax.

tax audit (3) A special review by the IRS of a tax return, usually in order to validate a taxpayer's income or deductions.

tax credit (3) An amount that may be deducted from a taxpayer's final tax obligation, for example, the earned income credit.

Tax Reform Act of 1986 (3) A major piece of tax legislation that eliminated or reduced many tax deductible items and tax shelters and, in turn, lowered tax rates.

tax shelter (3) An investment that provides losses for federal income tax purposes. The losses may only be paper losses due to high depreciation or tax credits.

tax withholding (3) The procedure by which the government withholds a regular amount from your paycheck in anticipation of tax obligations.

taxable estate (16) The value of an estate after reducing the gross estate for any debts and administrative expenses as well as deductions and exclusions.

technical analysis (12) The examination of a firm's prior price and volume data, as well as other market-related indicators, to project past trends into the future. Technical analysis does *not* call for examining the overall fundamental position of the firm in terms of earnings, management, etc.

term life insurance (10) Life insurance that promises to pay its face amount *only* if you die during its term of protection; it does not pay if you survive the term.

testamentary trust (16) A trust created by a deceased's will that can come into existence only after the will has been probated.

testator (testatrix) (16) The person making a will.

third-party coverages (8) Insurance coverages that pay others if you are responsible for injury to them or damage to their property.

threshold (8) A no-fault auto insurance loss measure beyond which you regain the right to sue the other party.

thrift plan (15) A retirement plan in which an employee makes a voluntary contribution which is then partially or wholly matched by the employer. Employee contributions are still treated as taxable income in this plan and do not provide immediate tax deductions.

title insurance (6) Insurance against any defects in the title passed along from the seller to the buyer in the purchase of a home.

total return (12) The current yield or income plus the capital appreciation.

total return on a fund (13) The change in the net asset value of a mutual fund plus dividends and capital gains distributions.

traditional brokers (12) Stockbrokers who not only buy and sell stocks for you but provide you with advice, supply you with literature on companies, and share their research with you; they tend to charge a full commission.

transactions costs (2) The costs of buying or selling an asset.

travel and entertainment credit card (5) A credit card, such as American Express, that is primarily used to pay for food, lodging, and entertainment expenses.

traveler's check (4) A type of check that is backed by a large financial institution and is accepted throughout the world.

Treasury bill (11) A short-term security issued by the U.S. Treasury, generally for 91 days, 182 days, or a year. T-bills are sold in minimum units of $10,000.

trust (16) A legal arrangement whereby one party transfers property to a second party to be managed for the benefit of a third party.

trust services (4) Services, normally offered by a bank, such as managing a client's assets, maintaining records pertaining to assets, and performing custodial services such as collecting dividends, interest, and royalty payments.

trustee (16) A person or institution that has been named to manage a trust for a beneficiary.

trusteed plan (15) A method of pension plan administration in which a commercial bank receives and manages pension contributions. The bank tries to earn a large enough investment return to ensure that the pension plan will have sufficient assets to meet payment obligations.

Truth-in-Lending Act (5) See *Regulation Z.*

Truth-in-Lending Simplification and Reform Act (5) A law passed by Congress in 1980 that reduced disclosure requirements and required lenders to use standard, easy-to-understand disclosure statements.

tutorial (7A) Computer programs that teach you how to make better use of the computer or use specific computer applications.

12b-1 plan (13) A plan in which a mutual fund may recover part of its selling and promotional expenses in the form of annual operating and management fees on the fund's shares.

umbrella liability policy (8) An insurance policy that fits over homeowner's and auto liability coverages and pays if those policies' liability coverages are exhausted.

unfunded pension plan (15) A pension plan in which no funds are set aside on a regular basis to provide for retirement income. Benefits are paid directly from general corporate funds.

unified tax rate schedule (16) A tax table used to determine the amount of tax owed for gift and estate taxes.

Uniform Gift to Minors Act (16) A law that permits an adult custodian to hold title to a minor's property and legally transact business on the minor's behalf. When the minor reaches majority, the property automatically transfers to the new adult.

uninsured/underinsured motorists insurance (8) See *reverse third-party coverages.*

unit benefit pension plan (15) A type of defined benefit plan under which employees receive benefits according to the number of units accumulated multiplied by a set dollar amount. The units are based on number of years of service, type of service, and so on.

unit investment trust (13) An unmanaged pool of securities, usually bonds, that may be federal government, corporate, or municipal issues. Once the securities in the unit trust are purchased, they remain in place until they mature.

universal life insurance (10) A modified form of endowment or whole life insurance. The policy provides both death protection, in the form of term insurance, and an investment component or cash value.

unmarried head of household (3) A federal income tax filing status that reflects that a single person is head of a household. It allows one to be in a preferential tax position in comparison to a single taxpayer.

unsecured bonds (11) Bonds that are not backed by the pledge of specific corporate assets as collateral.

VA loan guarantee (6) A guarantee made by a federal agency, the Veterans Administration, that the agency will reimburse the lender for any loss resulting from the borrower's inability to pay.

Value Line Investment Survey (12) A publication that ranks 91 different industries for probable performance over the next 12 months. *Value Line* also researches 1700 companies in the survey and ranks them as to timeliness and safety.

valued benefit (9) An insurance benefit where the insurer pays you an agreed amount of dollars if a particular occurrence stated in the policy takes place.

variable annuity (15) A type of annuity contract in which the payments fluctuate with the performance of the issuer's investments.

variable costs (7) Expenses that vary directly with volume.

variable life insurance (10) Life insurance designed to vary its face amount in order to create a relatively constant purchasing power, even during inflation.

variance from budget (2) The difference between the planned amount and the actual expenditure in a budget.

vesting (15) The process of meeting specified pension criteria and thus earning a nonforfeitable right to the money contributed by your employer on your behalf to a pension fund.

volatile interest rates (1) An environment in which interest rates move up and down by large amounts. Interest rates have been highly volatile in the 1970s and 1980s.

voluntary savings plan (13) An informal arrangement with a mutual fund in which the investor voluntarily agrees to place a certain amount in the fund monthly, quarterly, or annually.

waiting period (9) A disability income health insurance deductible; a period of time, starting when your disability begins, during which the insurer does not pay benefits.

waiver of premium (10) An inexpensive life insurance policy rider that keeps your policy in force if you are disabled and cannot pay the premium.

warranty deed (6) A deed in which the seller guarantees that there are no defects in the title to the property being sold.

whole life insurance (10) Life insurance that pays whenever you (the insured) die. It builds a cash value that pays the face amount at your age 100, if you live that long.

will (16) A legally enforceable declaration of a person's instructions about matters to be attended to after his or her death.

word processing (7A) A special software program that uses the computer as a typewriter to create, edit, duplicate, and store letters, records, and so on.

yield (11, 12) The effective rate of return on an investment.

zero-coupon bonds (11) Bonds that do not pay interest but are initially priced at a level sufficiently below par to pay a desired return to the investor.

Index

Note: n stands for footnote.